ANTHONY GIDDENS

Routledge Critical Assessments of Leading Sociologists

Already Published

ANTHONY GIDDENS
Critical Assessments

Edited by
Christopher G.A. Bryant and David Jary

VOLUME III

London and New York

First published 1997
by Routledge
11 New Fetter Lane, London EC4P 4EE

Simultaneously published in the USA and Canada
by Routledge
29 West 35th Street, New York, NY 10001

Typeset in 10pt Times by Solidus (Bristol) Ltd
Printed and bound in Great Britain by TJ Press (Padstow) Ltd, Padstow, Cornwall

British Library Cataloguing in Publication Data
A catalogue record for this book is available from the British Library

Library of Congress Cataloging in Publication Data
Anthony Giddens : Critical assessments / edited by Christopher G.A.
    Bryant and David Jary.
    p.   cm.
    1. Giddens, Anthony. 2. Giddens, Anthony—Bibliography.
    3. Sociology—Methodology. 4. Social structure.   I. Bryant,
    Christopher G. A.   II. Jary, David.
    HM24.A545   1996
    301'.01—dc20   96–1120

ISBN 0–415–11688–0 (Boxed Set)
ISBN 0–415–11689–9 (Vol. I)
ISBN 0–415–11690–2 (Vol. II)
ISBN 0–415–11691–0 (Vol. III)
ISBN 0–415–11692–9 (Vol. IV)

Contents

Bibliographies

Bibliography I: Works by Anthony Giddens, 1960–95 and Bibliography II: Works on Giddens or which use Giddens are placed at the end of Volume IV. Works cited in this General Introduction and in the eight section Introductions which are not included in Bibliography I or II are listed in a Select Bibliography at the end of the Introduction concerned. All works cited in reprints, including editions of Giddens, are always listed at the end of the reprint concerned.

SECTION FIVE:
Time–Space in Structuration Theory

Introduction

One of the most distinctive emphases in Giddens's structuration theory is his insistence on bringing 'time–space relations' into the very core of social theory. Above all, drawing in part on Heidegger, a recognition that time–space relations are 'inherent in the constitution of all social inter-action' avoids the 'repression' of time and agency associated with the sharp distinction between synchrony and diachrony favoured by structuralists and functionalists (Giddens, 1979a, p. 3).

The centrality – 'the ontological necessity' – of a space–time framework within Giddens's structuration theory, and the terms of the dialogue this involves with modern geography, are outlined with considerable clarity in our first reprint by the geographer, Tommy Carlstein (1981). Once again indicating Giddens's strong international and interdisciplinary appeal, this chapter first appeared in the *Swedish Geographical Yearbook*. Carlstein summarizes Giddens's view of structure 'as a relation between the past as a totality and the new moment of generation in which structure is perpetuated and modified as the result of human agency' (p. 41). The three-fold manner in which temporality is involved in Giddens's approach is outlined by Carlstein, who also indicates how Saussurean notions of *différence* are 'temporalised' to mean 'deferment and differentiation in time' (p. 47). As a geographer, Carlstein finds Giddens's general ideas 'very exciting and worthwhile', but it is evident that he remains unhappy with Giddens's concept of structure 'as simply a virtual order of differences' and he commends the use of graphical representations of time–space paths, as employed in human geography, as a means of bringing out how structures 'exist' and the 'basic constraints of mediation and resource limitation' they involve. For Carlstein, 'if structure is expressed only at the moment of constitution', this begs the question '*how long is a constituting moment?*' (p. 49).

The second item in this section is an interview with Giddens conducted by the Cambridge geographer David Gregory in 1983, who refers to structuration theory as 'one of the most vital junction-points between contemporary social theory and human geography'. Gregory notes the early influence on Durkheim of the geographer Vidal de la Blanche and *la géographie humaine*, but Giddens confirms that his own conception of the centrality of the 'temporal constitution of day-to-day life in time–space relations' – not just 'uninteresting' 'boundaries of social life' (pp. 126–27) – derived, in the first place, from phenomenology and from Heidegger. It was from this that Giddens was led back to geography, and then only indirectly 'through the influence of geographical thought on the *Annales* school' (p. 126). The value of the time-geographer Torsten Hägerstrand's conception of human agents as 'mobile bodies' is also discussed with Gregory, but it is the theoretical limitations of Hägerstrand's approach which are emphasized by Giddens and the 'more fundamental way' in which the conception of 'time–space distanciation' can be used in reworking previous conceptions of society and societal typologies. (For further discussions of these themes by Gregory and further replies by Giddens see Held and Thompson, 1989.)

While the 'particular importance to geography' of Giddens's placement of the 'spatiality of social practices' at the centre of social theory and historical analysis is noted, the third commentary from a geographer in this section – Michael Storper (1985) – is critical of key aspects of structuration theory. Although it is not clear that he has fully grasped all the nuances of Giddens's theory, Storper is successful in identifying a number of problems in structuration theory, not least the often 'arbitrary' and 'contradictory' way in which switches occur between voluntarism and determination in Giddens's work and the lack of systematization in structuration theory.

Nicky Gregson's (1986) concern, in the fourth discussion of structuration theory by a geographer, is to sound a warning about the possible limitations of structuration theory in empirical research. Ironically, the necessity which Gregson sees for this warning serves also as testimony to the wide influence achieved by Giddens's treatment of time–space within human geography and elsewhere. Gregson's article is also useful for its more extended discussion of approaches to time-geography, including Hägerstrand's.

Rather than a focus on space or space and time issues, Mark Elchardus's (1988) sophisticated discussion concentrates more specifically on 'the new role of *time* in sociological theory'. In a discussion of Luhmann as well as Giddens, what Elchardus refers to as the 'rediscovery of Chronos' involves the repudiation of the atemporal and invariant in social theory and a recognition of temporality as repetition and sequential order. Usefully reviewing previous conceptions of time in social theory, Elchardus regards structuration theory as doing little more than signalling the importance of 'an understanding of how societies constitute their temporality'. However, while he suggests that 'the search for a new concept of structure is still open', he accepts the value of Giddens's conception of structure as a move beyond the reworking of old concepts.

Like other commentators in this section, the town planning theorist Edward Soja (1990) acknowledges the importance of Giddens's contribution to the 'reconstruction of geographical thinking' but is also critical of it (see also Soja, 1983). For Soja, Giddens's 'infusion of power into an explicitly spatialized ontology of society and hence the interpretation of the making of geography alongside the making of history' (p. 155) is his major achievement. Soja indicates how Giddens's approach arises from an 'eclectic synthesis' of the work of social geographers and urban theorists, such as Lefebvre, Castells, Harvey, Mumford, Christaller and Sjoberg, amplified by 'a combination of Heidegger, Althusser and the work of the modern time-geographers'. Soja's criticism, however, is that Giddens, at least initially, is far stronger on time than on space, an imbalance which Soja sees as reproducing 'an imbalance also present in hermeneutics and structuralism'. 'Existential phenomenology, despite the inherently spatial quality of such concepts as *Dasein, Etre-là, Being*-there' is seen as continuing to concentrate on 'the temporality of Being and Becoming' (p. 144). For Soja, hemeneutics and structuralism 'opened new windows through which to re engage time–space relations' in greater symmetry, but failed to carry this through. In *A Critique of Historical Materialism*, Giddens is seen as 'edging closer' to the necessary reconceptualization, 'giving place to being'; and *The Constitution of Society* is described by Soja as 'the most rigorous, balanced, and systematic ontological statement currently available on the spatio-temporal structuration of social life'. For all this, Soja believes that the 'temporal chaperon' remains 'too protective' on occasions, which he explains by suggesting that Giddens 'is determined to acknowledge space without succumbing to the disciplinary biases' and the separatism of modern geography (p. 147). Nevertheless, Soja regards Giddens as having produced a 'seductive ontology', far more adaptable than others to analysis of 'the most fundamental contextual generalization about the spatiality of social life' – namely that 'the intelligible life-world of being is always and everywhere compromised by a multi-layered system of socially created nodal regions, a configuration of differentiated and hierarchically organized locales' (p. 148).

John Urry's (1991) chapter provides a further overall appraisal of the significance, applications and omissions of Giddens's time–space perspective, concentrating especially on what he sees as the limitations of Giddens's treatment of spatiality. Giddens's selective adoption of the work of the time-geographers is reviewed and the role of such key concepts as 'locale', 'power-container', and 'time–space-edges' in Giddens's work noted. Urry's verdict is that, although Giddens can be credited with making a vital contribution to a new emphasis on 'time–space' within sociology, this emphasis 'would probably have happened anyway'. The major weaknesses in Giddens's approach, according to Urry, include the one-sidedness of Giddens's focus on 'modernization through distanciation', the neglect of local context or 'place', and his failure to address fully issues raised by conceptions of 'post-modernity' or to discuss the 'disorganization' of modern capitalism. Urry also repeats his previous view (see Section Four), that Giddens fails to supply adequate accounts of the ways in which actors actually construct social structures and gives too little attention to the role of social movements.

Other commentaries on Giddens's treatment of time–space – especially including issues arising from Giddens's dependence on Heidegger and also Derrida – will be found in Joas (1987), Mendoza (1987), Thrift (1985a), Craib (1992a), Wagner (1993), reprinted in Section Four; Jary (1991), reprinted in Section Six; and Tucker (1993) and Thrift (1993), reprinted in Section Seven. Craib (1992a) in the selection we reprint and elsewhere, is useful on what he regards as a loss of the Heideggerian concern with 'authenticity' and the trivialization involved in Giddens's utilization of Laing's conception of 'ontological security' and 'insecurity' (see also Sections Six and Seven). Craib also questions Giddens's Goffman-inspired modification of Lockwood's (1964) distinction between 'social integration' and 'system integration' using Heideggerian conceptions of 'presence' and 'absence'.

Select Bibliography

Lockwood, D. (1964) 'Social integration and system integration', in Z. Zollschan and W. Hirsch (eds) *Explorations in Social Change*, London: Routledge & Kegan Paul.

The Sociology of Structuration in Time and Space: A Time-Geographic Assessment of Giddens' Theory*

T. Carlstein

*Source: *Svensk Geografisk Årsbok*, 1981, pp. 41–57.

Abstract

The sociology of structuration in time and space as envisaged by the well-known British sociologist Anthony Giddens is assessed from a time-geographic perspective. Structuration theory deals with the relation between individual *action* and social *structure*. Giddens objects to the lack of temporality both in traditional functionalism and structuralism. Moreover, he argues that structuralism as proposed by Lévi-Strauss neglects the acting subject, the person as a conscious being continuously engaged in action throughout life. From the aggregate perspective of how social forms and institutions are produced and reproduced, the lack of a time–space framework has been detrimental to deeper analysis of central problems in social theory and of human practice. Giddens regards structure as structural properties of social systems which are operational in the moment of generation in time, i.e. as time moves forward. Structure consists of *rules and resources* enabling the next moment of generation. Unlike in functionalism where structure is a set of static relations between the parts and the whole, Giddens looks upon structure as a relation between the past as a totality and the new moment of generation in which structure is perpetuated and modified as a result of human agency. The past totality forms an input into the structuration done in the succeeding moment added to the past. Giddens then applies this temporal/spatial scheme to various central problems of signification (meaning, ideas), domination (the application of resources and power as transformative capacity) and legitimation (sanctions, norms, rights and obligations, rewards). For reasons of brevity, Giddens's interesting theory can only be assessed here in terms of its time–space logic and its relations to time-geography.

Action and Structure

According to Gregory (1979), the lacking convergence of human geography and social theory has been due to the excess of spatiality in geography and the deficiency of it in the social theory of sociology and social anthropology. One effect has been that "social geography" remained something of an empty niche until the recent upsurge of neo-Marxist writings, another that human geography kept nicely out of touch with social theory. Structuralism, for instance, was almost unheard of in geography, thriving on its own brands of spatial functionalism.

A major tenet in time-geographic theory as an *integrative approach* has always been that our contact surface with the surrounding disciplines can only be broadened if human geography rethinks its temporally flat view of the world and becomes a true time–space science, placing activity systems analysis in time–space in the centre (cf. Hägerstrand 1970 ff.; Carlstein, Parkes and Thrift 1978; Carlstein 1980/81).

Given this point of departure, it is exciting to find a leading British sociologist outside the functionalist or time-budget study tradition writing a book on "Central Problems in Social Theory" in which he proclaims that:

> ... social theory must acknowledge, as it has not done previously, time–space intersections are essentially involved in social existence ... (Giddens 1979:54)

> An adequate account of human agency must, first, be connected to a theory of the acting subject [the human individual]; and second, must situate action in *time and space* as a continuous flow of conduct, rather than treating purposes, reasons, etc., as somehow aggregated together ... (1979:2)

When constructing a theory of action or agency, and in order to show the interdependence of action and structure, we "must grasp the time–space relations inherent in the constitution of all social interaction". These words sound as if they come straight from the time-geographic camp, and not from a sociologist reassessing the merits of the grand old masters like Marx, Comte, Durkheim, Weber, Pareto and others who have shaped the sociological heritage. Giddens not only reconsiders the merits of the central thinkers and problems of the 1800s but also those of the present century, of scholars like Lévi-Strauss, Parsons, Heidegger, and many other prominent figures.

Some of Giddens's constructive criticisms were presented in his "New Rules of Sociological Method" (1976) but his counterproposals are summed up in his "Central Problems ..." in what he calls a theory of *structuration*. Even this book is more programmatic than applied to some specific object, but an interesting turn in his project is that his later formulation places heavy stress on the logical (ontological) necessity of a time–space framework.

Unlike many functionalists and structuralists who bring time into the picture in relation to "social change", Giddens objects to the assumptions underlying this line of thought, e.g. the entrenched distinction between synchronic analysis as a "timeless snapshot" of how a society functions, and diachronic analysis as synonymous with social change. For all its other virtues, the structuralism of Lévi-Strauss even had the audacity to speak of "reversible time". To Giddens, specification and differentiation of social forms, practices and processes is without sense unless it is done with total reference to time and space. Temporality is *central* to the generation and perpetuation of social forms, not incidental to it, and temporality in turn makes no sense without concepts of spatial presence and absence.

The Structuralist Point of Departure

Many weaknesses of social science (including human geography) display themselves in the inability of many explanatory schemes to penetrate below the surface of observed phenomena, i.e. in an empiricist mode of scientific practice. The generative emphasis of structuralism and Marxist–structuralism tends to overcome this if well practised:

> In structuralism ... 'structure' appears in a more explanatory role ... Structural analysis, whether applied to language, myth, literature or art, or more generally to social relationships, is considered to penetrate below the level of surface appearances ... (Giddens 1979:60)

To Jonathan Friedman, who applies a Marxist–structuralist scheme,

> The principal contributions of structuralism to all this is the notion of 'system of transformations' which enables us to reduce superficially distinct structures to a set of variants which can be generated by a single underlying structure. (Friedman 1979:27)

A structuralist method thus codifies our knowledge of the world better. Lévi-Strauss, for instance, made his initial contribution to anthropology by showing how a great empirical variety of kinship systems spread throughout the world could be reduced to a few basic structures of how women were exchanged among groups. The division between structure (the pattern of a social system) and function (its operation) conventionally applied in function-alist analysis, is replaced in structuralist schemes by one between *code* and *message*. This paradigm was initially taken from linguistics, as developed by de Saussure (1916) in his distinction between *langue* (language as a code or syntactic structure) and *parole* (spoken language or discourse). We cannot understand the *generative principles* of language unless we know the code (grammar or syntax), and without knowledge of this code, no messages can be exchanged. It is the code which enables us to penetrate below the manifestations of language to its essence, its generative properties. What, then, is the code by which social phenomena are generated, the genetic code of society, if we so wish to phrase it, including both the rules of reproduction and mutation?

For all its potential virtues, the initial structuralist paradigm was too narrow,

> The structuralist can generate variants [of social forms], but it is only by embedding these in larger models of social reproduction that we can determine the way they are distributed in time and space. (Friedman 1979:28)

This pertains to all scales of time and space (micro-, meso- and macro-levels), from minute situations of social interactions to large blocks of historical geography. Another shortcoming of traditional structuralism was the implicit conceptualization of temporality and spatiality in conjunction with an overly deterministic perspective or one reducing social phenomena to the human mind. The structuralist scheme often reduced individuals to passive *objects* of generative principles or to 'victims' of structural determinisms. The latter is also typical of many forms of Marxism. In spite of some emphasis on individual consciousness and so on, individuals are neglected as active subjects, reflectively monitoring their action over time.

This latter point made by Giddens is not an idealist assault on a materialist ontology, but a recognition of the "strategic conduct" of individuals (in time-geographic language that individuals define and pursue projects of their own and that these projects are not simply handed down by tradition or structure). This proposition also goes beyond the fact that action is shaped by intentionality, as has been a theme greatly preoccupying social philosophers. Individuals have practical consciousness and know (within limits) what they are doing as members of a society. They can react to previous experiences and reflectively monitor their action over time. Incorporating this fact is not idealism but realism, as is the inclusion of the practical competences of actors, e.g. their use of language:

> 'understanding' ... *is the very ontological condition of human life in society as such* ... self-understanding is connected integrally to the understanding of others. Intentionality ... [should contrary to some phenomenological analysis be treated as] ... *necessarily* drawing on the communicative categories of language, which in turn presuppose definite forms of life. Understanding what one does is only made possible by

understanding, i.e. being able to describe what others do. .... it is integrally dependent upon the social character of language. (Giddens 1976:19–20)

This idea of strategic conduct of the individual(s) and reflexive monitoring of conduct by the individual, as well as his/her other practices introduces a duality (not a dualism) between individual and society, *a duality of structure*. This implies a two-way determination of agency and structure which structuralism tended to forget. Systems do not merely have structures (structural properties) which shape activity outcome, but the activity outcome of individuals alter the structural properties of the system in the next round. Structures are structured by individuals in their strategic conduct, and in the dialectic between individual and society, and between structure and system, determination works in both directions.

> To study the *structuration* of a social system is to study the ways in which that system, via the application of generative rules and resources, and in the context of unintended outcomes, is produced and reproduced in interaction. (Giddens 1979)

This scheme differs from several others previously employed, e.g. that of Durkheim, where norms as social constraints shape and confine the individual actor, society is reified in the individual. Or the voluntaristic countertheory of Max Weber, where society is shaped by individuals through intentional action. Or a two-way dialectic with implicit temporality, such as that by Peter Berger in which society is an externalization of man, and man a conscious appropriation of society, but where the articulation of the system is not spelled out. Structuration theory, by contrast, recognizes the continuous dialectic of individual and society as social systems unfold in time. Social structures are both the medium and the outcome of the activities or practices which constitute them. By emphasizing that social systems consist of institutions which are made up of actions/practices delivered by actors, time becomes central to the understanding of how the system is generated, maintained and altered, i.e. produced and reproduced.[1]

Institutions and Social Reproduction: The Case of Language

Let us now put the active subject and her/his strategic conduct in methodological brackets, and look at social systems from the aggregate perspective in which individuals become objective components in these systems. Another set of durable building blocks of society, its social forms, would be its *institutions*. "Institutions may be regarded as 'standardised modes of behaviour' which play a basic part in the time–space constitutions of social systems", to use the definition Giddens borrows from Radcliffe-Brown, the anthropologist. But the key note in structuration theory is to look upon institutions as composed of *practices*, recurrent *actions* forming habits and routines. Moreover, institutions are also reproduced over time in the form of practice.

Taking a fundamental example, a social institution typically reproduced through practice is human *language*. Already in his 1976 book, Giddens refers much to language "as a social form ... [which] exemplifies some aspects – and only some aspects – of social life as a whole."

Returning to the code-message paradigm of structuralism, language as a code forms an institution that is both reproduced and modified through active discourse. The code is there as a rule for generating sentences in the practical contexts of every-day life, i.e. language practices are "situated practices" in time and space. Language is a structure of *signification*, a (kind of cognitive) structure drawn upon, i.e. used as an input in human communication and exchange of ideas. Hence, language as reproduced practice serves as a *medium* for and (a generating moment later) as an *outcome* of reproduced practices (what Giddens refers to as the duality of structure, its two sides, in structuration).[2]

The Code/Message Linguistic Paradigm as a Model of Social Reproduction

Giddens's structuration theory 'dynamizes' the code-message paradigm by basing it on total temporality. Temporality enters into the reproduction of social systems in a three-fold way:

1. "In the *immediate nexus of interaction*, as contingently accomplished or 'brought off' by actors, social reproduction in its most elemental sense."
2. "In the *reproduction of personnel* of social systems, as beings with a finite life-span, Sein zum Tode, anchored in the course of biological reproduction."
3. "In the *reproduction of institutions*, sedimented in the *longue durée* of historical time." (Giddens 1979:96)

The code-message paradigm was also temporalized by extending Saussure's idea of *différance* to mean deferment and differentiation in time. Structure thus becomes, not a cross-sectional relation between parts and wholes, but a relation between generating moment and generated totality.

Structure is thus the mode in which the relation between *moment* and *totality* expresses itself in social reproduction. This relation is distinct from that involved in the relation of 'parts' and 'wholes' in the coordination of actors and groups in social systems as posited in functionalist theory. That is to say, the differences which constitute social systems reflect a dialectic of presences and absences in space and time. (Giddens 1979:71)

Hence, the theory of structuration implies that "life passes in transformation". This is the logic of the ever moving now-line across the time–space landscape. Along the now-line, a new present moment is generated at the same rate as the previous moment becomes a past one, adding a new link to the historical chain of moments.

> ... every process of action is a production of something new, a fresh act; but at the same time all action exists in continuity with the past, which supplies the means of its initiation. *Structure thus is not to be conceptualised as a barrier to action, but as essentially involved in its production* ... (Giddens 1979:70)

Structure is a *means*, not a constraint (cf. discussion on p. 17 below).

The Temporal Logic of Structuration Theory

Structure as structuring/-al properties thus has to have the paradigmatic status of a code, because how is it possible, in the temporal grammar Giddens chooses, to say that structure "exists" when it is different from one generating moment to the next. It is continuously restructured:

> structure is both the medium and outcome of the reproduction of practices. Structure enters simultaneously into the constitution of the agent and social practices, and 'exists' in the *generating moments* of this constitution. (Giddens 1979:5) [Italics added]

In this code-inspired generative theory of social forms and systems, we thus end up with the seeming paradox that "an understanding of social systems as situated in time–space can be effected by regarding structure [incessantly changing structural properties] as non-temporal and non-spatial", i.e. as a "virtual order of differences"! I must confess that I was confused by this at first, until I had cracked the code of Giddens's own paradigm. In the latter, each structure is unique to each moment, and alters as that moment is replaced by a new one. Hence, the output of two subsequent moments can never be the same, since life passes in *transformation* with time.

Of course, a structural concept of this kind must involve strong definitions of continuity, because a momentary structural input affecting something in spatial location A, cannot without further specification yield a structured output in spatial location B. Continuity with the past assumes some form of contiguity in space. Structure entails "binding of space and time".

I think these kinds of continuity constraints are beautifully brought out in the time-geographic notation system of paths of individuals and other entities (dead or alive) in time–space. In this sense, what has been done in time-geography so far is absolutely central to any structuration theory of the kind proposed by Giddens. However, it is not the verbal concept of path, which is so crucial, I would argue in relation to Pred's interpretation of Giddens, where Pred makes only incidental use of the time-geographic notation system as such. It is the *graphical* interpretation which allows one, not only to visualize the continuities of material existence and structuration, but also to see its material logic, since the model of paths in a three-dimensional time–space is not just a verbal conceptual model of reality, it is a *scale-model*, a mapping of reality through a direct and simple projection. This scale model talks back to us and tells us when we err in our assumptions of time–space-iality.

Consequently, when harnessing the time-geographic path model to our problems of structuration, we actually see the "time–space interactions, intersections" and "absences" or "presences". We also see "the binding of time and space". Because, it follows from Giddens own propositions about structure and structuration, that if "structure is both the medium and outcome of the reproduction of practices", and if structure is a code, some entities in the real world (e.g. human individuals) must serve as media for the code, as carriers of it. So the code itself must be localized in time and space. In the temporal grammar of my own choosing, structures would *exist*. And regardless of how paradigmatic we take structure to be, in the myriad of social situations making up social systems, we have a correspondingly vast number of lapsed structures embedded (albeit we may classify them into a fewer number of basic categories).

However, if structure is expressed only at the moment of constitution, *how long is a constituting moment?* What is, for instance, the shortest moment we perceive in our own strategic (or tactic) conduct?

The Fallacy of the Code and the Truth of Mediation

It would not be fruitful to argue that time does not reflect motion. Nor would it be of much use to deny that motion implies change, at least change in relative position. And it is the change in *relative* position which is the crux of the matter, not in absolute position. An advantage of the time-geographic notation system or the mapping of trajectories is that we can freeze the absolute coordinates of motion and look into its relations, ex post. This associates time with memory, with an anchorage in the past, with the durability of concepts so that we can transcend the ephemeral nature of time. Language was a great step forward in the cultural evolution of humankind, because through the memory function, through the durability of concepts, we could rid ourselves of the prison of the present moment and reflect upon our relative positions, where we came from and where we might want to go. In other words, the reflexive monitoring of action by the conscious subject, upon which Giddens places stress so rightly, assumes that durability is structured into the code as a cognitive structure. In strategic action, the concepts in the code are less ephemeral than the messages (re)produced in discourse.

What bothers me then, as a simple-minded time-geographer, is that in Giddens's paradigm of structuration, there is no *memory* to *structure*, the code of structuration is ephemeral and ever changing. Structures become "virtual" rather than material in Giddens's ontology. Now this to me seems to be a flaw in his choice of generative code itself, because it is not only that systems are structured as they unfold with time that is crucial, what matters equally are the *relative rates* of motion and unfolding. Structuration is based on the relative rates with which the mediating vehicles are able to regroup themselves into new constellations that form inputs into the next moment in line. If we define a moment as having duration, say, 24 hours, we may for some purposes of explanation have a much more relevant moment or interval of structuration. For other purposes, it may be a minute or a year. In fact, understanding the world around us at depth requires us to handle "messages" on a variety of interrelated wave-lengths of motion. This is to say that we must differentiate the relative rates of production and reproduction associated with different phenomena (cf. below).

Giddens's analytical code gets stuck in *the limiting case of the instant*. But what is the use of this concept or grammar when no change or motion is instantaneous? It is by practically knowing the relative rates of motion and mediation that we can understand and predict structuration. Hence it is of little avail to regard structural properties as ephemeral or to regard structure as a "virtual" order. I find Giddens's general ideas very exciting and worthwhile, but I fail to understand how he could retain the notion of virtual order. The latter is rooted in the implicitly temporal paradigms which he rejects at the outset.

Mediation as a Key to Structuration

It should follow from the logic of Giddens's scheme that the real code of structuration lies in understanding the time–space grammar of mediation. This in turn requires specification of the media and the medium, the agents and their habitat-environment.

> ... each of the three aspects of structure I have distinguished [signification, domination, legitimation] can be understood as ordered in terms of the *mediations* and *transformations* which they make possible in the temporal–spatial constitution of social systems. (1979:103)

Let us only initially note in the above formulation how the three aspects of structure (to which we shall return), are *enabling*, they "make things possible".

The most basic sense of mediation is that involved in the 'binding of time and space' themselves, *the very essence of social reproduction.* The binding of time and space [e.g. the continuity constraints on time–space trajectories as envisaged in time-geography] ... can be understood in terms of what can be called the 'presence-availability' of actors within social systems. All social interaction involves mediation in so far as there are always 'vehicles' that 'carry' social interchange across spatial and temporal gaps [e.g. distance]. In societies or communities of high-presence availability – in other words, where interaction is predominantly of a face-to-face kind – *the mediating vehicles* [*itals. added*] *are those supplied by the faculties of physical presence.* Writing and other media of communication (telephone, television, mechanised modes of transportation) *bind* much greater distances in time and space. (Giddens 1979:103).

This very key role of mediation in social reproduction cannot be interpreted in any other way than media being the "carriers" also of structural properties. The language of time-geography is one of the most effective languages for handling these intricacies of mediation by vehicles and carriers in social systems.

Giddens placed chief emphasis on the role of "practices" as mediating structure in social reproduction, and I think this sets things right from the outset. However, the "populations" involved in practices are neglected in his scheme. Social institutions are not just reproduced through practices or activities but also by the survival of individuals, and it is not only institutions as behaviour that are reproduced but composite situations involving artifacts, organisms (biofacts), materials and other elements of our terrestrial habitat ("terrafacts"), including the land base itself (space-ship earth as a medium). So if we say that society-habitat is reproduced in time–space situations following one another, we get closer to the time-geographic code of reproduction, brilliantly epitomized by Torsten Hägerstrand in the following simple but powerful sentences:

It is evident that the huge amount of situations which constitute societal life mutually regulate one another through the fact that the component people or objects which at a certain time and place cease to constitute a situation will later become components [input] in another situation at the same or in other places. Situations are thus linked to one another in a complicated web [of paths, human and non-human], *which is not without structure.* (Hägerstrand 1974: 226) [Transl. by T.C., itals. added.]

Now if a situation is defined as a specific configuration of divisible and indivisible entities/paths,

... it follows that there is an inevitable shortest time in which these entities can regroup themselves [in time and space] into a new constellation, i.e.

that there are definite *limits* to the *rate* at which different situations can *replace* one another [i.e. can be generated in time]. (Hägerstrand 1974) [Transl. by T.C. from unpubl. manuscript. Italics added.]

The "binding of time and space" is realistically speaking much stronger than Giddens tends to assume, and this aspect is brought out well in the language of time geography as a code of structuration.

On Structure as Constraint and the Essence of Allocation

The paradigm of structuration proposed by Giddens contains a long list of interesting points, which I will have to leave aside for a forthcoming publication, since the structure of this book forces me to be selective. I shall thus allocate remaining space to the topic of structure, constraint and allocation.

From a time-geographic assessment, a major drawback in Giddens's paradigm is that the *enabling* aspects of structure are not sufficiently balanced by *constraining* ones. There are too few principles of limitation, and by this I do not simply mean the moral–legal–normative social constraints emphasized by Durkheim and Parsons (1957), i.e. structures of legitimation. I am referring to *basic constraints of mediation and resource limitation* rooted in certain biotic-cum-physical realities of existence. Surely, structure must also imply limits to variation and to contingency in social systems (socio-environmental systems). Of course there is room for variation and human creativity. History has proven over again how the application of ideas and inventions in all realms of practice alters the received structure. But the latter is heavily biased towards the past, and imposes hard screening on things that are produced and reproduced and which ideofacts of human minds can be turned into accepted, integrated innovations and new viable institutions. These mechanisms of selection are by and large more strongly felt in the realm of "domination" (i.e. allocation of resources) than in that of "signification and legitimation", but Giddens's paradigm is biased towards the latter two, if not so much legitimation, towards signification.

To be able to deal with reproduction over time, we need realistic assessments of our limited capacity to act in relation to time. Since all social substance/form is, in reality, *encapsulated in media or carriers* (including the individual person caught in his own body), we must look into the structural constraints of limited carrying capacity in relation to time and space, as I have emphasized elsewhere (Carlstein 1980/81). This also impinges on any theory of *production*, whether the output is tangible like a book or intangible like the spoken word. Capability constraints and carrying capacity constraints define production possibility boundaries (limits to production variability), which are part of general living and activity possibility boundaries, i.e. structural properties. And to be able to construct a realistic theory of reproduction, we must have a corresponding one on production.

Let me illustrate this first by an example from evolutionary ecology. Already Darwin (whose work inspired Marx) discussed how production (foraging) and reproduction in nature took place within a framework of "struggle for existence" associated with limited life space and other structural properties of "the economy of nature". Natural *selection* took place in this context. It is interesting to note how modern evolutionary ecology has turned time-budgeting, space-budgeting and energy-budgeting into a central process in the structuration of biotic systems, i.e. processes of production and reproduction (Pianka 1978:257–59).

> Interactions and constraints between foraging [production] and reproduction have barely begun to be considered. A promising area for future work will be to merge aspects of optimal foraging with optimal reproductive tactics [cf. human strategic conduct] to *specify the rules* by which input is translated into output; optimal reproductive tactics ("output phenomena") surely must often impose substantial *constraints upon "input" possibilities* ...
> ... any organism has a limited amount of time, matter, and energy available to devote to foraging, growth, maintenance and reproduction. The way in which an organism *allocates these resources among various conflicting demands* is of fundamental interest. [My italics.]

Returning to the theme of limited rates of reproduction, nature has its own structural properties of rates and frequencies of reproduction. They vary extremely widely, but very systematically. Given intervals of reproduction in nature, from bacteria to man, are thus correlated positively to the time of production of the individual itself, as measured by the average size achieved (fig. 1). The larger the individual, the longer the "generation time", i.e. the average time between (the egg of) the parent and that of the offspring (which in turn reflects the life-span). Short-lived species reflect one strategy of adaptation to limited carrying capacities of the time-space niches/habitats that they occupy, but also a strategy of allocation in foraging and reproduction efficiency.

Giddens's structuration theory is still largely unspecified as far as selectivity of reproduction is concerned, and of course, many social forms and institutions fit well within received structural constraints on carrying capacity and so on. But *selective production and reproduction* can only be explained by much more explicit reference to structure as (resource and media-related) constraints. From this perspective, it is encouraging to note that Giddens rejected the "substantive" definition of economy as a sector of society, and adopted the "formal" definition of "equat[ing] the economic with struggles deriving from scarce resources". Although ironically most Marxists go by the

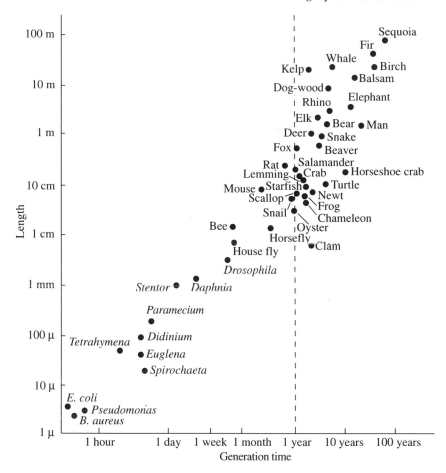

Figure I The plotting of body size (as a function of the time it takes an organism to get *produced*) in a double logarithmic graph against the 'generation tine' of *reproduction* for these organisms, the latter defined as the interval between the time that the parent becomes fertile to the time the offspring reaches fertile age (from 'egg to egg'). Source: J. T. Bonner 1965, quoted in Pianka 1978.

substantive definition, it is the scarce resources aspect which is closest to the materialist perspective of social reproduction. However, resource allocation is central to *all* human (and other biotic) activity. Hence it cannot serve to define a particular institution or sector of society (cf. Giddens 1979:108).

Even the structures of signification are embedded in and mediated by structures of resource allocation ("domination"). In linguistics this is illustrated by Zipf's rank-size rule applied to the reproduction of vocabulary (cf. Zipf 1949, Cherry 1961). The words most frequently used also are those that tend to be shortest or shortened (cf. the pronouns used to substitute for nouns, for instance). This is for reasons of economy in conversation. There are limits to mediation via spoken language or to how many words can be articulated per minute. If a person actually were to talk for 2000 hours per annum (the time it takes to reproduce *one* small delapidated family *house*), and produces 100 words per minute, he/she will produce 12 million words in that time. So even social phenomena (even a house *is social*) display a wide range of rates of production/reproduction, size, etc. as did biotic products. One gets a lot of value for time in verbal reproduction, so it may seem as if "signification" operates without much of resource constraints. How then, account for the shortening of the most frequent words or the tendency to select the shortest synonyms for most frequent use. Well, to me the answer would lie not at the phonetic, syntactic or semantic levels of language, but at the pragmatic and interactional. The "struggle among words" is displayed in dialectics or conversation due to the asymmetry of speech, between speaking and listening. A person can speak to many others at the same time, but only listen to one person at the same time, if meaning is to be put across. Hence, there are scale economies of speech, but none in listening. If there are many in the conversation, they have to *share* total time and cannot all speak at the same time but must do so in turns (cf. Carlstein 1974, 1978). Hence, mediation and interaction involves time allocation and selective production/reproduction. Even ideofacts have to be handled with economy, and even structures of signification are constraining structures.

Another aspect of selective reproduction is that as some new institutions enter as innovations, others may be displaced (due to resource shortages, e.g. of human time) and not reproduced. They become what I have previously called *exnovations* (Carlstein 1978a). The term reproduction should not be viewed so positively as to cloud processes of destruction, displacement and exnovation due to resource allocation and selection. These also account for a good many of the unintended consequences of action channelled in certain directions. We may, however, give the term constraint a more positive interpretation with respect to the projects and activities actually chosen or selected as a function of goals strived for in strategic action. Projects imply constraint by choice, in that once certain choices have been made, a number of constraining consequences follow. Positive choices made constrain action by channelling action in certain directions, to some alternatives among given sets. But constraints deriving from goal-seeking are positive in that they are not simply predetermined by structure but give room for contingency. Hence if we interpret "determination" in two ways, that *structures* determine action possibilities, and that individuals have their own determinations to pursue some possibilities rather than others, we see that there is not necessarily opposition between constraint and contingency, but that the two are mixed in ways amenable to investigation.

Notes

1. Cf. Gregory's discussion of structuration and humanistic geography (1981).

2. Even a particular word reproduced with a given frequency may be regarded as a minute institution which will "live" and "survive" as long as it is reproduced in discourse. The difference is that the institutionalized code of a language as a whole may often "outlive" many of its constituent pieces of vocabulary. Historically and culturally, however, the relation is not that simple. A language may be secularly transformed to such a degree that it becomes a new "species" through a kind of "genetic drift". We all know that Italian, French, Spanish and Portuguese emerged as full-fledged dialects within the Latin code. Latin thus lost most of its ground as a unified and wide-spread code. It got transformed and segmented, while a good many pieces of vocabulary survived and diffused far more widely than Latin grammar. Such a secular linguistic drift in the code is the result of language as mediated through *situated practices*. Pockets of more intensive communication develop at the cost of communication between regions. Hence the dialectics of action and structure produces dialects of language, that eventually reach autonomy, at the same time as new forms of communication may unify that which once had been split up. (I furnish this example as an illustration of how Giddens's concepts can be applied.)

References

Bonner, J.T. (1965): Size and Cycle: An Essay on the Structure of Biology. Princeton: Princeton University Press.

Carlstein, T. (1975): Regional or spatial sociology? In: A. R. Kuklinski, ed. Social Issues in Regional Policy and Regional Planning. The Hague: Mouton Publ.

——— (1978a): Time allocation, innovation and time–space packing. In: Human Activity and Time Geography, ed. by Carlstein, T., Parkes, D. and Thrift, N. (Timing Space and Spacing Time, Vol. 2). London: Edward Arnold.

——— (1978b): Time Allocation and Interaction in a Population System. Dept. of Social and Economic Geography, University of Lund.

——— (1980/81): Time Resources, Society and Ecology, vol. 1, Pre-industrial Societies. Meddelanden från Lunds universitets Geografiska institution, Ser. Avh. 86. Lund. Also publ. by: Allen and Unwin, London 1981.

Carlstein, T., Parkes, D., and Thrift, N. eds. (1978a): Making Sense of Time, London: Edward Arnold.

——— (1978b): Human Activity and Time Geography. London: Edward Arnold.

——— (1978c): Time and Regional Dynamics. London: Edward Arnold.

Cherry, C. (1961): On Human Communication. Cambridge, Mass.: M.I.T. Press.

Darwin, Ch. (1859): The Origin of Species by Means of Natural Selection.

Friedman, Jonathan (1979): System, Structure and Contradiction in the Evolution of 'Asiatic' Social Formations. (Social Studies in Oceania and South East Asia 2.) Copenhagen: The National Museum of Denmark.

Giddens, A. (1976): New Rules of Sociological Method – A Positive Critique of Interpretative Sociologies. New York: Basic Books.

——— (1979): Central Problems in Social Theory: Action, Structure and Contradiction in Social Analysis. London: Macmillan Press.

Gregory, D. (1979): Ideology, Science and Human Geography. London: Hutchinson University Library.

——— (1981): Human agency and human geography. Institute of British Geographers, Transactions 6, 1–18.

Hägerstrand, T. (1970): What about people in Regional Science? Papers of the Regional Science Association, 24, 7–21.

—— (1973): The domain of Human Geography. In: R.J. Chorley, ed. Directions in Geography. London: Methuen.

—— (1974a): Tidsgeografisk beskrivning – syfte och postulat. Svensk Geografisk Årsbok 1974.

—— (1974b): Ecology under one perspective. In: E. Bylund, H. Linderholm and O. Rune, eds. Ecological Problems in the Circumpolar Area. Luleå: Norrbottens Museum.

—— (1975): Space, Time and Human Conditions. In: Karlqvist, A., Lundqvist, L. and Snickars, F., eds. Dynamic Allocation of Urban Space. Farnborough: Saxon House.

—— (1978): A Note on the Quality of Life Times. In: Carlstein, T., Parkes, D. and Thrift, N., eds. Human Activity and Time Geography. London: Edward Arnold.

Lévi-Strauss, C. (1969): The Elementary Structures of Kinship. Boston: Beacon Press. (Orig. in French 1949).

Parsons, T. (1951): The Social System. New York: The Free Press.

Pianka, E.R. (1978): Evolutionary Ecology. New York/London: Harper and Row.

Pred, A. (1981): Social Reproduction and the Time-Geography of Everyday Life. Geografiska Annaler 63B, 5–22.

de Saussure, F. (1916): Cours de linguistique generale. (Course in General Linguistics.)

Zipf, G. (1949): Human Behaviour and the Principle of Least Effort. Cambridge, Mass.: Addison-Wesley Press.

46

Space, Time and Politics in Social Theory: An Interview with Anthony Giddens*

D. Gregory

*Source: *Environment and Planning D: Society and Space*, vol. 2, 1984, pp. 123–32.

This interview was recorded in Cambridge on 21 December 1983 and has been edited for publication.

Anthony Giddens is one of the most influential social theorists working in Britain today, and his programmatic theory of structuration provides one of the most vital junction-points between contemporary social theory and human geography. It was first sketched out in his *New Rules of Sociological Method*, but has since been extended and elaborated in *Central Problems in Social Theory* and in the first volume of *A Contemporary Critique of Historical Materialism*, subtitled *Power, Property and the State*. The second volume, subtitled *The Nation State and Violence*, and the third volume, subtitled *Between Capitalism and Socialism*, are in preparation, and a summary presentation of the theory as a whole, *The Constitution of Society*, will appear later this year. Anthony Giddens is a Fellow of King's College, Cambridge.

Derek Gregory   Throughout your work, it seems to me you repudiate the conventional separations between sociology and philosophy – ones which you say are possible only so long as each remains committed to some form of positivism. And on a number of occasions you anticipate a 'detailed reworking of preexisting formulations of realism' and propose that such a 'modified' version of realism 'may have most to offer' to the construction of postpositivist social theory.[1] In view, too, of the several points of contact between your own theory of structuration and Bhaskar's 'transformational model of social activity', which is itself connected to an avowedly realist programme,[2] could you elaborate on what you see as the significance of realism for social theory?

Anthony Giddens   There are two responses I would make to this question. One is about the relationship between philosophy and social theory. What I argue is that anyone practising social theory and interested in any one of the social sciences – sociology, geography, whatever – should be sensitised to philosophical problems. It's absolutely essential to be alert to philosophical debates, philosophical issues. But I don't think that's the same as collapsing social theory into philosophy. I don't think that the two are one and the same, so I don't make a case for arguing as, for example, a writer like Winch does, that there's some sense in which the social sciences are essentially philosophical.[3] So I don't think it's the case that one has in some way to resolve the most important philosophical debates to do interesting work in the social sciences. I simply make the case that one should constantly be alive to the connections between philosophy and social science from both directions – that philosophers should try in some part to study substantive social problems and that those working in the social sciences should have at least some cognizance of the philosophical debates that are going on. But I don't want to collapse one into the other. This therefore leads me to take a more reserved position with regard to epistemological debates than perhaps your question would tend to indicate. That is, although I'm sympathetic to realism, for example, especially the so-called 'new realism' of Bhaskar, Harré, and others, I don't think of myself as working in any innovative way on epistemological issues, and I try to 'bracket' them to some substantial degree. What I'm trying to do is to work on essentially what I describe as an *ontology* of human society, that is, concentrating on issues of how to theorise human agency, what the implications of that theorising are for analysing social institutions, and then what the relationship is between those two concepts elaborated in conjunction with one another. I think that it is true that any version of social theory presumes some kind of epistemological position, some position with regard to epistemological debates – for example, whether there can *be* an epistemology in a traditional sense, about which I'm still a bit unsure – but I don't think it either necessary or possible to suppose you could formulate a fully-fledged epistemology and then somehow securely issue out to study the world. So my idea is to fire salvoes into social reality, as it were; conceptual salvoes, which don't provide an overall consolidated epistemology. That's why I think of what I'm doing as rather different from the work of writers like Bhaskar, or even of more important writers like Habermas,[4] who are attempting to round out philosophical questions of that sort much more than I am.

Gregory   But one of the reasons that the 'new realism' has emerged, I think, is because of an increasing concern with just those ontological issues. Bhaskar, Keat and Urry, Sayer, and others[5] seem to be proposing that their engagement with realism is intended precisely to enable them to address ontological questions in a much more central way than the traditional formulations allowed.

Giddens   I don't think so – or what they mean by ontology isn't what I was just referring to. What I mean is a theory of social being, social existence; I don't mean by it a more generalised philosophical ontology of, as it were, what 'being' is in general. I am concerned to try to cope with certain issues of social theory that certainly are partly philosophical, but I think not wholly involved with the theory of knowledge. And if epistemology means the theory of knowledge – the foundations of potential claims to knowledge – then I don't think that what I'm doing is as fundamentally involved with that as the writings of the other authors you mention.

Gregory   Let's turn to some of those issues, then. The theory of structuration was developed, in part, through a critique of 'interpretative', and what I suppose we might call 'structural', sociologies. These two terms are no more than shorthand, of course, but the traditions which they represent are conventionally indexed by Weber and Durkheim. But in *New Rules of Sociological Method* you clearly regard much of Weber's work as 'obsolete' in the light of developments in the philosophy of method[6] – whereas elsewhere you return to Durkheim again and again. Do you regard Durkheim as somehow a more central, continuing presence in contemporary social theory than Weber?

Giddens   I don't really. If I said I regard most of Weber's methodological suppositions as open to question, I think that's partly because a lot of people have labelled me as a 'Weberian', and I react against that because I don't think it's accurate. I don't accept it as a derogatory label anyway – and it's usually used as one – but I don't think of myself as a Weberian. There are very few of the major themes in Weber's methodological writings that I would unhesitatingly accept as valid. But it wouldn't be accurate on the other hand to say that I've switched more attention to Durkheim. I maintain a lot of interest in both authors, partly because they've been so influential in the main traditions of social thought. I don't really think of them as alternatives. Durkheim's programme for social science is a fairly consolidated coherent one, and fairly forcibly advanced, and he more or less stuck to it for most of his career. Weber is a much more ambiguous figure, and his so-called methodological writings are not advocated as a normative methodology for the social sciences in quite the same way as Durkheim's *Rules of Sociological Method* are.[7] Weber, I think, is a person whose writings don't really fit neatly within the received tradition which most people – at least until recently – would have defined as 'sociological'. I think of Weber as a fundamentally more complex author than Durkheim: I'm not saying that to disparage Durkheim, because there's a good deal to be said for having a certain parameter of views and exploring those in some detail. But I don't really think of the two, therefore, as just providing alternatives, one 'interpretative' and the other 'structural' in some sort of sense; and I certainly think of myself as being just as critical of Durkheim as of Weber. My view on their methodological writings is that it doesn't make much sense to suppose that you can integrate one with the other, or take bits from one and add them to the other, because I think to a substantial degree developments in social theory have gone a long way beyond both sets of formulations. However, in some respects I do *substantively* follow Weberian themes, because I do think it important to recover notions of power as compulsion, of military power, of the state, and of territoriality. My recent interests in the city, too, are closer to Weber than to Durkheim.

Gregory   I mention Durkheim for two main reasons. One is that a major difference between your position and that of Bhaskar is over notions of 'emergence', which Bhaskar finds and applauds in Durkheim's work, whereas you seem to be much more sceptical.

Giddens   Yes. I think that depends on what the term 'emergence' actually means, however, because I certainly accept that there are structural properties of social systems that have to be analysed generically. That is, I certainly don't want to relapse into some kind of voluntarism and I take a lot of precautions not to do so. I don't really like the term 'emergence' too much, because it suggests that you have primitive elements, as it were, and when those come together you get emergent properties. I don't think this conforms to the basic idea of structuration theory, which is that structural properties of social systems are part and parcel of the ways in which human beings knowledge-ably do what they do. They're not emergent properties, they're built into the nature of even the most personal forms of knowledge that people have of their own selves. So although I don't favour the term 'emergent properties', I certainly wholeheartedly support the same theme – that is, that there are properties of social systems which are accurately defined as structural characteristics of those social systems.

Gregory   The other reason that I mention Durkheim is that he was evidently sensitive to concepts of spatial structure (in part, I think, through the connections which he sought to establish between 'emergence' and social morphology). His encounter with Vidal de la Blanche and *la géographie humaine* in the early twentieth century seemed to offer at the time the prospect of some cross-border traffic, if not a customs union, between sociology and human geography.[8] It's clear that in the theory of structuration you too are impressed by the centrality of time–space relations to social theory. But your interest didn't arise out of those classical debates, or even their contemporary counterparts, so much as from the contributions of Heidegger, Derrida, Foucault, and others: is that right?

Giddens   Yes, I think that's more or less correct. Certainly in terms of my own intellectual development that's an accurate characterisation. I came first of all to see problems of temporality as essential to social theory in some part via phenomenology. I came to the view that to analyse human intentions and the purposive character of human action, one must see human action as having a duration, not treating intentions as sort of closed, separable aggregates of psychical phenomena, in some sense, but as involved in the temporal constitution of day-to-day life. From there I came to the view that theorising temporality is basic to what social theory is all about; and that led me to be interested in Heidegger. In Heidegger, time is theorised in some sense as time–space, as 'presencing': and that led me back to looking at the origins of geography. So I came through a very circuitous route, actually, to the writings of geographers, and it's only very recently that I've been aware of the connection between Durkheim and the classical figures of geography. It's interesting how there were these two sets of 'founding fathers', as it were, in sociology and geography, in spite of the manifest connections between them.

Gregory   It's a very complicated paternity suit as far as geography is concerned . . .

Giddens   It is as far as sociology is concerned too. I just hadn't realised the connections that existed and therefore the possibilities that were latent there, I suppose, and I was only aware of them through the influence of geographical thought on the *Annales* school.[9] But when I was actually working on Durkheim ten or twelve years ago I didn't really pick up the connections between Durkheim and Vidal as a significant phenomenon.

Gregory   One contemporary geographer to whom you do pay attention is Hägerstrand, and several commentators have proposed that his time-geography has some affinity with Vidal's classical prospectus.[10] But you say that, although time-geography is appealing in various ways, and some of its notions are extremely important for the theory of structuration, there are certain objections you want to register against Hägerstrand's particular formulation of it. What are they?

Giddens   In my view it's conceptually fairly primitive, although methodologically quite sophisticated. It is relatively undeveloped with respect to theorising what human agents are like, because they are treated as mobile bodies having 'projects'; and it is fairly primitive theoretically as regards social institutions and their constitution. These shortcomings limit the degree to which one can incorporate Hägerstrand's ideas directly into the sort of work I have been involved with. So I have a pretty reserved attitude, as you do, to the usefulness of Hägerstrand's ideas in their unaltered fashion. I find them attractive insofar as, coming from a background in sociology, I am just not used to thinking in terms of concrete aspects of context. I've come to believe that contextuality of time–space, and especially the connections between time–space location and physical milieux of action, are just not uninteresting boundaries of social life, but inherently involved in its constitution or reproduction. I've found time-geography provides us with at least one way of approaching such issues in a preliminary way. I can envisage using some of the methodological ideas of time-geography, but I think they have to be conceptually elaborated within a more sophisticated theoretical framework than Hägerstrand uses.[11]

Gregory   Part of that elaboration has entailed the development of a concept of time–space 'distanciation'. This seems to me to have some continuity with Hägerstrand's theorems, because both of them are concerned – to some substantial degree – with changes in the mesh of time–space interactions. But you use time–space distanciation in a much more fundamental way, I think, and seek to establish its implications for a typology of social forms.[12]

Giddens   I conceive of the idea of time–space distanciation as quite fundamental to social theory. All social interaction is both contextual – 'situated' in time and space – and yet stretches across time–space 'distances'. In social theory, we have to try to grasp how it comes about that the situated action which is the 'materiality' of all social life intersects with the form of institutions which span large 'stretches' of time–space. For me, then, questions of time–space distanciation in some part replace traditional issues concerned with the nature of societal totalities. We can ask how social systems span time–space without supposing that 'societies' have easily defined or clear-cut boundaries. What a 'society' is has to be directly analysed.

Gregory   You've already said that you don't see the theory of structuration as in any sense a simple conjunction of Weber and Durkheim, and if any of the classical figures of sociology have moved centre-stage in your recent writings then it is surely Marx. I'm not referring here to the *Contemporary Critique of Historical Materialism* alone;[13] in *Central Problems in Social Theory* you say that Marx's writings represent the single most important fund of ideas that can be drawn upon to illuminate problems of agency and structure.[14] But here too your use is an avowedly critical one, and you describe your project as a 'deconstruction' of historical materialism. What do you mean by that?

Giddens   That's quite a complicated question, because it raises the influence of various aspects of Marx, and the complicated history of Marxism, and the two are obviously not entirely the same. As you know, I don't regard myself as a Marxist and have never thought of myself as a Marxist. I've always thought of what I do as using important aspects of Marx's writings and also important aspects of subsequent Marxist thinking, but in a highly critical way, and I would resist the idea that there's anything more than a generalised appropriation of the notion of *praxis* from Marx in structuration theory. That is, if historical materialism means a very generalised account of human beings making history, but in conditions which they don't choose – a theorem which is simple to set out but extremely complicated to elaborate – then in that sense I do indeed draw upon generalised aspects of Marx's ideas or certain interpretations of them. But I think historical materialism more specifically conceived has to be discarded. Historical materialism in this sense refers to a particular account of history in which the forces of production are somehow the most influential factors leading to social change. In other words, there is some kind of coordinated theorem explaining history (where 'history' means generic patterns of change). In the light of a hundred years of anthropology and archaeology since Marx, we have to say that this kind of approach is hopeless. I speak of 'deconstructing' it, because I think it's no longer possible to suppose that you can *reconstruct* an account of social change along those lines. I just don't accept that one can have a sovereign account of social change which can be reduced to a set of formulae; therefore my view of how one interprets and analyses social change is quite different from that of anyone who attempts to provide a coherent formulation of historical materialism understood in the second sense – such as Cohen.[15] I just think that kind of account doesn't work at all. Substantively, what I've borrowed from Marx is an account of certain key features of modern capitalism, and therefore I think of myself drawing on Marx more in respect of substantive notions than of methodological ones.

Gregory   At the same time, though, Marx was himself immensely suspicious of what he called "the *passe-partout* of a historical–philosophical theory whose chief quality is that of being suprahistorical".[16] And, certainly, one of the characteristic features of modern Marxism – if Anderson's *In the Tracks of Historical Materialism* is on the right lines[17] – is a return to the complexity of the concrete, a return which has involved the rise of history (in all its particularity) to a new prominence within historical materialism.[18] If one turns to writers like E P Thompson, for example, then it's surely clear that their work echoes many of the themes that you write about. That is, they would refuse any kind of economic reductionism, they would be very unhappy about any schematic form of structural Marxism which left scant space for human agency, and they would want to promote questions of culture and politics to an equal salience in their explanations. So in that sense aren't you closer to contemporary Marxism than you make out?

Giddens   It depends how you formulate that: you could argue that they are more distant from classical Marxism than they make out. It's quite right to say that my views of human agency and social institutions certainly are quite similar to some of Thompson's emphases – with reservations, because it does seem to me that the debate between Thompson and Anderson echoes the traditional sociological debates between those concerned with a more 'voluntaristic' standpoint on the one hand and those concerned with a more 'structural' standpoint on the other, and I don't unequivocally support Thompson's position in that debate.[19] Anderson scores a few points off Thompson quite effectively, I think, and that debate is actually a very good context in which to pick out some of the themes that can be elaborated out into a more general theoretical account. So the answer depends very much on how far you conceive of such authors as actually putting into practice methodological tenets which really are quite close to the classical theories and theorems of Marx.

Gregory   I'd like to pursue this, because one of the things that concerns me is your repeated insistence on a 'methodological bracketing'. Whereas, on the one hand, you're concerned to bring together agency and structure, or strategic conduct and institutional development, on the other hand you also accept the necessity of a 'methodological bracketing' of the two. In the *Contemporary Critique*, for example, you seem to be preoccupied with institutional analysis to such an extent that strategic conduct virtually disappears from any central place in the discussion. Is that because you see your interests as really rather different from the substantive issues which animate the historians we've talked about? Someone like Thompson would presumably want to address both 'agency' and 'structure' simultaneously, and that must raise a whole series of questions about how such a conjunction is to be effected: or whether you think it can be. It's one thing to grasp what the theory of structuration entails, it seems to me, but apparently quite another to incorporate its theorems into substantive accounts in such a way that one captures the engagements between agency and structure which are the fulcrum of the whole formulation.

Giddens   There are three aspects to that. First, the reason why I separate methodologically two aspects of doing social science, as it were, is that for many purposes, studies concentrate both empirically and theoretically on one aspect rather than on the other. The mistake is to suppose that what is a methodological bracketing is an ontological phenomenon – as someone like Blau does, for example, or even Durkheim did[20] – that the distinctive field of 'sociology' is where the analyst gets beyond individuals' purposes, intentions, and reasons and discovers social forces that somehow influence them outside of those purposes, intentions, and reasons. I don't think it's conceivable to suppose that all forms of social analysis are able to produce a wholly rounded account which would connect agency and structure in a systematic and satisfactory fashion, so I think it necessary to make a distinction between the theoretical stance that one has about that and the methodological limitations which doing particular forms of research involve one in.

The second issue concerns studying long-term institutional development. For the most part it seems to me that long-term institutional organisation and change happen through intentional action, but not intentionally: that is, I think it's highly important to see that most history is made 'unintentionally', even though all of it is done 'intentionally'. So I give a lot of attention to emphasising the importance of unintended consequences of intended actions, without slipping into some kind of functional interpretation. The sorts of issues that I was trying to analyse in a preparatory way in the *Contemporary Critique* fall into that kind of category. Most of the long-term developments that one analyses certainly couldn't be supposed to be the result of projects that any particular individual or aggregate of individuals have had. But I do try to insist in the book that in attempting to account for some of the important conjunctions in long-term processes of change one must also try to grasp the sorts of knowledgeability that people have had in particular contexts, so that, for instance, in theories of the origin of the state, or the origin of cities, or whatever it might be, the forms of available model that people have had in producing certain types of social change are specified. How far they've been aware of the existence of cities and states previously, whether or not the society in which they are living is the result of some kind of dissolution of preexisting urban forms – these things are important and cannot be compressed into a 'structural' account. So to say that long-term institutional change happens unintentionally isn't the same as trying to compress it into an isolated detached form of institutional analysis: I think there is a difference between the two.

The third consideration concerns the form of discourse in which one writes about these changes. All social research presumes what I call an 'ethnographic moment', which is the methodological correlate of the hermeneutic element in describing social action. So however statistical a given study might be, however abstract and remote it is, it presumes some kind of ethnography of individuals involved in the context which is being described. That ethnography is not, of course, always overtly written: in a statistical study, for example, it's largely a tacit taken-for-granted aspect of what's done, but it is necessarily there, I think, and it could in principle be written. So I don't accept that there's a distinction between two styles of research report. I think that even statistical studies presume a kind of ethnographic report which could be written, which is a description of the reasons, intentions, and contexts of action of the individuals presumably and presumptively involved in that statistical account. And that again is why I differ from structural sociologies, which repress that hermeneutic moment.

Gregory That has an important bearing on the political implications of this kind of theorising, doesn't it, because if you want to say – as you do – that the personal transient encounters of day-to-day life are inseparable from the long-term sedimentation or development of institutions, then the prospects for a transition from capitalism to socialism have to be bound up with the knowledgeability inherent in those encounters, just as much as they are in any long-term structural contradictions which, so you argue, underlie 'the possibility of progressive movement in history'.[21]

Giddens Yes. Again I would separate two aspects of this question. In *Sociological Investigations* I make a case for the notion that the social sciences are inescapably critical of the subject matter with which they are involved, but only in a very specific sense, which depends on the fact that social scientists claim to be delivering knowledge to individuals who already know a great deal about the conditions of their activity.[22] They therefore claim to know better than the individuals themselves why they act as they do; making that claim is manifestly in a broad sense a political claim, because the implication is that if the social scientists are right then the individuals involved will change their action. They will recognise that certain of the beliefs which inform that action are mistaken. That means that there is, as it were, a constant reciprocity between social sciences and their 'subject matter'. This gives social science a much more fundamental role than one would ordinarily think, because it means that the social sciences constantly enter and shape the discourse of the actions of the individuals and groups to which they refer. One of the best examples of this is economics, which in some part has created the discourse out of which modern industrial life has been born and shaped. That kind of constitutive encounter between the social sciences and their subject matter seems to me to suggest a nexus of problems to do with the formulation of social science as critical theory. And I don't really think that these can be analysed in terms of classical Marxism and its orthodox notions of contradiction.

These issues are all to do with one aspect of what a contemporary critical theory would look like. But the second is that, obviously, it must have some sort of substantive flesh. This depends on how a connection is made between the critical moment of social theory, philosophically elucidated, and the substantive institutional parameters of contemporary societies in relation to the traditional socialist project. This is a very complex matter, because there's no doubt in my mind that the traditional project of socialism is heavily compromised in the twentieth century. The existing so-called socialist societies are manifestly not very successful in respect to traditional socialist ideals, whether they are ideals of planning or ideals of creating a free and humane social order: and no one involved with socialism can afford to ignore that. Also, the twentieth-century world is so different from the nineteenth-century world which created the anticipated reality of socialism that it's necessary to bring back into the centre of political discussion issues that don't brook very large in traditional socialist debates. These include – for me anyway – theorems concerning the nation-state, the territoriality of states, the development of a nation-state system, and, above all, control of the means of violence. Traditional socialist ideas do not fit at all easily with the problem of how we should confront the problems inherent in living in a world in which there is constant escalation of the means of waging war in the hands of a fairly anarchic nation-state system. I think it necessary to develop an analytical account of the nature of the nation-state, of the nature and origins of military violence, and a philosophy of military power, as it were – or a philosophy of control of the means of violence – which would somehow address traditional problems of democratic theory. It's easy to see that it makes some sense to say that control of the means of production can be returned to workers through some kind of workers' self-management – that some kinds of ideal along those lines are at least plausible, within limits – but it makes no sense to speak of returning control of the means of violence to the mass of the population. The sorts of ideas that Marx had on that kind of issue are, I think, entirely obsolete. Marx believed that the workers had no country, and essentially held that an armed populace would be a democratically responsible populace in respect of the power of the state. That's manifestly not the case in respect of the modern nation-state. Here I see fundamental problems of political philosophy, as well as problems of social theory: and in fact these are the themes of *The Nation State and Violence* and *Between Capitalism and Socialism*.[23]

Gregory   And they return us to the concerns – if not necessarily the analysis – of Thompson and his involvement in the nuclear disarmament movement.[24] Presumably you would want to say that one of the most important 'time–space edges', to use your own terminology, between capitalism and socialism is the prospect of nuclear warfare?

Giddens   Yes. It seems to me that Thompson is quite right. It is the fundamental political problem of our times. We live in a world for which we are unprepared politically and in which the social sciences lack a conceptual vocabulary which can be readily focused on the relevant issues. It's extremely difficult to think through the implications of living in that world – one which we are the first generation to experience. We have to hope we won't also be the last. . . .

Notes

1. For example, see Giddens (1977, page 80; 1982a, page 14).
2. Bhaskar (1978; 1979).
3. Winch (1963).
4. For an indication of Giddens's views on Habermas – from whose writings he reckons to have learned more than from those of any other contemporary social thinker whose work he has encountered, and yet still finds himself in substantial disagreement with many of Habermas's major conceptions – see Giddens (1977, pages 135–164; 1982a, pages 82–116; 1982b).
5. Bhaskar (1978; 1979); Keat and Urry (1982); Sayer (1984).
6. Giddens (1976, page 23).
7. Durkheim (1895).
8. For a summary discussion, see Buttimer (1971).
9. For an account of the relations between (historical) geography and the *Annales* school of 'total history', see Baker (1984).
10. For example, see van Paassen (1981).
11. See Giddens (1984c) and Gregory (1984).
12. For a summary discussion, see Wright (1983, pages 17–22).
13. Giddens (1981).
14. Giddens (1979).
15. Cohen (1978).
16. Marx, cited in Giddens (1971, page 32).
17. Anderson (1983).

18. Anderson (1983, pages 21 and 24–26).
19. The debate has a complex genealogy, but the basic references are Thompson (1978) and Anderson (1980).
20. Blau (1964); Durkheim (1895).
21. Giddens (1979, pages 142–143); also see Giddens (1981, pages 230–252).
22. Giddens (1984b).
23. Giddens (1984a; 1985).
24. For example, see Thompson (1982); Thompson and Smith (1980).

References

Anderson P, 1980 *Arguments Within English Marxism* (New Left Books, London)
Anderson P, 1983 *In the Tracks of Historical Materialism* (New Left Books, London)
Baker A R H, 1984, "Reflections on the relations of historical geography and the *Annales* school of history" in *Explorations in Historical Geography: Interpretative Essays* Eds A R H Baker, D Gregory (Cambridge University Press, Cambridge) pp 7–21
Bhaskar R, 1978 *A Realist Theory of Science* (Harvester Press, Brighton, Sussex)
Bhaskar R, 1979 *The Possibility of Naturalism: A Philosophical Critique of the Contemporary Human Sciences* (Harvester Press, Brighton, Sussex)
Blau P, 1964 *Exchange and Power in Social Life* (John Wiley, New York)
Buttimer A, 1971 *Society and Milieu in the French Geographic Tradition* (Association of American Geographers, Washington, DC)
Cohen G A, 1978 *Karl Marx's Theory of History: A Defence* (Clarendon Press, London)
Durkheim, E, 1895 *The Rules of Sociological Method* (translated by W D Halls in 1982) (Macmillan, London)
Giddens A, 1971 *Capitalism and Modern Social Theory: An Analysis of the Writings of Marx, Durkheim and Max Weber* (Cambridge University Press, Cambridge)
Giddens A, 1976 *New Rules of Sociological Method: A Postive Critique of Interpretative Sociologies* (Hutchinson, London)
Giddens A, 1977 *Studies in Social and Political Theory* (Hutchinson, London)
Giddens A, 1979 *Central Problems in Social Theory: Action, Structure and Contradiction in Social Analysis* (Macmillan, London)
Giddens A, 1981 *A Contemporary Critique of Historical Materialism. Volume 1: Power, Property and the State* (Macmillan, London)
Giddens A, 1982a *Profiles and Critiques in Social Theory* (Macmillan, London)
Giddens A, 1982b *"Reason without revolution? Habermas's Theorie des Kommunikativen Handelns" Praxis International* 2 318–338
Giddens A, 1984a *A Contemporary Critique of Historical Materialism. Volume 2: The Nation State and Violence* (Polity Press, Cambridge) forthcoming
Giddens A, 1984b *The Constitution of Society* (Polity Press, Cambridge) forthcoming
Giddens A, 1984c, "Time, space and regionalisation" in *Social Relations and Spatial Structures* Eds D Gregory, J Urry (Macmillan, London) in press
Giddens A, 1985 *A Contemporary Critique of Historical Materialism. Volume 3: Between Capitalism and Socialism* (Polity Press, Cambridge) forthcoming
Gregory D, 1984, "Suspended animation: the stasis of diffusion theory" in *Social Relations and Spatial Structures* Eds D Gregory, J Urry (Macmillan, London) in press
Keat R, Urry J, 1982 *Social Theory as Science* second edition (Routledge and Kegan Paul, Henley-on-Thames, Oxon)

Sayer A, 1984 *Method in Social Science* (Hutchinson, London)

Thompson E P, 1978 *The Poverty of Theory and Other Essays* (Merlin Press, London)

Thompson E P, 1982 *Zero Option* (Merlin Press, London)

Thompson E P, Smith D (Eds), 1980 *Protest and Survive* (Penguin Books, Harmondsworth, Middx)

van Paassen C, 1981, "The philosophy of geography: from Vidal to Hägerstrand" in *Space and Time: Essays Dedicated to Torstein Hägerstrand* Ed, A Pred; Lund Series in Geography, Series B, 48 (C W K Gleerup, Stockholm) pp 17–29

Winch P, 1963 *The Idea of a Social Science* (Routledge and Kegan Paul, Henley-on-Thames, Oxon)

Wright E O, 1983, "Giddens's Critique of Marxism" *New Left Review* 138 11–35

47

The Spatial and Temporal Constitution of Social Action*

M. Storper

*Source: *Environment and Planning D: Society and Space*, vol. 3, 1985, pp. 407–24.

Abstract

A number of social theorists have attempted to elaborate poststructuralist analytics that capture the dialectics of social structure and human agency. Giddens proposes a 'general theory', centered on the notion of 'structuration'. He is particularly important to geography because he suggests that the spatiality of social practices belongs at the center of social theory and historical analysis. Systems of social practices are defined by their time–space characteristics. There are problems in the corpus of Giddens's work that require attention, however, before such a theory can be fully viable. These include: Giddens's derogation of intentional action in favor of practical knowledge; his notion that structure is 'instantiated', his concept of power; his treatment of material resources; and his lack of attention to discursive strategies. From an examination of these areas of Giddens's work, it can be seen that he advances several, inconsistent, theories of social change. In a reinvigorated theoretical human geography, based on the analysis of interaction in time and space, these problem areas must be tackled.

> Gambles rather than certainty line the paths through which social forces try to maintain or change structures. Briefly, in spite of structural 'determination', there is room for alternatives in history. Their actualization will depend not just on basic contradictions between interests, but also on the perceptions of new ways of turning a historical corner through 'a passion for the possible' (Cardoso and Faletto, 1976, page xi).

1 Introduction

The debate over the role of agency versus structure in social history is now celebrated, having touched all the social sciences. 'Structuralist' has become something of a pejorative because of its association with deterministic views of historical evolution in Marxism, and with convergence and functionalism in both Marxism and Parsonian sociology. There is renewed emphasis on the role that human action plays in creating history, and in generating the structures within which the actions of others are taken, in historical sociology and the 'new social history' (Thompson, 1978; Giddens, 1979; 1981; 1984; Tilly, 1981; Abrams, 1982). Structures appear to be contingent upon and modified by human agency. This has raised a concern with what is meant by the idea of social structure. How can the notion of structure be reconciled with the empirical variety which is found in concrete societies and which is apparently due to the exercise of human agency?

Giddens (1979; 1981; 1984) attempts to elaborate a viable 'general theory' to cope with the problem of human agency and historical contingency in the constitution and reproduction of social structures. He rejects functionalist causality, claiming that structures cannot have an historical telos, and so there is no place for evolutionary models in history. According to Giddens, Marx's inaccuracies regarding both non-Western societies and the path of capitalist development itself must be attributed to his implicit functionalism and evolutionism.

Giddens opts for a hermeneutic-interactionist theory of social 'structuration'. As opposed to the radical humanism of Thompson (1978), he advances the notion of 'system' to reintroduce agency, openness, and diversity to history. Systems are ensembles of social practices that are both medium to and outcomes of social structure, because they are composed of embedded social practices. Normally systems routinize action, but they do not prevent the exercise of agency or the unintended effects of purposive actions from generating system and structure changes.

Certainly Giddens is merely one of a number of social theorists who are attempting to capture and reformulate the various trends of 'poststructuralism', among whom the best known are Bourdieu, Habermas, and Foucault. But Giddens is particularly important to geography because he suggests that the *spatiality* of social practices belongs at the center of *social* theory and *historical* analysis (compare especially Giddens, 1984, pages 110–161 and 355–372.) The structural outcomes of social practices are premised upon their time–space characteristics, since these time- and space-defined practices serve simultaneously as patterns of interaction and, through their impacts on human experience, as foundations for the motivation to future practices. Power, which is the glue that holds institutions or structures together, is built from particular forms of time–space distanciation of social practice, because they make possible specific forms of control over allocative or authoritative social resources. In capitalist society, the city is the nexus of time–space distanciation (presencing and absencing) upon which control over allocative resources by the *bourgeoisie* is premised: the division of labor not only produces commodities, it also reproduces power by partitioning interaction in time and space.

It is essential that theories of action built on the time–space concept be subjected to the most critical scrutiny, since the prospects for elaborating a central role for space or territory in the explanation of social history – and not merely for space as another phenomenon that can be derived *from* the explanatory powers of *social* theory generally – depend on it. Harvey (1982) has suggested that the history of capitalism is impenetrable without the geography of capitalism. So that this goal is realized and powerful arguments to the contrary, such as those of Saunders (1981), are countered, considerable conceptual work remains to be done. I choose Giddens as the focus of this effort precisely because he has suggested the elements of a time–space-rooted general social theory. Although there are some portions of Giddens's voluminous writings which are more explicitly concerned with time–space relations, the entire corpus of his work is rooted in the time–space hermeneutic-interactionist paradigm. I will therefore concentrate here on the issues raised by his paradigm as a whole.

2 Systems and Structuration

Giddens's 'theory of structuration' comprises several interlinked concepts (compare Giddens, 1984, chapter 1). Among these are:

(a) structure and situated social practice, or systems;
(b) practice and action or the capacity for agency;
(c) action and routine/practical knowledge in systems.

Giddens begins with the observation that structures are not objective independent social forces, but the transformation rules among sets of concrete social practices.[1] Structures have only a 'virtual existence', because they exist in time–space as moments recursively involved in the production and reproduction of these *systems* of social practices. Different kinds of systems are related to specific institutional forms and modes of communication. At base, however, are their interaction patterns.

Most action is tracked into systems of routinized social practices. Individuals embody an implicit and practical savoir faire, which enables them to carry out these routines: they are 'knowing actors'. Giddens deliberately attempts to recenter the lay actor, as a reaction to the depreciation of routine action in much structuralist and functionalist social theory. Thus, the production of interaction qua systems of practice is the contingent accomplishment of knowledgeable social actors, and individual action is subsequently embedded in these practices.

Systems *change* because the purposive actions of individuals often have unintended effects, notwithstanding the fact that actors are knowledgeable; in turn, changes in situated social practices determine the survival of structures. The *reproduction* of systems is accomplished by the same knowledgeable actors: their choices to act or not to act mean that structures are reproduced only in the instant, in action. Structures exercise no functional control over individuals. They cannot provide the basis for an historical teleology, not even of a probabilistic character.

Giddens explicitly compares structure, system, and action with the architecture of Saussure's structural linguistics, in which *langue*, or generative grammar and syntax, is differentiated from *parole*, or the use of the grammar and syntax in individual action. Unlike Saussure, however, Giddens views individuals as knowledgeable actors who create social practices in using the grammar and syntax, and who in fact determine the evolution of the grammar and syntax itself. To Derrida's notion of a given nonrepresentational *différance*, Giddens proposes humanly created and representationally generated meanings to social practices which are subsequently embedded in routines.

Giddens's theory is logically appealing in that he attempts to inject a new humanism into social theory while recognizing the existence of power, structure, and direction in history. Nonetheless, it contains a number of unresolved tensions between agency and structure: Giddens vacillates between voluntarism, functionalism, and domination. I want to make three specific sympathetic criticisms of Giddens. First, Giddens does not advance a positive notion of the springs of human action. Giddens asserts that actors are able to go beyond situated practices because they are *knowing*. Important for geographers is Giddens's emphasis on the creation of knowledge in time- and space-differentiated practice (see Thrift, 1983). Still, his action theory is ambiguous, for routine is the basis both for situated social practices and for the knowledge that underlies free action. Since these phenomena are conflated, change is relegated to the realm of unintended effects and the systems come to appear as strongly functionalist structures (section 3).

Second, in the face of this weak basis for action, Giddens's rejection of functionalism and evolutionism rests on a radical denial of structure, that is, on the claim that structures do not do anything. He asserts that structure is merely instantiated in action. Since this voluntarist conception might appear to randomize history, Giddens introduces transcendent power as the glue that holds systems together – thus, we have voluntarism as possibility and domination as reality (section 4). Conversely, Giddens does not make it clear how some instances of human agency end up in the creation of reproduced properties, whereas others fall into the heap of trivial particularities of history. This is because action and interaction are self-referential and identical to his concept of structure: there is no signified–signifier difference. In contrast to this combination, action and structure, my third point is that the material foundations of structures are real and are to some extent autonomous from interaction (section 5). Moreover, we can see that institutions are reproduced through strategies, which admit of a role for *discursive* as well as practical knowledge (section 6).

3 Practical Knowledge or Strategic Intentionality?

Giddens takes structuralism – both linguistic and Marxist – to task for its implicit adoption of a functionalist model of social causality. Structuralism assigns the object (whether *langue* or society) a position prior to that of the subject, and treats society as if it were an emergent totality.

Yet, he does not subscribe to individualist action theories; he rejects both the intentionalist view of motivation as rooted in discursive conscious reasoning and the psychological conception of perceptions, interpretations, or motivations as completely unknown to the actor (the basis for functionalism and structuralism). Giddens is sympathetic to the notion that social action is structured since there are vast realms of individual action which cannot be explained by their authors discursively, and so much of social history seems to be intended by no one. His problem, then, is how social history can be ordered but not determined, and individual action free but not random. His solution is to propose a kind of 'unintentionally intentional' action, based on practical, or nondiscursive, knowledge.

> The reasons actors supply discursively for their conduct in the course of practical queries, in the context of daily social life, stand in a relation of some tension to the rationalisation of action as actually embodied within the stream of conduct of the agent. The least interesting or consequential aspect of this concerns the possibilities of deliberate dissimulation that exist: where an actor claims to have acted for reasons that he was not in fact guided by. More important are the grey areas of practical conscious-ness that exist in the relation between the rationalisation of action and actors' stocks of knowledge ... (Giddens, 1979, page 58).

Giddens advances the notion of intentionality as process.

> Such intentionality is a routine feature of human conduct, and does not imply that actors have definite goals consciously held in mind during the course of their activities (1979, page 56).

The knowledge underlying this type of action is

> not usually known to (those) actors in explicitly codified form; the practical character of such knowledge conforms to the Wittgensteinian

formulation of knowing a rule. The accounts actors are able to provide of their reasons are bounded, or subject to various degrees of possible articulation, in respect of tacitly employed mutual knowledge (1979, page 58).

This knowledge is the point at which the external, supraindividual, social world would impinge upon the formation of motivations and action. Because it is the key link in Giddens's 'structuration' model of social process, this concept of knowledge deserves very close scrutiny.

I want to argue here that Giddens does not adequately specify how human agency can be based on nondiscursive practical knowledge. Practical knowledge is itself a *product* of structured interaction in time and space. It is unclear how it can both produce interaction and be produced by it. As things now stand, his action theory is therefore potentially functionalist itself. To see this we must review the functionalism debate. This I do briefly in section 3.1, after which I return more directly to Giddens's knowledge/action (section 3.2).

3.1 Functionalism and Action

Functionalism differs from intentionalism in that the evolution of an institution, system, or behavioral pattern is *unintended* and *unrecognized* by the members of the beneficiary group, but is maintained by a causal feedback loop passing through the beneficiaries.[2] In functionalist biology, individuals compete according to the behavioral rule of 'local maximization' or 'gradient climbing'. This sets up a process of natural selection, the outcome of which is equilibrium. The social equivalent is maximization behavior in economics. Under the condition of perfect competition, individual maximization generates equilibrium outcomes.

Two basic mechanisms can underlie functionalism in sociology. In the 'strong' version of functionalist causality, the unintended and unrecognized consequences of behavior are generated by and contribute to the reproduction of structures. The 'weak' version is maintenance through feedback: a 'filter' mechanism is used to select and develop some of these consequences and eliminate those not functional to the structure. Wright (1978) advances a typical argument for the latter version of functionalist explanation in sociology. History, in this view, is characterized by all manner of 'creative' actions and intentional strategies, which are equivalent in sociology to random mutations in biology. For example, the structures of capitalism, through feedback loops, 'select' out nonfunctional forms and 'develop' functional ones, by allowing them to 'transform' existing institutions.

Since Giddens concentrates his critique on the implicit functionalism within much Marxist analysis, we may take as an example the reproduction of capitalist accumulation. Giddens holds that it is functionalist to claim that capitalism will fall as a result of the tendency for the rate of profit to fall.

Profit rates, after all, are restored with the resumption of each long wave of accumulation because of the introduction of new technologies and changes in capital–labor relations that are made possible during depressions (Mishra, 1979). Thus the downfall of capitalism as a result of the tendency for the rate of profit to fall must be contingent upon a *social–political crisis* in which *people* actively reject capitalism (Shaikh, 1980). Reproduction or failure would not be contingent only if action were filtered so as to make this social crisis inevitable. This is the 'class struggle' version of functionalist Marxism. Alternatively, failure might occur if, somehow, technological innovations were filtered so as to prevent those which offset the rising organic composition of capital from ever gaining popularity, even among the innovators themselves: this is the 'economistic' version of crisis theory. Giddens (and others, for example, Elster, 1979) points out that this logic involves a simplistic reification of structure because there is no intermediating action theory between the macroeconomic structures of capitalism and concrete outcomes. If the selection mechanisms themselves are contingent, then they are not mechanisms. If they are mechanisms, action is determined and reproduction is assured.

Giddens does not consider the 'strong' version of functionalism, however. In biology, there are instances of nonmaximizing behavior, as when individuals contribute fewer than the maximum numbers of offspring to a gene pool. This can be explained functionally as behavior that is *preadapted* to avoidance of the risk of exhaustion, sacrificing in the short run to make the attainment of a long-run *maximum* for the species more likely. Non-maximizing behavior leads to a structural optimum in the long run. Reproduction, in this case, is the consequence of 'dispositional facts' of the structure (or its necessary internal relations), that is, it is a property of the structure (organism in biology) prior to acquiring the trait that such traits would enhance its survival rate.

> Such dispositional facts make it possible to reconcile the normal meaning of 'causation' in which causes are temporally prior to effects, with functional explanation, in which effects are taken to explain the structures around them (Cohen, 1978, page 64).

Althusser (1969) extends the strong version of functionalism to social theory, but his task is even more complex than in biology, since he attempts simultaneously to account both for the stability of capitalism and for the certainty of its ultimate collapse, in the notion of 'overdetermination'. Capitalism has a strong tendency toward its own survival, but it is doomed to create the conditions in which its reproduction does not occur. For the latter to happen, a *series* of conditions must be combined; this is a 'threshold' theory of contradiction. How is this threshold crossed? If only by accident then preadaptation of individual actions may be perfectly functional, with contradiction activated only at the level of the macropolitical economy. Some coincidence in space and time would be necessary to activate the macro-contradiction in the face of functionalist preadaptation of the microcomponents of society. As a theory of history this type of probabilistic reasoning is philosophically meaningless, because it depends on random events.

Instead, structural overdetermination must mean that reproduction and failure (as a result of the series of conditions) are natural necessities of the structure, that is, they are inscribed in its *logic*. But how can a mechanism that today produces success tomorrow produce failure? In the case of over-determination, the preadaptation mechanism per se must perform *correctly*, but its underlying logic must be unworkable over the long run. The mechanism preadapts changes in forms, such as technology, but this maintains a drift toward catastrophe. This is possible in a game-theoretic sense, but only under the condition that the drift is essentially unidirectional. A slide toward catastrophe occurs with each move and countermove by the relevant actors, because the switching point from reproduction and toward failure is a mechanical event and not due to change in behaviors at the individual level. At the microlevel, in other words, overdetermination consists of something like a mathematical catastrophe model.

For example, in the strong functionalist view, a social crisis associated with the tendency for the rate of profit to fall is overdetermined to occur *because* technologies *cannot be found* to resolve the problem posed by the rising organic composition of capital; the tendency is a secular trend rather than a cyclical phenomenon (Dumenil et al, 1984a; 1984b). In this view there is some a priori reason why technologies can never be used to resolve the organic composition of the capital problem (either through the laws of physics or through microeconomic behavioral rules regarding knowledge and its application). Moreover, it must additionally be the case that, at some point in the process of rising organic composition, capitalists will cease to tolerate lowered levels of profits, and workers will simultaneously refuse to tolerate lower levels of wages. In other words, it must be shown that both the active and the latent sources of the crisis are overdetermined to occur. Althusser's nonmaximizing model of preadapted behavior differs from the biological model only in the *negative* outcome, but it is equally functionalist in its causal reasoning.

3.2 Practical Knowledge and Functionalist Behavior

Giddens asserts that, but does not make it clear how, structuration via practical knowledge differs from functionalism in which structural requirements preadapt action. His emphasis on practical knowledge as derived from routine activity, and as nondiscursive and implicit, resembles what is conventionally known as parametric rationality. The maximizing entrepreneur in a neoclas-sical economic model is just this kind of actor. In a pure equilibrium economy the individual is merely a 'decisiontaker' whose actions have unintended consequences. Under competitive conditions, they are selected and the outcome insures structural stability. This includes 'entrepreneurial' behavior as well as what might be thought of as routine decisions. Individuals cannot change the course of history.

Giddens's claim that actors really can exercise agency is based on the assertion that they go beyond parametric rationality to use practical knowledge of the rules in a *creative* way. There appear to be two sources of such creativity in Giddens's theory. First is the formation of motivations, which was touched on earlier. Although actors may not be able to supply accurate discursive descriptions of their motivations, they nonetheless are not guided by hidden or unconscious purposes. Second is something I have not yet mentioned, which is the actor's own reflexive monitoring and rationalization of subsequent actions.

Practical knowledge, however, is that which is necessary to 'get on' in a world which reflects supraindividual forces. Giddens does not tell us why practical knowledge itself is not a preadapted dispositional fact of the source structure, which would negate both of these sources of creativity by rendering them contentless. For example, neoclassical economics has been able to accommodate short-run 'satisficing' and reflexive monitoring of action (for example, long-run dynamic equilibrium via imperfect competition).

Sociological explanation in general is not restricted to the forms derived from the natural sciences. Conversely, Wright, a defender of functionalism, admits that if we reject functionalism in biology, then it certainly has no place in sociological explanation (Wright, 1983, page 16). Indeed, in biology, functionalism is being challenged by more historical forms of explanation. As Gould (1977) and others (for example, Thompson, 1978) have noted, a critical gap appears in the conception of change in natural selection theories. It seems impossible for important morphological jumps to occur in organisms under conditions of parametric stability or even under conditions of rapid parametric change.[3] These are explainable only as some type of 'self-evolution' through problem-solving behavior. This problem-solving behavior is the product of strategic action in which organisms must be capable of using indirect approaches and waiting now for a result later, thus possibly discovering a *new* way out of a dilemma. In natural history, gradualism has been challenged by the notion that order is temporary: it is the outcome of strategies formulated through the exercise of *non*parametric rationality. Here I am not referring to nonmaximizing behavior strictly of the submaximizing variety; I am including supermaximizing strategic effort. Occasionally, major new mutations (inventions) occur, and these are the outcomes of radical departures from past practices, not merely 'knowing how to do'.

Giddens rejects functionalism because of the way it derogates the lay actor in his/her routine state, but in turn he rederogates the lay actor by placing his greatest emphasis on the continuation of routines and on breaking them only as the unintended consequence of purposive action (compare Giddens, 1984, pages 293–295).

Strategic intentionality in social life is a product of the fact that individuals take account of the existence of other actors in the environment.[4] Human actors must

> not only make their choices on the basis of expectations about the future ... but also on the basis of their expectations about the expectations of others.... Each individual reflect(s) the totality from his point of view. The transparency and symmetry of this interaction ensures that the fate of the actors is in their own hands, whereas a community of parametrically rational actors will be in the grip of causal forces that elude them and that perpetually make their plans come to naught (Elster, 1979, page 19).

Intentionality implies neither maximizing behavior (as in rational expectations in neoclassical economics) nor a denial of the possibility for certain forms of collective solidarity (it does not necessarily conform to Mancur Olson's logic) (Elster, 1979). It does imply, however, that individuals can contribute to their own evolution, and to the evolution of their system, by trying to solve problems in a variety of ways. Moreover, there is a great diversity of motivations in solving problems and seeking gratification, which may involve internal conflict and contradiction as well as conflict between the actor and other actors or institutions. Giddens's notions of routine and practical knowledge must be integrated with a recognition of the complexity of biography formation and of the multiplicity and simultaneity of structuring processes at work.

People are structurally *enabled* to invent new forms of activity, technology, and commerce all the time because of the ways these complex motivations can be organized into projects by strategic actors and by collectivities with strategic leaders. This is a principal basis for institutional change. These projects may be in part the outcomes of prior routines, but they involve the ability to go beyond those routines, to take chances (Pred, 1984). Such projects may have unanticipated and unintended consequences but neither these consequences nor those which are intended are preadapted. A critical disagreement with Giddens, then, is the emphasis here on purposeful projects and their institutionalization (in the time-geographic sense used by Pred), as opposed to routines – the two are not identical although they may overlap.

In one sense, the criticism of Giddens advanced here is consistent with his overall perspective that social life is nonunitary, because it is rooted in time–space differentiated interaction systems in which practices are embedded. But, in my view, this time–space differentiation implies more than the reproduction of practical knowledge based on the routines associated with the interaction system. Complex strategies are possible, as people formulate projects based on the knowledge, motivations, and possibilities stemming from the multiple structuring processes present within any interaction system. It is necessary, then, to realize that practical knowledge in any interaction system refers not simply to the routine and nondiscursive, but to an extremely complex and contradictory set of inputs and impulses that give rise to strategic intentions. Two dimensions of this complexity are explored further in sections 5 and 6, but first we must turn to Giddens's notion of power.

4 Power and the Radical Denial of Structure

Giddens meets his weak action theory with its opposite, a radical denial of structure. This denial leaves intact the weak basis of human agency I identified in the previous section, but only by virtue of the lack of any strong structure to counter it. More problematically, he then introduces a non-structural notion of power which – *without functionalism* – results in a view of history-as-domination, completely in contrast to the voluntarism implied in his denial of structure.

Structures for Giddens "exist in time–space only as moments recursively involved in the production and reproduction of social systems" (1981, page 26). Giddens stresses that practices are 'instantiated' only in action, but in turn practices recursively instantiate structures: they are literally produced in the moment of action. Instantiation is therefore a 'radical' rejection of reified structure.

Giddens distinguishes his view from that of linguistic structuralism. In the latter, the generative grammar may force a certain coherence on the overall symbol structure by defining positions from which truth claims and meanings follow, but the content of symbols is entirely arbitrary. For Giddens, these truth claims and meanings are also intersubjectively defined, but the underlying properties and the possibilities for transforming them are rooted in human practical activity. Thus, the positions of symbols cannot be taken for granted when we move from unconscious motivations or mythical processes into practical activity. Giddens departs from the ideas of Saussure and Derrida and attempts to extend those of Wittgenstein, arguing for expanded notions of *différance* when analysing practical activity. Content and meaning are products of human agency because they result from social spacing (*langage* rather than *langue*). Moreover, signifier and signified cannot be combined: referents to practical activity are required and they imply some notion of 'practical spacing'. Giddens's hermeneutics are therefore embedded meanings which are referential, intersubjective, and subject to change.

Giddens's claims are contradictory: the generative grammar itself is instantiated, but it is based on *signified* as well as signifier. How can instantiation be possible if signified and signifier are different? The answer, it seems to me, is found in Giddens's analysis of power. The theme of power is touched upon in his 1979 book, *Central Problems in Social Theory*, but it emerges as the full-blown object of historical practice in *A Contemporary Critique of Historical Materialism* (1981), very much in keeping with the wave of interest in Foucault sweeping the anglophone world. Giddens preserves individual agency based on practical knowledge as a theoretical possibility, but he emphasizes that human history is really that of domination because the *object* of agency is power.

Power is "rooted in the very nature of human agency, and thus in the 'freedom to act otherwise'" (1981, page 4; 1984, page 14). It is the result of practices that produce interaction upon which structures of domination rest. These structures of domination-cum-interaction can take the form of control over allocative resources or control over authoritative resources. Interaction is regulated through time–space 'presenting and absencing' (1979, chapters 3–6; 1981, chapter 4; 1984, chapter 3). Giddens in his historical analysis characterizes capitalist society as control over allocation, and noncapitalist societies as domination through authority (1984, page 258). But, Giddens's recognition of the importance of the market system (allocative power) does not mean that he endorses the concept of mode of production as the basis of social analysis. Even the allocative power characteristic of capitalist society cannot be understood, for Giddens, independent of the increasing surveillance capabilities located in the state in these societies. This surveillance threatens us with totalitarianism (1984, pages 261–262). Indeed, Giddens (like Foucault) chastizes Marx for being naive with respect to power, claiming that it is a universal outcome of social practice, and not a specific outcome of private property. Thus, in capitalism, surveillance and mobilization are possible when interaction in time–space is appropriately arranged. Each mode of production is associated with a particular form of time–space distanciation and its attendant form of power (1981, page 155; 1984, page 119).

Notice that some people use their nondiscursive practices in time and space (as the source of subjective agency) to channel the interactions of others in order to perpetuate power and domination: some signifiers use the time–space differentiations of the environment to structure interaction to use, or deny, the agency of other actors. *Giddens advances a transcendental idea of time–space practice*: practice/interaction always leads to practice/power. There is no other independent referential base for the establishment of power in society. For those who are dominated, the pattern of interaction, or the signified, is what steers their lives. Their agency as signifiers has been eliminated (compare Giddens, 1984, pages 258–262).

Ironically, Giddens – the arch antistructuralist – falls into the same trap as do nonmaterialist or nonhistorical structuralists. Anderson (1983) demonstrates that the attack on the subject by putting the linguistic notion of structure at the center of historical and economic analysis ultimately *destroyed* any coherent definition of structure by rendering it arbitrary:

What Derrida had seen, acutely, was that the supposition of any stable structure had always been dependent on the silent postulation of a centre that was not entirely 'subject' to it: in other words, of a *subject* distinct *from* it. His decisive move was to liquidate the last vestige of such autonomy. The result, however, was not to achieve a higher-order, now entirely purified structure, but the very contrary: the effect was a radically *destructuring* one. For, once structures were freed from any subject at all, delivered over totally to their own play, they would lose what *defines* them as structures – that is, any objective coordinates of organization at all (Anderson, 1983, page 54).

This leads Anderson to conclude that the 'other side' of linguistic structuralism is not the evolutionary functionalism for which Marx has been criticized, but the 'randomization of history'.

Giddens appears, at first glance, to turn this around. He rejects structuralism and celebrates the subject. In replacing structure with instantiation he implies that interaction (like speech) is ultimately freely producible and it only subsequently comes to be routinized or embedded: "power is not a static quantity but expandable in relation to divergent forms of system property" (1984, page 260). Although interaction can be changed through the exercise of agency, in Giddens's schema, when Giddens's radical denial of structure is carried to its logical conclusion, there can be only one basis for the persistence of structures, and that is a universal will-to-power on the part of some actors who creatively use underlying rules to shape interaction, routines, and practical knowledge. With totalitarianism will there be an end to historical development through the total domination of time and space (compare Giddens, 1984, page 262)? The implicit view of history here is as a flat process, the drama eliminated through total domination. This is precisely the point on which Foucault has been roundly criticized (compare Dreyfus and Rabinow, 1982). Giddens leaves us with the voluntarism of instantiation alongside the transhistorical pursuit of power (compare Giddens, 1984, page 258).

5 The Realness of Structure 1: Instantiation versus the Material

There is a methodological inconsistency involved in Giddens's definition of structure. Structures are identified as the "transformation and mediation rules among sets of reproduced properties". Among the latter, Giddens counts resources (1981, page 26). Structures, then, can be inferred only from the existence of empirical regularities (things), but structures themselves are the rules, which in turn are instantiated in practice. Conventionally, the concept of social relations holds that 'rules' are not derived from empirical generalization, but through abstraction (compare Sayer, 1984). Giddens appears to go back on this, in deriving rules from patterns of interaction. It was noted in the previous section that the result is the radical denial of structural force to those rules. Yet, he simultaneously places those instantiated rules in a *position of primacy over the material world, or resources*. Let me quote at length:

> To say that rules are transformational, in the terminology I employ in this book, is to say that they generate an indefinite range of empirical contents, which have an identity with one another only in respect of their relation to those rules. While this may be obvious enough in respect of codes and norms, it is perhaps not so clear how resources involve either mediations or transformations. For resources (for example, property, wealth) might seem to exist in a temporal–spatial sense, in a way in which rules do not. But I want to say that the material existents involved in resources (a) are the content, or the 'vehicles' of resources in a parallel manner to the 'substance' of codes and norms, and (b) as instantiated in power relations in social systems, only operate in conjunction with codes and norms … The transformational character of resources is just as basic as that of rules: which is why I employ the term 'transformational capacity' as an intrinsic feature of human agency. Resources, however, provide the material levers of all transformations of empirical contents, including those involved in the operation of codes and norms (Giddens, 1979, page 104).

Giddens is obviously correct to point out that the social significance of resources is not given, but socially determined. But he implies that human agents use resources only for transformative purposes.

Giddens aptly notes – and this is one of his most important insights – that material resources may serve simultaneously as the foundation for the purposive activities of society and as a container for interaction in time and space. He claims that the city is the locus of authoritative power in noncapitalist societies but that in capitalist societies this is no longer the case. This is because authoritative power rests on dense human habitation with low time–space 'storage capacity', whereas the allocative power of capitalism has high storage capacity and thus no longer requires the city as such (1981, page 94). This is a provocative thesis, but it reduces the story of spatial integration and fragmentation to one of the interaction requirements for different forms of power and leaves out the material requirements of purposeful activities such as production. In attempting to reject the productionist emphasis of much Marxism, Giddens invents his own hyperbole with respect to the purpose of the forces of production: they are merely ways of organizing interaction.

> Irrigation schemes and other technical innovations usually do not so much increase average productivity as regularize and coordinate production (1984, page 259).

Giddens thus does not follow through on his own maxim that signifier and signified cannot be elided.

By contrast, the status of material objects as usable resources has a complex and often uncomfortable relationship to the ways they serve as a container for interaction: for example, cities are complex material products of commodity production in capitalist societies. They often are the loci of resistance to capitalism, yet it has thus far proved impossible to do away with them. And vice versa: the arrangement of interaction systems in real time and space often has an uncomfortable relationship with the production of material resources. The Marxist analysis of the labor process is an example of this tension.

This raises the broader question of Giddens's treatment of the domain of material artifacts in social history. Giddens notes that there are different 'layers of temporality' in social life, from *durée* to *Dasein* to the *longue durée* of institutions, and he 'brackets' the first two while devoting his attention to the latter (1981, page 28). The problem is that, since Giddens sees social history as the spread of interaction per se, his layers of temporality are exclusively concerned with the different endurances of rules and practices. However, history is not just the spread of rules and practices, but also of resources. Each of these has its own spatiotemporal dynamics. Even within the realm of material environments, there are very different temporal characteristics – think of the increasing durability of built environments as one goes from discotheques to factories and, finally, to cities. Each material environment carries with it certain patterns of interaction, and the interactions associated with one may help to change or impede a change in the others.

Resources may thus provide continuity and impede change. It would seem that even if people are endowed with a strong basis for action – the ability to break routines and invent new social and economic forms – there remain some combinations of these *elements* that are possible and others impossible. The *durée* of the material, although not imposing absolute constraints on system change, does mean that at any moment not everything is possible. For example, the acceptance of technological innovations is highly dependent on what else exists, no matter what technical path might represent long-run optimality (compare Nelson and Winter, 1982; Rosenberg, 1982). Whereas all actions contribute to history (trite but true!), some actions become more important to history than do others because they are imitated and come to be felt as external constraints by other individuals. They are 'totalized', in Sartre's words (Sartre, 1963). Giddens does not tackle the question of which impulses find a 'position' that permits them to create new ensembles of practical activity, because he associates this issue with functionalism. It is not functionalist to subscribe to some sort of principle of contradiction, by which the compatibility, or lack of it, among rules and resources may be understood.

We can readily see this by looking at historical materialism, one of the theories to which Giddens offers his own as a superior alternative. To take up

Marx's problem, let us (somewhat crudely) substitute 'relations of production' for rules and 'forces of production' for resources. Marx implied that productive forces 'determine' or 'condition' the relations of production, but he also repeatedly asserted that relations of production have a decisive effect on the forces, being successively forms of development and fetters on technical change. Much Marxist literature is, of course, simply an evasion of this question via the use of generalities such as 'determination in the long run', and 'dialectical processes'.

Cohen (1978), however, suggests that the relations of production are what they are because of their ability to promote the development of the productive forces, and they change when they no longer have this ability. In Cohen's functionalist view, the relations could 'select' the forces likely to perpetuate the existence of the structure, but this logic has already been rejected. Could it not be, alternatively, that the relations have a *causal* primacy over the forces, but the forces have an *explanatory* primacy over the relations? The relations are necessary to the full development of the productive forces, but there is *something else* which determines what relations actually arise historically and further develop the productive forces. The most likely candidate here is the set of concrete details of centuries of class struggle, which nothing can predict (think of the difference between England and France in the emergence of capitalist relations of production). Where such relations are perfected, they are extremely functional – so the historical evidence suggests – in promoting the development of the productive forces, which in turn reproduces the relations. In this sense, the forces can be said to explain the diffusion and dominance of the relations via a criterion of functionality (Elster, 1983). On the other hand, the formation of these relations cannot be derived functionally and, indeed, the existence of capitalist forces of production is not a sufficient condition for development and diffusion of relations: the state of capitalism in many Third World countries is a perfect example of the way that capitalist forces of production do not necessarily or easily cause perfected capitalist relations of production to come into being, and thus to diffuse throughout those societies the systems of interaction on which the full growth of capitalism is predicated. This calls into question Giddens's blithe assertions about the transformative capacity of resources.

Conversely, they may on occasion effectively insinuate property, technologies, and commodities (in the sense used by Marx, as unfetishized commodities that carry social relations) into societies, and this is bound to have powerful long-run impacts on the development of rules. This scenario resembles Giddens's portrait of the material existents of resources as vehicles of transformation, but differs in the critical respect that this relationship between resources, interaction, and rules is seen here as extremely *problematic*, *lagged*, and *differentiated* in time and space.

To sum the argument of this section: in Giddens's theory, interaction, practical knowledge, and power are all consequences of the same set of routines in any given system of practice. They are instantiated, and their reproduced properties are structures. This view, however, denies the realness of structures, for there are no outside referents or important lags and differentiations among these properties.

I have suggested, in contrast, that there are some nonself-constitutive bases of the possibilities and problems of practices, and this ground of possibilities makes the structure nonrandom and not merely instantiated. It also is the source of problems that gives any structure its openness and dynamism. One example of this referential ground of possibilities and problems is the set of material forces of production. This, in my view, makes structures more 'real' than Giddens implies in the term 'instantiation'. To claim that structures are more real is not to argue that there is *more*, or *less*, of a role for human agency than in Giddens's theory, but that there is a differentiated (and thus limited) topography for the exercise of that agency, rather than an endlessly recursive plain.

The use of the term 'real' immediately suggests, of course, the concept of realism in philosophy which is now associated with Bhaskar (1975; 1979) and most thoroughly articulated in geography by Sayer (1984). Bhaskar and Sayer refer to the 'natural necessities' of objects or structures, which are derived via scientific method of abstraction of their necessary internal relations. A formal separation is made between these necessary relations and external, or contingent, forces. Put in terms of the example presented above concerning the forces and relations of production, the forces and relations are internally related elements of capitalism. On an historical level, the relations are necessary to development of the forces, but *both* are contingent upon something else and thus not at all deterministically related in history. The realness of structure, as I have used it here, does not take issue with these dimensions of realism, but combines definitional and historical reasoning. The structure we identify definitionally *exists* only as a concrete totality both of the necessary relations and of the historically contingent processes, as they have actually developed. Here, I have concentrated on material things, whose nature Sartre so aptly described as 'practico-inert'. The inert artifacts of contemporary structures, as the concrete combinations of both necessary-internal and contingent-external from the past, will influence the *concrete* form of future social practices. This is quite a different sense of real from that which is contained in the theory of internal relations, although not necessarily in conflict with it.

6 The Realness of Structure 2: Discourse Reconsidered

Although Giddens does not seem to ascribe a sufficient role to the *durée* of the material, he does make the distinction between *durée*, *Dasein*, and *longue durée*, separating the quotidian acting out of institutional practices and the biological limits of human life and human memory from the *longue durée* of institutions and rules. Like many other social theorists (especially Habermas), Giddens agrees that this web of different temporalities is woven together through the process of *legitimation*: it is a key to transformation and mediation relations among practices, on the one hand, and rules and resources, on the other. Unlike others, for Giddens, legitimation is nothing more than the outcome of interaction. Practices are "situated within intersecting sets of rules and resources that ultimately express features of the totality" (1979, page 82).

Time and space are bridged through *communicative interaction* of various sorts:

> ... features of the relation between language and the 'context of use' are of essential importance to social theory. In the production of meaning in interaction, context cannot be treated as merely the 'environment' or 'background' of the use of language. The context of interaction is in some degree shaped and organized as an integral part of that interaction as a communicative encounter (1979, page 83).

There is a 'duality of structure' or structuration process at work in communication: on the one hand, "actors sustain the meaning of what they say and do through routinely incorporating 'what went before' and anticipations of 'what will come next' into the present of an encounter", but they also have some type of 'communicative intent', which is not necessarily discursively known to them. It is the interplay of communicative intent and context as *différance* that represents the duality of structure in this hermeneutic sense. The result is that "signification, as concerning generative properties of structure, is linked recursively to the communication of meaning in interaction" (1979, page 98).

I have just touched upon communicative interaction, but for Giddens, social practices cannot be explicated in terms of a single set of resources or rules. Practices instead are situated within intersecting rules and resources. To see what these intersecting rules and resources are, it is easiest just to reproduce Giddens's matrix below (Giddens, 1979, page 82; 1984, page 29):

Interaction	communication	power	sanction
(Modality)	interpretative scheme	facility	norm
Structure	signification	domination	legitimation

The columns are read as recursive processes: signification, domination, and legitimation depend respectively on interpretative schemes, facilities, and norms, which in turn depend on their forms of interaction – communication, power, and sanction. Each of the rows is also strongly interrelated. The various structures – signification, domination, legitimation – have particular theoretical domains and institutional forms. Each of the structures is imbricated in the institutional forms of the other structures (Giddens, 1984, page 33). Thus, legal institutions exist primarily for legitimation, but they also rest upon signification and domination, and their constituent communicative processes.

Giddens explicitly rejects 'substantivist' views of structures and institutions, that is, the notion that they are actually concretely differentiated, and he makes a good case for why this is so. The problem again comes back to the exclusive emphasis on interaction and practical knowledge as the basis of the communication upon which these institutions are founded. A certain circularity appears in the schema, for communication is tied, via its roots in interaction, to legitimation and domination, but the same interaction, and its practical knowledge, is the source of human agency. Thus, structures and institutions, as defined by Giddens, come to appear merely as different ways of abstractly describing the communicative processes which underlie them, according to the superficial institutional forms they take and by which we label them in official discourse. They do not appear to be different *real* structuring processes; there are no distinct temporal and spatial differentiations among them, not to mention material bases.

Giddens cannot fall back on psychoanalytic (for example, Lacan) or structuralist (Lévi-Strauss) explanations for the sources of hegemonic domination and legitimation. Interestingly, he therefore introduces *strategies* at the level of institutions, but does not tell us how they are connected to individual agency, in the form of the nondiscursive supply of meanings and intentions. In the matrix, Giddens has 'bracketed' institutional analysis, which is where the modalities of practice and structure are worked out.

> ... there is, strictly speaking, no such thing as *an* ideology; there are only ideological aspects of symbol systems.... To analyze the ideological aspects of symbolic orders ... is to examine how structures of signification are mobilized to legitimate the sectoral interests of hegemonic groups (1979, pages 187–188).

Here, then, is a clue to the riddle identified in the previous section: the way in which instantiated structures lead to domination. Somehow *discursive strategies* are being exercised to dominate.

The problem for Giddens's theory is that what is implicit in his methodological bracketing is *logically inadmissible* within the theory of structuration as it now stands. Giddens can admit that nondiscursive knowledge – leading to unanticipated and unknown results – can play a role in practice in the discursive sphere, but this is not the same as strategic action in discursive practice and thus in the production of what Foucault calls 'serious competence rules' (Dreyfus and Rabinow, 1982).

This raises the problem largely ignored by Giddens, that is, the 'relative autonomy of discourse' (Godelier, 1984). Both Foucault and Habermas, although from opposite positions, argue that discursive practice is an arena of direct production of social life, and that both nondiscursive and discursive practices are producers of discursive rules (Foucault, 1972; 1973; Habermas, 1979). Neither of them, of course, resolves all the difficulties surrounding the relationship of discursive practices to other social practices, in either hermeneutic or structural directions. Still, Giddens's emphasis on the nondiscursive and routine is not only a weak basis for practical action, but an unwarranted deemphasis on the discourse of lay and nonlay actors. His hermeneutic is passively involved with interaction to the exclusion of direct action in the interpretive sphere itself, and the complex relationship of the two.

The argument of section 3 can thus be extended to suggest that strategic intentionality can underlie discourse and the production of discursive systems, just as I pointed out that it underlies the production of interaction itself. Discursively supplied reasons or strategies need not be 'rational' in any mathematical sense to bear some real relation to action. And reasons *can* be causes, in the way that expectations may underlie real movements in the economy. Actors are not restricted to the production of meanings in given systems of *différances*; in taking account of the nature of the environment and using indirect as well as direct strategies, and by taking chances, they can conceptualize context and act to change it as well as its constituent terms. Thus, elements and contexts are simultaneously redefined, *not merely through the unintentional and unanticipated consequences of action, but also through intent*. To return to my original point, structures are more real, in yet another respect, than Giddens admits in his notion of instantiation: in addition to the real *durée* of the material, there is the intentional discursive arena of institutions. This discursive dimension of serious competence rules has its own *durée* as documented by Foucault (1972, page 115).

As I have already noted, there are many *longue durées*: practices, the forces of production, rules, and now discursive practices. How all of these *durées* interact cannot be known a priori, but it is more than likely that they do not simply coincide because of their recursive nature. They remain highly differentiated in time and in space. The problem is that Giddens's theory, even with its essential involvement with time–space differentiation, does not suggest these lines of inquiry, which should be of central importance to contemporary human geography and to all the social sciences.

7 Action, System, and Structure: Summary

This reexamination of Giddens's contribution is sympathetic to much of the theoretical agenda he identifies. It is necessary to resituate human action, and to reject explanations based on functionalism, the reification of structure, and evolutionism. Giddens's reformulation of action theory as a theory of practices situated in interaction milieux which are defined, in a large part, by their time–space characteristics is of seminal importance to contemporary human geography. His additional concern with hermeneutics and power is also of great interest, insofar as he sees these processes as grounded in time–space relations.

Several problems and inconsistencies arise in Giddens's reformulation, however. Although Giddens deplores the depreciation of the lay actor in structuralism, he does not go very far to recenter human agency, neglecting to consider the complexity of structuring processes and the diversity of strategies and intentions that arise – these are not conveyed in his emphasis on routines and practical knowledge. The result is a *weak* action theory that cannot meet the need identified in his own critique of structuralism. The weakness of the action theory is then apparently compensated for by a radical denial of the realness of structure. Structure is reduced to the recursive product of instantiated systems which are given no other substantive basis for their internal coherence, or for their grip on lay actors, than routine interaction.

This basic problem creates complications for the analysis of historical change using Giddens's theory. His copious writings include an explicit view of historical change, which he describes as the 'episodic' crossing of critical 'time–space edges' (1981, page 82; 1984, page 244). But the mechanics of the theory of structuration do not make explicit Giddens's view of how these thresholds are actually crossed, and thus why we should conceive of structure, practice, and change, theoretically, via the particular category of time–space distanciation. Indeed, the corpus of his theorizing contains several contradictory images of historical processes. When the human capacity for agency is referred to, and practical knowledge is emphasized, history appears as the gradual replacement of one set of routines by another. This view is consistent with Giddens's concern with the processes of daily life, which are also a major focus of research in the new social history and the new historical sociology. Like the impossibility in evolutionary theory in biology of getting from one morphology to another through changes generated by routine behavior, it is difficult to get from incremental change in Giddens's systems to the grand movements of history. On the other hand, when structure itself is considered, this capacity for agency is elevated to the point where history is completely open, the product of instantiation, and Giddens is a voluntarist. Where power and domination are involved, an idealist notion of history as power seeking implicitly reasserts itself. When material life is considered, it is subservient to the drive for power, and merely a byproduct of the attempt of the powerful to organize the time–space resources of society. Finally, when institutions are involved, strategies slip back in, but we are not told how.

In the critique of Giddens advanced here I add to routine action the variety of strategies that people exercise in undertaking projects, and thus provide a stronger basis for human agency and historical contingency. Coupled to this more vibrant view of human agency, however, is the possibility that structures may be more real than Giddens seems willing to admit. The practico-inert quality of the material and the role of resources in the transformation and mediation relations among reproduced properties were noted. Moreover, discursively supplied reasons, whether 'accurate' or not (and Giddens's own hermeneutics of suspicion are contrary to his emphasis on the centrality of the lay actor!), may be the consequence of direct historical action in the discursive sphere, and so they should be the focus of attention in their own right. The episodic crossing of time–space edges, then, is not a self-referential process: it is imbricated in a whole series of other purposeful social processes and domains of action.

These comments suggest that the reinterpretation of modern social life via attention to the time–space dimensions of interaction should not be reduced to a narrow concentration on routines, practical knowledge, and unintended outcomes. Strategic behavior, material resources and the inert quality of the material, and discursive institutional processes are prime candidates for the empirical research on the roles of time–space distanciation now emerging in human geography and the other social sciences.

Indeed, Giddens's concentration on interaction, practical knowledge, and unintended outcomes begins to sound neo-Weberian when scrutinized closely: society seems to emerge from the imperatives of some essential characteristics of human social interaction. The missing links in Giddens's analytics – strategic behavior, material resources, and discursive institutional processes – were, of course, not ignored by the Weberians. But they do raise all those questions about whether there are not, after all, some overarching structural relations within which these processes are enabled to unfold.

Acknowledgements

I wish to thank Allen Scott, Allan Pred, Susan Christopherson, Susanna Hecht, Richard Walker, and three anonymous referees for comments on previous drafts of this paper. I also thank participants in the California Social Theory Group Meeting, Monterey, 1984, for general stimulation. The usual disclaimers apply.

Notes

1. Thus, although Giddens intends the use of the term 'system' to carry a different meaning than its use in 'systems analysis', they end up with some similarities. Systems analysis is devoted to discovering the logic of stable systems, founded upon the principle of cybernetics. Here, systems are achieved forms of social practices, which emerge from particular historical circumstances and function via an achieved

internal logic. Both function as systems of interaction, and patterns of interaction are structures. This is very different than structures in the sense used by Marx, as sets of underlying relations, defined internally via each other.

2. The classic statements are found in Radcliffe-Brown (1952), Merton (1949), and Parsons (1951). Elster's (1979, page 28) definition of functionalism in sociology is that "an institution or a behavioral pattern *X* is explained by its function *Y* for group *Z* if and only if:

1. *Y* is an *effect of X*;
2. *Y* is *beneficial* for *Z*;
3. *Y* is *unintended* by the actors producing *X*;
4. *Y* (or at least the causal relationship between *X* and *Y*) is *unrecognized* by the actors in *Z*;
5. *Y* maintains *X* by a causal feedback loop passing through *Z*".

3. One of the major examples cited by Gould (1977) is the formation of wings on birds. If by natural selection, at what point does the terrestrial appendage turn into a wing? Would it not, long before that, have become *dysfunctional* for the species having it, causing it to disappear? It does not seem possible to get from the terrestrial appendage to the wing via gradualist natural selection.

4. For Giddens's views on intentionality, see Giddens (1984, pages 8–12).

References

Abrams P, 1982 *Historical Sociology* (Cornell University Press, Ithaca, NY)

Althusser L, 1969 *For Marx* (Penguin Books, Harmondsworth, Middx)

Anderson P, 1983 *In the Tracks of Historical Materialism* (Verso, London)

Bhaskar R, 1975 *A Realist Theory of Science* (Leeds Books, Leeds)

Bhaskar R, 1979 *The Possibility of Naturalism* (Harvester Press, Brighton, Sussex)

Cardoso F, Faletto E, 1976 *Dependency and Development in Latin America* 2nd edition (University of California Press, Berkeley, CA)

Cohen G A, 1978 *Marx's Theory of History: A Defense* (Oxford University Press, Oxford)

Dreyfus H, Rabinow P, 1982 *Michel Foucault: Beyond Structuralism and Hermeneutics* (University of Chicago Press, Chicago, IL)

Dumenil G, Glick M, Rangel J, 1984a, "La baisse de la rentabilité du capital aux États-Unis aux recherches et mise en perspective historique" *Observations et Diagnostiques Economiques* **6** 103–118

Dumenil G, Glick M, Rangel J, 1984b, "The tendency of the rate of profit to fall in the United States, part II" unpublished paper, OFCE, Université de Paris X (Nanterre), 92000 Nanterre

Elster J, 1979 *Ulysses and the Sirens: Studies in Rationality and Irrationality* (Cambridge University Press, Cambridge)

Elster J, 1983 *Explaining Technical Change* (Cambridge University Press, Cambridge)

Foucault M, 1972 *The Archaeology of Knowledge* translated by A M Sheridan Smith (Harper Colophon, New York)

Foucault M, 1973 *The Order of Things: An Archaeology of the Human Sciences* (Vintage Books, New York)

Giddens A, 1979 *Central Problems in Social Theory* (University of California Press, Berkeley, CA)

Giddens A, 1981 *A Contemporary Critique of Historical Materialism* (University of California Press, Berkeley, CA)

Giddens A, 1984 *The Constitution of Society* (University of California Press, Berkeley, CA)

Godelier M, 1984 *L'Ideel et le Materiel* (Fayard, Paris)

Gould S J, 1977 *Ever Since Darwin* (W W Norton, New York)

Habermas J, 1979 *Communication and the Evolution of Society* (Beacon Press, Boston, MA)

Harvey D, 1982 *The Limits to Capital* (University of Chicago Press, Chicago, IL)

Jay M, 1984 *Marxism and Totality* (University of California Press, Berkeley, CA)

Merton R K, 1949 *Social Theory and Social Structure* (Free Press, New York)

Mishra R, 1979, "Technology and social structure in Marx's theory: an exploratory analysis" *Science and Society* **43** 132–157

Nelson R R, Winter S G, 1982 *An Evolutionary Theory of Economic Change* (Harvard University Press, Cambridge, MA)

Parsons T, 1951 *The Social System* (Free Press, New York)

Pred A, 1984, "Structuration, biography formation, and knowledge: observations on port growth during the late mercantile period" *Environment and Planning D: Society and Space* **2** 251–275

Radcliffe-Brown A R, 1952 *Structure and Function in Primitive Societies* (Cohen and West, London)

Rosenberg N, 1982 *Inside the Black Box: Technology and Economics* (Cambridge University Press, Cambridge)

Sartre J-P, 1963 *The Search for a Method* (Alfred Knopf, New York)

Saunders P, 1981 *Social Theory and the Urban Question* (Cambridge University Press, Cambridge)

Sayer A, 1984 *Method in Social Sicnece: A Realist Approach* (Hutchinson, London)

Shaihk A, 1980, "The transformation from Marx to Sraffa" manuscript, New School for Social Research, 66 Fifth Avenue, New York City

Thompson E P, 1978 *The Poverty of Theory* (Merlin Press, London)

Thrift N J, 1983, "On the determination of social action in space and time" *Environment and Planning D: Society and Space* **1** 23–57

Tilly C, 1981 *As Sociology Meets History* (Academic Press, New York)

Wright E O, 1978 *Class, Crisis and the State* (New Left Books, London)

Wright E O, 1983, "Giddens' critique of Marxism" *New Left Review* **138** March–April issue, 11–35

48

On Duality and Dualism: The Case of Structuration and Time Geography*

N. Gregson

*Source: *Progress in Human Geography*, vol. 10, 1986, pp. 184–205.

A common feature of research in the social sciences is the diffusion of ideas or concepts, theories and methods. In this human geography is no exception. As Agnew and Duncan (1981) have observed, human geographers frequently import ideas from other social sciences and promote them within the discipline. However, as they go on to maintain, such procedures require cautionary use, at the very least an appreciation of the origins of ideas and their full implications. Indeed, without this knowledge it is but a short step to the type of situation described by Agnew and Duncan, in which ideas are transferred to human geography as they stand, in which little justification is given for their transfer, and in which evaluations of such procedures tend to be lacking. One recent import into human geography comes from social theory. This is Anthony Giddens's theory of structuration (Giddens, 1976; 1977; 1979; 1981; 1984). This paper provides an assessment of the import value of some of Giddens's ideas, something which is important for human geographers, not only because the number of references to structuration in the human geography literature is increasing but because Giddens himself has drawn increasingly on the work of human geographers, in particular that of Hägerstrand and his ideas regarding time geography.

I The Theory of Structuration and its Introduction to Human Geography

It is one thing to grasp what the theory of structuration entails . . . but quite another to incorporate its theorems into substantive accounts in such a way that one captures the engagements between agency and structure which are the fulcrum of the whole formulation (Gregory, 1984, 129).

Although complex in both its details and implications, the theory of structuration can be summarized as emphasizing the interdependence of human agency and social structure in time and space. There are two dimensions to this statement. On the one hand Giddens is arguing that individuals and society, two of the grand categories of social theory, cannot be theorized in isolation. Neither can they be construed as the individual *and* society. Instead both must be theorized together, as the individual *in* society and as society *in* individuals, or, as Abrams puts it,

> The problem of agency is the problem of finding a way of accounting for human experience which recognises simultaneously and in equal measure that history and society are made by constant and more or less purposeful individual action *and* that individual action, however purposeful, is made by history and society (1982, xiii).

The second point which Giddens stresses in his theory of structuration represents his most important and original contribution to social theory. This is to recognize that agency and structure are temporarily and spatially specific, that societies and individuals are embedded in a particular historical configuration of time and space which itself is the creation of history, society and individual action. In other words, Giddens is arguing that individuals and societies are not just located in linear time and absolute space but structure time and space socially such that they produce relative configurations of both specific to particular times and places. These relative configurations in turn provide a constraining influence on individual action. Structuration then is concerned with examining the connections between human agency, social structure, time and space in specific periods and places.

A theme which runs throughout the above discussion and which pertains closely to that which follows is that of duality versus dualism. Duality is central to the entire structurationist programme, figuring in both Giddens's presentation of the agency–structure relationship and the links between this and time and space. In this case it means that the interdependence between history, society and purposeful individual action is equal in weight; neither society, nor individuals are assumed to exert a greater influence on events than the other. The relationship between agency and structure in time and space is treated similarly: whilst temporal and spatial organisation limit individual action, they are, at the same time, the creations of history, society and individual action. Again, each exerts a determining influence on the other but this is again of equal weight. This duality based argument contrasts sharply with the more conventional dualisms found within social theory and social science. In this themes such as the individual and society, agency and structure, subject and object, macro and micro are treated both as opposite and as distinct. Furthermore, any proposed relationship between opposites, for instance, between individual and society, is presented in the form of a one-way directional arrow. Thus, in its most extreme forms, society can be seen either as conditioning all human activity (structural determinism) or as the product of unconstrained human action (voluntarism). The distinction between this type of argument and that of Giddens is total.

Beyond these points of clarification we can return to the comments of Gregory with which we began this section. To a degree such remarks run counter to the general tendency, and one which is particularly strong at present in human geography, which is to accept Giddens's structurationist arguments with little critical questioning. Although discussion here can only be selective rather than exhaustive, three examples will serve to substantiate this point. Thrift's (1983) paper 'On the determination of social action in space and time' provides a good indication of this trend. In this we find an argument which:

i) takes its inspiration for a discussion of human geography and social theory from Giddens's classificatory surveys of voluntaristic and structural determinist schools in social theory,
ii) accepts explicitly Giddens's argument that these tendencies need to be transcended, and
iii) states that the structurationist perspective, notwithstanding certain problems relating to determination, should play a central part in this transcendence. The problems which Thrift has in mind stem from Giddens's insistence that everything exerts an equal determining influence on everything else.

In a review of *A contemporary critique of historical materialism*, Sayer (1983) makes the following similar comment,

> (the) theory of 'structuration' ... parallel(s) similar ideas by Bhaskar (1979) ... and Bourdieu (1977), and in my view effectively resolve(s) the problem of structure and agency, and the associated poles of determinism and voluntarism ... the twin errors of voluntarism (actors act independently of constraints) and structuralist determinism (the conditions do the acting) are avoided (1983, 109).

Finally, we can take the example of Giddens's concept of determination and look at what human geographers have had to say so far about this. Thrift's (1983) comments in this respect have already been referred to: his proposed solution is to combine the structurationist perspective with Marxist theory which, of course, and contrastingly, has a very strong notion of societal determination. On the other hand, Gregory (1982a; 1982b), considering the same problem, returns to the intricate complexities of Giddens's own writing on structures of domination, signification and legitimation to seek determination there. In their different ways neither is really contesting in depth what Giddens has said. Each, whilst acknowledging gaps and deficiencies, ultimately accepts the merits of structuration theory, rather than expose its weaknesses in a sustained fashion. Furthermore, many other human geographers have recently made comments of an identical or similar nature to those of Thrift, Sayer and Gregory (Forbes, 1984; Johnston and Claval, 1984; Philo, 1984; Pred, 1981c; 1983; 1984; Soja, 1983; Thrift and Forbes, 1983). It seems reasonable therefore to suggest that both the argument concerning the need to avoid the pitfalls of voluntarism and determinism and that which stresses the necessity of an engagement with the structurationist perspective to effect the required change have become frequent features of methodological debate in human geography. The encounter between human geography and Giddens's work on structuration then can be summarized, at least thus far, as one in which certain ideas of current prominence in the social theory or sociological literature have been transferred into human geography as they stand; in which the origins and implications of these ideas have yet to be worked out fully and in which diffusion, one suspects, has been aided considerably by association with established figures, notably, in this case, Gregory, Pred and Thrift (cf. Agnew and Duncan, 1981).

The remainder of this paper is concerned with initiating the beginnings of a more critical approach to Giddens's theory of structuration and to his duality thesis in particular. In what follows two themes are pursued. The first of these investigates the links between structuration and time geography. In this considerable stress is placed on the constitution and construction of Giddens's own propositions using Hägerstrand's work on time geography and his more recent wider writing as examples (Section II). Second, in Section III, the serious difficulties encountered by the currently limited amount of structurationist-inspired empirical work are expanded upon. Both sections suggest and reveal substantial problems of a theoretical and empirical nature. Indeed, the second serves to undermine considerably one of Giddens's central propositions, namely his attempt to reconstruct social theory, social science and, by implication, human geography around the theme of duality. Furthermore, it is shown here that both Giddens's theoretical statements and the empirical work which has been influenced by these, do more to replicate existing tendencies towards dualism than to transcend these with the duality thesis; a conclusion which is echoed at the epistemological level in Foucault's work on knowledge and the social sciences.

II Time Geography and Structuration: Points of Convergence and Divergence

In line with the general tendencies disclosed in Section I, it has become something of a commonplace recently for some human geographers to seek affinities between their work and the structurationist programme. One of the most obvious examples of this trend is to be found in the time geography literature. Pred (1983; 1984), for instance, has argued that the central time geographic concepts of path and project provide the key to unlocking what he refers to as 'the material continuity of structuration' in time and space. Another example is provided by Carlstein (1981) who identifies two points of contact between time geography and structuration; first, the emphasis which both accord to time–space relations and, second, the importance of the graphical notation characteristic of time geography for visualizing the connections between everyday material life and structuration. Giddens too sees a considerable degree of convergence between time geography, particularly as presented in the work of Hägerstrand, and his own writing (Giddens, 1979; 1981; 1984). In this section it is suggested that such arguments are at best, misleading, at worst, plain wrong. Discussion is divided into two parts. In Section II(1) a short review of both time geography and Hägerstrand's recent writing is presented as a necessary prelude to a consideration of their portrayal within Giddens's work. This is outlined in Section II(2), wherein the marked dissimilarities between time geography, some of the more recent writings of Hägerstrand and structuration are made explicit. Together these sections serve to illustrate a central argument of this paper, that human geographers would do well to adopt a more critical attitude to the whole issue of structuration, including what Giddens has written about certain themes in the social sciences, before either aligning themselves solidly behind this thesis or seeking to identify their work with it.

1 Time Geography: From Paths and Projects to Diorama and Contextual Analysis

The fundamental intentions of Hägerstrand in creating time geography are made clear in his earliest statements on this theme and can be summarized as providing first, a critique of geography as spatial science and, second, an alternative view of the world to that presented in and by spatial analysis (Hägerstrand, 1970; 1973). In place of this characteristically atemporal and faceless geography, Hägerstrand proposed a geography which returned to the Vidalian themes of social life and habitat and which recognized and moved from three central principles:

i)   that human life is temporally and spatially ordered;
ii) that human life has both a physical (natural) and social dimension; and
iii) that the activities which constitute human life are limited by certain basic temporal and spatial constraints which condition various individual and group based activity possibility combinations (Carlstein, 1982; van Paassen, 1981).

These constraints, referred to in the time geography literature as capability and coupling constraints, are: the finite nature of human life; the indivisibility of human beings; the limited ability of people to engage in more than one activity at any one time; that every activity has a duration; that movement in space consumes movement in time; and the limited packing capacity of space.

These six constraints, together with the key path and project concepts (used to summarize individuals' movement through time and space and the intentions behind individual or group based activity respectively), provide the foundations of time geography. They also provided much of the focus for the early time geography literature, which dealt explicitly with exploring the limitations which these constraints impose on individual and aggregate path and project formation (Lenntorp, 1976; Martensson, 1977; 1979).

The early, essentially exploratory and descriptive, work which emanated from Lund in the 1970s has been the subject of considerable criticism (Baker, 1981; Gregory, 1982a; Rose, 1977; van Paassen, 1976), much of which has been instrumental in leading to a subtle and important shift in Hägerstrand's more recent writing. In this we can detect a movement away from the early time geography formulations and the analysis of constraints *per se* towards a broader concern with human life as association, with social life 'as it is' (Hägerstrand, 1982; 1983; 1984). Hägerstrand himself, in an autobiographical essay, documents this reorientation, possibly somewhat misleadingly, in terms of a response to the humanistic critique of early time geography and to the comments of Anne Buttimer in particular. Far from being about people, this early time geography, in Hägerstrand's reconsidered view, depicts a 'dance macabre', in which faceless individuals weave, almost as automatons, their paths through time and space (Hägerstrand, 1983). Indeed, he continues,

> In (the) existing system of concepts ... there lay hidden a blueprint of a world which neglected and ran over the more important part of human existence: the internal realms of experience and meaning (Hägerstrand, 1983, 154).

Such remarks, however, imply rather more in the way of radical reorientation than in fact has occurred to date in Hägerstrand's work. They suggest a shift to a concern with the inner worlds of significance, ideas, emotions and feelings, yet such dimensions are noticeably absent from the object-based, thingified, strongly physical world of Hägerstrand's most recent – and indeed, past – writing (Hägerstrand, 1970; 1975; 1982; 1984). Although influenced by the humanistic critique then, Hägerstrand's recent work has not reduced to this. It is, nonetheless, subtly different to previous formulations, and in at least two ways. The first of these reflects an increasing explicit concern on Hägerstrand's part with the issue of how we in fact conceptualize, or approach, the whole question of social life. The second difference is that time geography, rather than an end in itself, has become more of a means to an end. The end in this case is clearly Hägerstrand's vision of a *contextual* social science.

As regards the issue of social life, Hägerstrand's essential point is to stress the principle of neighbourliness: human beings live both in association with other human beings and within specific society-habitats (van Paassen, 1981).

Analysis within the social sciences and science generally, however, is constructed upon a quite different set of foundations, that is, it is organized specifically according to preconceived categories, the primary purpose of which is to order and interpret the world in terms of what are often isolated or abstract concepts. In place of this *compositional* analysis, Hägerstrand proposes a shift to contextual analysis. In the latter, togetherness, association and setting are central; it is the totality of what is (as well as what is not) 'there' within particular bounded time–space contexts which is important, not the categories which these can be slotted into (Hägerstrand, 1984).

The concepts which Hägerstrand uses to develop this notion of contextual analysis are diorama, path and project (Hägerstrand, 1982; 1984). Path and project, as established features of time geography, need no elaboration here (Carlstein, 1982; Pred, 1977). Henceforth, however, Hägerstrand employs them within the broader concept of diorama. By this concept he means to capture the 'thereness' of people and objects within their 'normal' environmental and social settings, in other words, to represent the totality of what is present (and what is absent) in bounded time–space situations. One such instance is the setting provided by the Swedish valley which formed Hägerstrand's childhood home. Here,

> Life received its somewhat halting rhythmicity by five pacesetters, partly coordinated, but largely not: the Bruk, the school, the railroad, the parish church and the cows ...
>
> The state made its presence felt in the area through the school. The flag on its high pole was widely visible on days of national celebration. Thus, school imposed a highly regular, almost mechanical, rhythm upon life – daily, weekly, yearly ...
>
> Equal in importance as a dominating pacesetter was the Bruk. It was privately owned, however. The factory whistle punctured the air four times a day, regulating the workers coming and going and telling everybody else about it. About half of the school children had to oscillate between the two worlds. The lunch breaks were reasonably well coordinated but not the beginning and end of the working day.
>
> The parish church did not interfere with the pace of the ordinary working day. But by six o'clock on Saturday evening the bells announced that all tools should be put away and the gravel-walk leading to the entrance door raked over. Then, on Sunday morning, the bells again called to service ...
>
> The farmers had also their regular routines. These were not imposed from the outside but were a traditional response to nature and habit. They used to milk the cows three times a day, still without machines ... (Hägerstrand, 1982, 329).

Diorama then provides the context, the physical associations, of social life;

paths and projects enable us to visualize the complex interweaving of these associations in time and space. Further, as dioramic configurations change, as what is present/absent alters, and as the routine, rhythmical elements of social life alter too, so it must be assumed that Hägerstrand intends to provide some form of analytical grip on the changing nature of social life itself through the twentieth century (Hägerstrand, 1982).

Time geography emerged from a critique of geography as spacial science. More recently, as time geography itself has undergone critique, Hägerstrand's own work has shifted perceptibly in orientation. In this it is now possible to see that time geography *per se* is but one element in a much wider and explicit concern with the whole issue of the totality of social life. Constraints, paths and projects, the fundamental concepts of time geography, are only partial dimensions to an understanding of the complexities of interaction between people and people and environment. Further, without the concept of association represented in the notion of diorama, they remain little more than the compositional categories to which Hägerstrand is opposed. In view of this it is obvious that time geography and Hägerstrand's contextual view of the world are some way from being one and the same thing. Instead, time geography has become a language for contextual analysis.

2 Time Geography and Structuration: Two Different Projects

Regarding time geography, Giddens makes the following observation,

> The interest of time geography in the theory of structuration is surely evident. Time geography is concerned with the constraints that shape the routines of day to day life and shares with structuration theory an emphasis upon the significance of the practical characteristics of daily activities in circumstances of co-presence, for the constitution of social conduct (1984, 116).

There are two dimensions to this statement which, along with a summary of the path, project and constraint concepts, brief comments on graphical notation and criticisms of the portrayal of the individual within time geography, constitute the bulk of Giddens's picture of both time geography and the work of Hägerstrand (cf. Section II(1)). On the one hand, Giddens isolates those areas of substantive interest common to both time geography and structuration; on the other, he implies, although does not develop, the idea that, notwithstanding these connections, structuration and time geography are fundamentally dissimilar in terms of their overall objectives. This second point is explored further here with reference to two issues: the differing conceptions of social life which appear in the writing of Hägerstrand and Giddens and their alternative approaches to the duality–dualism question. In more general terms the discussion illustrates Giddens's 'additive' approach to social theory (cf. Thrift, 1984). As with his approach to many 'schools' of social theory, Giddens's encounter with time geography and with Häger-strand's writing generally is fleeting. In this case Hägerstrand's arguments regarding time geography are summarized briefly, criticized for where they fail to coincide with the basic premises of structuration theory, praised for providing a novel form of notation and then dispensed with (cf. Coser, 1981). We are left with the distinct impression that for Giddens, it is the graphical language of time geography which is of lasting value but that ultimately this language represents little more than another interesting dimension to be added-in to structuration theory (Thrift, personal communication).

Hägerstrand's view of social life, the specific concepts which he uses to portray this and the role of time geography within this have already been discussed (Section II(1)). In contrast, Giddens's representation of social life is one framed not so much by the intention of presenting social life 'as it is' but by the abstract categories of social theory. Thus, far from being contextual in approach, much of the emphasis within Giddens's is on compositional analysis (cf. Thrift, 1983). Social life for Giddens is considered in three ways. The first two of these reflect two traditional categories within social theory, that is, the human subject and the individual–society (human agency–social structure) relationship. The third represents Giddens's main contribution to social theory – his argument that social theory needs to be about time and space right from the start (Section I). Social life in Giddens's terms is seen as hinging around the agency–structure relationship in time–space. It is, to corrupt Marx's famous and deceptively simple phrase, about people making history in temporal and spatial contexts, but not in the conditions or the time–space zones of their own choosing. Beyond this a further and important point of qualification needs to be made. Although Giddens's arguments concern social life, they have, at least so far, been more concerned with theorizing about this than with bringing this theory down to the level of social life 'as it is'. More precisely, we can identify three main theoretical strands here. The first is the need to develop a theory of human action which links the intentional, motivational and reflexive monitoring of individual activity to its unintentional, often societal, consequences. Second, Giddens has continually theorized the agency–structure relationship in terms of duality, arguing that social practices are both constituted by social structures and are (re)productive/transformative of these structures (Section I). The third theoretical point concerns time and space; social structures and practices are not just located in time and space but themselves reflect the societal organization of temporal and spatial resources (Section I). All of this is a very long way from social life itself and, indeed, from Hägerstrand's contextual approach to the same problem. Whereas for Hägerstrand social life is about the totality of all that is there within specific society-habitats, for Giddens it is something to be interpreted and understood by the categories of social theory, all of which, in addition, exclude the physical world which figures so prominently in Hägerstrand's writing. The difference between Hägerstrand

and Giddens then is considerable. They represent, quite simply, two different ways of interpreting the world. In view of this, the degree to which Giddens can coopt parts of Hägerstrand's work and incorporate them successfully within his own schema must be seen as fairly questionable.

The issue of duality versus dualism, as we have seen already, is a central theme in Giddens's writing (Giddens, 1976; 1977; 1979; 1981; 1984; Section I) and one which pertains to the proposed replacement of existing dualisms within social theory, by the duality-based structurationist argument (Abrams, 1982; Berger and Luckmann, 1966; Bhaskar, 1979; Bourdieu, 1977; cf. Giddens, 1979; 1981; 1984). As Giddens himself remarks,

> Structuration theory is based on the premise that ... dualism has to be reconceptualised as duality (Giddens, 1984, xx–xxi).

Central to this is the notion of the duality of structure, the concept which Giddens uses as the fulcrum between human agency and social structure and by which he ties the concepts 'structure' and 'system'. 'Structure' in these arguments refers to resources (both material and human) and the rules which relate to these. 'System', in contrast, is a shorthand term for social practices or interaction. 'Structure' and 'system' correspond, therefore, to the labels 'social structure' and 'human agency' respectively in Giddens's argument. The duality of structure, logically enough then, is defined by Giddens as a concept in which it is recognized that,

> the structural properties (rules and resources) of social systems become both the medium and the outcome of the practices that constitute those systems (1979, 69).

This same argument for duality between individual and society is reiterated in Giddens's approach to the traditional time–space and macro–micro dualisms. Thus, time–space, which is viewed in terms of both the 'presencing', or face-to-face interaction of individuals in time–space and the time–space horizons ('distanciation') of societies, is seen as produced by and (re)productive/transformative of society. Similarly, the duality based argument is used to collapse and merge the macro–micro scale distinctions characteristically made within social theory and social science. In Giddens's view these two scales are inextricably intertwined (Giddens, 1984, 139–44).

In contrast, the work of Hägerstrand does not problematize the issue of duality versus dualism. Nonetheless, it is still possible to interpret Hägerstrand's writing in terms of this question and here we can detect a fundamental difference between time geography *per se*. Hägerstrand's view of the world and Giddens's structurationist project. In the case of time geography, the specific sets of dualisms which appear are internal–external, individual–society, time–space and macro–micro. As the humanistic critique of time geography has emphasized, these resolved themselves in terms of individuals as objects rather than as subjects (as project governed paths through time and space), society (capability, coupling and regulative constraints), the timing and spacing of activity and primarily microscale studies respectively, in other words, precisely the resolutions which we would expect to find in work exploring activity limiting constraints (I(1), Carlstein, 1981; cf. Gregory, 1978). Unlike this, Hägerstrand's more recent work has stressed the individual in specific society-habitats, microscale study and the importance of contextual, as opposed to compositional, analysis. Thus, whilst time geography *per se* can be located towards the deterministic end of Giddens's social theory, Hägerstrand's wider view of the world is something which approximates more to the voluntaristic end of the spectrum. Both, however, can be seen as dualistic enterprises, rather than ones founded on duality; they focus on one side of these oppositional pairings rather than on the recursive relationship between the two.

In presenting a full picture of the development of the Lund school of time geography, its connections with the wider and more recent writing of Hägerstrand and some of the differences between both of these projects and structuration, one theme has been central, that a more critical engagement with Giddens's own work needs to take place. One form which this can take is to consider, as we have done here, Giddens's treatment of specific 'schools' or themes within social science. In this case it has been shown that Giddens's treatment of time geography and Hägerstrand's work generally is fairly superficial. Not only does he fail to place the development of time geography within the overall context provided by Hägerstrand's writing but he consistently chooses to emphasize either those features which coincide with and augment his own project (for instance, the constrained nature of human action and time geography notation), or those which flout key aspects of it (for example, the portrayal of human agency within time geography and the lack of an enabling dimension to constraint), rather than dwell on any fundamental points of divergence such as the duality–dualism issue or Hägerstrand's interpretation of social life and how this should be approached as an object of study. Furthermore, we can say that, in adding aspects of time geography to his time–space and agency arguments, Giddens is approaching the work of Hägerstrand in exactly the same way as he tackles the work of Goffman and Erikson on human agency, for instance, or Foucault on structure, time and space. In each of these cases, points which Giddens agrees with are harnessed to the general structurationist argument with apparently little regard as to whether they are either compatible concepts or, indeed, meaningful when combined together. In short, Giddens at times appears more concerned with analysing and extracting from what he portrays as dualistic work in social science than with developing fully his own duality thesis. This is a point which will be enlarged upon in the following section in which we move to confront a second area of critical engagement with Giddens's work, the connections between structuration and substantive empirical research. The points which have been made thus far, however, suggest that time geographers, as well as those sympathetic to Hägerstrand's broader concerns, would do well to adopt a more sceptical approach than hitherto to the structurationist programme and certainly one which emphasizes the distances, as well as the connections, between these projects and structuration.

III Structuration and Empirical Research

Giddens's overt concern with ontological issues in social science, specifically the nature of human action and the relationship of this to institutions, is something which is replicated in the very limited amount of substantive research carried out to date within the guidelines provided by structuration. Indeed, the detailed empirical work which has appeared so far has been concerned exclusively with the issues of human action, social practices and their wider relationship to institutions, rather than with Giddens's time–space arguments. Notwithstanding this point, this material does provide us with a means by which we can begin to assess the degree to which aspects of the theory of structuration actually illuminate empirical questions in the social sciences. Discussion here is divided into three parts. First, the nature of the type of research which has utilized the structurationist argument is considered. This enables us to make some speculative points concerning the future empirical domain of structuration and the relative strengths of Giddens's arguments relating to agency–structure and time–space. Second, the difficulties encountered in working with the key structuration concept of the duality of structure are made explicit. Third, we turn to look at the question of insight: just what types of insight does structuration produce? In all three areas fundamental problems appear.

1 Structuration: Substantive Research

That there is, at present, a general lack of empirical work using structuration theory is hardly surprising; Giddens's arguments have only attracted widespread attention since the appearance of *Central problems in social theory* in 1979. The work which has appeared, however, can be summarized as small scale, principally local studies concerned with analysing specific, situated social practices. Three examples will suffice to substantiate this point, two of which set out with the express intention of using structuration theory. The third is a study which Giddens (1984) presents as his major example of structuration theory in practice; it is, nonetheless, *not* an avowedly structurationist piece of work. We can begin with this particular example, Willis's (1977) study *Learning to labour*. In this Willis analyses the specific practices of a group of boys within a Birmingham school, the subculture which these practices produce and the unintentional consequences which this subculture has in terms of the future employment prospects and characteristics of this group. From a specifically structurationist perspective, Smith (1983) structures his research on American beef cattle production in terms of the social practices, as well as the intentions, meanings and unintended outcomes, implicated in specific beef farming ventures. Finally, Gregson (1984), in an analysis of the changing social relations of production within a particular area of northwest England over the period 1570–1800, focuses upon the specific practices and struggles of landlords and tenants within a large landed estate; the theoretical and practical consequences which these practices had for the changing nature of the property relation within this estate and the unintentional consequences of these practices for the future of individual 'peasant' production within this area. Although concerned with very different types of subject matter, and different time periods, these three studies all relate to the same distinctive scale of social inquiry. Furthermore, each stresses, although to varying degrees, the themes of human action, social practices and their consequences, intentional or otherwise.

It has to be emphasized that such themes are not the product of work conducted within, for example, an empiricist philosophy. Instead two of these studies share an explicit theoretical commitment to the structurationist perspective and to using this in a substantive research context. The third (Willis's) provides us with a clear indication of the type of study which Giddens himself sees as exemplifying the structuration thesis. They therefore provide us with a means of initiating a dialogue between Giddens's own, often extremely abstract, theoretical work and empirical research. Two points in particular are worth exploring here: the scale question and the themes which these particular studies have isolated as central to structuration theory.

Regarding scale, what each of the above studies appears to suggest – we might note, independently – is that the empirical domain of structuration may well turn out to be micro in focus. This is a conclusion which runs counter to Giddens's statements on this issue, in which no logical distinction is made between macro and microscale study. Structuration, at least according to Giddens, transcends the scale question. It is, nonetheless, a conclusion which is related strongly to Giddens's presentation of the agency–structure relationship. Although agency and structure form two distinct and conjoined categories in structuration, structure itself is only encountered as a category in Giddens's work at precisely the point of action; it has no prior existence. What this means in terms of empirical work guided by these arguments is that human action and social practices not only form the logical, although not prior, point of departure but that they must also be shown to be continually in evidence. This is something which can only be achieved realistically in smallscale studies. Indeed, to focus on structure *per se* would flout the admittedly rather implausible definition of structure within Giddens's work and, more importantly, risk losing touch altogether with the central notion of the reproductive and transformative capacities of human action. Thus, whilst

Giddens might argue in theoretical terms that structuration can be applied at any scale, the message from empirical work framed by this perspective suggests that this may not be the case, particularly if this work is to remain true to the specific form of agency–structure relationship which sits at the heart of Giddens's programme. It would appear then that, far from transcending the scale distinctions characteristic of social theory and social science, Giddens's argument in practice actually reinforces these.

As well as suggesting the empirical domain for structuration theory it is noticeable that the above three studies focus upon the agency–structure dimension within Giddens's arguments rather than upon his other two concerns, namely developing a theory of human action and the time–space constitution of society (II(2)). Given the short history of structuration theory and corresponding lack of empirical work in this vein, it would be premature to suggest that this characteristic will prove to be typical of structurationist work. However, it can be suggested that the focus in these three studies may be seen as a direct reflection of the relative emphases which each of these issues has received in Giddens's work. Of the three it is the agency–structure relationship which has been a constant preoccupation (Giddens, 1976, 1979, 1981; 1984). To a degree too, it is possible to interpret the emphasis accorded to the agency–structure relationship in these studies as symptomatic of the weaknesses of Giddens's arguments regarding human action and/or time–space.

With respect to time–space, the issue which impinges most closely on the concerns of human geography, we can make two points. The first is to suggest that, for all its apparent sophistication, Giddens's treatment of time–space says very little of real substance about the spatial and temporal constitution of present-day society. Thus Giddens considers, for example, how, in broad terms, different societies have constructed time–space in history, the 'stretching' of society's temporal and spatial horizons from the 'primitive, high presence, tribal societies' of the past to the 'low presence, impersonal, class-based society' of the present; the importance of developments such as writing and the invention of the clock in achieving this 'stretching'; and the durée of time as this relates to individuals, institutions and societies. Nowhere, however, does he integrate these ideas into a full and coherent account of how temporal and spatial resources are structured within contemporary capitalism (cf. Castells, 1977; Harvey, 1982). Indeed, in collapsing time and space to one concept, time–space, Giddens minimizes the importance of the separation of the temporal and spatial dimensions within capitalism. Furthermore, and at the micro level of individuals and groups, little attention is paid to the fact that individuals appear to experience time and space as distinct enabling or constraining dimensions of daily life, rather than as a single, all-embracing concept based upon the ease of face-to-face interaction (cf. Gross, 1982; Hägerstrand, 1970; 1982).

A second problem area in Giddens's writing on time–space is his stress on the routinized nature of human activity in time–space. For the individual, such activity is supposed to fulfil a basic role, that of security provision (Giddens, 1984). On a far broader scale, this same routine activity is seen as essential in the organization and reproduction of capitalist society, although the connections here remain to be worked out comprehensively (Giddens, 1979; 1984). Some fundamental objections can be made to this emphasis on routine. At the macro level, for instance, it needs to be recognized that, in order for capitalism to be reproduced, transformation, particularly in the form of the restructuring of existing modes of spatial and temporal societal organization, has to occur (Marx, 1967; Harvey, 1982; Massey, 1984; Wallerstein, 1974). This restructuring, in turn, has a not inconsiderable impact on the nature of routinized activity within specific places. Such arguments have yet to be tackled in detail by Giddens. Similarly, although on an altogether different scale, part of Giddens's central argument has always been to stress the reproductive *and* transformative dimensions within human action itself. At present, given Giddens's presentation of the individual within time–space and the particular emphasis which he places within this on routinized conduct, it is hard to see any indication of the creative, transformative facet of human agency.

In short, Giddens's basic arguments regarding time–space, although interesting and novel, as yet provide little in the way of analytical grip relating to either the societal or individual reproduction of temporal and spatial organization within contemporary capitalism. Neither do they probe the transformative dimensions within this setup. Not surprisingly, therefore, Giddens's concept of time–space remains peripheral, rather than central, to the human geography concerned with such issues. Furthermore, we can note that, of all Giddens's arguments, it is the agency–structure thesis which has received most attention in this work. This may, indeed, tell us something about the nature of 'critical' human geography, in which time–space relations have only recently been awarded parity with societal relations. However, it is also, almost certainly, just as informative about the strengths and weaknesses within Giddens's version of social theory. Either way, it is the agency–structure strand of Giddens's structuration theory which has been most readily assimilated within human geography.

2 Structuration: The Duality of Structure

A major problem faced by anyone working within the structurationist framework comes precisely at the point of embarking upon substantive work in this vein. As Smith (1983) expresses it,

> ... whilst theoretically attractive, the simultaneous and mutual 'causal' influences of agents on society and society on agents makes it difficult to apply this vision to concrete instances of social activities; it is difficult to know how one is to cut into the data (1983, 3).

The problem which Smith is referring to in this instance is one which traces to Giddens's central concept of duality and that of the duality of structure specifically. It is one encountered in all three of the studies mentioned above. Giddens himself speaks in this context of the 'methodological epoche', a term which relates to the bracketing-out of institutional analysis when focusing upon action and social practices, and vice versa. The above studies are all illustrative of this procedure; so too are Giddens's own examples of aspects of structuration theory (Giddens, 1979; 1981). What Giddens fails to make explicit, however, is that this bracketing exercise itself is little more than the substitution of methodological and empirical dualism in a situation where the central issue is supposedly duality. More specifically, in order to analyse the workings of the agency–structure duality we have to break in somewhere; the act of breaking itself automatically replaces a theoretical duality with a methodological and empirical dualism; the analysis itself is presented in terms of a dualism and the problem then becomes one of making the connections back to duality. Again, each of these studies faces this set of problems but, in the end, none gets beyond the type of statement reiterated countless times by Giddens, that social practices are produced and reproduced by the actions (intentional and unintentional) which, in turn, go to make up these social practices. Thus, to take the example of Smith's paper, it is stated that the social practices associated with American beef farming are produced and reproduced in action, but we only hear either about beef farming or about beef farmers' intentions and their understanding and experience of the beef business, not about in what specific circumstances action is (re)productive or transformative of these social practices. Similarly, in Giddens's own examples we find a focus on either the macroscale or the micro, not on the shading of the one into the other. His discussion of the city through history (1981) provides a clear illustration of this. Drawing heavily on the work of Jacobs, Sjoberg, Wheatley, Mumford and, to a lesser extent, that of Castells and Harvey, Giddens considers such issues as the pattern of spatial organization within 'classical' cities, the structuring of spatial and temporal resources within these, the central importance of the city in the process of the commodification of time and its role in the development of surveillance activities. In the latter case it is the inventions of writing and later printing, in particular, within the city which Giddens considers to be of crucial importance. Not only did these inventions extend each society's powers of surveillance over the population but they also led to an extension of the time–space horizons of these societies. They, and the city, therefore are seen by Giddens as essential planks in the development of capitalist society. Such comments, however, are directed strongly to the macroscale of world history. In all this, as we would expect, individual activity or social practices as such are 'bracketed' out yet nowhere does Giddens balance this with an impression of how human agency, in turn, fits into this picture. Thus we can suggest that whilst Giddens may argue in abstract terms that structuration is concerned with replacing dualism with duality, both his own examples and others' empirical work, at least so far, have failed to demonstrate this argument in practice. For all our endeavours, duality remains more a statement of intent than conclusively shown.

However, it is important to go a stage beyond this comment. Not only is this situation of dualism in the face of an argument for duality one which has been encountered in substantive work, it is also a situation which may well persist within the structurationist argument, for reasons which again relate to the duality of structure concept. In view of the central importance of this concept within his overall argument, it is surprising that Giddens himself devotes very little space to considering this notion fully. Instead, throughout his work, attention is focused upon examples of voluntarism and determinism in social theory, and upon harnessing aspects of these, either to the agency or the structure side of his argument. In other words, there has, so far, been little further development of the duality concept which is so central to his articulation of the agency–structure relationship. Thus, as Archer (1982) says,

> Rather than transcending the voluntarism/determinism dichotomy, the two sides of the duality of structure embody them respectively; they are simply clamped together in a conceptual vice (1982, 461).

A clearer demonstration of the penetrating depth of this statement than the existence of methodological and empirical dualism within research influenced by structuration theory, as well as the subsequent problems which have been encountered in trying to reincorporate the notion of duality, is hard to imagine. Furthermore, until Giddens himself sheds further light on this whole issue, particularly on how certain structural configurations reproduce or transform social systems and how social systems in turn reproduce or transform social stucture(s), it is difficult to envisage how this situation might alter. Nonetheless, some pointers in this direction can be suggested, of which three are perhaps paramount here. The first is a more thorough elaboration than hitherto of the concept of power within structuration. Second, a detailed appraisal is needed of the degree to which 'structure' can be defined usefully in terms of rules and resources. Evidently, this is a definition which is workable within microscale studies of human interaction but, at the same time, it is extremely simplistic when applied to such categories as modes of production. The third necessity is to work out fully the precise nature of the relationship between structure and system. This last point would need to take in both the first and second issues. In addition, it would require consideration of the following:

i)   whether structures and systems operate in a distinct one-to-one relationship, and

ii) the immense variety of types of social system, some of which, in the form of direct social struggle, have an obvious connection with either the reproduction or, more often, transformation of existing structures (Urry, 1982).

3 Structuration: The Insight Produced by Substantive Research

As the above examples indicate, whilst considerable insights can be achieved concerning, for instance, social practices, intentions, the knowledgeability of individuals and the constraining and/or enabling influence of specific sets of rules and resources on human action, these in themselves are not generated by the central pivot of structuration theory. Instead they can be seen as the product of Giddens's own harnessing of aspects of voluntaristic and deterministic social theory to his own project and, second, the methodological and empirical dualisms implicated in this type of research. For the specific, unique insights provided by structuration theory itself we need to focus on the duality concept. However, it is here, as we have seen, that major problems have been encountered. Indeed, it has proved impossible, so far, to do more than simply reiterate the essence of the duality of structure argument in empirical research (III(1); III(2)). This is something which is seen here as reflecting Giddens's portrayal of the link between agency and structure in terms of the duality of structure. In this, the connection between agency and structure is indeterminate in character; it states absolutely nothing about when and in what circumstances either agency or structure will dominate. This is an important point which has two main implications: that the methodological epoche has to be employed and that research, consequently, can only provide insight into either agency (human practices) or institutions, but not both together. Given this it is hardly surprising that the specific insights provided by structuration within substantive research have yet to progress beyond the level of simple relational, yet completely empty, statements concerning possible lines of connection between agency and structure. In this respect, empirical work is an accurate reflection of some of the considerable deficiencies which exist currently within Giddens's own theoretical statements. To date at least, substantive work suggests that the heart of structuration theory has yet to offer any fundamentally different insights to those which could be produced within alternative perspectives.

IV Conclusions

The primary concern of this paper has been to argue that human geographers need to be far more critical than hitherto in the nature of their engagement with the structurationist arguments of Anthony Giddens. Furthermore, it has been suggested here that such criticism can and needs to take two forms. The first, represented in this case by a detailed consideration of time geography and the writing of Hägerstrand, focuses upon how specific themes or 'schools' within social science are themselves considered by Giddens. The second strand of criticism provides a direct encounter with the problems which beset the structurationist perspective in the context of empirical research. Both lines of critique are important; the first because it demonstrates the tremendously varied origins and constitution of structuration theory; the second because it indicates, rather than obscures behind a cloud of special pleadings, the very considerable weaknesses of the central duality thesis within structuration. As regards the first, it is possible both to concur with and extend the remark of Hirst (1982), who says,

> I cannot accept that it is possible to put Adorno, Althusser, Derrida, Durkheim, Foucault, Freud, Goffman, Habermas, Heidegger, Lacan, Marx, Weber etc together in a rigorous theory (78).

Far from incorporating these into a rigorous theory, Giddens at times merely appears to bolt such arguments together using the central idea of duality of structure. Indeed, in support of this point we have seen that this central duality notion, when examined in detail at both the theoretical and empirical levels, collapses to little more than a consideration of either agency or structure rather than the fulcrum between the two (III(2)). The gaps in the duality thesis then are obvious. That they are there at all suggests that Giddens has not yet succeeded in integrating his vastly divergent sources.

Beyond this, we can suggest that the two strands of critique within this paper are perhaps not entirely unrelated. One of Giddens's major concerns has always been to provide a review of, and commentary on, developments within social theory. The critique and reconstruction arguments are things which, in strictly chronological terms, have followed on from this (Giddens, 1976; 1977; 1979; 1981; 1984). Nevertheless, the connections between these two aspects of Giddens's work are still extremely strong. Thus, for instance, even in *The constitution of society* (1984), supposedly the major summary of the structurationist position, we find commentary on, and criticism of, existing voluntaristic or deterministic tendencies within social theory and the social sciences (some of which, like the partial coverage of Hägerstrand's work, are marginal to Giddens's main concerns) and a working of some of these points into the agency–structure, time–space or acting subject arguments. The whole exercise therefore is one which is far more akin to a deconstruction and partial recombination of what already exists, that is dualism, rather than a genuine attempt at creating something else, that is duality. As we have seen, this is a point which has obvious implications for empirical research; it also has clear lines of connection to the epistemological level. Indeed, in arguing for duality and against dualism within social theory and social science, Giddens consistently comes up against, and consistently avoids, a fundamental epistemological question, namely, 'is it possible for social science and the knowledge which it produces to be reconstructed as a series of dualities?' In a society in which human beings are both subjects and objects and in which the social sciences were created to study both, so Foucault argues, dualism is both a central and necessary condition of existence. As Smart (1982) states,

> . . . sociological dualism is beyond resolution in the context of the epistemological configuration which provides the space for the human sciences and within a social order which produces the reality of the individual, but also provides for their representations (1982, 137).

Ultimately then it may not be possible to formulate the alternative, duality-based social theory, social science and, we might add, human geography which Giddens is seeking to create. Such epistemological conclusions have been echoed in both the empirical work framed to date by structuration theory and in Giddens's own theoretical formulations. In conclusion, it would seem that such points need to be borne in mind before human geographers take up the path of structuration theory. Undoubtedly, Giddens's work does provide much that is challenging and much that is of value. In contrast, some aspects of his work may turn out to be little more than cul de sacs. If we are to incorporate Giddens's social theory into human geography in the future a critical approach to his work will prove vital.

Acknowledgements

I would like to thank Nigel Thrift, Jim Lewis and an anonymous referee for their comments on an earlier version of this paper.

V References

Abrams, P. 1980: History, sociology, historical sociology. *Past and Present* 87, 3–16.
———— 1982: *Historical sociology*. Shepton Mallet: Open Books.
Agnew, J.A. and Duncan, J.S. 1981: The transfer of ideas into Anglo-American human geography. *Progress in Human Geography* 5, 42–57.
Archer, M.S. 1982: Morphogenesis versus structuration: on combining structure and action. *British Journal of Sociology* 33, 455–83.
Baker, A.R.H. 1981: An historico geographical perspective on time and space and on period and place. *Progress in Human Geography* 5, 439–43.
Baker, A.R.H. and Gregory, D. editors, 1984a: *Explorations in historical geography.* Cambridge: Cambridge University Press.
———— 1984b: Some terrae incognitae in historical geography an exploratory discussion. In Baker, A.R.H. and Gregory, D., editors, 1984a, 180–99.
Berger, P.L. and Luckmann, T. 1966: *The social construction of reality: a treatise in the sociology of knowledge.* London: Penguin.
Bhaskar, R. 1979: *The possibility of naturalism: a philosophical critique of the*

contemporary human sciences. Brighton, Sussex: Harvester Press.

———— 1983: Beef, structure and place: notes from a critical naturalist perspective. *Journal for Theory of Social Behaviour* 13, 81–95.

Bleicher, J. and Featherstone, M. 1982: Historical materialism today: an interview with Anthony Giddens. *Theory, Culture and Society* 1, 63–77.

Bourdieu, P. 1977: *Outline of a theory of practice*. Cambridge: Cambridge University Press.

Buttimer, A. editor, 1983: *The practice of geography*. London: Longman.

Carlstein, T. 1981: The sociology of structuration in time and space: a time-geographic assessment of Giddens' theory of structuration. *Svensk Geografisk Arsbok* 57, 41–57.

———— 1982: *Time resources, society and ecology: on the capacity for human interaction in space and time in pre-industrial societies*. Stockholm: C.W.K. Gleerup.

Carlstein, T., Parkes, D. and Thrift, N.J. editors, 1978: *Timing space and spacing time* Vols 1 and 2. London: Edward Arnold.

Castells, M. 1977: *The urban question*. London: Edward Arnold.

Coser, L.A. 1981: Review: Central problems in social theory. *American Journal of Sociology* 86, 1435–36.

Denzin, N.K. 1982: Review: A contemporary critique of historical materialism. *Sociology and Social Research* 67, 218–20.

Forbes, D.K. 1984: *The geography of underdevelopment*. London: Croom Helm.

Foucault, M. 1970: *The order of things: an archaeology of the human sciences*. London: Tavistock.

———— 1972: *The archaeology of knowledge and the discourse of language*. London: Tavistock.

Gane, M. 1983: Anthony Giddens and the crisis in social theory. *Economy and Society* 11, 368–98.

Giddens, A. 1976: *New rules of sociological method*. London: Hutchinson.

———— 1977: *Studies in social and political theory*. London: Hutchinson.

———— 1979: *Central problems in social theory*. London: Macmillan.

———— 1981: *A contemporary critique of historical materialism*. London: Macmillan.

———— 1982: *Profiles and critiques in social theory*. London: Macmillan.

———— 1984: *The constitution of society*. Cambridge: Polity Press.

Gould, P. and Olsson, G. editors, 1982: *A search for common ground*. London: Pion.

Gregory, D. 1978: *Ideology, science and human geography*. London: Hutchinson.

———— 1980: The ideology of control: systems theory and geography. *Tijschrift voor Economische en Sociale Geografie* 71, 327–42.

———— 1981: Human agency and human geography. *Transactions Institute of British Geographers* 6, 1–18.

———— 1982a: Solid geometry: notes on the recovery of spatial structure. In Gould, P. and Olsson, G., editors, 1982, 187–219.

———— 1982b: *Regional transformation and industrial revolution*, London: Macmillan.

———— 1984: Space, time and politics in social theory: an interview with Anthony Giddens. *Society and Space* 2, 123–32.

Gregson, N. 1984: Continuity and change in agrarian organisation in northwest England, 1570–1800. University of Durham, unpublished PhD thesis.

Gross, D. 1982: Time–space relations in Giddens's social theory. *Theory, Culture and Society* 1, 78–82.

Hägerstrand, T. 1970: What about people in regional science? *Papers of the Regional Science Association* 24, 7–21.

———— 1973: The domain of human geography. In Chorley, R.J., editor, *Directions in geography*, London: Methuen, 67–87.

———— 1975: Survival and arena: on the life history of individuals in relation to their geographical environment. *The Monadnock* 49, 9–29.

———— 1982: Diorama, path and project. *Tijdschrift voor Economische en Sociale Geografie* 73, 323–39.

———— 1983: In search for the sources of concepts. In Buttimer, A., editor, 1983, 238–56.

———— 1984: Presence and absence: a look at conceptual choices and bodily necessities. *Regional Studies* 18, 373–80.

Harre, R. 1980: *Social being*. Oxford: Basil Blackwell.

Harvey, D.W. 1982: *The limits to capital*. Oxford: Basil Blackwell.

Hirst, P. 1982: The social theory of Anthony Giddens: a new syncretism? *Theory, Culture and Society* 1, 78–82.

Johnston, R.J. and Claval, P. editors, 1984: *Geography since the second world war: an international survey*. London: Croom Helm.

Layder, D. 1981: *Structure, interaction and social theory*. London: Routledge and Kegan Paul.

Lenntorp, B. 1976: *Paths in space–time environments: a time-geographic study of movement possibilities of individuals*. Stockholm: C.W.K. Gleerup.

Martensson, S. 1977. Childhood interaction and temporal organisation. *Economic Geography* 53, 99–125.

———— 1979: *On the formation of biographies in space–time environments*. Stockholm: C.W.K Gleerup.

Marx, K. 1967: *Capital*. New York: International Publishers.

Massey, D. 1984: *Spatial divisions of labour*. London: Macmillan.

van Paassen, C. 1976: Human geography in terms of existential anthropology. *Tijdschrift voor Economische en Sociale Geografie* 67, 324–41.

———— 1981: The philosophy of geography from Vidal to Hägerstrand. In Pred, A., editor, *Space and time in geography*, Stockholm: C.W.K. Gleerup, 17–29.

Parkes, D. and Thrift, N.J. 1980: *Times, spaces and places: a chronogeographic perspective*. London: John Wiley.

Philo, C. 1984: Reflections on Gunnar Olsson's contribution to the discourse of contemporary human geography. *Society and Space* 2, 217–40.

Pred, A. 1977: The choreography of existence: comments on Hägerstrand's time geography and its usefulness. *Economic Geography* 53, 207–21.

———— 1978: The impact of technology and institutional innovations: some time-geographic observations. *Geographical Analysis* 10, 345–72.

———— 1981a: Of paths and projects: individual behaviour and its societal context. In Cox, K.R. and Golledge, R., editors, *Behavioural problems in geography revisited*. London: Methuen, 231–55.

———— 1981b: Production, family and free-time projects: a time-geographic perspective on individual and societal change in nineteenth century US cities. *Journal of Historical Geography* 7, 3–36.

———— 1981c: Social reproduction and the time geography of everyday life. *Geografiska Annaler* 63B, 5–22.

———— 1981d: Power, everyday practice and the discipline of human geography. In Pred, A., editor, *Space and time in geography*, Stockholm, G.W.K. Gleerup, 30–55.

———— 1983: Structuration and place: on the becoming of sense of place and structure of feeling. *Journal for Theory of Social Behaviour* 13, 45–68.

———— 1984: Structuration, biography formation and knowledge: observations on port growth during the mercantile period. *Society and Space* 2, 251–75.

Rose, C. 1977: Reflections on the notion of time incorporated in Hägerstrand's time-geographic model of society. *Tijdschrift voor Economische en Sociale Geografie* 68, 43–50.

Sayer, A. 1982: Explanation in economic geography, abstraction versus generalisation. *Progress in Human Geography* 6, 68–88.

——— 1983: Review: A contemporary of historical materialism. *Society and Space* 1, 109–14.

Shotter, J. 1983: 'Duality of structure' and 'intentionality' in an ecological psychology, *Journal for Theory of Social Behaviour* 13, 19–44.

Smart, B. 1982: Foucault, sociology and the problem of human agency. *Theory and Society* 1, 121–41.

Smith, C. 1983: A case study of structuration: the pure bred beef business. *Journal for Theory of Social Behaviour* 13, 3–18.

Soja, E. 1983: Redoubling the helix: space–time and the critical social theory of Anthony Giddens. *Environment and Planning A* 15, 855–66.

Thrift, N.J. 1981: Owners time and own time: the making of a capitalist time consciousness, 1300–1800. In Pred, A., editor, *Space and time in geography*, Stockholm: C.W.K. Gleerup, 56–84.

——— 1982: Towards a human geography. *Environment and Planning A* 14, 1280–82.

——— 1983: On the determination of social action in space and time. *Society and Space* 1, 23–57.

——— 1984: Review: A contemporary critique of historical materialism. *Progress in Human Geography* 8, 139–42.

Thrift, N.J. and Forbes, D.K. 1983: Review essay: A landscape with figures: political geography with human conflict. *Politial Geography Quarterly* 2, 247–63.

Thrift, N.J. and Pred, A. 1981: Time geography: a new beginning? *Progress in Human Geography* 5, 119–28.

Urry, J. 1982: Duality of structure: some critical issues. *Theory, Culture and Society* 1, 100–106.

Wallerstein, I. 1974: *The modern world system I*. London: Academic Press.

Willis, P. 1977: *Learning to labour*. Farnborough: Saxon House.

Wright, E.O. 1983: Review essay: Is marxism really functionalist, class reductionist and teleological? *American Journal of Sociology* 89, 452–59.

49

The Rediscovery of Chronos: The New Role of Time in Sociological Theory*

M. Elchardus

*Source: *International Sociology*, vol. 3 (1), 1988, pp. 35–59.

Abstract

This paper traces the new role of time in social theory, beyond the dissatisfaction with theories of change. This is done by identifying four developments: the clarification of historically independent processes, the new critique of positivism, the re-evaluation of 'micro sociology' and the emphasis on self-reference. These are specified on the basis of the work of Giddens and Luhmann, and related to the concept of time used by these authors. I argue that their predominantly naturalistic sui generis concept of time cannot do justice to the theoretical programmes they are implementing, and propose to focus instead on temporality and its conceptualisation. Temporality is defined on the basis of an invariant core that can be abstracted from the variety of operational culture-specific concepts of time. The paper closes with a discussion of some of the consequences of this shift from (naturalistic) time to social temporality.

Two very different ways of dealing with time can be distinguished in social science.

The first is concerned with the many ways in which human beings use time as a socially meaningful phenomenon: as a scarce resource, a measure of value, a medium for the coordination of action and for planning, a symbol of power and social importance, etc. . . .[1] Quite often the research dealing with these various uses of time fails to inquire about the way in which time comes to be constituted as meaningful. Secondly, time is dealt with as a core problem of social theory, one that has taken many different forms in the course of the history of social thought, and that concerns the relationship between the way in which time is conceived, on the one hand, and the way in which we try to understand history and social order, on the other.[2]

These two ways of dealing with time have existed independently of one another, as a largely empiricist and a mainly presuppositional endeavour respectively. With the present paper I hope to contribute to their inter-penetration using some of the findings of the empirical sociology of time to clarify issues of general social theory, while using the problem definitions of the latter to orient and explain the former.

Time and Social Change

Sociological theory has traditionally dealt with time in relation to the question of social change. The way in which this is done has profoundly altered over the last ten to fifteen years.

Until about ten years ago, and even more recently in some quarters and journals, one could hear sociologists lamenting the alleged static bias of their discipline and its lack of attention to the effects of the passage of time. Today it has become abundantly clear that such a charge does not stand up to close scrutiny. Both Martins (1974) and Kenichi Tominaga (1985) have amply documented sociologists' involvement with development, modernisation, social evolution and other modes of considering social change. More recently the question of change has been raised in a very different and more thorough way. The new mood is frequently one of failure. The statements pretending to be theories of change are being discarded as empirically invalid, overly and naively ambitious, and even as epistemologically ill-conceived.

Such criticism is, for instance, exemplified in the renewed popularity of the old proposition that the scientific study of social change is impossible, and that the phenomenon of social change can only be approached in the historian's way. That proposition has, for quite some time now, been forcefully defended by Robert Nisbet (e.g. 1969) and one finds it elegantly realised in the work of Reinhard Bendix.[3] Quite important for the future development of the discipline is, I believe, the growing number of sociologists who feel attracted to historical (comparative) studies and whose position is characterised by a scepticism towards theory and by a new sense of 'historical particularity' (e.g. Skocpol 1984).[4]

Methodological individualism, particularly its claim that a macro-sociological explanation of change is impossible, can be regarded as another, albeit quite different, expression of this critique (e.g. Boudon 1984).

The renewed interest in perspectives that imply a high degree of unexplainable variability in concrete courses of action that use less 'scientis-ing' methodologies, and attempt a return to the position of the old *Geisteswissenschaften*, express this same mood.

Irrespective of their theoretical import and merit, these criticisms indicate an important development. Thinking about social change now starts from the premise that the theory of history – whatever its form: theological, philosoph-ical, psychological or sociological – is dead.[5] Societies and social systems do change, but we have no theory to predict concrete courses of change: certainly not a general theory of change (whatever that would be), not even tenable special theories concerned with specific institutions. This loss of faith in theory is, however, much more than, and something quite different from, a recognition of ignorance. It is a definite position concerning the role of men and women in history, and leads to a different conception of time. It signals a renewed interest in what I would like to call *Chronos*, i.e. in time as a possibility for creation and destruction, and as a source of uncertainty and choice.[6]

Time and the Reconstruction of Social Theory

Today, time is increasingly recognised as an issue in its own right, and not just as a secondary factor that becomes relevant when the question of social change is raised. That recognition is carried by a number of notions and concepts that play an important role in contemporary theory debate. These will be traced here in the recent work of Luhmann and Giddens, particularly in the former's *Soziale Systeme, Grundriss einer allgemeinen Theorie*, and the latter's *The Constitution of Society*.[7] In these books one can identify at least four notions that are crucial for the new place of time in social thought.

Historically Independent Processes

The first of these crucial notions is the rejection of the static–dynamic difference, which has played a key role in the study of social change and in the older versions of system theory. Structures are no longer defined as stable relationships between the enduring elements of systems. Both Giddens (1979: 198) and Luhmann (1984: 471–2) reject the idea that structures can be conceived of as static, skeleton-like phenomena that can be studied through static or synchronic observation. Instead they conceive of social systems as continuously produced and/or reproduced as volatile elements, and of structure as either having virtual existence – as the order that makes such reproduction possible (Giddens) – or as consisting of expectations (Luhmann). System and structure, consequently, exist not only as processes in time (cf. Giddens 1979: 199) but also, in a sense that is of fundamental importance to Luhmann's *Grundriss*, by virtue of the passage of time (1984: 302–3, 383).

Beyond Positivism

Both the authors considered here show a readiness to draw radical philosophical conclusions from the (re)discovery of time as *Chronos*.

Giddens expresses these with regard to the possible influence of social theory on social life (e.g. 1982: 11–4). Social science 'laws' are historical and mutable; once formulated they can become norms and resources. This position leads him to a critique of positivism and of Marxist historicity, i.e. the belief that we can learn from the past to change the future (1984: 205).

Since all concrete activities partake in the uncertainty of time, and possibly form the occasion for a discontinuity, the crucial question, according to Luhmann, does not concern the causal explanation of a concrete state of affairs, but the possibility of abstraction, i.e. of the selection through abstraction of aspects of the fleeting reality that lead to the experience and understanding of duration (1984: 394–6).

Re-evaluating Micro-Sociology

A third, and very important characteristic of these theoretical developments, is the recognition of the accomplishments of phenomenology and ethnomethodology. Particularly pertinent in this respect are the notions of 'normalisation', 'standardisation as achieved' and 'negotiated identities', as well as the practices of 'let it pass', 'the waiting for something to happen which promises to clarify what has gone before' ... etc. (Garfinkel 1968: 220). These notions and practices refer to developments that necessarily take place over time, and that give interaction good continuity prospects, despite surprise, frustration and rule-breaking. They considerably clarify our understanding of the way in which events can be interpreted as consistent with rules and past experience, while at the same time they specify, reaffirm or even constitute rules and past experience as a basis for future expectation.[8] This sounds complicated: needlessly so, for nothing more mysterious is involved than the creative powers of looking back at what happened. After the passage of sufficient time, even the most unexpected and unlikely events can and often will come to be looked upon as self-evident and even inevitable.

Self-reference

The fourth crucial notion, that is in fact essential to the interpretation of the previous three, concerns the self-reference of the social system.

This is expressed by Giddens in his idea of the duality of structure, and in his insistence on the recursive character of reflexively monitored social practices (1979; 1982). Structure is seen as both medium and outcome of the reproduction of practices. These practices constitute recurrently both the subject or human agent, and the social object (society or institutions), while they are also practices of knowledgeable actors that can be institutionalised or followed by a majority of the members of a society (1982: 9).

The notion of self-reference is specified by Luhmann on the basis of the theory of autopoietic systems. That theory was initially developed as a definition of living systems. An autopoietic system is defined by Maturana and Varela as '... a network of processes of production (transformation and destruction) of components that produce the components which (1) through their action and transformations continuously regenerate and realise the network of processes ... that produces them; and (2) constitute it (the system M.E.) as a concrete unity in the space in which they (the components) exist by specifying the topological domain of its realising as such a network' (1980: 79).[9]

For Luhmann, who transfers this model to non-living systems, the components of the social system are acts. These are not given as such but self-referentially constituted as signified events through communication and attribution (1984: 191). The elements of the system – the acts – appear as a series of realised distinctions that divide the continuous flow of events (i.e. 'conduct') and achieve the self-simplification of the system to the point where a sufficient knowledge to operate adequately becomes possible. These acts are conceived of, by Luhmann, as 'passing', i.e. they create the occasion for other acts which are both new and prepared (*vorkategorisiert*) by the previous acts. This recursive production of action is structured in the sense of being monitored by expectations concerning the next appropriate or probable action.

The notion of self-reference always involves the seemingly paradoxical blending of operand and operator, subject and object. It conjures the image of systems being producer and product, and of elements producing the network that produces them. Strictly speaking we cannot represent something that is both and *at the same time* subject and object, operand and operator, unless we picture it in time as consisting of states that alternate in a circular sequence. 'Therefore', writes Varela, 'we find a peculiar equivalence of self-reference and time, in so far as self-reference cannot be conceived outside time, and time comes in whenever self-reference is allowed' (1978: 20).

Time and the Problem of Order

These various developments, particularly the emphasis on reflexivity, have made time a fundamental dimension of social theory (cf. Giddens 1984: 35; Luhmann 1984: 300–3). Both *The Constitution of Society* and *Soziale System* are largely devoted to the elaboration of a frame of reference and a consistent set of concepts that do justice to the new relevance of time.

The fundamental question for Giddens is how social systems come to be 'stretched across time and space' (1984: 35). This 'stretching' is equated with the existence of continuity which, in turn, is closely related to routine: 'routine is integral to both the continuity of the personality ... and to the institution of society' (1984: 60). This reconstructed problem of order is then translated into the question why actors 'follow the routines they do' (1984: 70). It is in answering this question that Giddens relies heavily on the work of Goffman, and, quite surprisingly after so much taunting of consensus theory, returns to the Parsonian solution for the problem of order. Indeed, he accounts for routine by the 'generalised motivational commitment to the integration of habitual practices across time and space' (1984: 64, cf. 70), and sees routine as grounded in tradition, habit and the need for security (1984: 86). At this critical junction, when structuration theory tries to answer a question it formulates as a critique of the so-called 'orthodox consensus', it fails to keep its promise of innovation, and returns full circle to the solution it initially seemed to reject. My critique does not concern the proposed solutions as such. Shared elements of culture, traditions, habits, needs, collectively held commitments ... are certainly worthwhile searching for and, when found, do render action intelligible. What has to be explained, or at least problematised, is, however, (1) the observation that interaction often continues even when not premised on a shared commitment to continuation, and (2) how and why interactions are opened, closed, bounded, continued, 'left behind', repeated ... One has, in other words, to show how a symbolic system can come to be shared, and to what extent it has to be shared in order to make it possible for instances of interaction to be repeated or continued. Quite a lot of what could be interpreted as commitment to continuation, and shared rules and meanings, might simply be the expectation that something sensible or good might 'yet come from it'.

Throughout his latest book Giddens emphasises 'the repetitive character of day-to-day life' as if this constitutes an explanation for, rather than an alternative formulation of, the problem of order. He thereby creates an image of society and reproduction as a boringly repetitive affair without room for innovation and change, except by unexplainable *caesura*.[10]

This failure is at least partly due to the use of a naturalistic concept of time, as well as to the failure to sufficiently clarify the relationships between (1) structure and time, and (2) structure and routine.

Giddens usually writes of time as of something *across* which social systems can be '*stretched*'. This is not a matter of unfortunate formulation. Giddens repeatedly uses 'time' in its present-day common-sense meaning (e.g. 1979: 199; 1984: XXVIII, 181, 201), which is a boiled down version of the metaphysical, absolute (Newtonian) specification of the concept of time.[11] As a consequence he does not investigate how and in what sense social and historical time can be considered a 'relation between ... events' or how social systems actively organise their temporal continuity. He does not ask how events, activities, or experiences can come to be seen as repetitions, and acted upon as such. Continuity and the possibility of repetition, recursiveness, etc. are instead treated as either unproblematical or realisable by virtue of a normative commitment.

Even though Giddens equates routine with institutional features of action (1984: 86), and hence with great time–space extension (1984: 17), and defines structure as '... the property which makes it possible for discernible similar practices to exist across varying spans of time ...' (1984: 17), he does not explicitly deal with the relation between structure and routine. Structure itself is seen by Giddens as standing 'out of time and space' (1984: 25), a view that is reminiscent of the neo-Platonic theory of time that distinguished between the eternal/atemporal and the temporal. That theory theologically sheltered

God from the activities of men and women. In a similar way, Giddens' atemporal view of structure seems to place both routine and structures out of time, beyond the reach of explanations that can be evaluated on the basis of historical and cross-cultural variations. Structuration theory, as it stands in the *Constitution of Society*, adds little or nothing to our understanding of how societies constitute their temporality. It merely signals the centrality of that problem to present-day social theory, and shows that a better understanding and a more precise conceptualisation of temporality is a condition for progress in theory-building.

Luhmann uses phenomenology and the contributions of micro-sociology in a much more radical and ambitious way than Giddens. While the latter changes the definition of the problem of order to finally give it a Parsonian solution, the former stays close to one of Parsons' definitions of the problem,[12] but tries to find a different solution. Implicitly referring to Parsons' emphasis on shared value commitments, Luhmann wonders whether time and history should not take their place as the foundations of social order (1984: 175). It is his attempt to outline such a solution, and his long-standing commitment to find alternatives to normative integration, that orient his approach to time. From the logical impossibility of conceiving of self-reference outside of time, Luhmann seems to conclude that time creates the possibility of the reflexive monitoring of action in complex self-referential systems (1984: 601), and defines time accordingly.[13]

His approach, and the way it differs from Giddens', can be illustrated by presenting his concept of structure and its relation to time.

For Luhmann, as for Giddens, the structure of social systems has to account for the way in which meaningful acts are related over or across time (1984: 383). For Luhmann it consists of expectations and, reflexively, of expectations of expectations. Structures thus conceived are moreover supported and protected by provisions for dealing with, as well as avoiding, frustrated expectations (magic, tact, belief in chance, politeness . . .). This view of structure is grounded in the conception of a social system as consisting of interpreted events that have a pointlike, timeless quality, and are constantly passing. The central problem of social systems, then, is to produce the next act, to follow up the previous one, without losing their identity. Structure is a selection of possible ways of following up and of connecting events and acts. As such it stands for selection – i.e. it excludes the possibility that everything can follow after everything – and it defines the identity of the system by the specific selections it entails. Within this view, a normative commitment becomes a way of structuring, rather than a ground or explanation for structure and routine. Similarly 'rules and resources' which for Giddens *are* structure and explain social practice, are 'merely' contingent structural elements that autopoietic systems use for their reproduction. At this point the contrast between the action-theoretical character of Giddens' approach, and the system-theoretical character of Luhmann's is particularly sharp.

Luhmann's *Grundriss* is largely devoted to ontology. Many sociological concepts that are usually regarded as fundamental are redefined by virtue of the role they can play in an inherently temporal process of autopoietic reproduction: 'commitment' comes to be seen as a mechanism for time-binding, i.e. as a way of creating non-random sequences of actions by limiting future choice (1984: 301);[14] 'structure' becomes a specification for the possibility of temporally relating elements of the social system (ibid.: 383); 'function' is considered as an abstraction that can make activities comparable and hence repetitive (ibid.: 408); 'roles' and 'values' are means to simplify expectations and make them operative in complex situations (ibid.: 416). Because of the dazzlingly conscious, creative, and consistent way in which this exercise is carried through, the *Soziale System* offers the basis of a conceptual scheme and a feasible programme to deal with the relation between time and social order in novel ways.

Both Luhmann and Giddens define structure in terms of time. For both, structure allows for the extension or reproduction of social systems over time. However, while time, and the relationship between time and social structure, occupy a central place in their theories, their conception of time remains highly ambiguous. Even though Giddens occasionally refers to time as a mode in which relations are expressed, and Luhmann sees it as the temporalisation of self-reference, both authors do in fact fall back on a naturalistic conception of time as something that exists independently of psychological and social systems. This naturalistic time is furthermore dealt with by negation. Giddens atemporalises the structure of systems, Luhmann their elements.

These ambiguities can be more clearly identified by distinguishing the three 'kinds of time' that are, usually implicitly, used in the literature.

Time, Temporal Meaning and Temporality

Time as a Concept

Time concepts and time awareness have a (Western) history that has been accounted for in a surprisingly consistent way by anthropology and sociology. Beginning with Durkheim (1968: 12–28, 627–36), the time concept has been described as evolving in the direction of ever greater abstraction, emancipating itself from local particularities in order to become, in the end, a mathematical concept that hides its history behind its apparently logical nature.[15] Subsequent scholarship has specified, qualified, but by and large confirmed, these propositions as an account of the Western history of time.

Time, as a concept used to interpret and give meaning to reality, has certainly not always been equally well distinguished or differentiated from what happens in time (cf. Hallowell 1937; Sorokin and Merton 1937; Evans-Pritchard 1940: 100–8): surface has been measured by the time it takes to till the land, and duration has been rendered by naming well known routine activities. Once such distinctions were reasonably well established, and for instance calendars could become more clearly differentiated from agendas, the concept of time was to become more abstract and universal.[16] Time came to be viewed as a very general code and medium – an abstract representation or measure of not yet committed possibilities of action. A premium was put on the regularity of time – time itself became absolutely, perfectly predictable – and this ideal was gradually approached by the technology of time measurement, up to the point where the earth itself could be declared a poor, hectic time-keeper. These developments – the differentiation of time from what happens in time and its mathematisation – have been related as both the consequence of and instrument to specific societal changes: increasing structural differentiation, the rise of the money economy and capitalism, the increase in structural complexity, uncertainty, and the load of coordination problems.[17] For modern European history, the most significant aspect of this mutually reinforcing process is the rise and diffusion of a mathematical conception of absolute time. This development manifests itself from the fourteenth century onward (Le Goff 1977, Pomian 1984: 253 ff.): it finds its crisp, formal expression in the realm of physics; it has philosophical and scientific critics from the moment it became clearly formulated (e.g. Berkeley, Leibnitz); and it has greatly increased the possibilities for coordination and control in many fields of activity.

As the use of absolute clock time spread, it raised strong feelings of resentment: '*Un Dieu sinistre, effrayant, impossible*', wrote Baudelaire about the clock. It would, however, have been more correct to address absolute time itself in that way. That conception of time is in fact, literally, an image and definition of God.[18] Absolute, mathematical sui generis time is a God concept that became Nature, second nature, common sense and commodity all at once.

The conception of time as something that 'flows equably without relation to anything external' and does so 'of itself and from its own nature'[19] is obviously so well suited to fit a highly differentiated world system into a common time frame (Zerubavel 1982; Luhmann 1982: 299–312) that its contingent nature was indeed, as Durkheim already suggested, hard to realise and even harder to keep in mind.

Time as Fact

Around the turn of the century the intellectual hold of absolute mathematical time had, nevertheless, been broken by the efforts of people like Bergson, Einstein, Mach and Poincaré.[20]

These authors no doubt contributed to the view prevalent today, that time 'as such' or 'as fact' need not be absolutely regular, flow equably, or have the other characteristics of a perfect, immutable interval scale. The natural character of time – the idea that it exists in a way that is relevant for social systems, yet independent of social and psychological systems – and its *sui generis* status – the idea that time cannot be influenced by social systems and their elements – seem, on the contrary, still generally accepted by sociologists.

A conception of time as natural and *sui generis*, though not absolute, is, however, not easy to formulate. One of the versions in which it manifests itself in sociology is the view that some 'kinds of time' are more natural than others. Usually 'clock time' is regarded as artificial, compared to the more 'natural' subjective perception of time or the temporality that results from certain kinds of adaptation to seasonal rhythms and other environmental or biological constraints. In general this proposition devalues the temporality of formal organisations and of a great many social systems, which depend on clock time for their coordination and functioning, in favour of temporalities that can be discovered in the organism and the psychological system and that are supposed to have been realised in the agrarian communities of yore. Whatever the normative and aesthetic merits of this position, it is also a beautiful illustration of how past contingent arrangements and selections can come to be considered as natural. It is, furthermore, plagued by the fact that in many cultures abstract mathematical time, as measured by the mechanical clock, has become the intuitive, everyday understanding of time. Access to other experiences of time has become very difficult.

Another way of dealing with non-absolute *sui generis* time consists in positing its existence, while skirting the problem of its specification. That is the strategy followed by Luhmann and Giddens. The former explicitly states that the time dimensions interprets something that *would nevertheless exist* even if it were neither interpreted nor given meaning (1984: 116, n.44) and that time is accordingly not just a concept but a fact of (macroscopic) nature (ibid.: 71). Luhmann declines, however, to specify what that 'fact' consists of.[21] In a similar vein Giddens states:

> It is in some part the lack of 'fit' between our unproblematic coping with the continuity of conduct across time–space, and its ineffable character when confronted philosophically, that is the very essence of the puzzling nature of time. I make no particular claim to elucidate this matter, St Augustine's problem.
>
> (Giddens 1984: 35)[22]

Temporality

A temporalised system is defined by Luhmann as a system that has learned to live with the inevitable and irreversible passage of time and that has done so because it has developed structures that are able to link elements (acts) that are constantly emerging and disappearing, constantly produced and decaying (1984: 77). The way in which a system achieves its temporality is system-specific. For the social system the process is mediated by meaning (1982: 291). In fact the whole reconstruction of social theory, as attempted by Luhmann, seems geared towards an account of the various ways in which social systems constitute themselves as temporal systems. His pressing the existence of time as fact of nature, seems at least in part a rather unfortunate consequence of a premature attempt at theoretical closure. Some kind of 'natural', pre- or subcultural, existence of time as an unspecified, meaningless and irreversible passage of not yet interpreted events has indeed to be assumed in order to ground social order in time and history, without recourse to either freely constituted subjects or value consensus (Luhmann 1979). Such a solution is only vicariously attractive, by virtue of the unattractiveness of its presently available alternatives. It is not imposing. The notion of a natural sui generis time that exists outside of our communication with the world is reminiscent of a science that conceived itself as observation from an imaginary outside and that was unable to see itself as a product of its subject matter. It is precisely this view that the reconstruction of social theory (and particularly the works focused on here) is trying to overcome. I therefore propose to bypass natural sui generis time, and to leave it as an object of inquiry to physicists. In social theory it is quite cumbersome anyway. Social systems have to be stretched across it, while it destroys their elements. It can, moreover, not be grasped, defined or specified. When natural time is no longer appealed to, the logic of Luhmann's and Giddens' theories demands a specification of (the function of) structure in terms of the *concept* of time and the temporality of systems. These can, moreover, no longer be defined or understood by reference to time as a (mysterious) fact of nature. The concept of time does not represent time-as-fact, and temporality does not cope with that fact. The questions 'what makes a system temporal?' and 'what does our concept of time stand for?' have to be answered in a different way. Here again it is possible to follow Augustine's lead, when, no longer baffled, he writes that '. . . if nothing were, there would be no present time'.

Sequence and Repetition

Instead of defining temporality as a system's ability to exist despite the (allegedly factual or natural) passage of time, I propose to define it as the property that is necessary and sufficient in order to meaningfully relate a system to the concept of time. What that concept is or involves cannot be specified without taking into account its uses: its different elaborations and various operationalisations, techniques, technologies and aesthetics. All these different uses concern, in one way or another, the measurement and designation of time, broadly conceived. The fact that such measurements, and with them the concrete operational concepts of time, do show great historical and cultural variation, does not exclude the presence of a more invariant kernel that can be considered as the core of the concept of time.[23]

For such a core to exist, all uses of the concept, however simple or complex, would have to share a number of identifiable properties that are necessary for the concept to be understood as a concept of time? Such a conceptual core has been sought by people studying the history of time-keeping and measurement. These scholars did indeed have to decide what they would consider as a measure of time. That task involves the identification of the properties a procedure must necessarily have (or that have to be embodied in some sort of contraption) for it to qualify as a measure of time. The answer given should, moreover, not suffer from ethnocentrism. It should not exclude any set of procedures, tools or machines that in any known culture are accepted (or experienced) to designate, tell or record time in a way that is intersubjectively understandable in terms of that culture. Their conclusion, in the words of Gerald Clemens, is that '*Any repetitive phenomenon, whatever, the recurrence of which can be counted, is a measure of time*' (1981: 406).[24]

Since time concepts must at least express the properties that are necessary and sufficient to experience, designate, tell, count or register time, this general definition of a measure of time can also be used to identify the necessary and sufficient core of the concept: the possibility to conceive of sequence and recurrence, and to conceive of sequence through recurrence, and of recurrence through sequence.

Only two properties are given by the definition: repetition (or recurrence) and sequence (or the possibility to count events). These can be formulated as general conditions.

In order for a system to be temporal the following two conditions must be simultaneously fulfilled:

−   *some, potentially unique, events must be constituted (classified) as, or taken to be, repetitions or equivalences (i.e. instances of a more general class of events); and*
−   *these events must be sequentially ordered, at least by the elementary distinction between before and after.*

A concept of time is a concept that expresses these properties and a temporal meaning is a dimension of meaning that interprets reality by using these properties.[25]

When these conditions are not fulfilled, a system cannot be related to time, except in the trivial sense of an observer who declares that a system he or she has arbitrarily defined, exists as a kind of chaos, while another system (e.g. a watch) indicates the passage of time.

The two conditions can be represented as dimensions. One of them being the familiar sequential dimension which, in its most abstract mathematical form, can be represented by the sequence of natural numbers. The other, less familiar, temporal dimension produces (the possibility to recognise) repetition or equivalence and hence the distinction between alternating states. This always involves what I shall call relative invariance: a change of state can only be observed when not everything is changing (at the same time and rate).[26]

These two dimensions can be analytically distinguished and experienced as different aspects of life. The sequential dimension underlies the linear aspect of time and the images of the irreversible flow of time and life to which Western literature has devoted so much attention.[27] The dimension of relative invariance underlies the cyclical aspect of time and the extremely powerful images of recreation, return, the recurrence of life and death, growth and decay. Such images gain their potency by emphasising one dimension of temporality to the detriment of the other. Concretely, these dimensions cannot be separated from each other. There is no such thing as a cyclical time or a linear time.[28] Time does not merely involve the creation of relative invariance (or classification) *and* sequence. These are not characteristics of reality that additively yield time. They have to be simultaneously implicated, so that also relatively invariant sequences of actions can emerge. The time concept captures this simultaneity of an event or a sequence of events as *both* a repetition and a phenomenon rendered unique by its place in a sequence and, more importantly, the discovery/invention of time gives every event the potential for both uniqueness and repetitiveness.

The classifications, and more generally, the relative invariances that are involved, can certainly not be conceived as determined by their own properties (cf. Goodman 1972: 443). They have to be made. And it is difficult to see how that production could take place without the simultaneity of relative invariance and sequence, i.e. without time. It is time that allows us to wait, to see whether the sequence of events clarifies the classifications, the relative invariances of the situation and the meanings that are involved. It is also time that allows us to emphasise either the uniqueness or the repetitiveness, as a function of our intentions, and of what happened afterwards. Yet the time in which such clarification can occur is not naturally given. It is rather a time constituted by relative invariance and sequential order. This view of time shifts our attention from the question of how systems live with time to the problem of the production of time and its use.

Since they are the necessary and sufficient conditions of a measure of time, it is obvious that the dimensions will be formally expressed in all time measurement technologies. These always present themselves as sequences of cycles. This, however, does not mean that these dimensions themselves are formal, abstract matters. Sequence or linearity and the cyclical are substantially involved in social organisation. The linear aspect of time expresses the belief that 'things will continue', 'that new events will occur' ... while the cyclical aspect expresses our ability to begin and to end, to delimit and to draw boundaries, to invent budgetary years and statutes of limitation, and to allow for the determination 'to start all over again' or 'to do it better next time'. This additive description does not do full justice to the social and emotional reality of the dimensions, for what is really involved is again not the ability to delimit *and* to continue, but the ability to begin and end *while* continuing.

The remainder of this paper will be used to clarify the temporal dimensions and the temporalist perspective, while, hopefully, illustrating their usefulness to both the sociology of time and general sociology.

Relative Invariance and Sequential Order

In clarifying and illustrating the use of the dimensions, I must limit myself to a few short, and quite general, remarks on four topics: structure, choice, the form of the interpretations of society and history, and the double task of the sociology of time.

Structures

Structures are usually defined as the properties that allow systems to exist in time, i.e. to continue to exist despite changes in their elements. Traditionally this was accomplished by viewing them as 'things' that lasted and stayed the same over time. More recently the concrete difference between 'thing-like' structures and processes has been abandoned. Both Giddens and Luhmann try to develop a concept of structure that makes duration intelligible without artificially separating structure and process. They do so by negotiating an escape from (factual) time. Giddens tries to accomplish this in a structuralist manner by placing structure 'out of time', while Luhmann, who sees structure as a selection of possible sequences of acts, relates the (relative) invariance of structure to the duration of the selectivity (1984: 386). None of these new conceptualisations has the clarity or intuitive attractiveness of the traditional view. It seems fair to say that the search for a new concept of structure is still open. From a temporalist perspective one can at least suggest the rethinking of some premises of that search.

Overcoming the passage of time, which is structure's theoretical function, does not have to be understood as dealing with natural sui generis time. It can, rather, be interpreted in the sense of creating a system's temporality. Structures, then, whatever else they do, would in one way or another create (the possibility of) relative invariance and sequential order. This conception establishes a strong Augustinian equivalence between the concept of structure and time. The one does not precede the other, explain it or negate it. The structure of a system realises the system's temporality, and the concept and semantics of time become one way of interpreting, reflecting upon, knowing and reproducing the structure. It is in this sense that the sociology of time can become a study of structure. Even though this concept of structure is still abstract and contentless, and cannot be much further specified without turning to concrete structural arrangements or specific systems, it allows for some theoretical and methodological remarks.

On the basis of this concept no a priori difference between structure and structuration (cf. Giddens 1984: 25) seems possible. The 'conditions governing the continuity or transformation of structures ...' cannot be dealt with as separate from structures themselves. They are part of the same process. *What keeps a system structured is not the presence of invariance of expected sequence (of rules, resources, expectations ...), but the maintenance of a difference between the more and the less invariant (or variant)*: not, for instance, fixed rules, but a difference between the game being played and the rules of the game. Similarly one cannot separate structure, as expected relations, from the mechanisms to deal with frustrated expectations. The latter are not supports of a structure that exists independently of them, but elements of the structure.

The Creation of Choice

The related concepts of choice and selection play a central role in the theories that emphasise the creative and destructive potentialities of time. To choose is, indeed, what actors are supposed to do when they are said to make history and reproduce society through meaningful selective action. To hold such a view of history and society implies that one should be able to specify the social conditions of choice. The temporal dimensions allow for such a specification, without seeing choice as either a property of freely constituted individuals or as an initially meaningless selection made necessary by the passage of time.[29]

The temporal dimensions can be seen as variable. There can be more or less temporal order, the ratio of what changes to what remains stable can vary, etc ... When seen in this way, the dimensions yield images of their limits. On the one hand, one can imagine a situation in which no sequential order whatsoever exists and everything changes at the same time. For this situation of complete randomness, in which foresight as well as hindsight is impossible and in which normalisation and rationalisation have as little place as expectations, our culture has developed the concept of chaos. Chaos is a temporal concept by negation. It creates the image of a situation from which time is excluded and that consequently must escape our understanding. On the other hand, one can imagine a perfectly predictable sequence of perfectly identical states. This is the kind of situation which has been expressed by the inter-related images of eternity, God and absolute time. Here too time is negated. In both of those extreme situations the concept of choice would have no sense. In a situation where there is no room for change, selection and choice are impossible. In a chaotic situation, choice, even if it could be imagined, would be without consequence and, hence, irrelevant. It is only when sequential order is taken to exist but to be potentially discontinuous *and* invariance is relative (i.e. not all sequential order is discontinuous at the same time) that the notion of choice becomes meaningful. 'Choice' would indeed have no meaning if it did not constitute a discontinuity or a non-determined selection, but it would be equally meaningless if this selection had no consequences, i.e. did not result in a sequel or constituted a sequence.[30]

Choice then is possible in a world of relative invariances, in which the discontinuity of sequence at one level, supposes the continuity at another level. If we choose to see human beings as making history by choice, then we also have to view them as living by self-imposed limits. Specifically by those limits or rules that are necessary to realise relative invariance and sequential order, and to make behaviour into selection and the initiation of a sequel. It is in that specific sense that the creation of sequential order and relative invariance constitute the conditions of choice and action.

The everyday Western experience of the world as a setting for choice, intentionally and purposefulness conflicts with the experience of that world as fact, constraint and external limitation. Even though these experiences constitute each other, one can make sense of that antinomy. There are, on the one hand, many situations in which relevant and significant events cannot be meaningfully related to intentions or purposes, i.e. in which the causal chains to do so would become impossibly long and complex. For these, the paradigms of fate, chance, God, nature and structural determinism offer good comfortable theories (while the notion of unintended consequences seems to offer a perversely disturbing account). On the other hand, action would become well nigh impossible if an actor would have to worry about all possible consequences and causes of his or her actions (including its conditions and the conditions of the reproducibility of these conditions). The possibility to act seems to be based on something like an 'enabling neglect' that is expressed and legitimated in the theories of the autonomous subject and the rational individual actor. In terms of a Freudian analysis, one can ground these theories in early childhood experience, when the infant 'learns' to attribute action, and later learns the use of the concepts of intention, motive and interest, to make sense of such attribution. Such an origin, however, must not obscure the later insight, typical of a more advanced and less enchanted age, that agency and intentions are attributed, and that the conditions that make intentions reasonable, and attribution workable, are quite fragile, and certainly beyond the control of single individuals. They are collective phenomena.

The practical relevance of these two frames or theories – the structural and the subjective – need not be called into question here. That practical value can, however, be distinguished from their theoretical or scientific merits. Many theorists, including Giddens and Luhmann, call for an integration of these theories or try to supersede the dualism their opposition embodies. One possible road along which this goal can be pursued, is indicated by the insight that time expresses the conditions of choice, while, as a concept it allows people to think and speak about these conditions. This should be correctly understood, and certainly not confused with Platonism. Relative invariance and sequential order are the abstract formulations of core conditions that are realised in many different ways. The ways of doing so can follow each other in history, and/or coexist, conflict and struggle for supremacy and self-evidence within the same culture. So, what is expressed when people talk about time and 'use' time, is not just the invariant core, but the specific way in which these conditions are realised in a concrete situation. It is for that reason that the empirical sociology of time should listen when men and women in concrete situations use the concept of time, and try to implicate some solution for the creation of relative invariance and sequential order in their dealings with each other.

Interpreting History and Society

Observation and interpretation are temporal activities. They suppose the capacity to distinguish and comprehend the difference between past and present, as well as the possibility to recognise repetition and equivalence. That does not make the conditions of observation and interpretation the ultimate explanation of reality, but implies that our interpretation will always be temporal. It will always move between the polar concepts of absolute invariance or fixed unique sequence (eternity, God, nature . . .), on the one hand, and chaos, on the other. Intellectual and scientific progress, especially conceptual progress, will to a large extent consist of the elaboration of ways in which to conceive of and explain relative invariance and sequential order without recourse to these extreme solutions.

The temporal self-interpretation of society can be studied by looking at the way in which the temporal dimensions are represented. The specification of the latter yields a ready checklist of pertinent questions: e.g. how are relative invariance and sequential order represented?, how is the relationship between the more invariant and the less invariant conceived?, how is the relationship between before and after understood? The history of these representations cannot be dealt with here.[31] Only some relatively recent shifts that are directly related to the reconstruction of sociological theory will be briefly sketched.

From the sixteenth century onward history lost its character of a programme and the possibility of conscious human intervention was gradually accepted (Lloyd 1953; Luhmann 1976; Pomian 1985). That development underlies the (re)discovery of *Chronos*

It problematises the very idea of sequence by establishing the distinction between a sequence of observed events and sequential order. To come to know and understand the latter a special kind of knowledge, not immediately given by sensory perception, is required: the kind of knowledge that would allow us to place a randomly presented series of fragments from an unknown biography, or a series of snapshots of the same unknown person taken at different ages, in the correct sequence. Social science has never been characterised by an exclusive focus on cause–effect relations in order to achieve such knowledge and understanding. Nevertheless, the alternatives, such as the emphasis on normalisation, means–end relations, the re-reading of history (Martins 1974: 266–7), or sensitivity to the ways in which people abandon themselves to events, and rationalise them afterwards as meaningful intersections of intended causal chains, figure much more prominently in sociological thinking today than they did a few decades ago.[32]

This problematisation of sequence should, however, not be interpreted to mean that the search for sequential order, and its use in the interpretation of history and society, has become less important.[33]

The distinction of levels of relative invariance, beyond the older God/ Man, essence/appearance and form/matter dichotomies, is a standard feature of such interpretations, at least since the Medieval introduction of '*aevum*' as a level of invariance between the atemporal '*aeternitas*' and the completely contingent '*tempus*'. *Aevum* was temporal, had a beginning and an end, but an unchanging essence (Pomian 1984: 44).[34] The distinction of levels of invariance has become an increasingly explicit feature of modern science, especially in system theory and the various forms of structuralism, e.g. organisation/structure (Maturana); function/structure (Parsons); *longue durée/conjoncture/événementiel* (Braudel); competence/ performance (Chomsky); *langue/parole* (de Saussure), rules/game.

Simplifying matters somewhat for the sake of brevity, one can say that natural science, and to a large extent social science, were until recently characterised by a view of reality and their respective subject matters, that privileged causal explanation, accorded priority to the past, assumed the existence of an unvarying master programme that was slowly discovered by science, and consequently saw the fulfilment of science in the search for the invariant, the atemporal and the negation of time (Monod 1970: 117; Wiener 1975: 26).[35] Today this view is being abandoned. That is one aspect of what has been called here the rediscovery of *Chronos*, and it is this shift in the conception of science that the reconstruction of sociological theory tries to assimilate. That shift does not mean – as some sociologists seem to think – that the concepts of cause and effect can be forgotten, that something relevant is said merely by calling perceived changes *caesura*, or that social systems only exist in the eyes of the beholder. It signals instead a greater degree of reflexivity in the use of time in the study of social systems. This reflexivity can be helped by the explicit recognition of the temporal dimensions and by the awareness that all social theory and all accounts of history will, if not explicitly then implicitly, contain as fundamental dimensions, first, a classification of social reality along the axis of relative invariance, secondly a set of assumptions about the sequential order that binds the observed reality. A temporalist perspective invites a specific kind of theoretical self-reflection. It induces us to look at theories with respect to the ways in which these conceptualise relative invariance and the nature(s) of sequential order. It is in the way theories combine and relate these dimensions to each other, that they give a substantive account of temporality.

The Sociology of Time

The sociology of time does not yet exist as a recognised specialism. Yet there are a number of research activities that can be grouped under that heading and that seem to share, at least to some extent, a body of research questions and an emerging set of criteria with which to judge research efforts.[36] The recent trends in general social theory, which have been sketched here, place this nascent sociological field in a rather strategic position and assigns it a double function.

Until now the sociology of time has been mostly involved with the study of the various ways in which time (as a general measure of possibilities) is used, as well as with the topics of scheduling and temporal organisation. The object of the sociology of time has even been described as the study of the institutions and mechanisms that control such uses of time (Zerubavel 1980). I think that object is considerably broader. The existence of temporal structures and temporal norms (Schöps 1980: 30 ff.; Zerubavel 1976, 1979, 1980) already imply that the timing and the duration of an event will be part of the complex of aspects on the basis of which the event will be interpreted, attributed to an actor and made into an act that calls for specific expectations and reactions. An early morning gathering is unlike to be(come) a party, and the meaning of a smile depends not only on its setting, but on its timing as well. In that sense time – as a dimension of meaning, or constitutive symbol – is crucially involved in the creation of sequences of events (= actions) through the interdependent processes of interpretation, communication and attribution.

The sociology of time should not limit its enquiry to those three areas of the use of time, its scheduling and the way in which temporal parameters function as constitutive symbols. It should also empirically study relative invariance and sequential order: not, of course, in the sense of a general study of structure, but specifically in relation to time. This involves at least two things. First, the study of the ways in which the creation of relative invariance and sequential order allows for the use of time: for its use as a generalised capacity or medium, as well as for the use of the parameters of time such as duration, timing, sequential position, cycle … The relationship between the way relative invariance and sequential order are realised, and the different ways of dealing with reality in a temporal frame, such as storing, preserving, forgetting, recalling, anticipating, planning … also belong here. Secondly, the sociology of time should study how specific concepts, semantics and technologies of time are involved in the (knowledgeable) creation of relative invariance and sequential order.

The way in which relative invariance and sequential order are realised, and allow for the use of time, involves knowledge that can be stored, improved upon, elaborated, and forgotten and discarded. Making explicit the reflexivity that is unavoidable when dealing with temporalisation, one can say that there are a number of socio-temporal technologies that are themselves time-dependent, but that constitute a level of invariance with regard to the way in which they are used in the realisation of the temporal dimensions.

These socio-temporal technologies can be used to solve specific problems. For instance, 'how to bring the future into the present, how to act now upon a situation that does not yet exist or how to make someone else do something now in view of what might happen later?'. Various solutions can and have been developed for such problems, going from social parenthood and artificial kinship to patronage and promise, to credit and contract ... Another ubiquitous temporal question concerns the preservation of present possibilities of choice and action for future use. This problem has been and is dealt with by the development of money and other media. The constitution is another well known example of a socio-temporal technology, one that is used to create a level of relative invariance which leaves ample possibilities for variation and choice. The sociology of time can certainly make a contribution by studying these and other institutions as socio-temporal technologies and arrangements that are used for the realisation of the temporal dimensions.

From Sui Generis Time to the Conditions of Temporality

From a temporalist perspective one can, self-reflexively, wonder what the explicit attention for the interplay of relative invariance and sequential order means. The operational concepts of time, which are related to the temporality of social systems, have in the past also oriented the development of socio-temporal technologies and hence the way in which sequential order and relative invariance were realised. The nexus of structural differentiation, the rise of capitalism, the mathematisation of time, the view of time as natural and sui generis, and the development of such socio-temporal technologies as modern credit systems, discrete transactional contract and constitutions, is more or less clear and seems quite obvious in retrospect. Much less evident are the social covariants of the demise of absolute, natural, sui generis time, which had begun in the nineteenth century.

One consequence of the shift from history in natural sui generis time to the temporality of systems is that the future can no longer be taken for granted. This disappearance of the future has nothing to do with pessimism. It is a consequence of the greater awareness of the fact that social systems create their own time and that the idea of a future is only meaningful to the extent the present and the future can be linked through some (relative) invariance and some sequence. In this sense, the future is no longer determined, contained in the past or open, but produced.

The developments in which such a shift becomes clearly apparent, and that constitute poles in the conflict with older conceptions and practices of time, manifest themselves at the level of social theory and of social exchange respectively.

In the realm of theory, classical nineteenth century sociology has abandoned the exclusive emphasis on freely constituted individuals with rights and duties that were grounded in a rational response to their natural appetites. It turned its attention to the social conditions of action. This shift, for instance, from methodological individualism to substantive voluntarism, does no longer allow for a (by now naive) exclusive focus on the question of how time, as a generalised medium or resource, can be used. It forces upon us the question of how time comes to be constituted as a resource.

At the level of organisation and exchange, this change takes the form of a shift from discrete transactions to relations that explicitly incorporate an awareness of, and a tolerance for, the effects of passing time on the definition of the relationship, as well as a sensitivity to the conditions of its reproducibility.[37] The clearest expression of this change is, no doubt, the growth of complex organisation and inter-organisational networks, or the shift away from 'timeless' market transactions towards temporal patterns of relatedness.

Acknowledgements

Revised version of a paper presented at the XIth World Congress of Sociology, New Delhi, August 18–22, 1986. Symposium 1, Sociological Theories and Social Change.

Notes

1. Such uses of time are, for instance, studied in time budget analysis, in research concerning scheduling and planning, in the analysis of queuing and waiting . . .

2. For a recent review of some of the major forms this relationship has taken, see Krzystof Pomian 1984, especially Ch. V. Our formulation should not be interpreted as suggesting that the relationship between conceptions of time and conceptions of order have been specialised from the outset, in the sense that the study of society was considered in need of a special conception of time. The contrary is true. When Augustine wrote '. . . if nothing passed, there would be no past time; if nothing were going to happen, there would be no future time; and if nothing were, there would be no present time' (Confessions XI: 14), he expressed a conception of ultimate reality that was at the same time a conception of man, nature and the nature of history.

3. For a balanced and insightful discussion of Bendix's position on the issue, see Rueschemeyer 1984.

4. The relationship between Clio and sociology has never been very easy. When, at the turn of the century, the traditional history of the purple patch, the linear time and the decisive Event, was losing its self-evidence, social scientists were among the first to attack it. In 1903 François Simiand proposed to smash 'the three idols of the historian's tribe'. One was the 'political idol', or the almost exclusive attention that was given to political events. The second, the 'chronological idol', stood for the belief

that something significant had been said when events had been ordered as simultaneous, anterior or posterior, without raising questions about correlations or causation. The third idol or the 'idol of particularism' referred to the historians' insistence on the unique and the particular to the detriment of the repetitive and the social (o.c. Pomian 1984: 74–6). Even though Simiand is approvingly cited by Lucien Febvre and Marc Bloch, and saw his conception of the historians' craft partly realised in the so-called Annales-school, the idols he attacked still seem with us today.

5. What is called here the 'theory of history' is sometimes referred to as social evolutionism (e.g. Giddens 1984: 237). This terminology should not blind us to the difference between the two. While a theory of history (historicism) is deterministic, the search for the logic and mechanisms of social evolutionary change is, and should be, perfectly compatible with indeterminism of the outcomes (cf. Shields 1986: 71–7).

6. Even though this insight can be presented as a recent critique of post-war sociology (coming from within as well as from outside the 'orthodox' tradition, e.g. Eisenstadt 1973: 22–116), one should not fail to see it as part of a long-term development that is characteristic of modernity and leads to the conception of the future as an open field of possibilities (Lovejoy 1953; Luhmann 1976). Consequently, it also manifests itself in other disciplines and in particular in the natural sciences (e.g. Prigogine and Stengers 1979).

7. For all the striking similarities with regard to the place they accord to time in their conceptual schemes, Luhmann and Giddens obviously differ dramatically on many central issues of general sociology. That causes some difficulties in presenting their ideas in a way that permits direct comparison.

8. For a critical appraisal of these developments and of the extent to which they are compatible with a collectivist position on the problem of order, see J.C. Alexander (1985: 33–7).

9. In that definition we find not only the idea of recursive, self-referential production, but also the requirement of a topological boundary which, of course, need not be a boundary in geographical space. In another paper (Varela et al. 1974) the authors give a key of six conditions which a system must meet in order to be autopoietic. Given the relative indeterminacy of such founding terms as boundary, interaction-relation, element-component and space-domain, this key can function as a glossary of terminology of autopoietic system analysis.

10. This critique of structuration theory was already formulated by Margaret Archer (1985) when she wrote that it characterised society by the counter-images of extreme volatility and chronic recursiveness. She was writing about *Central Problems in Sociological Theory* (1979). I fear that *The Constitution of Society* does not necessitate a revision of that critique.

11. One can find in Giddens' book a number of statements that would seem to contradict such an interpretation of the meaning he gives to time (e.g. 1984: 17, 34) or, when referring to Heidegger: 'We can only grasp time and space in terms of the relation of things and events: they are the modes in which relations between objects and events are expressed' (1981: 30–1). Such statements, however, remain isolated without noticeably influencing Giddens' approach.

12. As it was formulated in *Towards a General Theory of Action* in terms of the problem of the mutuality of expectations and the double contingency of interaction (1967: 15–6).

13. That is, as the temporalisation of a self-referential process: '*Zeit ist Asymmetrisierung von Selbstreferenz im Hinblick auf eine Ordnung von Selektionen, und im sozialen Bereich verzeitlicht sie die doppelte Kontingenz sozialen Handelns mit darin spielenden Selbstreferenzen, um zu ermöglichen, dass unwahrscheinliche Ordnung so gut wie zwangsläufig entsteht, wo immer doppelte Kontingenz erfahren wird*' (1984: 176).

14. A similar interpretation of 'commitment' was already proposed by Becker (1960), and used to explain the continuity of the life course (Elchardus 1984: 259–61).

15. Behind this grandiose Durkheimian tableau of the history of time, one suspects a simple but deeply felt idea: when you have less past in common, you must use a more abstract concept of time in order to coordinate the events you are going to share as a past. The feeling behind this idea is of course typically modern. It deplores the growing difficulty of integration and community, while simultaneously stressing the increased possibilities for communication, scale, interdependence and individual freedom.

16. The distinction between time and what happens in time is of course a matter of degree. Even though essential elements of the distinction are very old, Darwin still needed a few pages of his *Origin of Species* to explain to his readers that it is not time itself which causes evolution. Likewise, even though our calendars are far more clearly differentiated from our agendas than those of the Romans were, they are certainly not (yet) mere mathematical, purely formal tools for the coordination of action.

17. A very incomplete list of references would include: Sorokin and Merton (1937); Julkünen (1963); Luhmann (1968, 1982); E.P. Thompson (1968); Rezsohazy (1970); Inkeles and Smith (1974); Nowotny (1975); Zerubavel (1976, 1980, 1982); Heinemann and Ludes (1978); Schops (1980); Coriat (1981), Lewis and Weigert (1981); Bergmann (1983). Against the background of the consensus about the interactive relationship between societal developments and mathematisation and differentiation of time, the differences that exist between the authors mentioned here, however relevant in other respects, are of truly secondary importance. They concern, as could be expected, the relative importance of cultural or symbolic factors vs. matters of self-interest and control, and the importance of long-term development vs. the impact of more protracted periods of social change.

18. See, for instance, the contributions of the philosopher Henry Moore to the notions of absolute space and time (Dugas and Costabel 1969: 267 ff.).

19. Newton in *Mathematical Principles of Natural Philosophy* (1687).

20. The mathematical conception of time (i.e. the use of time as mathematical description) and time as fact (i.e. the object of inquiry into the nature of time) are now clearly distinguished by natural scientists (Nicolson 1980: 157). It was that distinction between mathematical description with the help of time, on the one hand, and the physical nature of time, on the other, that formed the starting point of Einstein's papers on relativity. For sociologists that difference does not always seem clear. One can still hear and read in print the observation that time budget research is ill-inspired because the precise temporal measure of behaviour implies a commitment to the view that social time is like absolute mathematical time.

21. 'We leave open what time is' (Luhmann 1984: 70). In an earlier article (1982: 299, originally 1975) Luhmann warned against the dangers of doing so.

22. The authority appealed to is formidable. The eleventh book of Augustine's confessions are still crucial reading for a student of time, and the following passage is probably the most quoted sentence in the literature on that subject: 'What, then, is time? I know well enough provided that nobody asks me; but if I am asked what it is and try to explain, I am baffled'.

23. I am certainly not claiming that this core or kernel constitutes the essential element of the concept of time. When studying cultures, rather than abstract and general characteristics of action, not this core but the variation would be both interesting and essential.

24. This definition covers the sociologically very interesting cases in which time is endogenously measured on the basis of recurrent social activities. In such cases

social life itself serves directly as a measure of time.

25. This definition should not be too easily accepted as self-evident. It differs from what is usually understood by time. When Prigogine and Stengers define the capacity to use time as a necessary property of observation, they only mention the capacity to distinguish between before and after (1979: 370). Luhmann too mentions only this capacity as a sufficient basis for the development of a more general time dimension (1984: 116). In general it is this sequential aspect of time to which explicit attention is devoted. That accounts for the habit of confusing conceptions of history with conceptions of time and of taking an interest in history as indicative of a temporal awareness (e.g. Needham 1981). One of the most developed aspects of the sociology of time concerns the time perspectives and the so-called past vs. future orientation of individuals, groups and cultures. I hope to make clear that both sequence and repetition are crucial for a good understanding of temporality. It should already be logically obvious that the one is not possible without the other. For a related, but still different view, see Leach (1961: 125) who holds that all aspects of time derive from the experiences of repetition and irreversible change.

26. In an earlier article (originally published in 1975) Luhmann gave a characterisation of time that came close to explicitly recognising relative invariance as a temporal dimension: 'Time is constituted as events are selected, for a selection is embodied in an event by its standing out from the background of an enduring structure of possibilities', and '... temporal consciousness is a response to the need for conceiving of constancy and change together' (1982: 299). Later (1984) this dimension of temporality almost comes to be equated with 'meaning'. This shift can be understood in the sense that it is very difficult to see how we could interpret and give meaning to reality if we did not view it in temporal terms.

27. For a collection of examples, see J.T. Fraser (1981: 56–8).

28. It is of course possible that a culture in its interpretation of life and history strongly emphasises one rather than the other dimension of time. Such emphasis is what is usually meant by the labels 'linear' and 'cyclical time', and it is often more correct to speak about cyclical and linear chronosophies (cf. Pomian 1985). Even such emphasis must necessarily be relative though, for both temporal dimensions are always involved in the experience and constitution of temporality. This explains why close scrutiny of a culture will invariably yield examples of both the linear and cyclical conceptions (e.g. Lloyd 1975).

29. The latter is the solution Luhmann tries to elaborate.

30. It is probably this paradoxical aspect of the concept of choice – the simultaneous presence of the assumption of continuity and its disruption – that accounts for the fascination it exerts: 'Must we not say that the asymmetry of choice, its character of origin and beginning, yet its setting in motion of a sequel, its uncaused power of causation, is essential to its filling the role that human craving, instinct, or intuition for dignity, responsibility, and free spontaneous pursuit of imagined glory ascribe to it' (Shackle 1979: 20). Whilst sharing the fascination and the enthusiasm, I think that the possibility of choice is 'simply' one of the marvellous products of temporalised systems.

31. For some remarks on their history in Western philosophy and science, see Elchardus (1985: 331–42).

32. This shift in emphasis is related to a growing focus on the present as a locus of decision, rather than on the past as the producer of the present. This change is, of course, related to an explicit critique of tradition and as such is part of a broad societal development. It is possible that George Herbert Mead's *Philosophy of the Present*, by proposing that the past and the future are reconstructed in each present, did play a role in incorporating that shift into sociological thinking (Bergmann 1981).

33. The search for sequential order and especially for the relative invariance of

sequential order under variable conditions, will emerge instead as an alternative to theories of history and grand social evolutionism. Such relatively invariant sequential order corresponds, for instance, to what Theda Skocpol calls 'causal regularities' in history (1984: 374–6).

34. The concept is not unlike the present day 'stages' or 'epochs'. See also Giddens on 'episodes' (1984: 244).

35. Examples of levels of invariance that are or were regarded as major discoveries abound: DNA and the genetic programme, the identity concepts in the study of personality, population in evolution theory ... In equating ultimate achievement with the negation of time, the positivist, scientific strand of modern thinking is in perfect accord with religious and mythical traditions: with the equation of utopia with the end of history and the localisation of paradise outside of time (Eliade 1952: 13).

36. Recent reviews: Lauer (1981); Bergmann (1983).

37. For a way in which this development manifests itself in legal theory and practice, see Macneil (1980, 1985) on discrete and relational contract.

References

Alexander, J.C. 1985. 'The 'Individualist Dilemma' in Phenomenology and Inter-actionism', in Eisenstadt, S.N. and Helle, H.J. (eds.), *Macro-Sociological Theory*, Vol. 1: 25–57. Beverly Hills: Sage.

Archer, M.S. 1985. 'Structuration versus Morphogenesis', in Eisenstadt, S.N. and Helle, H.J. (eds.), *Macro-Sociological Theory*, Vol. 1: 58–88. Beverly Hills: Sage.

Becker, M. 1960. 'Notes on the Concept of Commitment'. *American Journal of Sociology* 66: 32–40.

Bergmann, W. 1981. 'Handlung und Sozialität bei G.H. Mead'. *Zeitschrift für Soziologie* 10 (4): 351–363.

Bergmann, W. 1983. 'Das Problem der Zeit in der Soziologie'. *Kölner Zeitschrift fur Soziologie und Sozialpsychologie* 35 (3): 462–504.

Boudon, R. 1984. *La place du désordre*. Paris: P.U.F.

Clemence, G.M. 1981. 'Time Measurement for Scientific Use', in Fraser, J.T. (ed.), *The Voices of Time*. Amherst: The University of Massachusetts Press.

Coriat, B. 1981. *De werkplaats en de stopwatch: over Taylorisme, Fordisme en massaproductie*. Amsterdam: Van Gennep.

Dugas, R. and Costabel, P. 1969. 'Naissance d'une science nouvelle: La mécanique', in Bauer, E. et al. *Histoire générale des sciences*. Vol. II, La Science Moderne: 252–88. Paris: P.U.F.

Durkheim, E. 1968. *Les formes élémentaires de la vie religieuse*. Paris: P.U.F.

Eisenstadt, S.N. 1973. *Tradition, Change and Modernity*. New York: Wiley.

Elchardus, M. 1984. 'Life Cycle and Life Course, the Scheduling and Temporal Integration of Life', in Feld, S. and Lesthaeghe, R. (eds.), *Population and Societal Outlook*: 251 267. Brussels: Koning Boudewijnstichting.

Elchardus, M. 1985. 'Het Sociale Substraat van de Tijd' (The Social Substratum of Time). *Tijdschrift voor Sociologie* 6 (4): 317–353.

Eliade, M. 1952. *Images et symboles*. Paris: Gallimard.

Evans-Pritchard, E.E. 1940. *The Nuer*. London: Clarendon Press.

Fraser, J.T. 1981. 'A Mosaic of Metaphors of Time and Images of Transience in the Literature of the West, and, Notes Concerning Some Properties of Time', in Fraser, J.T. (ed.), *The Voices of Time*. Amherst: University of Massachusetts Press.

Garfinkel, H. 1968. 'Oral Contributions', in Hill, R. and Crittenden, K.S. (eds.),

Proceedings of the Purdue Symposium on Ethnomethodology. Purdue University.
Giddens, A. 1979. *Central Problems in Social Theory*. London: Macmillan.
Giddens, A. 1981. *A Contemporary Critique of Historical Materialism*. Vol. 1. London: Macmillan.
Giddens, A. 1982. *Profiles and Critiques in Social Theory*. London: Macmilan.
Giddens, A. 1984. *The Constitution of Society*. Cambridge: Polity Press.
Goodman, N. 1972. 'Seven Strictures on Similarity', in Goodman, N. (ed.), *Problems and Projects*. New York: Bobbs-Merrill.
Hallowell, A.I. 1937. 'Temporal Orientation in Western Civilization and in a Pre-literate Society'. *American Anthropologist* 39: 647–670.
Heinemann, K. and Ludes, P. 1978. 'Zeitbewusstsein und Kontrolle der Zeit', in Hammersich, K. and Klein, M. (eds.), 'Materialien zur Soziologie des Alltags'. *Kölner Zeitschrift für Soziologie und Sozialpsychologie* 20 (Special Issue).
Inkeles, A. and Smith, D.H. (1974) *Becoming Modern*. Cambridge, Mass.: Harvard University Press.
Julkünen, R. 1977. 'A Contribution to the Categories of Social Time and the Economy of Time'. *Acta Sociologica* 20 (1): 5–24.
Le Goff, J. 1977. *Pour autre Moyen Age, temps, travail et culture en Occident*. Paris: Gallimard.
Leach, E.R. 1961. *Rethinking Anthropology*. London: Athlone.
Lewis, J.D. and Weigert, A.J. 1981. 'The Structures and Meanings of Social Time'. *Social Forces* 60 (2): 432–462.
Lloyd, G.E.R. 1975. 'Le temps dans la pensée grécque', in Ricoeur, P. et al. *Les cultures et le temps*: 135–170. Paris: Payot/UNESCO.
Lovejoy, A.O, 1963. *The Great Chain of Being*. Cambridge, Mass.: Harvard University Press.
Luhmann, N. 1968. 'Die Knappheit der Zeit und die Vordringlichkeit des Befristeten'. *Die Verwaltung*, Vol. 1: 3–30.
Luhmann, N. 1976. 'The Future Cannot Begin: Temporal Structures in Modern Society', *Social Research* 43: 130–152.
Luhmann, N. 1979. 'Zeit und Handlung, eine vergessene Theorie'. *Zeitschrift für Soziologie* 8: 13–81.
Luhmann, N. 1982. 'World Time and System History', in Luhmann, N., *The Differentiation of Society*: 289–323. New York: Columbia University Press.
Luhmann, N. 1984. *Soziale Systeme, Grundriss einer allgemeinen Theorie*. Frankfurt: Suhrkamp.
Macneil, I. 1980. *The New Social Contract: An Inquiry into Modern Contractural Relations*. New Haven: Yale University Press.
Macneil, I. 1985. 'Relational Contract: What we do and do not know'. *Wisconsin Law Review* 3: 483–525.
Maturana, H.R. and Varela, F.J. 1980. *Autopoiesis and Cognition: The Realization of the Living*, Dordrecht: Reidel.
Monod, J. 1970. *Le hasard et la nécessité*. Paris: Ed. du Seuil.
Needham, J. 1981. 'Time and Knowledge in China and the West', in Fraser, J.T. (ed.), *The Voices of Time*: 92–135. Amherst: University of Massachusetts Press.
Nisbet, R.A. 1969. *Social Change and History*. London: Oxford University Press.
Nowotny, H. 1975. 'Time Structuring and Time Measurement: On the Interrelation between Timekeepers', in Fraser, J.T. and Lawrence, N. (eds.), *The Study of Time*, Vol. II: 325–342. Berlin: Springer.
Parsons, T. and Shils, E. 1967. *Towards a General Theory of Action*. Cambridge, Mass.: Harvard University Press.
Pomian, K. 1984. *L'ordre du temps*. Paris: Gallimard.
Prigogine, I. and Stengers, I. 1979. *La nouvelle alliance*. Paris: Gallimard.

Rezsohazy, R. 1970. *Temps social et développement: le rôle des facteurs socio-culturels dans la croissance*. Brussels: La Renaissance du Livre.

Rueschemeyer, D. 1984. 'Theoretical Generalization and Historical Particularity in the Comparative Sociology of Reinhard Bendix', in Skocpol, T. (ed.), *Vision and Method in Historical Sociology*. London: Cambridge University Press.

Shackle, G.L.S. 1979. 'Imagination, Formalism, and Choice', in Rizzo, M.J. (ed.), *Time, Uncertainty and Disequilibrium*: 19–31. Lexington, Mass.: Lexington Books.

Shields, M. 1986. 'Vision and Logic in Evolutionary Theory'. Ph.D. Thesis, Brown University.

Skocpol, T. 1984. 'Emerging Agendas and Recurrent Strategies in Historical Sociology', in Skocpol, T. (ed.), *Vision and Method in Historical Sociology*: 356–391. London: Cambridge University Press.

Skocpol, T. ed. 1984. *Vision and Method in Historical Sociology*. London: Cambridge University Press.

Schöps, M. 1980. *Zeit und Gesellschaft*. Stuttgart: Ferdinand Enke Verlag.

Sorokin, P.A. and Merton, R.K. 1937. 'Social Time: A Methodological and Functional Analysis'. *The American Journal of Sociology* 5: 615–29.

Thompson, E.P. 1968. *The Making of the English Working Class*. Harmondsworth, Middx.: Penguin.

Tominaga, K. 1985. 'Typology in the Methodological Approach to the Study of Social Change', in Eisenstadt, S.N. and Helle, H.J. (eds), *Macro-Sociological Theory*, Vol. 1: 168–196. Beverly Hills: Sage.

Toulmin, S. 1972. *Human Understanding*. Vol. 1. Oxford: Clarendon.

Varela, F.J. 1978. 'A Calculus for Self-Reference'. *Journal of General Systems* 2: 5–24.

Varela, F.J., Maturana, M.R. and Uribe, R. 1974. 'Autopoiesis: The Organization of Living Systems, its Characterization and a Model'. *Bio Systems* 5: 187–196.

Wiener, N. 1975. *Time Series*. Cambridge, Mass.: MIT Press.

Zerubavel, E. 1976. 'Timetables and Scheduling: On the Social Organization of Time', *Sociological Inquiry* 46: 87–94.

Zerubavel, E. 1980. 'The Benedictine Ethic and the Modern Spirit of Scheduling: On Schedules and Social Organization', *Sociological Inquiry* 50 (2): 157–169.

Zerubavel, E. 1982. 'The Standardization of Time, A Sociological Perspective'. *American Journal of Sociology* 88: 1–23.

50

Spatializations: A Critique of the Giddensian Version*

E.W. Soja

*Source: E.W. Soja, *Postmodern Geographies*, London: Verso, 1990, ch. 6. Cross-references citing chapters etc., relate to the original publication.

> [It] is ... as if each new aggression from the cosmic exterior appeared at the same time as a disparity to be absorbed and as the perhaps unique opportunity to recommence, on new grounds, the great totality-concocting which tries to assimilate ancient and indestructible contradictions, that is, to surpass them in a unity which is at long last rigorous – a unity which would be manifested as a cosmic determination. ... One may envisage the circular movement in a three-dimensional space, as a spiral whose many centers are ceaselessly deviated and ceaselessly rise by executing an indefinite number of revolutions around their starting point. Such is the personalizing evolution, at least up to the moment ... of sclerosis or regressive involution. In this latter circumstance the movement indefinitely repeats itself by passing the same places again or else is an abrupt fall from a higher revolution to some inferior revolution. (Sartre, *L'Idiot de la famille*, I, 1971, 656–57, trans. in Fell, 1979, 348)

Redoubling the Helix: Space–Time and Anthony Giddens

For more than a decade Anthony Giddens has been spiralling toward a critical reconceptualization of social theory in a remarkably linked sequence of books which have established him as one of the foremost contemporary interpreters of social theory writing in English. From his first critical reviews of the origins of sociology to his most recent theoretical syntheses, Giddens's project has evolved in the form of a helix. His arguments move persuasively forward through the accumulated antinomies that have traditionally divided social science and philosophy, but always curve back again to gain new perspective on the historical roots of sociological theory and analysis. This distinctive trajectory and style were set in his earliest works, where he attempted to recast social theory around a syncretic and critical appropriation and modernization of the classical theoretical programmes of Durkheim, Weber and Marx. With each new advance in his thinking, Giddens almost dutifully returns to evoke and reconsider this continental European inheritance from a different vantage point, somewhat more distant, but never so far as to lose sight of the enduring traditions.

In *New Rules of Sociological Method* (1976), for example, Giddens condensed his evolving critique around an analytical theory of meaning and action built upon a constructive reevaluation of interpretive sociology and hermeneutics. The helix path cut through broad realms of twentieth-century humanisms and action philosophies to centre on the creative force of human agency and praxis. It then curved back again to excoriate persistent functionalism (a recurrent theme in Giddens's work), resift through the Durkheimian legacy, and exorcise once more the ghost of Talcott Parsons, whose enervating theory of action so powerfully shaped post-war academic sociology and lingers in the background of most of Giddens's writings.

In *Central Problems in Social Theory* (1979) an important shift occurred. Giddens engaged his invigorated action theory with a sympathetic critique of the main currents of structuralist thought. Through this inflammatory conjunction of human agency and determinative structure, Giddens drew together two theoretical discourses which had developed through the twentieth century in explosive and unreconciled opposition. In *Central Problems* the dialectical engagement of agency and structure, subjectivity and objectivity, was assertively placed at the core of social theory, reconceptualized by Giddens in a budding theory of structuration which situated praxis and social reproduction in '*time and space* as a continuous flow of conduct' (1979, 2). This comprehensive confluence of ideas marked, for Giddens, the culmination of one spiral of critical reinterpretation and the beginning of another, more committed and constructive than the first.

Each of Giddens's books contains the seeds of its sequel, a pattern never more evident than in the link between *Central Problems* and his next major work, *A Contemporary Critique of Historical Materialism* (Volume I, 1981). *Critique* is much more than – and less than – an effective reinterpretation of Marx's historical materialism, an inching forward to glance back again to the nineteenth century. Although Marx, Durkheim, and Weber continue to fill more index space than any other authors, *Critique* became Giddens's most explicit and committed assertion of his own conceptualization of social theory, a constructive affirmation of the theory-generating capacity of the agency–structure nexus. It is cautiously offered as a propaedeutic, 'a stimulus to further reflection rather than ... approaching an exhaustive analysis of the major issue it raises' (1981, 24). Propaedeutic or not, *Critique* is Giddens's most original and therefore most vulnerable book, at once a cause for celebration and an invitation to critical reappraisal of the author's entire theoretical project.

Critique must be evaluated at both a substantive and a theoretical level, and as simultaneously a deconstructive critique and an attempted reconstructive affirmation. Giddens previews his approach to historical materialism in *Central Problems* (1979, 53), where he states that 'Marx's writings still represent the most significant fund of ideas that can be drawn upon in seeking to illuminate problems of agency and structure'. Their powers of illumination, however, must be brightened by selectively discarding an encumbrance of 'mistaken, ambiguous or inconsistent' analytical concepts and the many errors of subsequent Marxisms. Stripping away this encumbrance is the titular objective of *Critique*.

Many of the targets selected by Giddens are familiar themes of discussion within the contemporary Marxist literature: the inadequacy of Marx's evolutionary schema and outdated anthropology; the dangers of economism and structuralist determinism; the overuse of functionalist categories and explanation; the absence of appropriate theories of the state, of politics, of urbanization, of power. There is an attack on the mode of production as an analytical concept, a denial of the incessantly progressive augmentation of productive forces, a refusal to accept 'all history' as the history of class struggle. The phalanx of critical dismissals will no doubt anger and annoy some Marxist readers. Others will argue, with merit, that precisely the same issues have been addressed more effectively by critical theorists less averse to accepting the label 'Marxist' than is Giddens.

Yet, despite his grumblings, Giddens remains peculiarly accepting and sympathetic, committed to the centrality of historical materialism in the construction of critical social theory. Indeed, the critique of historical materialism he offers is primarily an accessory to the application and elaboration of Giddens's theory of structuration and, in particular, the embedded distinction between 'class-divided' and 'class' society posited in *Central Problems*. The substantive chapters of *Critique* revolve around this distinction in an attempt to address the specificity of industrial capitalism in comparison with prior phases in world history. The differences between class-divided societies (primarily agrarian states in which classes exist, but for which 'class analysis does not serve as a basis for identifying the basic structural principle of organization' – 1981, 7) and class society (that is, capitalism, wherein class-conflict, struggle, and analysis are essential and central) unfold in a series of critical essays which are stuffed with 'preliminary learning', loosely synthesized propaedeutic insights which I suspect would not easily withstand rigorous critical analysis, especially perhaps by Giddens himself.

Chapter 3, 'Society as time-traveller: capitalism and world history', is an analysis of the contradictions between Marx's evolutionary schema and the more guarded insights contained in the *Formen* section of *Grundrisse*. This is followed by 'Time–space distanciation and the generation of power' (an assertion of the importance of time–space relations versus relations with nature in a significantly reoriented materialist interpretation of history);

'Property and class society' (on the generation of class society in the interlocking of capital and wage-labour in a 'dialectic of control' shaped by the private ownership of property); 'Time, labour and the city' (on the commodification of time and space in everyday life under capitalism, an eclectic synthesis of Lefebvre, Castells, Harvey, Mumford, Wirth, Christaller, Sjoberg, et al.); 'Capitalism: integration, surveillance and class power' (a further exploration of the specificity of capitalism in terms of means of control, the role of the state, and the emergence of world systems of intersocietal integration); 'The nation-state, nationalism and capitalist development' (an interesting excursion from Montesquieu to the new international division of labour); and 'The state: class conflict and political order' (a creative, but limited, tour of the current debates on the theory of the state). *Critique* ends, characteristically, with the seeds of its projected sequels (*The Nation State and Violence* and *Between Capitalism and Socialism*), enmeshed in a discussion of 'Contradiction and exploitation'.

Before allowing Giddens to jump ahead to another stage in his helix path, however, some careful consideration must be given to the conceptualizing arguments which frame these substantive chapters and are presented in *Critique* (1981, 3) as 'elements of an alternative interpretation of history'. In particular, the *theory of structuration* must be submitted to the same 'positive critique' that Giddens has so successfully applied to others. In doing do, it can be argued that the spiralling trajectory which has marked Giddens's long project and propelled him into the perspicacious achievements of *Critique* may have become its own conceptual trap, constraining further theoretical development rather than generating it. A propaedeutic book perhaps deserves a propaedeutic evaluation, an invitation to further reflection rather than an exhaustive analysis.

Giddens's theory of structuration builds upon and elaborates Marx's pithy maxim that 'men make history, but not in circumstances of their own choosing', still the most evocative encapsulation of the agency–structure relation in social theory. To the making of history, Giddens adds, awkwardly at first and without full awareness of its implications, what can be described as the 'making of geography', the social production of space embedded in the same dialectic of praxis. *Critique* calls for the injection of temporality and spatiality into the core of social theory, and binds and brackets the theory of structuration in time–space relations. 'All social interaction', Giddens writes (1981, 19), 'consists of social practices, situated in time–space, and organized in a skilled and knowledgeable fashion by human agents'. Knowledgeability and action, however, are always 'bounded' by the structural properties of social systems, which are simultaneously the *medium* and *outcome* of social acts (forming what Giddens calls the 'duality of structure'). Social systems are thus conceived as *situated practices*, patterned (structurated) relationships socially reproduced across time and space, as history and geography.[1]

The theory of structuration is amplified through a combination of three discourses which serve to link the articulation of space–time relations directly to the generation of power and the reproduction of structures of domination. Heidegger's philosophy of Time and Being, Althusser's structuralist schemata, and the writings of modern geographers on such concepts as 'time-geography' and the subjectivity of distance, are recomposed by Giddens to describe 'how form occurs', how situated practices conjoin 'moments' temporally, structurally, and spatially in the constitution of social life. What comes through most clearly in the cloud of neologisms and revamped vocabulary (for which Giddens understandably begs indulgence) is an institutional emphasis on the operation of power, within which Giddens posits another definitive bifurcation. Power and domination are coupled in the structuration of allocative control (over the material world) and authoritative control (over the social world). Allocation and authority thus come to define, respectively, the realms of the economic and the political, and they connect the general theory of structuration to the themes and literature referred to in the subtitle of *Critique: Power, Property and the State*.

The theory of structuration outlined in *Critique* remains elusive, however, and much more appealing in intent than in execution. Part of the problem lies in the immensity of the task and in the disparate languages being unconventionally conjoined around the agency–structure linkage. In addition, Giddens's recurrent strategy in formulating theoretical arguments has been to spin off interlocking classificatory schema, a practice which becomes intractably dense in *Critique*, too often confusing rather than clarifying the argument. More fundamentally, however, the theory of structuration is built around a generative premiss which requires a more formidable adjustment in theoretical perspective than Giddens is able to achieve.[2] Although his repeated intention is to project both temporality and spatiality into the heart of critical social theory, presumably in the explicit balance of time–space, Giddens – very much like Heidegger – manages unintentionally to perpetuate the long-standing submergence of the spatial under the ontological and epistemological primacy of time and history. For Giddens, history and sociology become 'methodologically indistinguishable', but the analysis of spatial structuration remains peripheral, an insightful accessory.

Giddens's discovery of the 'writings of modern geographers' and the spatiality of structuration is, nevertheless, the most important new ingredient both in *Central Problems* and in *Critique*. It distinguishes these works more propitiously than anything else from all the author's earlier contributions, in which the spatiality of social life remained virtually invisible. Unfortunately, the growing contemporary debate on social theory and spatial structure, on the dialectics of society and spatiality, is barely seen by Giddens, who presents his discovery almost as if he were a lonesome pioneer. This leads him to draw upon disjointed pieces of the writings of such key contributors to this debate as Lefebvre, Foucault, Harvey, Castells, and Poulantzas, without recognizing that they have been providing the theoretical substance for an alternative conceptualization of the time–space constitution of social systems so central to *Critique*. In *State, Power, Socialism* (1978), for example, Poulantzas refocused his analysis of the institutional materiality of the state around the formation and transformation of 'spatial and temporal matrices', manifested in the themes of territory and tradition. As noted in the previous chapter, these matrices were defined as the 'presuppositions' (versus merely preconditions or outcomes) of capitalism, implied in the relations of production and the division of labour. Temporality and spatiality are presented together as the concretization of social relations and social practice, the 'real substratum' of mythical, religious, philosophical, and experiential representations of space–time. *Critique* would have been much richer had Giddens incorporated the explicitness and balance of Poulantzas's interpretation, both at the level of theory and in the substantive chapters on the state and nationalism, where their absence is most disturbing. Giddens's exposition of time–space distanciation, presencing and absencing, the commodification of time and space, allocation and authorization, would also have become clearer and more comprehensible. Instead, no mention is made of this crucial dimension of Poulantzas's last major work.

The irony of *Critique* is that Giddens misses what his helix path has so productively achieved over the past decade: an opportunity to reevaluate and reconstitute the classical contributions of Marx, Weber, Durkheim and the twentieth-century achievements of hermeneutics and structuralism. There is another helix of critical theory still to be written that would trace the history (and geography?) of the theoretical primacy of time over space to its generative roots. In this spiral, Durkheim, Weber, and Marx are again primary sources. It was in the anti-Hegelian wellsprings of historical materialism that revolutionary time and history displaced spatiality (in the spiritual from of the Hegelian state and territorial consciousness) and relegated it to the status of idealistic and diversionary fetishism. The development of an effective materialist theory of the state, of nationalism and regionalism, of the territorial collectivity and consciousness, has been constrained ever since. Similarly, the theoretical programmes of Durkheim and Weber, building a relatively spaceless social science based on differing interpretations of the link between individual action and collective consciousness, also peripheralized the spatial into an almost mechanical externality. Spatiality became a passive mirror/container to the forceful play of human agency and social process set free from 'environmental' determination.

Hermeneutics and structuralism reproduced much of this traditional imbalance. Existential phenomenology, despite the inherently spatial quality of such concepts as *Dasein*, *Etre-là*, Being-*there*, continued to concentrate on the temporality of Being and Becoming. For Heidegger in particular, the space of being remained a chronic problem, in more ways than one. Structuralism's celebration of the synchronic, in comparison, was filled with promising spatial metaphors but relatively little explicit spatial analysis.

Nevertheless, hermeneutics and structuralism both opened new windows through which to re-engage time–space relations in a more appropriate symmetry.

Persistently combative and procrustean as structuralism and hermeneutics have been, their recent and still tentative conjunction around the agency–structure relation (of which Giddens's work is but one major example) has demanded an appropriately dialectical nexus, with no enforced priority of agency over structure or the reverse. Significantly, this dialectical connection of agency and structure has been accompanied by increasing attention to another traditional duality, the spatial and the temporal, which calls for a similar conceptualization: epistemologically co-equal, dialectically related in their material expression, unified in praxis, and positioned at the very heart of critical social theorization.

Giddens edges close to this critical reconceptualization, certainly closer than any other contemporary sociologist writing in English. His theoretical 'space', however, remains too constrained. There is no mention in *Critique*, for example, of his Cambridge co-resident, Derek Gregory, whose work on social theory and spatial structure in the context of the agency–determination relation has so brightly illuminated the contemporary geographical literature.[3] There is also a too narrow and blinkered appropriation of French social theory. In particular, the extensive works of Lefebvre on the spatiality of social life and social reproduction, on the dialectic of agency and structure embedded in the social production of space, cannot be reduced to his commentaries on *le quotidien* and an errant reification of the 'urban', as Giddens does (following, as too many others have done, the voice of Castells in *The Urban Question*).

Although these weaknesses might be defined as 'structural', they are not, of course, conclusively determined, especially given the reflective and knowledgeable human agent involved. Soon after the publication of *Critique* and before the completion of its promised sequels, Giddens moved on to another level of theoretical development, passing the same places again but with greater clarity and a more formalizing intent. In *The Constitution of Society* (1984), Giddens simultaneously responded to his critics, laid bare the eclectic sources of his recent 'personalizing evolution', and carefully consolidated a totality-concocting theory of structuration. The propaedeutic seeds of *Critique* have now blossomed into a mature and orderly garden, with each flowering species carefully labelled as to its ontogenetic and phylogenetic heritage. *Constitution* thus offers another opportunity to consider the trajectory advanced by *Critique* and to reconstruct on firmer grounds the Giddensian version of the reassertion of space.

The Constitution of Society and the Reconstitution of Social Theory

In an interview with Derek Gregory in *Society and Space*, Giddens described his distinctive personal project:

> I don't think of myself as working in any innovative way on epistemological issues, and I try to 'bracket' them to some substantial degree. What I am trying to do is to work on essentially what I describe as an *ontology* of human society, that is, concentrating on issues of how to theorise human agency, what the implications of that theorising are for analysing social institutions, and then what the relationship is between those two concepts elaborated in conjunction with one another.... I don't think it either necessary or possible to suppose you could formulate a fully-fledged epistemology and then somehow securely issue out to study the world. So my idea is to fire salvoes into social reality, as it were; conceptual salvoes, which don't provide an overall consolidated epistemology. (Gregory, 1984, 124)

What emanates from these conceptual salvoes in *Constitution* is a reformulated theory of being, of the nature of social existence. Placed in proper perspective, *Constitution* stands out as the most rigorous, balanced, and systematic ontological statement currently available on the spatio-temporal structuration of social life. Its position and lineage within the discourse of critical social theory are obvious, but its accomplishment extends more broadly, via the philosophical tracks laid down by the efforts of Husserl, Heidegger, and Sartre, to give 'place' to being. This is where its primary achievements need to be located.

The intentional absence of a formal epistemology makes any simple and direct translation of Giddens's ontology into demonstrative empirical research rather difficult, while its necessary conceptual inventiveness continues to provoke misunderstanding, especially amongst those who seek such direct and simple empirical insight from Giddens's work. *The Constitution of Society* nevertheless provides illuminating, if complexly sinuous, guidelines to empirical analysis and, in particular, to a critical reinterpretation of the historical geography of capitalism. It does not present easy formulas and blueprints, nor does it propound rigidly categorical stances on the theoretical paths to be followed. But this is its strength, not its weakness.

The structuration theory in *Constitution* is an elastic synthesis of the almost endless concatenation of associated dualisms that has followed upon the too often frozen opposition of subjectivity and objectivity. Agency and structure, the individual and the societal, are flexibly combined by Giddens and this ontological flexibility and fusion is the primary message.

The key synthesizing concepts asserting this ontological balance can be lifted from the conveniently appended Glossary (pages 373–7). Our inherited concept language is so distorted with regard to spatio-temporal relations that it must be radically restructured to express the articulation of space, time and social being, a task which Giddens self-consciously takes on in *Constitution*. The resulting conceptual glossary is an artful balancing act that consistently inserts space adjoined with time, but never space alone, into the constitution of society.

Contextuality: The situated character of interaction in time–space, involving the setting of interaction, actors co-present and communication between them

Locale: A physical region involved as part of the setting of interaction, having definite boundaries which help to concentrate interaction in one way or another

Regionalization: The temporal, spatial or time–space differentiation of regions either within or between locales; regionalization is an important notion in counter-balancing the assumption that societies are always homogeneous, unified systems

Social integration: Reciprocity of practices between actors in circumstances of co-presence, understood as continuities in and disjunctions of encounters

System integration: Reciprocity between actors or collectivities across extended time–space, outside conditions of co-presence

Time–space distanciation: The stretching of social systems across extended time–space, on the basis of mechanisms of social and system integration

Despite the conceptual advances, the temporal chaperon becomes too protective on occasion, for Giddens is determined to acknowledge space without succumbing to the disciplinary biases of Modern Geography and their peculiar separatism. There is much less caution, however, with regard to history and its disciplinary inclinations. As a result, time and history often stand alone in *The Constitution of Society*, authoritative and allocative, much more 'established' than the less familiar geographical 'outsider'.[4] The enforced order is always 'time–space' connected in the same dominating to dominated sequence as 'core–periphery'.

Giddens thus fails again to initiate the necessary critique of historicism that must accompany the contemporary restructuring of critical social theory.[5] Nevertheless Giddens's reformulated conceptual vocabulary can be effectively appropriated to reconstruct the substance and meaning of spatio-temporal structuration. With some adaptive extension, the framework of concepts establishes a provocative social ontology conducive to the development of historico-geographical materialism, one that is far better suited to the task than any other that has emerged from the encounter between

Modern Geography and Western Marxism.

Giddens, to be more specific, comes closer than any other influential social theorist to uncovering what, in my view, is the most fundamental contextual generalization about the spatiality of social life: that the intelligible lifeworld of being is always and everywhere comprised of a multi-layered system of socially created nodal regions, a configuration of differentiated and hierarchically organized locales. The specific forms and functions of this existential spatial structure vary significantly over time and place, but once being is situated in-the-world the world it is in becomes social within a spatial matrix of nested locales. The topological structure is mutable and permutable, but it is always there to envelop and comprise, to situate and constitute all human action, to concretize the making of both history and geography.

Geographers and sociologists have peered at pieces of this existential spatialization and produced an impressive literature describing the particularities and hypothesized geometries of its real or expected empirical appearances.[6] The generative sources of the spatial matrix, however, have been both elusive and illusive. The failure of geography and sociology to recompose an appropriate ontology in which, to use a currently fashionable phrase, 'space matters' (rather than just being there) has kept the existential meaning of the spatial context hidden. Let us look more closely at how Giddens's approximation might be effectively extended to bring out more clearly the spatial generality and specificity of social being.

First there is the evocative concept of locale, a bounded region which concentrates action and brings together in social life the unique and particular as well as the general and nomothetic. As Giddens notes, it is a notion somewhat akin to 'place' as used in the writings of cultural geographers (where, I might add, it is often asserted as a favoured alternative to 'space' and 'region'). But it provokes even closer comparison to the use of 'place' in the ontologics of Heidegger and Sartre. For Giddens, locales refer to 'the use of space to provide the *settings* of interaction, the settings of interaction in turn being essential to specifying its *contextuality*' (1984, 118). These settings may be a room in a house, a street corner, the shop floor of a factory, a prison, an asylum, a hospital, a definable neighbourhood/town/city/region, the territorially demarcated areas occupied by nation-states, indeed the occupied earth as a whole. Locales are nested at many different scales and this multilayered hierarchy of locales is recognizable as both a social construct and a vital part of being-in-the-world.[7]

The concentration of interaction in locales is linked to another contextual specificity of social being which Giddens is hesitant to acknowledge. It might best be described as the nodality of social life, the socio-spatial clustering or agglomeration of activities around identifiable geographical centres or nodes. Nodality and centring in turn presuppose a social condition of peripheralness: for every centre there is a more or less boundable hinterland defined by a geographical diminution in nodality that is brought about mainly through controls over access to the advantages of agglomeration. Nodality and peripheralness exist to some degree in every locale, if only as a product of individual and collective efforts to contend with the ontologically given friction of distance immediately imposed on being-in-the-world. Existence, the very presence of being, means having to deal with the friction of distance whether it be on the level of the 'primal setting' or in the dull routines of everyday life. A distance-ordered space–time patterning thus pervades the existential setting of human interaction and cannot be ignored in theory construction.

But neither should the friction of distance be ripped out of its social contextuality and modelled as a quasi-Newtonian 'independent variable' determining the nodality of locales, as has so often been the case in quantitative or 'scientific' modes of Modern Geography. As Giddens implies in his too brief discussion of centre-periphery distinctions and 'uneven development', the operation of allocative and authoritative power regulates the formation of centres and peripheries across the whole range of locale-settings. Trying to avoid the obscurant tactics of spatial separatism, with its inherent depoliticization of spatiality, Giddens embeds nodality and its spatial extensions in the temporality of power relations, in an axis of antecedent 'establishment' of control over people and resources that subsequently defines the state of being 'outside'. This temporal axis of differentiation intersects with that between central and peripheral regions to form the baselines for Giddens's notions of time–space distanciation and region-alization, how human interaction is 'stretched' over time and space in a series of unevenly developed and differentiated settings.[8] Put more simply, the spatiality and temporality of locales are contextually intertwined and inseparably connected to relations of power from outset to outcome. Central and peripheral regions are thus homologous with the creation of a primordial social opposition between the in and out of power, to hark back to my earlier argument on the nature and necessity of geographically uneven development and the relations between spatiality and class (see Chapter 4).

Nodality, regionalization, and power are also involved in another con-textualizing feature of social being, the creation of bounded enclosures which demarcate what Giddens terms the 'presence availability' (presence/absence) of human interaction. Here two additional and closely related terms, 'territoriality' and 'regionalism', need to be included in the Giddensian glossary and woven into the theory of structuration. Both work, in many different ways, to segregate and compartmentalize human interaction by controlling presence/absence and inclusion/exclusion. Like the centre–periphery distinction, with which they are closely related, territoriality and regionalism express the allocative and authoritative power that operates in locales. To borrow from Foucault, they are products of the instrumentality of space/power/knowledge and provide the basis for making the operation of power both spatial and temporal.

Territoriality is the more general term and contains hints of such particularized notions as sovereignty, property, discipline, surveillance, and jurisdiction.[9] It refers to the production and reproduction of spatial enclosures that not only concentrate interaction (a feature of all locales) but also intensify and enforce its boundedness. Territoriality, almost by definition, is present in every locale at least at the outer boundary (where the absence of interaction begins). But this bounding can be more or less rigid or permeable and can change shape over time. It can also exist within the locale setting. This intra-locale territoriality may or may not coincide with central and peripheral regions but it is always associated with regionalization, with spatio-temporal divisions of activity and relation. Regional differentiation within and between locales is in turn the setting for a contingent regionalism, an active consciousness and assertiveness of particular regions, *vis-à-vis* other regions, as territorial and social enclosures. As an expression of the territoriality of locales, regionalism is grounded in the geography of power.

Material being in the form of the body is the first and prefigurative instantiation of this hierarchy of differentiated nodal locales. Ego is the primal tension-filled centring of being, and around it is formed a created region-alization that has escaped formal analysis until very recently, for it remained stubbornly outside what Giddens describes as our discursive (as opposed to practical) consciousness. Giddens turns primarily to Goffman's sociology of encounters and Hägerstrand's time-geography for insight into this ego-centred regionalization, but equally insightful conceptual salvoes can be found in the work of Edward Hall, Robert Sommer and others who helped to spatialize the ego through a cultural critique and the initiation of an environmental psychology of spatial cognition (Soja, 1971). What has become increasingly revealed in these writings is a remarkable micro-geography of human interaction hingeing around the portable bubbles of personal space zonation and 'proxemic' behaviour, a non-verbal and unwrit-ten ordinary language of spatial intersubjectivity.

But this is only the beginning, the first of many layerings of created locales and regionalizations rippling outward from the subjective spatiality of the portable ego to become imprinted on the humanized landscape. Nodality twines together collective activities around other centred and relatively fixed settings which are also regionalized and more or less territorially bounded. In the modern world, the place of work and the place of residence are the predominant nodal locales of social co-presence and their locational separa-tion and territoriality induces its own distance-ordered but socially produced patterning of human interaction and experience. In less modern contexts, these two locales are typically co-centred and reinforce one another to define more tightly bounded enclosures of social integration relatively impermeable to interaction at higher geographical scales, except through the agglomeration of nodal locales and individual micro-geographies into human settlements or what might usefully be called *localities*.

Localities – another term which Giddens does not use – can be defined as particular types of enduring locales stabilized socially and spatially through the clustered settlement of primary activity sites and the establishment of propinquitous territorial community. Like every locale, they are spatio-temporal structurations arising from the combination of human agency and the conditioning impact of pre-existing spatio-temporal conditions. They provide another created setting, a more elaborate built environment, for human interaction expanded in scale, density, social differentiation, and collective attachment to place. They are also generative locales for what Giddens defines as 'distanciation', the stretching of social systems over time–space from the co-presence of local social integration to the more encompassing and elastic collectivities and reciprocities of system integration. Localities are thus the building blocks of urbanization: the formation of nodally clustered and cohesive locales regionally differentiated internally (within the cluster), comparatively (one urbanized locale versus another), and hierarchically (positioned within a multi-level system of urban locales). Towns and cities may be described as localities which encompass contexts, enclosures and nodal concentrations of human interaction which are linked to both social and system integration, and hence to multiple networks of social power. In the context of the contemporary world, the locality can range from the smallest settlement or neighbourhood to the largest conurbation.

Urbanization, however, represents a break from ontological generality and forces a transition to a more concretely specified historical geography, a shift which Giddens fails to make sufficiently explicit. Every human society that has existed has been contextualized and regionalized around a multi-layered nesting of supra-individual nodal locales – a home-base for collective nourishment and biological reproduction, collection sites and territories for food and materials, ceremonial centres and places to play, shared spaces and forbidden terrains, definable neighbourhoods and territorial enclosures. But only in some societies have these locales been agglomerated into specifically urban settlements and only in the past two centuries has urbanization expanded to become the dominant life setting for a major portion of the world's population, even in areas conventionally defined as 'non-urban' or rural. This is the extended definition of the urban used by Lefebvre to describe the specific geography of capitalism.

Understanding urbanization and urbanism in the contextuality of hierarchically centred locales thus projects rather than rejects the Giddensian ontology. Giddens does not succeed in developing a rich and rigorous theory of urbanization, choosing instead to focus his projections on the nation-state (as if the state supplants rather than embodies urbanization as the primary locus of power). But he does insist on locating the urban at the heart of critical social theory and in the midst of time–space structuration. The specificity of the urban, that old question which so divided Marxist geographers and sociologists, is thus given a new look and significance.

Urbanization can be seen as one of several major accelerations of time–space distanciation that have extended the scale of human interactions without necessarily destroying their fundamental spatial anatomy. You and I still live within a hierarchy of nodal regionalizations emanating from our bodies, but social interaction and societal integration have now expanded to a world scale, a global reach in which the urbanization process has been a primary vehicle. The specificity of the urban is thus defined not as a separable reality, with its own social and spatial rules of formation and transformation; or merely as a reflection and imposition of the social order. The urban is an integral part and particularization of the most fundamental contextual generalization about the spatiality of social life, that we create and occupy a multi-layered spatial matrix of nodal locales. In its particularity, its social specificity, the urban is permeated with relations of power, relations of dominance and subordination, that channel regional differentiation and regionalism, territoriality and uneven development, routines and revolutions, at many different scales.

The descriptive generalities of the Chicago School and most of modern urban sociology and geography – claiming that cities are distinguished (presumably from the rural or non-urban) by their size, density, heterogeneity, anomie, functional solidarities, geographical concentricities and axialities – are not inaccurate. But they conceal the more fundamental specificity of the urban that arises from the conjunction of nodality, space, and power. Cities are specialized nodal agglomerations built around the instrumental 'presence availability' of social power. They are control centres, citadels designed to protect and dominate through what Foucault called 'the little tactics of the habitat', through a subtle geography of enclosure, confinement, surveillance, partitioning, social discipline and spatial differentiation.

The ability to control emanates in large part from nodality/centrality itself and extends outwards along at least two planes, one directly from centre to hinterland (a vicinal control which typifies social integration) and the second from one nodal centre to others (a hierarchical control characteristic of system integration). Together these urban and territorial emanations of power and control define the very nature of the state. They also define a contestable terrain of spatial politics and civic struggle over *le droit à la ville*, the 'rights to the city' in Lefebvre's terms, the power of citizens to control the social production of space.[10]

As Giddens writes, the city is 'far more than a mere physical *milieu*. It is a "storage container" of administrative resources' around which states are built (1984, 183). He notes the dramatic shifts in the contextuality of the city which come about with the rise of capitalist industrialization and its commodification of time and space at the end of a chapter on 'Time, Space and Regionalization'. He then turns, appropriately enough, to Foucault for critical insight into the 'timing and spacing' of disciplinary power, building these insights into a subsequent analysis of the structural principles of Tribal,

Class-Divided, and Class (capitalist) Society. Here an important distinction arises between the dominant locale organization of class-divided societies, rooted in the symbiosis of city and countryside, the 'axis relating urban areas to their rural hinterlands'; and the dominant locale organization of capitalism, the 'sprawling expansion of a manufactured or "created environment"'. How close this is to focusing our attention on the problematic and instrumental spatialization that has marked the historical geography of capitalism, that Lefebvre unmasked and tied so closely with urbanization, that others have begun to identify as the key to understanding contemporary capitalist society.

But Giddens again spirals right up to the edge of the Lefebvrean version, only to refuse to take the next (lateral?) step. In the second half of *Constitution*, the Giddensian helix begins an almost regressive involution, repeating itself without advancing very far forward. The vivid and central significance of spatiality seems to be stripped away piece by piece until we are left, in a long chapter on the application of structuration theory to empirical research and social critique (which follows another exorcism of Talcott Parsons!) with almost no space at all. There is a brief mention of uneven development as having 'a broader application than has ordinarily been recognized' (319), followed by several, almost Wallersteinian, sentences on regionalization both producing and diffusing social contradictions. But the explicit advice given to the 'social analyst' seems to have omitted the forceful assertion that 'space matters' after all. It is no wonder that the sociological response to Giddens, both pro and con, has almost entirely failed to recognize the significance of his pronounced spatial turn, for Giddens himself seems to cover it up at the most critical moments.

Giddens, at the very end of *Constitution*, tries hard to recover his geography after stashing it away for the previous 150 pages. Posed as the ultimate afterthought, he writes:

> The phrase might seem bizarre, but human beings do 'make their own geography' as much as they 'make their own history'. That is to say, spatial configurations of social life are just as much a matter of basic importance to social theory as are the dimensions of temporality. (1984, 363)

These are the last sentences of the text:

> Space is not an empty dimension along which social groupings become structured, but has to be considered in terms of its involvement in the constitution of systems of interaction. The same point made in relation to history applies to (human) geography: there are no logical or methodological differences between human geography and sociology! (368)

Whether these terminal and exclamation marked statements on 'Social Science, History and Geography' will remain Giddens's last words on the subject or become the seeds for another spiralling sequel, it is difficult to foretell.

Looking back over *The Constitution of Society*, there remains much to be praised. In my view, the infusion of power into an explicitly spatialized ontology of society and hence into interpretations of the making of geography alongside the making of history is Giddens's major achievement. Similar arguments are there in the work of Foucault, Lefebvre, Poulantzas, Sartre and perhaps others I have missed. But in *Constitution*, Giddens brings almost everything together in a monumental synthesis which provides, for the first time, a systematic social ontology capable of sustaining the reassertion of space in critical social theory.

The easiest criticism of Giddens is the most complicated and possibly the most futile, for he has set up such strong armour against it in his personalized evolution. By leaving epistemology to others and concentrating on social ontology, Giddens frees himself to dip into empirical analysis at will and without commitment to any but his own framework of interpretation, his own 'cosmic determination' (to capture again the head quotation from Sartre). This is, of course, not uncommon among the best social theorists and philosophers. But it makes Giddens vulnerable to missing the particularities of the contemporary moment, its new possibilities and its breaks with the past. As the sociologist and theoretical realist John Urry writes:

> [Giddens] tends to neglect the problems of explaining the causes and consequences of recent transformations in the spatial structuring of late capitalism. Moreover ... this omission is particularly serious since it is space rather than time which is the distinctively significant dimension of contemporary capitalism, both in terms of its most salient processes and in terms of a more general social consciousness. As the historian of the *longue durée*, Braudel, argues 'All the social sciences must make room for an increasingly geographical conception of mankind'. (1985, 21)

This is essentially a call for both a more empirical and more spatially centred application of critical social theory to the perplexities of the present day. And it takes us into another round of *restructuring*, a deeper and more radical deconstruction and reconstitution of critical social theory than Giddens has apparently contemplated.

Making sense of contemporary modernity, or postmodernity if you will, cannot be done by simply announcing the logical and methodological equivalence of history, geography, and sociology in their Modernist guises, and extolling the fruitfulness of their nascent reconnections. The whole fabric of the Modern academic and intellectual division of labour that has defined, enclosed, and reified these disciplines since the late nineteenth century must be radically reshaped. Giddens's residual sociologism thus takes on a new significance, for the Sociology that has been so richly consolidated and expanded by Giddens stands today as one of the many reified disciplinary monuments that need to be deconstructed before we can successfully do anything new.

Notes

1. It is interesting to note that Giddens consistently emphasizes the combination 'time–space' but never explicitly uses 'historical geography'.

2. Given the discussion in the previous chapter, it might be more accurate to describe this generative premise as an *ontological* assertion derived primarily from Heidegger, whose works have been particularly influential in Giddens's theorizations.

3. See Gregory (1978) in particular. After the publication of *Critique* there is much more contact between Giddens and Gregory. See Gregory (1984), Gregory and Urry (1985), and Gregory's entry on 'structuration theory' in *The Dictionary of Human Geography* (Johnston et al., 1986).

4. Giddens's glossary includes an entry for *historicity*: 'The identification of history as progressive change, coupled with the cognitive utilization of such identification in order to further that change. Historicity involves a particular view of what "history" is, which means using knowledge of history in order to change it.' There is no equivalent entry for *spatiality*.

5. But so too, it must be added, has every one of the spatializing social theorists I have discussed, from Foucault and Lefebvre (who come the closest) to Harvey, Mandel, and Jameson.

6. Central place theory, for example, describes an idealized geometry of the spatial matrix under conditions in which market relations and distance minimizing behaviour with regard to the provisioning of social services are assumed to dominate the social production of space. Its models occasionally bear some fortuitous resemblance to the actual geographical landscapes of capitalist societies, largely because they too are structured around an assumed spatial matrix of nested locales. They represent one of the very few attempts in the history of social theory to address selected aspects of this existential spatialization.

7. Scale and hierarchy must also be seen as social constructs, not simply as existential givens. For some recent discussions of the distinctive spatial scales associated with capitalist development (at the level of the global, the nation-state, and the urban), see Taylor (1981) and Smith (1984). These works, however, are little more than initial probes into a very complex and understudied subject.

8. Giddens presents a simple diagram (1984, 131) to describe these relations. The vertical axis has 'established' on top, 'outsiders' at the bottom. It is crossed by a horizontal axis running from 'central regions' to 'peripheral regions'.

9. I began to explore the concept of human territoriality and its relation to the political organization of space in the late 1960s (see Soja, 1971). Much of this work had to be purely defensive, for the then prevailing view of territoriality was filled with bio-ethological imperatives which obscured any socio-political interpretation. For a recent attempt to recover and recast the debates on human territoriality, see Sack, 1986. Neither my earlier work nor Sack's, however, provide a satisfactory social ontology of territoriality.

10. See Michael Mann, *The Sources of Social Power* (volume 1, 1986) for the beginnings of what promises to be one of the few explicitly geographical analyses of the state and social stratification. Mann starts out with the following underlined assertion: '*Societies are constituted of multiple overlapping and intersecting socio-spatial networks of power*' (1). He goes on to note that 'Most theorists prefer abstract notions of social structure, so they ignore geographical and sociospatial aspects of societies. If we keep in mind that "societies" are *networks*, with definite spatial contours, we can remedy this' (9).

References

Castells, M. (1977) *The Urban Question*, London: Edward Arnold; trans. of *La Question urbaine* (1972) Paris: Maspero.

Fell, J. (1979) *Heidegger and Sartre: An Essay on Being and Place*, New York: Columbia University Press.

Giddens, A. (1984) *The Constitution of Society: Outline of the Theory of Structuration*, Cambridge, Polity Press; and Berkeley and Los Angeles: University of California Press.

Giddens, A. (1981) *A Contemporary Critique of Historical Materialism,* London and Basingstoke: Macmillan; and Berkeley and Los Angeles: University of California Press.

Giddens, A. (1979) *Central Problems in Social Theory*, London and Basingstoke: Macmillan; and Berkeley and Los Angeles: University of California Press.

Giddens, A. (1976) *New Rules of Sociological Method*, New York: Basic Books.

Gregory, D. (1984) 'Space, Time and Politics in Social Theory: an Interview with Anthony Giddens', *Environment and Planning D: Society and Space* 2, 123–32.

Gregory, D. (1978) *Ideology, Science and Human Geography*, London: Hutchinson.

Gregory, D., and Urry, J. (eds) (1985) *Social Relations and Spatial Structures*, London: Macmillan; and New York: St Martin's.

Johnston, R.J., Gregory, D., and Smith, D.M. (1986) *The Dictionary of Human Geography*, Oxford: Basil Blackwell.

Mann, M. (1986) *The Sources of Social Power Volume I: A History of Power from the Beginning to A.D. 1760*, Cambridge: Cambridge University Press.

Poulantzas, N. (1978) *State, Power, Socialism*, London: Verso.

Sack, R. (1986) *Human Territoriality: Its Theory and History*, Cambridge: Cambridge University Press.

Sartre, J.-P. (1971 and 1972) *L'Idiot de la famille*, Paris: Gallimard.

Smith, N. (1984) *Uneven Development*, Oxford: Basil Blackwell.

Soja, E. (1971) *The Political Organization of Space*, Washington DC: Association of American Geographers, Resource Papers.

Taylor, P. (1981) 'Geographical Scales in the World Systems Approach', *Review* 5, 3–11.

Urry, J. (1985) 'Social Relations, Space and Time', in Gregory and Urry (eds), 20–48.

51

Time and Space in Giddens' Social Theory*

J. Urry

*Source: C.G.A. Bryant and D. Jary (eds), *Giddens' Theory of Structuration*, London: Routledge, 1991, ch. 6.

In this chapter it will be shown that Giddens has placed the analysis of time and space at the very heart of contemporary social theory. There is now a sense in which any such theory cannot be oblivious to the ways in which social activities are temporally and spatially organized. Giddens' various writings have authorized such a concern and provided some of the terms in which the debates are now cast. However, these concerns would probably have developed anyway since a wide variety of social processes would have forced the analyses of time and space onto the social theoretical agenda, in particular, through making clear just how historically and spatially specific is the concept of 'society'. It will be shown that Giddens' own formulations are highly frustrating, in the sense that they index some important issues but do not provide the basis for developing a really worked-out position. In particular, Giddens does not interrogate the concepts sufficiently. Time and space paradoxically remain for him as 'structural' concepts demonstrating not the duality of agency and structure but their dualism. No real account is provided as to how human agency is chronically implicated in the very structuring of time and space. They are viewed as essential to the context of human actions but as such they channel or structure such actions from the outside. By contrast, I shall argue that time and space should be seen as produced and producing, as contested and determined and as symbolically represented and structurally organized. Indeed, it will be argued that there are a variety of times and spaces, that they intrude at different levels within an adequate social theory and that Giddens' formulations do insufficient justice to the complexity of the resulting studies.

This chapter is organized into three sections. First, an exposition is provided of the key concepts that Giddens introduces to deal with the temporal and spatial ordering of human activity. Second, a number of deficiencies are outlined, particularly in relationship to the more general project to develop the theory of 'structuration'. Some claims are developed that attempt to remedy certain of the deficiencies in Giddens' study of time and space. Finally, there is a brief conclusion.

Exposition

Time and space first surfaced in Giddens' work in 1979 in a wide-ranging and innovative chapter in *Central Problems in Social Theory* (1979a, Ch. 6). In subsequent works many of the themes were to reappear, although the analysis of time rather than space has normally been more central. By the later 1980s he was devoting less explicit attention to matters of time and space. They were absolutely central themes in his writings in the early and mid-1980s, particularly within his major work *The Constitution of Society* (1984a). Detailed expositions of certain more specialized topics, such as Heidegger's philosophy of time, are also to be found in various chapters and articles written in the same period.

Thus, in a number of works Giddens attempts to demonstrate how time and space are absolutely central to social life. This has involved a quite profound attempt to redraw conventional academic boundaries, particularly between sociology, geography and history. Conventionally, sociology had been taken to be the study of social structures that are then seen as operating within the 'environments' of time and space. To the extent to which time was considered, this was something investigated *only* to the extent to which societies were thought to be undergoing change. By contrast, Giddens' theory of structuration treats time–space relations as constitutive features of social systems, implicated in the most stable as well as the rapidly changing aspects of social life (Giddens, 1981a: 30). Time–space is not, then, a contentless form in which objects exist but it expresses the very nature of what objects are (see Gregory, 1989. 7).

He is well aware that there is an extensive philosophical literature concerned with establishing just what can be understood by the notions of time and space. Surprisingly, he does not address the literature debated within geography, which has concerned itself with whether time and particularly space are to be viewed as absolutes, possessing their own natures or particularities, or whether they are merely relative, expressing the relations between objects or events (see Urry, 1985). Instead Heidegger is employed to demonstrate the irreducibly temporal character of human existence (Giddens, 1981a: 3ff). Heidegger (1978) repeatedly stressed in *Being and Time* that philosophy must return to the question of 'Being', something that had been obscured by the western preoccupation with epistemology. Central to Heidegger's ontology of Being was that of time, which expresses the nature of what subjects are. Human beings are fundamentally temporal; that they find their meaning in the temporal character of human existence. Being necessarily involves movement between or the 'mutual reaching out and opening up of future, past and present' (quoted in Giddens, 1981a: 32). However, the nature of time (and space) should not be confused with the ways in which it is conventionally measured, such as intervals or instants. Giddens' commentary on Heidegger ceases at this point and he sets out five ways in which, because of their temporal character, human subjects are different from material objects.

First, only humans live their lives in awareness of their own finitude, something reinforced by seeing the death of others and of how the dead make their influence felt upon the practices of the living. Second, the human agent is able to transcend the immediacy of sensory experience through both individual and collective forms of memory; through an immensely complex interpenetration of presence and absence. Third, human beings do not merely live in time but have an awareness of the passing of time, which is embodied within social institutions. Furthermore, some societies have developed an abstract concept of rational, measurable time, radically separable from the social activities that it appears to order (by contrast with the 'reversible time' of, say, the Nuer; discussed in Giddens, 1981a: 36). Fourth, the time-experience of humans cannot be grasped only at the level of the intentionality of consciousness but has also to be located within each person's unconscious in which past and present are indissolubly linked. And fifth, the movement of individuals through time (and space) is to be grasped via the interpenetration of presence and absence, which results from the location of the human body and the changing means of its interchange with the wider society. This particularly involves new communication and transportation technologies, such as writing, printing, telegraphs, telephones, railways, cars, jet planes, electronic transmitted information and so on. Each of these transform the intermingling of presence and absence, the forms by which memories are stored and weigh upon the present, and of the ways in which the long-term *durée* of major social institutions are drawn upon within contingent social acts. In order to investigate particularly these latter processes more fully, Giddens draws upon the work of Hägerstrand's 'time-geography'.

The starting point here is the routinized character of much daily life and the manner by which we can both characterize and explain it. Hägerstrand's approach is based upon identifying sources of constraint over human activity given by the nature of the body and of the physical contexts in which human action occurs (see Giddens, 1984a: 111ff.). There are six critical determinants here: the indivisibility and corporeality of the body; the movement of the life span towards death; time as a fundamentally scarce resource; the limited capability of human beings to participate in more than one task at once; the fact that movement in space is also movement in time; and the limited packing-capacity of time–space so that no two individuals can occupy the same point in space. These factors condition the webs of interaction formed by the trajectories of the daily, weekly, monthly and overall life paths of individuals in their interactions with each other. Individuals moving through time–space meet at 'stations' and comprise 'bundles'. Hägerstrand talks of individuals pursuing 'projects' that have to use the inherently limited resources of time and space. These consist of 'capability constraints', such as the need for regular sleep or food, and 'coupling constraints', which constrain activities that are undertaken with others at least for part of the time.

The result of these constraints is that daily conduct is not simply bounded by physical or geographical boundaries but by 'time–space walls on all sides' (quoted in Giddens, 1984a: 114). Obviously, though, there have been major changes in the character of such walls, particularly as a result of 'time–space convergence', namely the shrinking of distance in terms of the time taken to move from one location to another. The journey from the East Coast to the West Coast of the USA would take two years by foot, four months by stagecoach, four days by rail (in 1910) and five hours by air (ibid). Thus, at least for some people, the constraints on mobility and communication are much reduced, although Giddens also notes that such time–space convergence has a 'palpitating' character that may generate problems of appropriate 'coupling' (*sic*).

Giddens' reservations about the time-geography of Hägerstrand, that it has a defective conception of the individual, that it overly emphasizes constraint as opposed to enablement, and that it presents no developed theory of power, leads him to develop a partly alternative set of claims (see Giddens, 1984a: 116–9; and Gregory, 1985 on Hägerstrand's work much more generally). These can best be understood through a number of novel concepts that present what Giddens terms 'sensitizing devices' (ibid: 326) by which to think through just how the life processes of individuals, including their daily, weekly and monthly paths, are linked to the *longue durée* of social institutions.

1. *Locale*: refers to the use of space to provide the settings within which interaction occurs. Locale is not to be described merely in terms of its physical properties but how it is used for human activities, how it provides for the contextuality of social life. Locales may range from a room, a house, a street corner, a shop floor, a town, a city, to the territory occupied by a nation-state.

2. *Regionalization*: locales are typically regionalized and these are critical in constituting contexts for interaction. Regionalization refers to the zoning of time–space in relationship to routinized social practices. Rooms in a house are, for example, zoned both spatially and temporally. There are obviously huge variations in such zoning between societies and over time. In the latter case, Giddens gives two examples: the development of powerful forms of artificial lighting that has dramatically expanded the potentialities of interaction settings within the 'night'-time; and the changing zoning of social activities as more 'specialized' rooms have developed in the houses occupied by the mass of the population (see Giddens, 1984a: 119–22).

3. *Presence-availability*: the degree to which, and the forms through which, people are co-present within an individual's social milieu. Communities of high presence-availability include almost all societies up to a few hundred years ago. Necessary co-presence resulted from the corporeality of the agent, the limitations upon daily mobility because of existing transportation technology and the physical properties of space (see Giddens, 1984a: 122–4). Presence-availability has been transformed in the past century or two. On the one hand, there has been the development of new transportation technologies and especially the separation of the media of communication from the media of transportation. The invention of the electromagnetic telegraph was a stunningly important invention that meant that communication between people who were spatially distant did not have to involve the literal mobility of the human body. And on the other hand, there has been an exceptional commodification of social life resulting from the development of money and its power to bridge distances and hence to bring about forms of interaction between people spatially distant.

4. *Front regions, back regions*: regionalization encloses zones of time–space that actors employ in the organizing the contextuality of action and the sustaining of ontological security. Contrary to Goffman, Giddens argues against the claim that it is only what happens backstage that is properly authentic (see Goffman, 1959; Giddens, 1984a: 122–9). The sustaining of ontological security could not be achieved if front regions were mere façades. Front regions are where much routinized daily life takes place, life in which people are often affectively involved. And backstage is not merely where the solitary individual prepares for his or her performance in a state of distracted anxiety, it is where people's basic security system is restored, particularly through dissipating the tensions derived from the demands of tight bodily and gestural control in other settings of day-to-day life.

5. *Time–space distanciation*: this refers to the processes by which societies are 'stretched' over shorter or longer spans of time and space. Such stretching reflects the fact that social activity increasingly depends upon interactions with those who are absent in time–space. From the eighteenth century onwards, society is increasingly organized via system integration rather than social integration through immediate presence-availability. Time–space stretching occurs via two sets of resources, the authoritative and the allocative and the particular forms and patterns in which power in each is stored (see Giddens, 1981a: 92–7). Giddens emphasizes a number of factors that structure such patterns of time–space distanciation: the changing control of information, via the invention of writing, then printing and, recently, of electronic information, which separates presence in time from presence in space; the development of the city as a religious, ceremonial and commercial centre and power container;

the development of the more modern urban form, as a created space through the commodification of land and the disruption of the ties of the city with nature; changes in transportation and communication technologies, especially the stagecoach system, the railway and particularly, the timetable, with its choreographing of activities in time–space, the car and lorry, the telegraph, the telephone, postal services and so on; the development of the territorially bounded nation-state with its expanded powers of documentation and surveillance; and the commodification of time so that it becomes separated from lived experience and actual social activities and appears like money as a universal and public measure (see Giddens, 1981a, Chs 4 and 6; 1985a, Ch. 7).

6. *Time–space edges*: this refers to the forms of contact or encounter between types of society organized according to different structural principles. This notion is part of a battery of concepts and arguments used by Giddens to emphasize the inadequacy of evolutionary theories based upon an endogenous or unfolding model of social change. Rather, it is essential to investigate *inter* societal systems, of the time–space edges by which, for example, a tribal society is confronted by a class-divided society. Episodes of social change also depend upon the emerging structures of world-time, that is the particular conjunctural phase of world development (see Giddens 1981a, Ch. 7; 1984a, Ch. 5).

7. *Power-containers*: time-span distanciation is integrally bound up with domination and power. There are, as we have seen, two types of resources, each of which is crucial to the possible forms of time–space distanciation and hence to the character of power in different types of society. Centrally important here is the storage capacity of different societies, particularly storage across time and space. In oral cultures human memory is virtually the sole repository of information storage. In class-divided societies it is, Giddens says, the city, especially with the development of writing, which becomes the primary crucible or container of power (see Giddens, 1981a, Ch. 5; 1984a, Ch. 6; Mumford, 1960). Particularly significant is how religious, military and administrative power is conjoined literally within the walls of the city to give physical shape to this crucible of power. By contrast, within capitalist societies it is the territorially bounded nation-state that is the dominant time–space container of power. The city loses its distinctiveness as such (as the walls come tumbling down!). A number of conditions have conspired to consolidate the unified administrative power of the nation-state: the mechanization of transportation and its separation from communication; the invention of printing and later of electronically recorded information, which expands the spatial power of the state; the enormous expansion of the documentary activities of the state, beginning with the keeping of official statistics; and the development of much more effective 'internal' pacification including in part the 'disciplinary power' of various total institutions (see Giddens, 1985a, Ch. 7).

These are, then, the array of concepts Giddens employs to make sense of time and space, concepts designed to problematize any easy assumption about the necessary coherence and closure of individual societies.

Critique

There is little doubt that Giddens' work represents a most important contribution to constructing a sociology of time. Less impressive is his contribution to current writing on space, to the degree to which the two topics can be separated. In the following I shall consider initially the limitations of his attempt to construct a sociology of time. I shall not here present an alternative formulation since this can be found in part elsewhere (Urry, 1985; 1987). Nor shall I say much about how these concerns relate to the rest of his theory since that is covered elsewhere in this book (and see the reviews in Thrift, 1985a; Gregory, 1989).

First of all, the status of time-geography in his argument is not made clear (for discussion, see Gregory, 1989). Once he has introduced some key notions it drops out of subsequent discussion. The analysis of time–space edges/ distanciation is not obviously dependent upon time-geography. Indeed, such studies have been most significant in the analysis of 'place' (see, for example, Pred, 1985). And yet Giddens systematically avoids any analysis of place as such. This seems to be because, as we shall see later, the processes of time–space distanciation are seen as gradually over time eroding the importance of separate places, and indeed, contains a covert evolutionism (see Bagguley, 1984). Thus while many of the substantive analyses within time-geography have involved showing how changes in the structuring of time have affected the geography of place, this is precisely what Giddens does not examine. He implicitly operates with a modernization thesis couched in terms of a variety of time-saving processes that erode distance and transform presence-availability. As he says: 'Position upon an evolutionary scale becomes replaced by distance or proximity in time–space' (Giddens, 1981a: 91; see also Bagguley, 1984, especially pp. 20–1).

Curiously though, not only does Giddens not consider the time–space organization of particular places, he also does not analyse the varying organization of time within different societies, except in two rather limited respects. These are, first, the reversible time of the Nuer, and second, the way in which in modern societies a rational and abstract time ('clock time') has developed through, especially, the generalization of the timetable. However, what he does not examine is how and especially why a different structuring of time is found in some industrial countries rather than others (for extensive discussion of such changes at the turn of the century see Kern, 1983). For example, the weekend is a time-zone implying also a particular organization of space (in, for example, the family home, or at church, or at sports events).

It is more important as a time-zone in some countries than others. For example, in New Zealand until recently, shops did not open on Saturday or Sunday, much of the industrial labour force worked a set five-day week, and the weekend was mainly spent in the space of one's home with one's family. Two factors that appear to have produced such a zoning were the considerable strength of the labour movement to prevent the temporal flexibilization of the labour force; and the power of the churches to protect the sanctity of the weekend (that is, the family) from commercialization. One should also note the importance of the Judaic tradition in the artificial construction of the 'week' in the first place, this being the only important time-zone that is not derived from nature (see Colson, 1926).

Giddens seems to regard the organization of time as given, somehow embedded within the structuring of rules and resources that characterize modern societies in general. The organization of time is not seen to vary greatly between modern societies or to stem from the particular powers of social forces concerned to 'produce' different ways in which time may be zoned. In Britain the attempt in 1987 to transform the traditional Sunday by allowing all shops to open was met by furious opposition that was successful in sustaining Sunday as a distinct time-zone. The production and reproduction of zones of time, as with the production and reproduction of spaces or places, is unanalysed in Giddens' work. There is in effect what Mouzelis (1989) terms the dualism rather than the duality of structure.

A further aspect of time that is curiously absent is any serious examination of travel. Giddens does discuss some of the changes associated with new forms of transportation technology. But there is no examination of why people travel and hence why saving 'time', or covering more 'space', might be of 'interest' to people. One obvious reason for travel is for pleasure. It is a kind of liminal zone where some of the rules and restrictions of routine life are relaxed and replaced by different norms of behaviour, appropriate to being in the company of strangers. Travel is also pleasurable because it enables one to visit other places and people. Giddens' conception of human activity is too routinized, too boring, and it is difficult in his framework to conceptualize pleasure-producing activities such as travel, leisure, holiday-making, sight-seeing, shopping, playing sport, visiting friends and so on. Much social activity indeed involves semi-routines in which travel is an important element. What are involved are disruptions to everyday patterns that are nevertheless recognizably acceptable. In travel and related activities, the maximizing of time–space distanciation may often be irrelevant. People want to transcend particular distances via specific forms of transportation. And often there are well-established connections between certain forms of travel and resulting social activities (travelling by train to English seaside resorts, by air to European holiday destinations, by car to theme parks and so on). Travel is an irreducibly social phenomenon rather than merely a means of transcending distance.

This can be seen by briefly considering the nineteenth-century development of the railway, certain aspects of which Giddens rightly stresses.
However, his emphasis is all upon how the railway permitted phenomenal
increase in time–space distanciation in mid- to late-nineteenth-century
Britain. As a commentator at the time wrote: 'As distances were thus
annihilated, the surface of our country would, as it were, shrivel in size until
it became not much bigger than one immense city' (quoted Schivelbusch,
1986: 34). But what this ignores is a whole series of further changes that the
railway generated in transforming social practice and consciousness (see
Schivelbusch, 1986; Mackenzie and Richards, 1986). These included: the
bringing of machinery into the foreground of people's everyday experience
outside the factory; new methods of building that were not mimetic of nature
but involved its flattening and subduing; the perception of landscape as a
swiftly passing series of framed panorama; the development of new public
areas, the stations, which were a partially liminal space; the potential
heightening of new forms of worker organization and consciousness; the
provision of the basis for the growth of mass holidays; and the development
of new ways of maintaining social distance as a result of people finding
themselves with large numbers of strangers in the enclosed space of the
railway carriage.

Thus, the effects of particular modes of overcoming what geographers term
the 'friction of distance' are complex and by no means reducible to the
extension of time–space distanciation. Giddens does not examine in any detail
how time–space changes will often have the consequence, not merely of
heightening distanciation, but also of helping to encourage resistance,
opposition, pleasure, autonomy or a sense of deprivation. Giddens views
many of these developments in a rather one-dimensional fashion, as in effect
'modernization' through distanciation. This he sees as becoming more and
more extensive and is, first, making people more oriented to the future and to
the further progressive extension of such distanciation; and second, gradually
dissolving the significance of specific spaces or places as people are able to
move through time and space in increasingly rapid fashion. On the first point,
it is curious that Giddens barely addresses the concept of post-modernism and
the way in which it involves a re-evaluation of past, present and future. In
particular, there is a 'panic' about the future and a collapse of social historical
projects and narratives that bound together the past, present and future (see
Kroker and Cook, 1986). Jameson talks of the headlong rush into pastiche
rather than parody – a fragmented, arbitrary and wide-ranging juxtaposition
of various kinds of signs that have little or no connection with anything
substantive or real; time is fragmented into a series of 'perpetual presents'
(see Jameson, 1984; Lash and Urry, 1987, Ch. 9). In this free-floating
economy of the sign, those from the past have become exceptionally highly
valued, constructing various kinds of nostalgia for a range of historical images
(see Stauth and Turner, 1988). Post-modernism thus involves the disruption

of the relationships between past and future in which signs from the former have become widespread, a process involving a 'new nostalgia', including the heritage industry, which poses immense problems for, amongst others, socialist parties that were organized around a particular historical project and narrative (see Edgar, 1987; Hewison, 1987). Frampton summarizes: 'We live in a paradoxical moment when, while we are perhaps more obsessed with history than ever before, we have, simultaneously, the feeling that a certain historical trajectory, or even for some, history itself, is coming to an end' (Frampton, 1988: 51).

Thus, there are a number of features of contemporary western societies that involve transformed temporal relations that Giddens does not address, issues that involve treating time as more than a structural property of societies. I shall now consider some of the more spatial elements of his structurationist theory. Again it will be shown that these elements are not viewed in terms of their production and symbolization, but only in terms of the structural effects *upon* human action. This can be seen, first, by considering the notion of 'co-presence'. This often looks as though this is *the* most important element in his analysis of space and time. It seems essentially to consist of face-to-face interaction between people, albeit extended by letter, telegraph and telephone (and one may add answerphone; see, for example, Giddens, 1979a: 332ff.). Co-presence is thus viewed in a literal sense, of all those with whom actual interaction is or could take place. But what this ignores is what could be termed 'imaginary co-presence'. David Cooper once talked of one's 'imaginary family', the family that one carries around with one even when the actual members of it are geographically distant or even dead (Cooper, 1972). In terms of one's contemporary conduct it is often this imaginary family, its likes and dislikes, its jealousies and hostilities, its warmth and passions, that are of great emotional significance. Giddens, as we noted, talks of each person's unconscious linking together past and present. But he does not tie this together with his more general analysis of time–space relations, which are viewed in a resolutely literal manner. Indeed, in the case of space this seems to involve, as Gregory (1989) points out, his reconstruction of the programmatics of a spatial science.

Some related problems with his 'spatial' analyses can be seen with respect to a number of key distinctions employed, namely, frontstage/backstage, time–space regionalization between home and work and core/periphery. On the first of these some such separation conceived of at least in a partly spatial sense is treated as ontologically necessary for human existence and the main question is taken to be the way in which such a distinction enables human activity to be sustained. However, what this ignores are the more interesting sociological questions, namely: how such a division between front- and backstage varies within and between societies; how such a division is set up and sustained and the *degree* to which it depends upon a spatial separateness; how the resulting pattern may involve complex interconnections between a number of determinants, viz capital accumulation, land markets, regimes of surveillance, regimes of pleasure and so on; and how such a division may be struggled for or struggled against by individuals or larger-scale social forces. Elsewhere it has been shown how the mass media has served to undermine the information systems that are specific to particular social groups..Such systems had, in a sense, constituted a repository of meanings 'backstage' and they were separate from how that group acted 'frontstage'. Television has, however, made all backstages public property and hence served to undermine such a demarcation (see for further detail, Lash and Urry, 1987: 297–8).

Similar points can also be made with regard to the process of time–space regionalization between 'home' and 'work'. Giddens treats this as a factual or structural characteristic of certain types of society. Such a division and the resulting allocation of women to the former and men to the latter is seen as being inscribed within the structuring of capitalist societies. However, this is not an appropriate way of understanding such a division. Rather, the pattern should be seen as resulting from the intersection between new forms of social organization, viz factories and large urban settlements, *and* collective struggles, especially by male workers to exclude women from the workplace and force them back *into* a much more domesticated sphere of the home (see Walby, 1986, for extensive documentation of this). After all, the earliest factory workers were women textile workers and there was a considerable intermingling of the relations of paid work and of domestic/familial organization. Time–space regionalization is not something that should be taken as fixed and given.

This can also be clearly seen in the main distinction Giddens employs to characterize larger-scale time-space regionalization, namely, that of core and periphery. He seems to regard this division as given, fixed and structural (paralleling what he says about the south/north divide). It is not something that historically changes, nor is the division viewed as being more-or-less important depending upon a number of complex determinants. What is particularly strange is that there is no discussion of the literature that has particularly addressed and confronted the notion of a fixed, ahistorical and functional core/periphery, namely that of 'restructuring' (see for the clearest account, Massey, 1984: Bagguley *et al.*, 1989). In this alternative approach it is argued, first, that there are a number of patterns by which industries come to be sociospatially reorganized and core/periphery is most definitely not the only pattern. Second, it is shown that the pattern actually adopted within a given industrial sector is the result of complex determinants, including in part at least the role of the organization of labour as a collective agent. Third, the resulting social and spatial organization within a given society is highly complex, since it depends upon the overlapping effect of the spatial divisions of labour found within each of the industrial sectors that have been present. And finally, in more recent restructuring literature, it is demonstrated that there are forms of organization within civil society, particularly those of gender relations, which are not reducible to the patterns of industrial restructuring but nevertheless are centrally important to the structuring of social relations within particular places (see, for much more detail, Bagguley *et al.*, 1989).

And that brings us back to the point noted earlier, namely that Giddens really says nothing about place as opposed to space. When he talks of place as such it is seen as given or fixed rather than socially constructed and contested. Locale is viewed as the context for action rather than as the outcome of action, particularly that resulting from what one can term 'collective knowledgeability'. Giddens' argument is, if anything, reductionist (as well as partly evolutionist) since he emphasizes with particular force the commodification of space, that space becomes entirely 'created' through the commodification of time. As Marx argued, the development of capitalist relations had the effect of overcoming spatial barriers. However, what both Marx and Giddens ignore is that this annihilation can only be achieved through the production of new, fixed and relatively immobile spatial configurations. As Harvey says: 'spatial organisation is necessary in order to overcome space' (Harvey, 1985: 145). There are a number of important points to note about such old and new forms of spatial organization. First, people are highly attached to different spaces – the threatened destruction of which is often bitterly resisted. Much politics is, in effect, a defence of existing spatial arrangements, such as a particular neighbourhood, a given town centre, a factory located within a community, an unspoilt landscape and so on. Such a politics stems from the fact that 'space' comprises a set of physical and built forms that conveys a plethora of signs and meanings to observers. Such meanings although often ambiguous are none the less important in their effects. Spaces thus are redolent with signs and a variety of possible meanings. There is to put it simply a politics of landscapes and townscapes – a politics of space (see Daniels and Cosgrove 1988: 7).

Second, even the apparently simple, two-dimensional spaces found on maps are social. This is so both in the sense that they 'speak' about the social world and because they result from particular social and political forces. Maps are thus to be seen, not primarily as inert records of townscapes or landscapes, but as discourses, as ways of conceiving, articulating and structuring the human world that are biased towards, promoted by and exert influence upon particular sets of social relations (see Harley, 1988: especially pp. 278–80). Maps may be almost as important as timetables, as involving forms of control, surveillance and the determination of property through space, central in fact to the extension of time–space distanciation. Harley talks of maps contributing to the development of 'space-discipline', which parallels the development of capitalist 'time-discipline' (see Harley, 1988: 285; Landes, 1983). Maps, moreover, have the effect of 'desocializing' territory, fostering the notion of a socially empty space when in fact they are discourses about the social and involve the language of social power.

Third, one crucial point about places is that they are often symbolized by particular features of the built environment. They stand for that particular place (such as King's College Chapel in Cambridge, Canterbury Cathedral, the Royal Pavilion in Brighton, the Ford works in Dagenham and so on). Such individual buildings connote a range of social, historical and spatial features. Buildings stand for that particular place – they are in a sense *the* place and help to construct what people feel and think about it. Such buildings are almost sacred (even when they are not literally so), so that it would be unimaginable for them to be destroyed. To demolish such a building would be, symbolically, to demolish the whole place.

Fourth, places are important as repositories of knowledge. It is important to consider the changing availability of knowledge and the manner in which certain kinds of place either limit what can be known or permit knowledge to be enhanced. There are a number of senses though in which a social group can be said not to have 'knowledge': first, the knowledge that is literally unknown because of the group's position in time and space; second, there is that knowledge that a group cannot understand; third, there is knowledge that is undiscussed because the social world is taken for granted; and fourth, there is knowledge that is concealed or hidden because of the distorted character of dominant social relations (see Thrift, 1985b). In order to decipher the 'geography of knowledge', what needs to be undertaken is an analysis of just how different places affect these different forms of 'unknowing'. And this involves two breaks with Giddens' project. On the one hand, knowledge is not seen simply in terms of surveillance but also in terms of its capacity to empower social groups. And on the other hand, cities are to be seen as not simply constraining but as also enabling, to use Giddens' terminology. Cities may permit the rapid diffusion of all sorts of knowledge often of a quite disruptive sort, including new technologies (see Gregory, 1989: 12), new social and political beliefs (see Lane, 1982), or new forms of profession-alization strategy (see Lash and Urry, 1987, Ch. 6).

Conclusion

There are therefore a range of issues concerned with the analysis of, especially, space that Giddens fails to address. Without considering the more philosophical issues involved here (see Urry, 1985, for my views thereon), it should be noted that there is really no 'space' as such – only different spaces. This is because there are at least three different levels at which space (and time) can be seen as intruding into social analysis. First, empirical events are distributed in space and time. Second, social entities are built around particular spatial and temporal structures, including the forms of stretching across space and time. And third, social entities are temporally and spatially interrelated with each other, interrelationships of immense complexity over time and across space. Giddens' principal concept of 'time–space distancia-tion' is too blunt an instrument to capture the temporal and spatial interdependencies between social entities, which possess immense and yet historically and spatially contingent causal powers.

Giddens' thesis also fails to capture important features of contemporary social development. It will be remembered that he maintains that in each type of society there is a single power container, the city in class-divided societies and the nation-state in capitalist societies. Both of these raise problems. On the first, although he correctly notes how cities in different kinds of society differ, he seems to treat them entirely in terms of their power-containing capacity. So although he also asserts that the analysis of urbanism should occupy a central position in any empirical programme deriving from 'structurationism', he in fact ignores such research that has been undertaken on the changing functions of the city. Recently, it has been asserted that many cities have become not centres of production but increasingly centres of consumption (see Zukin, 1988). As such they may be centres of important resources, but not the authoritative or allocative resources that Giddens concentrates upon, but of what could be called symbolic resources of 'distinction' or 'status' (see Bourdieu, 1984; Turner, 1988; Zukin, 1988).

On the second point, he does not show just why the nation-state will continue to be the dominant power container in the future. He notes after all extraordinary increases in time–space distanciation of a *supra*-national sort which would seem on the face of it to suggest that the power container of the nation-state has perhaps had its day. Elsewhere I have argued more generally that contemporary capitalist national societies are being dislocated or disorganized, from 'above' via internationalization, from 'below' via decen-tralization and from 'within' via the growth of a powerful middle class (see Lash and Urry, 1987). In such a dramatic transformation of the previously organized capitalist societies, it is hard to see why the organization of time and space means that the nation-state will remain as *the* dominant power container in disorganized capitalist societies.

Giddens' opening up of the issues of time and space within social research has thus revealed a veritable Pandora's box of topics of investigation. But his own formulations are too blunt and insufficiently integrated with the other supposed characteristics of structurationism to provide that much assistance in unravelling the paths of time and space travelled by knowledgeable social actors.

References

Bagguley, P. (1984) 'Giddens and historical materialism', *Radical Philosophy* 38: 18–24.

Bagguley, P., Mark-Lawson, J., Shapiro, D., Urry, J., Walby, S., and Warde, A. 1989) *Restructuring. Place, Class and Gender*, London: Sage.

Bourdieu, P. (1984) *Outline of a Theory of Practice*, Cambridge: Cambridge University Press.

Colson, F. (1926) *The Week*, Westport, Conn.: Greenwood Press.

Cooper, D. (1972) *The Death of the Family*, Harmondsworth: Penguin.

Daniels, S. and Cosgrove, D. (1988) 'Introduction: iconography and landscape', in D. Cosgrove and S. Daniels (eds) *The Iconography of Landscape*, Cambridge: Cambridge University Press.

Edgar, D. (1987) 'The new nostalgia', *Marxism Today*, March: 30–5.

Frampton, K. (1988) 'Place-form and cultural identity', in J. Thachara (ed.) *Design after Postmodernism*, London: Thames & Hudson.

Giddens, A. (1979a), *Central Problems in Social Theory*, London: Macmillan.

Giddens, A. (1981a) *A Contemporary Critique of Historical Materialism, vol. 1: Power, Property and the State*, London: Macmillan.

Giddens, A. (1984a) *The Constitution of Society*, Cambridge: Polity Press.

Giddens, A. (1985a) *The Nation-State and Violence – Vol. 2 of Contemporary Critique of Historical Materialism*, Cambridge: Polity Press.

Goffman, E. (1959) *The Presentation of Self in Everyday Life*, New York: Doubleday.

Gregory, D. (1989) 'Space, time and politics in social theory: an interview with Anthony Giddens', *Society and Space* 2: 123–32.

―――― (1985) 'Suspended animation: the stasis of diffusion theory', in D. Gregory and J. Urry (eds) *Social Relations and Spatial Structures*, London: Macmillan.

Harley, J. (1988) 'Maps knowledge and power', in D. Cosgrove and S. Daniels (eds) *The Iconography of Landscape*, Cambridge: Cambridge University Press.

Harvey, D. (1985) 'The geopolitics of capitalism', in D. Gregory and J. Urry (eds) *Social Relations and Spatial Structures*, London: Macmillan.

Heidegger, M. (1978) *Being and Time*, Oxford: Blackwell.

Hewison, R. (1987) *The Heritage Industry*, London: Methuen.

Hägerstrand, T. (1953) *Innovation as a Spatial Process*, Chicago: University of Chicago Press (1976).

Jameson, F. (1984) 'Postmodernism and consumer society', in H. Foster (ed.) *Postmodern Culture*, London: Pluto Press.

Kern, S. (1983) *The Culture of Time and Space, 1800–1918*, London: Weidenfeld & Nicolson.

Kroker, A. and D. Cook (1986) *The Postmodern Scene*, New York: St Martin's Press.

Lane, T. (1982) 'The unions: caught on an ebb tide', *Marxism Today*, September: 6–13.

Landes, D. (1983) *Revolution in Time: Clocks and the Making of the Modern World*, Cambridge, Mass.: Harvard University Press.

Lash, S. and Urry, J. (1984) 'The new Marxism of collective action: a critical analysis', *Sociology* 18: 33–51.

Lash, S. and Urry, J. (1987) *The End of Organised Capitalism*, Cambridge: Polity Press.

Massey, D. (1984) *Spatial Divisions of Labour*, London: Macmillan.

MacKenzie, J. and Richards, J. (1986) *The Railway Station. A Social History*, Oxford: Oxford University Press.

Mouzelis, N. (1989) 'Restructuring structuration theory', *Sociological Review* 37: 613–35.

Mumford, E. (1960) 'Universal city', in C. Kraeling and R. Adams (eds) *City Invisible*, Chicago: University of Chicago Press.

Pred, A. (1985) 'The social becomes the spatial, the spatial becomes the social; Enclosures, social change and the becoming of place in the Swedish province of Skane', in D. Gregory and J. Urry (eds) *Social Relations and Spatial Structures*, London: Macmillan.

Schivellbusch, W. (1986) *Railway Journey: Industrialisation and Perception of Time and Space*, London: Berg.

Stauth, G. and Turner, B. (1988) 'Nostalgia, postmodernism and the critique of mass culture', *Theory, Culture and Society* 2/3: 509–26.

Thrift, N. (1985a) '"Bear and mouse or bear and tree?" Anthony Giddens' reconstitution of social theory', *Sociology* 19: 609–23.

Thrift, N. (1985b) 'Flies and germs: a geography of knowledge', in D. Gregory and J. Urry (eds) *Social Relations and Spatial Structures*, London: Macmillan.

Turner, B. (1988) *Status*, Milton Keynes: Open University Press.

Urry, J. (1985) 'Social relations, space and time', in D. Gregory and J. Urry (eds) *Social Relations and Spatial Structures*, London: Macmillan.

—— (1987) 'Society, space and locality', *Environment and Planning D: Society and Space* 6: 435–44.

Walby, S. (1986) *Patriarchy at Work*, Cambridge: Polity Press.

Zukin, S. (1988) *Loft Living*, London: Constable.

SECTION SIX:
Capitalism, Historical Materialism, Class, Power and the Nation-State

Introduction

As noted in the General Introduction, Giddens has indicated that the construction of a new basis for social theory has always been a central objective in his work, and that we are thus entitled to treat this work as a whole, from the earliest of his exegetical writings and engagements with classical social theory down to the present. Nowhere is this continuity more strongly evident than in his treatment of the themes of the present section. The ideas of Marx, Durkheim and Weber on capitalism, class, power, and the nation-state, and the associated critiques of functionalism and evolutionism, which are the central focus of Giddens's earliest writings, retain their prominence in the two volumes of *A Contemporary Critique of Historical Materialism* and in later works, even if they increasingly share the stage with ideas drawn from a far wider range of twentieth-century social theories.

More recent theorists to influence Giddens include Foucault, whose theories of administrative power and surveillance, albeit with significant modification, do much to shape the reworking of conceptions of power at the heart of Giddens's thinking. As Cassell (1993) suggests: 'Power is arguably the axial concept in Giddens's entire repertoire. It is at the centre of his "structuration theory" and his analysis of modernity' (p. 11) (see also Section Four). As well as a conception of power which recognizes a 'dialectic of control' in which 'the less powerful can exert control over the more powerful in power relationships' (Giddens, 1984), Giddens distinguishes crucially between 'allocative power' and 'authoritative power'. He also sets out to overcome sociology's inattention to such features of modernity as the growth of the administrative power of the state and the industrialization of warfare. Finally, of course, Giddens is interested in the complex ways in which different patterns of 'time–space distanciation' involve the operation of power, and in the ways different types of 'locale' – such as 'cities' as 'power containers' – and both nation-states and capitalism exercise domination over both nature and persons.

The two short reviews of *Class Structure of the Advanced Societies* (1974) by the prominent sociologists W.G. Runciman (1974) and Ralf Dahrendorf (1975) which begin this section illustrate well both the continuities in Giddens's work and the celebrity as a social theorist which, even at this early point, he was beginning to achieve. Runciman notes how Giddens is 'quite explicit about Marx's misleading assimilation of capitalism and industrialism' (cf. Held, 1989), and Dahrendorf recognizes the originality of Giddens' 'non-static' structurationist analysis of class, although, anticipating later critics, he finds Giddens's willingness to see change as a matter only of 'specific constellations' 'oddly sceptical'.

As we have outlined in Bryant and Jary (1991), Giddens's chief contentions in the two volumes of *A Contemporary Critique* are that:

1. there exists no necessary overall mechanism of social change, no universal 'motor of history' such as 'class conflict' – contingency not teleology sums up human history;
2. no universal periodizations of social development are possible, these being ruled out by intersocietal systems and 'time–space edges' (the ever-presence of exogenous variables) as well as by human agency;
3. societies do not have needs other than those of individuals, so notions such as 'adaptation' cannot properly be applied to societies;
4. 'class conflict' *is* central in capitalist society compared with pre-capitalist societies, but there is no teleology that guarantees the emergence of the working class as the universal class, and no ontology that justifies denial of the multiple bases of modern societies represented by capitalism, industrialism, surveillance and the industrialization of warfare;
5. sociology, as a subject concerned pre-eminently with modernity, addresses a reality in which, unlike earlier societies, reflexive monitoring is inherent.

In his discussion of these themes, Giddens makes clear both the similarities and the dissimilarities between his theory and that of Marx. Similarities are evident, for example, in Marx's statement in the *Grundrisse* that:

> The conditions and objectifications of the process [of production] are themselves equally moments of it, and its only subjects are the individuals, but individuals in mutual relations, which they equally reproduce and produce anew ... in which they renew themselves even as they renew the world of wealth they create.
>
> (Quoted in Giddens, 1977i, p. 129)

Giddens's ambivalence towards Marx, however, is revealed in his warning that 'there are no easy dividing lines to be drawn between Marxism and "bourgeois social theory"', and that 'no one today ... can remain true to the spirit of Marx by remaining true to the letter of Marx' (Giddens, 1979a: 1).

The major responses generated by Giddens's critique include the following: counter-critiques which point to the limitations of his treatment of historical materialism (e.g. Hirst, 1982; see also Callinicos, 1985; 1987) and of Giddens's general conception of time–space (see also Section Four); a defence of developmental and evolutionary theories against Giddens's strictures (Wright, 1983; Jary 1991a); concern over the limited empirical grounding of aspects of Giddens's historical narratives (Hirst, 1982; Smith, 1982a; Skocpol, 1987; Breuilly, 1990; Jary, 1991a); the identification of understated elements in Giddens's treatment of modernity (Knöbl, 1993; Held, 1989; Shaw, 1993), in one case even the suggestion that such understatements arise from an overdependence on Marx (Collins, 1983); continued scepticism about the feasibility and benefit of Giddens's overall project as a syncretic or synthesizing 'social theory' (Hirst, 1982; see also Craib, 1992a).

As a leading figure in the English Althusserian reinterpretation of Marx of the period (see Hindess and Hirst, 1975), Paul Hirst's (1982) description of Giddens's theory as 'a new syncretism' is not surprising. Hirst is unhappy with any conception of theory that attempts to put together such diverse theorists as Marx, Heidegger and Derrida, preferring instead a strategy of developing productive theoretical divergence. Nor is he satisfied with Giddens's polarization of capitalism and pre-capitalism, or very much impressed by the significance claimed for Giddens's new emphasis on time.

Dennis Smith's article, reprinted from the same *Theory, Culture and Society* symposium, takes a different tack, providing a useful location of Giddens's treatment of history alongside other leading examples of historical sociology which have attracted major interest, Barrington Moore's *Social Origins of Dictatorship and Democracy* (1966), Immanuel Wallerstein's *The Modern World-System* (1974) and Perry Anderson's *Passages from Antiquity* (1974a) and *Lineages of the Absolutist State* (1974b). (Compare Anderson, 1990, for his own extended comparison of historically-oriented social theorists.) Although finding *A Contemporary Critique of Historical Materialism* 'thoroughly stimulating', Smith's major challenge to Giddens is that his account too often pursues a ruthless dichotomous logic and understates historical complexity (see also the later discussion of Giddens in Smith's *The Rise of Historical Sociology*, 1993).

Both Ira Cohen's (1983) and Randall Collins's (1983) short reviews derive from a further review symposium on volume 1 of *A Contemporary Critique* in the US reviews journal, *Contemporary Sociology*. As the author of a monograph on Giddens, Cohen's review benefits from a greater awareness of the overall direction of Giddens's work, and is the more favourable of the two. In Cohen's eyes, Giddens's general stature – along with Habermas, Foucault and Jeffrey Alexander – as 'one of the few vitally important contemporary theorists' is in no doubt. Even Cohen, however, notes that Giddens 'is more intent on breaking new ground than upon systematising his insights'. While impressed by Giddens's telling phrase 'society as time-traveller', and persuaded by Giddens's emphasis on 'real actors in time and space' as moving in the right direction, Collins's main judgement on Giddens's treatment of historical time is that it is 'hopelessly romantic'. He rejects Giddens's suggestions that pre-capitalist societies involved less alienation and more 'ontological harmony' (cf. Craib, 1992a, in Section Four) and that exploitation is confined to capitalist societies. In Collins' view, Giddens makes the necessary criticisms of Marx but does not go far enough. Features of capitalism which are insufficiently grasped by Giddens include the primacy of markets and the centrality in modern societies of a class conflict based on the attainment and maintenance of monopoly privileges in occupations.

Eric Ohlin Wright's (1983) far more extended discussion of Giddens's critique of Marxism (also included in Thompson and Held, 1989; cf. Wright, 1984) is a defence of Marxism – and a defence of some significance. 'It is tempting', Wright suggests, 'to opt for Giddens' solution, to reduce the theoretical ambitions of Marxism in favour of a more contingent causal pluralism' (p. 32). However, in Wright's view three main considerations render such a move unnecessary: (1) 'property relations impose ... limits on the overall process of social change', (2) 'capacity for control' continues to depend upon 'control over allocative resources', and (3) 'the motivational basis of developments of the forces of production are more plausible than the parallel claims of autonomous development of control over authoritative resources' (pp. 32–33). In these circumstances Marxian developmental models retain their utility (see Jary, 1991 in Section Six for further discussion). (It is also relevant, as Cassell (1993) notes, that Giddens is indebted to Lefort's (1978) reading of Marx's *Formen*, which provides a model of Marx as a 'discontinuist' in which capitalism is a major disjunction, and does so, moreover, without undermining the strong developmental perspective which Giddens considers essential.)

Joseph Smith and Bryan Turner's (1986) review article, which discusses *The Constitution of Society* (1984) as well as *The Nation-State and Violence* (1985), marks the important next step in the development of Giddens's analysis of capitalism, class and power, in which the nation-state and violence make their fullest entrance as the major understated elements in both classical sociological theory and Marxism. Smith and Turner's assessment of *The Nation-State and Violence* is mainly negative, its insubstantial empirical grounding being seen as a particularly telling weakness. To Smith and Turner, Giddens's status as a major theorist is 'an enigma'. If it is not the quality of his exegetical writings (see also Turner, 1992), what is it that gives his writings their appeal? In part, Smith and Turner address similar general issues to those raised by Stewart Clegg (see Section One) and, drawing a distinction between theory which is 'significant' and theory which is 'influential', they must be counted among those who in the mid-1980s believed Giddens's influence and reputation were then far greater than his ultimate significance would prove to be.

Two further brief reviews of *The Nation-State and Violence* by Roger Friedland (1987) and Theda Skocpol (1987) again address a number of 'weaknesses' in Giddens's approach, but in general they are much more welcoming than Smith and Turner. As a well-known comparative historical sociologist in her own right, Skocpol points out how in going for the theoretical 'big picture' Giddens will disappoint those 'who might want pointed causal explanations or empirically grounded historical general-ization'. Nevertheless, the overall focus on 'a transnational *system* of states' which is the central element in Giddens's argument in *The Nation-State and Violence* receives a strong welcome from Skocpol, although, like others, she has reservations about the sharpness of some of Giddens's typological contrasts between 'traditional' and 'modern' states. Friedland's 'Golden Gloves' (1987) is a refreshingly boisterous review which conveys how Giddens's central argument proceeds as a series of exigetical 'bouts' with contenders whose ideas are selectively incorporated into his own overall theoretical and substantive account. Although impressed by Giddens's range, Friedland regrets both that 'the human subject is barely visible', and that specification of the conditions for the emergence of 'arenas of historicity' is absent.

Hugh Ward's (1987) article carries the discussion back to the wider methodological issues and difficulties in Giddens's treatment of power (see also Clegg, 1989). Writing from within a political science tradition, Ward's article is useful in reviewing Giddens's conceptions of power and structure alongside Marxian notions of 'structural power' (especially Jessop, 1983; cf. Jessop, 1982, in Section Six) and those of Steven Lukes (1973 and 1977; see also Layder, 1985, in Section Four). Ward's article illustrates once again how difficult Giddens's conception of 'structure' and 'power' and 'duality of structure' can be to grasp fully. Although Ward suggests otherwise, it is arguable that Giddens's conception of power and of structures *is* compatible with Ward's view of the distinctions that need to be drawn between 'structural power', 'non-structural power' and 'structural constraints'.

David Held (1989) deals with the treatment of 'citizenship and citizen rights' within Giddens's work. Closely linked with the issues of individual agency which have from the start been utterly central in structuration theory, these issues have become increasingly prominent as Giddens has explored both issues of power and the potential for new political movements in modern societies – sometimes in critical engagement with the thinking of Foucault and T.H. Marshall as well as Marx. Held concentrates particularly on the historical processes by which citizenship rights and duties have been established. His contention is that there are ambiguities at the very heart of Giddens's project. Giddens's identification of the roots of the transformation of subjects into citizens in the expansion of state sovereignty is accepted by Held. However, according to Held, not only does Giddens misrepresent Marshall as 'evolu-tionist' when differentiating his own work, but he also fails to capture the extent to which citizenship grows in ways that both expand and limit membership rights, and he understates the part played by social movements apart from the labour movement, including ethnic movements and the women's movement. While recognizing the value of Giddens's emphasis on a mutual interplay between capitalism and the rise of the nation-state, Held sees a crucial ambiguity in Giddens's account of whether the 'capitalist state' or 'modern' pluralism is the central feature of modern societies. Giddens's 'range of insight' is acknowledged by Held, but he suggests that the task of social and political theory is to 'think through' the relations explored by Giddens with greater precision and a more grounded comparative analysis.

Christopher Dandeker's (1990) and John Breuilly's (1990) chapters provide contrasting overall evaluations of Giddens's treatment of the nation-state and the modern world system. While Dandeker underlines the value of Giddens's 'neo-Weberian' emphasis on the role of war and the military in his reworking of social theory, Breuilly is more critical of Giddens's approach, not least his over-simple dichotomized typology of state forms. Dandeker describes Giddens as 'an open-minded realist concerned to push social theory in new directions' (p. 269). Despite finding Giddens 'highly stimulating in places', Breuilly regrets a lack of continuity in the concepts employed in the two volumes of *A Contemporary Critique* and complains about the difficulties of relating *The Nation-State and Violence* to Giddens's general approach and 'criticizing it as an independent work' (p. 273). He is also particularly critical of Giddens's explanatory historical accounts, which he sees as unreconciled with the research principles of structuration theory.

David Jary (1991a) provides a holistic view of Giddens's overall treatment of historical change, historical materialism and the nation-state in world society. While recognizing the flair and interest of much of Giddens's structurationist treatment of history, he questions whether Giddens's assumption that social change is episodic and contingent must follow from his central structurationist argument. Too often Giddens seems content to provide empirical illustrations rather than more developed theoretical and empirical demonstrations. Jary also argues that Giddens may have cut himself off from a more grounded and systematic treatment of social change by too sharp a differentiation of structuration theory from earlier evolutionary and development theory, including Marxism. (For further discussion of evolutionary issues and consideration of differences and similarities between Giddens and Habermas see McCarthy (1978), Ashley (1982), Habermas (1982), Joas (1987), Strydom (1992) and Outhwaite (1994); see also Giddens (1977c, d; 1982j; 1985d).)

The final articles in this section are once again an illustration of the breadth of interest and application of Giddens's work, despite the criticisms it attracts. Wolfgang Knöbl (1993), reprinted in the original German, emphasizes the importance of a renewed focus in sociology on the nation-state and warfare. Comparing the contributions of Mann (1986), Hall (1985) and Giddens, he finds Giddens's approach by far the most valuable. In addition, he suggests that more sociologists should follow Max Weber's lead and do more to seek to communicate and to apply sociological understanding as widely as possible. (This is, of course, something that Giddens himself recommends in his methodological writings and has in fact recently attempted to do.)

Martin Shaw (1993) focuses on 'security' as an increasingly prominent sociological topic, and notes the paradox – in the work of Skocpol and Mann as well as Giddens – of an increased sociological interest in the state as an actor (the traditional state-centred, 'realist' approach of international relations) at a time when international relations is moving away from this view. In our view, Giddens is perhaps somewhat unfairly selected as an initial target for Shaw's concern. Given his opposition to unitary conceptions of society and his emphasis on relations at a distance at many levels, a fairer view of Giddens might be that his work always represented only a partial incorporation of realist conceptions designed simply to bring the state 'back in' to sociological analysis. It is, after all, the multi-layered emphasis on security and risk within sociological analysis favoured by Shaw which has become central to Giddens's most recent work – see Section Seven – as Shaw concedes. Indeed, he seeks, in the final part of his article, to apply Giddens's extended discussions of risk and trust in *The Consequences of Modernity* (1990a) and *Modernity and Self-Identity* (1991a) to international relations theory.

Select Bibliography

Anderson, P. (1974a) *Passages from Antiquity*, London: New Left Books.

Anderson, P. (1974b) *Lineages of the Absolutist State*, London: New Left Books.

Hall, J. (1985) *Powers and Liberties: The Causes and Consequences of the Rise of the West*, Oxford: Blackwell (also Penguin Books, 1996).

Hindess, B. and Hirst, P. (1975) *Pre-Capitalist Modes of Production*, London: Routledge & Kegan Paul.

Jessop, B. (1983) 'On the commensurability of power and structural constraint', paper to the EGOS Symposium on Power, University of Bradford, May.

Lefort, C. (1978) 'Marx – from one vision of history to another', *Social Research*, 45.

Lukes, S. (1973) *Power – A Radical View*, London: Macmillan.

Lukes, S. (1977) 'Power and structure', in *Essays in Social Theory*, London: Macmillan.

McCarthy, T. (1978) *The Critical Theory of Jürgen Habermas*, London: Hutchinson.

Mann, M. (1986) *The Sources of Social Power – A History of Power from the Beginning to AD 1760*, London: Macmillan.

Moore, B. (1966) *Social Origins of Dictatorship and Democracy*, New York: Beacon Press (1967, London: Allen Lane Press).

Outhwaite, W. (1994) *Habermas: A Critical Introduction*, Cambridge: Polity Press.

Strydom, P. (1992) 'The ontogenetic fallacy: the immanent critique of Habermas's developmental logical theory of evolution', *Theory, Culture and Society*, 9, 3: 65–93.

Thompson, J.B. and Held, D. (1982) *Habermas: Critical Debates*, London: Macmillan.

Wallerstein, I. (1974) *The Modern World-System*, New York: Academic Press.

52

Review of *The Class Structure of the Advanced Societies**

W.G. Runciman

*Source: *British Journal of Sociology*, vol. 25, 1974, pp. 108–11.

The Class Structure of the Advanced Societies, Anthony Giddens. Hutchinson University Library, 1973, 336 pp. £3.50.

The title of Anthony Giddens's interesting new book is a little misleading: it would be more accurate to call it a discussion of how far the (or a) *theory* of class structure can be applied to *some* advanced societies. But it is at the same time much more than a textbook. Although the first seven chapters are largely taken up with a summary and assessment of the views of Marx and his principal commentators, they are followed by six chapters on the workings of capitalist industrial society, two chapters on state socialist society and two concluding chapters on 'Classes in Contemporary Society' and 'The Future of Class Society'. Giddens's avowed aim is to revive the notion of 'class' as fundamental to the understanding not only of capitalist society but also of the nature of the difference between capitalist and state socialist society. The book suffers, in this reviewer's opinion, from three minor failings and one major limitation. But it deserves to be closely read by anyone interested in the organization and structure of advanced industrial societies.

Of the three minor failings, the first concerns the relation of Marx's theory, as Giddens expounds it, to Giddens's own analysis of twentieth-century industrial societies. Giddens's summary of Marx and his critics is admirably done, and his short, clear accounts of the views of Dahrendorf, Bell and Touraine will not merely encourage but justify his student readers in the belief that they can afford to neglect the originals. But how far does an understanding of what is happening in present-day Yugoslavia or Japan really depend on an understanding of a century-old theory concerned principally with mid-Victorian Britain and France? Giddens, although he convincingly defends Marx against some of the oversimplified criticisms levelled against him, is quite explicit about Marx's misleading assimilation of capitalism and industrialism, which led him to a mistake so fundamental – the belief that, as Giddens puts it (p. 136), 'the transcendence of class society either necessarily leads to, or even provides a basis for, radical change in those aspects of the division of labour which are involved in the sphere of paratechnical relations' – as to make the reader wonder why Giddens then devotes so much space to the theory which embodies it. Is it not, on Giddens's own argument, time to forget the founders? Where Marx's views can be adapted to fit a mid-twentieth-century capitalist society, this is because, as Giddens points out, its history has been a special one: contemporary French Marxism, interesting as it is, fits the actual course of events in France only at the cost of increasing irrelevance to the actual course of events in the United States. Holding this view, might not Giddens be expected to have devoted more of his space to comparing the histories of those countries and less to expounding the history of Marxism?

The second minor failing concerns the use of numerical evidence in comparisons of social structure. Most of Giddens's comparisons are qualitative. He makes it clear that, for example, the distinguishing feature of capitalist society is the significance of market relations within it. No international comparisons are offered in terms of, say, value of fixed assets held in the public sector, or proportion of full-time adult workers in self-employment, or distribution of net personal wealth; and the unexpected fact that nearly a third of the East German labour force continued in the private sector after 1945 is cited only to point the contrast with Czechoslovakia after 1948. The reader is on the whole left to make what he chooses of such broad distinctions as whether 'the ultimate criteria regulating production are determined by political decisions' (p. 155) or 'the major part of the economic system of a society' is ordered according to the pursuit of private profit in a monetary labour market (p. 142). Yet in other places, Giddens appears to rest his argument on quantitative differences whose significance is at best questionable. Thus, an American survey of 1964 which showed that 'no more than 20 per cent' of non-Southern white manual workers supported Goldwater is cited as telling against 'the conventional view that prejudiced attitudes are concentrated among the white working class' (p. 281). But an isolated statistic like this is almost worthless as an aid to understanding the complicated interplay between race and politics in the United States in the 1960s, as Giddens himself more or less admits on the following page. The point may not be of great importance to his general argument. But such seemingly haphazard use of figures is bound to raise a mild suspicion that he is trying not so much to test his case as to bolster it.

The third minor failing concerns Giddens's choice of historical examples. As I have already implied, the list of 'advanced' societies discussed or even mentioned is by no means exhaustive. Giddens is at pains to correct the tendency of writers on these topics to take a single country as the paradigm for one social type. He rightly insists that the United States, which he sees as different in no less than five significant ways from Western Europe or Japan, no more furnishes the model of capitalist development than does the Soviet Union of the evolution of state socialism. But this only makes it the more surprising that several of the most distinctive of the advanced societies are mentioned only in passing (such as Sweden) or not at all (such as Israel). Giddens is careful to distinguish, for example, between the Yugoslav system of 'workers' control' and the rather different schemes of this kind which were tried out in Poland after 1956 and Czechoslovakia after 1966. But is not the more interesting comparison in this area that between the management of industrial enterprises in Eastern Europe generally on the one hand and in China on the other? Giddens may (although he does not say so) omit China from consideration because so many of its workers are still on the land. But by this measure, neither Yugoslavia or Poland are yet fully industrialized. In any case, this does not make China any less interesting from the standpoint of Giddens's own concern with what he calls 'generic aspects of the position of workers in state socialist society'. The account given, for example, in Chapter 4 of Franz Schurmann's *Ideology and Organization in Communist China* raises questions at least as crucial to Giddens's thesis as those raised by the contrast between Yugoslavia, Czechoslovakia and Poland. It is perfectly legitimate for Giddens to say, as he does (p. 20), 'I shall concentrate upon a limited number of societies as a source of empirical reference in order to illustrate my case'. But he has then to beware of allowing any implication later on that they are enough not merely to illustrate his case but to establish it.

These deficiencies, however, do not diminish the interest of the two principal themes which Giddens develops with reference to capitalist and state socialist society, respectively. His analysis of present-day capitalism leads him to two linked conclusions which merit particular attention. Giddens argues first, that the present state of the industrial countries of the West is not 'late' but, on the contrary, 'mature' capitalism; and second, that the separation of industrial and political conflict is a consequence not of evolution to a new form of social organization but only of the incorporation of the labour movement and the redirection of its aims towards pay and security rather than political control. This process is linked in its turn with the formation of a relatively isolated underclass – or strictly, two underclasses of men in unskilled manual jobs and women in routine non-manual jobs – and the growth of a middle class of diminishing specific social and cultural influence. These tendencies are modified, if not overridden, by such particular circumstances as the overlap of class and race in the United States or the pattern of enterprise unionism in Japan. But Giddens insists, and persuasively so, that the working class in a capitalist industrial society will be 'revolutionary' only where there has been an abnormal prolongation of the initial confrontation between 'progressive' capitalism and 'retroactive' semi-feudal agrarianism. There has been such a prolongation in France as a result of what happened (or did not happen) after 1789. But this is a deviation from the 'general principle, which applies to the emergence of capitalist-industrialism in any given country, that the mode of rupture with post-feudal society creates an institutional complex, within which a series of profound economic changes are accommodated, *that then becomes a persisting system, highly resistant to major modification*' (p. 214; author's italics). On this argument, neo-Marxist diagnoses of the contradictions of *Spätkapitalismus* are no less mistaken than the diagnoses of those (chiefly American) sociologists who confuse this relative stability with an 'end of ideology' and a dissolution of class conflict.

In his discussion of state socialist society, Giddens is primarily concerned to insist not merely, as many others have done before him, that the substitution of a political elite for an upper class does not abolish the exploitation of man by man, but also that the industrial order characteristic of state socialism is inherently less stable than that of mature capitalism because of the way in which it is 'subject to the occasional, but much more deep-rooted, eruption of worker antagonism involving an orientation to control' (p. 269). He therefore disagrees not only with orthodox Soviet apologetics on the one hand but also with Djilas on the other. On Giddens's view state socialist societies are characterized by an endemic tension deriving precisely from the changed relation between the economic and the political order which marks them off from capitalist industrial societies. Indeed, this tension parallels the unresolved contradiction in socialist theory between the proposed 'rationalization' of social organization and the supposed elimination or transcendence of 'exploitative' social relations. Giddens is therefore very sceptical of the view that state socialist societies are moving towards a more decentralized and less overtly political mode of social control. Predictions of 'technocracy' he dismisses altogether, partly because those who make them confuse the indispensability of experts with their (often nugatory) influence and partly because even if economic expertise is decentralized within the overall control of the Communist Party this will merely arouse the local antagonism of workers who cannot, in the nature of the situation, be channelled towards 'economism' and will therefore seek to press their own demands for control. The tension is thus inescapable; and Giddens's own cautious forecast is that 'The most probable cause of development of the state socialist societies, in the near future at least, will be one veering from the relaxation of political controls over the economic order back to the reimposition of a tight hierarchy of political command' (p. 253).

It remains, however, for me to state my own major doubt about what is in many ways a very good book. As I have already brought out in this review, Giddens bases his whole discussion on the fundamental distinction between capitalist industrial society on the one hand and state socialist industrial society on the other. Thus, Sweden is assimilated to the rest of Western Europe on one side just as Yugoslavia, for all its differences from the Soviet Union on which Giddens insists, is bracketed with the rest of Eastern Europe on the other. But does this imposed classification hold? Or does the analysis of the social organization of the advanced societies of the 1970s not call for an altogether fuller and more flexible taxonomy? It may be that Sweden, about whose ostensibly distinctive features Giddens says disappointingly little can nevertheless be best explained on the same 'mature capitalist' model as Britain. But what about Israel? Or China? Or South Africa? Or Mexico? And what about the histories of pre-war Germany and Japan? The only reason why Fascist industrial society (for want of a better term) finds no exemplification in the contemporary world is that these two countries went to war and then lost it: they didn't collapse through any internal dialectic which renders Fascist industrial societies inherently unviable. Giddens says openly in his introduction that he is not attempting an exhaustive classification of differences in the socio-economic infrastructure of the advanced societies. But he agrees that it needs to be done; and it seems to me that his own approach may be as likely to retard it as to bring it about.

There may, despite what I said earlier, be nothing wrong in starting once again from Marx if Marx's theory is still, for all its shortcomings, the most illuminating, or at least the most suggestive, that we have. But there is a risk that to do so will lead to a too ready an acceptance that the capitalist/socialist distinction is indeed basic and that all variations between industrial societies are to be subordinated to and expressed in terms of it. Giddens makes a strong case for the continuing significance of the distinction for the particular purposes which he has set himself, and in questioning his emphasis on it I am not attempting any covert resuscitation of 'convergence theory'. I merely venture the question whether, as more and more countries reach the stage of advanced industrialization, differences of other kinds among both capitalist and state socialist systems will not turn out to be more useful in explaining both their initial development and the subsequent modifications in organization and structure which await them.

53

Review of *The Class Structure of the Advanced Societies**

R. Dahrendorf

*Source: *Sociology*, vol. 9, 1975, pp. 134–37.

Anthony Giddens, *The Class Structure of the Advanced Societies*. London: Hutchinson University Library, 1973, 336 pp., £3.50 (£1.80 paperback).

Anthony Giddens has written an intelligent and thoughtful book about class; and since the title of his book has been called a misnomer, let me add that in my view it describes subject and intention of this study quite well. It is about the *Class Structure of Advanced Societies*, notwithstanding the point that for Giddens not all advanced societies have a class structure, and that not-so-advanced societies may in any case have to be described in terms other than those of class. In other words, Giddens uses the term 'class' to distinguish; for him, classlessness and non-class conditions are necessary notions if class is to make any distinctive sense at all; perhaps it can be said therefore that his method is somewhat conceptual. Class is a socio-economic category, not merely a nominalist decision.

Giddens's definition of class is original. Class refers, he says (p. 192) 'to a cluster of forms of structuration based upon commonly shared levels of market capacity'. The statement includes two notions which are central for Giddens. One is that class, and class structure, are not to be understood in a static manner. Classes and class structures do not simply exist, but they develop under specified conditions; there are, in certain societies, processes of class structuration. Such processes are particularly probable in capitalist societies with their characteristic methods of mediating the relations between economy and polity. In a totally bureaucratic, indeed in a state-socialist society, class structuration is less likely, if only because 'market capacity' is replaced under such conditions by more authoritative structures of the organization of life chances. The market capacity of groups – a most useful and intriguing term – is the set of trump cards which they bring to the bargaining game, property, organization, leadership, intelligence, many other things. Where there is no market, there is no relevant market capacity, and thus no class structuration. Where class structuration is far advanced, as in what Giddens would call early capitalism, and others high capitalism, class structuration takes on the form of conscious organization and action.

One part of Giddens's book is concerned with a polemical development of these (and several other) concepts. The thrust of Giddens's polemics is directed against critics of Marx among modern social scientists, not because they have criticized Marx, but because they have criticized him for the wrong reasons. My own youthful contribution figures prominently in this context (along with distinguished authors like Aron and Ossowski, later in the book Marcuse), and I shall take up the challenge presently. By far the greatest part of Giddens's book however consists of discussions of socio-political, and at times socio-economic developments in advanced societies. These are often a pleasure to read, even where one may not entirely agree, and they shed much light on specific problems of France, of Japan, of several state-socialist countries, of the new working class, the intelligentsia, the white-collared and white-bloused. Indeed, after so much intelligent discussion of differences, one wonders how much there is to the discipline of sociological theory, except that it provides a language to describe the undiscipline of social reality.

But despite such justified scepticism, a few general, mostly critical comments about Giddens's book may be in place. And here I would begin with his treatment of Marx, because it is relevant to the analytical force of class analysis.

I must admit today that when I wrote *Class and Class Conflict* in 1957, I underestimated Marx in at least one important respect. While his political economy may at times be little more than Hegelian philosophy (turned upside down, of course) couched in economic language, he did go some way from the philosophy of historical dialectic through the sociology of class struggles to the economics of the real basis of politics and society. Economic conditions do not only impose certain constraints on class structuration, or on the market capacity of groups, but there is, for Marx, an underlying reality: men, in seeking to improve their life chances, sometimes find it possible to visualize and expect solutions which are prevented by the legal, organizational, political conditions of their time. Forces of production, permanently changing, can be stifled by given relations of production. It is this underlying tension which gives class relations their force and anchor, so that class analysis is not a concern suspended in sociological mid-air, but part of a more comprehensive socio-economic or politico-economic analysis: ruling classes are invariably the defenders of existing relations of production, indeed these provide the substance of their class interests, whereas rising classes borrow their rhetoric and their hope, thus their class interests, from new forces of production.

I said that I have underestimated this point. Giddens probably does not underestimate it. His discussion of Marx's own theory of forces and relations of production (p. 85 sq.) is imprecise, even in the use of terms, in the light of both the *Critique of Political Economy* and the *Grundrisse*. But Giddens states that revolutionary class consciousness presupposes a condition of 'contradiction' (p. 114), and clearly the concept of market capacity relates social groups to conditions facilitating or constraining their actions. But at the end of his book, I still feel that Marx was superior not only to me, but also to him in his ability to come to grips with the dialectic of existing social and economic structure on the one hand, and the potential of solving problems which given structures are incapable of realizing on the other.

That Marx was superior does not mean that he was right. My own thinking today – as may be apparent from the wording which I have used here – revolves around ways of identifying social structures and problem-solving capacities without dogmatizing the specific experiences of the industrial revolution, *i.e.* of a human and technical potential of (factory) production fettered by a persistent structure of (feudal) rules and rights. Indeed I am surprised that Giddens finds it as difficult as he does to abandon the production bias of Marx which surely is outmoded even if it remains true that half the labour force is, in some countries, employed in manufacturing. As Freud has to be stripped of the dated elements of his theories – the super-ego as the internalized father presupposes a Victorian family organization – so does Marx. And of course, he himself gives indications of the direction in which we might look; for example, when he speaks of the 'social production of our lives'. I cannot say that I have finished my own reflections on this matter, but I had wished that Giddens would have helped more than he does.

One of the weaker parts of Giddens's book is his discussion of elites. For one thing, it does rather less than justice to the literature on the subject; surely, Pareto and Mosca need to be taken rather more seriously. For another thing, however, it fails to cope with one of the more obvious problems of social conflict. Conflicts are in fact not carried out by great armies of people, organizing the two sides of the combat, and originating from identifiable groups whose wives send supplies to the fighters and weep about victims – at least, this is not the way in which intra-societal conflicts occur. Even civil wars involve an element of elitism, that is, of relatively small groups in contest, with the large majority being used in argument rather than in the fight itself. The rhetoric and imagery of the class struggle presents a very misleading picture of what is actually going on in human society: indeed I would suggest that it is no accident that even revolutionary leaders are often worried about the contradiction between their own position and their claims.

The problem posed here is probably not solved by classical elite theories. That there is a small group of leaders and a large apathetic mass is certainly not the whole truth. But there is a lot to be said for looking very closely at the drama that is acted out at the top of the socio-political pyramid of countries. The phenomenology of conflict presents more examples of struggles within elites, or between elites and counter-elites, than of comprehensive class battles. And it is therefore necessary to assess the relationship between these acting elites and those for whom they claim to act in considerable detail: perhaps the first problem of class structuration!

What is needed here may be some kind of a theory of legitimacy, or to imply one of its elements, of the constraints imposed upon actors in positions of great impact. For class structuration may well be an essentially negative phenomenon, a reminder of what the powerful cannot do, or can no longer do, a heightened visibility of the limits imposed on political action. This in turn might mean that the antagonisms of competing elites have a lot to do with the traditional subjects of class analysis. I find it at least conceivable that new forces of production are recognized and advocated by small and highly skilled groups – elites – rather than large social categories, classes. If this should be so, however, then there is a whole new set of problems to be solved around the subject of class *vs.* elite theory.

I do not want to become too abstract in reviewing a book which in many parts is so refreshingly specific. But there is one general point which has to be made. It is true that Giddens's approach renders more dynamic an analysis which is often conducted in unsatisfactorily static terms. Classes are not entities to be described and assessed as such, but class is a process, a tidal process almost, with periods of high structuration and others of receding articulation. While I can agree with this thesis, it does change the subject of class analysis somewhat. The fact that the title of Giddens's book is not a misnomer, is also an indication of its limitations. My own subject was, and continues to be, change: what is it that makes modern societies tick? When do they move, how fast, how comprehensively, and of course above all, in what direction? In answering these questions, one has to look at the moving forces of history, and one of them is conflict. Giddens says as much in the last chapter of his book (p. 283). But it makes a difference whether the dynamics of class structuration is seen predominantly in its impact on conflict and change, or whether it is made a subject of its own.

Anthony Giddens, although quite obviously interested in understanding advanced societies, and contributing much to such comprehension, is oddly sceptical about change as a subject of inquiry. At several points, he casts doubt on the very possibility of a theory of revolution, for example (p. 153: '... if such a theory is conceivably possible at all'!), and seems to hand over the subject to the study of history, *i.e.* of specific constellations (cf. p. 211). I wonder whether this is not an unnecessarily defeatist approach, and what is more, one that robs the analysis of class of much of its vigour. The often-quoted, apparently symbolic fact that the chapter on classes in *Das Kapital* remained unfinished might mean after all that the subject was but of limited interest to its authors who were looking for the 'law of development of capitalist society', and for classes only in so far as they influence this law. This, in any case, was my subject, so that my own book may in fact have been misleadingly described as being about class when it was in fact about conflict and change in modern societies. There is a sense, in other words, in which Giddens's book and mine are about different subjects rather than different approaches to the same subject.

It would be easy to go on discussing aspects of the book by Anthony Giddens, and this fact testifies to the quality of the book. This is a rare quality, for it combines information with originality in a way which I have not seen very often. Students can read it and find most of the necessary information about other authors on the subject; these other authors can read it and find much to think, to rethink and to respond. I for one am glad and thankful that Anthony Giddens has written this important book on class structuration.

54

The Social Theory of Anthony Giddens: A New Syncretism?*

P. Hirst

*Source: *Theory, Culture and Society*, vol. 1 (1), 1982, pp. 78–82.

Giddens has written a number of works with the common aim of reorienting something called "social theory". His latest book, *A Contemporary Critique of Historical Materialism*, attempts to assess what is of enduring value in Marx's work and to integrate it as part of a larger theoretical synthesis. Let me begin by saying that Giddens is right to claim that Marxism is in need of radical theoretical reconstruction and a root and branch critique which challenges those aspects of it which are imprisoned in nineteenth-century metaphysics. Giddens will, rightly, have nothing to do with evolutionism and functionalism, with "iron laws" and historical necessity, with economic determinism, and so on. In this respect he is concurring with the massive body of non-orthodox Marxist theoretical work over the last twenty or so years, and, with all due respect, is saying little that is new or surprising in the course of his critique.

The problems with Giddens' new book begin when we consider what we are asked to regard as valuable in Marxism and how this residue is to be incorporated into the synthesis which produces a new "social theory". Giddens' whole theoretical project from *Capitalism and Modern Social Theory* onwards has been syncretic and eclectic, seeking to bring together the distinct strands of theorising he regards as valuable in a new synthesis. This is one reason for his popularity; he appears to offer a way out of the chaos of competing theories and conceptions of work in the social sciences. I must confess I am deeply suspicious of the category "social theory"; it offers the prospect of a unified theory of a single object – "society", "social life", the products of, and conditions for, "human praxis", or whatever. I would argue, on the contrary, that the concepts of distinct theoretical fields cannot easily be abstracted from those fields and synthesised; they depend upon other (perhaps less assimilable) concepts and upon distinct (and non-syncretistic) methods of theoretical work. I would further argue that the objects these distinct theoretical fields attempt to construct are by no means as compatible as Giddens seems to think they are. They are not partial stabs at a greater object "society", rather they differentiate social relations and human subjects. I would prefer a strategy of accepting theoretical difference and divergence, pursuing distinct methods of work seriously and living with the, perhaps, productive incompatibility. This is not to argue for dogmatism and the perpetual tendency struggle of opposed domains of theory – rigorous work *within* a field need not imply an ignorance of, or unwillingness to work in other fields.

I cannot accept that it *is* possible to put Adorno, Althusser, Derrida, Durkheim, Foucault, Freud, Goffman, Habermas, Heidegger, Lacan, Marx, Weber, etc, together in a rigorous theory. I must confine myself to some limited remarks about Giddens' use of three of these authors – Marx, Heidegger and Derrida.

Giddens does not examine "historical materialism" as a theoretical field, rather he criticises Marx and Marxists extensively and also attempts to retain what he sees as being the bits of Marx's theories of greatest relevance to contemporary society. It appears that, due to his concern with time and with the radical break capitalism produces with all hitherto existing modes of social life, Giddens (1981, p. 119) accepts some version of the theory of value. He says: "the calculation and coordination of exchange values by labour time is a specific feature of the commodification of economic relations introduced by the convergence of money capital and the formation of wage-labour characteristic of capitalism". But the law of value is not merely something that "happens" in capitalism; the "calculation and coordination of exchange values by labour time" is the most hotly debated aspect of Marx's theory as presented in *Capital*. Marxists and non-Marxist economists and philosophers have rejected various constructions of the "law" on technical and on conceptual grounds. The defences offered by those Marxists committed to the concept of "value" seem less than compelling. In the absence of the *means* by which it is argued, it seems difficult to assert the existence of the "phenomenon". But this is what Giddens seems to do, he is silent on these debates, offers no theoretic defence, and seems to conclude that Marx drew the right conclusions about the "phenomenon" and so we can adopt these conclusions whilst neglecting the means by which they were produced. The same can be said about the "tendencies" in capitalism Marx identifies – again Giddens concludes that Marx was by and large right about these phenomena and is therefore able to ignore both the conceptual problems with the notion of "tendency" itself and the problems with the construction of specific laws of tendency, such as the law of the declining rate of profit.

Giddens draws the strongest possible contrast between capitalism and pre-capitalist societies. But it is difficult to see how he can sustain this if he rejects the Hegelian–Marxist notion of "totality" – if societies are not wholes with structural limits and governed by a single determinative principle, it is impossible to draw this contrast in a Marxist sense. Indeed, Giddens (1981, p. 104) goes so far as to say that pre-capitalist societies are not modes of production. In fact the contrast Giddens draws is in most respects closer to such distinctions as status-construct, *Gemeinschaft–Gesellschaft*, as we shall see below in our remarks on time and "presence".

In order to examine Marx's views on pre-capitalist societies Giddens relies more or less exclusively on *The German Ideology* and the *Grundrisse*. Giddens draws a rigid distinction between pre-capitalist societies in which exploitation is based on direct political coercion and in which the labourer has direct access to the means of production, and capitalism, in which exploitation works through a strictly economic necessity which is separated from the political realm and in which workers are separated from direct access to the means of production. Now whilst Marx gives voice to such a view in *Capital*, that text unlike the earlier ones, contains the means to subvert such a view. This is because unlike the earlier ones it contains his developed theories of surplus value and rent. As Barry Hindess and I have argued in *Pre Capitalist Modes of Production* (1975), Marx *does* regard slavery and feudalism as modes of production in *Capital* and that, to be consistent with such a view, the process of exploitation in such modes must involve distinct economic forms and mechanisms which are not reducible to direct coercion. This, as we have shown, involves definite forms of separation of the direct labourer from the means of production in both the slave and the feudal systems. Thus the general contrast capitalism-economic exploitation, pre-capitalism-political exploitation cannot be sustained if the theoretical possibilities in the discourse of *Capital* are to be developed. Without such development we are driven into a position where we contrast wage slavery based upon the dull compulsions of propertylessness and hunger with more or less legitimated forms of banditry on the other side. Hindess and I may have subsequently challenged some of our own concerns in *PCMP* and, indeed, the concept of "mode of production" itself (in its technical Marxist sense of a social totality), but the above aspect of our book I would still adhere to and would claim it to be consistent with certain of the key concepts in *Capital*.

Almost any simple and radical contrast between "capitalism" and "pre-capitalism" will not do, as Giddens knows when he struggles with the exceptions. The European Middle Ages were technically innovative (if we are to believe a writer Giddens cites like Jean Gimpel), medieval monastic life was governed by time and conduct patterned according to the hours of the day, in Tokugawa Japan Edo offers the model of an urban metropolis (approximately one million inhabitants in the early eighteenth century) with a degree of pornography and sex obsessions found probably only in the contemporary USA. Once we reject concepts of societies as "totalities" or evolutionary schemes it is difficult to sustain the contrasts derived from them. Even with such concepts things were difficult enough. Marxists still earnestly debate when in Europe between the fifteenth and the eighteenth centuries the transition between feudalism and capitalism was accomplished.

To conclude my remarks about Marxism, we may note Giddens (1981, p. 177) is less than fair to Marxists on the matters of the national question and of war. To argue that war is neglected in social theory and that Marxists "usually only touch upon violence as revolutionary violence, or as counter insurgency", is unjust and misleading. Marx and Marxists have stressed the necessary role of war and violence in the creation of a capitalist labour force, in the slave trade and in the foundation and maintenance of European empires generally. Lenin, Bukharin and others were at pains to link World War I to the antagonisms between the great powers created by inter-imperialist competition. Mao Tse-Tung constructed the theory of the people's war. Clausewitz was always a central theoretical text for those in the Marxist–Leninist tradition, and Trotsky, Mao, Giap, etc consider war not merely from a narrow political standpoint or as technical military specialists, but regard themselves as writing in the tradition of Clausewitz as theorists of war. Indeed, probably the best modern book on war in general is the volume edited for the Soviet General Staff by V D Sokolovsky, *Military Strategy* (1963). Giddens (1981, p. 179) claims: "No great Marxist work on the nation state or nationalism emerged of comparable status with, say, Hilferding's *Das Finanzkapital* in the realm of economic theory". Giddens knows that Marxists wrote on the "national question" – he mentions Otto Bauer. Lenin's work on this "question" is indeed comparable to Hilferding in subtlety and theoretical complexity. At the turn of the century the "question" of nationalism had a quite specific meaning, none of the great powers were nation states, rather all were supra-national empires which held subject peoples in check. England, far from being a "nation state", was perceived by Marxists as an enslaver of peoples, not merely beyond the seas but in the British Isles. The national question turned on the right of nations to self-determination and what was to count as a "nation". Lenin linked the (national) revolt of the subject peoples in the colonies with the assertion of the rights of small nations within the European empires' own terrains. These two processes have produced the world of "nations" we see today – the dismembering of the British, Russian and Austro-Hungarian empires in Europe and the rise of the subject peoples of Africa and Asia. The Leninist tradition can fairly claim not merely to have understood nationalism rather well but to have played a great part in producing the world of "nations" we see today. Marxism has always paid recognition to the specificity and complexity of national oppression. "Social theory" is something distinct from Marxist political theory, quite clearly, but Marxism, as a political theory, has taken war and nationalism seriously.

Moreover, Marxists have asserted that capitalism far from being a supra-national economic system must take the form of definite national economies. How else are we to comprehend Lenin's work on uneven-development and on the agrarian question in Russia? In practice there is an irreconcilable tension in Marx's own work between the universal abstractions of the capitalist mode of production and the fact that capitalist production takes a definite social form in a state territory. Marx was, ambiguously, aware that what constituted the labour force, the working day, the form of property and the institutional organisation of production and trade were matters of struggle and determination within a definite state territory. Does not Gramsci's (1971) account of the uneven development of Italian capitalism and of the "Southern Question" make clear that capital always exists in definite territorial state forms. Marxism has not adequately *theorised* national economies as objects of analysis, nor is Marx's concept of the CMP as a generality compatible with such theorisation. But within Marxism the connection between capitalistic production and a definite state territory has not been ignored. Giddens probably has little time for the Leninist tradition within Marxism; I would argue on the contrary that Leninism *and* the Marxism of the Second International (Lenin's conceptual point of departure) have a great deal to offer which has been ignored by the philosophical Marxist critics in Western Europe. Giddens would not lay claim to the title "Marxist"; I would – however heterodox my own work might be regarded. Marxism has glaring theoretical weaknesses but these do not consist in inattention *per se* to certain problems like war, nationalism or the national economy.

Let us turn from Marx to Heidegger. Giddens makes a great play in this book and in the previous one with the neglect of space–time relations in social theory. Again it depends on how the question is perceived. Clearly in one sense Hegel's *Philosophy of History* could be taken to be intimately concerned with the perceptions of space and time on the part of different peoples. Only with the development of the concept of the subject in Ancient Greece does history become a conscious phenomenon, a province of change and meaning. Are not the featureless plains of Asia without difference, without location and therefore without identity? Giddens argues that we must not consider space–time as a neutral set of coordinates in which social relations are situated. Rather we must move toward a fusion of the Heideggerian conception of time and the social geographer's conception of space. The problem with this is as follows. Heidegger's time is always *time for a subject*, time is experienced and is an irreducible aspect of existence. Yet society is not a subject. Giddens concurs in this – it has no experience as such. Now we may refer to discourses on time, and practices of measuring and utilising times in different forms of society but not to "time" as an existential phenomenon. Societies construct time differently and this is indeed consequential, but the consequence is that the "times" in question are different and have no common referent or standard of measure. It is therefore impossible to refer to a common spatio-temporal aspect of social systems as a phenomenon neglected by social theory – this would only be possible if time–space were both a supra-societal set of coordinates *and* something more than a mere means of location, a material envelope of and limit to human social action. Giddens hints at this by pointing out as Parsons did to the temporal limitations of human life. Parsons saw this as part of "ultimate reality", an environment above action and outside of empirical knowledge – something perceived and handled by belief systems like religions. Now belief systems can tell us that "life is a dream" or orient us to the Second Coming and, to the extent we believe them, construct ultimate realities apart from or beyond death. Giddens (1981, p. 34) makes time a mode of Being: "the temporality of *Dasein* is finite, as a being that is born, lives and dies. This characteristic is shared, of course, with the animals. But only human beings live their lives in awareness of their own finitude". It is distressing to see Giddens swallowing whole some of the cloudiest bits of German metaphysics. Humans have squandered their lives as if they were nothing – not merely Zulu *impis* or Mahdist fanatics but sober Christian industrial workers on the first day of the Somme. Chimpanzees, by contrast, do seem to get very upset when one of their number dies in front of them. In Heidegger's day intelligent men did not sit in the bush watching apes. I accept that there is some value in Heidegger's *negative thought*, his critique of Western metaphysics. This I take to be what Althusser, Derrida and Lacan have found to praise in him. The position from which he makes this critique, for example, his views on "Being", leads one to accept Adorno's and Sartre's strictures, that his philosophy taken as a whole amounts to a reactionary, religious and essentialist metaphysics.

To turn from Heidegger to Derrida. Giddens makes willful play with the term "presence". Giddens uses "presence" as a key category in a contrast, which (for all his talk about space–time distinctions) means little more than societies in which face-to-face interaction predominates versus those in which division of labour, mobility and impersonal media of exchange predominate. A re-run of the *Gemeinschaft–Gesellschaft* opposition. This will only work if we privilege "presence" in another sense, and one which Derrida is rightly critical of, that of the spoken, the direct, the immediate as the real and authentic. Giddens (1981, p. 48) says: "The telephone, and television video techniques, do not of course achieve the full presence of parties to interaction characteristic of ordinary 'face-to-face' encounters." Here we have the idea of mediation versus the immediate, whether the media be money or information technology. Now Giddens continually insists that pre-capitalist societies in general and hunting and gathering societies in particular are marked by greater "presence" – i.e. less "space–time distanciation". But the model of what counts as "distanciation" is a highly Westernised one, one which harbours an idea of the immediate and intimate and our movement away from them in spatio-temporal techniques like clock-time and division of labour between places. But the lost intimacy and immediacy are a myth if we take the categories and practices of non-Western societies seriously. Taboos, age-sets, the kin-based division of space all create social distance between persons and can set up temporal and physical distributions: cadets who look forward to becoming elders, patterns of huts, sacred places, etc. The Kula ring becomes another of Giddens' (1981, p. 162) "exceptions". One is constantly surprised by statements like "... in all non-capitalist civilisations, if one discounts mass migrations of populations in times of warfare, plague or famine, travel was a specialised affair" (Giddens 1981, p. 147). This is like saying, 'if one discounts holidays and business few people travel in the modern West'. It is unclear what "specialised" means, but ordinary people *did* travel, for example, on pilgrimages – travelling was difficult indeed before railways and steamships but a common experience as works like J.J. Jusserand's *English Wayfaring Life in the Middle Ages* (1974) testify. The danger of Giddens' syncretism is that layer upon layer of incompatible ideas are superimposed, categories like "presence" upon sociological chestnuts like community and association.

Finally, I want to take up one point that Giddens has repeated for several years and which seems to me wholly misguided, the claim that Althusser and those influenced by him neglect "human agency". Althusser is accused in effect of conceiving social agents as determined and deluded automata, "cultural dopes" (Giddens 1981, p. 18), and is coupled with Parsons in doing so. However, for Giddens (1981, p. 224) "to be a human agent is to have the capability of 'making a difference' in the world, which is the same as saying that the agent 'could have acted otherwise'". Agents are characterised by choice – indeed, all "agents" and all relatively complex animals have choices in behaviour. Several courses of action are open to any organism or organisation which behaves as a result of some non-instinctual means of decision – whether it be a chimpanzee or a business corporation. Complex social organisations necessarily require human agents, but they involve them in a division of labour which has "emergent properties" as an agent and they involve the formation and construction of specific capacities on the part of the human agents involved. To couple someone with Parsons these days is to attempt to give them the kiss of death, but Giddens' linking is not inapposite. Althusser and Parsons do not regard human agents as automata, what they do ask, however, is *how is it possible* for men to function as agents. Agency is not a mere given. The *answers* both give may be less than satisfactory, but they do ask pertinent *questions*. If human agents were wholly determined by the structure of a mode of production then the questions Althusser asks in his paper on "ISA"s – how is the subject constituted as an agent? how is its conduct patterned although not pre-determined? – would make no sense whatever.

Bibliography

Althusser Louis (1971), Ideology and Ideological State Apparatuses in *Lenin and Philosophy and Other Essays*, London: New Left Books.

Giddens Anthony (1971), *Capitalism and Modern Social Theory*, Cambridge: Cambridge University Press

Giddens Anthony (1981), *A Contemporary Critique of Historical Materialism*, London: Macmillan

Gramsci Antonio (1971), *Selections from the Prison Notebooks*, edited and translated by Q Hoare and GN Smith, London: Lawrence and Wishart

Hindess Barry and Hirst Paul Q (1975), *Pre-Capitalist Modes of Production*, London: Routledge and Kegan Paul

Jusserand JJ (1974), *English Wayfaring Life in the Middle Ages*, London: Corner House (orig. 1888)

Sokolovsky VD (1964), *Military Strategy: Soviet Doctrine*, London: Praeger

55

'Put Not Your Trust in Princes'*

D. Smith

*Source: *Theory, Culture and Society*, vol. 1 (2), 1982, pp. 93–99.

In the decade during which Giddens has been exploring the nature of structuration a major revival has occurred in the sphere of historical sociology, stimulated in part by the resounding success of Barrington Moore's *Social Origins of Dictatorship and Democracy* (1966). In 1974 Perry Anderson published *Passages from Antiquity to Feudalism* (1974a) and *Lineages of the Absolutist State* (1974b). In the same year Immanuel Wallerstein's *The Modern World-System* (1974) appeared. To this swelling tide Moore added his *Injustice* (1978). *States and Social Revolutions* (1979) made its appearance shortly afterwards, soon to be followed by Wallerstein's second volume, *The Modern World-System II* (1980). Historians and sociologists have been coming to grips once more with the problem of the transition between commercialised agrarian bureaucracies and modern industrial nation-states. They have been wrestling with the various logics of exposition associated with comparative sociology and narrative history (Runciman 1980; Smith 1983, pp 156–65). At least one chronicler of these events argues that Giddens' work in the latter part of the decade has caught the spirit of this movement, that *Central Problems in Social Theory* (1979) with its emphasis upon 'the problematic of structuring', is 'a manifesto for a new time-centred enterprise' (Abrams 1980, pp 13–14).

Moore, Wallerstein, Anderson and Skocpol have been concerned with the interpretation of specific sequences of historical change. The first two named above have also been explicitly interested in specifying morally desirable and politically feasible goals for human action. Indeed, as I have argued elsewhere, Moore's intellectual enterprise culminating in *Injustice* has important affinities with the work of critical theorists and especially with that of Habermas (Smith 1983, pp 163–4, pp 169–73). Against this background, the publication of *A Contemporary Critique of Historical Materialism* in 1981 offered an exciting possibility. After several years of developing his ideas on structuration, was Giddens going to be able to integrate this intellectual scheme with a convincing strategy of historical analysis and a well-founded normative theory? For the answer to the second part of that question we must probably wait for publication of the second volume which has yet to appear. However, a provisional answer can be given about Giddens' attempts at historical analysis. It must be said straightaway that after years in the theoretical stratosphere the re-entry problems have been considerable.

In the immensity of its ambition and the complexity of its logical constructions Giddens' sociological synthesis as outlined over several books reminds me of certain aspects of the work of both Herbert Spencer and Talcott Parsons. All three writers attempt to give due weight both to the creativity of human actors and the constraining effects of social structure. If this parallel is accepted it is perhaps not surprising that Giddens should express his distinctiveness by heavily criticising both functionalism and evolutionism as modes of explanation. The case against each is made in *A Contemporary Critique of Historical Materialism*. Giddens' views on functionalism are familiar. The heart of his objection to evolutionism is contained in his counter-assertion that although solutions to structural contradictions may be 'immanent' within social orders such solutions exist only as 'possible futures' and are not bound to appear. It is intriguing to notice that this view is shared by, among others, Barrington Moore. The latter, however, has been prepared to incorporate aspects of evolutionary and functionalist approaches in a historical methodology which gives considerable weight to human agency (Smith 1983, pp 61–2).

The comparison with Moore is relevant because it allows me to contrast two approaches to the interplay between theoretical and empirical materials. Moore candidly and explicitly tolerates in his work a number of partially competing sociological or philosophical approaches, such as functionalist, evolutionist, cyclical, Transcendentalist, Hegelian and Utilitarian schemes of explanation. Giddens, on the other hand, reveals a powerful drive towards conceptual closure, usually in terms of a rigid dichotomous logic. When applied to empirical historical analysis Giddens' consistency is achieved, in the work being discussed, at the expense of a certain crudity in his treatment of data. I want to explore this aspect of Giddens' work shortly with particular reference to his discussion of absolutism. However, the general point is that Moore, for all the 'loose ends' and occasional inconsistencies in his theoretical approach to human nature and social structure, often tells me important things I did not know before. Giddens, on the other hand, often seems to ignore or deny important things which I continue to think are the case. Rather than engage in random sniping, which would be a churlish response to a thoroughly stimulating book, I am going to discuss some aspects of Giddens' analysis of what he calls 'class-divided societies', especially absolutist states.

Class-divided societies contain classes but 'class analysis does not serve as a basis for identifying the basic structural principle of organisation'. Such societies are normally to a great extent integrated through military power.

Within them there is 'a deep-seated differentiation between city and countryside'. The city plays a strategic role in system integration within class-divided societies, which are predominantly agrarian. The city is a 'storage container', a crucible of power, a 'generator of the authoritative resources out of which state power is created and sustained'. This capacity is not purely, or even mainly, economic. It is religious, military and bureaucratic. The exercise of this capacity 'permits time–space distanciation well beyond that characteristic of tribal societies'. In other words, 'regularised transactions' are possible with others who are not physically present in time and space (Giddens 1981, p 7, pp 93–4, pp 144–5, p 163).

Cities are, in Giddens' view, a precondition for the existence of both the state and classes in class-divided societies. The dominant class located in the city uses its control over the means of violence to extract surplus from the agricultural producers. However, this class relationship between producers and those who extract the surplus does not intrude into the process of production itself, argues Giddens. In his view, peasant labour is intimately tied in with traditional communal practices and expresses a close relationship with nature.

The transition from class-divided agrarian societies to capitalist societies entails a profound re-ordering of relationships in a number of respects: for example, in relations between humankind and the natural world, between 'the economic' and 'the political', between authoritative and allocative resources, and between existential and structural contradictions. Without going into details, one aspect of this change will be noticed here. In class-divided societies the coordination of authoritative resources, especially through the religious and military arms of the state, 'forms the determining axis of societal integration and change' (Giddens 1981, p 4). This situation reflects the structural discontinuity between economic production, which is based on the village, and the political organisation of the state which is centred upon the metropolitan city and whose operation is society-wide. However, in capitalist societies authoritative resources cease to play a leading role since the key mechanism, the labour contract, is in the sphere of allocative resources.

Giddens argues that the principal characteristics of capitalist society are related to the capitalist labour contract through whose agency class relations enter into the very process of production. Supervision of wage-labour is assigned to management alone. The wage-labourer is denied participation in 'the authoritative apparatus of decision-making within the enterprise'. Similarly, the capitalist state is unable to determine through its monopoly of violence the process whereby surplus is extracted by business elites. The state thus depends for its own revenue upon a process occurring outside its proper sphere which is 'the political'. Within this political sphere the wage-labourer exercises his citizenship rights. Insulation between the economic and the political spheres within the nation-state is thus, in Giddens' view, mediated by the capitalist labour contract. The differentiation between the city and the countryside thus ceases to be structurally significant.

How does the transition between class-divided societies and capitalist societies occur? Translated into other terms, this is the problem which has preoccupied many of the historical sociologists referred to above. Giddens has remarkably little to say about the process of transition but a crucial passage is the following:

> There are many ways ... in which post-feudal Europe differed from other class-divided civilisations (just as those differ widely among themselves). So there is no question of 'explaining' the emergence of capitalism, or of characterising its cardinal features, in terms of a single set of processes. But *one* historical conjunction of decisive significance was the central-isation of power in a context of a class alliance with rising bourgeois elements. The monopolisation of the means of violence went along with the extrusion of control of violent sanctions from the exploitative rela-tions involved in emergent capitalism (Giddens 1981, p 180; italics in original).

The above passage has been quoted complete with its initial disclaimers. This is because I want to argue that Giddens's model of class-divided society actually misdescribes post-feudal absolutist Europe. I also want to argue that class alliances between absolutist rulers and 'rising bourgeois elements' were far less significant than Giddens implies, particularly in the later stages of absolutist regimes in the period associated with the appearance of 'emergent capitalism'.

By the term 'absolutist state' Giddens means a political order which is 'dominated by a sovereign ruler, monarch or prince, in whose person are vested ultimate political authority and sanctions, including the means of violence'. Such political orders are to be considered as 'part of a class-divided order' (Giddens 1981, p 186). In his opinion they are to be distinguished from the class-divided imperial societies of America and Asia by the absence of a single pan-European state power, by 'certain residues of feudal society' (which remain unspecified) and by the ideological inheritance of Roman law (Giddens 1981, pp 184–5).

Giddens stresses the location of absolutist states within a European system of states. Although the argument is expressed in a very condensed manner, Giddens (1981, pp 188–90) seems to be suggesting that the alliance between centralising monarchs and 'natural bourgeoisies' (beneficiaries of the 'polit-ical revolutions of seventeenth- and eighteenth-century Europe') was complementary to the struggles between European states within the con-tinental arena. It has already been noted that Giddens believes that this alliance was 'of decisive significance' in explaining the emergence of, and structuration of, the capitalist nation-state.

It will be recalled also that within class-divided societies surplus product is extracted from rural labour through the application of authoritative resources by a dominant *urban* class integrated through the administrative order of the state. In Giddens's (1981, p 176) words, in such societies 'the exploiter is in some sense (variable in different systems) an agent of the state'.

At this point, in this reader's mind at least, some nagging questions arise. What about the landed aristocracy? Were the great landowners 'agents of the state'? Were they an urban class? The questions lead on to two observations. First, apart from brief references to 'urban communes' and 'deliberative assemblies' Giddens (1981, p 185) pays scant attention to the opponents of rulers *within* absolutist states as opposed to their external opponents. Second, there is a large *hiatus* in the argument which is the virtual neglect of relations between the centralising monarchy and the great aristocratic landowners.

In order to elaborate these points it is necessary to indicate some important differences, overlooked by Giddens, between class-divided societies in Meso-America, Asia and Europe. A distinction should be recognised between 'horticultural' societies (such as the Aztec and Inca empires) and more technologically advanced 'agrarian' societies which were able to exploit the combined resources of iron, the wheel and animal power. The relevance of this distinction (which is explored, for example, in Lenski 1966) is that the transition from the shifting 'slash-and-burn' agriculture of the horticultural society to the more intensive and potentially more productive agrarian technology is typically associated with the development of land tenure as an important aspect of class relations or, more generally, of structuration. Jack Goody (1963), for example, has emphasised this contrast. In agrarian, as opposed to horticultural, societies property in land becomes a political base which is potentially independent of – and may be used in resistance to – the state bureaucracy.

By focusing upon the contrast between city walls in class-divided societies and the exact boundaries of the nation-state (the supposedly equivalent 'power container' in capitalist societies) Giddens has neglected an important third factor: the precise demarcations of the great landed estate in agrarian societies. The great estate could be a 'power container' in its own right, even in the age of absolutism. As Wallerstein (1974, p 311) points out, citing an extreme example, in the course of the sixteenth century the landed estate in East Elbia become 'something like a small political unit within the state: its inhabitants (were) only indirectly subjects of the territorial prince'.

A further distinction, some of whose implications are under-stressed by Giddens, is between the Chinese Empire and Europe. The dramatic reduction in the importance of political bureaucracies in the European feudal period following the demise of the Roman Empire produced an arena in which, to borrow Giddens's expression, the 'power containers' were the manorial estate and the Papacy. The revival of state apparatuses and the renewed appearance of vigorous commercial activity – processes of which the 'absolutist state' was a latter-day expression – occurred in the context of an entrenched religious bureaucracy and great landowners securely settled upon their estates. By contrast, in China, which had not undergone this historical sequence, land tenure and the magical or religious powers of the *literati* were much more closely bound up with the authority of the state itself.

I would stress, to a much greater extent than Giddens, that 'absolutist' claims made by European princes were a kind of radical propaganda directed against the powerful reserves of legitimacy and influence vested in the religious and feudal spheres. Some of the most significant developments in the theory of absolutism occurred, as Quentin Skinner (1978b) has shown in his remarkable survey, during the sixteenth century at a time when the Valois monarchy was attempting to loosen the restraints imposed upon it by France's feudal ruling class whose influence was deeply entrenched in the *parlements*. One expression of the battle being fought was the publication in 1519 of Claude de Seyssel's *The Monarchy of France*. Seyssel, who had served in the Parlement of Paris, argued that the king's authority was held in check by 'la police' (very crudely, the obligation to respect the existing social order), 'la justice' and 'la religion' (Skinner 1978b, pp 254–61). Twenty years later, this argument was undermined by the publication of Claude Du Moulin's *Commentaries on the Customs of Paris* (1539), which Skinner (1978b, p 263) describes as 'an epoch-making attack on the pyramidal structure of legal rights and obligations characteristic of feudalism'. In 1576 Jean Bodin, much of whose political experience was of weak kings and warring nobles, published his *Six Books of a Commonweal*. This work made a massive contribution to a movement through which 'By the end of the religious wars, the foundations had ... been firmly laid for the ideology which was subsequently used to legitimate the mature absolutism of *le grand siècle*' (Skinner 1978b, p 301).

At any point between the sixteenth and the eighteenth centuries we would be wise not to take an absolutist ruler's claims about the extent of his (or her) power at face value: in that sense, at least, we should 'not put our trust in princes'. The monarch's political claims and his search for allies were very often indications of his weakness, not his strength. Royal taxes and feudal rents were *competing* claims upon the surplus product, a cause for contention rather than cooperation. The court and the manor house were in conflict, not in collaboration. The differentiation between city and countryside in the absolutist state represented not the domination of the former over the latter but the conflictual interdependence of two social orders – royal and manorial – competing for political space.

Cutting across this conflict between major interests in the town and rural society was another conflict, centred upon the city, between the managers of the state apparatus and the manipulators of commercial networks linked through the cash nexus. Merchants and bureaucrats respectively had vested interests in maximising the influence of forms of domination and resource appropriation which were to a significant extent in competition with each other. While the operations of each power grouping were made easier by the existence of the other, each resisted any tendency for the other to become stronger. To overgeneralise, the weaker party always feared that the stronger might usurp the former's share of social resources and add to the prestige of a hostile normative order.

These cross-cutting conflicts were complicated further by the expansion of the urban market for agricultural products, as Barrington Moore (1966) has shown. The penetration of the cash nexus into the countryside had the effect of linking together closely the fate of three interests: the urban bourgeoisie, the monarch (with his bureaucracy) and the great landowners. Just as state bureaucrats and merchants derived both benefits and penalties from their exchanges, so did royal officials and landowners. For example, the flow of cash into aristocratic coffers depended to an increasing extent upon well-regulated urban markets, on the peace which that otherwise unwelcome tax-gatherer, the state, alone could provide. There were similarities in the relationship between the bourgeoisie and the aristocracy. On the one hand, both derived profit from the existence of the market for food among town-dwellers; on the other hand, the price of grain was an issue which set urban employers against rural landowners.

In order to understand how relations developed within this quarrelsome triangle of interlocking interests it should be noticed that, unlike his partners-cum-antagonists, the power of the landowner was to a considerable extent based upon immobile assets, his rural estates. In some cases, as in parts of Russia and Prussia, this control was extended to rural labour, immobilised through serfdom. By contrast, monarchs and merchants manipulated mobile resources through the extension of market networks and the reaching out of bureaucratic administration (cf. Smith 1978, pp 181–4). These networks, which were based upon the city, extended up to and beyond the boundaries of the absolutist polity. The capacity of absolutist states to survive *in spite of* the persisting lack of cohesion between the rural localised order of the great estates and the more far-flung urban order of the merchant and the bureaucrat was due, to some extent at least, to the fact that the latter two interests were able to tap the resources of a rapidly expanding colonial hinterland. Despite his references to relations between absolutist states in Europe Giddens lays insufficient stress on the significance of the global economic and political context. It is too easily forgotten that the balance-of-power diplomacy of the seventeenth and eighteenth centuries was to a steadily increasing extent, the local manifestation of a sea-borne scramble for empire.

In this wider context the potential conflict flowing from the 'internal' contradictions between the localised feudal order and the competing urban regime could to a significant extent be (not so much resolved as) by-passed. Colonial expansion and foreign trade provided pickings for many. The predatory relationship of an expanding Europe to its global environment also had consequences for the other, cross-cutting, contradiction mentioned above.

Since the inflow of external resources made it possible to 'buy off' potential opponents (a bribe to a customs officer here, a sinecure at court for a merchant's nephew there), it was possible to defer the fundamental and deeply contentious issue of how relations between the market-oriented order of the bourgeoisie and the bureaucratic order of the state were to be institutionalised. This issue, which was resolved (temporarily at least) in one direction through the American Revolution and in the other through the establishment of the Napoleonic order, did not become really pressing until *after* the almost simultaneous occurrence, in different European societies, of two radical changes which would ramify throughout the West and beyond. The first was industrialisation. The second was the release, for potential mobilisation by the state, of human energies previously confined within the parochial limits of the feudal moral and political order.

In a post-feudal epoch, managers of the state could (as in France) reach out directly for the allegiance of peasants and urban workers in the name of citizenship. The bourgeoisie could seek to command the energies of the populace through the capitalist labour contract. However, these claims upon the people were as likely to be competing as complementary and the boundaries between them depended to a great extent on the balance of influence achieved between private property and public bureaucracy. A crucial mediating factor in the latter-day absolutist state and the developing nation-state has been the disposition of the landed aristocracy. The form of articulation which has developed within urban industrial nation-states in the capitalist West between the market and bureaucratic orders has depended to a significant degree upon the great landowners' tendency to support one side rather than the other in the relationship – which is as much conflictual as cooperative – between rulers and 'rising bourgeois elements'.

These remarks will now be summarised. First, it has been argued, *contra* Giddens, that the differentiation between city and countryside supposedly characteristic of class-divided societies had fundamentally different structural implications depending upon whether or not land tenure constituted a source of power resources which could be opposed to bureaucratic domination. Second, it has been argued, *contra* Giddens, that the absolutist state manifested chronic structural contradictions between, on the one hand, a localised feudal order and, on the other hand, bureaucratic and market-based orders focused upon the city. Third, the conflictual aspects of relations between rulers and bourgeois elements and the contradictions inherent in relations between market and bureaucratic structures have been emphasised to a much greater extent than in Giddens's book. Fourth, it has been argued that the capacity of absolutist polities to cohere to a considerable degree in spite of these contradictions was to a significant extent due to the inflow of resources from outside the territorial boundaries defended by the absolutist states within Europe itself. Fifth, it has been suggested that, partly as a consequence of the growth of urban markets and colonial expansion, the conditions of existence of the aristocracy were to an increasing extent determined within bureaucratic and market networks which were outside its sphere of influence. Finally, it has been suggested that members of the aristocracy were in these circumstances gradually driven, usually unwillingly, into alliance with either 'rising bourgeois elements' (as in England) or elements within the state apparatus (as in France, Prussia and Russia). *Contra* Giddens, the strategic alliance which was to be of 'decisive significance', especially in determining how 'the economic' and 'the political' would relate to each other, was not between the ruler and bourgeois elements but between the landed aristocracy and *either* bourgeois elements *or* the ruler. This latter alliance was, as implied above, by far the most common. It is interesting to note that a similar – or at least compatible – conclusion should be found in *The Class Structure of the Advanced Societies*. Giddens (1973, p 165) writes in this book:

> any analysis of the development of modern capitalism from the latter part of the nineteenth century to the present time must recognise the protracted significance of 'traditional' land-owning groups within the class structure. The reaction of such groupings, first to commercialisation, and subsequently to industrialism, is the key factor which has influenced the form taken by the structuration of the upper class in all societies – except in the case of the United States, which did not come to capitalism through the dissolution of feudalism.

Finally, it may be objected that I have provided little more concrete evidence for my counter-assertions than Giddens furnished himself in the book being criticised. That would be an excellent response if it directed attention back to the historical data and stimulated further investigation exploiting the interplay between empirical and theoretical work.[1]

Note

1. These comments are based upon part of a paper that was presented to the seminar on 'patterns of history' organised by the Department of Philosophy, Logic and Scientific Method of the London School of Economics. I was grateful for the comments of those present, especially Michael Mann, Ernest Gellner and John Hall.

Bibliography

Abrams P (1980), History, sociology, historical sociology, *Past and Present*, 87, pp 3–16

Anderson P (1974a), *Passages from Antiquity to Feudalism*, London: New Left Books

Anderson P (1974b), *Lineages of the Absolutist State*, London: New Left Books

Giddens A (1971), *Capitalism and Modern Social Theory*, Cambridge: Cambridge University Press

Giddens A (1973), *The Class Structure of the Advanced Societies*, London: Hutchinson

Giddens A (1979), *Central Problems in Social Theory*, London: Macmillan

Giddens A (1981), *A Contemporary Critique of Historical Materialism*, London: Macmillan

Goody J (1963), Feudalism in Africa? *Journal of African History*, 4, pp 1–18

Lenski G (1966), *Power and Privilege*, New York: McGraw-Hill

Moore B (1966), *Social Origins of Dictatorship and Democracy*, Boston: Beacon Press

Moore B (1978), *Injustice*, London: Macmillan

Runciman WG (1980), Comparative sociology or narrative history? *European Journal of Sociology*, 21, pp 162–78

Skinner Q (1978a) *The Foundations of Modern Political Thought. Vol. 1: The Renaissance*, Cambridge: Cambridge University Press

Skinner Q (1978b), *The Foundations of Modern Political Thought. Vol. 2: The Age of Reformation*, Cambridge: Cambridge University Press

Skocpol T (1979), *States and Social Revolutions*, Cambridge: Cambridge University Press

Smith D (1978), Domination and contamination: an approach to modernisation, *Comparative Studies in Society and History*, 20, pp 177–213

Smith D (1982), *Conflict and Compromise: Class Formation in English Society 1830–1914. A Comparative Study of Birmingham and Sheffield*, London: Routledge and Kegan Paul

Smith D (1983, forthcoming), *Barrington Moore: Violence, Morality and Political Change*, London: Macmillan

Wallerstein I (1974), *The Modern World-System*, New York: Academic Press

Wallerstein I (1980), *The Modern World-System II*, New York: Academic Press

56

Breaking New Ground in the Analysis of Capitalism*

I.J. Cohen

*Source: *Contemporary Sociology*, vol. 12, 1983, pp. 363–65.

A Contemporary Critique of Historical Materialism, Vol. 1: Power, Property, and the State, by ANTHONY GIDDENS. Berkeley: University of California Press, 1982. 294 pp. $24.50 cloth. $10.95 paper.

Giddens is one of only a handful of contemporary theorists who do not produce free-standing works but are committed to long-term projects within which separate works are conceived and executed. His overall goal is nothing short of a fundamental reorientation of the theoretical agenda, the problems no less than their resolutions, that originated in the nineteenth- and early-twentieth-century classical traditions, and that, through various permutations, has continued to shape the development of sociological analysis up to the present era (see Giddens, 1971:246ff.; 1976a; 1976b:7; 1977:9–29; 1979:1–2). It is an uncommon virtue of Giddens's project to incorporate an extraordinary range of scholarly perspectives, extending far beyond conventional sources (see Walker, 1979). But unlike Parsons, Giddens does not seek prefigurations of a theoretical consensus in these works. And – to make a point that is crucial for an adequate appreciation of the present work – unlike orthodox Marxists, he has no interest in establishing a direct continuity with canonical texts. Rather, Giddens's strategy is to develop concise critiques of the foundations of previous approaches to theoretical dilemmas. In each critique he abstracts elements of enduring value while departing from much that he argues to be misguided or incorrect. As he proceeds, each new critique synthesizes and moves beyond points previously established. In the end this tacking process permits Giddens an approach to the foundations of social theory that preserves and unites the ambit and ambition of his many different sources while retaining a great latitude of intellectual autonomy. Giddens thus is one of the few vitally important contemporary scholars – Habermas, Foucault, and Jeffrey Alexander also come to mind – whose mission it is to introduce a new era of "classical" sociology.

This work represents a new point of departure in Giddens's larger project.

Previously he has devoted three volumes (1976b; 1977; 1979; see also 1981) to the establishment of his remarkable new methodological–analytical framework, the theory of structuration. While the framework remains of absolutely integral importance to the present work, Giddens's focal concern now shifts over to more substantive issues. His point of origin is a critique of Marx, but this is no ordinary critique of Marx's thought. Giddens's objective is to identify the errors and vacuolae in the foundations of Marx's thought, to extract what remains of value, and to reconfigure the latter in a new orientation to the nature of modern capitalism. The result is a series of innovative arguments that are among the most important to be published on either Marx or capitalism in quite some time.

Unrestrained by Marxist loyalties (p. 1), Giddens is able to bring to bear on his efforts both non-Marxist and Marxist resources, ranging beyond social theory to incorporate pertinent findings from contemporary archeology, geography, and history. These resources permit him to criticize Marx and synthetically to establish his own arguments against a "long view" of history. (A companion volume is proposed to shift this focus to the transition from capitalism to socialism.) In turn, what allows Giddens to take this "long view" without a predetermined partisanship regarding any of the works on which he draws are the analytic principles provided by his theory of structuration (see chap. 1).

In this work Giddens is more intent on breaking new ground than upon systematizing his insights. While he covers far more terrain than can be summarized here, the foundation of his position rests upon his retention of Marx's concern for the analysis of domination, exploitation, and alienation, as he radically overhauls the historical materialist principles of Marx's thought.

Giddens's theory of structuration is premised upon analytically interrelated conceptions of *praxis* and social structure, and a non-teleological orientation to history that are far more comprehensive and precise than anything Marx envisioned (cf. 1979:150–55). In chaps. 2, 3, and 4 he applies elements of this framework to reject *and* reconstrue both the analytical elision of labor-power and *praxis* that often appears central to the materialist foundations of Marx's thought, as well as Marx's class-struggle conception of the *telos* of history. While Giddens continues to maintain that a capitalist society (but not its predecessors; see chap. 4) is a class society (see also 1973), a pause to consider how many of the theoretical, methodological, and ethico-political foundations of Marx's thought intrinsically depend upon these points will indicate how far reaching are the implications of their rejection and reconstruction for the development of Giddens's own views.

Having profoundly reoriented the historical materialist foundations of Marx's thought, Giddens is now free to turn to his central interest in the analysis of capitalism (chaps. 5, 6). As a point of departure Giddens emphasizes more emphatically than either Marx or theorists of industrial society how radically distinct are the nature of capitalist domination and the characteristics of day-to-day life that it engenders from all earlier forms of social organization. The foundation for this argument is provided by the remarkably original and important analytical conception of the time–space constitution of social systems developed by Giddens in the theory of structuration (see chap. 1; also 1979: chap. 6 passim; 1981). Giddens uses this position to reinterpret the theory of surplus value, emphasizing more extensively and precisely than Marx that the historically unprecedented nature of capitalist domination and exploitation is intrinsically connected to the commodification of time, i.e., the separation of its form from its content. This provides a basis for new conceptualizations of capitalist entrepreneurial authority and the labor contract, as well as the valorization and accumulation of capital. Moreover, the commodification of time, together with the related concept of the commodification of space that Giddens also develops, provide him with a unique vantage point from which to assess the dramatic differences between day-to-day social relations in capitalist societies and all preceding forms of social relations.

Space precludes an account of the significant innovations that, in chaps. 7, 8, and 9, Giddens introduces into the ongoing discussion of the state in capitalist societies, as well as the nature and the historical emergence of the relationship between the modern nation-state and the capitalist economy. But mention should be made of his analysis of modern nationalism (pp. 191–96)[1] and his absolutely refreshing discussion of the significance of liberal democracy and citizenship rights (pp. 220–29, 251) because both topics remain unincorporated within most theoretical accounts of capitalism.

This book is packed with insights that defy condensation in this review. Overall it is a work of great importance, as suggestive and ambitious as Marx's own *Critique of Political Economy*. For those who seek a new theory of capitalism along classical lines, Giddens's groundbreaking arguments will be consulted and discussed for many years to come.

Note

1. It cannot be emphasized too strongly that a full appreciation of the innovative character of Giddens's arguments throughout this book requires a sound grasp of his previously developed methodological–analytical framework. With specific regard to nationalism, readers are advised to acquaint themselves with his theory of the acting subject, and in particular his conception of ontological security (see pp. 34–37, 193–94; 1979:55–59). An appreciation of these arguments also serves to moderate and augment the emphasis on the importance of unintended consequences that is ascribed to Giddens's theory of structuration in a recent commentary (Knorr-Cetina and Cicourel, 1981:27–28, 40, 161).

Other Literature Cited

Giddens, Anthony. 1971. Capitalism and Modern Social Theory: An Analysis of the Writings of Marx, Durkheim and Max Weber. Cambridge: Cambridge University Press.

———. 1973. The Class Structure of Advanced Societies. New York: Barnes & Noble.

———. 1976a. "Classical social theory and the origins of modern sociology." American Journal of Sociology 81:703–29.

———. 1976b. New Rules of Sociological Method: A Positive Critique of Interpretative Sociologies. New York: Basic Books.

———. 1977. Studies in Social and Political Theory. London: Hutchinson.

———. 1979. Central Problems in Social Theory: Action, Structure and Contradiction in Social Analysis. Berkeley: University of California Press.

———. 1981. "Agency, institution, and time–space analysis." In Advances in Social Theory and Methodology: Toward an Integration of Micro- and Macro-Sociologies, ed. K. Knorr-Cetina and A. V. Cicourel. Boston: Routledge & Kegan Paul.

Knorr-Cetina, K., and A. V. Cicourel, eds. 1981. Advances in Social Theory and Methodology: Toward an Integration of Micro- and Macro-Sociologies. Boston: Routledge & Kegan Paul.

Walker, David. 1979. "Sociology's 'theoretical babel': An interview with Anthony Giddens." The Times Higher Education Supplement, December 14.

57

Society as Time-Traveller*

R. Collins

*Source: *Contemporary Sociology*, vol. 12, 1983, pp. 365–67.

This is an ambitious book. It combines two intellectually popular themes, Marxian and cognitivistic *praxis* philosophy, and out of them attempts to build a general theory of societies and their historical changes. Marx is a reliable analyst of capitalism only, Giddens asserts; the theory of precapitalist societies must be totally redone. And in the process one must stay clear of the errors of evolutionism and functionalism, for which Giddens takes a number of Marxists to task.

The core of Giddens's theory is an attempt to ground all of society in the action of conscious and knowledgeable human agents located in space and time. History has its major breaks when the modes of space–time presence are shifted. There are two such breaks: the first occurs when tribal societies give way to agrarian states; the second when the latter are transformed into modern capitalism. In the first transformation, the local kinship system with its traditionalism based on high presence-availability among persons locally, gives way to an impersonal system of controls based on "information storage" at the level of the state: i.e., writing and record-keeping make the city a center of power over the countryside. In capitalist society, in turn, direct coercion by the state is replaced by the indirect compulsion of economics. This is due to the further time–space transformations involved in money-capital, and the vastly increased surveillance powers of modern organizations, both in the factory and the state.

I must admit I am predisposed to agree with Giddens regarding the importance of casting sociology in terms of real actors in time and space; in a recent article (1981) I pointed out that if one subtracts the micro components of explanatory theory, what is left as macro structure consists only of the variables of time, physical space, and number of persons. What Giddens says about space is by and large in the right direction, although I think it could go a good deal further in the direction of already existing theories of the world system and of geopolitics. Giddens's treatment of time, however, strikes me as hopelessly romanticized. He draws upon Heidegger's existentialism (the human *Dasein* as being-towards-death) for a picture of the human bedrock of time as the very essence of being. How is this to be reconciled with Giddens's stress upon the quasi-Parsonian evolutionary (pardon the expression) media inventions (writing, money-capital) which make the crucial breaks between historical societies? The connection is via the Marxian theory of alienation, with a generous helping of mass-society theory and the critique of capitalist everyday life thrown in. Thus we find that capitalism has commodified time itself, destroyed public space, enforced privatization, made surveillance anonymous, and removed meaning from the world of work.

The pathos is in the contrast between modern life, denuded of moral meaning and carried out under dull economic compulsion, and the pre-capitalist society in which "the producer relates to nature as part of, and yet at the same time as an active contributor to, natural processes and events" (p. 77). Or to up the rhetorical ante, "in the world that capitalism has originated, time is no longer understood as the medium of Being" (pp. 251–52).

But this is rank romanticism. Agrarian or even tribal societies were hardly exemplars of an unalienated Eden from which we were rudely thrust by capitalism. Giddens would have us believe that peasant producers in agrarian societies carried out their work with little reference to the exploiting classes except to hand over their surplus production, and hence remained on the daily level in a condition of ontological harmony with the universe. But in fact agrarian societies contained the highest amount of daily humiliating deference to authorities of any society that has ever existed; and this is especially true of the women who made up most of the household labor and produced most of the usable commodities by their spinning and weaving. Even for the relatively unsupervised farm laborer, where *he* existed, his life consisted largely of boredom, dust, and the smell of manure – features which have always made rural workers willingly flee the sylvan countryside for the "alienated" excitements of the big, bad city. Nor do I think Giddens's argument is true even for tribal societies, where nature is more likely to be experienced as a dangerous and anxiety-provoking force than as a satisfying world-womb. As Lévi-Strauss (1969) argued, tribal myths stress people's separation from nature rather than merging with it.

At the modern end, I think Giddens's argument is just as wrong. Despite the pronouncements of Braverman, Lefebvre, and others, it is fairly clear that people in capitalist society are on the average no more alienated than people were in most other types of society. Intellectuals as heirs to elite traditions have looked down upon the private lives of the masses for several hundred years now, and this has been a stock theme of twentieth-century highbrow literature. In the Marxian version of this argument we are told that the old meaningful public ceremonies are gone and replaced by the alienated meaninglessness of the mass media. But just because intellectuals like ourselves don't like TV does not mean that the people who watch it four hours or so per day do not find it meaningful. In fact one could argue that most people now spend more of their daily lives in meaningful activities than they ever did before: people who carry around cassette-recorders or radios blaring out popular music are literally wrapping themselves in a cocoon of self-chosen meaning, whereas in every premodern society they would have to wait days if not months for a big public celebration to get their dose of "meaning fix." One wishes Giddens had punctured prevailing clichés a little further.

In any case, the argument about alienation is tangential, because the important facts about any society have to do with conflicts that go on whether people are alienated or not. For Giddens, this brings us to the economics of capitalist exploitation. The central point is that capitalism is uniquely based on the expropriation of labor from the means of production, leaving propertyless workers who are driven to subordinate themselves to the discipline of an employer in return for wages. This Marxian theme seems to me based on the antithesis between modern workers and a romanticized myth of the past. Property is not all-or-nothing, anyway; it is a set of socially negotiated behaviors that can be exercised over all kinds of activities, not merely over physical things, and which can be split up into different packages of advantages and disadvantages. The peasant serf had certain access to the means of sustenance that a modern worker lacks, but also certain property debilities, such as the possibility of being sold along with the land. The traffic in slaves in traditional societies is another instance, not to mention the interfamily-alliance market of women in kinship-based societies. All of these we would certainly call "exploitative" in the popular sense of the word, though Giddens wants to reserve it for its technical Marxist meaning in which "exploitation" refers only to the expropriation of surplus value from the laborer.

As usual, Giddens makes some of the necessary criticism of Marx, but fails to go far enough. He points out that in precapitalist societies the concept of exploitation does not mean anything definite, except whatever those in power manage to squeeze out of those under them (p. 111). But this brings us back to the popular sense of the word; and in this sense, virtually all societies have exploitation. When it comes to capitalist societies, though, Giddens blandly accepts exploitation in the surplus-value sense, and indeed makes this their key feature. But even in capitalist societies, I would say, the concept of exploitation is misleading. It is not literally true that capital is equivalent to surplus value extracted from workers. There are other ways to generate capital: banks loan out several times more funds than they have, speculative markets like real estate or stocks may burgeon, and indeed every time someone extends credit they are freeing up some capital that can be put to use at least temporarily in investments. The modern financial system depends to a considerable extent upon the endless rollover of these kinds of time-bound transactions, and both Böhm-Bawerk (a favorite among some contemporary Marxists) and Schumpeter proposed a model that made this time-delay the key to capitalist profit (see Schumpeter, 1934).

To say this, of course, is heresy from the orthodox Marxian viewpoint. It is the error that has been charged against both Wallerstein and Weber, of basing capitalist stratification upon the market instead of upon the relationship to the means of production. Nevertheless, Marx's neo-Ricardian economic scheme never did work very well in the real historical world, and there is no reason why, apart from its rhetorical glorification of workers, it should not be replaced by something more realistic. I would say that, contrary to the theme of current *praxis*-oriented Marxism, Marx's major contribution was to point to economic cycles and crises as the central phenomenon of capitalism, which is something that neither Giddens nor most current Marxists pay much attention to. But Marx's own technical scheme was incapable of handling this dynamic realistically. Instead, what we need is to see how conflicts and crises emerge from capitalism precisely as a set of markets, and above all from *capital as a credit market* with very definite self-destructive tendencies. We not only don't need the concept of surplus value; it gets in the way of seeing the essence of capitalist dynamics as they happen right around us.

The primacy of capitalism as markets (rather than as extraction of surplus value) applies even to the case of propertyless workers. Giddens's argument is: If people were not stripped of their own productive property, why would anyone work for someone else for wages? But in fact plenty of small farmers have left their autonomous property (where they could have at the worst eked out a subsistence of food) to work in factories; and plenty of small business owners have sold out and gone to work for a corporation. The reason they left was often as not economic compulsion, but it did not require *absolute* propertylessness to make people go to work for wages. The farmer who could not stand the price competition with other farmers would find his standard of living dropping to the point where it was more remunerative to sell his labor instead. Thus to get capitalism going originally, it was not necessary to expropriate the peasants; it was only necessary to amass some capital (including in the form of credit) and to get a market going, which eventually drove people into the labor force all by itself. Marxists fail to see this because Marx's archaic economics deduced that wages under capitalism would always be as low as possible, and hence could never be an attraction in their own right.

But I think this misses the location where the major struggle goes on under capitalism. Workers fight to make property out of their job-positions, to institute some degree of tenure, to win long-term wage provisions (e.g., salaries instead of wages), and to cut down the amount of labor effort their bosses can get out of them. These tactics have been especially successful in the white-collar sector of the labor force. Hence modern class dividing lines do not fall where Marx classically had them (between owners of traditional capital vs. possessors of nothing but their labor), but between numerous classes fighting to get or maintain monopoly privileges upon the labor market itself (see Collins, 1979). Relative degrees of monopoly among organizations, similarly, enable bigger businesses to pay more in the form of "sinecure benefits" to their own workers. It is no wonder, then, that big rich organizations are often more attractive places to work than small individually owned businesses of the sort which Marx idealized.

In short, the essence of capitalism is the struggles that take place in markets. Its dynamics are the boom-and-bust cycles that occur, not in relation to a fictional construct of surplus value but in the circulation of several media: monetary credit, position-monopolizing credentials, as well as the cultural currencies passed around in the conversational markets of everyday life. Giddens is on the right track in a very abstract sense, in his attempt to ground society in the experience of human beings in everyday time and space. But concretely I think he has missed precisely the forms which these take that are most important for a theory of capitalist dynamics.

There were times when reading this book that I felt I was vainly searching for points I could agree with that I didn't already know. This mood was too harsh. The value of the book, though, is mainly on the negative side. Giddens produces first-rate critiques of many current theories, such as the barely veiled Marxist functionalism of Poulantzas, or the historical writings of Foucault. And Giddens is an excellent, clean-boned writer, rare enough qualities among the people whom he is discussing. He gets off an occasional telling phrase, like the one that makes up the title of this review. At the same time, he accepts too many of the trendy errors of current Franco-German Marxism to get as much as he could out of his initial leads. On the whole, Giddens is, I think, on the side of the angels. He promises us a sequel to this book, on the transition from capitalism to socialism. We ought to wish him well on future ambitious ventures.

Other Literature Cited

Collins, Randall. 1979. The Credential Society. New York: Academic Press.
————. 1981. "Micro-translation as a theory-building strategy." In Advances in Social Theory and Methodology: Toward an Integration of Micro- and Macro-Sociologies, ed. Karin Knorr-Cetina and Aaron V. Cicourel. Boston: Routledge & Kegan Paul.
Lévi-Strauss, Claude. 1969. The Raw and the Cooked. New York: Harper.
Schumpeter, Joseph. 1934. The Theory of Economic Development. Cambridge: Harvard University Press.

58

Giddens's Critique of Marxism*

E.O. Wright

*Source: *New Left Review*, no. 138, 1983, pp. 11–35.

Critiques of historical materialism tend to be one of two types: either they are hostile attacks by anti-Marxists intent on demonstrating the falsity, perniciousness or theoretical anachronism of Marxism, or they are reconstructive critiques from within the Marxist tradition attempting to overcome theoretical weaknesses in order to advance the Marxist project. In these terms, Anthony Giddens's book, *A Contemporary Critique of Historical Materialism*, is a rare work: an appreciative critique by a non-Marxist of the Marxist tradition in social theory. While finding a great deal that is wrong with basic assumptions and general propositions in Marxism, Giddens also argues that 'Marx's analysis of the mechanisms of capitalist production ... remains the necessary core of any attempt to come to terms with the massive transformations that have swept the world since the eighteenth century.'[1] Indeed, there are certain specific discussions in the book – such as the use of the labour theory of value and the analysis of the capitalist labour process – in which Giddens's position is closer than many contemporary Marxists' to orthodox Marxism. The book is thus not a wholesale rejection of Marxism, but rather an attempt at a genuine 'critique' in the best sense of the word – a deciphering of the underlying limitations of a social theory in order to appropriate in an alternative framework what is valuable in it. While, as I attempt to show, I think many of Giddens's specific arguments against historical materialism are unsatisfactory, the book is a serious engagement with Marxism and deserves a serious reading by both Marxists and non-Marxists.

Overview of Giddens's Argument

The critiques elaborated in *A Contemporary Critique of Historical Materialism* are rooted in Giddens's general theory of social structure and agency, his theory of 'social structuration'. This framework involves complex, and sometimes obscure, prescriptions about what a good social theory must contain. Among other things, Giddens argues, social theories must recognize the knowledgeability and competence of actors; they must be built around a concept of the 'duality of structure', in which social structures are viewed as both the medium and outcome of the practices which constitute social systems; temporality must be treated as an intrinsic dimension of social processes; human action must be understood as involving conscious intentionality as well as 'practical consciousness', practical knowledge of the workings of society that are discursively inaccessible to actors; and all action must be situated within the unacknowledged conditions of action and the unintended consequences of action. These guidelines to theorizing constitute the heart of Giddens's ambitious attempt at building a radical critical sociology.

This general framework is laid out in the Introduction and first two chapters of the book. Many readers will find parts of these chapters extremely dense. Very few readers, I imagine, will understand what is meant by a sentence like: 'The chronic interpenetration of presence and absence, the symbolic interpolation of the absent within the presence of the continuity of everyday activities, is a peculiar characteristic of human social life as contrasted to that of animals'.[2] Giddens directs the reader to his earlier work, *Central Problems of Social Theory*,[3] for clarifications of this conceptual apparatus, but unfortunately that earlier book is even more difficult to decipher than *A Contemporary Critique of Historical Materialism*. Fortunately, once the more schematic conceptual discussions at the beginning of the book are finished, most of the rest of *A Contemporary Critique* is clear and engaging. And while the arguments throughout the book do draw on concepts introduced in the more opaque discussions, nevertheless the book can be fruitfully read even if the introductory conceptual material is not fully understood.

In this essay I will not attempt a general assessment and summary of the theory of social structuration itself. Instead I will focus on the core theme of the book: the critique of the Marxist account of the forms and development of societies and the elaboration of some of the essential elements of an alternative macro-structural theory.

The heart of Giddens's argument revolves around three interconnected problems: (1) The methodological principles for analysing the interconnectedness of different aspects of society within a social whole or 'totality'; (2) the strategy for elaborating classification typologies of forms of societies; and (3) the theory of the movement or transition of societies from one form to another within such a typology. Giddens criticizes what he considers to be the Marxist treatment of each of these issues: *functionalism* in Marxist analyses of the social totality; economic or class *reductionism* in the typologies of societies rooted in the concept of mode of production; and *evolutionism* in the theory of the transformation of social forms. In place of these central errors, Giddens offers the rudiments of his general theory of social structuration: instead of functionalism, social totalities are analysed as contingently reproduced social systems; instead of class and economic reductionism, forms of society are differentiated on the basis of a multidimensional concept of 'space–time distanciation'; and instead of evolutionism, transformations of social forms are understood in terms of what Giddens calls 'episodic transitions'. These critiques and alternatives are summarized in Table 1.

To anticipate briefly my assessment of each of these general arguments: (1) Giddens's critique of functionalism in Marxism is largely correct, although his discussion is somewhat misleading in ignoring the growing Marxist critique of functional explanations in historical materialism. (2) Giddens's critique of class reductionism in social typologies is less satisfactory. On the one hand, his own proposal is not as sharply different from traditional Marxist treatments of social forms as he imagines, and on the other, his rejection of the Marxist typology rests on a characterization of the Marxist concept of 'class' which many Marxists do not share. (3) The critique of evolutionism is the least satisfactory. While Giddens is correct in rejecting strong forms of teleological evolutionary theory (in its Marxist and non-Marxist incarnations), I think his general rejection of weaker forms of evolutionary theory is unjustified. Indeed, as I shall argue, Giddens's own approach to social change should be viewed as a type of evolutionary theory. What is at issue, then, in his critique of historical materialism is two competing evolutionary arguments. Those will be my central conclusions. Now let us look in some detail at each of the arguments.

I. Functionalism and the Social Totality

Giddens correctly observes that much Marxist work can be characterized as covertly functionalist. This functionalism takes a variety of forms. In classical Marxism the base–superstructure metaphor is essentially a type of functional explanation: the state, for example, is explained by the functional requirements generated by class relations. In the work of Althusser, functionalism is

Table 1 Summary of Giddens's critique of historical materialism

	Central Marxist Concept	*Giddens's Critique*	*Giddens's Alternative*
1. Logic of Interconnection of Social Whole	Functional Totality	Functionalism	Contingently Reproduced Social System
2. Typology of Social Forms	Mode of Production	Class and Economic Reductionism	Level of Space–Time Distanciation
3. Logic of Transformation	Dialectic of Forces and Relations of Production	Evolutionism	Episodic Transitions

smuggled in under the rubric of 'reproduction' and 'structural causality'. The form of ideological apparatuses, for example, is explained by the require-ments for reproducing the relations of production. In many current Marxist discussions, explanations of racism and sexism take the form of functional arguments about their beneficial effects for increasing the rate of profit or dividing the working class. In somewhat more obscure ways, analyses of society as an 'expressive totality' or attempts by Marxists in the 'capital logic' school to 'derive' properties of capitalist society from the category 'capital' can also be viewed as implicit functional explanations, since the logic of 'expression' or 'derivation' is essentially based on the requirements for reproducing the social whole. The fact that most of these analyses also contain discussions of contradictions and conflicts does not negate the fact that in all of these cases, various properties of society are explained by their functions within the social totality.

Giddens criticizes such functional explanations on a variety of familiar grounds: functionalist explanations rest on a false division between statics and dynamics; they tend to turn human actors into mere bearers of social relations, lacking any knowledge or intentionality; and, most importantly in Giddens's view, they falsely impute 'needs' to social systems. Thus, for example, Giddens criticizes attempts by Marxists to explain unemployment in terms of the 'needs' of capitalism for a reserve army of labor.[4] The only way Giddens feels in which functional arguments can be legitimately employed in social science is when such arguments are treated in a strictly *counterfactual* manner: 'We can quite legitimately pose conjectural questions such as "What would have to be the case for social system *x* to come about, persist or be transformed?"'[5] But stating such conditions of existence does not constitute an explanation of anything; they merely point the direction towards what needs explaining.

Giddens is, I believe, substantially correct in both his assessment of the functionalist tendencies within Marxism and in his critique of those tendencies. Social reproduction should always be understood as a contingent reality in need of explanation rather than as an automatically guaranteed process. While in some cases functional *descriptions* may be heuristically useful – i.e. descriptions of how a particular institution or structure in fact does reproduce class relations – such descriptions are never in and of themselves explanations.

Selection Mechanisms and Feedback Processes

In spite of my agreement with the main thrust of Giddens's arguments about functionalism, nevertheless his discussion of the problem is in certain respects misleading. First of all, he writes as if Marxists have largely ignored this problem, whereas in fact a great deal of the critical debate within Marxism in the past decade has resolved around the problem of functionalism. This has been the case in the discussions of work by Althusser and other 'structuralist'

Marxists, but the problem of functionalism has been raised in numerous other contexts as well. It is particularly surprising in this context that Giddens does not discuss in this book the most sustained defence of functional explanations in historical materialism, G.A. Cohen's *Karl Marx's Theory of History: A Defence* (1978), or the debate over functionalism and Marxism which this book has inspired.[6]

Secondly, while I think that Giddens is correct in being suspicious of the way writers slide from functional descriptions to functional explanations, I think he is wrong totally to dismiss the term 'function' from explanations of social phenomena. While the functionality of a given institution or practice is never a *complete* explanation of that institution, I see no reason why arguments about functionality cannot constitute an aspect of a proper explanation. Take the problem of the state, for example. Marxists often attempt to explain particular state policies in terms of their 'function' for capital accumulation. Giddens would not deny that many policies do reproduce conditions favourable for accumulation; what he objects to is the functional form of the explanation of such policies. The explanation, he would argue, should be sought in the practices and strategies of actors who intentionally create such policies with an eye to their consequences. While of course there may be unintended consequences to state policies, and it may even happen that such unintended consequences are reproductive, the unintended consequences cannot ever be explanations of the policies themselves; the explanations always have to work through intentional practices of actors.

The fact that intentionality is always implicated in such explanations, however, does not mean that there cannot also be nonintentional causal 'feedback' processes at work which reinforce or undermine a given state policies unfavourable to private profits and private accumulation, a causal what they are. For example, given the institutional separation of the state apparatuses from production in capitalist societies, if the state engages in policies unfavorable to private profits and private accumulation, a causal chain will be set in motion: economic conditions will deteriorate, unemployment will tend to rise, the tax base of the state will tend to erode and thus fiscal pressures on the state increase, etc. These conditions, in turn, will shape the kinds of intentional strategies in which actors will engage, and these strategies (including the strategies of state actors) will tend to produce changes in the disruptive state policies. The critical point is that while intentions play a central role in this process, the fact that the intentions of actors take this form is itself explained by the structural properties of the system, and thus there is a meaningful sense in which one can say that these structural properties, and not just the intentions, 'explain' why state policies in fact tend to favour private accumulation. Thus, given a specification of the institutional context of state policies, functional arguments within explanations are not in principle illegitimate.[7]

The critical step in this argument is the specification of the institutional context within which such functional explanations are made. The argument is that institutions may be organized in such a way that they have built in to them certain 'negative selection mechanisms', to use Claus Offe's formulation. Such mechanisms, once in place, provide for the causal feedback processes needed to generate functional relationships. Of course, such institutional forms are themselves the result of intentional practices. But this fact does not mean that once in place they cannot filter policies in a manner that is, in an on-going way, not regulated by intentions and which nevertheless is systematically functional. In such contexts, a functional element within the explanation of a given policy seems entirely appropriate.

To say this, of course, does not prejudge the question of whether or not in any particular case a functional argument is correct. In fact, there are good reasons to be suspicious of such arguments. In general it seems to me that the 'filter mechanisms' inscribed in institutional forms of the state are much less effective, much more internally contradictory and much more contingent upon particular forms of class conflict than is suggested by Marxists who adopt such functional reasoning. I would thus agree with Giddens that functional arguments are often dubious. But this is because they are substantively wrong, not because a priori no explanation can legitimately contain functional reasoning.

Indeed, it is possible to identify some social contexts within which full-fledged functional explanations are possible in social science. Jon Elster, himself a vigorous opponent of functionalism, gives a clear example in his discussion of profit-maximizing strategies of capitalist firms. Elster argues that it is appropriate to use a functional explanation to answer the question, 'Why do capitalist firms adopt on average profit-maximizing strategies?'[8] His argument is that the market acts as a selection mechanism which eliminates firms that adopt sub-optimal strategies. After a sufficiently long operation of the market, only those firms which happened to adopt profit-maximizing strategies will survive. Thus, even though the decision-making procedures within capitalist firms operate on 'rough-and-ready rules of thumb', only those particular rules of thumb which happen coincidentally to maximize profits will survive over time. The end result, therefore, will be a distribution of strategies among firms which are generally functional for the reproduction of those firms, even though such a distribution was not intended by any actor within the system. Of course, it may empirically happen that some capitalists consciously attempt to adopt profit-maximizing strategies. Elster's point is that we need not assume that they do so in order to understand how the functional outcome is possible. Conscious profit-maximization may improve the efficiency of the selection mechanisms, but the functional relationship is itself structurally ensured through the operation of the market. A functional explanation of profit-maximizing strategies by firms (profit-maximization is explained by its consequences for the survival of firms) is thus justified in this case.

As Elster stresses, there are relatively few social processes which have the properties of firms acting in a competitive market, and thus it is generally not the case that genuine selection mechanisms operate to produce functional relations. Functional explanations by themselves are usually unsatisfactory precisely because no plausible mechanism for regulating the functional outcome can be posited. Giddens is therefore quite justified to be suspicious of functional explanations. His categorical rejection of any use of functional arguments within social explanations, however, is unwarranted.

II. Typologies of Social Forms

At the heart of Marxist theory lies a particular strategy for classifying societies. In one way or another, all Marxists root their typologies of social forms in the concept of class structure, which is itself based on the concept of mode of production. While there are substantial disagreements over how the concept of mode of production should be defined and precisely how class structures should be distinguished, there is a general agreement among Marxists that these concepts provide the central principle both for differentiating types of societies and for providing a road map of the historical trajectory of societal transformations. Even where Marxists allow a great deal of room for the autonomy of relations of domination other than class (e.g. ethnic, gender, national), they nevertheless characterize the overall form of society primarily in terms of its class structure. A great deal of Giddens's book is devoted to challenging this principle of social typology. The accusation that historical materialism is an economic or class reductionist theory is, of course, a standard criticism. What is unusual about Giddens's position is that he rejects class-based typologies of societies without challenging the importance of class analysis in general.

Giddens raises the critique of reductionism in two contexts: first, he insists that only in capitalism can class be viewed as the central structural principle of the society as a whole, and thus class structure provides an inadequate general basis for specifying the pivotal differences between social forms; and second, he argues that societies are characterized by multiple forms of domination and exploitation which cannot be reduced to a single principle, class. The first of these can be termed the critique of *intersocietal class reductionism*; the second, of *intrasocietal class reductionism*. Since Giddens spends so much more time discussing the first of these, I will concentrate on it below.

(A) Intersocietal Class Reductionism

Societies should not be primarily classified in terms of their class structures, Giddens argues, because only in capitalism is it the case that class constitutes the basic structural principle of the society. Only in capitalism does class permeate all aspects of social life. While various forms of noncapitalist society may have had classes, class relations did not constitute their core principle of social organization. This argument forms the basis of the pivotal distinction Giddens makes between *class society* (a society within which class is the central structural principle) and *class-divided society* ('a society in which there are classes, but where class analysis does not serve as a basis for identifying the basic structural principle of organization of that society').[9]

Giddens's defence of this proposition revolves around his analysis of *power* and *domination*. Power, in Giddens's theory of 'social structuration' is defined as a subcategory of transformative capacity, in which 'transformative capacity is *harnessed to actors' attempts to get others to comply with their wants*. Power, in this relational sense, concerns the capacity of actors to secure outcomes where the realization of these outcomes depends upon the agency of others.'[10] This relational transformative capacity rests on specific kinds of resources which are used to get others to comply. In particular, Giddens distinguishes between *allocative* resources (resources involving control over nature) and *authoritative* resources (resources involving control over social interactions of various sorts). *Domination* is then defined as 'structured asymmetries of resources drawn upon and reconstituted in such power relations'.[11] On the basis of these concepts societies can be classified along two principal dimensions:

(1) Which type of resource domination, allocative or authoritative, is most important for sustaining power relations. Giddens argues that it is only in capitalism that control over allocative resources *per se* is of prime importance. In all noncapitalist societies 'authoritative resources were the main basis of both political and economic power'.[12]

(2) The magnitude of control over each of these resources in time and space. This is the core of Giddens's complex concept of 'space–time distanciation'. The control over any resource can be specified in terms of its extension over time and space. This is easiest to understand in terms of allocative resources. Hunting and gathering societies involve rather limited control over allocative resources in both time and space: food is continually acquired in the present with relatively short time horizons, and trade over long distances (spatial extension of allocative resources) is very limited. On both of these counts, settled agriculture involves greater space–time 'distanciation'. And industrial capitalism, of course, extends this to historically unprecedented levels: production is organized globally and allocative time horizons extend over decades in some cases. In terms of authoritative resources, the central basis for the extension over time and space is the increasing capacity of a society for *surveillance*: for the gathering and storing of information and for the supervising of subordinate groups. The basic institutional sites for this extension of authoritative resources in time and space are initially the city and subsequently the state.[13]

Taking these dimensions together produces the general typology of societal forms in Table 2. This is certainly a different kind of typology from the usual Marxist typology of modes of production. But are the two really completely incompatible? Giddens certainly believes that they are. Nevertheless, I think that the distance may not be quite so great as Giddens imagines.

The central qualitative break in Giddens's typology occurs between capitalism and all noncapitalist societies. Only in capitalism are allocative resources the central basis of power, and thus only in capitalism can class be viewed as the organizing principle of the society. Only in capitalism is it the case that the direct control over allocative resources (private ownership of the means of production) in and of itself confers general social power. In feudalism, and indeed in all 'class-divided societies', the control over authoritative resources was the central issue. While peasants often controlled the means of production, this did not confer general power to the peasant class, because it did not have access to the central authoritative resources of the society. This seems to run directly counter to the Marxist thesis that class structures (or modes of production) are the basic structural principle of all societies. On closer inspection, however, I think that the difference may not be quite so significant for two reasons.

First of all, we can ask: *why* is it that in noncapitalist societies authoritative resources are the basis of power, whereas in capitalism allocative resources are the basis? One response, of course, is to say that this question is illegitimate. The authoritative/allocative resource distinction could be treated strictly as the taxonomic criterion for specifying the different types of society, and thus there would be no theoretically meaningful answer to the question (any more than there is a theoretically meaningful answer to the question: 'Why do mammals nurse their young while birds do not?', since in the absence of nursing a mammal wouldn't be a mammal). Giddens, however, does not seem to reject this question, and when he does attempt to explain the differences between the two types of society, he tends to emphasize the causal importance of differences in their economic structures: the importance of agrarian production, the degree of economic autonomy of communities, the

Table 2 Giddens's typology of social forms

| | | TYPE OF RESOURCE WHICH IS THE PRIMARY BASIS OF POWER | |
		Authoritative	*Allocative*
LEVEL OF	*Low*	Tribal Societies	
SPACE–TIME	*Medium*	Class-divided Societies	
DISTANCIATION	*High*		Capitalist Societies
	Very High	Socialist Societies	

existence of free wage labour, the alienability of different forms of property, and so on.[14] While Giddens emphasizes noneconomic factors in his explanations of the *genesis* of capitalism (e.g. the specific character of the European state system), he consistently argues that it is the distinctive property relations of capitalism that explain why class becomes such a central organizing principle of capitalist societies. Such an explanation, however, is symmetrical: the distinctive property relations of feudal society (in contrast to capitalism) explain why in feudalism the control of authoritative resources is the central axis of power.

This argument comes quite close to Marx's argument in *Capital* that the economic structure of society is 'determinant' even if in specific types of society other aspects of society may be 'primary': 'One thing is clear: the Middle Ages could not live on Catholicism, nor could the ancient world on politics. On the contrary, it is the manner in which they gained their livelihood which explains why in one case politics, in the other Catholicism, played the chief part.'[15] This idea is also at the heart of Althusser's notion of society as a 'structured totality' within which the form of economic structure determines which aspect (instance or level) of the society is 'dominant'. To be sure, Giddens emphatically, and I think correctly, rejects the functionalist logic underlying Althusser's argument. But nevertheless it appears that when Giddens tries to explain the differences in the relationship between allocative and authoritative resources in capitalist and noncapitalist societies he relies heavily on differences in the system of property relations.

Giddens's Definition of 'Class'

A second reason why Giddens's position may not be quite so distant from some Marxist formulations centers on the concept of class itself. Giddens very narrowly ties the concept of class to 'sectional forms of domination created by private ownership of property,'[16] where 'ownership' is taken to mean the direct control over the use and disposition of property, and 'private' is meant to designate legally guaranteed *individual* (or family) rights of disposition over that property. This means that where an individual or group appropriates surplus through directly coercive means without controlling the actual use of the means of production, this appropriation is treated as a result of the control over authoritative resources (command over military personnel and activity), not ownership of private property. The *result* of such coercive appropriation is still class division since it produces differential access to allocative resources (i.e. rich and poor), but the *basis* for the appropriation itself is not the class structure, but the structure of authoritative domination. It is for this reason that Giddens insists such societies should be termed class-divided rather than class societies.

This formulation by Giddens depends heavily upon his definition of 'class'. Many Marxists, myself included, define classes in terms of the mechanisms by which surplus products or surplus labour is appropriated, not by private property in the means of production as such.[17] Such appropriation of surplus always involves specific combinations of economic and political mechanisms (i.e. relations to allocative and authoritative resources in the present context). In feudal societies this mechanism involves the direct use of extra-economic coercion; in capitalist societies the political face of class relations is restricted to the guarantee of contracts and the supervision of the labour process. In both societies, however, the mechanisms of surplus extraction specify the character of class relations.

What this suggests is that the disagreement between Giddens and many Marxists is at least partially of a terminological nature. Marxists draw precisely the same descriptive contrast as Giddens does between the economic mechanisms of class relations rooted in the labor contract of capitalist society and the extraeconomic coercive mechanisms of noncapitalist class societies. And many Marxists agree completely with Giddens that this qualitative distinction between capitalist and precapitalist (or noncapitalist) societies is a much more fundamental break than any distinctions among the range of precapitalist societies (G. A. Cohen in particular stresses this point). Where they differ is in how the term 'class' is to be employed with respect to the use of authoritative and allocative resources in surplus appropriation.

Now, terminological disputes are rarely innocent. It is generally the case that drawing the boundary criteria for a concept in one way or another opens up or closes off lines of theoretical inquiry. When Marxists treat the mechanism of appropriation (exploitation of labour) as the pivot for specifying class relations they are doing so because, at least implicitly, they feel that: (1) these mechanisms determine a set of social actors or collectivities with opposing interests and thus tendencies towards struggle; (2) the typological distinctions among these mechanisms constitute the basis for distinguishing societies with different dynamics, forms of social conflict, trajectories of development; and (3) the different elements within these mechanisms do not have an autonomous logic, but instead form at least a loose kind of *gestalt*.

This last point is, I think, the most fundamental in the present context. By combining the control over allocative and authoritative resources in the specification of class relations, Marxists are at least implicitly arguing that these two forms of resource control are not just contingently interconnected. They are systematically linked one to the other so that only certain forms of combination can occur stably. By excluding the relation to authoritative resources from the concept of class, Giddens is, in contrast, affirming his view that the social organization of authoritative resources and their development and transformation is autonomous from allocative resources. (This is not to say, of course, that the development of forms of control of authoritative resources has no effects on allocative resource control, but simply that those effects are contingent rather than necessary.) The implications of this difference in claims about the relationship between allocative and authoritative resources will become clearer when we discuss the problem of evolutionism below. But first we must briefly turn to the issue of intrasocietal class reductionism.

(B) Intrasocietal Class Reductionism

Historical materialism is class reductionist, Giddens argues, not only in its treatment of the central differences between societies; it is reductionist in its treatment of the various forms of domination within given societies. In addition to class relations, Giddens argues that relations between states, between ethnic groups and between sexes constitute 'axes of exploitative relationships'.[18] None of these are reducible to class exploitation. Marxists, however, have often attempted to explain the existence and forms of these axes of domination or exploitation as 'expressions' of class, typically by recourse to functional explanations. If such reductionist accounts are illegitimate, then the attempt at characterizing the overall form of society strictly in terms of modes of production is clearly inadequate, since interstate, ethnic and sexual relations of domination within societies have sources of variation independent of class structures.

Many, perhaps most, contemporary Marxist theorists accept much of this argument. In general there is a recognition that at least ethnic and sexual domination are not simply reflexes of class domination, and some Marxists would add interstate domination to this as well. How much autonomy such relations have and precisely how their articulation with the class system should be understood are, of course, matters of considerable disagreement. While tendencies towards functional reductionism continue in the Marxist tradition, it is nevertheless the case that the thrust of much contemporary Marxist thinking has been against attempts at intrasocietal class reductionism.

Where Marxists would tend to disagree with Giddens is in the implication that such irreducibility of sex or ethnicity or nationality to class implies that these various forms of domination/exploitation are of potentially equal status in defining the differences between or dynamics within societies. Most Marxists would continue to argue for a general primacy of class, even if other relations are not simple reflections of class. In particular it is often argued that the class determines the limits of possible variation of other forms of relations, even if it does not functionally determine the specificity of those relations. If such arguments are correct, class relations do not simply 'illuminate' the analysis of sex, ethnicity or nationality, as Giddens suggests; they determine the basic structural parameters within which these other relations develop.

This kind of argument, of course, can be reversed. It can be argued, as many feminist writers have argued, that gender relations impose limits on forms of variation on the class structure. And it is certainly plausible to argue that the interstate system of political and military relations imposes real limits on the possible forms of development of class relations. If the relations of limitation are symmetrical, then it is rather arbitrary to claim any primacy for class relations. Yet Marxists continue to argue for such primacy, if sometimes covertly or apologetically. Three kinds of arguments are used to defend the primacy of class. First, it is sometimes argued, if only implicitly, that while various nonclass forms of domination are irreducible to class, class most systematically and deeply structures the forms of consciousness of actors. This does not imply that individuals are necessarily 'class conscious' in the sense of being aware of their class position and class interests, but simply that their forms of social consciousness are most systematically shaped by their class location. Class, therefore, is viewed as having the greatest *existential* impact on human subjectivity, and therefore should be accorded primacy.

Giddens endorses this view for capitalism – and thus his designation of capitalism as a class society, a society within which class permeates all facets of social life – but he rejects it as a general thesis about the effects of class in all societies. In this, I think Giddens is correct. Indeed, I would argue that even for capitalism there is no necessity for class to be existentially primary in all cases. It is entirely possible, for example, for racial domination more pervasively to shape the forms of consciousness of an oppressed racial group than class domination. And at least in some advanced capitalist societies, the same might be said for gender domination. In any event, the thesis is at most valid for capitalism, and thus cannot effectively serve as a defence for the primacy Marxists accord to class in general.

A second argument for class primacy, therefore, shifts the attention from the consciousness of actors to the objective constraints under which they act. Here the argument is that class relations, by structuring the access to social resources of various sorts (particularly the surplus product), most pervasively determine the limits on capacities for action of different groups, including groups defined by nonclass relations. Thus, for example, racial domination may be irreducible to class domination, and yet the condition for blacks to struggle effectively against racial subordination may be gaining control over more of the surplus product. Thus, even if the interests or motivations for struggle are irreducible to class interests, the conditions for successful pursuit of those nonclass interests are fundamentally structured by class relations.[19]

This argument seems much sounder than the first. Nevertheless, it could still be argued that there are many necessary conditions for successful struggle, including ideological and political factors which are themselves not simply reflections of relations of control over the surplus product (i.e. class structures), and there is no compelling reason to privilege any of these multiple necessary conditions. While it may be the case that transformation of the class structure is part of the process of black liberation, it is also the case that transforming racial consciousness is a necessary condition for transforming the class structure. It is therefore arbitrary to assign one of these 'necessary conditions' a privileged position, and thus to accord class a general primacy over other relations.

This, then, leads to the third argument in defence of the primacy of class. While it may be the case that different forms of domination reciprocally condition each other as suggested above, Marxists have generally argued that only class relations have an internal logic of development, a logic which generates systematic tendencies for a trajectory of transformations of the class structure. This trajectory has a general directionality, it is argued, because of the way class relations and class struggles are articulated to the development of the forces of production. The apparent symmetry in the relationship between class and gender or class and race, therefore, is disrupted by the developmental tendencies of class relations. No such developmental trajectory has been persuasively argued for other forms of domination. This third argument seems to me to be the most compelling. To assess it we must turn to the third critique Giddens raises against historical materialism: evolutionism.

III. Evolutionism

Throughout *A Contemporary Critique of Historical Materialism* Giddens attacks all forms of evolutionary thinking in social theory. He does so for two principal reasons, one methodological and the other primarily empirical. Methodologically, most evolutionary perspectives in sociology are based on some notion of *adaptation*, particularly of adaptation of society to its material environment. But, Giddens insists, it is meaningless to talk about 'societies' adapting to anything: 'the idea of adaptation falls in the same category as the functional "needs" to which I have already objected. Societies have no need to "adapt" to (master, conquer) their material environments.'[20] Societies are not organisms and it is an inadmissible use of language to see them as evolving adaptively in the manner of biological organisms. The tacit teleology of such arguments must be rejected.

An alternative is to reconstruct the theory of social evolution on the basis of a theory of individual human adaptation. Human individuals, it could be argued, adapt to their environment and through such adaptation the societies within which they live may be pushed along some evolutionary path, even though the mechanism is not really lodged in 'society' *per se*. Such a reconstruction, Giddens argues, simply fails empirically. While it no longer rests on the methodological sin of reifying society, it is now based on a false empirical generalization, namely that there is a transhistorical tendency for human beings to improve their material conditions of existence. Furthermore, no alternative transhistorical principle of adaptation can be found: in Giddens's view there simply are no transhistorical individual drives or motives which could provide the basis for a general theory of social development.

The Marxist theory of history is thus doubly unsatisfactory. It is, in Giddens's view, empirically false. It is simply not true that there is any general tendency for the forces of production to develop throughout history, and thus the 'dialectic' of forces and relations of production could not possibly be the basis for a general trajectory of historical development. And it is methodologically flawed in its presupposition that societies have transhistorical adaptive imperatives.

In place of such evolutionary schemas, Giddens offers a view of social change in terms of what he calls *episodic characterizations* and *time–space edges*. 'Episodes,' Giddens writes, 'refer to processes of social change that have definite direction and form, and in which definite structural transformations occur'.[21] The critical point is that the directionality and dynamics of such change are specific to each episode, each historically specific form of social transition. There is no general dynamic or direction to social change. There are no 'episodes of episodes'. 'Time–space edges' refer to the 'simultaneous existence of types of society in episodic transitions'.[22] Giddens feels that evolutionary theories imply successions of societies in sequences of stages, whereas in fact social change is always a process of overlapping of different forms of society. Instead of a theory of social evolution, Giddens thus envisions social change as a set of qualitatively distinct transitions involving overlapping forms of society and which have no overall pattern or logic of development.

I will criticize Giddens's treatment of evolutionism on several grounds: first, while he is correct in rejecting teleological forms of evolutionary theory, he is wrong to characterize evolutionary theory as necessarily teleological; second, when a proper specification of evolutionary theory is made, it does not have the flaws attributed to it by Giddens; and third, Giddens's own theory of space–time distanciation and episodic transitions should be viewed as a variety of evolutionary theory in these terms. My conclusion will therefore be that the challenge Giddens poses to Marxist theory is not so much anti-evolutionism vs. evolutionism, but two substantively different theories of social evolution.

Giddens is on firm ground when he rejects theories of social evolution which are built on teleological arguments, arguments that societies inexorably develop towards some end-state of increasing adaptation to environmental or material conditions. And he is correct that one finds such images of social development in many social theories employing evolutionary arguments, Marxism included. In contrast to Giddens's claims, however, I would argue that this is not the essential structure of evolutionary theory. For a theory of society to be evolutionary three conditions must hold:

(1) The theory involves a typology of social forms which *potentially* has some kind of directionality to it. Evolutionary theories are not built simply around taxonomies of societies, but typologies capable of being ordered in a nonarbitrary way.

(2) It is possible to order these forms of society in such a way that the probability of staying at the same level of the typology is greater than the probability of regressing.

(3) In this ordered typology, there is a positive probability of moving from a given level of the typology to the next higher level. This need not be greater than the probability of regressing, but once a movement up occurs, the probability of staying there is greater than the probability of moving back. However weak the tendency towards development is, the typology is thus 'sticky downward'. This implies that there is some process, however weak and sporadic, which imparts a directionality to movements from one form to another.

Several things are important to note about this way of defining evolutionary theory. First, there is no claim that societies have needs or teleologically driven tendencies towards achieving some final state. Teleological arguments would be one way of elaborating conditions *2* and *3*, but not the only way. Second, this way of defining evolutionary theory does not imply that there is a rigid sequence of stages through which all societies *must* move. There is no statement that the probability of skipping a stage is zero. The only claim is that there is some positive impulse for movement. Third, it does not follow from this specification that all, or even most, societies necessarily evolve. Regressions are possible, perhaps in some situations even more likely than progressions. And in most societies, long-term steady states may be more likely than any systematic tendency for movement in the typology. All that is implied in the criteria for evolutionary theory is that given enough time, *some* societies will evolve in the manner indicated in the evolutionary typology.

Finally, this definition of evolutionary theory does not imply a metatheory of history, in the sense of claims for a universal mechanism of transition from one form of society to another. There is, to be sure, a claim about a universal logic to the typology of social forms in the evolutionary process, but the actual mechanisms which might explain movement between adjacent forms on the typology need not be the same at every stage of the typology. The theory specifies the roadmap of history and specifies which kinds of movements are likely to be stable or unstable, reproducible or unreproducible. But it does not necessarily postulate a universal process for each actual transition.[23] Obviously, this specification of evolutionary theory is clearly nontrivial. There is no logical reason why every taxonomy of societies should meet these criteria and it may be impossible to order social forms in this way.

The Development of the Forces of Production

The Marxist theory of social change meets these three criteria. While it is certainly true that before capitalism there were no strong impulses for the development of the forces of production, nevertheless it was the case that (a) there was in general a positive probability of the forces of production developing, if only very sporadically and slowly, and (b) the probability of regression was less than the probability of retaining given levels of productivity.

The defense of such claims need not rely at all on theses about the goals or needs of society. What is needed is a general argument for why the development of the forces of production should be 'sticky downward'. A number of such arguments can be found in Marxist writing: First, and perhaps least contentiously, there are in general no groups in a society with interests directly in reducing the level of productivity of labour. People may have interests which have the unintended consequence of reducing the productivity of labour (e.g. they may have interests which lead them to engage in military activity which results in a destruction of forces of production) or, in specific circumstances, they may intentionally strive to reduce productivity to accomplish some other interest (e.g. workers may want to reduce productivity if they feel this will protect their jobs). But no one has an interest in reducing labour productivity *per se*. This means that once a level of productivity is reached there will not in general be groups organized to reduce it.

Second, the key aspect of the development of the forces of production is the development of knowledge of productive techniques, not the physical hardware as such. As G. A. Cohen has argued, with any luck if a society can retain the knowledge of production it can restore a given level of productivity even if the physical means of production are destroyed, whereas if the knowledge is lost, then those physical means of production are useless even if they are in working order. Knowledge, in general, has a 'sticky downward' character. This does not mean that technical knowledge is never lost, but simply that it will have tendencies towards being retained.[24]

Third, as Marx and Engels argued in *The German Ideology*, once a given level of the forces of production is reached by whatever route, it tends to engender needs in people which are dependent upon that level of development of the forces of production. This means that in addition to there being no groups (in general) with strong interests in the reduction of labour productivity, there will be groups with strong interests in the preservation of a given level.

Fourth, specific arguments can be made for why there are also interests in enhancing labour productivity, and thus developing the forces of production (and not simply preventing their decline). Under conditions in which increases in labour productivity have the consequence of reducing the toil of direct producers, direct producers will in general have interests in developing the forces of production. Direct producers may not have any particular interest in increasing the surplus product as such, but they will have interests in reducing unpleasant labour. This means that in preclass societies, in which improvements in productivity generally imply lesser toil, direct producers will have interests in increasing productivity. This does not mean that people will feel under any great *pressure* to reduce toil, but simply that when innovations which reduce toil occur for whatever reasons and however sporadically, they will tend to be adopted rather than rejected.[25]

In societies with class exploitation, however, there is no longer any necessary link between the development of the forces of production and the reduction of toil. On the contrary, in many cases technical changes may be associated with the intensification of toil of direct producers. There will thus no longer be any universal interests in developing the forces of production. Ruling classes, however, will generally have at least weak interests in adopting changes which increase the level of labour productivity. They certainly have class interests in maintaining or enhancing the level of surplus appropriation, since this is critical to their reproduction as a ruling class. And except in peculiar circumstances where increasing productivity undermines their ability to appropriate surplus, this implies that they will have some interest in the development of the forces of production. This certainly does not mean that in precapitalist class societies, ruling classes experience systematic pressures to encourage such innovations, but simply that they will tend to adopt them when they occur.

To be sure, this is a very weak impulse throughout much of human history. It took hundreds of thousands of years of virtually stagnant forces of production before some of the basic innovations which marked the transition from hunting and gathering societies to settled agriculture occurred. And many societies continued without such innovations at all. The argument is simply that there is at least a weak impulse for such improvement and that when such achievements are made, they are not willingly relinquished.

The Marxist theory of history, of course, is not simply a technological typology of societies. The heart of the theory is a specific argument about the interconnection between the tendency for the forces of production to develop and the social relations of production within which those forces of production are used. Two pivotal claims are made: (1) That for a given level of the forces of production, only certain types of production relations are possible. Other forms, if they were to occur through historical accidents, would be highly unstable and would be more or less rapidly transformed into a 'compatible' form. (2) Within a given form of production relations, there is a limit to the possible development of the forces of production. There is thus a relationship of reciprocal limitation between the forces and relations of production. However, as argued above, there is at least a weak impulse for the forces of production to develop, and this creates a dynamic asymmetry in their interconnection. Eventually the forces of production will reach a point at which they are 'fettered', that is, a point at which further development is impossible in the absence of transformations of the relations of production.

Distanciation and Power

Now, the classic Marxist argument is that when such fettering occurs, the relations will be transformed, and thus societies will necessarily move from one societal form to another. As I have argued elsewhere this claim presupposes that social actors with interests in such transformations will necessarily have the capacity to accomplish the qualitative change in social relations of production.[26] Marxism, however, lacks a developed theory of class capacities, and thus the strong claims about the *inevitability* of progression cannot be sustained. This, however, does not call into question the argument about the tendencies towards progression or the directionality of the ordering of social forms. And this is all that is needed for the theory to retain its evolutionary structure.

Not only does Marxist theory generally meet these three criteria for evolutionary theory, so does the framework elaborated by Giddens in *A Contemporary Critique of Historical Materialism* and elsewhere. Giddens formulates a typology of social forms which has a clear quantitative ordering along the dimension of space–time distanciation. But does this ordering meet the second and third criteria of evolutionary theories? Giddens insists that the mechanisms or dynamics of movement from one form to another are specific to each transition; there is no transhistorical impulse to move from tribal societies with low space–time distanciation to capitalist societies and eventually socialist societies with high space–time distanciation.

On closer inspection, however, Giddens's own detailed accounts seem to suggest a general logic to such progression. 'Space–time distanciation' is a concept which captures the ability of people in a society to control allocative and authoritative resources in time and space for use in power relations. Expanding allocative space–time distanciation involves (among other things) the development of the forces of production; expanding authoritative space–time distanciation involves developing the means of surveillance. Increases in such distanciation are human achievements: they increase the capacities of certain agents to act. But if those are indeed capacities, then it follows that the people whose capacities are enhanced by a given level of distanciation will not willingly accept lower levels of space–time distanciation once a given level is achieved.

Of course, there may be other agents who would like to see the level of distanciation reduced. This is particularly the case for space–time distanciation of authoritative resources. Is there any general reason why we might suppose that the capacities of actors with anti-distanciation interests will generally be weaker than those with pro-distanciation interests? The answer to this question depends upon how we conceive the relationship between the *level of* space–time distanciation and the degree of *inequality of access to* the resources in question. There are two principal possibilities:

(1) If there is complete equality in access – radically egalitarian distributions of access to allocative and authoritative resources – then all agents would have an interest in preventing reductions of distanciation, since this would reduce their capacities to act. They might not have interests in actually increasing distanciation, since increases might have negative consequences

for the initial egalitarian distributions, but they would in general have strong interests in opposing reductions.

(2) If, on the other hand, there is unequal distribution of access, then in general those with the greatest access to the resources in question will have an interest in preventing a decline in space–time distanciation with respect to those resources. And, since by virtue of their greater access to the resources they also have greater capacities to secure their interests, they will, in general, be able to prevent such regression from occurring. The only exception to this would be the peculiar circumstance in which people with the greatest access to authoritative and/or allocative resources would have their control of resources *increased* by a *decline* of distanciation. This could occur if regression increased inequality more than it reduced overall space–time distanciation. In general, however, agents with privileged access to resources will have both an interest in preserving a given level of distanciation and the capacity to secure that interest. This does not mean that distanciation will never regress, but simply that it will tend to be sticky downward in both the egalitarian and inegalitarian situations.[27]

What can we say about the third criterion? Is there a positive probability however weak of forward movement? Clearly there is in capitalist society, but is there any such general impulse towards *increasing* space–time distanciation (not just preventing its decline)? I think that it is possible to read such an impulse from Giddens's analysis. Essentially, the impulse towards expansion of space–time distanciation comes from different forms of conflict and competition in different societies. In class societies (capitalism) this is impelled primarily by conflicts over allocative resources in the form of economic competition between capitalist firms; in class-divided societies it is rooted in conflicts over authoritative resources, primarily in the form of military and territorial competition. The leading edge of space–time distanciation thus varies, depending upon which kind of resource is the 'basis of power' in the society, and accordingly which dimension of distanciation will be most implicated in social conflicts.[28] Because of the link between conflict, power, resources and distanciation, there will be at least some impulse for increasing space–time distanciation throughout history. Again, this is not equivalent to claiming that there will be universal *progress*, a universal tendency for all societies to actually increase space–time distanciation; it is simply a claim that there is a universal, if often weak, impulse towards such increase, and thus a positive probability for such increases to occur.

Giddens's Causal Pluralism

If this reconstruction of Giddens's argument is correct, then what is novel in Giddens's argument is not that it is necessarily anti-evolutionary (although it is anti-teleological), but that it proposes a dual logic to evolutionary development: the evolutionary trajectory is animated by the autonomous impulses for the expansion of space–time distanciation with respect to allocative and authoritative resources. Stated in more conventional terms (which Giddens would probably disavow), social evolution is the result of autonomous evolutionary dynamics rooted simultaneously in political and economic structures. While in specific historical cases one may be justified in saying that one or the other of these constitutes the central locus of impulses for social change, there is no general priority of one over the other and their interconnection is best characterized as historically specific and contingent.

What we have, then, are two contending evolutionary theories.[29] The debate over these alternatives is not, I would argue, fundamentally a methodological one, but a substantive one. On the one hand there is the view, shared by most Marxists, that the developmental tendencies with respect to political power and economic structures are intrinsically linked, with economic structures having primacy. While there may be a 'relative autonomy' of one with respect to the other in the sense that a range of variations in forms of political power can coexist with a given form of economic structure, the relation is not simply a historically contingent one. They form a loose *gestalt*. And within this *gestalt*, the most *systematically* dynamic element is rooted in the organization of production itself. Giddens, on the other hand, insists that the developmental tendencies of these two structures are autonomous and no general principles govern their interconnection. In different historically specific situations one or the other may be most important.

This debate underlies the specification of the concept of class as well as the claims about the relationship between class domination and other forms of domination discussed earlier. The Marxist claim that the concept of class combines the relations of economic exploitation and authoritative domination is implicitly a rejection of the claim that these have genuinely autonomous logics of development; Giddens's restriction of class to relations of domination with respect to allocative resources affirms his view that allocative and authoritative domination are autonomous processes. The adjudication of these contending class concepts and the typologies of social forms to which they are linked, therefore, ultimately hinges on these different substantive claims about the process of transformation of economic and political (allocative and authoritative) aspects of social relations.

It is not, of course, an easy task to build a convincing case one way or the other on this issue. Particularly once the simple functionalist version of the base–superstructure model is abandoned, it is difficult to argue systematically for the structural unity of economic and political relations within the theory of social development and the concept of class. It is tempting, therefore, to opt for Giddens's solution, to reduce the theoretical ambitions of Marxism in favour of a more contingent causal pluralism. This solution has been pursued in different ways by a number of Marxist theorists such as Barry Hindess and Paul Q. Hirst in England and Robin Hahnel and Michael Albert in the United States.[30]

This temptation, I think, should be resisted. Even though it is in need of modification in a number of crucial ways, there are, I believe, compelling intuitions for why the Marxian account of evolutionary trajectories should be retained. I will mention only a few of these in closing:

(1) As discussed earlier, Marxists generally share Giddens's view that in precapitalist societies the appropriation of surplus labor (or products) relied on the use of extra-economic coercion (control over authoritative resources). There is therefore no disagreement that the concrete relationship between control over allocative and authoritative resources varies across social forms. Marxists, however, insist that the *explanation* for the primacy of authoritative resources in precapitalist societies must be sought in the nature of the economic structure of such societies. If this is correct – and nothing in Giddens's analysis directly challenges this point – then it should be expected that the key to understanding changes in the relationship between allocative and authoritative resources lies in understanding the trajectory of development of economic structures. This does not imply that an autonomous political process of change is absent, but simply that the dynamics centered in property relations impose more fundamental limits on the overall process of social change.

(2) Any theory of social change that recognizes the importance of social actors must contain, among other things, an account of the interests implicated in different processes of social change and the capacities of actors for translating such interests into outcomes. In these terms, there is a clearer link between interests and the evolutionary tendencies around allocative resources than around authoritative resources. Throughout most of human history there have been systematic interests in increasing the productivity of labour either in order to reduce toil or to increase actual surplus products, and this underwrites the sustained, if often weak, impulse towards the improvement of the forces of production. There is no such general interest in the expansion of social control over authoritative resources. Such expansion is pervasively contested, and thus there is a less sustained generic impulse for its continual development. To the extent that in spite of this contestation there is a net evolutionary tendency for 'space–time distanciation' with respect to authoritative resources, it is because the social actors supporting such expansion have greater capacities (power) to accomplish their objectives. But this greater capacity itself depends upon their control over allocative resources: the means of paying troops and retainers, of building the infrastructures of surveillance and communication, etc. Thus again, there is an asymmetry between allocative and authoritative resources, with the former providing a more systematic basis for explanations of evolutionary tendencies.

(3) Finally, the motivational assumptions underlying claims about the development of the forces of production are more plausible than parallel claims about the autonomous development of control over authoritative

resources. It is easy to see why people wish to reduce toil or increase surplus – or at least, why they are reluctant to have labour productivity decline (i.e. why the changes are sticky downward). But why should people want greater 'space–time distanciation' over authoritative resources? One answer is that this contributes to their material wellbeing, either by increasing consumption or reducing toil even further. The beneficiaries of increasing space–time distanciation of authoritative resources are typically ruling classes who use their increased command of authoritative resources to increase their material welfare.[31] Such an answer, however, has the effect of subordinating the development of authoritative resources to motivations structured by allocative resources. This kind of subordination is more consistent with the Marxist account of their intrinsic structural interconnection. An alternative answer is that people want power for power's sake, not because it increases their material welfare. This could then provide the motivational basis for an autonomous development of political power, of domination with respect to authoritative resources. However, while there are undoubtedly specific cases of such noninstrumental power motivations (i.e. power as an end in itself rather than as a means to some other end), this seems hardly a satisfactory motivational basis for a general argument of the autonomous logic of development of authoritative resources.

Conclusion

It is important not to overstate the differences between much of what Giddens proposes and the basic tendencies of current Marxist theorizing. While Giddens's general theory of action may run counter to mechanistic and functionalist reasoning in the Marxist tradition, it is largely compatible with most of the *substantive* claims of both classical and contemporary Marxism. There is no intrinsic incompatibility between the substantive claims Marxists make about the importance of class structures and class struggle, about the role of the state and ideology, etc. and Giddens's methodological stress on the knowledgeability of actors, the 'duality of structure', the analysis of social processes in terms of the unacknowledged conditions of action and the unintended consequences of action, and so on. Many of the criticisms of functionalism and class reductionism which Giddens makes from this methodological standpoint are also accepted by many, if by no means all, contemporary Marxist theorists.

Even on more strictly substantive matters, Giddens's position is not generally the polar opposite of Marxist positions. The actual structural typology of societies Giddens elaborates is much closer to conventional Marxist typologies than either are to typologies in 'modernization' theory, for example. And on many specific topics, such as the analysis of the capitalist labour process, the developmental dynamics of capitalism or the structural contrast in forms of surplus extraction in capitalism and feudalism, Giddens's analysis hardly differs at all from most current Marxist formulations.

What is less easily meshed with contemporary Marxism are Giddens's arguments of the duality of power rooted in the autonomous logic of control over allocative and authoritative resources. This leads Giddens to reject the possibility of any general theory of history, any general principles of historical development, in favour of more limited epochal theories of particular transitions. Most Marxists retain a commitment to constructing an overall theory of historical development, based in some version of historical materialism, within which the development and contradictions of class relations provide the central framework for analysis. Giddens not only rejects the substantive propositions of this project, he rejects the project itself.

What are the stakes in Giddens's critique of the possibility of a theory of history? Some Marxists have argued that the Marxist *theory* of history can in any event be abandoned without prejudicing Marxist class analysis. In this view Marxism provides a range of general *concepts* with which to analyse historical development, but provides no general theory of that development. There are specific theories of specific social formations, but no general theory of the overall historical trajectory of social forms. Can the Marxist theory of history be dispensed with so easily without serious ramifications for Marxism in general?

I think not. Specifically, I think that the justification for Marxian class analysis largely rests on the theory of history in which it is embedded. There are three kinds of arguments for the Marxist preoccupation with class: a functional defence, a structural constraint defence, and what I have termed a dynamic defence. Each of these potentially provides a defence of Marxist claims for the primacy of class in the analysis of social structure and social change. If the functional defence is rejected as unsatisfactory, and the structural defence is viewed as only contingently correct, then we are left with the dynamic argument: class relations have a specific primacy in that dynamics rooted in class relations provide an overall directionality to the trajectory of historical change. If this argument is also rejected, then there is no longer any general justification for Marxist class analysis as such. Without the theory of history and without a general theory of class analysis, it is hard to see what remains as the distinctive theoretical core of Marxism as such.[32]

It would still be possible, of course, to adopt insights from Marxist class analysis, as Giddens enthusiastically does. And it would even be possible to say that in a particular instance, say the analysis of capitalism, class does have a form of primacy as characterized by Marxist theory. But there would no longer be any grounds for class analysis being the core of a general social theory. This is the central challenge posed by Giddens's critique. It is a challenge which should be taken seriously by Marxists.

Notes

1. Macmillan, London 1982, p. 1 (hereafter cc).
2. cc, p. 35.
3. University of California, Berkeley 1979 (hereafter cp).
4. cc, p. 18.
5. *Ibid*, p. 19.
6. For contributions to this debate, cf. Jon Elster, *Ulysses and the Sirens*, Cambridge 1979; and 'Cohen on Marx's Theory of History', *Political Studies* XXVIII:1 (March 1980), pp. 121–28; Joshua Cohen, 'Review of *Karl Marx's Theory of History: a Defense*', *The Journal of Philosophy*, 1982, pp. 253–73; and Andrew Levine and Erik Olin Wright, 'Rationality and Class Struggle', NLR 123 (September/October 1980). Subsequent to the publication of *A Contemporary Critique*, Giddens did directly address this debate in a special issue of the journal *Theory and Society* (July 1982).
7. This assertion, of course, presumes that functional explanations are not in principle illegitimate on philosophical grounds. There are, of course, philosophers of science who reject functional explanations in general, even in biology. Functional explanations in biology generally take the following form: a particular trait of an organism is explained by the functions it fulfills for the organism, i.e. by the beneficial effects it has on the probabilities of the organism surviving (or more precisely, reproducing). Such explanations rest on what G.A. Cohen has called 'dispositional facts' about the organism, namely that it is a property of the organism prior to acquiring the desirable trait that such traits would enhance its survival rate. Such dispositional facts make it possible to reconcile the normal meaning of 'causation' in which causes are temporally prior to effects, with functional explanations, in which effects are taken to explain the structures which produce them. If one rejects such reasoning for biology, then functional explanations of any sort are impermissible in social science. Giddens, however, does not appear to reject functional explanations in biology, since his critique of sociological functionalism is precisely that it treats societies as 'organisms' with 'needs'.
8. Elster, *Ulysses*, p. 31.
9. cc, p. 108.
10. cp, p. 93.
11. cc, p. 50.
12. *Ibid*, p. 108.
13. In addition to the distinction between the type of resource which is most important and the *degree* of space–time distanciation with respect to resources, Giddens makes a number of other typological distinctions in his discussion of social forms. In particular, he distinguishes societies in terms of the degree and forms of asymmetries in the control over allocative and authoritative resources. This provides the basis for Giddens's analyses of despotism, totalitarianism and democracy. Since these distinctions are clearly embedded in the more basic dimensions indicated above, and since they are given less sustained treatment in the book, I will not consider them systematically in the discussion which follows.
14. See, for example, cc, pp. 114–15.
15. Volume I, Harmondsworth 1976, p. 176.
16. cc, p. 107.
17. For an important dissenting view which attempts to build a Marxist concept of class strictly in terms of property relations, see John Roemer, *A General Theory of Exploitation and Class* (Cambridge [Mass.] 1982), and the special issue of *Politics and Society* (11:3, 1982) devoted to a debate on his work.

18. CC, p. 242.

19. This argument rests on the distinction between the 'interests' groups may have and their 'capacities' for realizing those interests (see Wright, *Class, Crisis and the State*, NLB, London 1978, pp. 98–108). Functionalist attempts at reducing nonclass relations to class relations typically involve a translation of nonclass interests into class interests. The 'interest' whites might have in dominating blacks is explained in terms of the 'interests' the bourgeoisie has for dominating workers: the former is functional for the latter. Here, nonclass interests are viewed as radically irreducible to class interests, but the capacities for realizing those interests are dependent upon class relations.

20. CC, p. 21.

21. *Ibid*, p. 23.

22. *Ibid*.

23. In a somewhat different way, the same point can be made concerning biological evolution. For example, there is no implication in evolutionary theory that climatic change universally explains why evolutionary development accelerates to the point of constituting general transitions between evolutionary epochs, even though this might be the basic explanation for certain specific transitions.

24. G. A. Cohen, *Karl Marx's Theory of History: A Defence*, Oxford 1978, p. 41.

25. Cohen's arguments for the tendency for development of the forces of production revolves around the problem of toil (see *ibid*, esp. pp. 302–307).

26. See Levine and Wright (1980).

27. The argument actually needs to be made more complex since the increase in space–time distanciation with respect to authoritative and allocative resources is not in general a unitary process in Giddens's analysis. In contemporary capitalism, for example, it could be argued that capitalists have interests in a reduction in space–time distanciation with respect to authoritative resources – i.e. reducing the planning capacities of the state – precisely because their control over allocative resources tends to be eroded by the expansion of state-centered control over authoritative resources. Capitalists, therefore, use their power, rooted in the inequalities of access to allocative resources, to prevent declines in allocative space–time distanciation by trying to reduce authoritative space–time distanciation. There is still a sticky downward property to distanciation, but it has a more uneven character to it than suggested above.

28. Giddens insists in *A Contemporary Critique* (p. 50) and in *Central Problems in Social Theory* (p. 94) that the concepts of domination and power do not necessarily imply *conflict*, although they may be universally implicated in conflicts. Giddens, in effect, wants to leave the door open for the possibility that there is no opposition of interests between dominators and dominated within power relations: in a Rawlsian sense, inequalities in access to allocative and authoritative resources could conceivably be in the interests of those agents with the least access to those resources. Nevertheless, in more historical terms, inequality of access to resources does generate opposing interests and thus conflicts, and such conflicts can be viewed as providing impulses towards increasing distanciation.

29. To these a third evolutionary principle could be added, as elaborated in the recent work of Jurgen Habermas (*Communication and the Evolution of Society*, Boston 1979): the claim that normative structures also have an autonomous logic of development producing a typology of societies based on their level of moral development (a kind of moral space–time distanciation, where 'meaning' can be seen as an action-relevant resource).

30. See in particular Anthony Cutler, Barry Hindess, Paul Q. Hirst and Athar Hussain, *Marx's Capital and Capitalism Today*, 2 volumes, London 1979 and 1980; and Michael Albert and Robin Hahnel, *Unorthodox Marxism*, Boston 1979.

31. It is interesting in this regard that many of the earliest historical advances in surveillance which Giddens stresses so heavily were advances precisely concerned with the tallying of tribute. See, for example, his discussion of the early forms of writing in Sumer (CC, p. 95). The content of these lists are all centered on allocative resources.

32. Two other ways of defining the distinctiveness of Marxism could be adopted, but neither seems satisfactory. One is to say that Marxism has no distinctive substantive theory at all; its distinctiveness is entirely one of 'method'. This is the stance adopted by Lukacs in his famous essay, 'What is Orthodox Marxism?' (in *History and Class Consciousness*, Cambridge [Mass.] 1971). The other is to say that the distinctiveness of Marxism lies in its political project – socialist revolution, the emancipation of the proletariat, the liberation of humanity (or some related formulation) – rather than in either its specific methodological prescriptions or its substantive propositions. The first of these seems unsatisfactory because when 'Marxist method' is properly specified and its tendencies towards Hegelianism eliminated, then in general its prescriptions are no longer unique to Marxism. And the second is unsatisfactory, for without a substantive theory, there is no reason to believe that this political project is possible, or, perhaps more significantly, that socialism – a particular form of transformation of class relations – is the necessary condition for human emancipation in general. While the political project of Marxism is crucial, it cannot be viewed as an autonomous justification of Marxism outside of the substantive theory to which it is linked.

59

Constructing Social Theory and Constituting Society*

J. Smith and B. Turner

*Source: *Theory, Culture and Society*, vol. 3 (2), 1986, pp. 125–33.

The Constitution of Society, Outline of the Theory of Structuration by Anthony Giddens. Cambridge, Polity Press, 1984, pp 402, £19.50

The Nation-State and Violence, Volume Two of A Contemporary Critique of Historical Materialism by Anthony Giddens. Cambridge, Polity Press, 1985, pp 399, £19.50

Anthony Giddens is now widely regarded as an influential thinker in modern social theory, but his status within the social sciences remains an enigma. For a writer of such widespread influence, it is interesting to observe that his work has not yet been subject to systematic or extensive criticism and evaluation. Indeed the main debate about the character of Giddens' social theory has occurred in the pages of *Theory, Culture & Society*. The other aspect of Giddens' status in the sociology discipline is that there is no clear view as to the precise contribution of his work to the content and development of sociology. Giddens' influence depends partly on his contribution to the exegesis of classical sociology, especially the works of Marx, Durkheim and Weber. We might note however that the solid achievement of *Capitalism and Modern Social Theory* (1971) was not reinforced or extended in subsequent exegesis of the main contributors to classical sociology, since for example Giddens' treatment of Durkheim is slight and conventional (1978). Giddens has also produced some interesting introductions to sociology, but *Sociology, A Brief but Critical Introduction* (1982) could not be regarded as a central or definitive text on sociology as a discipline. While Giddens is noted for his introductions and interpretations of classical sociology, it cannot be said that he has generated an innovative and coherent perspective on classical sociology. There is nothing in Giddens' interpretations of classical sociology which would correspond to Talcott Parsons' notion of the convergence of classical thought on a so-called voluntaristic theory of action (Parsons 1937). He has not produced a systematic analysis of sociological theory which could compare with Jeffrey Alexander's (1982–84) *Theoretical Logic in Sociology.* Giddens' treatment of major sociologists has often assumed a merely introductory character and can be challenged for its compression of complex issues. For example, his account of Durkheim could not be compared with Steven Lukes' *Emile Durkheim, His Life and Work* (1973).

Giddens' impact on the teaching of sociology probably also rests on a number of edited collections on sociological theory which have enjoyed widespread use and appreciation (Giddens and Held 1982; Giddens and Mackenzie 1982). In this respect he has played an important entrepreneurial role in the promotion of social theory in relation to a number of key publishing companies in the British context. In this area the entrepreneurial activity of Giddens possibly resembles that of Durkheim at the turn of the century in relationship to Alcan and the journal *L'Année Sociologique.*

Substantial and enduring reputations in sociology are rarely based merely on introductory texts, interpretive schema and collected editions of essays for the purposes of undergraduate courses. A substantial reputation may be delayed by lack of public scrutiny as in the case of Norbert Elias whose massive contribution to the cultural sociology of Western civilisations has only recently received appropriate evaluation. Few sociologists have had the pleasure of a substantial reputation and appreciation during their own lifetimes; academic acclaim usually follows retirement and death, as in the case of Benjamin Nelson. An enduring contribution in sociology has to be organised around a new perspective, generating explanatory frameworks and new conceptual schemes which develop research and theory along new and influential lines. Thus the stature of Parsons depends in part on the development of an action-system framework which provided theoretical coherence to a diversity of studies in American sociology in the 1950s and 1960s. Similarly the importance of Weber rests to some extent on the application of interpretive sociology to a wide variety of issues in order to grasp the significance of the emergence of rational industrial societies. Alternatively a reputation might be grounded in a major empirical research project which transforms some existing assumptions within a discipline and thereby opens up whole new areas of inquiry and theorisation. The field work of Malinowski or Evans-Pritchard would be examples of empirical inquiry which transformed not only anthropological method but the whole per- spective on religious ritual in human societies. One obvious feature of Giddens' sociology is the absence of a systematic empirical inquiry illustrating or developing the theory of structuration. The empirical content of Giddens' sociology is typically second-order, providing illustrative features for his conceptual elaboration of sociology.

It is over the issue of theoretical contribution that there is a great uncertainty and division amongst both the critics and admirers of Anthony Giddens. Giddens has been criticised for his analytical eclecticism (Hirst 1982), for his failure to solve the deep lying problems of agency and structure

(Urry 1982) and for his inability to solve the issue of time and space in social theory (Gross 1982; Ashley 1982). These earlier criticisms of Giddens amounted to the position that Giddens' social theory held no promise of replacing historical materialism in any way that could be regarded as satisfactory. In a more recent commentary on Giddens, McLellan has suggested that Giddens' terminological and conceptual contribution to sociological theory turns out to be largely metaphorical and analogical rather than substantial. That is, Giddens has provided a set of neologisms (time–space edges, social distanciation, presence and storage capacity) which is interesting but not necessarily important in extending the scope of real social analysis; they do not appear to offer distinctive sociological propositions (McLellan 1984). While these criticisms of Giddens were quite common, the publication of *The Constitution of Society* and *The Nation-State and Violence* had been welcomed by many as the solution to issues raised in both classical sociology and Giddens' version of social theory. These studies are seen to be the final synthesis of the structuration theory providing a coherence to Giddens' work as a whole and demonstrating the fruitfulness of his theoretical position for the analysis of empirical social processes. Indeed these books have been welcomed as the most important example of grand sociological theory in the past decade. Other writers have suggested that the new publications by Giddens silence previous criticism and establish his reputation on an unambiguous and secure footing. In this review we take the opposite position, namely that these two volumes merely compound the existing range of problems in Giddens' theory and are largely reiterative in simply reworking well known issues in the social theory of Giddens. *The Constitution of Society* has the leading hallmark of his previous work (scope, generality and diversity), but it also brings out the existing confusion concerning the status of structuration theory. Much of *The Nation-State and Violence* is a summary of his existing views on the character of contemporary capitalism.

Although there is much disagreement as to the value and character of Giddens' social theory, there is at least some agreement that his sociology is important because it has provided a modern defence of the notion of agency and knowledgeability of human agents. The core of Giddens' contribution to social theory appears to lie therefore in the notion of structuration – a contribution which is signified in the sub-title of the new volume. Although Giddens' view of the relationship between agency and structure has been criticised (Dallmayr 1982; Urry 1982), there is a general consensus that the idea of structuration is an original contribution to the development of a key area of sociology and that the theory of structuration represents Giddens' most important and coherent contribution to modern social theory. Under the notion of structuration, Giddens has made a spirited defence of certain components of classical sociology against modern forms of structuralism which emphasise the determination of the individual by structure and he has also used structuration as a critique of certain aspects of neo-Nietzschean sociology (Giddens 1982). The structuration argument has also been mobilised by Giddens to challenge the deterministic assumptions of some theories of modern industrial sociology, for example the uni-dimensional emphasis on the determination of workers by the process of de-skilling (Giddens and Mackenzie 1982). Against this existing consensus, we will show that Giddens' theory of structuration is untenable as ontology and vague as sociology. We also argue that structuration incorporates much common sense thought which has been under-developed from a theoretical point of view. Thus no satisfactory contribution has been presented to the action/structure dilemma by Giddens' theory of structuration. We argue that *The Constitution of Society* goes no way towards resolving these problems but simply restates them with further empirical illustration.

To understand Giddens' theory of structuration, we need to understand how he conceives of the ontology of societies. Unlike Bhaskar's position, with which Giddens' theory of structuration has been compared, Giddens carefully distinguishes between *societies* and *social structures*. Societies are analysable by means of the notion of a *social system*. Social systems for Giddens are not particulars or entities, but are reproduced relationships between either individual actors or collectivities, or between both, throughout "time–space" (Knorr-Cetina and Cicourel 1981). Thus unlike Bhaskar (1979), Giddens does not take social systems to be structures, but rather social systems have structural properties and relationships. Structures are recursively organised generative rules and resources. The modes through which social systems are reproduced by agents via the use of such generative rules and resources constitute the structuration of a social system. Social systems as such are structured only in and through their continual reproduction in day-to-day social life: this is Giddens' notion of the *duality of structure*. As he puts it, "social structures are both constituted by human agency, and yet at the same time are the very *medium* of this constitution" (Giddens 1976, p 121). In the new study, Giddens renders this notion in the following statement that "the constitution of agents and structures are not two independently given sets of phenomena, a dualism, but represent a duality. According to the notion of the duality of structure, the structural properties of social systems are both medium and outcome of the practices they recursively organise" (Giddens 1984, p 25). The duality of structure is seen in the case of one social entity, human language. Language exists as syntactical and semantical structures only insofar as there are syntactical and semantical linguistic rules. The rules of syntax "govern" the reproduction of "like elements", and yet at the same time, the rules of syntax generate the totality of speech acts which thereby constitute language: "it is this dual aspect of structure as both inferred from observation of human doings, and yet also operating as a medium whereby those doings are made possible, that has to be grasped through the notions of structuration and reproduction" (Giddens 1976, p 122). In the new study the same use is made of language and language rules to illustrate the idea of a duality of structure.

The notion of the duality of structure seems to us to involve a vitiating circularity. According to Giddens, social structures are constituted by human agency as well as simultaneously being the medium of such constitution. We will show that action is taken as a (prior) necessary condition for structure and structure as a (prior) necessary condition for action, so that we are forced to turn in an impossible circle. Now social structures are said to be a medium of their constitution or construction, but Giddens nowhere tells us that he is giving terms such as "medium" and "constitution" a theoretical sense which is substantially different from their natural language sense; so we assume in what follows that he is using these terms in their natural language sense. So let us ask what is involved in x being a medium for y to occur. In pre-relativistic physics, the aether was thought to be a medium for the propagation of electromagnetic radiation. This aether pre-existed the propagation of the waves. Air and other material substances are said to be a medium for the propagation of sound. Air certainly can pre-exist the occurrence of a particular sound. Now if social structures are also a medium for the propagation of social action, then they must also pre-exist occurrence of any particular social action. Giddens agrees with Wittgenstein that social actions are individuated by reference to contexts which are often defined by social structures or "forms of life" (Giddens 1976). In the new study Giddens attempts to give an account of the notion of seriality in encounters through the use of Wittgenstein's notion of forms of life which Giddens associates with the notions of keying and management in Goffman's sociology of everyday life (Giddens 1984, p 74). If this is so then for any individuation to occur, the context or medium must be predefined. On the other hand, that the context or medium is itself constituted by social action is a basic proposition of the notion of the duality of structure. We fall into a vicious circle: to have action we must first have structure, but to have structure we must first have action. The metaphor of a "medium" presents us with no other option. Despite the extensive discussion of structuration in the first section of the new study, these basic problems of circularity have not been resolved.

This conceptual antinomy is presented in the view of causality of Harré (Harré 1970; Smith 1972). Giddens is very much in debt to the post-positivist philosophy of science of Harré, although his acknowledgements of this debt are parsimonious. Bhaskar has also accepted that social structures do not exist independently of the activities they govern, so that societies exist only in their effects. If we reject a Humean ontology of events, as Bhaskar and Giddens believe we should, causal relationships must be impossible, since one of the relata of the causal relationship is missing and therefore the concept is ill-defined. If we are correct in this criticism, then Giddens' theory of structuration is undermined because as a matter of logic it can be shown to be conceptually untenable. In our opinion the theory of structuration can therefore have no positive value and should be discarded.

We have criticised Giddens' solution to one of the central problems of social theory (the action–structure dilemma) from the side of structure. Critical comments will now be made on Giddens' theory of action. In the history of sociological theory there has been considerable debate around such notions as "social institution", "social system" and "social structure" (Giddens 1979; Giddens 1982, p 207 ff). There has also been an endless debate about the notion of "action" and "agency" (Dawe 1978). Furthermore, the relationship between agency and structure has been the focus of a continuing tradition of analysis. We have suggested that Giddens' notion of structuration does not help solve these somewhat separate dimensions of the agency–structure dilemma. Briefly there are three positions with respect to the agency–structure question. Some sociological theories take up a position which gives primacy to structure in determining or enabling action; structural Marxism in the work of Louis Althusser would be an illustration. Other positions such as methodological individualism and ethnomethodology have given centrality to the notion of individual action as bringing about significant differences in social relations. The social is brought about by the continuous interaction of social individuals in their everyday exchanges (Wallace 1969). The majority of sociological theories either by design or accident collapse towards the middle, where both structure and agency are seen to be causally significant. People create social relations in an ongoing fashion, but in turn these social relations react back upon the agents to limit or shape their agency (Berger and Luckmann 1967). The problem with these positions, including that of Giddens, is that very few theories systematically ask the question: what or who is the agent in agency? That is, there is a taken-for-granted assumption that, while agency and structure may be conceptually problematic, whatever constitutes the agent is relatively certain. While Giddens has been concerned with the problem of the subject (Giddens 1979), he has not strenuously pursued the question of the constitution of the agent. In short, his assumptions about the capability and knowledgeability of the subject are based on a common sense view that there is an equation between the human subject and the agent. Giddens' previous work incorporated unwittingly a large dosage of methodological individualism into the debate about structuration because in the last analysis the agent in Giddens' notion of agency is the real empirical human subject. However, in recent social theory and philosophy, what constitutes the subject is extremely problematic.

One important contribution from modern structuralism and discourse analysis, especially in the work of Michel Foucault, has been to raise questions about Cartesian dualism and it is interesting that Giddens (1982) has been especially critical of this development in social theory, while not properly recognising its contribution to the analysis of the human subject. It may be that Giddens' rejection of writers like Foucault is a response to the pessimistic and deterministic interpretation of the body and agent in such studies as *The History of Sexuality*. When Giddens talks about agency, he is essentially thinking about the individual exercising resistance through knowledge and action, but this is a somewhat primitive notion of both agent and agency. Theories of agency and resistance will have to address themselves more significantly to the question of human embodiment and the phenomenology of embodied experience since one aspect of human agency is the resistance of the embodied person to power and social constraint. An elaborated notion of resistance would have to consider the individual as empowered, embodied and enselfed. This more elaborate notion of agency and resistance would thus draw upon the developing tradition of phenomenology and existentialism where a sophisticated view of conscious embodiment has been developed in the French and German traditions. The irony is that Giddens, at least in his previous publications, appeared to accept implicitly a Cartesian dualism which failed to address itself to the significance of the human body in the debate about agency (Smith 1984; Turner 1984). Despite his interest in the philosophy of Heidegger, Giddens has not developed an adequate hermeneutic of being. Giddens' notion of action and resistance appears to be essentially cerebral; it is not able to grasp the character of our embodied resistance. We need a theory of how social structures operate on bodies and how resistance is worked out against knowledge and power through the "lived body" (Lash 1984).

There are a number of points at which Giddens in *The Constitution of Society* promises to provide a theory of the body as a significant contribution to the modern analysis of agency through the theory of structuration. For example, there is a discussion of the body and time where Giddens (1984, pp 34–37) tells us that the body is "the locus of the self" and also that there is an apparent contradiction between the *durée* of daily life and of biological time. Daily life is in "reversible time"; the life of the individual is irreversible. The reason for this contradiction, which is never fully given by Giddens, is that because of the body, individual life must be being-towards-death. Further, there is an obvious interaction between "reversible time" and "irreversible time"; try as we may, the cycle of the body ultimately grinds on the *durée* of daily life in death. Apart from these brief comments, Giddens gives no theory of embodiment and has in fact no theory of the agent.

The body appears against in Giddens (1984, pp 174–179) work in the discussion of constraint where he informs us that the physical capacities of the human body place a limitation upon the options open to the agent. However, this is a uni-dimensional view of the body since we need a theory which will show how the body is simultaneously enabling and constraining. We experience our bodies as phenomena which we have but also as phenomena which we do. We need our bodies as an environment by which to experience our environment and so it is never simply the case that the body is constraining. These arguments were of course developed quite early in social anthropology by Marcel Mauss under the notion of body techniques (Mauss

1979). The complexity of the notion of the body in recent social theory was brilliantly illustrated by Scott Lash's (1984) commentary on the "genealogy and the body". This tantalising commentary on the body in *The Constitution of Society* is typical of Giddens' work as a whole, namely that it often appears to be a collection of preparatory notes rather than a systematically worked out position. A collection of comments on the body will not constitute a theory of embodiment which is a necessary component of any theory of the agent and therefore an essential basis for a theory of structuration. Having been critical of the Nietzsche–Foucault fashion in sociology, Giddens appears to have adopted wholesale the Foucaultian notions of surveillance (of populations and bodies) as an aspect of pacification in *The Nation-State and Violence*.

Of course this gap in Giddens' treatment of the agent is not peculiar to Giddens' sociology, since few sociologists have addressed themselves to the problem of what constitutes the agent in the notion of agency and as a result most sociologists are based upon a common-sense assumption about the human being equalling the agent. This assumption has on occasion been questioned as when, for example, Hirst (1979) in criticising Marxist theories of law noted that in late capitalism there is no necessary correspondence between the human person, the legal subject and the economic agent. This raises important questions about whether, for example, economic corporations are agents, whether social classes exercise agency, whether women in pre-modern societies are agents and finally whether embryos are agents. It is obvious that this has been the subject of very long philosophical enquiries, but the issues have not been resolved adequately inside sociology. This is somewhat paradoxical given the long debate over questions of methodo-logical individualism versus collectivism. Giddens does not address himself systematically to these issues and it is not clear from his account of structuration as to whether social classes might be agents exercising agency. There are obviously difficulties with the notion that social classes are knowledgeable in the same sense that one might say an individual human being is knowledgeable. Our argument is that the theory of structuration does not answer these questions and to some extent does not even address them, despite Giddens' interest in the legacy of methodological individualism versus holism.

We have argued that *The Constitution of Society* does not provide a significant addition to Giddens' existing approach to structuration which remains logically confused and under-developed with respect to the notion of the agent. However, a seemingly new concept is added to the theory of structuration in the concept of structural principles (Giddens 1984, pp 180–185). Despite Giddens' (1984, pp 181–182) discussion of the classifi-cation of societies, structural principles turn out to be no more than "principles of organisation of societal totalities" (1984, p 185). Structural principles cannot explain why various social totalities are as they are, because to do so must be to explain the genesis of the organisation of these totalities themselves – mere internal structural principles do not account for the genesis of totality. In any case this concept says very little and its application to historical study is doubtful.

The main thrust of Giddens' work is therefore to defend the notion of effective agency against various forms of deterministic structural theory which would render the human agent knowledgeless and incapable of significant action. Although we would applaud this objective, much needs to be done within Giddens' idea of structuration before it can be made fully useful in the canon of modern sociology. We have already indicated that a full theory of agency would require a theory of embodiment and furthermore we would suggest that Giddens' emphasis on knowledgeability has to be supported by a fully fledged theory of the limitations of ideology. Although the critique of ideology played some minor role in Giddens' (1979, 1981) earlier publications the problem of ideology is strangely absent from *The Constitution of Society*. In order to defend the idea of knowledgeability of the actor, it is necessary to show clearly how ideological incorporation is limited and what grounds there are for believing that the idea of "false consciousness" is inappropriate in sociological research. Giddens appears to take for granted the limitations of ideological distortion and incorporation but does not provide the general theory by which that position could be secured. If *The Constitution of Society* is intended as a general theory of structuration then it would be important, indeed necessary, to provide a specific theory of ideology since there is a long tradition in both Marxism and sociology which would see ideology as limiting or undermining knowledgeability.   .

In *The Nation-State and Violence*, the issues of structuration, agency and knowledge are unimportant. Instead, this new volume follows through a number of themes in Giddens' analysis of space, power and the state (Giddens 1981 and 1984). The relationship between this volume and the critique of historical materialism often appears to be largely accidental; that is, the primary purpose of this study does not appear to be to demolish Marxism and provide a valid alternative. The idea of critique appears more as a pretext to write about the transformation of the state through three stages: absolutism, nation-states and the rise of the administered society. In the course of this inquiry, Giddens takes us over a lot of familiar territory from his previous exposition: the city and countryside (Giddens 1982 and 1984); time and space (Giddens 1981 and 1984); capitalism, industrial society and socialism (Giddens 1971, 1973, 1981 and 1984); and the character of the modern state and nationalism (Giddens 1978, 1981, 1982a and 1984). As a result, the new volume on the state appears to be repetitious.

Although this volume is impressive in terms of its scope and moral seriousness, it is frustrating in a number of key areas. Giddens wants to criticise the classical tradition in sociology (primarily Marx, Weber and Durkheim) because it neglected issues which have become central to modern society; the industrialisation of war, the threat of global violence and the decline of liberal-democratic policies in conjunction with the emergence of panoptic surveillance. As a broad generalisation this criticism may have some validity, but to sustain it we are forced to do considerable injustice to the classical legacy of sociology. Since Giddens is recognised as a leading commentator on sociological theory, these sweeping claims are less than inspiring. A more complex view of the history of sociological thought in relation to militarism, war, violence and the state would have to consider the writing of Jacques Novicow, Ludwig Gumplowicz, Franz Oppenheimer, Friedrich Engels and the Austro-Marxists. In contemporary social thought, Giddens does not reflect upon the contributions of C Wright Mills (*The Causes of World War III*) and Barrington Moore (*Reflections on the Causes of Human Misery*). Although Giddens discusses the impact of war on the growth of citizenship, he neglects much of the important literature on modern politics and war (which has been considered in, for example, D Gallie, *Social Inequality and Class Radicalism in France and Britain*). The real problem with Giddens' exegesis is, however, his curious treatment of Weber.

While Giddens makes extensive use of Weber, he does not believe that Weber provided an adequate analysis or basis for a sociology of war, violence and militarism. Giddens suggests that the Nietzschean element in Weber gave rise to a view of violence as part of the human condition, but this influence did not produce the framework for a social theory of the state and violence. This interpretation is of course somewhat dubious (Eden 1983; Strong 1975; Turner 1982). In fact, the issue of military organisation, the state and violence was very central to Weber's sociology; we can argue that his sociology was about the relationship between the ownership of the means of production and the means of violence. This contrast was essential to his discussion of feudalism and prebendalism (Turner 1981, p 203 ff). In specific terms, Giddens wants to make a close connection between the history of warfare and the emergence of citizenship within the boundaries of the nation-state. In the chapter on citizenship in his *General Economic History*, Weber argued that the growth of citizenship was connected with the peculiar features of the western city and the nature of military discipline, especially the democratic impact of an organised infantry. Finally, Giddens wants to criticise T H Marshall for treating citizenship in an evolutionary framework and for neglecting the impact of war on citizenship rights. Unfortunately, Giddens neglects to discuss two of Marshall's most important books (*Social Policy* and *The Right to Welfare*) where Marshall argued that British social policy and the growth of welfare rights could not be understood without a grasp of the impact of total war on welfare. This viewpoint laid the basis for the work of R Titmuss on war and welfare.

We have called into question Giddens' exegesis of various traditions in sociological theory, but the most significant gap in *The Nation-State and Violence* is the scant consideration of Norbert Elias. Giddens' general thesis is that modern societies have transformed the relationship between city and countryside, pacified the internal population and created an extensive machinery of surveillance. These pacified communities, however, are situated in a global context of total violence which is in turn connected with an industrialisation of war. The major theorist of surveillance, pacification and the civilisation of violence is of course Elias who is mentioned once on page 195. We can see Elias' work as precisely the study of the evolution of restraint on violence and men-at-arms. In addition, Elias has offered a powerful interpretation of the spectacle of sport in a social system based on interpersonal restraint (Dunning 1971). An explanation of the cultural significance of violent sport would have been an important theoretical and empirical addition to Giddens' most recent study.

So far we have addressed a number of theoretical and exegetical issues in Giddens' sociological publications. We have not asked whether his account of modern societies is valid. The empirical evidence would appear to call into question his perspective on modern societies. Although he recognises the problem of political violence, he does not provide an adequate account of the nature of violence in capitalist democracies; it is difficult to reconcile urban terrorism and movements for regional and national autonomy (in Northern Ireland, Spain, Italy and Germany) with his views on surveillance and internal pacification. However, the major issue for Giddens would be the United States of America, where, because of constitutional arrangements for a free militia, the population remains armed for self-defence. The USA is clearly a nation-state with undisputed boundaries, but it might be difficult to argue that the population is pacified and de-militarised. The irony is that the USA is possibly the only modern democracy in which the ownership of the means of violence is entirely socialised.

In sociology it is valuable to make a distinction between significant and influential theory. The former would include theories that open up new theoretical terrain and revolutionise sociological research and theory by identifying and partly solving new problems. Significant social theory grows out of a radical transformation of paradigms and/or the establishment of new research areas which generate a range of innovative issues and questions. Influential theories by contrast are theories which are well known within a scholarly community and are influential in the sense of directing students towards well rehearsed issues and well established problems. Influential theory summarises concepts and problems rather than generating paradigms. Our argument is that *The Constitution of Society* summarises Giddens' existing contribution to the theory of structuration rather than developing or elaborating the theme of structuration. Although in this new study Giddens draws upon a wide range of empirical issues in sociology, Marxism and modern geography, he does not develop an essentially new perspective. *The Nation-State and Violence* does not adequately reflect the complexity of sociological studies of violence; it does not provide a valid treatment of empirical issues in modern politics; it is a work of synthesis. Giddens clearly has a great facility for synthesis but the effect is to reaffirm a position he has taken in many previous publications rather than to extend his or other people's theoretical perspective. Giddens' sociology is often based upon the development of metaphors and neologisms which are clever rather than significant. Since in our view structuration is neither wholly original or wholly successful, we would have to conclude regretfully that Giddens' contribution to social theory so far is influential without being significant.

References

Alexander J C (1982–84), *Theoretical Logic in Sociology*, London: Routledge and Kegan Paul

Ashley D (1982), 'Historical Materialism and Social Evolutionism', *Theory, Culture & Society*, 1, 2, pp 89–92

Bhaskar R (1979), *The Possibility of Naturalism*, Sussex: Harvester Press

Dallmayr F (1982), The Theory of Structuration: A Critique in Anthony Giddens, *Profiles and Critiques in Social Theory*, London: Macmillan, pp 18–25

Dawe A (1978), Theories of Social Action in Tom Bottomore and Robert Nisbet (eds), *A History of Sociological Analysis*, pp 362–417

Dunning E (ed 1971), *The Sociology of Sport*, London: Cass

Eden R (1983), *Political Leadership and Nihilism, a study of Weber and Nietzsche*, Tampa: University Presses of Florida

Giddens A (1971), *Capitalism and Modern Social Theory*, Cambridge: Cambridge University Press

Giddens A (1973), *The Class Structure of the Advanced Societies*, London: Hutchinson

Giddens A (1976), *New Rules of Sociological Method*, London: Hutchinson

Giddens A (1977), *Studies in Social and Political Theory*, London: Hutchinson

Giddens A (1978), *Durkheim*, London: Fontana

Giddens A (1979), *Central Problems in Social Theory: Action, Structure and Contradiction in Social Analysis*, London: Macmillan

Giddens A (1981), *A Contemporary Critique of Historical Materialism*, London: Macmillan

Giddens A (1982a), *Sociology, A Brief But Critical Introduction*, London: Macmillan

Giddens A (1982b), *Profiles and Critiques in Social Theory*, London: Macmillan

Giddens A and Held D (eds 1982), *Classes, Power and Conflict, Classical and Contemporary Debates*, London: Macmillan

Giddens A and Mackenzie G (eds 1982), *Social Class and the Division of Labour*, Cambridge: Cambridge University Press

Giddens A (1984), *The Constitution of Society*, Cambridge: Polity Press

Giddens A (1985), *The Nation-State and Violence*, Cambridge: Polity Press

Gross D (1982), Time–Space Relations in Giddens' Social Theory, *Theory, Culture & Society*, 1, 2, pp 83–88

Harré R (1970), *The Principles of Scientific Thinking*, London: Macmillan

Hirst P (1979), *On Law and Ideology*, London: Macmillan

Hirst P (1982), The Social Theory of Anthony Giddens: A New Syncretism?, *Theory, Culture & Society*, 1, 2, pp 78–82

Knorr-Cetina K and Cicourel A V (eds 1981), *Advances in Social Theory and Methodology*, London: Routledge and Kegan Paul

Lash S (1984), Genealogy and the Body: Foucault/Deleuze/Nietzsche, *Theory, Culture & Society*, 2, 2, pp 1–18

Luke S (1973), *Emile Durkheim: His Life and Work*, London: Allen Lane

Mauss M (1979), *Sociology and Psychology*, Essays by Marcel Mauss, London: Routledge and Kegan Paul

McLellan G (1984), Critical or Positive Theory? A Comment on the Status of Anthony Giddens' Social Theory, *Theory, Culture & Society*, 2, 3, pp 123–129

Parsons T (1937), *The Structure of Social Action*, New York: Free Press

Smith J W (1982), A Reply to Frankel's Criticism of Harre's Theory of Causality, *Philosophy of Science*, 49, pp 282–289

Smith J W (1984), *Reductionism and Cultural Being*, The Hague: Nijhoff

Strong T B (1975), *Friedrich Nietzsche and the Politics of Transfiguration*, Berkeley: University of California Press

Turner B S (1982), Nietzsche, Weber and the devaluation of politics; the problem of state legitimacy, *The Sociological Review*, 30, 3, pp 367–391

Turner B S (1984), *The Body and Society, Explorations in Social Theory*, Oxford: Basil Blackwell

Urry J (1982), Duality of Structure: some critical issues, *Theory, Culture & Society*, 1, 2, pp 100–106

Wallace W L (1969), *Sociological Theory, An Introduction*, London: Heinemann

60

Giddens' Golden Gloves*

R. Friedland

*Source: *Contemporary Society*, vol. 16, 1987, pp. 40–42.

The Nation-State and Violence: Vol. 2 of a Contemporary Critique of Historical Materialism, by Anthony Giddens. Berkeley: University of California Press, 1985. 399 pp. $35.00 cloth.

This is Giddens' second bout with Marx. If Karl is the principal contender, Tony uses the occasion to square off with Immanuel, swipe at Michel, and even gently rebuke his real trainer, Emile. Or is it Max? I can't tell. The last bell has just rung. The judges are counting points. And I don't know about you, but I'm sweating like a pig.

The Punches

Contrary to the evolutionary monism of historical materialism, Giddens argues that the development of capitalism, industrialism, and the nation-state each shape each other's fortunes in a symbiotic, historically contingent fashion. Each has its own independent logic and cannot be reduced to the other.

Modernity is marked by distanciation, the stretching of social practices across time and space. The accumulation of administrative, and particularly state, power is the dominant force driving distanciation. The rising administrative power of the state derives from its capacities both to code information and to supervise activity. As a result, the state can increasingly control the timing and the spacing of human activity. Writing, with its decontextualization of communication and its fixity across time and space, emerged out of administrative notation. The walled city, the preeminent "power container" of precapitalist society, derived from state power, not economic exchange. So too, its demise follows from the development of artillery, which reduced its strategic importance and thereby allowed monarchs to cede it increased administrative autonomy, paving the way for capitalist expansion. The diffusion of road and rail networks, telegraphy, aviation, and finally computers were all driven by the requisites of state power, particularly warfare. Innovations in military technology drove civilian technological change much more than the reverse.

Giddens distinguishes between allocative resources, or control over material facilities, and authoritative resources, control over human beings. Marxists, he argues, derive the latter from the former, power from class. It is not just the commodification of labor power, a systemic outcome of dispossession from the means of production, that makes the development of the productive forces possible. Surveillance in the workplace is equally important. Marxists are bereft of a theory of organization, of workplace surveillance. Ultimately, he argues, the concentration of allocative resources depends upon authoritative resources. And if this is so, then the productive forces don't develop endogenously out of capitalism alone.

The development of capitalism, with its extrusion of violence from the labor contract, depended upon the emergence of a centralized state capable of pacifying the population, enforcing a calculable law subject to neither the caprice of kings nor noble exemption. This was accomplished through the expanding administrative power of absolutist states in the sixteenth and seventeenth centuries, driven in large part by the exigencies of changing modes of warfare. Demands for resources for war led the state progressively to monetize the economy and stimulate its growth, to extract monetary resources, and to secure mass conscription. The armies grew larger, war became ever more total, and the mass graves became deeper. When the battlefields cleared, only those states that controlled the entire population in a continuous territory remained. If the emergence of the "strong" modern state made capitalism possible, it cannot, Giddens insists, be explained by the external predations made necessary by that self-same capitalism.

It is fanciful, he argues, to suggest that class conflict drove precapitalist history. Class conflict was uncommon, because the vast bulk of producers were free from the surveillance of the dominant class in production or of the state in community governance. The distance – geographical, social, symbolic – between the peasantry and the dominant class was too vast, primarily because the state did not control the territory over which it ruled. As a result, military forces were used both for internal control and external conquest. States had frontiers, not borders. Only the modern state has been able to monopolize violence over its territorial domain, and only when that monopoly was achieved was it able to create a "private" civil society, and to bring into existence the sociologists' untheorized object – society.

By replacing structuralism with structuration, based upon the subject as agent whose knowledge is necessary for the reproduction of social systems, Giddens provides an opening for integration of structural and interpretative approaches. Actors achieve structure in a self-aware, or reflexive, manner in light of two kinds of knowledge they possess – both tacit "practical consciousness" and explicitly articulated "discursive knowledge." In this volume, the reflexivity of social practice is not revealed through the ethnomethodologists' paradigmatic conversations, but through the emergence of nation states that periodically cast a shadow of death across the world and nationalist ideologies that mobilize millions willing to sacrifice all for the great leader.

The state is an organization that, like others in its genus, reflexively uses knowledge about the conditions of its reproduction in order to modify them. The nation state has technical preconditions, such as the possibilities of coding, storage, and transmittal of information that expand the scope of surveillance and permit the administrative unity of a territorial domain. However, the formation of a modern state is not simply a matter of choreography of the movements of its population. On the contrary, the collection of information involves the creation of social categories – citizen, deviant, conscript, mad, poor, divorced, criminal – constitutive of the phenomenon to which the information pertains. And expansion of state surveillance is impossible without mass knowledge of the conceptual apparatus of the sovereign state, a symbolic order not only necessary to its power but integral to its existence.

Thus expansion of participation in the discursive world of the dominant class, a prerequisite for class struggle, depends upon the extension of state power which – at the same time that it creates an urbanized citizenry into whose most private life it increasingly intervenes – becomes increasingly vulnerable to the vagaries of its faith and compliance. Thus the mechanization of communication opened up a discursive arena at the same time it expanded the power of the state. The emergence of official statistics, mass media, and a public are simultaneous developments. Civil rights evolve out of the impersonality of the state's administrative, and particularly police, powers, not as "bourgeois" rights outside it. Nationalism is predicated upon the territorial "historicity" of the Western nation state, its "controlled use of reflection upon history as a means of changing history" (212).

Giddens argues that the formation of the state cannot be understood solely as an endogenous process. Its organizational structure is shaped by a body of discursive knowledge – first balance of power and later sovereignty – that states use to regulate the relationship between them. The sovereignty of the nation state, its universal equivalence and unit character, is derived not only from endogenous processes but from the progressively widening interaction of several states around this discourse. The discourse constitutes the emerging state, it does not simply describe it. Absolutist France was the first state to play a directive role in Europe without becoming an empire and the first to develop a diplomatic corps. That diplomacy, that "reflexive monitoring" of the conditions of state reproduction, did not undermine the sovereignty of the state. It constituted it. Contrary to those who argue that inter-state inter-dependencies regulated through diplomacy, modern warfare, sphere of influence, and international organizations erode state sovereignty, Giddens contends that national sovereignty is achieved and universalized through these cross-national ties. The ruling ideas are not those of the ruling class; they are the ideas of rule.

A cut is opening over Karl's left eye. There are, Tony insists, no laws of motion, only the structural affinities of institutional forms, contingently distributed in time and space. Thus capitalism became the dominant world mode of production because industrialization of warfare took place first in nations that were capitalist. The nation state emerged because of the superior military power of the world region where it was born relative to the imperial powers hegemonic elsewhere. The contingent outcomes of military contest shaped the emergence, structure, and diffusion of institutional forms.

The Points

The fight's over. It was a clean match, no rabbit punches. Tony won on points. Karl was on the ropes for rounds at a time. He should have retired long ago. You should see it for yourself, but I've got some commentary of my own.

Despite Giddens' disclaimers about the dialectic of control, that to be human is to have power, the historical panorama is dominated by agents of the state – policemen, scribes, soldiers, kings – whose expanding means of surveillance first crush and then codify a malleable population. Indeed, the human subject is barely visible. While Giddens argues that social movements arise in the "arenas of historicity" produced by the organizational structures they oppose, he never specifies the conditions under which they emerge or are successful.

This problem is related to his insistence that routinization by tacitly knowledgeable agents is the key to reproduction of "institutionalized practices." Thus the conditions necessary for state "governability" depend not on legitimacy or the "justifiability of its policies," but on mass acceptance of the daily routines shaped by administrative power (322). In this volume, only the disruption of daily life, the rupture of routine, makes the masses available for new symbols of solidarity, including nationalism. In short, ordinary people live in a behaviorist world where the discursive knowledge of elites is appropriated as practical consciousness. Without discursive knowledge, ordinary people cannot make history. Given the centrality of social move-ments for the transformation of the meanings of organizational historicity, an adequate social theory must comprehend why and how dominant symbols are refashioned or challenged.

Giddens cannot analyze conflict within institutions in part because of his view of the relationships between them. Conflicts and contradictions between institutions are absent from an analysis dominated by the symbiotic com-plementarities of industrial capitalism and nation-state formation. The conditions for action lie in part in those interinstitutional contradictions. But equally important, Giddens' account is institutionally restrictive. Neither family nor religion is even mentioned in his explanation of the genesis of these institutional forms.

Surely class conflict in capitalism derives not simply from the efforts of workers to regain control of the work place, but from families whose orientation to use-value periodically comes into conflict with the commodification of capitalism. Religion penetrates deeply into daily life, and as he himself acknowledges, this is nowhere more transparent than in Christianity. So too the peculiar association between Protestantism and national parliamentary democracies lies in part in the theology of election with its emphasis on voluntary choice and the unmediated individual relationship to God.

If, as Giddens argues, the segregation of sexuality and death is the requisite of bureaucratic routine, then marginalizing religion and family, which construct the discourse that makes them meaningful, is inadmissible. If regression to prepubertal object identification provides the template for mass allegiance to an authoritarian leader, then the family must be brought to the center of the ring. Ontological security derives not simply, as Giddens seems to emphasize, from the routines of market and state, but from the symbolic and deeply existential worlds constructed in these two institutions.

Giddens points to the discursive construction of territorial sovereignty and national historicity. Nonetheless, time and space are primarily analyzed via distanciation, that is as technical constraints of distance decay or as enabling locations. The interpretative dimension is largely lost. Here the hand of the Swedish geographer Hägerstrand weighs heavily. Time and space are not just resources to be used, but have different qualities depending on the historically specific institutions through whose discourse they are understood. The development of new institutional structures which permit new forms of control over the timing and spacing of human activity are bound up with new interpretative frames by which time and space are understood. These interpretative frames, which are again as central to the logic of kinship and religion as to state and capitalism, must be integrated into the analysis in order to understand the historically variable pattern of distanciation.

Finally, although Tony throws a mean uppercut, he jumps around the ring quite a lot. Beyond the conceptual profusion (modes of domination, modes of control, rule, power, authoritative resources, administrative power – all that by p. 19), there is a turgidity to the prose. Part of the problem is that the fellow has a global agenda, and with his productivity, the internal referentiality is building geometrically. Part of it is that he doesn't like substantive footnotes. Part of it is that he is a master of distanciation himself, jumping over centuries and civilizations by the paragraph. And part of it is that he works through crescive iterations, where not only does each of the volumes build upon and modify those that come before, but unfortunately so do the chapters. We have to work to find out how smart he is.

Like most of his North American audience, I have left Giddens' public lectures mesmerized by their coherence, elegant phrasing, and perfect timing. And all this without a shred of paper in front of him and with the customary British elocution. If he wrote more as he speaks than as he thinks, he would, in the words of that other great pugilist, "float like a butterfly, sting like a bee."

61

Review of *The Nation-State and Violence**

T. Skocpol

*Source: *Social Forces*, vol. 66 (1), 1987, pp. 294–96.

The Nation-State and Violence: Volume Two of a Contemporary Critique of Historical Materialism. By Anthony Giddens. University of California Press, 1985. 399 pp. $35.00

A visitor to Highgate Cemetery in London will find Karl Marx and Herbert Spencer lying just across a path from one another. Perhaps, therefore, it is fitting that Britain's grandest sociological theorist of today has written this volume in critical dialogue with certain metahistorical presumptions shared by the revolutionary-socialist Marx and the evolutionary-liberal Spencer. However much they were otherwise at odds, Marx and Spencer agreed that European societies of the nineteenth century were leading the way toward a world dominated by pacific pursuits, leaving behind the vainglorious militarism of previous "feudal" or "militant" societies. Brave dreamers, they, at a relatively pacific European interlude in the history of "civilization."

The modern social sciences, and especially sociology, have incorporated the nineteenth century's pacific vision of social change into theories of "industrialism" or "capitalism." But, Giddens asks, how valid are contrasts to past militaristic societies "given that the current era is one stamped by the impact of war and by the intensive development of sophisticated weaponry?" Hasn't the bloody twentieth century, pivoted on two World Wars, belied the benign projections of nineteenth-century modernization theorists? Typically for Giddens, a sharp question is posed – and an eclectic, heavily exegetical set of answers is given. Giddens borrows from every major interpreter of modern Europe from Comte and Spencer, and Marx and Weber, to Hintze and Foucault, in effect arguing that all should be added together to give contemporary "critical social theory" the correct big picture. Those who might want pointed causal explanations or empirically grounded comparative historical generalizations must look elsewhere. Instead, this book offers a quintessential Giddensian exercise in macrosociological "theorizing," spinning a world view about modernization and a menu of concepts to characterize modern national states.

One basic line of argument is convincing. From their origins in early modern European times down to the present, modern national states have always existed within a transnational *system* of states. Nor has this "system" been only one of recurrent warfare. It has been that, but it has also been a set of culturally embodied understandings about what a "sovereign" state is, and how it should be recognized and dealt with by other sovereign states. In effect, Giddens is combining insights about war-making states (in the fashion of theorists like Charles Tilly and Randall Collins) with insights about world-wide cultural tendencies toward "rationalization" (in the style of theorists like John Meyer). Giddens further underlines an important implication: inter-national organizations of the twentieth century are updated embodiments of the sorts of transnational rules of the game that have always accompanied and enforced competing national sovereignties. Thus, we should not imagine that the spread of multinational corporations, or the emergence of the United Nations, or the operations of the International Monetary Fund will bring about the demise of national states. Instead, all function to reinforce the prerogatives of such states.

This transnational-systemic picture contradicts linear evolutionist views of societal modernization. Yet Giddens also aims to update venerable contrasts between "traditional" and "modern" societies, for he concludes that the nineteenth-century theorists were not entirely wrong. Modern societies, according to Giddens, are invariably "national states" that contrast fundamen-tally with "traditional," "class-divided" societies. The latter were constantly at war, not only among themselves but also within. They had coercive and administrative organizations that could *not* penetrate or transform local, popular socioeconomic and cultural life; yet their elites engaged in violent conflicts over who would sit atop the rural masses, siphoning revenues into administrative cities. In contrast, says Giddens, modern national states are "internally pacified." They have strong, penetrating administrative organiza-tions, especially the state, that can exercise "surveillance" over all citizens and most aspects of life. Violence is "extruded" from daily life, centered in professional militaries that engage in more and more deadly "industrialized" warfare, while pacified political dialectics of management and participation are played out among the civilian citizenry at large.

For Giddens, modernity thus conceived has both a benign and a horrific side. When modern states are not at war, life may be nicer. But war becomes more and more of a threat to humanity, as first total war and then nuclear weapons evolve. And whether at war or not, all industrialized national states are at risk to become "totalitarian," because of the control potentials built into their surveillance mechanisms.

As an overall gloss on what has changed in the world's polities from the fifteenth century to the twentieth, this is reasonable. It also makes considerable sense as a guide to the kinds of horrors that critically minded twentieth-century people should be worried about. Giddens wants us to realize that working through class-based movements for the "transcendance of capitalism by socialism" may not be as pressing a task as engaging in peace movements or ecological crusades, or opposing the practice of terror by a variety of present-day national regimes. With this it is hard to quarrel, and I do not.

But I am more worried about the *The Nation-State and Violence* as a theoretical guide for macroscopic sociology, for both empirical and conceptual reasons. I am far from convinced that all "modern national states" (and Giddens does not tell us how to operationalize this type) are more internally pacified than all "traditional class-divided" empires. What would happen if we juxtaposed, say, Italy with its *banditti* and *mafiosi*, to Imperial China in one of its unified and Confucianist epochs? Surely putting most of today's Third World into the picture would create even greater complexities. We would soon find ourselves identifying various dimensions of "pacification," of "state control," and so forth.

All to the good: this could open the door to a more nuanced analysis of the social structural, political, and cultural conditions that underpin more or less pacification in traditional and modern societies alike. In my view, this would be preferable to the Foucault-like reification and over-generalization of "surveillance" that lies at the heart of Giddens's conception of pacified modern states. Other critical theorists like Alvin Gouldner (also taking issue with Marxism) have agreed that the activities of managers and professionals should be conceptualized separately from class exploitation. But they have not focused on information-gathering and discipline to the exclusion of other intellectual, cultural, and organizational functions. And they have not written in such systemic–essentialist terms. Reading Giddens, it is hard to tell where exactly to look, and whose activities to trace, to get a handle on various patterns of surveillance in modern nations.

Giddens admits that he makes "no claim to offering an exhaustive analysis of variations among states in today's world." Indeed, *The Nation-State and Violence* offers only limited help in conceptualizing where we should look to describe and explain such variation. Instead, this book concludes (one hopes!) a sociological dialogue with the pacific illusions about modernization held by Marx and Spencer. It explains very clearly what the twentieth century has cruelly taught: modern national states are more than frameworks for class relations, trade, and industrial production; they are purveyors of deadly violence and potent agencies of social control. This is a valuable point. But it leaves a lot of analysis and explanation yet to be done, and I doubt that we will be well served by assuming at the outset sharp contrasts between "traditional" and "modern" states. Sociology has been getting away from such ideal-typical classifications, and it is sad to see Giddens (cheered on by the ghost of Foucault) working to reestablish them.

62

Structural Power: A Contradiction in Terms?[*]

H. Ward

[*]Source: *Political Studies*, vol. 35, 1987, pp. 593–610.

Abstract

The idea that capital possesses structural power over the state is of growing importance. Yet the theoretical literature on power has argued that this concept is either a contradiction in terms or is conceptually redundant. This paper seeks to show that a coherent distinction can be made between structural power, non-structural power, and structural constraints. These distinctions are based upon a concept of human agency which draws attention to the peculiar pasts of those individuals occupying the same type of structural position. It is argued that these distinctions are both widely applicable and 'empirically' relevant.

In recent years increasing use has been made of the concept of structural power in discussions of the relations between capital and the state.[1] Yet little or no effort has been made to define explicitly structural power or the concept of non-structural power which is implied by it. However, it is clear that a thorough discussion of these concepts is needed, for some theorists have often denied the coherence of this distinction. Structural Marxists like Poulantzas argue that power is a product of the interaction of various structural levels operating through social classes rather than individuals: for them all power is structural.[2] Moreover, authors who, unlike Poulantzas, pay serious attention to the actions of individuals in constructing social explanations, have also denied that a coherent distinction can be made here. On the one hand Steven Lukes has argued that structural power is a contradiction in terms because power operates within structural constraints.[3] On the other hand, for Anthony Giddens, the conceptual distinction between structural and non-structural power is redundant since all the resources on which power is based are definitionally part of the social structure.[4]

It is important to show that a clear distinction can be made between these two sorts of power. Without this, little further progress seems possible in more detailed 'empirical' studies of structural power. It will be argued here that the distinction between structural and non-structural power is of crucial explanatory importance, and that it is possible to define the ideas of agency, social structure, and power in such a way that we can talk without contradiction or redundancy about both structural and non-structural power. In the first section of this paper, it is argued that structuralist theories which make no reference to the actions of human agents will only provide relatively incomplete explanations, even in situations which favour the structural position.[5] A hypothetical example will be constructed to introduce the central concepts of this paper and to show that we may sensibly talk of the structural and non-structural power of capital.

Power in Structural Marxism

Although Poulantzas' notion that 'power is located in the field of social relations and it specifies the effects of those different levels or structures on the ability of a given class to realise its specific objective interest' has often been interpreted as dispensing completely with ideas of action and human agency, this interpretation is probably incorrect.[6] As Jessop has argued, Poulantzas does retain a space for the intervention of individuals within the constraints imposed by social structure, but only as members of social classes 'whose situation is determined by their members' specific function in production'.[7] Rather than being rational subjects, individuals are constituted through 'a complex overdetermined ideological practice'.[8] But even in circumstances in which economic and class pressures are intense, it is implausible to suggest that individuals' actions are merely a function of their class positions.

Consider a dealer working in the market in foreign currency or in the secondary government bond market. These markets approximate the model of perfect markets in neo-classical economics. Thus, those who operate in them are each under some competitive pressure and, indeed, it is a necessary condition for their long-run survival in the market, that they maximize profits, for competition drives down abnormal profit rates. In their everyday dealings in the market in pursuit of short-term profit, the dealers continually make decisions which not only have a bearing upon their solvency but also affect the relationship between capital and state. As an unintended consequence of numerous bargains made within those financial markets the state may be prevented from pursuing certain policies.[9] For example, if the state decides to increase public expenditure, dealers in foreign currency markets may feel that this move would inflate the domestic currency and its value may fall. Also, increased public expenditure is often financed through the issue of government bonds, and as these flood onto the market the price at which they are taken up will fall, provoking an increase in interest rates which may have the second-order consequence of deflating investment by industry. Either a run on the currency or the fear of crowding out industrial investment may be enough to make the state resort to deflationary policies, and the state may, indeed, anticipate market reactions.

Now the structuralists' argument would suggest that dealers are merely calculating machines translating the competitive constraints under which they operate into decisions over transactions: what they do is merely a function of their position in the mode of production – they are mere bearers of social structure – and the way in which the state is constrained is the result of the interaction of structures not individuals. But such an argument would be highly implausible, both on theoretical and on empirical grounds.

The theoretical point is that even in perfect markets, economic decision-makers are not just calculating machines translating preferences and constraints into choices.[10] Economists have long known it to be the case that even if individuals have well-defined preferences, a clearly discernible set of constraints and perfect information about prices, there are many situations in which it is impossible to specify an optimal course of action. Furthermore, empirical work strongly suggests that, even if they have perfect knowledge of prices, individuals seldom possess all relevant information and do not have the time and capacity to process it.[11] Financial markets can plausibly be assumed to present a decision problem for financiers which has no well-specified optimal solutions, for there is extreme uncertainty about the future and about how others will react to their moves in the market.

The point here is not that this indeterminacy necessarily introduces an element of randomness into dealers' behaviour. Clearly dealers develop routines, standard operating procedures, and institutionalized forms of action for coping with the problem.[12] But the choices any dealer makes will be crucially influenced by the particular heuristic methods they employ when making decisions about whether to enter or leave the market, so that the market pressures upon them are not all that matters.

It is generally accepted that heuristic methods develop through time and undergo continuous modification. If this is so, it seems theoretically implausible to suggest that each dealer will use the same methods even if competitive pressures tend to produce some convergence.[13] Averaging over the different buyers and sellers in the market, the heuristic methods used generate a tacit 'market view' of government economic policy. But what this view is, and thus the scope and extent of the constraints under which the state operates, will depend on who is at present in the market and the whole history of how the market has developed through time.[14] In this sense the market brings its past to bear upon the present. Moreover, dealers in the market have a degree of autonomy from structural constraints and their actions in the market may be said to affect the state: they are not mere bearers of social structure. The current economic structure does not completely determine this aspect of the relationship between capital and the state.

In many respects the perfect market exemplifies the view of social structure taken here. The crucial point about such a market is that it relates buyer and seller in an impersonal way: the price charged, the quality of the goods and other features of the transaction do not vary when different buyers and sellers are involved. So far as any buyer is concerned, sellers are interchangeable, and vice versa.

Capital may be said to possess both structural and non-structural power resources, and, thus, structural and non-structural power over the state. Any British government is going to be dependent on the bond market for borrowing: this is one aspect of the structure relating capital and the state which is invariant with respect to which government is in power or who is in the market. Capital derives resources from this dependence which it may use deliberately to constrain state policy or which may have the side-effect of so constraining the state when used for other reasons. If the argument above is correct, the way these structural resources affect the state will depend upon who is in the market and their history. It might plausibly be argued that the various links which the City has with British government are more useful to the City when a Conservative government is in power. The increased utility of these links is a non-structural resource for the City: rather than being dependent on the impersonal structures of the relationship between the British state and financial markets, it is contingent upon which particular government happens to occupy a crucial location within the state and, probably, upon which individuals occupy crucial financial roles.[15]

Structural constraints are impersonal, equally preventing any particular agent who happens to occupy a certain structural location from acting in certain ways. If my argument is correct, financiers are not completely constrained by economic structures because we would expect them to react in a range of ways to the same market conditions. Nevertheless they face some constraints which make certain acts impossible. For example, no financier can consistently charge more than the going rate and stay in the market. It is also argued below that all British governments face certain economic and organizational constraints which make certain policies impossible.

It has been suggested that the constraints governments face may, in part, be the unintended consequence of actions made by dealers in the pursuit of short-term profits. Nevertheless, for the purposes of social explanation, financiers should be regarded as agents exercising power over the state and deploying structural resources. In the minimal sense in which the term agency is used here, agents need not be conscious of what they are doing, responsible for outcomes, or personally autonomous as individuals. All that is needed is that we can show that what they did was not completely determined by structure, a condition which is satisfied in the case of financiers.

In this section it has been argued that social explanations will often have to refer to the actions of individuals.[16] Similar arguments could be made in relation to collective agents.[17] This is not to say that social structures always leave space for action: sometimes they leave open only one possibility. But, in general, the structuralists' argument for seeing all power as structural fails. Moreover, in a preliminary way, a possible method has been illustrated of distinguishing the structural and non-structural power of capital. In subsequent sections, this position will be contrasted with those of Giddens, Lukes and Jessop, and the argument put forward that they cannot adequately deal with both structural and non-structural power, even though, unlike the structuralists, they take the actions of agents seriously.[18] An attempt will also be made to illustrate the utility of the concepts deployed outside the confines of the debate on capital and the state, although some criticisms will be made of the literature on the structural power of capital.

Social Structure, Structural and Non-Structural Resources

It is a central feature of our intuitive understanding of social structures that they are independent of the particular individuals related by them – they are impersonal. As Cohen argues,

> One may know what the structure of an argument is without knowing what its statements are, and one may know what the structure of a bridge is while being ignorant of the character of its parts. One may, moreover, remove the original statements and replace them with others without changing the argument's structure, and the same applies to the structure of the bridge, though the second operation requires great caution.[19]

Social structure includes relations between people and relations between people and things, but changes in the 'bearers' of social relationships do not imply changes in structure. 'Suppose A owns a factory and B works for him. Then the economy might be said to change slightly if A and B switched roles. ... But these changes even if [they are] changes in the economy, entail no change in its structure.'[20]

Besides being intuitively plausible, Cohen's definition is useful in social explanation. If social structures are impersonal this allows us to distinguish non-structural resources from structural resources which are inherent in the structure of the situation, and are independent of the particular agents related by that structure. However, agents may also bring non-structural resources to bear upon the outcome which are independent of the structure of the situation and relate to the particular agents involved.[21] Between them, Giddens, Lukes and Jessop cover the major alternatives to the way of defining social structure used here. Yet these alternative definitions cannot make sense of the distinction between structural and non-structural power.

The central concern of Giddens's theory of structuration is to overcome the view that the actions of agents and social structures are two different things. For him, structure and action are two sides of the same coin: social structure is continually reconstituted by, and is only perpetually observable through, human action, while the resources agents deploy in using their 'causal powers' derive, at the same time, from structures. Thus Giddens believes that his central focus upon 'the duality of structure and agency' demands that

> the resources which the existence of domination implies and the exercise of power draws upon are seen to be, *at the same time structural components of the social system.*[22]

Clearly it would be redundant to talk of *structural* power within this framework. There is no definitive listing of types of resources in Giddens's work. However, reference is made to institutions, norms, rights and obligations, interpretative schemes, regularized social practices and social rôles. These are typical of the items which we are liable to regard as part of the social structure (as independent of the particular agents bearing it) but they are not the only, nor necessarily the most important, bases of power. For example, a prosecuting lawyer may derive certain resources from standard legal procedures, rules of evidence, methods of choosing jurors, and so on, which have become 'regularized' in British courts. But it is a commonplace that some prosecuting lawyers are better than others, and can obtain convictions where others would not. They deploy personal resources such as verbal skills, memory, contacts with the legal profession, and so on. Or again, consider an employer bargaining with an employee. Certain of his bargaining resources are available to any similar employer: knowledge of the tightness of the national market for labour, the level of social security provision, and so on. But certain resources are non-structural: the employer's own bargaining skill, any personal knowledge of the particular circumstances of the employee which give some bargaining leverage, for instance.

Presumably what Giddens means when he says that all resources are structural components of the social system is that it is possible to account for how they arise and are sustained through time in terms of the interaction of structure and agency. However, it seems unlikely that the non-structural resources of individuals would be completely accounted for in this way because there is much in the lives of individuals and in the rôles they come to occupy which is inexplicable or seems random and accidental. Nor is it any easier to provide complete accounts of the macro-political events which may give resources to collective agents.[23] For example, if part of the power of capital over the state turns upon which party is in power, it seems much more plausible to treat this as contingent rather than socio-structural, for election results may, in turn, depend upon such 'random shocks' as the date of the outbreak of the Falklands War.[24] What cannot be accounted for in terms of the theory of structuration cannot be socio-structural in Giddens's sense.

Lukes's essay 'Power and Structure' is much nearer to the mainstream analysis of structure for, like many authors, he defines social structures in terms of the constraints they place upon agents. This has important implications.

> The first corollary is (somewhat surprisingly) that, on this account, *the notion of a power structure becomes a self-contradiction, since power operates within structures.* However the matter is not so simple, since the possession and exercise of power by some can be a structural fact of the situation for others – so that what is structural with respect to the recipient may not be so with respect to the exerciser. The point, however, is that to the extent to which the explanation of a given outcome is structural, the claim being made is that to that extent the agents involved in bringing it about were powerless to act otherwise.[25]

Whereas Giddens cannot talk of non-structural power, Lukes believes that to talk of structural power is self-contradictory.[26] However, it is not self-contradictory to talk about structural power if agents normally act within structural constraints yet also derive resources from social structure: this is the view advocated here. In fact Lukes wishes to deny the existence of structural resources, although this is not a logical consequence of his other beliefs about structure and agency. However, the examples used here suggest that the idea of structural resources does possess plausibility and explanatory utility.

Of the three authors discussed here, Jessop is the only one whose conceptual framework could be naturally developed to define both structural and non-structural resources, so that his view of structure deserves some attention. Jessop's view of structure taps the common idea that what is structural is more 'permanent' than what is non-structural. The basic distinction is between the 'structural' and 'conjunctural' moments.

> The 'structural' moment can be defined as those elements in a social formation that cannot be altered by a given agent (or set of agents) during a given time period ... The 'conjunctural' moment may be defined as those elements in a social formation that can be altered by a given agent (or set of agents) during a given time period.[27]

What is viewed as structural is relative to the time period under consideration and also to the particular agent under consideration, for what is structural for one agent may be conjunctural for another. Within the limits set by any structural constraints upon them agents might be seen as both producing effects from resources derived from what is structural in a situation on the one hand and from what is conjunctural on the other hand.[28] The problem with this way of defining what is structural is, of course, that everything depends upon how the 'given time period' is defined.[29] Supposing that NATO's reliance on 'theatre' nuclear weapons cannot be changed overnight, the USA's control of the relevant technology and knowledge gives it a certain power within NATO.

From both sides of the Atlantic this dependence might be viewed as structural in Jessop's sense.[30] However, there are endemic disputes about how fast NATO could convert to conventional deterrence even among those who believe this to be desirable. A more workable distinction between structural and non-structural power might be made along the lines advocated in this paper. The fact that each of the European allies is somewhat dependent on the US military gives it a certain structural power. But in order to obtain use of bases from which to attack Libya, Reagan had to deploy crucial non-structural resources derived from the US's 'special relationship' with Britain and his own personal links with Thatcher. As this case illustrates, it is generally easier to agree on what is and is not invariant across a set of actors located in a structure than to arrive at a widely accepted definition of the long term.

It will now be argued that structural constraints may be defined in a useful way if we accept the view of structure suggested in this section.

Structural Constraints and the Social Structuring of Preferences

Lukes is right to hold that social structures may constrain action, although his account of how such constraints operate may not be acceptable. However, Giddens seems to believe that one must drop the idea that social structure blocks action if the opposition between structure and agency is to be dissolved. Giddens has criticized Lukes's position because it involves the idea that structures constrain.

> In representing structure as placing limitations or constraints upon the activities of agents, however, Lukes tends to repeat the dualism of agency and structure that I have spoken of in earlier papers. Hence he talks of 'where structural determinism ends and power begins' and is unable to satisfactorily deal *with structure as implicated in power relations and power relations as implicated in structure.*[31]

Although Giddens is right in thinking that structures facilitate and are continually reconstituted through action, these ideas do not demand that we drop the notion that structures may constrain.[32] In contrast to Giddens, it will be argued here that social structures may make certain acts unthinkable or physically impossible, and in contrast to both Giddens and Lukes, it will also be argued that social structures may make certain acts so costly that actors are structurally constrained from carrying them out.

It might be argued that if social structures are reproduced through and are only apparent in action they may change at any time, and cannot permanently block action. For, at any time, the emergent consequences of a set of actions may transform the structure. As Giddens puts it

All reproduction (of social structures) is necessarily production, however: and the seed of change is there in *every act* which contributes towards the reproduction of any 'ordered' form of social life.[33]

The implicit contrast here is with physical structures which need not be continually reproduced through human actions and are often highly resistant to attempts to change them. Giddens may be correct that some social structures like language are continuously open to change and are not barriers to competent users. But consider the case of ideological structures. It is certainly true that ideological structures need to be propagated through the socialization process, and continual minor modifications occur within them as the unintended consequence of the numerous political uses to which they are put: they are continuously reproduced in and through action. But, in some cases, it is impossible to imagine this reproduction failing, and they may constrain political action for long periods by making certain changes unthinkable.

Up until the late 1960s the constitutional settlement forged around the turn of the century was, with minor exceptions, extremely stable and very widely accepted. In particular, the ideas of strong government from the centre and the dominant position of the cabinet were hardly questioned. Yet they played a crucial role in legitimizing an élitist political tradition in which secrecy and a high degree of centralization of power were the norm. Successive governments have derived crucial structural resources from this tradition.

Since the end of the sixties these constitutional ideas have come under a three-fold attack: from members of the judiciary arguing for stronger constitutional limitations on government with a view to reducing the extension of the rôle of the state; from the Liberal Party and later the SDP for electoral unfairness and for the economic consequences of adversary politics; from the left of the Labour Party for blocking radical change.[34] However, it is difficult to see how the British constitution could have undergone failure of reproduction in, say, the fifties. With the partial exception of the Liberal Party, all organizations which might have provided a platform for the articulation of alternatives had too strong an interest in the status quo. It took major structural change elsewhere in the system – Britain's continuing relative decline and the partial breakdown of the two-party system – for this to occur.

Giddens's approach fails to allow for the crucial stabilizing rôle of such institutional gatekeepers of political discourse. He wishes to downplay the importance of ideology.[35] The importance of ideology can be over-emphasized, but it is clear that certain ways of thinking can become taken-for-granted parts of our world and may constrain our thought by, as Lukes puts it, making certain thoughts impossible for certain agents.[36]

Giddens also wishes to argue that social structures do not make acts impossible in the way that some physical barriers do. Social structures are not felt as barriers to action by agents.

The anatomy of a body or the girders of a building, the sort of imagery that is involved with this conception of structure [as analogous to physical structure], are perceptually 'present' in a sense in which 'social structure' is not.[37]

However, social structures do make certain acts physically impossible for certain individuals. To deny this is, for example, to deny the social patterning of illness in our society.

Consider the case of individuals severely malnourished in childhood, exposed to a carcinogen at work, or subject to dirty working conditions. There are social structures which relate diseases to particular occupations: certain poor peasants to stunted development; workers in the nuclear industry to cancer of the prostate; coalminers to black-lung. Individuals in these occupations certainly become perceptually aware of such disease structures either through their own or their workmates' suffering. Moreover, these structures make politically significant collective actions physically impossible for many of those who suffer their effects: it is wrong to argue that the *disease* makes those actions impossible not the social structure, since this would be to ignore entirely the social patterning of disease.[38]

Another concrete example may help illustrate the way in which social structures make certain actions impossible, while raising another important issue about structural constraints. In his essay 'Do artifacts have politics?' Langdon Winner argues that certain freeways in New York designed by Robert Moses embody both racial and class biases for they were deliberately designed so that bridge underpasses were too low to enable buses to use the freeways. Winner argues that certain freeways in New York designed by Robert Moses embody both racial and class biases for they were deliberately designed so that bridge underpasses were too low to enable buses to use the freeways. Winner argues that

Many of (Moses') monumental structures of concrete and steel embody a systematic social inequality, a way of engineering relationships among people that after a time, *becomes just another part of the land-scape.*[39]

Certain bus journeys are physically impossible in New York's transport system. The bridges are bearers of part of the community power structure which relates the transport system to particular bureaucratic rôles. This structure physically rules out certain acts through the medium of the road system.

However, Moses' bridge designs are of social significance not so much because they make certain bus journeys physically impossible as because New York's 'transport poor' find alternatives like the option of buying a car or hiring a cab coercively costly, so that access to certain parts of the city is effectively ruled out. Giddens might wish to argue that the 'transport poor' are not hemmed in to certain parts of the city because it is possible, even if costly, to travel.[40] Certainly Lukes would argue that no structural constraint operates here. But such arguments are implausible.

For Lukes what distinguishes structural constraints from other constraints on agents is that structural constraints reduce agents' freedom. A basic conceptual distinction is made between structural constraints and rational constraints.

> Rational constraints determine, that is set limits to, the options of agents by providing them with relevant and sufficient reasons not to act in certain ways ... The paradigm case are economic constraints ... By contrast, structural constraints do not operate through the agents' reasons, and they may, indeed, prevent certain reasons from being reasons for *him*: they may limit his capacity to have certain desires or hold certain beliefs.[41]

For Lukes rational constraints do not limit the agents' freedom and power to act otherwise whereas structural constraints do.

> The key point here is that such [rational constraints] can be compatible with the agents' freedom to overcome them ... Rational constraints will not, therefore, be structural, that is limiting the power of agents; the agent is seen as retaining the power to overcome the constraint however high the price.[42]

Further Lukes argues, 'structural constraints limit the agent's freedom or power to act otherwise by precluding (rather than putting a price tag on) such a possibility'.[43] The distinction made here is partially coincident with accounts of freedom like those of Steiner where only physical constraints are seen as limiting liberty. Steiner argues that once it is allowed that costs may limit liberty, any cost, however trivial, does so, so there is no natural cut-off point on what limits liberty.[44] (Of course Lukes also includes limits on what can be thought of as possible actions as well as physical constraints, and this is in line with his emphasis on the third dimension of power.) Lukes seeks to identify the notions of power and *moral* responsibility for outcomes. He says as much in his book *Power: A Radical View*.

> The point, in other words, of locating power is to fix responsibility for consequences held to flow from the action, or inaction, of certain specifiable agents.[45]

An agent is held responsible if he was not structurally constrained and could, at least potentially, have known what would be the consequences of his action or inaction. If we seek to use the ideas of power and structural constraint to explain social outcomes, this position is distinctly unhelpful. As Saunders argues, the crucial question when we are using power in an explanatory way is whether the agent has a causal impact on the outcome, and such impacts may occur whether or not the agent may be held responsible.[46] It is obvious that there are cost penalties which 'no reasonable man' would incur in a given situation.[47] Many authors would argue against Lukes and Giddens, that such coercive cost penalties limit liberty, and constrain in a manner directly analogous to physical constraints.[48]

If certain actions are equally ruled out for all agents located in a certain position in a social structure, the constraint is impersonal in its operation and we might talk of a structural constraint.[49] We can never be certain what level of cost penalties is so great that 'no reasonable man' would bear them – and Lukes holds to the approach of the extreme view that such penalties do not constrain. However, if we can identify costs which bear upon all who occupy a certain structural location, and none is willing to bear those costs, a structurally imposed outer limit upon action has been found. To identify such an outer limit is often a very helpful step in social explanation, for it shows what was *socially* ruled out.[50] The abstract possibility that some might have borne the costs is both irrelevant for explanatory purposes and meaningless to all whose options are foreclosed by coercive costs.[51]

Now it could be argued that this notion of coercive costs is too narrow. It might be the case that, although the cost penalties associated with some given action are unlikely to be completely compelling, we cannot imagine 'many' occupants of a certain rôle incurring those costs. Conceptual clarity demands that we retain this strong notion of constraint. Nevertheless, we certainly need some way of thinking about the degree to which social structure patterns the costs and benefits at a less than determinant level.

The difficulty is that we need to distinguish the *social patterning* of these costs and benefits, to be seen as independent of the particular actor occupying a position, from other determinants of actors' perceived costs and benefits. These perceptions might vary because of the peculiar pasts of the actors, variation in other social positions which they occupy, and variations in their perceptions of the costs and benefits due to differences in the degree to which experience in that rôle has enabled them to learn the 'true values' of the costs and benefits.

There seems to be no simple way in which we can empirically disentangle the effects of this variation from any underlying social patterning of costs and benefits invariant across agents. Nevertheless, in certain cases, there may be such great similarities between preference rankings of the actors that there is a strong presupposition that such social patterning exists. Further, if a certain option, or small range of options, stand out in the preference rankings of all the actors involved, whether positively or negatively, we might speak of a *strong social patterning* of agents' preferences. Conversely, if the preference rankings of agents varied widely and no options stood out we might say that agents' preferences were only weakly socially patterned (if at all).

Although the recent Marxian theory of the state tends to argue that there are no determining economic constraints upon the state, certain options are liable to be ruled out of court. The more socialist variants of the Labour left's Alternative Economic Strategy would probably result in such extensive economic dislocation, as financial capital was withdrawn from Britain, that the very ability of the state to control civil society would be brought into question. It seems incredible that any individual who actually or potentially occupied a position of power within the state or, for that matter, any Labour government would risk such loss of control. Clearly, though, not all areas of economic policy are as constrained as this. While the macro-economic policies of post-war governments have been rather similar, suggesting strong social patterning, there have been major differences in industrial policy between governments.[52]

It would be mistaken to assume that the structural power of capital is merely the result of economic structures or that individual industries do not possess structural power.[53] Structural power may result from organizational structures within the state which are partially sustained through links with a certain industry, and prevent certain policy alternatives arising.[54] For example, Weir and Skocpol have shown that the failure of the British state to develop a coherent Keynesian response to the pre-war economic crisis was due to lack of organizational capacities and constraining organizational ideologies which were not present in Sweden where social Keynesianism was more successful.[55] It could be argued that the City benefited from these organizational constraints and, particularly through its relations with the Treasury, actively helped to sustain them.[56] Thus, in pre-war Britain, there is evidence to suggest that organizational structures led to strong social patterning of the macro-economic views of the political parties, these views being strikingly similar.

The structure of centre–local relations under the Thatcher government may provide another example of strong social patterning. Although two groups at least – the Labour leaderships in Liverpool and Lambeth – appeared to be prepared to incur local bankruptcy, personal penalties and central takeover in the pursuit of policies practically opposed and ideologically orientated against the present government, few other local authorities were willing to go this far. The Liverpool leadership did back down, but this does not imply that it was structurally constrained by centre–local relations. Rather, it was pressure from within the Labour movement which resulted in this behaviour. However, it would seem reasonable to say that the leadership in Liverpool did not, in the last resort, need that much pushing and that the perceived costs they faced were similar to, though not identical with, those of other groups. The preferences of local politicians were strongly patterned by a relationship of dependence upon central finance and by new legal initiatives to control local politicians.

To conclude this section, it is reasonable to argue that social structure facilitates action and may constrain action by making certain acts unthinkable, physically impossible, or coercively costly. If the idea that social structure is invariant with the particular agents related by it is accepted, it is possible to say that a structure constrains in any of those three ways so long as a certain act is equally ruled out for all located in a certain position in the structure. It is also possible to talk of the strong social patterning of preferences.

Power, Autonomy and Agency

Outside the structuralist literature, power is normally only said to be exercised if an actor has made a difference to some social outcome.[57] An actor who has exercised power is an agent in the sense that he has brought something about which would not otherwise have occurred. To be an agent exercising power is, then, to have some sort of autonomy: as Lukes and Giddens put it, an actor has exercised power only if she 'could have acted differently',[58] for the actor who could not do so is merely translating structural constraints into a choice and is not an agent. Lukes's and Giddens's view that power should be conceptually linked with agency is right, but their accounts are neither conceptually nor empirically helpful.

As we saw above, Giddens does not believe that social structures block action, hence structural factors never prevent actors from doing otherwise. For Giddens all competent individuals are agents *by definition*, for they may always act differently and may deploy their 'causal powers' to affect outcomes.[59] For Giddens, what matters is that the agent has a degree of autonomy from structural constraints and this is guaranteed by high-level arguments rather than being something which we need to demonstrate empirically on a case-by-case basis. However, as shown above, it is implausible to argue that social structures *always* leave some space for autonomous action, and it must be demonstrated that such a space exists.

In contrast to Giddens, Lukes believes that actors often have 'a certain relative autonomy' but this needs to be demonstrated rather than assumed.[60] For example, Lukes suggests that we look for evidence that other agents in a similar structural location acted differently or that the same actor acted differently in similar circumstances at another point in time.[61]

This sort of evidence is certainly crucial to showing that the actor had some autonomy from social structure. The major problem with Lukes's position is, though, that he goes on to link power not just with autonomy from social structure but also with personal autonomy.[62] As we saw above, Lukes suggests that an actor has exercised power only if he can be held responsible for his actions, and this presupposes that the actor was potentially conscious of what he was doing and was not 'inner driven' by some compulsion. However, as Giddens points out, domination is often maintained as an unintended consequence of action.[63] Although Giddens's agents have many of the characteristics of actors who are personally autonomous on standard liberal definitions, they may, moreover, do things because of unconscious motives.[64] In using power to explain social outcomes what matters, as was pointed out above, is an actor's capacity to make a difference to outcomes not their degree of personal autonomy.

For the purposes of social explanation, we can bypass the knotty conceptual and empirical problems associated with personal autonomy. In a minimal sense (which makes no reference to personal autonomy, responsibility or consciousness), an actor can be said to be an agent who has had a causal impact on a social outcome if there is evidence that some other agent or agents similarly located within the social structure acted differently at some time t.[65] In contrast, if all similarly located actors acted in the same way at time t, there is a *strong presumption* that what they did was structurally determined – that they were not agents at this point in time.[66] Of course, the temptation will always be to go beyond this empiricist way of identifying agency and power to try to explain why agents acted differently. Often we might refer to the peculiar pasts and histories of the individuals occupying particular locations – for instance, the history of the 'special relationship' between the US and Britain which led Thatcher's government to allow use of British bases. In this manner we may sometimes be able to account for personally autonomous acts in which agents step outside their normal selves, critically examine their rôles, beliefs, and motives and do the unexpected. However, even if we have to take the variation in the behaviour of a set of agents in a given location as an unexplained residual, we may have a useful, although incomplete, explanation.

Conclusion

This paper has tried to show that if an 'impersonal' view of social structure is accepted, definitions of structural and non-structural resources, structural constraint, and agency naturally follow. It has been argued that social structures will usually be implicated in two ways in social explanations: first they set up constraints on agents; secondly they provide resources which agents use in various ways. Despite the importance of social structures to explanation, actors often have some room for manoeuvre, and in explaining outcomes we will often need to draw attention to, and explain if possible, the variation in the actions of similarly placed agents. It is neither self-contradictory nor redundant to talk of the structural power of capital, and the distinction between structural and non-structural resources points towards two distinct types of powers and areas of capital's power, both of which deserve fuller attention than they have received here. At the same time, the idea of structural power is of wide applicability outside the debate upon capital and the state.

Notes

1. The essence of the argument that capital has structural power is that capital's control over investment leads to state officials, in the pursuit of their own goals, either deferring to, or anticipating the reactions of, the capitalist class. This argument is well reviewed in D. Marsh, 'Interest group activity and structural power', in D. Marsh (ed.), *Capital and Politics in Western Europe* (London, Frank Cass, 1983). See especially C. E. Lindblom, *Politics and Markets* (New York, Basic Books, 1977), Ch. 13. For the clearest theoretical statement of Marxist accounts of structural power, see F. Block, 'Beyond relative autonomy: state managers as historical subjects', in R. Miliband and J. Savill (eds), *The Socialist Register 1980* (London, Merlin, 1980).

2. See especially N. Poulantzas, *Political Power and Social Classes* (London, Verso, 1978), Ch. 3. For a structuralist critique of Lukes and Giddens see S. Clegg, *The Theory of Power and Organisations* (London, Routledge and Kegan Paul, 1979), Chs 5, 6.

3. S. Lukes, 'Power and structure', in S. Lukes, *Essays in Social Theory* (London, Macmillan, 1977).

4. A. Giddens, *Central Problems in Social Theory: Action, Structure and Contradiction in Social Analysis* (London, Macmillan, 1979), Ch. 2. Giddens has presented similar arguments in earlier works but refers the reader to this statement in his latest book, *The Constitution of Society* (Cambridge, Polity Press, 1984), which I sometimes refer to for clarity. But also see A. Giddens, *New Rules of Sociological Method* (London, Hutchinson, 1976).

5. There now seems to be a general movement towards giving Marxian theory microfoundations in explanations of individual action. See, for example: J. Roemer, *A General Theory of Exploitation and Class* (Cambridge, Mass., Harvard University Press, 1982); I. Steedman, *Marx after Straffa* (London, New Left Books, 1977). For a more general argument about the need for microfoundations in Marxism covering these topics see: J. Elster, *Making Sense of Marx* (Cambridge, Cambridge University Press, 1985); B. Jessop, 'The state and political strategy' (paper given at the Conference of IPSA, Paris, 1985), p. 36.

6. B. Jessop, 'On the commensurability of power and structural constraint' (paper presented to the EGOS Symposium on Power, University of Bradford, 6–7 May 1976), p. 19.

7. Jessop, 'On the commensurability', p. 20.

8. Jessop, 'On the commensurability', p. 15. See also P. Saunders, *Urban Politics: A Sociological Interpretation* (London, Hutchinson, 1983), p. 59.

9. For detailed discussions of the effects of the operation of financial markets on governments in Britain see, for example: B. Fine and L. Harris, *The Peculiarities of the British Economy* (London, Lawrence and Wishart, 1985), pp. 71–9; J. Coakley and L. Harris, *The City of Capital* (Oxford, Blackwell, 1983), Part 3; G. Ingham, *Capitalism Divided* (London, Macmillan, 1984), Ch. 1. I do not wish to take up the debate about whether the structural power of the City of London harms industry in Britain. On this also see F. Longstreth, 'The City, industry and the state', in C. Crouch (ed.), *State and Economy in Contemporary Capitalism* (London, Croom Helm, 1979).

10. In Spiro Latsis' terminology, the capitalist's choice is situationally deter-mined. See S. Latsis, 'A research programme in economics', in S. Latsis (ed.), *Method and Appraisal in Economics* (Cambridge, Cambridge University Press, 1980). Latsis' point is that situationally determined, single-exit models of decision-making used in neo-classical economics lead to a degenerating research programme in Lakatos' sense. Many decisions are multiple exit, and one needs to invoke psychological

models of decision-making to explain choice rather than the thin theory of rationality of neo-classical theory.

11. See H. Simon, 'A behavioural model of rational choice', *Quarterly Journal of Economics*, 69 (1955), 99–118. Or, more recently, H. Simon, *Reason in Human Affairs* (Oxford, Basil Blackwell, 1983).

12. Simon, 'A behavioural model of rational choice'.

13. As Nelson and Winter put it in their discussion of evolutionary pressures on firms: 'given the assumption [of imperfect information] one would expect a diversity of firm behaviour in real situations. Firms facing the same market signals respond differently, and more so if the signals are relatively novel.' See R. Nelson and S. Winter, *An Evolutionary Theory of Economic Change* (Cambridge, Mass., Belknap Press, 1982), p. 276.

14. That there is variation in the methods dealers use is indicated by the fact that the short-term rate of profit is far from uniform in financial markets. The 'markets' view' of British economic policy has also changed with the growing inter-nationalization of the London markets, and especially the entry of US financial institutions with different modes of operation. See Coakley and Harris, *The City of Capital*, Ch. 3 on the effect upon government policy of the growth and inter-nationalization of the Eurodollar market.

15. It is, however, mistaken to suggest that the non-structural power of capital is exercised in its relations with the state through interest groups and corporatist structures while its structural power involves the 'automatic' operation of markets and the state's reaction to them. (See, for example, Marsh, 'Interest group activity and structural power'.) Clearly representatives of capital may employ the *explicit threat* of a run on currency or a capital strike in their bargaining with the state through their interest groups. But this resource derives from the structure of the situation, though the effectiveness is somewhat dependent on the contingencies of who is in office.

16. For the idea that the notion of subconsciously motivated behaviour subverts structural determinism, see T. Benton, *The Rise and Fall of Structural Marxism* (London, Macmillan, 1984), p. 213. For a discussion of the impact of the phenomeno-logical argument that social action cannot be explained independently of the meaning agents attach to it and the relation of this to structuralism see Saunders, *Urban Politics*, pp. 50–3.

17. For example, neither economic nor military structures seem to lead to the complete convergence in industrial societies predicted by some post-industrial society theorists. See C. Kerr, *The Future of Industrial Society: Convergence or Continuing Diversity* (Cambridge, Mass., Harvard University Press, 1983).

18. Other useful discussions of these problems which will be alluded to briefly below are: G. Debnam, *The Analysis of Power: A Realist Approach* (London, Macmillan, 1985); T. Baumgartner, W. Buckley, T. Burns and P. Shuster, 'Meta-power and the structuring of social hierarchies', in T. Burns and W. Buckley (eds), *Power and Control: Social Structures and Their Transformation* (Beverly Hills, Sage, 1976).

19. G. Cohen, *Karl Marx's Theory of History: A Defence* (Oxford, Oxford University Press, 1978), p. 36.

20. Cohen, *Karl Marx's Theory of History*, p. 36.

21. Because the concept of a power resource is relational – the resource is useful in relation to some specified set of others – to talk of any kind of resource is to imply some sort of structure. The point is that this need not be *social* structure. Cohen is wrong to suggest that *all* structures are independent of their bearers, though this is true of *social* structures.

22. Giddens, *Central Problems in Social Theory*, p. 91, emphasis added.

23. It is sometimes argued that there are collective resources held by collective agents which are irreducible to the resources held by members of that collectivity. See,

for example, Debnam, *The Analysis of Power*, Ch. 2. Debnam cites the image of a collectivity as the only coherent example, but others would define these more widely: D. H. Wrong, *Power: Its Forms, Bases and Uses* (Oxford, Basil Blackwell, 1979), pp. 130–45. Are all collective resources structural? While they are independent of the particular agents who happen to be members of the collectivity at that time, some collective resources might be available to any *collectivity* which occupied its position within some structure. Thus part of the corporate image of all large American corporations derives from their importance in the economy rather than their particular line of business, history, and so on.

24. On the electoral impact of the Falklands War see H. D. Clarke, M. C. Stewart and G. Zuk, 'Politics, economics and party popularity in Britain, 1979–83', *Electoral Studies*, 5 (1986), 123–41. As Goldman has shown, there is no logical connection between the idea that human actions might be the result of the operation of universal laws and antecedent conditions and the *actual possibility* of predicting action. See A. Goldman, *A Theory of Human Action* (Princeton, N.J., Princeton University Press, 1970), Ch. 6, and particularly pp. 178–9. Behaviour may not be contingent, but some elements of it must needs be treated as contingent.

25. Lukes, 'Power and structure', p. 9, emphasis added. It is clear from the context that Lukes is not talking about power structures in the sense of élite theorists like Floyd Hunter but in a broader manner.

26. In fact Lukes could say that *A* has structural power over *B* if he can place a structural constraint on *B* and non-structural power if he can affect *B* in some other way. For a related view see Baumgartner *et al.*, 'Meta-power', which refers to this as 'meta-power' or, sometimes, as 'generative structural power' (p. 264).

27. B. Jessop, *The Capitalist State* (Oxford, Martin Robertson, 1982), p. 253. Jessop's position has changed significantly since his earlier work cited above.

28. Jessop does not himself distinguish non-structural from structural power although this is one way he might have done so. Another is to say that structural power involves placing long-term restrictions on another while conjunctural power involves placing short-term restrictions. In fact this suffers from the same problems as the extension discussed in the text.

29. Another problem is that Jessop is wrong to suggest that structures always have a degree of permanency. Sometimes they do and sometimes they do not as is suggested in the next section.

30. Perhaps the US derives conjunctural resources from the particular short-term reliance on certain weapons systems like Cruise missiles.

31. Giddens, *Central Problems in Social Theory*, p. 91, emphasis added. Lukes does argue, though, that power may be exercised within structures in a way which eventually dissolves a constraint. But at any given time structures constrain; Lukes, 'Power and structure', p. 29.

32. See R. Bhaskar, *The Possibility of Naturalism* (Brighton, Harvester, 1979), pp. 49–50. Bhaskar's position is similar to Giddens's, yet he believes social structures may constrain.

33. Giddens, *New Rules of Sociological Method*, p. 102, emphasis in original.

34. J. Dearlove and P. Saunders, *Introduction to British Politics* (London, Polity Press, 1984), pp. 80–115.

35. Giddens, *Central Problems in Social Theory*, pp. 71–3.

36. Lukes, 'Power and structure', p. 13.

37. Giddens, *Central Problems in Social Theory*, p. 62.

38. Within a realist perspective there is no problem with the notion of structures being causally effective. See Bhaskar, *The Possibility of Naturalism*, pp. 39–47 and R. Keat and J. Urry, *Social Theory as Science* (London, Routledge and Kegan Paul, 1975), Ch. 2.

39. L. Winner, 'Do artifacts have politics?', *Daedelus*, Winter 1980, pp. 121–36, p. 124, emphasis added.

40. This would certainly be consistent with Giddens's criticism of Durkheim's view that social structures are constraining. In one of his crucial examples, Durkheim argued that social structures constrain entrepreneurs from adopting old vintages of technology. I take it that Durkheim's point was that this was physically possible but coercively costly. See Giddens, *New Rules of Sociological Method*, p. 2. Giddens does make the isolated comment that 'structure is both enabling and constraining' (Giddens, *Central Problems in Social Theory*, p. 69), although his work is full of such remarks as 'structure (thus) is not to be conceptualized as a barrier to action' (Giddens, *Central Problems in Social Theory*, p. 70). I think that what Giddens is implying is that cost penalties do not make things impossible: a similar point to Lukes!

41. Lukes, 'Power and structure', pp. 12–13.

42. Lukes, 'Power and structure', p. 13.

43. Lukes, 'Power and structure', p. 13.

44. H. Steiner, 'Individual liberty', *Proceedings of the Aristotelian Society*, LXV (1974–75), pp. 33–50.

45. S. Lukes, *Power: A Radical View* (London, Macmillan, 1974), p. 56.

46. Saunders, *Urban Politics*, pp. 61–5. Saunders also provides a good example of how power may be exercised through the unintended consequences of numerous small actions in urban politics. See Saunders, *Urban Politics*, pp. 53–7.

47. See, for example, B. Gertz, 'Coercion and freedom', in J. R. Pennock and J. W. Chapman (eds), *Coercion: Nomos* XIV (Chicago, Aldine, 1972). Gertz argues that only threats are coercive in this sense, but offers may set up *opportunity cost* of refusing to accept them that no reasonable man would bear. These, too, may be coercive and may be seen as constraints. Goldman, *A Theory of Human Action*, pp. 215–21 provides a general account of constraints upon individuals in which things which make certain options costly or difficult, not just impossible, are seen as constraining. But, in contrast to the position advocated here, he talks of different degrees of constraint and does not limit the word constraint only to those penalties high enough to be compelling to any agent facing them.

48. See D. Miller, 'Constraints on freedom', *Ethics*, 94 (1983), 66–86, although Miller would argue that the liberty of another is only impaired if the agent imposing the coercive cost penalty is responsible.

49. As in my example of the social patterning of disease, structural constraints may operate in a probabilistic sense. Not every miner gets a physically disabling case of black-lung but, other things being equal, all have *about equal chances* of being disabled, and in this sense, the disease structure constrains impersonally.

50. It might be argued that to infer the existence of constraints from actions and then use those constraints to explain the action is tautological. But this may be overcome if past evidence is used to explain later actions.

51. I think that coercive cost penalties are crucial to the closure of social classes. Closure strategies do not aim to make it physically impossible for some others to enter a certain class, but rather coercively costly. See F. Parkin, *Marxism and Class Theory: A Bourgeois Critique* (London, Tavistock, 1979), especially on the credentialist strategies of professionals.

52. See A. Gamble and S. Walkland, *The British Party System and Economic Policy 1945–1983: Studies in Adversary Politics* (Oxford, Oxford University Press, 1984).

53. Marsh, 'Interest group activity and structural power', associates structural power with economic structure, although he points out that the structural power of the financial sector is important.

54. R. Alford and R. Friedland, *Powers of Theory: Capitalism, the State and*

Democracy (Cambridge, Cambridge University Press, 1985), pp. 169–75 make the opposite mistake of defining structural power as only arising from organizational structures within the state. By organizational structures I mean aspects of organizations which are invariant with the particular individual who happens to occupy the various bureaucratic roles within them.

55. M. Weir and T. Skocpol, 'State structures and the possibility for "Keynesian" responses to the Great Depression in Sweden, Britain, and the United States', in P. Evans, D. Rueschemeyer and T. Skocpol (eds), *Bringing the State Back In* (Cambridge, Cambridge University Press, 1985).

56. See Longstreth, 'The City, industry and the state'. It is wrong to say that a social group has power if it benefits from constraints it has no part in creating or sustaining. For an example of this error see Parry and Morris's discussion of the 'consequential power' the Orange Order supposedly derives from political routines in Ulster which it did not create or sustain: G. Parry and P. Morris, 'When is a decision not a decision', in I. Crewe (ed.), *British Political Sociology Yearbook, Vol. I* (London, Croom Helm, 1974). Some might argue that the City has had very little to do with the origins or reproduction of the ideology and organizational power of the Treasury from which it has benefited. See Ingham, *Capitalism Divided*, especially Ch. 6. If Ingham is correct, the City benefits from organizational constraints, but the City's power is not implicated in them.

57. Much of the opposition to structuralism comes from those who believe that individuals and social groups are capable of autonomous acts which shape history. See, for example: T. Benton, *The Rise and Fall of Structural Marxism* (London, Macmillan, 1984), p. 213; E. P. Thompson, 'The poverty of theory', in his *The Poverty of Theory and Other Essays* (London, Merlin, 1978).

58. Giddens, *The Constitution of Society*, p. 9; Lukes, *Power: A Radical View*, p. 54.

59. Giddens, *The Constitution of Society*, p. 14.

60. Lukes, *Power: A Radical View*, p. 54.

61. Lukes, 'Power and structure', pp. 24–25.

62. Also see the discussion linking the question of whether individuals could have acted otherwise with the way in which agents are to be conceptualized in Lukes, 'Power and structure', pp. 26–9. Lukes argues that individuals can normally be seen as having a range of possible sets of preferences, beliefs, and so on, not just the ones they actually hold at any time and that, through time, the agent might be envisaged changing in various ways. This openness of the individual's personality is, of course, a necessary condition for personal autonomy.

63. Giddens, *The Constitution of Society*, pp. 10–14.

64. For instance, Giddens's agents 'reflexively monitor' their actions to see whether the consequences conform with their aims (*Central Problems in Social Theory*, pp. 57–8); they are not the mere 'cultural dupes' of Parsonian Sociology, nor are they 'mere bearers of the mode of production', and they have a 'worthwhile degree of understanding of the social world' (*Central Problems in Social Theory*, p. 71); they are able to rationalize their actions, and have motives which supply 'overall plans or programmes' for their lives (*The Constitution of Society*, pp. 6–7). However, especially in *The Constitution of Society*, Giddens emphasizes the unconscious. For the relation of this to the theory of structuralization see *The Constitution of Society*, Ch. 1.

65. Of course, it may be extremely difficult, as Lukes notes, to say whether individuals *are* located in the same position: Lukes, 'Power and structure', p. 24. But it is always easier to establish autonomy from social structure than it is to establish personal autonomy, for the former is a necessary, but not a necessary and sufficient condition for the latter. By asking the counterfactual question 'Did other agents do the

same?', we can often make some headway in saying how *relatively important* structures and agency were to an outcome. If all agents acted very similarly, then presumably the structural effects were very important.

66. This can never be more than a presumption, unless further evidence is adduced. A set of actors may happen all to do the same, *even though* they did not have to do so because of structural effects. The point is that so long as the number of actors similarly located is 'large' it is *highly unlikely* that they would all act the same way unless structures constrained their actions.

63

Citizenship and Autonomy*

D. Held

*Source: D. Held and J.B. Thompson (eds), *Social Theory of Modern Societies: Anthony Giddens and His Critics*, Cambridge: Cambridge University Press, 1989, ch. 8.

In this chapter, I wish to cut a particular path through Anthony Giddens's work by focusing on the way in which he interprets the relationship between citizenship, capitalism and the possibilities of a new 'progressive' politics. I believe this to be a particularly fertile domain in which to assess his writings because it is in exploring the interconnections between class, citizenship and related phenomena that Anthony Giddens analyses some of the key features of modern society and evaluates some of the key contributions of the major traditions of political and social theory: above all, those of liberalism and Marxism. It will be my contention that there are ambiguities at the very heart of Anthony Giddens's project. While he unquestionably makes a major contribution to rethinking social and political theory today, there are a number of essential questions which remain unanswered in his work – questions which cast doubt on the coherence of central parts of his project as it is currently formulated.

The chapter has a number of sections. In the first part, I examine T. H. Marshall's classic study, 'Citizenship and Social Class'.[1] In a number of his works Giddens focuses attention on Marshall's contribution; for Marshall's work is a – if not the – classic treatment of the relationship between class and citizenship, capitalism and democracy (see *CCHM*, pp. 226–9; *PCST*, pp. 164–80; *NSV*, pp. 198–209). In the second part I shall argue that Giddens is right to focus attention on Marshall, but that many of Giddens's specific criticisms of Marshall are misconceived. After elaborating elements of Giddens's attempt to move beyond Marshall's views in the third part, I will contend in the fourth that the entire framework through which Marshall and Giddens examine the relationship between class and citizenship is partial and limited. The terms of reference of their analysis are such that they exclude from view a whole range of substantive problems, conflict areas and struggles. In the fifth and final part, I will explore some of the implications of this position. Focusing in particular on Giddens's recent work, I shall show that the failure to examine class and citizenship in broader terms has created ambiguities in his characterization of rights, of the political realm, of social structure, and finally of the political choices that face us today. I shall argue that there are fundamental ambivalences in Giddens's account of central elements of contemporary society.

Citizenship and Class

By citizenship, Marshall meant 'full membership of a community', where membership entails *participation* by individuals in the determination of the conditions of their own association.[2] Citizenship is a status which bestows upon individuals *equal* rights and duties, liberties and constraints, powers and responsibilities.[3] While there is no universal principle that determines what exactly the citizen's rights and duties shall be, societies in which citizenship is a developing force create, Marshall contended, an image of an 'ideal citizenship' and, thereby, a goal towards which aspirations can be directed. Within all such societies, the urge to attain the ideal is 'an urge towards a fuller measure of equality' – an enrichment of the stuff of which citizenship is made and an increase in the number of those upon whom the status of citizenship is bestowed.[4] If citizenship is a principle of equality, class, by contrast, is a system of inequality anchored in property, education and the structure of the national economy.[5] According to Marshall, class functions, among other things, to erode and limit the extent to which citizenship creates access to scarce resources and participation in the institutions which determine their use and distribution. Class and citizenship are contrary principles of organization: they are basically opposed influences.

The concept and reality of citizenship are, Marshall argued, among the great driving forces of the modern era. There has been a long, uneven, but persistent trend towards the expansion of the rights of citizenship which for analytical purposes can be broken down into three 'bundles' of rights; civil, political and social. [*Terminological note:* By civil rights Marshall meant 'rights necessary for individual freedom', including liberty of the person, freedom of speech, thought and faith, the right to own property and enter into contracts and the right to be treated equally with others before the law. Political rights refer to those elements of rights which create the possibility of participation in the exercise of political power 'as a member of a body invested with political authority or as an elector of the members of such a body'. Social rights are defined as involving a whole range of rights 'from the right to a modicum of economic welfare and security to the right ... to live the life of a civilized being according to the standards prevailing in ... society'.[6] The adequacy of Marshall's categories will be discussed in several places in the chapter and additional rights categories – the economic, reproductive and those deriving from international law – will be examined.

The meaning of the latter categories will be set out as they are introduced.] Essentially, he maintained, political reform in each of these domains can modify the worst aspects of economic inequality and can, therefore, make the modern capitalist system and the liberal polity more equal and just, without revolutionary activity. The dynamic of class inequalities stemming from the capitalist market system can be moderated to some degree: the excesses of class inequality can be contained, or in his word 'abated', through the successful development of democratic citizenship rights. Citizenship can remould the class system.

Marshall's discussion is explicitly focused on Britain and, although he sometimes generalizes beyond this context, he does not claim that his argument can be applied with equal cogency to other countries.[7] With respect to Britain itself, his argument is that the three elements of citizenship developed at different rates over the past two or three centuries. He sought to show that civil rights were the first to develop, and were established in something like their modern guise before the first great Reform Act in 1832. Political rights developed next, and their extension was one of the main features of the nineteenth century, although it was not until 1928 that the principle of universal political citizenship was fully recognized. Social rights, by contrast, almost vanished in the eighteenth and early nineteenth century, but were revived in the latter part of the nineteenth century.[8] Their revival and expansion began with development of public elementary education, but it was not until the twentieth century that social rights in their modern form were fully established. Marshall's principal evidence for this is the history of the modern welfare state. The great redistributive measures of the postwar welfare state, including measures introducing the health service, social security, new forms of progressive taxation and so on, created better conditions and greater equality for the vast majority of those who did not flourish in the free market. And they provided a measure of security for all those who are vulnerable in modern society, especially those who fall into the trap of the 'poverty cycle'. Marshall's proposal is that social rights form a vital element in a society which is still hierarchical, but which has mitigated the inequalities – and mellowed the tensions – deriving from the class system.

While Marshall interpreted the development of modern citizenship rights as an uneven process, he conceived each bundle of rights as a kind of step or platform for the others.[9] The eighteenth century was the main formative period for civil or legal rights, when the rights of liberty of the individual, and full and equal justice before the law, became firmly established. Civil rights created new freedoms – although initially, of course, it was the male property-owning individual who was to benefit from them directly. The new freedoms gradually allowed the male citizen liberty from subservience to the place in which he was born and from the occupation to which he was typically tied by custom or statute. While these freedoms (and others relating to them) threatened the traditional forms of power and inequality imposed by feudal society, they did not strain the new forms of inequalities created by the emergence of the competitive market society; on the contrary, Marshall argued, they were 'indispensable to it'.[10] The fundamental reason for this is that the new rights 'gave ... each man ... the power to engage as an independent unit in the economic struggle'. They created individuals who were 'free and equal in status' – a status which was the foundation of modern contract. Paradoxically, then, 'the single uniform status of citizenship', in its early form, provided the foundation of equality on which the [modern] structure of inequality could be built'.[11]

The slow but progressive achievement of civil rights was a prerequisite for the secure establishment of the liberty of the subject. It was also an indispensable first stage in the development of political rights: for, as Giddens usefully explains it, 'only if the individual is recognised as an autonomous agent does it become reasonable to regard that individual as politically responsible' (*NSV*, p. 203). The establishment of political rights belongs above all to the nineteenth century and involves a growing interest in equality as a principle to be applied to a range of domains. It involves, moreover, an appreciation of a tension between, on the one hand, the formal recognition of the individual as 'free and equal' in civil matters and, on the other, the actual liberty of the individual to pursue his interests free from political impediment. Political rights were gradually recognized as indispensable to guaranteeing individual freedom. Since there is no good reason for believing that those who govern will act ultimately in anything other than a self-interested way (as will those who are governed), government must, to avoid abuse, be directly accountable to an electorate called upon regularly to decide if their objectives have been met.

The establishment of 'political liberty' involved a process whereby the political rights which had previously been the monopoly of the privileged few were extended to the adult population as a whole. The rise of the trade union movement and of the labour movement more generally was a critical factor in the development of political citizenship. If citizenship was an entitlement, it had to be an entitlement to full political membership of society. Thus, the search for citizenship became the search for the conditions under which individuals could enjoy a sense of equal worth and equal opportunity. The scene was set for struggle over the enactment of political rights, and of social rights as well.

The ascendance of industrial capitalism created massive disparities in wealth, income and life conditions. Those who were unsuccessful in the marketplace experienced profound inequalities in all aspects of their lives. With the establishment of the universal franchise, the organized working class was able to secure, Marshall argued, the political strength to consolidate welfare or social gains *as rights*. While citizenship and class have been 'at war' in the nineteenth and twentieth centuries, the labour movement has succeeded in imposing modifications on the capitalist class system. In the twentieth century, demands for social justice have, in Marshall's words, 'contained contract'.[12] The preservation of economic inequalities has been made more difficult by the expansion or enrichment of the notion of citizenship. Class distinctions certainly survive, Marshall recognized, but there is less room for them today, and they are more under pressure and are more likely to be challenged. As he eloquently put it, the expansion of social rights

> is no longer merely an attempt to abate the obvious nuisance of destitution in the lowest ranks of society ... it is no longer content to raise the floor level in the basement of the social edifice, leaving the superstructure as it was. It has begun to remodel the whole building, and it might even end by converting the skyscraper into a bungalow.[13]

Contract has been challenged by status, and the rule of market forces has begun to be subordinated to social justice.[14] Marshall's view of the likely progress of social democratic reforms (unsurprisingly perhaps, given that many of his ideas were formulated in the late 1940s) is decidedly optimistic.

Giddens versus Marshall

While Anthony Giddens affirms the significance of Marshall's analysis of citizenship for contemporary social and political theory, he has a number of criticisms to make (see *CCHM*, pp. 226–9; *PCST*, pp. 171–3; *NSV*, pp. 204–9). In the first place, he is critical of what he sees as the teleological and evolutionary elements in Marshall's analysis (see especially *PCST*, p. 171). Giddens criticizes Marshall for treating the development of citizenship as if it were something that unfolded in phases according to some inner logic within the modern world. In Giddens's account, Marshall tends to overstate the extent to which citizenship rights can be understood in terms of a threefold staged process. In addition, Giddens sees in Marshall's account an over-simplification of the role of politics and the state. Marshall, according to Giddens, understood the unfolding of citizenship rights from the eighteenth to the twentieth century as a process which is supported and buttressed by 'the beneficent hand of the state'. In Giddens's analysis, Marshall seriously underestimated the way 'citizenship rights have been achieved in substantial degree only through struggle' (*PCST*, p. 171). Furthermore, Giddens argues, Marshall underestimated the degree to which the balance of power was tipped to the underprivileged only during times of war, particularly during the periods of world war.

   These criticisms are, in my view, misleading in a number of respects.[15] Far from suggesting a general evolutionary framework for the explanation of the development of citizenship rights, Marshall, in my assessment, takes a more contingent view of historical change.[16] There seems little, if any, evidence to suggest that his scheme rests on the assumption of an evolutionary logic. Marshall emphasized that institutions and complexes of rights developed at their 'own speed' and under the direction of varying forces and principles.[17] The development of rights by no means followed, he stressed, a linear path in any one time period; there were often losses as well as gains. Further, the chief factor which he saw underpinning the development of rights was, in fact, struggle – struggle against hierarchy in its traditional feudal form, struggle against inequality in the market-place and struggle against social injustice perpetuated by state institutions. Rights had to be fought for, and when they were won they had to be protected. At the root of these processes was (and is) the delicate balance between social and political forces. When Marshall discussed citizenship and class, and when he described the relationship between the two as one of 'warfare', he was addressing himself explicitly to some of the major social movements which have shaped the contemporary world. In writings after 'Citizenship and Social Class', Marshall is even more explicit about the formative role of political and social conflict.[18]

A second area of criticism voiced by Giddens concerns Marshall's treatment of the expansion of citizenship rights as a purely 'one-way phenomenon' (*PCST*, p. 173). Marshall is criticized for regarding the development of citizenship as an 'irreversible process'. There are passages in Marshall which certainly justify this criticism. However, it seems in general to be misplaced. For instance, Marshall documented the way in which primitive forms of social rights – rooted in membership of local communities and functional association (guilds) – existed prior to the eighteenth century and yet practically vanished in the latter half of the eighteenth century and the early nineteenth century. He argued that their revival began with the development of public elementary education, but that this process of revival itself had by no means a stable history, and depended on the particular strength of the various social movements supporting reform.[19] More fundamentally, Marshall pointed to the emergence of nationalism – 'modern national consciousness', as he put it – as a critical factor in the stimulation of the demand for the recognition of equal social worth.[20] Nationalist movements inspired a direct sense of 'community membership' and the aspiration that all nationals become full and equal members of the community. Marshall did not develop this insight, and he did not provide a detailed analysis of the international context within which the demands for citizenship rights developed. Nonetheless, he did not ignore this context, and in various writings stressed the significance of nationalism and warfare to the history of rights, particularly social rights.[21] Moreover, Marshall concluded his reflections on class and citizenship by arguing that the balance achieved between these two great forces in the twentieth century by no means promised a simple stable future. In Marshall's view, how long the current balance lasts cannot easily be determined. And, he concluded, 'it may be that some of the conflicts within our system are becoming too sharp for the compromise to achieve its purpose much longer'.[22] Marshall appears to have been quite sensitive to the potential instabilities which might wreck any period of social equilibrium. Written four decades before the epoch of Reagan and Thatcher, and the New Right's attack on welfare rights, this certainly was an insightful observation.

A third set of criticisms Giddens makes is concerned with Marshall's threefold classification of rights. Giddens objects in particular to Marshall's treatment of civil rights as a homogeneous category. He emphasizes that the civil rights of individual freedom and equality before the law were fought for and achieved in large part by an emergent bourgeoisie. These rights helped consolidate industrial capitalism and the modern representative state. As such, they are to be distinguished from what Giddens calls 'economic civil rights' (or 'industrial citizenship', as Marshall put it). This latter group of rights had to be fought for by working-class and trade union activists. The right to form trade unions was not gracefully conceded, but was achieved and sustained only through bitter conflicts. The same applies to the extension of the activities of unions in their attempt to secure regularized bargaining and the right to strike. All this implies that there is 'something awry in lumping together such phenomena with civil rights in general' (*PCST*, p. 172). If individual civil rights tended to confirm the dominance of capital, economic civil rights tended to threaten the functioning of the capitalist market.

More fundamentally, Giddens maintains that each category of citizenship right should be understood as an arena of contestation or conflict, each linked to a distinctive type of regulatory power or surveillance, where that surveillance is both necessary to the power of superordinate groups and an axis around which subordinate groups can seek to reclaim control over their lives (see *NSV*, pp. 205ff). For instance, he writes,

> Civil rights are intrinsically linked to the modes of surveillance involved in the policing activities of the state. Surveillance in this context consists of the apparatus of judicial and punitive organizations in terms of which 'deviant' conduct is controlled ... [Like the other kinds of rights] civil rights have their own particular locale. That is to say, there is an institutionalized setting in which the claimed universality of rights can be vindicated – the law court. The law court is the prototypical court of appeal in which the range of liberties included under 'civil rights' can be both defended and advanced.　(*NSV*, pp. 205–6)

Table 1 shows the type of classificatory scheme of rights, and the modes of power and institutional sites to which they are related, which is suggested in Giddens's writings.

It is hard to be sure that the scheme in Table 1 is exactly what Giddens has in mind because he is inconsistent in his use of key terms. In some

Table 1 Rights, surveillance and locales

Types of right	Civil	Economic civil	Political	Social
Type of regulatory power or surveillance	Policing	Control of work-place	Political	'Management' of population
Institutional centre or locale where rights are championed and fought over	Law courts	Work-place	Parliament or legislative chamber	(State administrative offices?)[a]

[a] This category is particularly underdeveloped in Giddens's writings

publications, for example, economic civil rights figure prominently, while in others they do not; in some writings social rights are themselves referred to as economic rights, although in others they are not. The same can be said about the treatment of the locale of rights (see *PCST*, ch. 12 and *NSV*, ch. 8). In addition, while Giddens recognizes that the struggle for types of rights is not restricted to one particular setting, the precise connections that are drawn (and the significance of them) remains vague. For instance, the category of civil rights includes a variety of important rights ranging over matters as diverse as marriage, religion and economic affairs. This involves 'bundles' of rights which have quite different origins, conditions of existence and institutional mechanisms of support, from the local community to the courts or Parliament.[23] Why, and in what particular ways, types of rights are linked to particular forms of power and locale is not sufficiently elaborated. And while there is much to recommend Giddens's emphasis on the achievement of rights through contestation, it does not separate him as decisively from Marshall as he claims: Marshall does grant conflict a central place in the achievement of rights.

However, underpinning Giddens's concern with conflict, and the domains in which it is located, is a wider concern to develop a new explanatory framework for the development of rights. It is worth dwelling on this for a moment; for it has a number of advantages over Marshall's account although, as I shall show, it is itself by no means fully satisfactory.

The Roots of Modern Citizenship

In Giddens's view, the development of citizenship and of modern democracy in general has to be linked to the expansion of state sovereignty or the build-up of administrative power from the late sixteenth century. The development of the state's 'apparatus of government' was made possible to a significant extent by the extension of the state's capacity for surveillance; that is, the collection and storing of information about members of society, and the related ability to supervise subject populations (*CCHM*, pp. 169ff.). As the state's sovereign authority expanded progressively and its administrative centres became more powerful, the state's dependence on force as a direct medium of rule was slowly reduced. For the increase in administrative power via surveillance increased the state's dependence on co-operative forms of social relations; it was no longer possible for the modern state to manage its affairs and sustain its offices and activities by force alone. Accordingly, greater reciprocity was created between the governors and the governed, and the more reciprocity was involved, the more opportunities were generated for subordinate groups to influence their rulers. Giddens refers to this 'two-way' expansion of power as 'the dialectic of control' (*NSV*, pp. 201f.)

The struggle for rights, Giddens argues, can be understood in this context. The expansion of state sovereignty helped foster the identity of subjects as political subjects – as citizens. As Giddens puts it, 'the expansion of state sovereignty means that those subject to it are in some sense – initially vague, but growing more and more definite and precise – aware of their membership in a political community and of the rights and obligations such membership confers' (*NSV*, p. 210). Nationalism is a critical force in the development of this new identity. In fact, Giddens contends, nationalism is 'the cultural sensibility of sovereignty' (*NSV*, p. 219). The conditions involved in the creation of the modern state as a 'surveillance apparatus' are the same as those that help generate nationalism. Nationalism is closely linked to the 'administrative unification of the state'. And citizenship mediates this process. The development of citizenship, as pertaining to membership of an overall political community, is intimately bound up with the novel (administrative) ordering of political power and the 'politicization' of social relations and day-to-day activities which follows in its wake (see *NSV*, ch. 8).

The pursuit of equal membership in the new political communities reconstituted the shape of the modern state itself. Although the struggle for citizenship took a variety of forms, the most enduring and important was, Giddens claims, class conflict: first, the class conflict of the bourgeoisie against the remnants of feudal privilege; and, second, the class conflict of the working classes against the bourgeoisie's hold on the chief levers of power. These conflicts shaped two massive institutional changes, respectively. The first of these was the progressive separation of the state from the economy. It was the establishment of civil and political rights by the bourgeoisie which first and foremost helped free the economy, and more generally civil society, from the direct political interference of the state. The 'separation' of the state from the economy remoulded both sets of institutions. As Giddens explains it, the new rights and prerogatives

should not be seen as being created 'outside' the sphere of the state, but as part and parcel of the emergence of the 'public domain', separated from 'privately' organised economic activity. Civil rights thus have been, from the early phases of capitalist development, bound up with the very definition of what counts as 'political'. Civil and political citizenship rights developed together and remain, thereafter, open to a range of divergent interpretations which may directly affect the distribution of power.

(*NSV*, p. 207)

The development of polyarchy (rule by the many, or liberal democracy as it became in the West) can be understood against this background. The new 'public' domain became concerned in principle with protecting the space for citizens to pursue their activities unimpeded by illegitimate state action and with ensuring the responsiveness of government to the preferences of its citizens considered as political equals.[24] The 'public' and the 'private' spheres were formed through interrelated processes.

The second massive institutional change was linked, after the general achievement of the franchise, to the success of the working classes in the late nineteenth and twentieth century struggling for 'social rights', or for what Giddens sometimes prefers to call 'economic rights'. This second set of struggles produced the welfare order – the modern welfare interventionist state. Social or economic rights cannot be regarded as a mere extension of civil and political rights, for they are in part the creation of an attempt to ameliorate the worst consequences of the worker-citizen's lack of formal control of his or her activities in the work-place.

In sum, in Giddens's assessment, class conflict has been and remains the medium of the extension of citizenship rights and the basis of the creation of an insulated economy, polyarchy and the welfare state. The forging of state sovereignty was a critical impetus to the struggle for rights and to the remoulding of citizenship. The increase in state administrative power led to the creation of new aspirations and demands, and to the development of institutions which were responsive to them. These were major historical changes. But there is nothing inherent about them, Giddens notes, which would prevent their erosion in different political or economic circumstances. They remain fragile achievements.

There is much that is compelling about this position. In particular, Giddens's emphasis on the way in which an increase in state power led to the progressive reliance of the state on new relationships with its subjects – relationships based on consent, rather than force – has much to recommend it as a basis for explaining why new forms of political relations were called into being in the modern era. Likewise, his emphasis on the contingent nature of these developments has much to be said for it, especially if one is seeking to explain the different forms citizenship has taken, and the complex articulation of these forms with industrial capitalism.[25] Nonetheless, it is my view that the value of Giddens's analysis is weakened considerably by a number of difficulties. It will be my contention that problems in Giddens's position derive from accepting too much of Marshall's initial terms of reference, and from lack of precision in central formulations. The upshot of these problems is a fundamental underestimation of the complexity of citizenship: its multidimensional roots and the way the struggle for different types of rights is 'inscribed' into, or embedded in, changing conceptions of citizenship. A few reflections on the nature of citizenship provided a useful starting point from which to highlight these shortcomings.

Citizenship, Rights and Obligations

From the ancient world to the present day, all forms of citizenship have had certain common attributes. Citizenship has meant a certain reciprocity of rights against, and duties towards, the community.[26] It has entailed membership, membership of the community in which one lives one's life. And membership has invariably involved degrees of participation in the community. The question of who should participate and at what level is a question as old as the ancient world itself. There is much significant history in the attempt to restrict the extension of citizenship to certain groups: among others, owners of property, white men, educated men; men, those with particular skills and occupations, adults. There is also a telling story in the various conceptions and debates about what is to count as citizenship and in particular what is to count as participation in the community.[27]

If citizenship entails membership in the community and membership implies forms of social participation, then it is misleading to think of citizenship primarily in relation to class or the capitalist relations of production. Citizenship is about involvement of people in the community in which they live; and people have been barred from citizenship on grounds of gender, race and age, among many other factors. To analyse citizenship as if it were a matter of the inclusion or exclusion of social classes is to eclipse from view a variety of dimensions of social life which have been central to the struggle over citizenship. In the light of this fact, the debate about citizenship initiated by Marshall requires elaboration and modification.[28]

The argument against Marshall and Giddens can, thus, be put as follows. Class conflict may well be an important medium for the development of citizenship rights, but it is by no means the only one which requires detailed examination. If citizenship involves the struggle for membership and participation in the community, then its analysis involves examining the way in which different groups, classes and movements struggle to gain degrees of autonomy and control over their lives in the face of various forms of stratification, hierarchy and political oppression. The post-Marshall debate needs to extend the analysis of citizenship to take account of issues posed by, for instance, feminism, the black movement, ecology (concerned with the moral status of animals and nature) and those who have advocated the rights of children.[29] Different social movements have raised different questions about the nature and dimensions of citizenship. As one commentator aptly put it, 'citizenship rights are the outcome of social movements which aim either to expand or to defend the definition of social membership ... The boundaries which define citizenship ... ultimately define membership of a social group or collectivity.'[30] The struggle over the nature and extent of citizenship has *itself* been a, if not the, central medium of social conflict – the medium through which various classes, groups and movements strive to enhance and protect their rights and opportunities. The very meaning of particular rights cannot be adequately understood if the range of concerns and pressures which have given rise to them is not properly grasped.

Now, it is the case that Giddens does acknowledge a range of movements which have been significant in shaping the struggle for citizenship rights. But this acknowledgement has come 'late' in the sense that it leaves the impression of being tacked on to his existing explanatory framework. This is the case for at least two reasons. First, whenever Giddens offers substantive explanations of the development of citizenship, class conflict is the major determining factor (*PCST*, pp. 171–2; *CCHM*, pp. 227–9; *NSV*, ch. 8). Second, little attention is devoted to understanding the nature and activities of social movements, and particular movements' advocacy of certain rights is not properly explained.[31] Giddens's attempt in his most recent work to provide a 'conceptual map' that links together diverse sources of social protest with particular sets of institutions and particular forms of rights does not solve the problems (*NSV*, pp. 310–25). Significant movements are missed out altogether (such as the anti-racist movements),[32] and the connections between those that are there and particular struggles for rights seem tenuous. For example, many would argue with the view taken within Giddens's scheme that social rights[33] are the prime objective of the labour movement, that political rights are the prime concern of the 'free-speech movement' (a dubious catch-all category itself), that civil rights are the main focus of the peace movement and that 'moral imperatives' are the preoccupation of the ecological movement. Moreover, different movements changing orientations over time (from civil concerns to perhaps wider political and social issues), their different institutional locations at any given moment (economy, polity, local community, etc.) and their different views of the meaning of rights cannot be accommodated on a map which essentially plots static relations between phenomena. In short, although Giddens acknowledges different clusters of movements and rights in the struggle for citizenship, this is not elaborated into a coherent framework. If Giddens is serious about the necessity to encompass a diverse range of groups and movements in his account of citizenship, then he will have to depart decisively from the terms of reference of his debate with Marshall, which affirms class as the key variable affecting, and the determining influence on, citizenship rights.

It is important to be clear about the meaning of rights if a more adequate account of citizenship is to be developed. The type of rights which are central to the Marshall–Giddens discussion can be defined as *legitimate spheres of independent action (or inaction)*.[34] Accordingly, the study of rights can be thought of as the study of the domains in which citizens have sought to pursue their own activities within the constraints of community. If the early attempts to achieve rights involved struggles for autonomy or independence from the locale in which one was born and from prescribed occupations, later struggles involved such things as freedom of speech, expression, belief and association, and freedom for women in marriage. The autonomy of the citizen can be represented by that bundle of rights which individuals can enjoy as a result of their status as 'free and equal' members of society. And to unpack the domain of rights is to unpack both the rights citizens formally enjoy and the conditions under which citizens' rights are actually realized or enacted. Only this 'double focus' makes it possible to grasp the degrees of autonomy, interdependence and constraint that citizens face in the societies in which they live.[35]

There is insufficient space in this chapter to elaborate fully a new classificatory scheme of rights which would do justice to the range of rights which have been established or advocated in the struggle for citizenship. But it is important at least to indicate that the set of rights compatible with citizenship in modern societies has to be conceived more broadly than either Marshall or Giddens has allowed. The broad cluster of rights Marshall refers to under the headings 'civil', 'political' and 'social', and Giddens refers to as 'civil', 'economic civil', 'political' and 'social', can usefully be thought of as pertaining to four distinct spheres which I prefer to call civil, economic, political and social. Giddens's reasons for not lumping together civil and economic civil rights are sound, but little is gained by retaining the label 'civil' in this category. Accordingly, economic rights means all those rights which have been won by the labour movement over time and which create the possibility of greater control for employees over the work-place. Removing this category from civil rights distinguishes usefully those rights which are concerned with the liberty of the individual in general from those sub-categories of rights which seek to recover elements of control over the work-place, and which have been at the centre of conflicts between labour and capital since the earliest phases of the Industrial Revolution.[36] The category of political and social (or welfare) rights can, following Marshall and Giddens, be treated as fairly unproblematic for the purposes of this chapter.

But apart from these broad sets of rights, there are other categories which neither Marshall nor Giddens develops, linked to a variety of domains where, broadly speaking (non-class specific) social movements have sought to re-form power centres according to their own goals and objectives. Among these is the area of struggle for reproductive rights – at the very heart of the women's movement.[37] Reproductive rights are the very basis of the possibility of effective participation of women in both civil society and the polity. A right to reproductive freedom for women entails making the state or other relevant political agencies responsible not only for the medical and social facilities necessary to prevent or assist pregnancy, but also for providing the material conditions which would help make the choice to have a child a genuinely free one and, thereby, ensure a crucial condition for women if they are to be 'free and equal'. Giddens's lack of attention to reproductive rights is symbolic of his disregard of the whole question of the social organization of reproduction, and of women and gender relations more generally.[38] He has not made the latter an integral component of his work and the inevitable result, I believe, is major lacunae in his conception of the conditions of involvement of women (and men) in public life.

Marshall's and Giddens's accounts of rights suffer, in addition, from a further limitation: a strict focus on the citizen's relation to the nation-state. While this is unquestionably important, the whole relation of rights to the nation-state has itself become progressively more problematic in the twentieth century For a gap has opened up, linked to processes of globalization, between the idea of membership of a national political community, i.e. citizenship, and the development of international law which subjects individuals, non-governmental organizations and governments to new systems of regulation.[39] Rights and duties are recognized in international law which transcend the claims of nation-states and which, whilst they may lack coercive powers of enforcement, have far-reaching consequences. For example, the International Tribunal at Nuremburg (1945) laid down, for the first time in history, that when *international rules* that protect basic humanitarian values are in conflict with *state laws*, every individual must transgress the state laws (except where there is no room for 'moral choice'). The legal framework of the Nuremburg Tribunal marked a highly significant change in the legal direction of the modern state; for the new rules challenged the principle of military discipline and subverted national sovereignty at one of its most sensitive points: the hierarchical relations within the military.[40] In addition, two internationally recognized legal mainstays of national sovereignty – 'immunity from jurisdiction' and 'immunity of state agencies' – have been progressively questioned by Western courts. While it is the case that national sovereignty has most often been the victor when put to the test, the tension between citizenship, national sovereignty and international law is marked, and it is by no means clear how it will be resolved.

A satisfactory account of the meaning and nature of citizenship today must transcend the terms of reference which Marshall and Giddens have set down. The study of citizenship has to concern itself with all those dimensions which allow or exclude the participation of people in the communities in which they live and the complex pattern of national and international relations and processes which cut across these. Neither Marshall nor Giddens has provided an adequate basis for such a study.

Rights, States and Societies

The restricted conception of citizenship in Marshall's and Giddens's work has serious sociological and political implications for central areas of inquiry. The section below will explore these implications in relation to Giddens's treatment of the ideological nature of rights, the critical dimensions of the state, the social structure of postwar society and contemporary political directions.

Rights: Sham or Real?

When setting out the meaning of citizenship rights, Giddens criticizes Marshall from a Marxist perspective and then uses Marshall against Marxism, pursuing the question: are rights an ideological sham or of real significance? In recent writings, Giddens has affirmed that capitalism is, as Marx argued, a class society. Pivotal to Giddens's analysis is the capitalist labour contract, the basic concept, he suggests, for analysing the class structure of capitalism from the eighteenth century to the present time.

The creation of a marketplace for both labour power and capital involved two fundamental developments. The first of these was the progressive separation of the economic from the political, referred to earlier. The creation of a distinctive sphere of the political was established by the overthrowing of feudal, courtly power, and by its progressive replacement by parliamentary representative government (*PCST*, p. 173). The struggle for civil and political rights consolidated this development, giving distinctive form to the public domain. While the separation of the economic from the political was in many respects a progressive development in political terms, it served also to undercut the new-won freedoms. For although the new freedoms were universal in principle, they favoured the dominant class in practice. The rights of the citizen to elect or stand as representatives were not extended to work and, accordingly, the sphere of politics was not extended to industry. Once citizens entered the factory gates, their lives were fully determined by the dictates of capital. To quote Giddens: 'the capitalist labour contract ... excludes the worker from formal rights over the control of the workplace. This exclusion is not incidental to the capitalist state, but vital to it, since the sphere of industry is specifically defined as being "outside politics"' (*NSV*, p. 207). 'In substantial degree', Giddens argues, 'Marx was surely right' (*PCST*, p. 173; *NSV*, p. 207). Many of the new freedoms were 'bourgeois freedoms' (CCHM, p. 228; *PCST*, pp. 173–4).

In prior types of society it was taken for granted that the worker or peasant had a significant degree of control over the process of labour. But with the birth of industrial capitalism this substantial degree of control was lost and had to be won all over again. The formation of the labour movement, and of trade unions in particular, created a minimum basis of power for workers in the industrial sphere. Labour and socialist parties were able to build on this despite often bitter opposition. Together, unions and socialist parties took advantage of and fought for the development of political and social rights. It is very important, Giddens concludes from this, to see the different kinds of citizenship rights distinguished by Marshall as – contra Marx and Marxism – 'double-edged'. Citizenship rights do serve to extend the range of human freedoms possible within industrial capitalist societies; they serve as levers of struggle which are the very basis on which freedoms can be won and protected. But at the same time they continue to be the sparking points of conflict. In the final analysis, therefore, citizenship rights have not simply been bourgeois freedoms. To use Marshall against Marx is, according to Giddens, to recognize that Marxism has failed to understand, and anticipate, the very way in which certain types of citizenship rights have been actualized within the framework of liberal industrial capitalist society. As he puts it:

> Among the industrialized societies at least, capitalism is by now a very different phenomenon from what it was in the nineteenth century and labour movements have played a prime role in changing it. In most of the capitalist countries, we now have to speak of the existence of 'welfare capitalism', a system in which the labour movement has achieved a considerable stake and in which economic [social] citizenship rights brook large.
>
> *(NSV, p. 325)*

Citizenship rights helped cement the industrial capitalist order while at one and the same time creating new forms of politics linked to new rights for all its citizens.

There is a fundamental ambiguity in Giddens's analysis. This ambiguity derives from his attempt to reconcile three different positions. First, he wants to argue that Marx was right: citizenship rights have been so much ideology – a sham (*CCHM*, p. 228). Giddens affirms the view that citizenship rights have for long periods largely been the province of the bourgeoisie and can legitimately be referred to as 'bourgeois freedoms' (*CCHM*, pp. 227–8). Secondly, he argues that Marx was only partially right. Marx was right about the extent to which citizenship rights served to legitimate and cement the industrial capitalist order. But Marx was wrong as well, because citizenship rights have proven to be 'double-edged'. Thirdly, Giddens argues that Marx was simply wrong about the nature of rights. The fact that rights are double edged – the fact that citizenship rights can be actualized within the framework of liberal democracy – seems to him to imply that the revolutionary socialist project is quite unjustified. To support this view Giddens singles out the fact that citizenship rights have been actually developed and extended within the sphere of industrial capitalism modifying and altering industrial capitalism itself. Giddens's overall equivocation on this issue, and the consequences this equivocation has, can be highlighted by considering his appraisal of the political significance of the separation of the 'political' and 'economic'.

For Giddens, the separation of the political and economic is linked fundamentally to the nature of modern domination – the rule of capital. While he is surely right to stress the way the institutionalized separation of the economic from the political creates the very basis for the development and expansion of capital – and secures the interests of the capitalist class – his analysis fails to explore systematically the ways in which this separation also creates a significant space for the realization of political rights and freedoms. The relative separation of the political and economic means that there is a realm in which the citizen can enjoy rights unavailable to those in societies where this separation has not been established. What this amounts to, among other things, is the necessity to recognize the fundamental liberal notion that the 'separation' of the state from civil society is (and must be) a central feature of any democratic political order; for without it, a number of critical modern political innovations – concerning the centrality, in principle, of an 'impersonal' structure of public power, of a constitution to help guarantee and protect rights, of a diversity of power centres within and outside of the state, of mechanisms to promote competition and debate between alternative political platforms – cannot be enjoyed.[41] While one consequence of the differentiation of the economic and political is to give the economy relative freedom and, thereby, to produce and reproduce massive asymmetries in income, wealth and power, as Giddens rightly maintains, another is to create a space for the enjoyment of civil and political rights.[42] The significance of this requires detailed comparative investigation (between countries West and East, North and South) which is missing in Giddens's work.

An additional problem of analysing and assessing citizenship rights primarily in terms of their ideological significance for class relations and capitalist society is that the very diverse origins of rights and the distinctively modern conception of citizenship get put aside. The modern conception of citizenship is inseparable from a series of multiple and complexly overlapping conflicts. Struggles between monarchs and barons over the domain of rightful authority; peasant rebellion against the weight of excess taxation and social obligation; the spread of trade, commerce and market relations; the flourishing of Renaissance culture with its renewed interest in classical political ideas (including the Greek city-state and Roman Law); the consolidation of national monarchies in Europe (England, France and Spain); religious strife and the challenge to the universal claims of Catholicism; the struggle between church and state – all played a part in the emergence of the modern idea of the state, the citizen and citizenship.[43] The idea of the individual as a citizen is, moreover, an idea deeply connected with the doctrine of freedom of choice, a doctrine which raises questions about choice in matters as diverse as marriage, economic and political affairs.[44] If the modern idea of citizenship crystallized at the intersection of a variety of struggles, it did so in the context of struggles concerned with rights which are fundamental to most aspects of choice in everyday life. The significance of these rights goes far beyond that which can be embraced in an analysis which simply places class first.

Giddens's emphasis on separating out the formal rights that people enjoy from the actual capacities they have to enact rights is important. But this insight is not original, and his use of it is marred by terms of reference which are too narrow and do not permit the adequate specification of the diverse range of rights that emerge with the development of modern citizenship. The right to freedom of choice in marriage, the right to choice about one's religion – these and many other rights cannot simply be understood or their meaning explicated within the framework of concerns: rights – sham or real? They suggest a diversity of issues, and a diversity of conditions, which need much more careful analysis than Giddens has hitherto provided. They also require a much more sophisticated classificatory scheme of rights if many of them are to be given adequate treatment at all. A satisfactory theory of rights, which attends to the diverse range of rights which have been essential to the shaping of the modern world, will require an analysis which goes far beyond that provided by Marx, Marshall or Giddens.

State: Capitalist or Modern?

In modern Western political thought, the idea of the state is often linked to the notion of an impersonal and privileged legal or constitutional order with the capability of administering and controlling a given territory.[45] While this notion found its earliest expression in the ancient world (especially in Rome), it did not become a major object of concern until the late sixteenth century.[46] It was not an element of medieval political thinking. The idea of an impersonal and sovereign political order, i.e. a legally circumscribed structure of power separate from ruler and ruled with supreme jurisdiction over a territory, could not predominate while political rights, obligations and duties were closely tied to religious tradition and the feudal system of property rights. Similarly, the idea that human beings were 'individuals' or 'a people', with a right to be citizens of their state, could not develop under the constraining influences of the 'closed circle' of medieval intellectual life.

These notions are sometimes argued to be constitutive of the very concept of the modern state. There are passages in which Giddens seems to share this view, and as a corollary an emphasis on the extraordinary innovatory power of these notions, recognizing that they provided a critical impetus to the form (constitutional, representative) and limits ('separation' of state and civil society, division of powers) of the modern 'apparatus of government' (see *CS*, ch. 6). From this perspective it follows that an understanding of the state requires a detailed appreciation of its institutional and legal bases – a 'state-centered' perspective.[47] While Giddens sometimes seems to recognize this, there are other passages in his work where the very idea of the modern state is eclipsed by the idea of the 'capitalist state'.

By the 'capitalist state' Giddens means, following Claus Offe, a state

'enmeshed' in class relations (see especially *CCHM*, pp. 210–14, 219–26).[48]
The following points are central to the position:

(1) The state in capitalism 'is a state in a class society' – a society in which
     class relations (via control over allocative resources) enter into the very
     constitution of the productive process; class struggle is a chronic feature
     of everyday life, and class conflict is a 'major medium' of the internal
     transformation of society (*CCHM*, pp. 214, 220–1).

(2) Unlike other ruling classes in history, 'the ruling class does not rule' in
     capitalism; that is, the 'capitalist class does not generally compose . . . the
     personnel of the state' (*CCHM*, p. 211). Nonetheless, 'the state, as a mode
     of "government", is strongly influenced by its institutional alignments
     with private property and with the insulated "economy"' (*NSV*, p. 136).

(3) The state is dependent upon the activities of capitalist employers for its
     revenues and, hence, operates in the context of various capitalist
     'imperatives' (*CCHM*, p. 211). It has, accordingly, to sustain the process
     of accumulation and the incentives for the private appropriation of
     resources while not undermining belief in itself as an impartial arbiter of
     all class interests, thereby eroding its power base.

(4) The state is 'directly enmeshed in the contradictions of capitalism'. In so
     being, it is 'not merely a defender of the status quo' (*CCHM*, p. 220). For
     if it is enmeshed in the contradictions of capitalism, it can in some part
     be seen as a force able to shape the very nature of interests and policies.

In this analysis, the explanatory and political axis 'class/state' is once again
granted the central role. Class and state power are directly linked and class
power is held to be the basis of political power. Such a position clearly grants
primacy to the capitalist nature of modern societies *and* states.

While there is some scope within this framework for understanding the
political or strategic intelligence which government and state agencies often
display, the general emphasis is one which denies what is central to the idea
of the modern state, i.e., that the state apparatus itself has sufficient primacy
over social classes and collectivities that the nature and meaning of political
outcomes – constitutional forms, particular institutional structures and the like
– cannot be inferred directly from the configuration of class relations.
Giddens's account of the capitalist state sits uneasily with his recognition of
the *sui generis* powers of the modern state, and of the necessity to see the state
as 'a set of collectivities concerned with the institutionalized organization of
political power' (*CCHM*, p. 220). Further, it sits in some tension with his own
argument that Marx's treatment of the capitalist state is deficient because it
generally ignores the non-capitalist features of the state and fails to separate
out the institutional elements of modern politics from the broad pattern of
social relations (see *NSV*, pp. 141, 160).

Giddens's equivocation on the critical dimensions of the modern state is
related to his equivocation about rights. It is one thing to argue that the

modern state has (as do civil and political rights) central 'functions' for the reproduction of capital – an argument, however, that would need very careful elaboration (see the contribution by Jessop in this volume [*sic*]). But it is quite another thing to stress the capitalist character of the state to the point at which the significance of the institutional, constitutional and legal innovations of the modern state tends to be eclipsed from view altogether. A systematic treatment of the idea of rights, and of the new freedoms they formally allow, and a systematic understanding of the relationship between formal rights and the actual possibilities of their realization require a much more substantial account of the modern state than can be found in Giddens's work. Only such a treatment could do justice to the fact that the modern state developed partly in response to the demand to articulate and protect a range of rights and interests which cannot be reduced to issues of property and property relations.

Society: Pluralist or Class-Ridden?

In *A Contemporary Critique of Historical Materialism* and other texts, Giddens argues at length that capitalism is a class society. In fact, it is his view that capitalism is the only social formation to which the concept of 'mode of production' is applicable. As he puts it, 'I do … want to claim that capitalism is the first and only form of society in history of which it might be said with some plausibility that it both "has" and "is" a mode of production' (*NSV*, p. 134).

However, there are many other places in Giddens's work where he rejects (even in the case of capitalism) the direct connection Marx made between the history of classes, exploitation, conflicts of interest and the political power of the state. Here he argues that there are multiple routes of domination and different types of exploitation within and between classes, states, the sexes and ethnic groups. He suggests it is a mere delusion to imagine that the end of capitalism means the end of oppression in all its forms. In a typical passage he writes,

> The validity of much of what Marx has to say in analysing the nature of capitalist production need not be placed in doubt … However, Marx accords undue centrality to capitalism and to class struggle as the keys to explaining inequality or exploitation, and to providing the means of their transcendence.
>
> (*NSV*, p. 336)

The difficulty here is that ultimately Giddens has not resolved the issues posed by the debate between Marxism and pluralism – and no amount of elaborate syntheses seems to have resolved the matter.[49] Giddens wishes to affirm the centrality of class in the determination of the character of contemporary society while at the same time recognizing that this very perspective itself marginalizes or excludes certain types of issues from consideration. This is true of all those issues which cannot be reduced, as Giddens himself recognizes, to class-related matters. Classic examples of this are the domination of women by men, of certain racial and ethnic groups by others, and of nature by industry (which raises ecological questions). Other central concerns include the power of public administrators or bureaucrats over their 'clients' and the role of 'authoritative resources' (the capacity to co-ordinate and control the activities of human beings), which build up in most social organizations.

Giddens's affirmation of class analysis is certainly not unqualified; he argues strenuously on behalf of class analysis in social theory, but does not grant class relations primacy over many critical areas: from ecology to the military. Further, he recognizes, of course, the social and political significance of a number of social movements (*NSV*, ch. 11). But how exactly these movements are to be linked into the overall emphasis on class is not clarified. As one critic has remarked: 'Giddens wants to affirm the centrality of class while not giving up pluralist insights.'[50] Earlier equivocations and ambiguities are reflected in the decisive issue of how he characterizes the very nature of contemporary society. There are fundamental unresolved tensions in Giddens's account of the core relations and conflicts of modern life.

Political Choices: Liberalism or Socialism or . . . ?

These problems are carried over into the political dimension of Giddens's work. Giddens does not see himself as a champion of liberalism, but neither does he stray far from some of liberalism's central prescriptions. He does not straightforwardly advocate socialist positions, but neither does he wish to jettison central socialist ideals. He is critical, in addition, of a variety of intermediate positions, for example pluralism, and of 'reformist' political views like those of Marshall's. Yet he shares some of the terms of reference of the 'middle ground'. In *The Nation-State and Violence*, Giddens appears to advocate the necessity to go beyond liberalism, pluralism and Marxism. The contemporary world, he argues, is far more complex than any of these doctrines anticipated, and it has left none of them with their 'hands clean' (*NSV*, ch. 11). He maintains, moreover, that there are trends at work in the late twentieth century – particularly global trends – which render incoherent most contemporary conceptions of the political good (*NSV*, pp. 325ff.).

Traditionally, concepts of the political good have been elaborated at the level of state institutions, practices and operations; the state has been at the intersection of intellectually and morally ambitious conceptions of political life.[51] The challenge facing these traditional concepts is daunting today, as Giddens stresses. The dynamics of a world economy which produces instabilities and difficulties within states and between states and which outreach the control of any single 'centre'; the rapid growth of transnational links which have stimulated new forms of collective decision-making involving states, intergovernmental organizations and an array of international pressure groups; the build-up of military arms and the general means of warfare as a 'stable feature' of the contemporary political world – all these developments raise, I believe, fundamental questions about the terms of reference of liberalism, pluralism and Marxism. It is, of course, important to recognize the new questions on the political agenda. But it remains a, if not the, central task of political and social theory to think them through. One cannot be wholly optimistic about Giddens's future contribution in this area while there is such ambiguity at the heart of his critique and reconstruction of social and political theory. On the other hand, if Giddens fails here, we will all almost certainly be the losers, for there are very few with his scope and range of insight.

Notes

1. T. H. Marshall, 'Citizenship and Social Class', in Marshall, *Class, Citizenship and Social Development* (Westport, Conn.: Greenwood Press, 1973), pp. 65–122. Marshall's later work altered some of the emphases of his earlier essay. See, for instance, 'The Welfare State – a Comparative Study', in the same volume, pp. 277–95.

2. Marshall, 'Citizenship and Social Class', p. 70.

3. Ibid., p. 84.

4. Ibid., p. 84.

5. Ibid., pp. 84–5.

6. Ibid., pp. 71–2.

7. Ibid., p. 72.

8. Ibid., p. 83.

9. See ibid., 71–83, 95–6. See also Giddens, *NSV*, pp. 203–5, for a succinct statement of this issue.

10. Marshall, 'Citizenship and Social Class', p. 87.

11. Ibid., p. 87.

12. Ibid., p. 111.

13. Ibid., pp. 96–7.

14. Ibid., p. 111.

15. I am by no means the first to make this observation. See Bryan S. Turner, *Citizenship and Capitalism: The Debate over Reformism* (London: Allen & Unwin, 1986), pp. 45–6 for a particularly helpful discussion.

16. This is not the emphasis, it should be acknowledged, which has generally been put on Marshall's work in recent times. The chief reason for the discrepancy lies in the way Marshall's ideas were incorporated and popularized by writers who dominated sociological thought in the 1950s and 1960s such as Seymour Martin Lipset, Reinhard Bendix and Daniel Bell. Some of the latter's concerns and perspectives, in my view, distorted the reception of Marshall's key notions. While Marshall's writings are not without some ambiguity on these matters, they cannot, for reasons set out below, simply be interpreted as offering an 'evolutionary' account of citizenship rights.

17. Marshall, 'Citizenship and Social Class', pp. 73–4.

18. See, for example, *The Right to Welfare and Other Essays* (London: Heinemann, 1981), particularly pp. 104–36.

19. Marshall, 'Citizenship and Social Class', pp. 79–83, 95ff.

20. Ibid., p. 92.

21. See Marshall, *Social Policy in the Twentieth Century* (London: Hutchinson, 1975), especially part 1.

22. Marshall, 'Citizenship and Social Class', p. 122.

23. I shall return to this point at some length below.

24. *NSV*, pp. 198–201. Giddens's conception of polyarchy is directly informed by Dahl's and Lindblom's views. See R. A. Dahl, *Polyarchy* (New Haven: Yale University Press, 1971) and Charles E. Lindblom, *Politics and Markets* (New York: Basic Books, 1977).

25. See Göran Therborn, 'The Rule of Capital and the Rise of Democracy', *New Left Review*, 103 (1977), 3–41; and Michael Mann, 'Ruling Strategies and Citizenship', *Sociology*, 21, 3 (1987), 339–45.

26. See Carl Brinkmann, 'Citizenship', in *International Encyclopaedia of the Social Sciences* (New York: Macmillan, 1968), pp. 471–4.

27. For an account see my *Models of Democracy* (Cambridge: Polity Press, 1987).

28. This argument has been stated very usefully by Turner. See his *Citizenship and Capitalism*, especially chs. 1, 2 and 4.

29. Ibid., pp. 88–9 and pp. 85–92 for a fuller discussion of these issues.

30. Ibid., pp. 92, 85.

31. The women's movement, for example, typically gets half a paragraph in *NSV* (p. 321). In addition, the contemporary women's movement is connected, without explanation, to concerns with civil and political rights. Some of the difficulties involved in such a view – above all, the neglect of the struggle for reproductive rights – are discussed below.

32. Giddens would counter this criticism by arguing that all social movements can in principle be located on his 'map' (see *NSV*, p. 318). It is quite unclear, however, how movements concerned with matters such as racial prejudice or sexual freedom can be fitted into his categories. The same kind of consideration is raised in the note above about the prime orientation of the women's movement.

33. Giddens actually uses the term 'economic rights' here instead of 'social rights'. I have stayed with Marshall's term in order to help keep clear the key concepts under discussion.

34. Not all types of rights can, of course, be reduced to this conception. But it is, I believe, the pivotal notion underpinning the issues raised by Marshall and Giddens. I discuss this and related conceptions of rights further in my *Foundations of Democracy* (Cambridge: Polity Press, forthcoming).

35. For an elaboration of the issues underpinning the necessity of a 'double focus' in the analysis of citizenship rights see my *Models of Democracy*, ch. 9.

36. Separating these categories in this way also helps illuminate why certain types of rights may not always be complementary (as illustrated, for instance, in recent controversy over whether 'the closed shop' undermines the individual's freedom of choice).

37. Cf. Rosalind P. Petchesky, *Abortion and Women's Choice* (London: Verso, 1986).

38. On this point see the chapter by Linda Murgatroyd in this volume [*sic*].

39. See R. J. Vincent, *Human Rights and International Relations* (Cambridge: Cambridge University Press, 1986).

40. For an excellent discussion of these issues see Antonio Cassese, *Violence and Law in the Modern Age* (Cambridge: Polity Press, 1988).

41. I trace the importance of these issues at some length in *Models of Democracy*, chs. 2, 3, 8 and 9.

42. See Turner, *Citizenship and Capitalism*, pp. 37–44. Turner offers an illuminating discussion of some of the key theoretical issues involved here.

43. See, for example, Gianfranco Poggi, *The Development of the Modern State* (London: Hutchinson, 1978); Charles Tilly, 'Reflections on the History of European State-making', in C. Tilly (ed.), *The Formation of National States in Western Europe* (Princeton: Princeton University Press, 1975); Theda Skocpol, *States and Social Revolutions: A Comparative Analysis of France, Russia and China* (Cambridge: Cambridge University Press, 1979); Reinhard Bendix, *Kings or People* (Berkeley: University of California Press, 1980); S. I. Benn and R. S. Peters, *Social Principles and the Democratic State* (London: Allen & Unwin, 1959); John Keane, *Public Life and Late Capitalism* (Cambridge: Cambridge University Press, 1983), essay 6; and my *Models of Democracy*, ch. 2.

44. Cf. C. B. Macpherson, *The Real World of Democracy* (Oxford: Oxford University Press, 1966), ch. 1.

45. See Quentin Skinner, *The Foundations of Modern Political Thought* (2 vols., Cambridge: Cambridge University Press, 1978).

46. See ibid., vol. 2, pp. 349–58.

47. For a discussion of this perspective see Peter B. Evans, Dietrich Rueschemeyer and Theda Skocpol (eds.), *Bringing the State Back In* (Cambridge: Cambridge University Press, 1985).

48. Cf. Claus Offe, *Contradictions of the Welfare State* (London: Hutchinson, 1984).

49. See Gregor McLennan, *Pluralism, Marxism and Beyond* (Cambridge: Polity Press, 1989) for an excellent discussion of this issue.

50. Ibid., ch. 6.

51. See John Dunn, 'Responsibility without Power: States and the Incoherence of the Modern Conception of the Political Good', lecture delivered to the IPSA, Paris, July 1985. Forthcoming in M. Banks (ed.), *The State in International Relations* (Hassocks, Sussex: Wheatsheaf).

64

The Nation-State and the Modern World System*

C. Dandeker

*Source: J. Clark, C. Modgil and S. Modgil (eds), *Anthony Giddens: Consensus and Controversy*, London: Falmer Press, 1990, ch. 20.

Anthony Giddens: Critique and Renewal in Contemporary Social Theory

Since the publication of *Capitalism and Modern Social Theory* in 1971 (Giddens, 1971a) and in a series of subsequent works, Giddens has sought to reconstruct the intellectual foundations of contemporary social theory. Three related themes can be identified in his writings: first, an attempt to synthesize agency and structure in a theory of 'structuration'; second, a critique of evolutionary models of explanation in the social sciences; third, an evaluation of the two pre-eminent paradigms in the development of sociology – the theory of industrial society (with its functionalist underpinnings) and Marxism – as accounts of the nature, emergence and current prospects of modern societies.

Giddens's writings have always encompassed abstract methodological questions as well as the more substantive issues of modern societies, such as class structures and the distribution of power (Giddens, 1973). In his earlier work and in keeping with the wider currents of modern sociology, Giddens tended to ignore the fundamental part played by war and military power in social life. However, in his more recent work Giddens has sought to address explicitly the issue of the nation-state and violence (the title of his recent book, Giddens, 1985a) and the wider connections between the nation-state and the modern world system. Giddens contends that in order to understand these issues, social theory has to break with the two paradigms of modern sociology mentioned above and incorporate a third tradition into the mainstream of contemporary social analysis. Depending upon the context, Giddens refers to this as Nietzschean, right-liberal or conservative. In a related discussion Mann (1984) has described this strand of social theory as militarist, and the present writer has revived the term 'neo-Machiavellian' to make a similar point (Ashworth and Dandeker, 1987). When one turns to the discourse of political science, the conventional way of referring to this tradition is to use the term 'neo-realist' (Waltz, 1988).

The argument to be defended here is that Giddens's recent concern with the nation-state and violence comprises one aspect of a broader reorientation in modern social theory, as those who seek to comprehend the nature of the contemporary world find it necessary to break with many of the assumptions of liberal and Marxist sociologies.

Modernity and the Nation-State: Conflicting Interpretations in Social Theory

Giddens's analysis of the nation-state and the modern world system should be located in the broader context of his discussion of modernity and the ways in which his account draws on each of the three traditions of social theory indicated above. The roots of these can be traced in part to the writings of Marx, Durkheim and Weber.

For Giddens the modern era is defined by a clustering of four institutional elements: 1) the significance of 'heightened surveillance' through bureaucratic administration in what are increasingly formally organized societies (by surveillance is meant activities concerned with the supervision of subject populations and the gathering of information about them); 2) the modern capitalist enterprise with its market oriented dynamism and asymmetrical relations between capital and labour (this organization is also a major site of surveillance); 3) industrialism, that is, the application of modern technology to both the control of nature and human populations; 4) the concentration of administrative and military power in the nation-state as a territorially bounded sovereign entity. Of these four institutional orders, Giddens suggests that 'only two have received sustained attention within the social sciences' (1985a, 294).

While Marxism has focused on the development of capitalism and the strategic part played by class struggles in social change, theorists of industrial society have been preoccupied with the (supposedly progressive) impact of technology on social structure. As Giddens argues, 'with some notable exceptions, neither the expanded role of surveillance nor the altered nature of military power with the development of the means of waging industrialised war has been made central to formulations of social theory' (*ibid.*, 294–5).

This situation is not the result of neglect or simple oversight: rather, Giddens is pointing to the ways in which the two pre-eminent traditions of social theory are characterized by reductionist accounts of military and administrative power. With regard to war and military organization both Marxism and the theory of industrial society contend that the significance of these phenomena will decline with the maturation of modern societies. For the theory of industrial society, the normal development of the division of labour in and between societies will ensure that peaceful activities of production and exchange supplant warfare as dominant social activities. The networks of global interdependence established by market exchange provide conditions under which a peaceful concert of liberal nation-states can thrive. Aggressive nationalism will wane with the rise of a united humanity and the triumph of reason over tradition and the affectual aspects of human behaviour. So argued Durkheim, Spencer, Cobden and Bright (see Howard, 1981; Ashworth and Dandeker, 1987).

In contrast, Marxist social theory regards war and military organization as aspects of the development of political struggle in class societies. Far from being a constitutive feature of a world of competing states – or in the modern age, nation-states – war is contingent upon the existence of class divisions. Socializing the means of production or the abolition of class divisions, preferably on a world scale, would remove the socioeconomic basis of war and military organization and preface the establishment of a peaceful confederation of socialist states. This view constitutes a mirror image of the liberal vision to be found in the theory of industrial society: for one capitalism is the root of war, for the other it is the basis of peace.

The reductionist accounts of war and military organization offered by these two theories are also linked with similar approaches to the problem of surveillance and administrative power. Surveillance as a means of domination over other people is viewed as a transitory phase of human history. With the maturation of modern societies, the administrative coordination of social life will be performed either by a technocratic élite acting to supplement the operations of the market in pursuit of the common interest, or by socialist planners establishing a framework of regulations within which many administrative functions will be devolved to the local population in the form of direct democracy. In both scenarios the abolition of economic scarcity, albeit by different means, heralds the end of fundamental human conflict and the beginning of an era of the administration of people over things rather than over other people.

These two interpretations of modern societies also hinge on teleological conceptions of social change: the dialectic of class struggle on the one hand, and the development of scientific and technological progress on the other. The possibility that war between states and asymmetrical relations of administrative power, together with conflicts between rulers and ruled, are not contingent upon economic scarcity or economic class division, but are independent elements in the structuring of human societies, is hardly recognized.

Along with other writers Giddens has suggested that in order to understand properly the nature of military and administrative power in social life, modern sociology should revive its interest in right-liberal or, as I term them, neo-Machiavellian thinkers, such as Weber, Hintze (see Gilbert, 1975), Mosca (1939) and Aron (1954, 1958, 1981). These writers did focus on the importance of the state as a war-like entity. They were also reluctant to consider the relations between rulers and ruled exclusively in economic terms, preferring to regard struggles for power within societies and the division of modern humanity into competing and potentially warring nation-states as inevitable. In addition, these writers often stressed that warfare has played an important part in the expansion of the surveillance capacities and very identity of the modern nation-state. This theme is in sharp contrast with more liberal writers such as Bendix and Marshall, who preferred to view the modern state as 'a political community within which citizenship rights may be realised, not as a bearer of military power within a world of other nation-states' (Giddens, 1985a, 29).

Although Giddens does not discuss this point directly, it should be noted that although right-liberal social theory, particularly in the nineteenth century, was often linked with evolutionary, social Darwinist models of history, there was nothing inevitable about this connection. Indeed, Weber and Mosca, for instance, were sceptical of the argument that history could be viewed in terms of some teleological schema according to which humanity, with the West in the vanguard, was advancing towards a terminus of peaceful global industrialism or socialism. In their writings one can detect a conception of history as fundamentally a contingent, reversible social process: different societies made advances or regressions from one type to another in different periods. This was because, in the absence of any internal process of 'unfolding', contingencies relating to actors' choices under bounded conditions could be decisive for the nature of historical outcomes. This is the methodological context in which Weber's famous discussion of the battle of Marathon and his arguments about the historical role of charisma, together with Mosca's views on the 'accidents of war', should be viewed (see Ashworth and Dandeker, 1987).

The significance of this line of argument is that Giddens too has taken exception to evolutionary models of social change. As will be observed later, his analysis of the nation-state and world system is linked to a view of history and world-time which in substantial respects breaks with the evolutionary assumptions of orthodox sociology and expands on the notion of 'reversibility' indicated above.

It should be stressed that although he recognizes the importance of this third tradition of social theory as providing the basis of an overdue corrective to the drift of contemporary sociology, Giddens has three serious reservations about right-liberal ideas. These can be stated briefly here and their implications explored in the more detailed discussion of Giddens's analysis of the nation-state presented below. The first concerns their inadequacies in respect of identifying the peculiar features of the modern nation-state and the ways in which these are connected with capitalism and industrialism. Here Giddens stresses that this is where liberal and Marxist social theory have advantages in showing how modern technology and the process of commodification introduced quite new sources of social change and provided the basis for the distinctively modern organization of the democratized nation-state. The second weakness of conservative ideas is that they are associated with a view of violence and war as inescapable features of the human condition. The struggles between absolute values can only be resolved by the ultimate arbiter – force. The third criticism of conservative social theory is that the supposed inevitability of war and violence in human societies is linked with an equally pessimistic view of the necessarily oligarchical nature of the relationships between rulers and ruled: power is normally exercised selfishly by an élite which also has a tendency towards the self-recruitment of new members. In contrast with the political optimism of liberal and Marxist social theory, there is little scope in the conservative-inspired analyses of Weber and especially Foucault for considering the ways in which shifts in economic relations and the organization of political structures can effect genuine advances in the democratization of organizations such as the modern state and capitalist enterprise (see Giddens, 1985a, 26–31; 1982a, 215–30).

Notwithstanding these reservations about conservative ideas, both Giddens's account of the nation-state and the world system and his critique of alternative positions such as that of Wallerstein indicate his indebtedness to them. This is evident from the following themes that can be discerned in his analysis.

1. The modern world comprises a network of competing nation-states. The now universal appeal of the nation-state as a type of human community shows no sign of attenuation in the face of either the global market or socialism.
2. The means of violence and military power are fundamental features of human societies and will not 'wither away' with the maturation of modernity.
3. Although capitalism and industrialism have had a dramatic impact on modern societies, and in particular, on the relationships between states and their subject populations, systems of administrative power should not be conflated with those of economic class relations. By implication, power and conflict more generally should not be viewed as contingent upon economic scarcity. As Weber and Mosca suggested in their critiques of Marxism, the economic, political and cultural aspects of societies should be regarded as interdependent phenomena and not as derivative of one key variable.
4. Modern social theory should break with its tendency to study societies as isolated entities and instead locate them in the wider context of the emergent world system. It is only in the context of the interplay between intra- and intersocietal processes that the development of the nation-state as a reflexively monitored organization and its connection with the capitalist economic system can be properly understood.
5. Contemporary social theory should break with evolutionary assumptions and recognize the contingent or conjunctural nature of history. In this

context two of Giddens's suggestions are of particular importance; first, all notions of teleology should be abandoned in the social sciences, whether in the guise of progress through the logic of technology or the dialectic of class struggle; second, Giddens defends a 'discontinuist' conception of modern history, that is, in crucial respects the rise of modern societies involved a radical break with the past.

The Modern Nation-State as a Power Container

The Nation-State and Class Societies

In drawing on elements from the three traditions of social theory considered above, Giddens analyzes the nation-state by linking it with each of the other components of modernity, but seeking to avoid doing so in a reductionist manner. For Giddens 'societies' are in large part the products of modernity. If by 'society' one means a clearly demarcated and internally well articulated social entity, it is only relatively recently (within the last 200 years) that populations have lived under such arrangements. These are associated with: 1) the formation of the nation-state as a well demarcated system of administrative and military power focused on the maintenance of territorial sovereignty; 2) the generation of resources by modern capitalism as an economic system based on the self-expanding process of commodification. On the one hand, these resources provided the material basis for the modern state's mobilization of administrative power through its taxation and military bureaucracies. On the other hand, this administrative power of capitalist states played a strategic part in the rise of the West and the global extension of the process of commodification from the sixteenth century onwards; 3) the ways in which the technologies of industrialism undermined the barriers to social interaction posed by time and space, as, for instance, in the revolution in transport and communications initiated in the nineteenth century by the steamship, railway and electric telegraph; 4) bureaucratic surveillance as a mode of administrative power, which provided the rulers of modern states with the means of supervising subject populations and gathering information about their activities in ways denied to the rulers of non-modern states.

It is in this broad context of the elements of modernity that Giddens's definition of the modern nation-state should be viewed: 'the nation-state, which exists in a complex of other nation-states, is a set of institutional forms of governance maintaining an administrative monopoly over territory with demarcated boundaries (borders), its rule being sanctioned by law and direct control of the means of internal and external violence' (1981a, 190; 1985a, 121).

There are three related issues arising from this definition which require analysis. The first relates to Giddens's contention that the nation-state is a 'bordered power container' and indeed, the 'pre-eminent power container' of the modern era. This will involve a discussion of the process of internal pacification and the consequent emergence of the distinct fields of internal and external relations of the nation-state as a reflexively monitored organization. The second concerns the place of the nation-state in the modern world system and Giddens's more general discussion of 'world-time' and the deficiencies of evolutionary theory. The third issue relates to the prospects of war and peace and the future of the nation-state in a world system which is not simply rooted in asymmetrical relations of economic exchange but also comprises a competitive system of military power.

Power containers are 'circumscribed areas for the generation of administrative power' (1985a, 12–17). A locale or setting of interaction can be converted into a power container if it 'permits a concentration of allocative and authoritative resources' (*ibid.*, 13), i.e. if it is a means of controlling nature and people respectively. This process of concentration depends upon four factors: whether activities can be confined within bounded settings and thus watched and supervised; whether administrative officials not directly involved in material production can be deployed; the extension of the 'scope and intensity of sanctions and above all the development of military power' (*ibid.*, 16); and the development of ideology, or the extent to which the symbol systems of ruling authorities can gain hegemony. These conditions are of relevance in Giddens's analysis of the nation-state as a power container. The first three concern the institutional organization of the nation-state, while the fourth relates to the social psychology of nationalism.

The borders of the nation-state are strictly demarcated. As Giddens suggests, this was a modern development and at first confined to western Europe and the USA from the late eighteenth century onwards. The drawing of boundaries was one aspect of the differentiation of external and internal relations of the nation-state and a corresponding division of labour between the emergent bureaucracies of the professional armed forces on the one hand and agencies of police surveillance on the other. This process of differentiation was also one of concentration and consolidation of administrative and military power, the roots of which lay in the military revolution and organization of the absolutist state system of the seventeenth century. By the end of the seventeenth century the principal features of the modern military had been established: 1) a state machine responsible for and capable of maintaining full-time forces in war and peace; 2) a specialized military subculture set apart from society; 3) the imposition of military discipline and the creation of a military machine which became the instrument of foreign policy. 'War was no longer the unrestrained clash of societies that was characteristic of warfare in the ancient and medieval worlds' (Gilpin, 1988, 607; see also Howard, 1976, 38–55).

The military revolution involved the concentration of force under state control and thus the pacification of domestic populations. It is in this context that Giddens points to the valid element in liberal social theory: that modernity and peace are connected. A distinctive feature of modern nation-states is that the primary focus of military power is on the external relations of the state, not on the internal control of subject populations. Here, in contrast with non-modern states, the subject populations do not provide significant sources of armed opposition to the rulers. The error of liberal social theory is to extrapolate from the process of internal pacification to the intersocietal context.

The concentration of military power and its 'retreat' from the internal sphere with the advance of police surveillance were both connected with the social changes wrought by capitalism and industrialism. With regard to the impact of capitalism, Giddens links the development of the nation-state with the shift from class-divided to class societies and the contrasts between these and tribal societies.

Tribal societies are defined in terms of the fusion of social and system integration – the primacy of face-to-face interaction and the 'absence of separate agencies of political administration or legal sanctioning' – and the significance of tradition and kinship as 'the basic media of societal integration' (1981a, 161). In class-divided societies 'the existence of a differentiated division of labour within the non-capitalist city and the more deep-seated differentiation between city and countryside foster modes of economic interdependence that are rare or unknown in tribal societies' (*ibid.*, 163). Here the emergence of propertied and ruling classes is more strongly defined and whose power lies in the city not the countryside. However, these societies still remain largely segmental structures in which the face-to-face basis of local communities remains 'relatively untransformed by the mecha-nisms of state administration and surplus product exploitation' (*ibid.*, 162). Notwithstanding the development of central tax and military bureaucracies, the surveillance powers of the central authorities are limited: in the larger and imperial types of these societies military power remains a crucial mechanism for overcoming internal dissent.

In the class societies of modern capitalism the differentiation between system and social integration is most strongly defined and bureaucratic surveillance is the principal means of societal integration. As an economic system rooted in the transformation of western Europe and its relations with other societies from the sixteenth century onwards, modern capitalism is defined in terms of the principle of commodity production (Giddens, 1985a, 122–37). The features of this system which mark it out as distinctively modern are the extent to which commodification has overcome social barriers to market operations such as the alienability of property rights and restrictions on the use of labour power. Modern capitalism creates class societies. The differences between class and class-divided societies concern both the impersonality of social relations characteristic of class societies (due to the primacy of contractual relations) and the impact of horizontal and vertical relations of solidarity. Although both class-divided and class societies are characterized by inequalities of power stemming from property relations, in the latter these inequalities are mediated by the market which constitutes them simultaneously as horizontal ties of solidarity and vertical relations of antagonism. In class-divided societies the hierarchy of power is normally rooted in the horizontal rivalries and vertical connections of deference and patronage (Giddens, 1973, 132–5; Perkin, 1969, 16–72).

The emergence of class society is linked with the primacy of bureaucratic surveillance as a medium of societal integration. Here there is an institutional differentiation of, and insulation between, the economic system based on private property and the state. The characteristic relationships between state and society are conceptualized in terms of the principles of separation and surveillance. Thus the modern state is a quite distinct legal and administrative order yet at the same time able to control society through mechanisms of police surveillance in ways quite unmatched by non-modern polities. This is because in the modern era the technologies of industrialism permit such a compression of time and space and the consequent expansion of the surveillance capacities of the nation-state.

The Nation-State and Nationalism: Class Power and Geopolitics

From the preceding discussion it is clear that for Giddens the class societies of modern capitalism are only 'societies' at all because of the institutional combination of commodification, industrialism, surveillance and the consolidation of the military power of the modern nation-state. This argument provides the basis for a view of the capitalist state as an autonomous political actor.

While modern capitalism has become a global system of commodity production and exchange, capitalist societies are bordered entities. Yet as Mann has also argued (1984, 40), there was nothing inevitable about the development of capitalist societies. The process of commodification and the industrial technologies spurred by capitalist production were harnessed by ruling authorities for geopolitical and strategic ends which can in no way be considered as derivative of the class relations between capital and labour. Marxist theory has paid too little attention to the fact that capitalist development and the social changes it engendered occurred in the context of a pre-existing geopolitical and military framework of the absolutist state system. This peculiarly Western intersocietal system – comprising competing and warring states no one of which could establish a durable and European-wide despotism – provided the geopolitical crucible in which the modern nation-state was formed (see J. A. Hall, 1985; McNeill, 1983; Ashworth and Dandeker, 1987; Mann, 1986).

The autonomy of the nation-state as a political actor is rooted primarily in its external relations and its character as a reflexively monitored organization. The reflexivity of the state is based on the use of rational bureaucracy to monitor its internal and external conditions of operation. Here Giddens is drawing on conservative theory which has always stressed the coordinating or 'brain'-like functions of the state. Giddens uses this argument about reflexivity to analyse the interplay between internal and external relations in the formation of sovereign nation-states. He contends that 'international relations are not connections set up between pre-established states which could maintain their power without them; they are the basis upon which the nation state exists at all' (1985a, 263–4). To speak of a sovereign state is a misnomer; from the outset sovereignty 'depends upon a reflexively monitored set of relations between states' (*ibid.*, 263). By the same token the expansion of international organizations is not to be regarded as indicative of the waning of the nation-state but the reverse; as the institutional basis for the global universality of the nation-state as a political form (*ibid.*, 264–6).

While Giddens locates the autonomy of the state primarily in the context of the differentiation of its internal and external relations, he also wishes to draw on Marxist theory in regarding the structures and policies of the capitalist state as class conditioned. In this attempt to link internal class relations with external geopolitics one can observe remarkable parallels with Max Weber's analysis of the Wilhelmine state. Weber attempted to develop an argument that steered between two tendencies in German social theory: the Marxist claim that the state was the agent of the dominant class; and the conservative riposte that the state was the bearer of the national interest and seat of absolute values (Weber, 1978, 1381–461).

Although conservative theory offers an important corrective to liberal and Marxist perspectives on the nation-state, it also has serious deficiencies. These concern the issues of nationalism and the human propensity for warfare. Here the focus is on nationalism and Giddens's contention that, in its view of humanity as being divided eternally into competing peoples or nations, conservative theory fails to comprehend the ways in which modern nation-states are quite different from non-modern political forms. Put another way, nations and nationalism are products of modernity (1985a, 116–21; 1981a, 191–6).

Giddens draws an important distinction between these two phenomena: nations comprise aspects of institutional organization. What makes the nation a component of the nation-state 'is not the existence of sentiments of nationalism but the administrative control over territory permitted by the displacement of the segmental organisation of class divided society by modern capitalism' (1985a, 190). Nationalism is a social psychological phenomenon rooted in two aspects of modern societies. The first of these is the 'polyarchic' character of modern states; that is, following Lindblom (and Tocqueville), the relations between rulers and ruled are democratized, or grounded in the generalization of rights of citizenship. Thus Giddens accepts Kohn's argument that 'nationalism would not have emerged without the bourgeois idea of popular sovereignty . . .' (*ibid.*, 192).

Giddens rejects any crude attempts to regard nationalism as an ideology simply imposed on subject populations by the dominant class. It is in part a spontaneous outcome of democratization. Of course, this is not to deny the impact of class power on the genesis and propagation of nationalist ideologies. Yet there is more to Giddens's view of nationalism than this: he does not totally depart from conservative social theory. Following Geertz, he accepts that the lineages of modern nationalism lie in the 'primordial sentiments' characteristic of tribal societies in which tradition and kinship are the basic media of societal integration. What Giddens wishes to stress is that the sentiments of nationalism are rooted not only in popular sovereignty but also in the routinization of everyday life produced by commodification, pacification, urbanization and the impact of the 'created environment'. With this process of routinization, the spheres of 'meaningful existence' retreat to the most intimate on the one hand – the areas of personal and sexual relations – and to the larger-scale realms of political ceremonial and spectator sports. If nationalism provides a focus for the attachment of primordial sentiments and thus 'ontological security' in a 'rationalized world', Giddens also suggests that this solution to the 'problem of meaning', as it were, is a far more fragile one than is the case in societies suffused with tradition. Moreover, in modern societies, when routinized structures are threatened with breakdown, these sentiments can become focused on authoritarian solutions to the 'problem of order'. Here Giddens is suggesting that there are fruitful links to be forged between theories of nationalism on the one hand and those of charisma and group psychology on the other.

The Nation-State and the World System

For Giddens all societies are elements of intersocietal systems and consequently there are links between internal and external social processes. No causal primacy is accorded to either of these. Thus the rise of modernity and the nation-state involved not simply a transformation of Western societies but also the creation of a quite novel intersocietal system which provided other tribal and class-divided societies with conditions of 'development' that the West itself had not faced.

Giddens argues that Wallerstein has provided an important corrective to sociological orthodoxy. He has challenged the assumptions of social evolutionists and comparative sociologists by both placing intersocietal relations as a central problem of social analysis and characterizing the distinctive features of the 'modern world system'. The latter is viewed as quite distinct from the imperial intersocietal systems in the immediately pre-capitalist phase of world history. Its peculiarities derive principally from the ways in which relations of military power and economic interdependence are organized. As Giddens argues (echoing Spencer as well as Wallerstein), in the imperial systems comprising class-divided and tribal societies 'the scope of military sanctions basically determines the boundaries of economic relations both within and between societies' (1981a, 197).

In the modern era the reverse applies: the capitalist state secures a monopoly of political and military power within its own boundaries, but the world system which it has promoted 'is fundamentally influenced by capitalist processes on a world scale' (*ibid.*, 197). As J. A. Hall has put it, in the modern era capitalism is 'bigger' than the nation-state (1985, 158–62). Within the context of this emergent world system, which emerged from the sixteenth century onwards, three related regions can be distinguished: the capitalist (and exploiting) core, comprising the USA, western Europe and more recently Japan; the semi-periphery of societies which are simultaneously exploiting and exploited (e.g. much of Latin America); and at the bottom in power terms, the peripheral exploited areas involved in the production of cash crops.

Giddens identifies a number of deficiencies in this type of analysis. First, he argues that the modern world system constitutes a break with previous phases of world-time not only in respect of the organization of military and economic power but also in the sheer scale of the activities involved. It is the first intersocietal system to be truly global in scope, whereas all previous intersocietal systems were relatively speaking confined to regional areas.

Second, the modern world system is defined as a capitalist system, yet this formulation ignores the significant part played by state socialist societies in the global economy. While admittedly comprising relatively insulated trading areas, they are connected with the economies of the capitalist world with significant consequences for both types of society, e.g. note the importance of eastern Europe for West Germany and vice versa. Thus the world system cannot be defined simply as capitalist in character. Giddens extends this line of argument to question the utility of the concepts of core, periphery and semi-periphery, except as general orienting ideas. This is because they tend to conceal important empirical differences among the societies they group together. For example, the metropolitan core includes one society, Britain, which having once been 'the core of the core' (1981a, 201) has steadily declined in world power, and its future European significance is an open question. In addition, the core of the USA, Japan and Europe is itself developing into an emergent triad of power and competition that will provide much of the substantive basis of world history for the next few decades at least (see Kennedy, 1988, 395–437).

It is at this point that Giddens makes a major theoretical criticism of Marxist accounts of the modern world system: they are characterized by an economic reductionism. Here Giddens applies his non-reductionist view of modernity to intersocietal relations and suggests that the modern world system comprises a cluster of institutional elements, of which the economic is only one. They are: the global information system; the nation-state system; the world military order; and the capitalist system (1985a, 276–7). Of particular importance here are the political and military orders, and these will be considered briefly together.

Giddens argues that Wallerstein fails to consider how modern capitalism emerged within the context of the pre-existing European state system and 'underplays the role of military power and warfare in shaping the world we live in today' (1981a, 197). Here, as was observed earlier, Giddens is defending the idea of the nation-state as an autonomous political actor, thus echoing Mann's suggestion that geopolitical struggles between states. both pre-date and would post-date modern capitalism. What capitalism does is to alter the forms and social organization of such struggles by providing the material basis of the nation-state as a power container. This more 'Machiavellian' perspective on the world system leads Giddens to classify the societies which comprise it not just in economic terms but also in relation to the organization of world politics and consequent distribution of political and military power. Here Giddens develops two classifications of nation-states: one concerned with their position in the present bipolar world of super powers; the other with the ways in which those nation-states originated, and in particular their connections with the processes of modernization, colonization and decolonization (1985a, 267–76).

Although Giddens uses Hintze and Weber to counter Wallerstein's perspective on the modern world system, it should be remembered that these intellectual relationships are also reversed in both his suggestions that nations are products of modernity and that war and violence between peoples are not inherent features of the human condition. These issues of war and peace and the future of the nation-state in the world system are taken up in the conclusion.

War, Peace and the Future of the Nation-State

For Giddens, notwithstanding the existence of different types of nation-state together with shifts in the organization and distribution of world politics – as, for example, in the emergence of the triad of world power within the capitalist sector of the world system indicated earlier – there is every reason to expect the nation-state to continue to provide the organizational basis for human societies. Three reasons are adduced in support of this contention (*ibid.*, 225–7). First, as was illustrated by the case of Prussia/Germany in the nineteenth century, the institutional combination of military power and industrialism within the democratized nation-state provided a means of geopolitical power which other states were forced to defer to or copy; many have done so, and will continue to do so successfully. Second, the nation-state, as a power container, provides an institutional organization of authoritative resources that is indispensable for the operation of the money economy. The political preconditions of economic life include not only the process of internal pacification, but also the reflexive monitoring and management of external relations between states. Here one can note that there is something in the liberal argument that, at least in the capitalist sector of the world system, societies acquire a material interest in the perpetuation of peace by virtue of their participation in free trade systems. For example, aspects of

British foreign policy in the nineteenth century have been interpreted in these terms (Kennedy, 1982, 441–63), as has the cooperation between those capitalist states involved in the treaties to abolish privateering at sea (O'Malley, 1988). However, a free trading world system depends upon the existence of a hegemonic power and its military infrastructure to 'underwrite' it, as was the case with Britain's role in the nineteenth century and the USA's in the twentieth. Indeed without this condition there is a drift to protectionism and war.

The third reason for the persistence of the nation-state relates to conditions which are not generic to it but are peculiar to the history of the (old) core of the modern world system. One of the most important of these has been the legitimation and celebration of the nation-state as the appropriate form for the expression of democratic sovereignty, epitomized, for instance, in the Treaty of Versailles. Given Giddens's views on the social basis of nationalism, the democratic impulse is hardly likely to depart from a focus on national identities. In addition to these considerations, it should be stressed that for Giddens the evidence indicating the apparent transcendence of the nation-state actually suggests the reverse (1985a, 281–7): the increased number of intergovernmental organizations, and particularly the UN itself, are means for the operation of nation-states: world business corporations usually have a parent company based in a particular (core) nation-state; most important of all, it can be argued that we are witnessing the breakup of a bipolar world and a shift to more complex structures as both superpowers undergo relative decline (Kennedy, 1988, 395–412). Thus any moves toward the political unification of Europe (which in any case face huge obstacles), even if successful, have to be placed in the context of likely events in, say, the Soviet 'empire'. To say the least, it would seem that the nation-state is here to stay.

If the prospects of world government and thus the abolition of the nation-state appear remote, what of the prospects of peace and war? Here Giddens seeks to avoid both the utopianism of Marxist and liberal social theory on the one hand, and the dark pessimism of conservative theory on the other. Thus he rejects the view that the dialectic of class struggle will lead to a peaceful world, and in particular doubts that a return of the military power of the state to the people is consistent with the value of peace. As Michael Howard, drawing on Hobbes, has argued in respect of liberal and Marxist social theory, to abolish the state as a monopolizer of military power might abolish wars but it would abolish peace too (Howard, 1983, 7–22). On the other hand, Giddens rejects the Weberian view of war and violence in social life as stemming from the irreconcilable conflicts between human values. The philosophical basis of this argument lies in using network theory to contend that ultimate claims in both science and ethics are equally dependent upon rational and empirical arguments (Giddens, 1977d). This allows Giddens to view the prospect of war as neither inevitable nor destined to wither away, but as open to human choice and management. This is the context for his comments on detente, the control of nuclear proliferation and other forms of arms control (1985a, 325–35).

These are arguments of an open-minded realist, concerned like a number of other writers to push modern social theory in new directions by placing the issues of the nation-state and world system together with the prospects of peace and war as central to its concerns. In the 1970s Giddens's analysis of the nature of modern societies was inspired in large part by the debate between Marxism and Weber's sociology. At the conclusion of the 1980s it will be apposite if the results of Giddens's attempt to synthesize the three traditions of social theory in order to understand the place of the nation-state in the contemporary world are once again described by commentators as 'neo-Weberian'.

References

Aron, R. (1954) *The Century of Total War*, London: Derek Verschoyle.

Aron, R. (1958) *War and Industrial Society*, Oxford: Oxford University Press.

Aron, R. (1981) *Peace and War*, Malabur: Krieger.

Ashworth, C. and Dandeker, C. (1987) 'Warfare, Social Theory and West European Development'. *Sociological Review* 35:1–18.

Giddens, A. (1971a) *Capitalism and Modern Social Theory*, Cambridge: Cambridge University Press.

Giddens, A. (1973) *The Class Structure of the Advanced Societies*, London: Hutchinson (revised ed. 1981).

Giddens, A. (1977d) 'Max Weber on Facts and Values', in Giddens, A. *Studies in Social and Political Theory*, London: Hutchinson, pp. 89–95.

Giddens, A. (1981a) *A Contemporary Critique of Historical Materialism, Vol. 1: Power, Property and the State*, London: Macmillan.

Giddens, A. (1982a) *Profiles and Critiques in Social Theory*, London: Macmillan.

Giddens, A. (1985a) *The Nation-State and Violence, Vol. 2 of A Contemporary Critique of Historical Materialism*, Cambridge: Polity Press.

Gilbert, F. (ed.) (1975) *The Historical Essays of O. Hintze*, New York: Oxford University Press.

Gilpin, R. (1988) 'The Theory of Hegemonic War', *Journal of Interdisciplinary History* 18:591–613.

Hall, J.A. (1985) *Powers and Liberties: The Causes and Consequences of the Rise of the West*, Oxford: Blackwell (Harmondsworth: Penguin, 1986).

Howard, M. (1976) *War in European History*, Oxford: Oxford University Press.

Howard, M. (1983) *The Causes of War*, London: Counterpoint.

Howard, M. (1987) *War and the Liberal Conscience*, Oxford: Oxford University Press.

Kennedy, P. (1982) *The Rise and Fall of the Anglo-German Antagonism*, London: Unwin Hyman.

McNeil, W. (1983) *The Pursuit of Power: Technology, Armed Force and Society Since A.D. 1000*, Oxford: Blackwell.

Mann, M. (1984) 'Capitalism and Militarism', in M. Shaw (ed.) *War, State and Society*, London: Macmillan.

Mann, M. (1986) *The Sources of Social Power, Vol. 1: A History of Power from the Beginning to A.D. 1760*, Cambridge: Cambridge University Press.

Mosca, G. (1939) *The Ruling Class*, New York: McGraw-Hill.

O'Malley, P. (1988) 'The Discipline of Violence: State, Capital and the Regulation of Naval Warfare', *Sociology* 22:253–70.

Perkin, H. (1969) *The Origins of Modern English Society*, London: Routledge and Kegan Paul.

Waltz, K. (1988) 'The Origins of War in Neo-realist Theory', *Journal of Interdisciplinary History* 18:615–28.

Weber, M. (1978) *Economy and Society*, 2 vols. ed. by G. Roth and C. Wittich, Berkeley, California: University of California Press.

65

The Nation-State and Violence: A Critique of Giddens*

J. Breuilly

*Source: J. Clark, C. Modgil and S. Modgil (eds), *Anthony Giddens: Consensus and Controversy*, London: Falmer Press, 1990, ch. 21.

This chapter begins with an outline of the general project on which Giddens is engaged, of which the book *The Nation-State and Violence* forms a part; it then examines how Giddens develops these ideas for an understanding of the modern state; and finally discusses some of the prospects and problems raised by his approach.

The General Approach

In much of his work, and especially in the series of volumes on *A Contemporary Critique of Historical Materialism* of which *The Nation-State and Violence* is one, Giddens is seeking to develop a general framework within which one can analyze societies and understand how they work and change. Negatively he wishes to avoid what he sees as various flawed approaches, above all the assumption that there are unitary objects which one can call societies. If one refuses to make that assumption, a whole range of sociological perspectives is called into question. Functionalist explanations which consider that particular actions or institutions perform a function for 'society' are rejected because they depend upon an assumed part (specific function)–whole (society) relationship which is not acceptable. Evolutionary social theory is rejected because there is no appropriate object (society) which can evolve within its environment. Forms of determinism which argue that actions/institutions at one level determine the character of actions/institutions at other levels fail because they are based upon assumed part (level)–whole (society) relationships. Giddens argues that the same point can be made about pluralist models which analyze interaction between various levels, even if in a non-determinist way. Hegelian views which take society to be an 'expressive totality' (or indeed any idealist approach which depends upon the notion of an essence, a *Zeitgeist*, a *Volksgeist*, a 'spirit of the people') are likewise unacceptable. Instead any valid theory must stress the loose fit between different elements of human organization, the contingency of outcomes, the significance of agents' intentions and actions, and the episodic, accidental, open ended nature of history.

Many historians, myself included, would agree wholeheartedly with these comments. Many would assume that it meant the abandonment of futile attempts at general social theory. For a sociologist to begin by giving up the concept of society is rather like an historian giving up the concept of the past: it seems to involve denying the existence of the very thing which it is the purpose of one's discipline to explore. However, Giddens sees himself at this stage as clearing the ground of the refuse of sociological theorizing. The task he sets himself is to construct *valid* general social theory which avoids the mistakes of these various approaches, but which does not see history and the ways in which human beings organize their affairs simply as an eclectic collection of particularities.

Giddens draws attention to the *efforts* people make to give meaning to their world, to pattern their activity, to connect together different kinds of action, to organize, etc. This effort is undertaken on the basis of unacknowledged conditions (by which I assume Giddens means conditions which are real but unknown to the agents) and leads to unintended outcomes (though I imagine that Giddens would accept that not all conditions are unacknowledged and not all outcomes are unintended). There are relationships between people which extend beyond their knowledge and which can act both as resources and constraints, though one should not reify those relationships (as structuralist approaches do) in order to deny the role of agency altogether. Instead Giddens develops the concept of *structuration*, the idea that structure has a *duality*, both as *medium* and *outcome* of social interaction. Such structuration occurs at a number of levels: face-to-face and at more extensive (system) levels; and along a number of dimensions: those of meaning, control over material goods and authority, and the operation of sanctions. Giddens stresses that the ways in which these interactions take place vary from one kind of social division to another. For the modern period Giddens stresses the distinction between the class-divided societies of agrarian empires and the class societies of capitalism or state socialism. Giddens also develops ideas about how these societies are 'bound' together in time and space, e.g. the importance of written records, routines, the practical understandings people develop in order to operate in institutional settings, the concentration of particular activities into certain regions and locales, the characteristic ways in which material goods are produced, exchanged and distributed, and the power employed in different kinds of social organization.

Giddens objects to traditional Marxist analysis on the grounds that it is evolutionary, teleological, determinist, and stresses the internal class relations of unitary 'societies' as the motor of history at the expense of other factors.

At the same time Giddens concurs with Marx's approach to capitalism as a dramatic break with previous forms of economic organization, based on the transformation of labour into the commodity labour power, as well as with his understanding of capitalism as an inherently dynamic economic system in which class conflict is of central importance. The problem for Giddens is how to retain only the valid aspects of the Marxist approach.

My own evaluation of Giddens's general theory is that it is highly stimulating in places but, like all such theory, rather arbitrary in its positive assumptions and concepts. Furthermore, I cannot see that *The Nation-State and Violence* as Volume 2 of *A Contemporary Critique of Historical Materialism* really builds systematically upon Volume 1. The two volumes overlap in style and characteristic concerns, but many of the key theoretical notions of Volume 1 (as well as other of Giddens's writings) are barely employed in *The Nation-State and Violence*. For example, all the ideas about 'regions' and 'locales' are absent in *The Nation-State*. Conversely in that book Giddens develops other concepts, such as that of 'surveillance'. There is a double problem when one criticizes *The Nation-State and Violence*: relating it to Giddens's general approach and criticizing it as an independent work.

Specific Concerns

In *The Nation-State and Violence* Giddens begins by noting that the classic sociological tradition has neglected the state as an autonomous agent, especially in its administrative, legal, bureaucratic and coercive forms, and as an actor in a system of competing states. The dominant emphasis of that tradition has been upon the leading role of 'society'. The state was derived from internal social analysis. Marx considered the state either as an instrument of class domination or having autonomy in situations where different classes were in balance (Rigby, 1987, Ch. 2). In either case the state is conceptually subordinate to society. Durkheim was interested in the coordinating function of the state in the context of varying types of the social division of labour. Writers such as Spencer and Comte assumed that the growth of industry and commerce signalled the end of the militarist and coercive state, products of earlier epochs. Classical liberals constructed the state normatively from the idea of a social contract, and assumed that the free market and a private civil society would reduce state functions to a minimum.

These are justifiable criticisms. Giddens does not ask why the sociological tradition took this form. Without such an assumption sociology itself might never have developed, any more than would have political economy without the assumption of an autonomous market whose principles of operation could be theoretically grasped without reference to power and the state. Furthermore, the dominant role of first Great Britain and then the USA in the world encouraged a neglect of the state. In both cases it might appear superficially that the state was not a very powerful agent, predominance resting rather upon the free workings of civil society. The long peace from 1815 to 1914 obscured the role of state violence in shaping economic and social development in the eyes of many social theorists. The shift of global dominance to the USA enabled some theorists to attribute the resurgence of large-scale state violence to the continuing influence of reactionary forces within Europe (Skocpol, Evans and Ruschmeyer, 1985, esp. 4–7).

There were in Europe theorists who never succumbed to these illusions (see *ibid.*, 7–9; also Dyson, 1980; and for a nice juxtaposition of contrasting perspectives, Poggi, 1978, Ch. 1). But precisely because they did not, they generally failed to develop general *social* theories. They operated like Clausewitz and his successors as military theorists; or like Hintze and Ranke as historians of state bureaucracy and international relations; or like Schmoller and von Roscher they developed historical treatments of economics or law or state bureaucracy which resisted generalization. The one towering exception was Max Weber. But typically Weber, as initially made known to twentieth century English language readers, was not Weber the political scientist concerned with the irreducibility and irrationality of power and struggle, but rather Weber the sociologist, founder of 'social action' theory and analyst of the relationship between Protestantism and capitalism.[1] Only in recent years, along with the rediscovery of the state, has the other side of Weber been more widely advertised (see Mommsen, 1984, published in English thirty years after the original German edition; and Mommsen and Osterhammel, 1987; esp. Parts 3 and 4).

It is, above all, real historical change which has compelled this rediscovery. The continuation of war, combined with the frightening increases in the military capacities of states and the continued growth of state organizations with massive powers of internal control – the police, social welfare agencies, educational institutions, etc. – all have made it impossible to think of the state as a derivative and declining entity. Increasingly theorists are turning back to the state and trying to understand it as a dynamic and autonomous agent.[2]

To these general considerations Giddens adds specific concerns. He pinpoints key developments in the modern period: the growth of world capitalism; the subjugation of nature through industrialization; the construction of massive systems of surveillance (Giddens is much indebted to Foucault; see *idem.*, 1977); and the creation of technologically advanced military systems (especially the nuclear capability). Giddens then considers why all these developments have converged on the nation-state, which has become the dominant political unit of the modern world, the prime source of political loyalty and identity, indeed, ironically, the unit which furnishes the boundaries of what is often described as 'society'. These are the central concerns of *The Nation-State and Violence*.

It would be pointless to try to summarize the book. Rather I shall pick out the central arguments and then subject these to two kinds of criticism: first, an *internal* criticism: how effectively does Giddens put his argument and how does it relate to his more general theorizing? second, an *external* critique: what is deficient in Giddens's arguments and what is omitted?

The Central Arguments

Giddens identifies four dimensions or institutional clusters around which his analysis is organized. Two are economic: capitalism and industrialism; one is administrative–political: surveillance and 'internal pacification'; and the fourth is military power. Before considering these concepts in detail, it should be noted that they can be related only obliquely to the four dimensions of analysis used by Giddens in his general theory. Capitalism and industrialism *can* be related to the dimension concerned with economic authority. Surveillance and military power *could* perhaps be linked to political authority and the operation of sanctions, though that would be rather strained. There is no provision for the analysis of meaning, of social symbols, the fourth of Giddens's general dimensions.

Capitalism understood as the dominant economic system which rests upon the use of free wage labour is regarded by Giddens as clearly modern. It brings in its train the private economy and extensive class conflicts between wage earners and owners of capital which are endemic in the modern world. Industrialism, that is, the shift to large-scale units of production employing inanimately powered machinery, is also clearly modern. Surveillance involves the gathering, storing and use of information in order to exert power. The enhanced power of modern surveillance rests upon methods of communication which are much faster than methods of transportation and physical human movement. In such a situation 'messages' can be detached from and move ahead of the transmission of people and material goods from one place to another. The construction of electric and then electronic means of transmitting information has made this a standard feature of the modern world. In addition, bureaucratic organization and modern information storage systems enable state institutions to hold and to use far more information than was ever before possible. Finally, the industrialization of war, involving massive investment in basic scientific research, has culminated in the mass production of nuclear weapons and rocket delivery systems, equipping the modern state with unprecedented powers of destruction.

According to Giddens, and this fits in with his basic approach, none of these developments can be regarded as an 'expression' or a 'determination' of any other development. For example, the arms race between the two superpowers cannot be seen in terms of the manipulation of a military–industrial complex or as an expression of certain capitalist or state socialist imperatives. However, Giddens can relate these developments to one another in two ways: by considering, first, the political forms on which they all converge and, second, the way in which they mutually condition one another.

All four dimensions of change converge on the political form of the nation-state and the international system of competing nation-states. Military conflict is the expression of conflict between nation-states, although since 1945 these have formed broader international blocs dominated by the two superpowers. Surveillance is conducted by the nation-state more intensively and effectively than by any other organization. Although capitalism and industrialism are international in scope, nevertheless their patterns vary greatly from one state to another, states are closely involved in shaping those patterns, and when we use the terms 'society' and 'economy', we normally refer to units defined by the inhabitants of a nation-state.

Giddens also argues that the nation-state and the international state system are distinctively modern. Nation-states have clear boundaries, borders rather than frontiers to use his terms. Nation-states are *polyarchic*, by which Giddens means that large numbers of people are involved in the political process. The state is not the affair of small élites set above the mass of subjects who themselves are regionally segmented and whose connections to the state weaken as one moves towards frontier regions, as is typical of agrarian empires (see Gellner, 1983, 1988). Nation-states claim sovereignty over their sharply defined territories and base this claim on being the secular, impersonal (though often symbolically articulated) expression of the society they rule – that is, the 'nation'. Finally, nation-states build up elaborate methods of coordinating their relations with one another. The concept of international relations, along with the diplomatic codes and coordinating organizations that sustain that concept, are essentially modern (see Giddens's very illuminating analysis of the role of international agencies in strengthening rather than limiting the sovereignty of nation-states (1985a, 10)).

Giddens also considers the mutual connections between the four kinds of change. Capitalism provides the dynamic economic base upon which industrialism can be generated. Capitalism and the institutions of the modern state provide the two poles of the separation and specialization of the economic and the political. The modern state performs key functions for capitalism, e.g. creating stable monetary and legal systems. Industrial establishments generate the information transmission and storage methods which the modern state can utilize in its surveillance systems. Industrial capability forms the basis of modern military technology and production, and that in turn compels the state to organize certain economic sectors to ensure adequate support for military requirements (see Pearton, 1982, to which Giddens refers). The breakdown of the 'segmental' societies of pre-modern times means not merely that the state is able to penetrate further into everyday life, but equally that large numbers of people react to that penetration, thus extending the basis of political participation. Giddens stresses that modern class relations are one base upon which extensive political participation rests.

Increasingly, therefore, political activity and social movements focus upon the nation-state, so much so that it becomes accepted as the 'natural' basis of political life and identity and loyalty.

Giddens goes on to develop the links between the four institutional clusters and the social movements which react to them. Thus he sees the labour movement as the central response to the growth of capitalism; ecological movements as a response to industrialism and the 'created environment'; peace movements as a response to the threats of mass destruction; and civil rights movements as a response to the increased capacities of state surveillance. These different movements may conflict with one another as well as with the interests which dominate within the four institutional clusters. At the end of the book Giddens argues that this modern state develops the conditions on which totalitarianism can flourish, regarding this as a type of rule exercised by the regimes identified with Hitler and Stalin and (more weakly) Mussolini. That type of rule builds upon modern surveillance, national identity and powerful social movements.

Throughout the analysis Giddens does not resort to teleology or determinism to make connections. The relationships between the various kinds of changes and the forms that they take depend upon a wide variety of contingent developments (e.g. specific kinds of scientific breakthroughs and technological innovations). There is, however, a pattern about the way these changes are organized and converge on the modern state. Giddens concludes that one should neither blindly condemn nor welcome 'progress' or assume that any group or institution is its privileged vehicle. In resisting the anti-human features of the modern state and state system, above all in the fight against the threat of nuclear destruction, Giddens argues we should combine utopian ideals with realistic, even pessimistic analysis of modern conditions. Historical analysis rightly makes us aware of the constraints upon us, but also makes us realize that our destinies are not predetermined. The message is that of Gramsci: pessimism of the intellect, optimism of the will.

This is a sweeping perspective. It apparently proceeds according to the methodological canons laid down by Giddens. It is neither reductionist nor teleological. It gives equal weight to military and administrative as well as economic forces. It stresses the open-ended nature of history and the role of accidents (e.g. the role of the First World War is seen in these terms as not merely hastening pre-existing trends but actually creating new ones). Yet Giddens has also constructed a systematic theoretical framework within which the central features of modernity are connected together without committing the cardinal sins of evolutionism, determinism and functionalism. But can one accept the case that Giddens has made?

Internal Critique

First, there are problems with the way in which the argument is presented. We are confronted with certain basic 'types' which Giddens uses to measure the changes which have taken place on the road to modernity. The principal types are the tribe, the city-state, the agrarian empire with its class-divided society, and the modern state with its class society. These are presented statically, with their main features being almost logically derived from the type to which they are assigned. 'Facts' are introduced in a passive illustrative way. Evolution in the sense of constant development is certainly not asserted; instead one is presented with various static situations which, by means of unspecified mechanisms, give way to other situations. The picture is one of 'episodic evolution' whereby the structure of the state type largely determines the routine operations of that state until the whole thing breaks down. At no point does Giddens inform us as to the status of these types, whether they are ideal types or empirical generalizations.[3] Their internal differences are not considered, nor are the ways in which different kinds of polity react upon one another, nor whether other features of these different political types have been omitted to further the analysis. It would be interesting, for example, to ask to what extent the city-state represents a different kind of polity in medieval and modern Europe from that of the territorial monarchy, and how concepts of sovereignty, techniques of surveillance, forms of political participation, etc. varied from one state type to another. Arguably the ideas and forms of the modern nation-state derived as much from the historical interactions between these various types of state and the kinds of political consciousness and culture to which they gave rise as they did from the convergence between Giddens's four institutional clusters (for a development of some of these points see Chapter 1 [*sic*] and the conclusion to Breuilly, 1982). Furthermore, the historical treatment of these pre-modern state forms omits issues such as the role of religion, which are not merely empirically important in the development of absolutism but are central to the very notion of absolutism. One simply cannot understand how the political community of the nation-state came into being without making religion a central concern. Giddens's general dimension of systems of meaning would seem to lend itself to a consideration of this aspect of modern state-formation, but it is not raised in the analysis of *The Nation-State and Violence*.

The same criticism can be made of the way in which the relationships between these four clusters is handled. Certain events are simply taken as read – e.g. the transformation of labour into a commodity which is an essential condition of the development of capitalism. Certain connections are juxta-posed by simple fiat, e.g. the assertion that the phase of absolutism accompanies the transformation of land and products into capital, while the phase of the nation-state is linked to the transformation of labour into a commodity (Giddens, 1985a, Ch. 6). The events which are asserted to have accompanied one another are then 'explained' in terms of Giddens's analytical scheme. On the one hand, there is the citizenry which both controls and is controlled by the nation-state. This is the political aspect of the modern division between the political and the economic. On the other hand, there is the free wage labour force which is formed under capitalism and which constitutes the economic aspect of that modern division. Describing two processes and then turning them into two aspects of a larger process is frequently how Giddens claims to 'explain' changes. Here is a typical example:

> The creation of a perceived need for 'law and order' is *the reverse side* of the emergence of conceptions of 'deviance' recognised and categorised by the central authorities and by professional specialists. They *are intrinsic* to the expansion of the administrative reach of the state, penetrating day-to-day activities – and to the achievement of an effective monopoly of violence in the hands of the authorities. (1985a, 184; emphasis supplied)

There are problems with this procedure. First, the 'factuality' of the assertion is misleading. It is debatable whether events of this kind did accompany one another. The construction of France as a nation-state long preceded the creation of a national free wage labour market; on the other hand, the construction of nation-states in much of east and central Europe came long after the formation of extensive free wage labour forces. There is no indication that Giddens is employing definitions in a loaded way, so that what counts as a nation-state must include the transformation of labour into a commodity. Anyway, that would convert the connection to be explained into a definitional claim, and one cannot do both of these things at the same time. There is also no indication that Giddens appreciates that statements of the kind he makes (as well as the counter-statements I have made) are not 'factual' in any straightforward sense, but can only be valid as the outcome of complex analysis.

How can one proceed beyond complex description to providing any kind of explanation of these sorts of connections? A functionalist or determinist argument might claim that the modern nation-state 'functions' to create free wage labour forces. A determinist or pluralist account might view these as different 'levels' of development within a unitary 'society'. An evolutionary explanation might regard these as two types of specialized adaptation to a changing environment. An Hegelian account might see these two features as parts of the 'totality' which is modern society. But Giddens has rejected as invalid all explanations or accounts of these kinds. All he is left with is an open-ended historical account, a complex narrative which makes events more understandable, even if it does not provide any kind of causal or intentional explanation. Unfortunately, Giddens furnishes us with phrases such as 'reverse-side' and 'intrinsic to' rather than an illuminating contextual account, of which narrative is one kind. The result is that Giddens neither properly describes the events with which he is concerned nor provides any kind of explanation of how those events are connected with one another.

It is difficult to see how to reconcile Giddens's historical accounts with his notion of structuration, in particular his emphasis upon the intention of the agent. Indeed, the way in which he uses typologies, ascribing a simple historical factuality to them, is rather akin to the way other theorists employ the notion of structure. There may be 'skilled, knowledgeable actors', but it seems that their skill and knowledge can only fruitfully be employed speaking lines and acting out parts which are given under the rules on which the different types operate. Louis XIV has to operate according to the rules set down by the 'agrarian empire' type.

Yet there are alternative historical accounts upon which Giddens could have drawn which would be more amenable to his type of theorizing. For example, there are many historical works which assert the importance of changes in the values of key political élites in modern Europe which led to the construction of rationally organized, secular institutions pursuing policies designed to increase population and production, and in which the 'freeing' of the economy and the 'bureaucratization' of the state went hand in hand (see, for example, Gagliardo, 1968). Obviously one should not go too far and interpret such consequences solely as the intended result of the efforts of such 'skilled, knowledgeable actors', but it would provide some grounding for the argument about the connection between modern state forms and free wage labour as well as correcting a one-sided emphasis upon structures. Yet Giddens does not avail himself of this literature, or indeed anything from the 'state-building' or 'deliberate modernization' approaches.[4] Thus Giddens interprets the development of constitutions, of modern forms of policing, and even of the elaboration of statistical techniques and investigations, all as *responses* to more basic kinds of change as states had to handle mobilized subjects or novel kinds of social and economic transformation. But in part these were also deliberate constructs designed to guide precisely such 'basic' change.

Even more importantly, such accounts might also have led Giddens to appreciate the way in which limited types of explanation of such events can be offered which go beyond the use of mysterious phrases such as 'reverse-side' and 'intrinsic to'. It is both possible and necessary to employ a modest form of functionalism in historical explanation. The form is modest because the focus will be on how one discrete practice functions for another discrete practice. That leaves aside all the problems which Giddens rightly exposes when a particular practice is regarded as functioning for the 'whole' society. Second, insofar as the functional relationship is not an intentional one (after all, people do sometimes successfully design practices which are functionally related), it is necessary to specify the 'feedback' relationship which maintains and extends that relationship. An example of such an account concerns the political implications of the development of free market economic relationships out of a prior economic system in which economic and political capacities were formally connected, as with the operation of guilds in urban manufacturing or noble privilege within the agrarian economy. Once the economic part of the privilege has been diffused into free market relationships, this has the effect of 'hollowing-out' the political part of the privilege. Yet one can point to ways in which the economic actors 'need' to be able to operate within a context of political stability. If that is a genuine need, then if it is not met that will have economic consequences. Obviously 'needing' something does not, in itself, explain why that something is provided. But the need does explain why such an economic change will stimulate attempts to reconstruct new forms of political authority and also why the defenders of the older type of political authority will be in a weak position. Insofar as those new forms of political authority are institutionally detached from economic capacities, they will appear to have a more specialized character than the older forms of political authority. Furthermore, one can identify ways in which these new principles of economic and political organization create 'feedback' relations which reinforce their existence and serve to reduce the extent and significance of older principles. The mechanism of bankruptcy in a free market economy provides an obvious example. Less obvious is the development of bureaucratic and/or representative forms of political authority in place of corporate institutions such as guilds and seigneurial courts. In these ways one can point to a certain 'logic' in an intentional chain which moves from developing free market economic relations to constructing new forms of specialized political authority, and one can also provide some limited causal explanation of why such intentions, in certain circumstances, enjoy a large measure of success. By rejecting in principle any employment of functionalism, and by failing to build intentionality into his historical descriptions (though one would expect this from his theory of structuration), Giddens deprives himself of any kind of explanatory account.

Such accounts would take a non-determinist form. However, there is no very lively sense in Giddens's detailed accounts of the contingency of history, of the possibility of alternative developments. Yet this recognition is central to his general approach. For example, Giddens points out that the First World War could only have taken place on the basis of certain initial conditions – the mobilizing capacity of the state, the advanced forms of military technology, etc. In turn the war gave rise to further change such as mass democracy and the generalization of the form of the nation-state to most of Europe. If war had been avoided or if the Central Powers had won it (though Giddens does not raise the latter possibility), such developments might not have taken place, or at least have taken a very different form.

Yet such an account does not really stimulate a sense of open-endedness or represent a disciplined way of exploring alternatives. Rather it creates a sense of 'episodic evolution'. Certain forces unfold and then a cross-road is reached; a certain turn is taken and further forces unfold until the next cross-road is reached. However, episodic evolution is as incompatible with Giddens's general approach as any other kind of evolution. Instead of this he should have explored how constantly unpredictable innovation creates new possibilities (which admittedly are only realized given certain 'unacknowledged conditions'). He should have also paid attention to the way in which certain 'failures' can suggest real alternative historical possibilities. These points are best supported with examples.

In 1866 Prussia defeated Austria, and in 1870/71 France, and went on to construct a German nation-state. First, one has to see how even the possibility of those events was only created by means of unpredictable innovations that had occurred only since mid-century. Railway construction, the exploitation of the mineral resources of the Ruhr region, the development of new kinds of weapons – these are all examples of such innovations. Even then such innovations could only have been employed effectively in the context of other changes in the international balance of power which weakened Austria at the expense of Prussia. Even then choices had to be made by key actors and pursued with varying levels of competence before the particular outcomes occurred.

The second point follows on from this. German unification, which was so closely tied up with Italian unification, established the 'model' of nation-state formation. Yet what if Königgratz had gone the other way? Would it have been possible for a multinational empire such as the Habsburg Empire to have shaped the political and economic forms of modernity? The question is unanswerable as a purely counter-factual one. But insofar as we are dealing with the *failure* of political systems other than the nation-state, not the *non-existence* of such systems, then some historical exploration of the question is possible. Certainly there are impressive modern attempts to provide an alternative to the model of a Europe made up of nation-states. Napoleon's short-lived empire which embraced virtually all of non-Russian continental Europe between 1807 and 1812, and Hitler's which had about the same extent and duration, are the obvious examples. But so too was the Habsburg pre-eminence in central Europe between 1815 and the mid-1850s. What an examination of these 'failures' can do is give us some clues as to what is *essential* in the success of the modern nation-state. After all, one might seek to explain the failure of Napoleon or the Habsburgs or Hitler in terms of the balance of power without paying much attention to the kinds of states competing with one another. Alternatively, and more fruitfully, one might try to show that in modern times states which develop a legitimacy integrally connected to the ideas of nationality and citizenship can mobilize human and material resources more effectively than states which are not able to develop those ideas at all or to the same degree.

One can then connect the two points together. Certain innovations and changes in balances of power might appear at first glance rather arbitrary. Yet it may be that only modern principles of social organization can handle those innovations effectively and, by so doing, undermine older principles of social organization. Thus to explain why and how the nation-state is the key political unit of modernity, one has to examine the 'failures' of other kinds of state.

An examination of Giddens's detailed arguments suggests that they do not develop on the theoretical lines which he explicitly advocates. A static state typology is asserted as though it was a direct expression of some large historical fact. From this is constructed the peculiar features of the modern nation-state. That procedure alone robs most of human history of a sense of contingency or agency, except for the odd traumatic moment like the First World War, when Giddens argues that things might have turned out differently. The particular elements which converge on the modern nation-state are also treated as if they were basic kinds of events which actually happened and their relationships are characterized as ones of mutual reinforcement. But, having deprived himself of any model of teleological or evolutionary or functional or structural causality, Giddens is compelled to rely upon that of actual historical relationships, and in the absence of a serious treatment of those relationships, he finds himself reduced simply to asserting that history has taken the forms which fit his particular framework of analysis. At best what he offers is a defensible empirical generalization of what did happen. But such an account does not seem to require any kind of theory and does not indicate why modern history has taken the direction it has.

External Critique

So far I have criticized the way in which Giddens conducts his argument and uses historical evidence in support of that argument. I want now to discuss some problems about his definition and use of certain concepts and also the importance of what is omitted from his account of the modern state.

First, there are criticisms to be made of the four key concepts of capitalism, industrialism, surveillance and military capacity. They are different kinds of concept and their value for historical analysis varies greatly. Recently there has been a great deal of historical criticism of the idea of industrialism. At best the idea only makes sense for some parts of the world from the later nineteenth century. The factory as a new unit of production dominated the imaginations of contemporaries, and some of the major social theorists projected the image of the factory into the heart of their understanding of modern society. But they exaggerated the pace and extent of its development, and subsequent economic change has rather reduced the centrality of that kind of production. Furthermore, some of those writers, and subsequently both Foucault and Giddens, have exaggerated the idea of the 'factory as barrack'; this calls into question much of what Giddens has to say about the development of the notion of surveillance in industrial society. Clearly the application of technology and large-scale organization to production has transformed our world, but the notion of industrialism turns out to be very slippery (see Breuilly, 1985; Kumar, 1978).

There is less objection to the notion of capitalism because Giddens is much more aware of the debates surrounding the use of this term. However, he is not perhaps fully aware of the very halting and late development of the transformation of labour into a commodity.[5] Beyond certain parts of western Europe and the USA, by 1900 it would be difficult to argue that the bulk of labour took the form of free wage labour; and from the onset of the Stalinist revolution large parts of the world have developed industrial capacity without transforming labour into a commodity of the kind defined by capitalism. Furthermore, as already argued, industrial capitalism has also developed in non-nation-states, and one cannot assert as simple and direct a relationship as Giddens does.

Giddens's idea of military capacity is less a concept than an historical observation. What especially impresses him is the nuclear capability, but it is not clear how far one should regard this as simply the 'highest' expression of a more general increase in modern military capability. Indeed, in certain respects nuclear capability has reversed or undermined certain modern features of military development. Arguably the major advance in military capacity from the early modern period stemmed from organizational rather than technological innovations – the capacity of the absolutist state to mobilize greater human and material resources than had been possible since the destruction of the Roman Empire, followed by the leap from professional to popular armies that was made in the French revolutionary and Napoleonic era. Certain weapons, communications and transportation innovations enabled this vastly expanded capacity to mobilize men to be put to more concentrated use in the Austro-Prussian, Franco-Prussian and American Civil Wars (though with a very different outcome in the last case). The First World War was marked more by a further expansion in this mobilizing capacity than by any dramatic technological innovation. Indeed, much of the historical debate revolves round the 'failure' to exploit innovations such as the tank, the aeroplane and the aircraft carrier. Only in the naval sphere had military men become obsessed with the problem of technological innovation and its dreaded converse, obsolescence.

After 1918 such hopes and fears were extended to other fields of warfare. The Second World War was the forcing ground for many innovations, culminating in the (as yet separate) abilities to make nuclear weapons and rocket delivery systems. But ironically those very capacities, though involving massive mobilization of scientific, technical and production capacities, have reduced the need to mobilize, organize and equip large bodies of men, the principal trend from the early modern period until 1918. That dubious distinction has passed on to states such as Iran and Iraq, which have recently fought a war reminiscent of Europe seventy years ago. It is precisely this very recent freeing of one kind of military capacity from the general modern ability to mobilize massive amounts of manpower and material resources for war which has apparently emancipated the state from social constraints, at least in the sense that in principle a few people in government can unleash sufficient force to destroy the societies they govern without having to involve those societies in implementing such decisions. That is unique, but it can hardly be seen as the culmination of modern military development. In fact, this development perhaps better fits Giddens's notions of contingency and accident in history than the changes comprehended by his other three concepts. However, just because that is so, it is difficult to understand how it can be related to other facets of modern life or even to earlier phases of military development. Rather it appears as a 'spin-off' of scientific research which has fairly arbitrary connections to anything else. That is also how the nuclear threat is experienced – as something unreal, a shadow hanging over everything else (for a general overview of military changes see Howard, 1976).

The most dubious of all four concepts is that connected with the ideas of surveillance and internal pacification. Giddens's basic argument is that violence has played a decreasing role in the maintenance of state control. People work 'freely' for a wage, and generally employers do not need to apply physical force or the threat of such force, either directly or through agents of the state, to maintain control over their labour forces. It is frequently argued that in capitalism the state/economy separation has led to an extrusion of violence, or 'extra-economic-coercion' from economic relationships. Instead control is now ensured by a mixture of 'internalization' of consent and surveillance. First, through institutions such as the family and school, people have learnt to accept the required values and forms of behaviour. This has largely eliminated the need to use violence or the threat of violence to maintain order. Second, where the internally generated consent fails, there has been a growth in surveillance to monitor and control deviant values and behaviour. Analysts such as Foucault begin by stressing the role of surveillance in prisons and asylums as an alternative to the infliction of pain as a punishment and deterrent for offenders and deviants. Along with the development of these institutions has gone the advocacy of a third purpose beyond that of punishment and deterrence, namely that of rehabilitation. Some writers have taken these notions of surveillance and rehabilitation and extended them beyond specific institutions to the whole of society. Giddens suggests that it is this surveillance capacity which is at the heart of the growth of state power relative to those of its subjects.

There are many problems about the historical application of these ideas. First, it is not clear that violence has been extruded in the way that is claimed. The state itself has not been able to employ much violence against most of its subjects directly before the modern period, simply because the means of violence at the disposal of the state were not very great. Of course, one should not identify violence with state violence (or conversely with a restricted view of the state which confines it to central government). Violence applied by masters to journeymen, noble landowners to their serfs, or Justices of the Peace to petty offenders was of greater significance than that applied by central government to its subjects.[6] The threat of violence in the form of executions and the infliction of pain was part of the penal process and was dismantled only during the nineteenth century. But the importance of such violence is often exaggerated. Conversely one can exaggerate the degree to which it was dismantled. One historian has claimed that Prussian troops played a larger role in dealing with 'civil' disturbances in the period after 1815 than before (see Lüdtke, 1979). Another has argued that only with the Third Reich did professional differentiation within the military élite undermine its capacity to exercise general political power (see Müller, 1987). One argument questions the idea of the declining role of the military in the maintenance of order, the other the dating of its decline as a major political force.

Foucault's work has been heftily criticized for exaggerating the role of institutions such as prisons in modern society and for confusing some visions of how prisons should be organized with how they actually were organized, let alone experienced.[7] On the other hand, violence clearly continued to play a part, for example, the use of police and soldiers to handle strikes (something which appears to increase significantly in late nineteenth and early twentieth century USA), as well as the growth of private security services to fill in where state agents are unable or unwilling to act. Such developments clearly limit the idea of the end of 'extra-economic' coercion.

There are even more problems with the extension of the idea of surveillance beyond these 'total' institutions. It is undoubtedly true that bureaucratic organization and the techniques of information storage, linkage and retrieval confer huge potential powers upon those who can control this mass of information. But such potential can only be realized if there are other resources to back up that information, i.e. the capacity to punish or reward those about whom there is 'bad' or 'good' information. This has happened, e.g. with the increased importance of credit-ratings and legal records for those wishing to obtain loans or jobs. But Giddens tends to study surveillance simply as a set of spying techniques isolated from these other matters. That is how many people experience surveillance, but that does not make it a central feature of the modern state. Furthermore, it may be neat to treat the type of social movement concerned with civil rights as a response to the growth of surveillance, but historically it is quite inaccurate. Arguably civil rights movements were far more stimulated by the failure to make liberal constitutional advances as rapidly as was expected. It has far more to do with 'polyarchy' (to use Giddens's own term) and pressure for the extension of individual freedom than with surveillance.

Generally there is a problem that Giddens only focuses explicitly on surveillance and military capacity for a detailed consideration of the modern state. Yet elsewhere his arguments suggest that these should not be given such prominence. His points about class societies and the polyarchic nature of the modern state point to the idea of considering the modern state as a way of handling the extension of political participation. But there are two crucial failures on Giddens's part to take this argument any further.

First, his preoccupation with surveillance and nuclear capability excludes an analysis of those features of the modern state which deal with this extension of the political community. It seems incredible that one can write a book about the modern state without including sections on the role of parliament or other kinds of elective or representative bodies and the role of parties and other organizations which mobilize large numbers of people for politics. That in turn would need to be linked to arguments about the role of classes or social interests in the working of the modern state. Only thus can one get to grips with the notion of polyarchy. Although there are chapters which suggest that Giddens is going to deal with these issues, in fact they are neglected. For example, bureaucracy as anything other than an instrument for surveillance is only considered in relation to absolutist states. But bureaucracies have to be understood as one instrument for the realization of many of the claims associated with 'social' citizenship, e.g. for the provision of medical and educational goods and income supplements. Only within this context can one understand the power of modern state bureaucracy.

Second, Giddens's definitions of the nation, nationalism and the nation-state prevent him advancing his analysis to any great extent. He defines the nation as the body of subjects under the modern state and nationalism as 'the affiliation of individuals to a set of symbols and beliefs emphasising communality among the members of a political order' (1985a, 116). These are purely formal ideas without any content. Is any body of subjects under the modern state a nation, and is any sense of communality among members of a political order nationalism? Armenians are subjects of the modern Soviet state, as are Estonians. Does that make them all members of the Russian/Soviet nation? Iranian politics is dominated by commitment to certain Shi'ite beliefs. Does that make it nationalism? Precisely the same point applies when we come to Giddens's definition of the nation-state.

> The nation-state, which exists in a complex of other nation-states, is a set of institutional forms of governance maintaining an administrative monopoly over a territory with demarcated boundaries (borders), its rule being sanctioned by law and direct control of the means of internal and external violence. (1985a, 121)

Weber offered a definition of this kind of the *modern* state. Clearly it cannot be used of the state *per se* (leaving the problem of whether the term 'state' can be applied to pre-modern forms of authority), but it is a definition which can be applied to states which are multinational in character. To use the definition as one applying to the nation-state is therefore misleading because it fails to grapple with the specific role of nationality in modern state development. Nationality and nationalism are then formally derived from this misapplied definition, although to that formal derivation are added some rather speculative remarks about the social–psychological basis of national consciousness under modern conditions.

One could respond that this does not matter. We can leave aside the terms 'nation-state' and 'nationalism' and simply analyze the modern state in terms of the four institutional clusters to which Giddens draws attention. But it is not as easy as that.

Giddens believes, I think rightly, that the sense of political community based on ideas of history, belonging, homeland, etc., as well as the more purely political beliefs based on modern notions of citizenship, are crucial to the modern state, the nation-state. I agree that the creation of an ideological political community called a nation is central to the task of holding together the extended political communities of the modern state. But Giddens nowhere analyzes how this creation proceeds. Although one of the key dimensions of his general theory is concerned with symbol systems and meanings, the four concepts used for analysis in *The Nation-State and Violence* do not cover this area. The only concept that might do this, that concerned with surveillance, has nothing on this issue. There is no consideration of traditions of political thought and their impact on state forms. There is no consideration of how the interaction of new forms of centralized political control in modern Europe with earlier traditions of political liberties helped shape modern state forms and the ideologies which sustained those forms.

This leads one to an even more glaring hole in Giddens's analysis. The modern state is dominated by the institutions of bureaucracies, parliaments and parties. Bureaucracies are not simple agents for surveying and controlling the population, as already argued. Parties and parliaments are crucial to the modern construction of a 'public sphere', so central to the modern state and the idea of the nation-state, yet Giddens says nothing at all about this. It is as if he is so preoccupied with the threat of nuclear war and the growth of the 'secret state' that he can only consider these aspects of the modern state. These are then juxtaposed fairly arbitrarily alongside the standard sociological concerns with capitalism and industrialism.

This in turn vitiates his analysis of the only specific form of modern state he considers, namely the totalitarian state. Here he does not take much note of the large recent literature which has challenged the use of the term for Hitler's Germany and/or Stalin's Russia.[8] If the concept has any validity at all, and I doubt it, it must include an account of how subjects respond to the totalitarian state and how their values and interests shape or at least constrain the operations of that state. But Giddens approaches the matter in terms of 'control from above', an approach which has largely been discredited by recent historical analysis.

Conclusion

Giddens begins with some very telling critical comments. His general theory criticizes dubious assumptions about 'society', and *The Nation-State and Violence* is rightly critical of the failure to take proper account of the 'state'. In his specific analysis of the state some searching points are made about the significance of new forms of information transfer and handling, types of military capacity, and the functions of international agencies in a world of sovereign nation-states. But when measured against the claim to provide a general framework for an understanding of the modern nation-state, this is inadequate.

Classical theories of the state have been divided into those concerned with 'why' and those concerned with 'what'. Giddens cannot belong to the first camp because of its functional or teleological implications. His approach is of the 'what' kind. His definition is in the tradition of Weber, focusing on the monopoly of legitimate violence in a demarcated territory. But as already noted, this is given as a definition of the nation-state, not the modern state. With this definitional sleight of hand, Giddens makes it impossible for us to identify what is modern about the state independently of the idea of nationality, simultaneously depriving himself of any independent theory of nationalism which can then be connected to (rather than defined as part of) modern state development.

The one historical typology Giddens offers – tribal states, agrarian empires with class-divided societies, nation-states with class societies – focuses on the social settings within which states operate. These types are crude, historically dubious, and are used in the spirit of 'structuralism' rather than 'structuration-ism'.[9] The four specific concepts used for analysis of the modern state are only arbitrarily linked to the 'dimensions' of Giddens's general theory. Two are again concerned only with the social setting of the modern state (capitalism, industrialism). The other two refer to rather narrow aspects of modern state activity, although the nuclear capability in particular has the potential to overshadow everything else. The concept of surveillance is in any case of little use unless linked to increases in the state's capacity to reward or punish on the basis of the information obtained, which in turn should be linked to Giddens's notion of polyarchy. In many ways the nuclear capacity reverses many trends in the development of modern military capabilities.

According to Giddens's theoretical canons, the relationships between the concepts can only be demonstrated through actual historical linkage, but this is rarely provided. The general patterns of change with which they are associated are handled implicitly through a model of 'episodic evolution' rather than the kind of ever-open historical exploration of alternative possibilities which Giddens's general approach demands. The concepts exclude many of the most central problems for the analyst of the modern state, above all the connections between the expansion of state power, the active political community, the institutions which handle those expansions of both power and participation, and the political ideologies which justify these developments and help people handle them effectively. These are the concerns which should be at the heart of any analysis which asks why the modern state is a nation-state.

Finally, if a concept of 'society' with distinct processes and modes of development is to be rejected, why should one be less sceptical of the concept of the 'state'? In principle one must either accept both or neither as theoretical constructs. To accept both could take one into some fruitful analysis of how, in modern times, there have appeared clear and distinct notions of 'state' and 'civil society', even if these are more difficult to accept and apply now than during the heyday of liberalism. To accept neither takes one towards the highly impressive approach of Michael Mann (1986), which focuses on different forms of social power, which may or may not be organized through state institutions. But what Mann also demonstrates is how open one has to be in practice to the complexity and contingency of history if this approach is to work at all.

Giddens has identified some of the major questions facing the contemporary analyst of the nature of political and military power in the modern world. However, his own approach as exemplified in *The Nation-State and Violence* does not go very far towards answering these questions, above all because, rather strangely for a sociologist, he fails to consider the nation-state as a political community.

Acknowledgment

I would like to thank my colleague Steve Rigby for his useful comments on an earlier draft of this chapter.

Notes

1. One of the early translators of Weber's work was Talcott Parsons (Weber, 1930). After 1945 typical translations were by A. Henderson and Talcott Parsons (Weber, 1947) and by Edward Shils and Henry Finch (Weber, 1949).

2. For a recent set of theoretical considerations see Skocpol, Evans and Ruschmeyer (1985). A major general historical treatment of the closely related subject of power is Mann (1986), with two more volumes planned to complete the historical analysis and a fourth volume of a more theoretical kind. Mann shares Giddens's scepticism about the concept of 'society' but approaches the problem of the state in a very different way. I return to this question at the end of the chapter.

3. For scepticism about the very sharp distinctions which Gellner (1983) makes between these types of polities and the kind of political consciousness to which they give rise see A. Smith (1986, esp. Ch. 4).

4. For 'state building', on which there is a large literature, see two of the volumes in the *Studies in Political Development*: Tilly (1975) and Grew (1978). Tilly has taken the notion of state building in an interesting direction recently in his essay, 'War Making and State Making as Organized Crime', in Skocpol, Evans and Ruschmeyer (1985, 169–91). For examples of 'deliberate modernization' see Wehler (1987), especially Part 2 on the idea of 'defensive modernization'.

5. For the case of Germany, for example, see the essay by Kocka (1986). Some of the other essays in this volume [*sic*] touch upon the same problem, though not as systematically. An illuminating account of the complexity of wage and non-wage elements in a worker/employer relationship is provided by Sonenscher (1983).

6. There is sometimes the danger that Giddens equates 'state' with 'central government', in which case clearly the modern state has far more power over its subjects than earlier states. However, if one regards guild masters or church courts or privileged landowners as sharing with central government in the exercise of political authority over subjects, then the trend is less clearcut. Indeed, there is no 'trend', which implies growth within a given structure, but rather structural transformation. That should be Giddens's position in theory, but he does not take that position in practice.

7. Foucault was criticized for his determinism by Ignatieff (1978); and Ignatieff in turn by Laqueur (1981). The development of modern policing is far more complex in its causes and patterns than the notions of 'surveillance' and 'internal pacification' allow. For a good comparative treatment of the issue see Emsley (1983).

8. The concept of totalitarianism has a large literature. Broadly there is the approach which centres on the precise analysis of the institutions of regimes and that which focuses on the political consequences of the development of 'mass society'. A lucid exponent of the first kind of approach is Schapiro (1972), and the best known of the second kind is Arendt (1951). Both have been severely criticized in recent historical analyses of Germany and Russia, especially the former, on which there is voluminous evidence. See Kershaw (1986) for a survey of much of this material for Germany. The essays in Lewin (1985) provide a rich antidote to the simplistic views of Stalinism as totalitarianism. Even if one wishes to continue to defend the concept, it will have to involve the broader analysis of the popular base of totalitarianism, and not a narrow focus on the workings of police and bureaucracies. Even then it will be clear that the ideas of atomized societies, the one-way transmission of initiative from the top down, and a monolithic regime, and much else will have to be abandoned. No complex modern society operates in that way.

9. They have most recently been employed to stimulating effect by Gellner (1988). But Gellner's explicit acceptance of a 'trinitarian' view of history and the way in which he uses these three types is very different from that of Giddens.

References

Arendt, H. (1951) *The Origins of Totalitarianism*, New York: Harcourt Brace.
Breuilly, J. (1982) *Nationalism and the State*, Manchester: Manchester University Press.
Breuilly, J. (1985) 'Artisan economy, artisan politics, artisan ideology: The artisan contribution to the 19th Century European labour movement', in C. Emsley and J. Walvin (eds), *Artisans, Peasants and Proletarians 1760–1860*, London: Croom Helm, pp. 187–225.
Dyson, K. (1980) *The State Tradition in Western Europe*, Oxford: Martin Robertson.
Emsley, C. (1983) *Policing in Its Context 1750–1870*, London: Macmillan.
Foucault, M. (1977) *Discipline and Punish: the Birth of the Prison*, New York, Vintage Press.

Gellner, E. (1983) *Nations and Nationalism*, Oxford: Blackwell.

Gellner, E. (1988) *Plough, Sword and Book: The Structure of Human History*, London: Collins Harvill.

Giddens, A. (1981a) *A Contemporary Critique of Historical Materialism, Vol. 1: Power, Property and the State*, London: Macmillan.

Giddens, A. (1985a) *The Nation-State and Violence, Vol. 2 of A Contemporary Critique of Historical Materialism*, Cambridge: Polity Press.

Grew, R. (ed.) (1978) *Crises of Political Development in Europe and the United States*, Princeton N.J.: Princeton University Press.

Howard, M. (1976) *War in European History*, Oxford: Oxford University Press.

Ignatieff, M. (1978) *A Just Measure of Pain: The Penitentiary in the Industrial Revolution*, London: Macmillan.

Kershaw, I. (1986) *The Nazi Dictatorship*, London: Edward Arnold.

Kocka, J. (1986) 'Problems of Working-Class Formation in Germany: The Early Years, 1800–1875', in I. Katznelson and A. Zolberg (eds) *Working-Class Formation: Nineteenth Century Patterns in Western Europe and the United States*, Princeton N.J.: Princeton University Press, pp. 279–351.

Kumar, K. (1978) *Prophecy and Progress. The Sociology of Industrial and Post-Industrial Society*, Harmondsworth: Penguin.

Lacquer, T. (1981) 'Review' of Ignatieff (1978), *Social History*, vol. 6, 1981, pp. 384–6.

Lewin, M. (1985) *The Making of the Soviet System*, London: Methuen.

Ludtke, A. (1979) 'The role of state violence in the period of transition to industrial capitalism: The example of Prussia from 1815 to 1848', *Social History* 4, pp. 175–221.

Mann, M. (1986) *The Sources of Power, Vol. 1: A History of Power from the Beginning to A.D. 1760*, Cambridge: Cambridge University Press.

Mommsen, W. (1984) *Max Weber and German Politics 1890–1920*, Chicago, Ill.: Chicago University Press.

Mommsen, W. and Osterhammel, J. (1987) *Max Weber and his Contemporaries*, London: George Allen and Unwin.

Muller, K. (1987) *The Army, Politics and Society in Germany, 1933–45*, Manchester: Manchester University Press.

Pearton, M. (1982) *The Knowledgeable State*, London: Burnett Books.

Poggi, G. (1978) *The Development of the Modern State*, London: Hutchinson.

Rigby, S. (1987) *Marxism and History: a Critical Introduction*, Manchester: Manchester University Press.

Schapiro, L. (1972) *Totalitarianism*, London: Pall Mall Press.

Skocpol, T., Evans, P., and Ruschmey, D. (eds) (1985) *Bringing the State Back In*, New York: Cambridge University Press.

Smith, A.D. (1986) *The Ethnic Origin of Nations*, Oxford: Blackwell.

Sonenscher, M. (1983) 'Work and wages in Paris in the 18th Century', in M. Berg *et al.* (eds) *Manufacture in Town and Country before the Factory*, Cambridge: Cambridge University Press.

Tilly, C. (ed.) (1975) *The Formation of the National States in Western Europe*, Princeton N.J.: Princeton University Press.

Weber, M. (1930) *The Protestant Ethic and the Spirit of Capitalism*, London: Allen & Unwin.

Weber, M. (1947) *The Theory of Social and Economic Organization*, New York: Oxford University Press; new edn 1964, New York: Free Press.

Weber, M. (1949) *The Methodology of the Social Sciences*, Glencoe Ill.: Free Press.

Wehler, H.-U. (1987) *Deutsche Gesellschaftsgeschichte*, vol. 1 *Vom Feudalismus des Alten Reiches bis zur Defensiven Modernisierung*, Munich: C.H. Beck.

66

Society as Time-Traveller: Giddens on Historical Change, Historical Materialism and the Nation-State in World Society*

D. Jary

*Source: C.G.A. Bryant and D. Jary (eds), *Giddens' Theory of Structuration*, London: Routledge, 1991, ch. 5. Cross-references citing chapters, etc., relate to the original publication.

Introduction

In more senses than one, the scope of Giddens' aspirations for his structuration theory is utterly global. In *Central Problems in Social Theory* (1979a) and *The Constitution of Society* (1984a) the goal was no less than to provide a total framework for the union of interpretative and structuralist sociologies. In the two volumes that are the main focus of this chapter, *A Contemporary Critique of Historical Materialism* (1981a) and *The Nation-State and Violence* (1985a) (and in a promised further volume on socialist societies), his objective is to realize the possibilities of a comprehensive reassessment of historical change first sketched in *Central Problems*.[1] His aim is to provide a theoretical and empirically based analysis of past, present and possible future societies that can replace both historical materialism and social evolutionary theories, each of these being seen as possessing serious weaknesses, not least their dependence on functionalism. Others, like Parsons and Habermas, have attempted a synthesis of theoretical perspectives as sweeping as Giddens'. There have been historical sociologists recently – notably Perry Anderson (1974a,b) and Michael Mann (1986) – who have supplied accounts of the development of the state and society that in their range and depth of historical analysis obviously outstrip Giddens. But no one has quite matched Giddens' integration of historical analysis and attention to theoretical foundations. Giddens is at one with Abrams (1982) who has suggested that sociology and history are methodologically speaking ulti-mately one subject, and that a proper attention to theory is essential. Undoubtedly, considerable advantages flow from Giddens' attention to theoretical bases. The value to macro- and historical sociology of his subtle discussion of the interrelation of action and structure – the conception of a 'duality of structure' at the heart of his structuration sociology – has been widely acknowledged, even by those unable to accept all its aspects (e.g. Urry, 1982; Thrift, 1983; Callinicos, 1987). The craftsmanship and clarity of his perceptive and highly systematic reworking of many of historical and political sociology's main typological concepts – a synthesis of Marxian and non Marxian approaches – has also been much admired (e.g. Wright, 1983). In addition, the relative novelty of his analysis of historical change in terms of the general concept of 'time–space distanciation' – the 'stretching of social relations across time and space' – brings interesting new insights. Finally, if Giddens is to be believed, this approach can also lead us not only to a better understanding, but also to some prospect of influence on a world that, as he puts it, at present 'totters on the edge of nuclear disaster' – a world in which the analysis of the role of nation-states within a worldwide nation-state system must be made central, alongside the more conventional analysis in sociology of unitary societies and economic forces.

Aims of this Chapter

The aim of this chapter is twofold:

1. to outline the main elements of Giddens' structurationist account of historical change, no easy task when he himself covers much ground;
2. to confront a number of issues that can be raised about this approach, seeking to assess its strengths but also its possible limitations.

While I hope to show that room exists for suggesting that Giddens is sometimes overzealous in this repudiation of 'rival' approaches, and over-assertive in advancing aspects of his own model of historical change, this will not be seen as detracting from the many virtues of his analysis in charting the terrain of macro-sociological analysis. Since he himself sometimes insists that structuration theory is an 'approach' rather than a tightly formulated theory, I would see my criticism as operating within the spirit of Giddens' own work, as an attempt to get the best from all existing approaches. My argument will be that efforts such as his should be seen as part of a broader 'reform' movement already well established in comparative historical sociology (cf. Tilly, 1981; Abrams, 1982; Anderson, 1974a, b; Mann, 1986; Collins, 1986; Eisenstadt, 1987), and that it is far from clear that Giddens' version of theoretical bases or his substantive account of historical change should simply be accepted.[?]

Focus and Main Themes of Giddens' Historical Argument

As Giddens expresses it in *The Constitution of Society*:

> the fundamental question of social theory – the 'problem of order'

conceived in a way quite alien to Parsons' formulation when he coined the phrase – is to explicate how the limitations of individual 'presence' are transcended by the 'stretching' of social relations across space and time.

(Giddens, 1984a: 35)

If such a 'stretching across time and space' is a feature of all societies – i.e. is intrinsic to all social institutions – it reaches its greatest extent in contemporary societies, which truly can be said to exist as part of a 'world-system'. In pre-historical 'band societies' regularized transactions with (live) others who are physically absent occurred only rarely. But in modern societies not only have interconnections grown, transportation dramatically improved and distances been bridged, but communications across space have become instantaneous. Moreover an increased capacity to organize time and space might seem of the essence of the greatly increased economic and political power exhibited by modern societies. How has such a time–space distanciation of social relations come about? What organizations, what logics, has this process involved? These are Giddens' questions. If Giddens' questions are relatively simple, his answers are more complex and involve an amalgam of empirical, theoretical and epistemological and ontological arguments concerning the implications of human agency, time and space and political and economic power that it is not always easy to unravel. However, four key elements in his overall argument can perhaps be initially identified.

1. If historical change is marked above all by time–space distanciation, then the accumulation of political power, especially the administrative and military power of modern states, is at least as significant as economic forces, and may even be more decisive.
2. Accounts of historical change must recognize its multicausal basis, eschewing all attempts at monocausal explanations. In line with his D–D–L–S model of institutions (see Figure 3), Giddens identifies four interrelated institutional bases of social order and social change.
3. It is essential that societies should be seen as connected by 'intersocietal systems' and influenced by their location in 'world-time', i.e. by the variety of social forms that cross-cut societal boundaries, and by particular geopolitical contexts and particular historical conjunctures.
4. Partly because of the complexities arising from (1), (2) and (3), but more generally because of human knowledgeability and the 'reflexive nature of human social life', 'episodic characterizations' of historical change, in which change is recognized as 'discontinuous' and 'historically contingent', are the only ones appropriate. This is to say, that social change always consists of *non*-evolutionary 'historically located sequences of change', each having 'a specifiable opening, trend of events and outcome' but *not* a part of any necessary sequence of social development (Giddens, 1984a: 374). Giddens' reasoning here would seem to be that any simple

law-like explanation of historical change is ruled out, first, by the existence of 'time–space edges' – i.e. connections between, rather than any simple linear sequence of societies of different structural types – and secondly by the 'reflexive monitoring' carried out in this context, particularly by state elites. More generally, as Giddens puts it: 'there is no mechanism of social organization or social reproduction identified by social analysts which lay actors cannot also get to know about and actively incorporate into what they do' (Giddens, 1984a: 284).

If the first and second of these four points are directed especially against historical materialism, the third and fourth count equally against both historical materialism and evolutionary theory (and also functionalism). It is in this context that Giddens speaks of his thinking as 'deconstructing' rather than reconstructing historical materialism and evolutionary theory (Giddens, 1984a: 243). 'We live in a world', he suggests, 'for which traditional sources of theory have left us unprepared' (Giddens, 1987a: 166). The alternative he proposes is a multidimensional, non-evolutionary and non-functionalist analysis of historical change that he believes can be grounded in structuration theory.

In what follows we first note aspects of the general location of Giddens' historical thinking within structuration theory, then trace in more detail the main lines of his historical account before concluding with a critical discussion.

The Location of Giddens' Account within Structuration Theory

Complaints are made that Giddens' books present increasing problems of internal self-reference (Friedland, 1987). The extent of recapitulation and sheer repetition can also be a source of irritation, although doubtless this is intended to help the reader who dips into only parts of the ever-expanding corpus. What this leaves in no doubt, however, is how strikingly cumulative has been the development of Giddens' structuration theory. The theories and empirical accounts of others are endlessly mined, concepts are added, but relatively little is given up. Though always stressing the uncompleted nature of the enterprise, Giddens is evidently well pleased with the cogency of the framework of concepts accumulated over more than a decade. Concepts, when added, only supplement or enlarge the framework, rarely if ever changing it in fundamental ways.

'Time–Space' in the Constitution of Society and in Historical Change

The analysis of time and space, and historical change, is integral to structuration theory. Actions and structures must both be seen as continuously in process. As Giddens remarks, quoting Rilke, 'Our life passes in transformation' (1979a: 3).

The emphasis on 'process' and 'transformation' in structuration theory may ease the transition between accounts of 'order' and accounts of 'change' (see Figure 1), but it would be a mistake to assume that 'process' and 'transformation' are simply *equivalent* to 'historical change' as conceived in Giddens' historical sociology. Plainly this is not so. 'Prehistorical' band societies, for example, though continuously 'in process' and obviously existing in time, do not because of this *automatically* undergo 'historical change'. Certainly, the 'two most essential characteristics of human social life', are: (a) what Giddens terms, the 'transformative capacity' – the 'could have done otherwise' – inherent in all human action, and (b) 'the variety of ways in which, in social systems, interaction is made possible across space and time'. However, Giddens makes a point of contrasting what he terms the 'historicality' – i.e. the potentiality for historical change – of all societies, and the actual historical change and conceptions of 'historicity' that occur only in some. What Giddens means by historicity in this context is the existence within a society of conceptions that involve 'the identification of history as progressive change', and coupled with this 'the cognitive utilization of such identification in order to further change' (Giddens, 1984a: 374). In societies – such as many tribal societies – entirely pervaded by conceptions of 'reversible' rather than 'irreversible' time (see also Chapters One and Six, this volume) conceptions of historicity do not exist and do not readily develop. Only in some societies, principally for Giddens those societies that also become states, do such conceptions begin to appear and become associated with the stretching of societies across time and space.

	Structuralist or voluntarist theories	*Giddens' structurationist alternative*
Characterization of structure	structure *or* agency	'duality of structure' the interrelation of action and structure
Characterization of actor	agents as supports of structure ('cultural dopes') *or* as purely voluntaristic	knowledgeability of actors/conscious intentionality – but in context of structure as medium and outcome of agency and interaction
Characterization of historicality	ahistorical structures: synchrony *versus* diachrony, statics *versus* dynamics	time (and space) and 'historicality' as integral to action and structure, with 'historicity' as an emergent feature leading to 'time–space distanciation' as intended but also unintended consequence

Figure 1 Structure, agency and historicality in Giddens' sociology

This is *one* very general sense in which the development of human societies can be seen as 'episodic'. The existence of such a two-phase notion in Giddens' historical thinking has a similar force to Michael Mann's assertion that while general evolutionary theory may be applied to the Neolithic Revolution, 'general social evolution ceased (with) the emergence of civilization' (Mann, 1986: 39), when distinctively 'historical' change takes over.

Giddens and Time-Geography

It is the time-geographer Stig Hägerstrand who suggests that the life of the individual might be represented as 'movement through time–space' (Giddens, 1981a: 38). His work is also of value in 'identifying sources of constraint over human activity given by the nature of the body and the physical contexts in which activity occurs' (Giddens, 1984a: 111). Another time-geographer, Donald Janelle, is credited with introducing the notion of 'time–space convergence', 'the shrinking of distance in terms of the time needed to travel between different locations' (Giddens, 1981a: 38; 1984a: 114).

Giddens is critical of the time-geographers, however, in four key respects: (1) a tendency to view the constitution of the individual independently of social settings, a dualism of action and structure; (2) lack of reference to the 'essentially transformative character of human action'; (3) 'concentration solely on the constraining properties of the body'; (4) the lack of a well-developed theory of power (Giddens, 1984a: 117).

One difference of significance between Giddens and the time-geographers is his replacement of the concept of 'place' with the concept of 'locale' – a concept of special importance subsequently because it leads on to the crucial notion of historically decisive 'power containers' (including cities and states) as special kinds of locale. Giddens prefers the term locale because it can be given more than a positional reference (Giddens, 1981a: 39). Locales refer to the use of space to provide the 'settings' of interaction, these settings in turn being seen as essential to specifying the 'contextuality' of action – in time and space – in a fully sociological way.

It is from Goffman that the concept of 'social setting' is drawn, and it is Goffman who also provides a further vital element in Giddens' thinking, specification of the 'profound difference' that exists 'between *face-to-face interaction and interaction with others who are physically absent*' (Giddens, 1979a. 203, emphasis in original). This distinction possesses a multiple significance within Giddens' historical macro-sociology (as it does within structuration theory in general – see Figure 2), first, in underlining that 'the study of day-to-day life is integral to analysis of the reproduction of institutionalized practices' (Giddens, 1984a: 282) and, second, in indicating how far-flung connections in social life should be understood as involving an interpenetration of 'social integration' and 'system integration'. More generally, it is found valuable in bringing an explicit focus on 'the extension

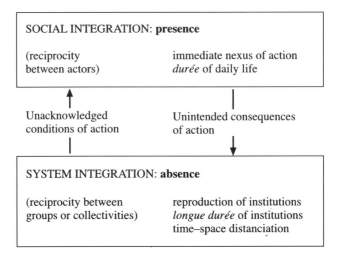

Figure 2 Social integration and system integration
Source: Adapted from Giddens, 1984a; Spybey, 1987

of social systems in space and time' as 'an evident feature of the overall development of human society' (Giddens, 1979a: 20). In general, Goffman's work is taken as showing how different kinds of social setting arrange time and space (including the body) differently. Finally, it is within this general conceptual framework centred on time and space that further key concepts such as 'time–space edges' or 'world-time' can be readily incorporated. The latter of these concepts derives from the historian Eberhard (1965).

'Power' and 'Surveillance' in Structuration Theory

For Giddens:

> 'Power', along with 'agency' and 'structure', is an elementary concept in social science. To be human is to be an agent – although not all agents are human – and to be an agent is to have power. 'Power' in this highly generalized sense means 'transformative capacity', the capability to intervene in a given set of events so as in some way to change them. The logical connection between agency and power is of the first importance for social theory, but the 'universal' sense of power thus implied needs considerable refinement if it is to be put to work in the interests of substantive social research.
>
> (Giddens, 1985a: 7)

If power is involved in all areas of action and institutions identified by Giddens (cf. Figure 1.3, p. 10), two conceptual refinements can be seen as playing a pivotal role within his treatment of historical change: (1) the

Signification (S)	Domination (D)		Legitimation (L)
Symbolic orders/ modes of discourse	D (auth) Political institutions	D (alloc) Economic institutions	Law/modes of sanction
[S–D–L]	[D(auth)–S–L]	[D(alloc)–S–L]	[L–D–S]

Figure 3 Giddens' D-D-L-S model of institutions
Source: Versions of this model appear in Giddens, 1981a and 1984a and elsewhere

distinction between power based on 'allocative resources' (domination over the material world, including material facilities) and that based on 'author-itative resources' (domination over human beings) (see Figure 3) and (2) his concept of 'surveillance', a term he borrows from Foucault (1975) but considerably reformulates. For Giddens, 'surveillance' refers to two aspects of modern state power and the power of organizations that vastly extend their effectiveness: (1) the collection and collation of information, greatly expan-ded in modern times by all manner of information technologies; and (2) the direct 'watching over' of human activities, made increasingly possible by the existence of many specialist 'bounded locales'. The latter include, as well as the state directly, the 'new ways of enforced regularizing of activities in time and space', including prisons and workplaces, referred to by Foucault as 'sequestration'.

Contrary to Foucault, Giddens stresses that the outcome of domination and surveillance is 'enabling' as well as 'constraining', and not only 'negative'. In addition, since it is always mediated by a 'dialectic of control', power is never 'absolute'. Giddens does not neglect the unacknowledged conditions or the unintended consequences of the exercise of power – as seen in Chapter One, this volume, he accepts that some of the most important tasks of social science are the investigation of the significance of these in system reproduc-tion. Notwithstanding this, the main thrust of his general argument is that sociology has frequently overemphasized the decisiveness in history of allocative power, while underestimating the enormous significance, for good and ill, of authoritative power.

Giddens' Historical Account

It will not be possible to provide more than a sketch of Giddens' historical account. This is a pity, because he is often perceptive on historical points of detail, irrespective of how one may ultimately judge his overall theory.

However, in order to make a general assessment of the applicability of structuration theory to historical analysis it is the broad lines of his account that it is important to grasp.

The 'City' and 'Traditional Empires' as 'Power Containers' and 'Prime Carriers' of the Time–Space Distanciation of Societies

The first step in Giddens' account, for which his analysis of both power and time-geography prepares the way, is the entry of the 'city' and of states on to the stage of history as new kinds of 'locale', as centres for the 'storage' of power, as 'power containers'. Although 'the storage of "material" or allocative resources' (for example, in grain stores or irrigation systems) may seem more obvious, in the end it is the storage of authoritative resources that Giddens categorically states as 'more significant' (Giddens, 1984a: 94). While even the storage of material resources 'involves far more than *merely* the physical containment of material goods', what storage of authoritative resources crucially entails is *'the retention and control of information or knowledge'* (ibid: 94, emphasis in original). In this respect, writing is a 'decisive development', creating a storage 'container' beyond human memory. It is this that brings the capacity for time–space distanciation that is simply lacking in preliterate societies. First, listings and administrative records, and then 'recorded history' – and with this the possibility of 'historicity' – make their appearance in this way.

It is in these terms – here reviving the work of Lewis Mumford – that Giddens regards the 'city' as the first distinctive power container in modern history. Its role within early 'civilized' societies in beginning the process of extensive time–space distanciation is crucial. When Spengler wrote, 'world history is city history', Giddens mainly agrees (Giddens, 1984a: 96). The city, in creating a new division (but also new relations) between an urban environment and the countryside, becomes a 'crucible for the generation of power on a scale unthinkable in non-urban communities'. 'The enclosure of cities by walls' may enhance 'the metaphor of the "container"', but walls are only the physical expression of a more significant intramural power, the power of the city as a 'religious, ceremonial, and commercial centre' and as a centre of political power: the arrival of 'city-states'. The issue of whether the 'agricultural revolution' and the expansion of 'productive forces' is the underlying factor in the rise of cities and the chief mobilizer of social change is not ignored by Giddens. However, he dismisses Gordon Childe's long-standing thesis that a 'neolithic revolution' *preceded* the emergence of cities. Nor does he accept Jacobs' (1970) view that it was the purely 'economic' power generated by cities that was most significant (Giddens, 1981a: 94–100).

The historical step that, according to Giddens, provides the next significant power container is 'the fusion of several cities to form *empires*'. This again represents a 'qualitative break between two types of social organization'

(Giddens, 1981a: 100). Although limited developments in transport and communications restrict their power in comparison with modern states, empires constitute 'the only examples of large scale centralized societies before the establishment of capitalism'. They reflect the 'conscious attempts' of rulers to establish 'homogeneous modes of administration and political allegiance within particular territories' (ibid: 102). If military power (including developments in military technology) plays the decisive role in the creation and continuity of these new political forms, two further factors are also acknowledged as important: the legitimation of authority *within* the apparatus of government and the 'formation of economic ties of interdependence'. What Giddens insists, however, is that economic factors were the 'least important'. Again the message is clear, 'the first territorial states' become established *without* economic forces being decisive. Furthermore, Giddens goes on to assert that for all sorts of traditional state societies prior to capitalism the same is so, 'coordination of *authoritative* resources forms the determining axis of societal integration and *change*' (ibid: 4, emphasis added). Thus on Giddens' assessment, 'noncapitalist societies are definitely not modes of production, even if modes of production are obviously involved'. Nor do these societies possess any obvious inherent tendency to evolve.

If such statements as these would appear to conflict with historical materialism this, of course, is exactly what Giddens intends. However, as he is well aware, they do not conflict in the same way with much that Marx actually wrote, in the *Formen* and elsewhere, about 'pre-capitalist' forms of society. It is clear that Marx entertained many doubts about the 'dynamic' character of economic forces and class relations in these forms of society. What Giddens concludes about pre-capitalist agrarian states is that although they can appropriately be described as 'class-divided societies' – in contrast with earlier 'tribal societies' – they are not 'class societies' in that their central dynamic is not class. Above all, their subordinate classes, while remaining in control of the means of production as immediate producers possess insufficient 'spatial stretch' to sustain class organizations or class conflict. In Giddens' view, therefore, these forms of society must be sharply contrasted with modern forms of capitalist 'class society' (see Figure 4), in which class is the central axis of order and change.

What Giddens suggests about Marx's work at this point is summed up by him in the following way:

> that it is the themes of the *Formen* which are worthy of further elaboration rather than those involved in Marx's evolutionary interpretation of history. The forces/relations of production dialectic is not a miraculous device that somehow holds the answer to disclosing the underlying sources of social change in general. Nor can the contradictory character of social formations be understood in these terms – except in the case of capitalism.
>
> (Giddens, 1981a: 89)

	CLASS-DIVIDED SOCIETIES	CLASS SOCIETIES (Capitalist societies)
	'Symbiosis of the city and countryside'	Commercially created 'built environment'
		Formal separation of economic and political spheres
MODES OF DOMINATION/ PREDOMINANT SANCTIONS	Local, relatively autonomous communal production – 'allocative power'	Private ownership of capital; 'asymmetrical' capitalist labour contract – 'allocative power'
	Centralized political and military power – 'authoritative power'	State surveillance – 'authoritative power' and violence extruded from the labour contract
	Predominant sanction: control of means of violence	Predominant sanction: economic necessity of employment
ROLE OF CLASS AND CLASS CONFLICT	Class divisions, but class conflict not the central dynamic – peasant rebellions, but only the dominant class possess spatial stretch	Class divisions and class conflict a central dynamic (although not alone decisive)

Figure 4 Class-divided societies and class societies

Giddens' Non-Evolutionary Societal Typology

Unlike some critics, Giddens writes about Marxism neither as an 'implacable opponent or a disillusioned ex-believer' (Giddens, 1981a: 1). Instead, though making plain that he is not a Marxist, he is eloquent in his 'belief' that 'Marx's analysis of the mechanism of capitalist production ... remains the necessary core of any attempt to come to terms with the massive transformations that have swept through the world since the eighteenth century' (ibid.). Elements of Marx's analysis of human *Praxis* are also accorded considerable value. Marx's 'evolutionary scheme', however, remains fatally flawed.

Reduced to essentials, Giddens' critique of historical materialism – a relatively conventional one – has two aspects. First, the focus of historical materialism on *Praxis* and human agency is undermined by an unjustifiable 'elision' of 'praxis in general' with 'labour' in particular (Giddens, 1981a: 54)

(i) **Tribal society** (oral culture):
– Tradition (communal practices)   [Fusion of social and
– Kinship   system integration]
– Group sanction
Dominant locale organization: band groups or villages

(ii) **Class-divided society:**
– Tradition (communal practices)   [Differentiation of social and
– Kinship   system integration]
– Politics/military power
– Economic interdependence
 (high lateral and vertical   STATE
 interdependence)
Dominant locale organization: symbiosis of society and countryside

(iii) **Class society:**
– Routinization   [Differentiation of social and
– Kinship (family)   system]
– Surveillance
– Politics/military power   STATE
– Economic interdependence
 (high lateral and vertical
 interdependence)
Dominant locale organization: the 'created environment'

Figure 5 Typology of societies
Source: A modified version of figures that appear in Giddens, 1981a and 1984a
Note: In the 1984 version of this figure politics/military power is a feature of 'class society'; in the 1981 version it is absent.

– the reduction of the 'transformative capacity' of human agents ultimately to merely economic agency. Second, evolutionary and functionalist arguments – Marxist and non-Marxist versions of these – are rejected so long as they continue to invoke untenable explanatory conceptions of 'societal needs' and societal 'adaptation'. What this second criticism boils down to is that there exists no 'evolutionary' operation of social contradictions and no functionalist 'autoproduction' of social systems (though 'counterfactual' forms of functionalist argument, asserting what would be required for a particular system to exist or reproduce, are accepted as legitimate by Giddens). For Giddens, such biologically derived concepts as 'adaptation' or 'need' are too lacking in precise content to possess any useful purchase faced with the complexities of social development. In any case, Giddens agrees with Gellner (1964) – from whom he also borrows the term 'episode' – that: 'Human history is not … a "world-growth story"', in that it is a record that involves neither the continuous nor the unilinear development implied by historical materialism or social evolutionism (Giddens, 1984a: 237 *et seq.*).

In these circumstances, Giddens' own typology of main types of society – Figure 5 – is a typology only of historically existing societies, not intended as an evolutionary scheme. Its focus is on the extent and kind of differentiation exhibited by different forms of society, as well as on the time–space distanciation of societies, but as an uneven historical sequence not a necessary evolutionary progression. Thus first there is 'tribal society', in which political and economic institutions remain undifferentiated and where the time–space is severely limited. Second, there is 'class-divided society', in which the differentiation of political and economic institutions takes the form of a 'symbiosis of city and countryside', and where social integration and system integration also become separated and the time–space stretch of society begins. And third, there is 'class society' (and 'nation-state') with its far more formal separation of political and economic 'spheres', and highly extended distanciation and lateral and horizontal interdependence. The historical and 'non-evolutionary' nature of this sequence of societal development is underlined by Figure 6, which indicates the intersocietal systems and time–space edges existing in world-time. What such a world-historical context for individual societies reinforces, according to Giddens, is that, though societal typologies have their uses, there can be no question of a simple sequence of 'endogenous' societal development.

Capitalism, Absolutism and the Nation-State

As is clear both from his remarks and his typologies, Giddens does not dispute the very great importance of capitalism in the time–space distanciation of societies. However, in line with his rejection of the evolutionary monism of

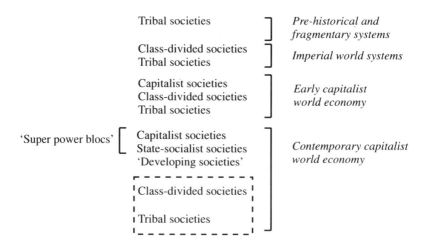

Figure 6 Intersocietal systems in 'world-time'
Source: Giddens, 1981a: 161

historical materialism and his view of social change as episodic, he insists: (1) that the development of capitalism and the nation-state (and also industrialism) must be seen as interrelated phenomena with no one determining factor; (2) that these interrelated developments were historically contingent and *distinctively European*, leading to an ascendancy of the west finally confirmed only in the latter half of the seventeenth century; and (3) that this happened only in a geopolitical context in which, for the first time, Europe was no longer threatened militarily from the east and when its naval technology had also achieved a worldwide supremacy. That there was much that was not inevitable or 'evolutionary' about these developments, Giddens declares, is confirmed by noting how very different history might have been, for example, had Charlemagne succeeded in his goal of a new European empire or if the European powers had suffered lasting defeat at the hands of the Ottoman Turks in the seventeenth century.

For Giddens, the undoubted historical significance of western capitalism is that it involves the commodification of land, labour-power and the means of production, as well as the abstraction of surplus value by capitalists, 'on an altogether new scale'. This is turn led on to the commodification of time and space generally in modern societies. If as is widely recognized, money, including new means of credit and accounting, plays a particularly vital role in 'disembodying social relations, in detaching these from time and space', then:

> Marx has to be given very great credit for first showing that it is the *commodification of time* that forms the underlying connecting link between the massive expansion of the commodity form in the production of goods, on the one hand, and the commodification of labour (as labour power) on the other.
>
> (Giddens, 1981a: 130, emphasis in original)

Thus, to this extent in a manner broadly consistent with Marxism itself, Giddens sees the entire process of commodification in modern societies as a systematic outcome of the dispossession of workers from the means of production and the 'extrusion' of violence from the labour contract.

This said, however, it is a decisive element of Giddens' argument that the capitalist extraction of surplus value could not have occurred without the part played by the 'coterminous' emergence of new state forms in pacifying populations and enforcing the rule of law, or without new means of surveillance in the workplace – forms of authoritative rather than merely allocative power. Giddens quotes from Foucault as follows:

> If the economic take-off of the West began with the technique that made possible the accumulation of capital, it might perhaps be said that the methods for the accumulation of men made possible a political take-off in

relation to traditional ritual, costly, violent forms of power, which soon fell into disuse and were superseded by a subtle, calculated technology of subjection.

(Foucault, 1975: 220–1)

Among the new methods in the workplace, of course, were the coordination of machinery and labour power by 'clock-time' and more general control over the labour process, described so vividly by E.P. Thompson (1967) and Braverman (1974). These replaced the self-control and more natural rhythms that had previously governed work in traditional societies. Thus, as Giddens puts it, 'struggle over time becomes the most direct expression of class conflict in the capitalist economy' (Giddens, 1981a: 120), and the 'policing' of society a crucial factor in the effectiveness of capitalism.

For Giddens, however, the new state forms involve far more than the policing of civil society envisaged by orthodox Marxism or by liberal thought. Crucially in Giddens' view, the modern European nation-state is a 'bordered power container', enclosing far greater administrative intensity than traditional states. It can be sharply distinguished from its predecessors by its clearly demarcated borders and its existence within a state-system of similarly constituted states in which warfare and the preparation for war plays a fundamental constitutive role. In Giddens' own summary:

Nation-states only exist in systematic relations with other nation-states. The internal administrative coordination of nation-states from their very beginnings depends upon reflexively monitored conditions of an international nature. 'International relations' is coeval with the origins of nation-states.

(Giddens, 1985a: 4)

Figure 7 indicates in outline the overall developments considered important by Giddens, who particularly criticizes Weber and other theorists for not stating more clearly the sharpness of division between traditional and modern states and the distinctiveness this gives to modern societies – their more unitary character than previous state societies.

In these developments it is the transitional 'absolutist' states of fifteenth- and sixteenth-century Europe as well as the fully fledged nation-states of modern times that, according to Giddens, must be regarded as an integral part of capitalist development, providing both 'some of the conditions for its early development' as well as the means of its later expansion. Essential to this view is that capitalist *societies* came into being as territorially bounded states and as part of a *state-system*. Central to absolutism is the idea of 'sovereignty', first as personal power but later as impersonal administrative power. In Giddens' view, it was the successful institutionalization of new concepts of sovereignty that did much to ensure 'the dissolution of the city/

	TRADITIONAL STATE	ABSOLUTIST STATE (a transitional form)	MODERN NATION-STATE
CHARACTER OF BOUNDARIES OF STATES	No clear boundaries: frontiers not borders	Forerunner of modern nation-state	Clearly defined and highly administered borders
	State and society not coextensive: multisocietal states	Concept of 'sovereignty', at first 'personal' then linked to nationalism	State and society coextensive: the 'nation-state'
		State system in which war and preparation for war central	Existence (and definition) as part of a well-defined 'state-system' of nation-states
MONOPOLY AND ROLE OF VIOLENCE	*Internal*: violence as a routine feature of administration; limited pacification	*Internal*: obsolescence of city walls symbolic of new state power and unification of town and country	*Internal*: internal pacification largely accomplished, with the threat of violence mainly in the background
	External: military force and military technology as the basis of territorial domination	*External*: warfare and preparation for warfare central to state formation	*External*: industrialization of warfare – application of technology: standing armies; conscription, etc. – leading to 'total war'
		Naval superiority over non-European states	
SCOPE AND INTENSITY OF ADMINISTRATIVE REACH	Wide territorial control but low administrative intensity and limited penetration of many areas of life	Increasing administrative control – especially fiscal and in relation to needs of military. New legal order☐	High administrative intensity: surveillance – control of information and sequestration
CENTRAL INTERNAL CONFLICTS	Intra-elite conflicts (dynastic change)	Varying alliances between state and traditional and emerging elites	Class conflict between capital and labour and class conflict a central dynamic, but class conflict not alone decisive
	Peasant revolts, but no centrality of class conflict		Polyarchy; citizen rights

Figure 7 Traditional, absolutist and modern nation-states

countryside relations' that characterized the traditional state. In a heterodox but not unMarxist way, Giddens presents the development of absolutism as an alliance of traditional local and state elites in which traditional feudal power was reorganized rather than entirely replaced (cf. Anderson, 1974b). Thus, it is not strictly true to say, as does Friedland (1987: 41), that for Giddens, the 'ruling ideas are not those of the ruling class, they are the ideas of rule'. However, contrary to historical materialism (at least as he sees it), Giddens' portrayal of the relation between capitalism and the new state forms is one that emphasizes reciprocal causation, so that in neither origins nor outcomes can the role of the state be reduced to economic factors.

At one level, for example, the suggestion is that the process of state development can be seen as driven in large measure by the demands of ever-changing modes of warfare. If, as Clausewitz the famous theoretician of modern warfare suggested, 'war is politics by other means', then for Giddens, economics must often be recognized as driven in large part by politics and by warfare. Thus, it is the geopolitical conflicts of states, first on a European scale and subsequently on a world stage, that he presents as frequently uppermost in influencing economic developments. In this way, for instance, the monetization of the economy arises as much from the fiscal demands posed by the ever-escalating costs of warfare as from the more general requirements of production and exchange. Likewise, many innovations in administration can be seen as having occurred first in connection with military needs, for example, the new forms of military discipline, that Giddens refers to as the 'Taylorism of this sphere'. Innovations in military technology also frequently predated advances in civilian technology. Giddens goes so far as to suggest that capitalism may even have become the dominant world mode of production *primarily* because of the military power possessed by the nation-states with which it was associated. For, while the imperial power of traditional empires might have resisted capitalism, these empires were unable to match the military power – more specifically perhaps the naval power – of the west. In more general terms, many of the technical inventions usually thought distinctive to modernity and often associated particularly with capitalism – improvements in transportation by sea, road, rail and air, and advances in communications and information technology such as telegraphy and computers – are as much driven by the strategic (and reflexive) requirements of state power, particularly the requirements of warfare, as by any logic of capitalism (or industrialism) alone. It would be wrong to suggest, as does Hall (1984), that internal relations play only an unimportant part in Giddens' analysis. But Giddens does insist that an economic- or a class-reductionist account of state power can only mislead as to the true role of the state in shaping both the internal and external relations of modern societies. Even nationalism, as Thrift (1984: 141) puts it, is seen as a 'psychological outproduct' of state power. Rather than the initial cause of the rise of nation-states, nationalism involves the state creation of new 'traditions'.

Giddens sums up his own view of the importance of state power when he describes the nation-state as the '*preeminent* modern power container'. While there are historians (notably Tilly, 1975) who claim that the association of capitalism and the nation-state is largely fortuitous (e.g. that the Hanseatic League had no association with a major state, that Spain and Portugal, though major powers, were not capitalist states), Giddens' reply is that this is true only of the earliest forms of capitalism, that thereafter the nation-state and capitalism require each other to survive and expand. Thus, the core of Giddens' argument would seem in fact to relate relatively little to the origins of capitalism. On the matter of such origins Giddens in fact says surprisingly little – a possible weakness of his argument *vis-à-vis* historical materialism we take up subsequently. Rather his argument is that it is in the establishment of capitalist societies that the role of the state must *certainly* be seen as crucial. In line with his multidimensional conception of historical causation, what Giddens concludes about modern societies is that in all four interdependent 'institutional clusterings' must be seen as associated with modernity: 'heightened surveillance, capitalist enterprise, industrial production and the consolidation and centralized control of the means of violence'. Moreover, 'none of these is wholly reducible to any of the others' (Giddens, 1985a: 5).

Contemporary 'World-Society' and the 'World Capitalist System'

The multidimensional, contingent and non-evolutionary, character of social development, with politics and the state playing a central role, is no less in evidence in Giddens' thinking when he brings his story up to date and turns his attention to the twentieth century and the contemporary world-system. So much is indicated by his assertion that: 'We live in what Wallerstein has called a "world capitalist economy", in which capitalist economic relations pertain on a world scale. *Even more important*, we live in a *world nation-state system* that has no precedent in history' (Giddens, 1987a: 166, emphasis added). For Giddens, it is a decisive feature of the modern world-system that 'From the state system that was once one of the peculiarities of Europe there has developed a system of nation-states covering the globe in a network of national communities' (Giddens, 1985a: 255) and that in this process: 'the military involvement of states also strongly influences the developments of . . . other features of societal organization, in ways that can be fairly readily traced out, even if they are missing from most sociological discussions' (ibid: 233).

The multiple developments that Giddens regards as significant in this process include:

1. the 'industrialization of warfare' – new weapons of destruction, the impact of new forms of communication and transportation – and 'total war'; in which both the old constraints of social convention and time and space have progressively diminished and in which entire populations are engaged either as conscripted participants or as targets;

2. the triumph of 'sentiments of nationalism' over internationalism in this process, signalling the new importance 'that the connection of sovereignty and citizenship had assumed and which would, henceforth, dominate the global community' (Giddens, 1985a: 232);
3. the aftermath, in particular, of two World Wars, in which the concept of the 'independent unity of each state' finally replaces both the 'older type of imperial system' and the more recent forms of European colonialism.

That the contingent nature of these developments remains emphasized by Giddens, however, is indicated by his insistence, for example, that:

> If the course of events in the Great War, including the participation of the USA in the hostilities and the peace settlement, had not taken the shape they did, the nation-state in its current form might not have become the dominant political entity in the world system.
>
> (Giddens, 1985a: 234–5)

Given his focus on the time–space distanciation of societies, it is no surprise to find that Giddens is strongly influenced by theorists of the 'world-system' such as Wallerstein. He praises especially the latter's strong emphasis on the 'regionalization of political and economic systems (and) upon spatial features of social organizations and change' (Giddens, 1985a: 166). However, the 'ever-increasing abundance of global connections' and international organizations, Giddens insists, 'should not be regarded as intrinsically diminishing the sovereignty' of states, but rather seen as 'in substantial part the chief condition of the worldwide extension of the nation-state system in current times' (ibid: 5). Moreover, within this state-system warfare and the threat of war remains a significant factor; indeed its importance is in many ways increased by the arrival of nuclear weapons. Reflecting the continued importance of Marx's thinking within his overall analysis, Giddens does sometimes refer to the world-system in general as a 'world capitalist economy' (e.g. Figure 6). Thus, Wallerstein's account of the origins of 'core' and 'peripheral' national economies – explained by him in terms of the presence or absence of strong states – is obviously accepted by Giddens. As often with Giddens' appropriation of the work of others, however, Wallerstein's account – seen as marred by functionalism as well as economic reductionism – becomes the butt of criticism, clearing the way for Giddens' own preferred model, which is that the contemporary world system will be fully understood only if it is seen as made up of four interrelated systems, corresponding to his D–D–L–S model of social institutions (see Figure 3):

1. *world capitalist economy* (corresponding to D alloc);
2. *nation-state system* (corresponding to D auth);
3. *world military order* (corresponding to L);
4. *global information system* (corresponding to S).

A critic might suggest that many of Giddens' formulations made using this framework – e.g. 'a military order that substantially cross-cuts the division between the First, Second and Third worlds of the world capitalist economy' – amount to little more than a loosely textured synthesis of much that is already accepted within the disciplines of political science, international relations and sociology. But Giddens appears content that such distinctions make apparent the relative complexity – and unpredictability – of the forces operating in the current world-system compared with the picture that emerges from more reductionist and more determinate models. Giddens presents as his 'main emphasis' in *Nation-State and Violence* the provision of 'an interpretation of the development of the nation-state in its original, i.e. "Western, habitat"', and a tracing out of 'why this form has become generalized across the globe'. He states clearly that he makes 'no claim to offering an exhaustive analysis of variations among states in today's world' (ibid: 5).

Contemporary Western Societies

In characterizing contemporary western capitalist societies, Giddens' account is fuller, though it still depends heavily on the application of general categories. Again, it is the contingent character and the political dimensions of development – including the effects of war – that Giddens points to as relatively neglected and misunderstood by sociologists. For example, it was not the endogenous development of industrialism but war 'that dissolved the power of traditional elites in Germany and Japan, and it was not internal processes of political change that resulted in liberal democracy in these states' (Giddens, 1985a: 243). In addition, Giddens' insistence on a multidimensional account is underlined by his rejection of the idea, much favoured in modern sociology, that western societies must nowadays be seen either as 'capitalist societies' or as 'industrial (or "post-industrial") societies', that these can be characterized by a single determining dialectic or dynamic (Bleicher and Featherstone, 1982).

For all this, one important 'generic' feature of modern western nation-states is stressed by Giddens: power is 'double-edged'. The 'polyarchic character' of modern states derives from 'administrative concentration' ('achieved via the expansion of surveillance') and from the 'altered nature of the dialectic of control that this produces' (Giddens, 1985a: 5). Thus if the routine penetration of political power into the daily lives of citizens is increasingly evident in western societies – a tendency sometimes leading also to 'totalitarianism' – the other side of the coin, according to Giddens, has been a steady expansion of the arena for public discourse and political participation. Commentators such as Hall (1984) or Smith and Turner (1986) who categorize Giddens as only repeating a 'neo-Nietzschean' thesis about modern surveillance are therefore wide of the mark. Instead, seeking strenuously to steer a course between a view of modern societies as involving either a 'primacy of class interests over civil rights' ('the Marxian view'), or a 'primacy of civil rights over class' (cf. Bendix, 1978, or Marshall, 1973) Giddens proposes that the 'generic association' that exists between the modern nation-state and polyarchy – the rule of the many – provides increasing scope for *various* forms of agency, but primacy for none. This discussion of 'rights' and 'social movements' in modern societies can be seen as a particularly crucial part of Giddens' entire argument for it also leads on to the 'critical analysis' of the main dynamics and prospects for change in modern society with which he concludes his analysis.

First, Giddens follows T.H. Marshall (1973) in identifying three distinct categories of citizen rights within modern societies: (1) *civil rights*, including freedom of expression and organization; (2) *political rights*, including the right to vote and to run for office; and (3) *economic rights*, including the right to welfare and social security. But whereas for Marshall the expansion of rights in all three areas greatly reduced the intensity of class conflict, for Giddens class continues to have major significance within contemporary western societies as *one* pervasive basis of conflict as a consequence of the 'asymmetry' of the capitalist labour contract. 'Class conflict' remains a 'threat' to the 'integration' and 'governability' of modern societies, given that 'class compromise', 'based firmly on an "effort bargain" between the labour force and the state', depends upon the continued 'delivery of adequate economic performance' (Giddens, 1985a: 322). For Giddens, however, concentration on class as the only basis of significant social movements, or on 'the transcendence of capitalism by socialism as the sole objective of future social transformations' (ibid: 5), can no more be justified than can Marshall's view. Instead Giddens suggests that each of Marshall's three categories of rights corresponds to a distinct arena of 'surveillance and contestation' in modern societies, as follows: (1) civil rights, corresponding to 'surveillance as policing'; (2) political rights, corresponding to 'surveillance as reflexive monitoring by the state'; and (3) economic rights, corresponding to 'surveillance as "management" of production'. Finally, reformulating these distinctions in terms of his D–D–L–S model, Giddens suggests that in all, four bases of social movements are significant: labour movements; democratic movements; peace movements, and ecological movements (see Figure 8). (As well as these movements, in a more *ad hoc* way, the importance of the women's movement and ethnic movements is also noted by Giddens.) Of these areas, the 'ecological' – although something of a mixed-bag, including debates about industrialism and all aspects of the 'created environment' – would appear crucial, for Giddens here locates the most general discursive and critical social debates about modern society – including sociology itself!

Some striking parallels exist between Giddens' thinking in these terms and the role seen for emancipatory discourse in the critical theory of Jürgen Habermas. But there are also important differences, for, as Giddens expresses it, Habermas's thinking remains bound up with the very evolutionary

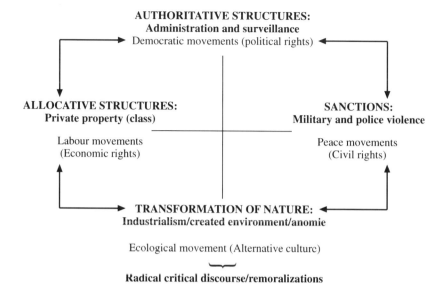

Figure 8 Modern social movements
Source: This combines a number of separate 'maps' provided by Giddens in
Nation-State and Violence (1985a), which he suggests can be superimposed

assumptions that must be avoided. Instead, in Giddens' view, critical theory today, while influenced by Marx, 'must be post-Marxist', recognizing that four main institutional axes of modernity are 'world-historical', and that stripped of 'historical guarantees, critical theory reenters the universe of contingency' (Giddens, 1985a: 335–7).

In summary, then, the world revealed in Giddens' historical sociology is a world of competing social movements and competing nation-states as well as a world of capitalism, with no predictable outcomes. And not the least reason for this uncertainty – although plainly not the only reason – is a nation-state system: 'in which a fragile equality in weaponry of the two major super-powers is the only brake upon the political anarchy of the international order' (Giddens, 1987a: 166). In these circumstances, Giddens restates his case for a structurationist historical sociology thus.

Those who have wanted to model sociology upon natural science, hoping to discover universal laws of social conduct, have tended to sever sociology from history. In breaking with such views, we have to go further than simply asserting that sociology and history – or more accurately the social sciences and history – are indistinguishable, provocative though such a claim may appear to be. We have to grasp how history is made through the active involvements and struggles of human beings, and yet at the same time both forms those human beings and produces outcomes which they neither intend nor foresee. As a theoretical background to the social sciences, nothing is more vital in an era suspending between extraordinary opportunity on the one hand and global catastrophe on the other.

(Giddens, 1982d: 165–6)

But how adequate is Giddens' view, and the scaling up of sociology's focus and the scaling down of sociological aspirations that this involves? More particularly, how far must this be seen as the only possible outcome of the adoption of a structurationist focus on structure and agency?

Commentary and Evaluation

With so much ground covered by Giddens, the task facing any assessment of his work is no less daunting than its summary. Such an assessment is bound to be selective. I want first, therefore, to say something about the general orientation of what follows before passing on to a number of more particular points of criticism and evaluation.

Giddens' 'World-View'

A common criticism of Giddens' work (e.g. Urry, 1982; Gregson, 1986) is that many of his proposed additions to sociological theory, including crucially the concept of 'duality of structure', are conceptual and terminological only, although very interesting and valuable at this level. Other commentators (e.g. McLennan, 1984; Smith and Turner, 1986), while far from entirely hostile to Giddens' work, have suggested that some at least of his more specific conceptual and terminological additions – including many of his time–space concepts such as storage capacity or time–space edges – are merely metaphorical and analogical rather than making a truly original theoretical contribution. Regarding *Central Problems* and *Contemporary Critique*, the observation often voiced was that judgement must be suspended until the ideas therein had been more tried and tested in empirical inquiry (e.g. Gregson, 1986). Moreover, the publication of *Constitution of Society*, with its identification of preferred forms of research, did little to assuage such doubts since most of the examples of research accorded the structurationist seal of approval by Giddens were neither carried out under the auspices of structuration theory nor, equally importantly, did they always conspicuously *combine* accounts of structure and agency. *Nation-State and Violence* with its potentially more empirical focus might have been expected to resolve the issue. But not so. As Skocpol remarks:

Those who might want pointed causal explanations or empirically grounded comparative historical generalizations must look elsewhere. Instead, this book offers a quintessential Giddensian exercise in macro-sociological 'theorizing', spinning a *world-view* about modernization and a menu of concepts to characterize modern national states.

(Skocpol, 1987: 295)

As in *Contemporary Critique* so in *Nation-State and Violence* what Giddens presents is an appraisal of the relevant literature in terms of the general principles of structuration theory, rather than any stricter testing of proposi-tions. Both works, therefore, must be judged in this light. The central question about Giddens' historical theory, then, is how justified is this 'world-view'?

There are questions to raise in five main areas: (1) the value of the concept of time–space distanciation; (2) the interpretation and operational use of the conception of the duality of structure; (3) the distinction drawn between 'allocative' and 'authoritative' resources, and the cogency of Giddens' critique of historical materialism and evolutionary theory; (4) the character of Giddens' 'empirical' accounts; (5) problems associated with his approach to critical theory.

Time–Space Distanciation

Turning first to Giddens' reconceptualization of historical time–space, I do not intend to detract from its many sharp insights and considerable general interest. Undoubtedly, the concept of time–space distanciation illuminates Marx. As Gregson (1986: 91) jokingly says, Marx's famous aphorism must now be rephrased to refer to: 'people making history in temporal and spatial contexts, but not in the conditions or in the time–space zones of their own choosing'.

The concept of time–space distanciation – with its focus on 'regions' in time–space and on 'intersocietal' relations – brings a fresh slant to the analysis of societal development. It is useful in synthesizing and integrating previously diverse accounts of social development and it has stimulated further research – especially perhaps in the new symbiotic relations this has established with geographers, although there are also reservations (see Thrift, 1983; 1985a; Gregory, 1984; Carlstein, 1981; and as well as Urry, this volume). As Thrift puts it, partly but not only as a result of Giddens' work, and 'even if the implications are only now being thought through',

there is little doubt that it is becoming rare to find social action in space and time treated by social theorists as simply an afterthought or as the mere imprint of social structure or as belonging, in some way, to an autonomous realm of existence.[3]

(Thrift, 1983: 49)

The other side of the coin, however, is that many of Giddens' new concepts are metaphorical and analogical (cf. McLennan, 1984), often re-presenting the known facts about social development, even if to some extent in a new light. Thus, for instance, while the historical significance of the rise of cities and states is illuminated by their discussion within Giddens' time–space frame of reference – as specialist locales, and power containers, etc. – equally it is not the case that the significance of these is seen for the first time or in a wholly novel way using this framework. It is not the case therefore that Giddens can be said to have unequivocally established a decisively new theoretical perspective – still less the entirety of his historical theory – simply by his formulation of the concept of time–space distanciation.

Agency and Structure in Giddens' 'World-View'

In order for him to be able to claim a decisive theoretical breakthrough for the entirety of his theoretical package, Giddens would need to establish unequivocally what I take to be the two most crucial aspects of his overall argument:

1. Theoretically, that his particular perspective on time–space distanciation – including its particular emphasis on historicity, 'episodic' transitions and the frequently decisive role of political agency – arises as a necessary outcome of the adoption of the basic tenets of a structurationist perspective with *no* alternative;
2. Empirically, that such an extended interpretation of structure and agency is also confirmed by the historical record.

A schematic reconstruction of what I see as the various elements in Giddens' argument in these terms is given in Figure 9.

Since Giddens, neither in whole or in part, subjects his overall historical theory to systematic comparative testing, and would at times even appear to find such systematic testing inappropriate, this would perhaps suggest that he does regard the justification of his historical sociology as more a matter of his having demonstrated its general theoretical basis in structuration theory and the general fertility of this in historical analysis, e.g. in providing 'sensitizing concepts'.

The first problem I see with Giddens' approach here, however, is that it is hard to escape the conclusion that a number of his decisive interpretative stances regarding historical change would appear to depend upon particular (i.e. contentious) interpretations of the interrelation of structure and agency. This problem we must sum up as a general ontological and epistemological 'bias' towards 'open agency' and against lasting lawlike structuration – an assumption that because agents construct and can and do reconstruct social arrangements, the assumption must also be made that they always will reconstruct these in ways that cannot be captured by lawlike propositions or general mechanisms (cf. Layder, 1981, who suggests that in Giddens' work,

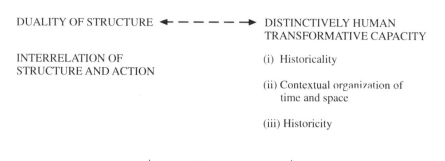

DUALITY OF STRUCTURE ◄ ─ ─ ─ ─ ► DISTINCTIVELY HUMAN
                                  TRANSFORMATIVE CAPACITY

INTERRELATION OF   (i) Historicality
STRUCTURE AND ACTION
                                  (ii) Contextual organization of
                                       time and space

                                  (iii) Historicity

(i)   Time–space distanciation as an outcome

(ii) Information and communication as a major
      factor in time–space distanciation/convergence

(iii) Reflexive monitoring (and storage of
      information) carried out particularly within   CONTINGENT
      states   SOCIAL REALITY
                                                            AND 'EPISODIC'
(iv) 'Episodic' transformations rather than   CHANGE,
      evolutionary pattern, given that individuals   WITH POLITICS
      can always behave differently and act with an   AS A MAIN
      awareness of world-time   ELEMENT

(v)   Potentiality for discursively grounded social
      critique informed by sociology, but a
      'post-modern' world in which there are no
      certainties, and where social actors achieve
      ontological security via 'routine'

Figure 9 Duality of structure in Giddens' 'world-view'

structure 'collapses into agency').[4] Thus, although in many places in his work Giddens shows no reluctance to employ what, on the face of it, are general models – e.g. his reference to 'axes of structuration', 'circuits of capital', 'acceptable' forms of functionalist argument, etc. – in the end an objection to 'vulgar' evolutionary or materialist developmental models often gets transmuted into the assertion of an equally 'vulgar' assumption that sociological generalities and general models *will* always be undermined.

It is difficult to accept, however, that there is no alternative to such a simple dichotomous view as this, that this is not too sweeping and that it fails to do justice to the variety of forms in which general models and lawlike tendencies can be seen as central in both social and physical science (cf. Martins, 1974). Giddens does sometimes qualify his position, stating as the goal of sociology the generation of 'systematically coherent explanatory models' (Cohen, 1986:

127). But in the event, his general concern to preserve agency – and contingency – usually means that he shows relatively little inclination to develop such models very fully or to explore systematically the range and possibilities of the many different kinds of general model, statements of general tendency, etc. that exist in the social sciences (cf. Turner, 1986b; Craib, 1986; Layder, 1981; Thrift, 1983; 1985a; Stinchcome, 1986; and McLennan, 1988 – who from their different perspectives, whether positivist, realist, or Marxist, agree on this and complain of the relatively weak sense of 'determination' in Giddens' work).

At times, Giddens has written perceptively on epistemological issues and is well aware of the highly contested character of discussions of the role and status of scientific laws in modern-day, 'post-empiricist' philosophy (e.g. Giddens, 1977j). At one level, therefore, it is surprising to find him apparently content to operate with so hard-and-fast a distinction between physical science 'laws' and social science 'contingency'. But this would appear to be the ontological and epistemological interpretation of the implications of agency often made by him. In this respect, Giddens declares himself mainly happy to follow Weber's lead on such general issues. Giddens is, of course, right that in key respects the difference between agents and physical objects does represent a distinction of kind. But, with so many controversies in the philosophy of science and social science, and such variety in the forms of lawlike tendencies, general 'mechanisms', etc. actually claimed within the physical as well as the social sciences, I cannot see that he can be regarded as having eliminated alternatives, or even that he could ever hope to do so in this manner. In today's ontological and epistemological climate – and in better keeping, I would argue, with the requirements of a structurationist focus on agency *and* structure more broadly viewed – it would seem to me that the question of what kinds of generalizations are possible is one better left open, to be settled only in particular cases, rather than in a once-and-for-all way.[5]

A further crucial reason for arguing thus is the general 'operational' problems of Giddens' formulation of a 'duality of structure' already alluded to (and well documented by Urry, 1982; Thrift, 1983; Gregson, 1986; Smith and Turner, 1986, among others), which is that this is above all a programmatic statement and *not* automatically an operational model or one from which a single set of answers can ever be expected.

One indication of this, of particular significance in relation to Giddens' emphasis on the state, is that on Giddens' own admission, accounts in terms of structure usually involve different methodological *épochés*. Thus, Friedland (1987: 41–2) is able to complain that in *Nation-State and Violence* (Giddens, 1985a) the 'human subject is barely visible ... the interpretative dimension is largely lost'. If this may seem paradoxical in view of my earlier claim of an 'agency bias', at one level the apparent paradox *can* be resolved by showing this particular structural bias arises from the combination of two sources. The first is the ontological assumption made by Giddens that 'individuals could always have acted differently'. The second is the difficulty of operationally accomplishing analysis in terms of both agency and structure, when these involve different *épochés*. Thus, the outcome of the combination of Giddens' ontological assumption with the inevitability at some point of providing a structural account would seem to be the assertion that it is state elites with their peculiar capacity for reflexive monitoring who must often possess the decisive historical role. It is significant in this respect that some commentators (e.g. Hall, 1984) have even suggested that Giddens' work, like that of Raymond Aron and others, can be viewed as part of a movement to *entirely* reverse the replacement of the political by the 'social' (and economic) that occurred in social theory with the rise of sociology. This allows, Hall suggests, in certain circumstances, even for an 'absolute autonomy of politics'. To a lesser degree, both Skocpol (1987) and Friedland (1987) reach a similar conclusion about the near primacy of the political within Giddens' historical sociology. Obviously, this is at odds with the more balanced approach that Giddens states as his goal. However, it is a reading of Giddens' work that at some points has some substance. And if we look for further explanations of the high profile of, and possible 'bias' towards, the political in his work, it is not hard to find these. The most prominent is the greater scope this leaves for human agency, but with paradoxical and questionable conclusions such as those indicated, which reference merely to the duality of structure cannot resolve.[6]

It is in such circumstances as these that alternative interpretations of the duality of structure seem bound to arise. Thus, Callinicos (1987) (cf. also Bhaskar, 1979; 1986) though attracted by Giddens' definition of 'structure': (1) as unanticipated conditions and unintended outcomes; and (2) as enabling and constraining, nevertheless wants to see this as leaving scope for analysis in terms of structural conditions and 'structural capacities' – including class locations – in excess of those seen by Giddens. None of this prevents Callinicos (or Bhaskar) from agreeing – in fact, an almost universal verdict among sociologists – that Giddens' discussion of structure and agency is of very great value. But this only underlines that valid alternative interpretations are bound to arise, and that Giddens goes too far in implying that any one set of implications necessarily follow from his structurationist view. Thus in terms of Figure 9 what can be suggested is that room exists for other world-views (cf. Kilminster, in this volume).[7]

'Allocative' and 'Authoritative Power' and the 'Evolutionary' and the 'Episodic'

More specific, but still significant, general questions concerning Giddens' overall historical world-view involve the cogency of his distinction between 'allocative' power and the role of this in establishing his 'non-evolutionary view' – a topic taken up with some élan especially by Wright (1983) and also by Thrift (1983) and Craib (1986). In this respect, Wright's position is of particular interest because, although a Marxist, he is fulsome in his praise of many aspects of Giddens' thinking – including the critique of historical materialism in its 'vulgar' forms – while dissenting from any acceptance that either historical materialism or evolutionary thinking are eliminated by Giddens' argument. In this context, at least two strong objections to Giddens' view arise:

1. that Giddens' use of his concepts of allocative and authoritative power leads to an unduly restrictive conception of the 'economic' (and of class), which would be simply unacceptable to many Marxists, and must therefore be seen as suspect in any claims to have eliminated historical materialism;

2. that whereas for most Marxists, class is defined – and 'economic primacy' claimed – in terms of the *overall* mechanism by which surplus products or surplus labour is appropriated, for Giddens, class is defined, and questions of economic primacy appraised in terms only of 'private property in the means of production'.

Thus, for example, when Giddens represents traditional agrarian empires as domination of authorative power over allocative power, and as therefore inconsistent with historical materialism, such a conclusion is unacceptable to Marxists since, as Wright puts it, the 'appropriation of surplus value *always* involves specific combinations of economic and *political* mechanisms (i.e. relations to allocative and authoritative resources)' (Wright, 1983: 21, emphasis added). And so, claims about the importance of class structures and class struggle – its presence or absence – which Marxists make central to social analysis are not seen as overturned by Giddens' attempt at 'elimination'.

In general, Giddens' category of allocative power is so narrowly drawn compared with authoritative power that finding a more decisive role for the latter would sometimes appear almost an inevitable outcome of the use of his terminology. I am not suggesting that this utterly overturns all of Giddens' claims about the relative importance of political power, merely that it raises questions about his claim to have eliminated historical materialism, and once again he is far from establishing the overall superiority of his own view. As Wright stresses: 'When Giddens tries to explain 'the differences in the relationship between allocative and authoritative resources in capitalist and noncapitalist societies he relies heavily on differences in the system of property relations' (ibid: 20). Thus at one level there exists 'no *intrinsic* incompatibility between the substantive claims Marxists make about the importance of class structures and class struggle, and about the role of the state and ideology' (ibid: 34). Nor in a wider way does any overall incompatibility exist with 'Giddens' methodological stress on the knowledge-ability of actors, the "duality of structure", the analysis of social processes in terms of the unacknowledged conditions of action, and so on' (ibid: 34).[8] In general, therefore, what Wright suggests, correctly in my view, is that:

> While Giddens' general theory of action may run counter to the mechanistic and functionalist reasoning in the Marxist tradition, it is largely compatible with most of the *substantive* claims of both classical and contemporary Marxism. Many of the criticisms of functionalism and class reductionism which Giddens makes from his methodological standpoint are also accepted by many, if by no means all, contemporary Marxist theorists.
>
> (ibid: 34)

The decisive difference, however, is that Wright along with many theorists like him (including other theorists generally quite sympathetic to Giddens, e.g. Thrift, 1983, 1984, 1985a, as well as leading Marxist historical sociologists such as Anderson): (1) retain a wider view of the 'economic' than Giddens' model of historical materialism, and (2) see no reason to give up an evolutionary or an historical materialist approach.

For a theory of society to be evolutionary, according to Wright (1983: 26), three conditions must hold:

1. a typology of social forms 'which *potentially* has some kind of directionality';
2. 'the probability of staying at the same level' in terms of this typology is 'greater than the probability of regressing';
3. 'there is a positive probability of moving to the next higher level', although such a probability need 'not be greater than the probability of regressing'. However, once such a movement has occurred, 'the probability of staying there must be greater than the probability of moving back'; thus, 'however weak the tendency towards development', the typology is 'sticky downward'.

In terms of such a model, in Wright's view, not only has Giddens not succeeded in eliminating the possibility of an evolutionary theory, but his own framework with its 'clear quantitative ordering along the dimension of time–space distanciation' (ibid: 29) must also be seen as such a model. Thus, the situation we face, according to Wright, is one in which there must be seen to exist two 'contending' evolutionary theories! In Wright's estimation, historical materialism must still be seen as the stronger theory, in that: (1) 'the dynamics centred in *property relations* impose *fundamental limits* on the overall process of social change'; (2) 'capacity for control' *depends upon* 'control over material resources'; (3) the 'motivational' basis for such development of the forces of production is plausible, and more plausible than in connection with 'authoritative resources' (ibid: 32–3, emphasis added). Against such suggestions, Giddens' point remains well made that societal development is less easily captured by simple evolutionary principles and far more open-ended than often previously suggested, but this is altogether a different matter from unequivocally establishing his own view of the merely 'contingent' relation between political and economic factors or his overall 'episodic' view.

Thus none of Giddens' arguments would seem decisive in seeing-off the *real* alternatives to his own view. Certainly his point is well taken that political as well as economic factors play an important role, but this is not effective in eliminating Marxist – or broader – notions of primacy of material factors or the tendency of these to develop, as suggested by Wright, Thrift or Anderson.

Empirical Historical Issues

If the arguments by which Giddens claims to have eliminated methodological alternatives to his own view remain contentious, many of the more straightforwardly theoretical and empirical arguments within his historical account can also be challenged. Obviously, it is beyond the scope of this chapter to confront such detailed points of criticism very fully. However a number of specific empirical and theoretical points do merit consideration for the general light they throw on Giddens' overall historical project.

Critics – including historians, but not only these – have remarked about the *ex cathedra* character of many of Giddens' historical assertions (e.g. Hechter, 1987), his lack of respect for (ordinary) chronology (Friedland, 1987), his lumping together in his societal typologies of very different kinds of societies and states, and different eras (Hirst, 1982; Smith, 1982a) and so on. If any historical macro-sociology on Giddens' scale and generality is to be possible, a certain amount of criticism of this kind is, of course, only to be expected. In Giddens' case, however, rather more than the 'usual' level of concern has been registered about the corners that have been cut. Compared with Michael Mann or Perry Anderson, who cover broadly similar ground to Giddens, and often impress historians and other specialists by their generalists' grasp of the historical sources, Giddens can be said to skate over the surface.

A general indication of the problem here are the numerous 'caveats' of the following kind that punctuate Giddens' account:

> Nor is it my purpose (at any point in this book) to enter into endless debates about the weightings of contributory factors to the rise of capitalism.
>
> (Giddens, 1981a: 134)

> I have already commented briefly about absolutism, I do not wish to enter more than marginally upon such a contested terrain.
>
> (Giddens, 1981a: 184)

As well as omissions highlighted in this way, there is also surprisingly little reference to feudalism, or to ancient society and slavery, both areas where a fuller consideration might have been expected in any historical account, especially one so much couched in terms of a debate with historical materialism. Such purely empirical omissions in Giddens' work obviously raise with redoubled force the question of his entitlement to decide on such issues as the various forms of the primacy thesis or his 'episodic character-ization' of change. Thus, this lends weight to the earlier suggestion that he does regard such questions as decidable on methodological grounds, and that his accounts are often 'illustrative' rather than involving decisive 'testing'.

Undoubtedly, Giddens' response would be that his assessment is based, not only on methodological argument, but also on a general examination of the historical record and the conspicuous lack of clear-cut laws. But we have already seen that what counts as 'primacy' or 'lawlike' regularity in such interpretations is also a contested matter. Thus the absence of detailed examination of key historical transitions can be taken to considerably weaken Giddens' case – particularly so given that his emphasis is so much on the relative uniqueness of historical episodes. Whatever the view ultimately taken on such general methodological issues, because of such empirical omissions in Giddens' account, ambiguities undoubtedly remain as to what Giddens is or is not claiming about crucial periods of transition between societal types. Thus, it is the overall symbiotic relationship between capitalism and the nation-state that has pride of place rather than any detailed unravelling of the complex causalities involved in the *rise* of capitalism. Concerning the transition from traditional empires to modern European society, for instance, Giddens would appear to follow something like Anderson's (or for that matter Weber's or Collins') account that a 'concatenation of antiquity and feudalism' was decisive. Likewise, on the social basis of 'absolutism' Giddens again follows Anderson. Yet in neither of these cases does he make any sustained attempt to enter the complex debates that surround such highly controversial accounts (cf. Fulbrook and Skocpol, 1984; Hindess and Hirst, 1975) or to explore the implications of Anderson's own continued attachment to histor-ical materialism (cf. also Runciman, 1980).

In these matters the contrast between Mann and Giddens is instructive. Mann's broadest rhetorical questions are substantially the same as Giddens'.

Of all the issues raised by sociological theory over the last two centuries, the most basic yet elusive is that of ultimate primacy or determinacy. Are there one or more core, decisive, ultimately determining elements, or keystones, of society? Or are human societies seamless webs spun of endless multicausal interactions in which there are no overall patterns? What are the major dimensions of social stratification? What are the most important determinants of social change?

(Mann, 1986: 3)

His general answers to these questions also echo Giddens:

> Economic power relations do not assert themselves as 'finally necessary in the last instance' (to quote Engels); history is not 'a discontinuous succession of modes of production' (to quote Balibar); class struggle is not 'the motor of history' (to quote Marx and Engels). Economic power relations, modes of production and social classes come and go in the historical record. In occasional world historical moments they decisively reorganize social life; usually they are important in conjunction with other power sources; occasionally they are decisively reorganized by them. The same can be said of all power sources, coming and going, weaving in and out of the historical record.
>
> (ibid: 523)

Mann's overall model of social change in terms of four main sources of social power (his IEMP model, Figure 10), though not identical with Giddens' own fourfold model, overlaps significantly with this. My own view for what it's worth, however, is that Mann's categories are framed in an empirically more straightforward manner than Giddens' equivalents. (Is this perhaps because they are unencumbered by the need to carry the more diffuse links with a general theory of structuration theory that are involved in Giddens' approach?) For whatever reasons, Mann's general categories are perhaps rather more unambiguously applied in historical analysis. But far more important – and in this he is perhaps more true to his episodic view than Giddens – Mann gives far more attention to detailed testing of his historical accounts (albeit usually *not* comparative testing, since he is wary of the implications of intersocietal connections, and claims that there are simply too few genuinely autonomous cases). It should also be noted in this respect that Anderson (1986: 1405) has much praise for Mann's 'comprehensive concern' with what he calls the 'exact infrastructures' of each kind of power. And there is little doubt but that Mann's general framework is one that is proving highly productive.

At best also, Giddens' kind of framework promises the same kind of results. However, the same can also be said of Anderson's own approach, which in developing more systematic comparisons between multiple European routes also goes further than either Giddens or Mann with their concentration mainly on a single Western European route. Furthermore, even if heterodox in the eyes of many Marxists, Anderson's approach remains materialistic, and he also wants to insist that Mann's study can be seen above all as amounting to an 'organizational materialism', in which possibilities of developmental models – substantially of Wright's kind – cannot be ruled out. Indeed, despite Mann's fondness, like Giddens', for portraying his own sociology – 'episodically' – as involving a 'radical break' with most previous approaches,[9] continuities, if some differences of emphasis, are also in

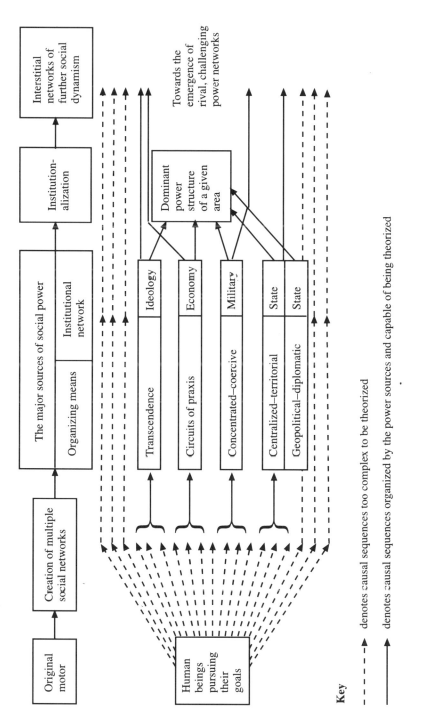

Figure 10 Causal IEMP model of organized power
Source: Mann, 1986: 29.

evidence. Both Mann and Giddens offer more scope for rejection of a dichotomy between lawlike and non-lawlike accounts in sociology than they are prepared to admit. Thus, even if change occurs as the result of 'accidental conjectures', 'unevenly', or in a 'geographically shifty way', we find Mann asserting that:

1. Stratification is the overall creation and distribution of power in society (Mann, 1986: 10).
2. Human capacities for collective and distributive power have increased quantitatively throughout the historical period (ibid: 524).
3. Once invented, the major infrastructural techniques seem almost never to have disappeared from human practice, [resulting] in a broadly one-directional, one-dimensional development of power (ibid: 524).

Giddens as 'Critical Theory'

Where does all this leave Giddens' claim to have provided, as well as a new historical account, a new basis for 'critical theory'? Despite his different interpretation, Giddens' conception of 'historicity' draws on Marx. There are also obvious similarities between what Giddens refers to as his 'dialogical' model of critical theory and Habermas's more overtly neo-Marxian and evolutionary view of the implications of the inconstrained application of discursive will-formation in judgements of the effectiveness and legitimacy of economic and political institutions. For Habermas and Giddens alike a dialogical interaction between social science and lay actors in reaching such judgements is regarded as essential.[10] What Smith and Turner (1986) refer to as the 'moral seriousness' of Giddens' sociology is in no doubt. The difference is that for Giddens, there are no guarantees, only contingencies.

There is some truth in the comment that Giddens' overall account of the 'discursive constitution of territorial sovereignty and national historicity' (Friedland, 1987: 41–2) provides no more than scant basis for any expectation that such a dialogic relation between social science and social movements might succeed when so much of that historical account suggests only a codified, malleable population. Thus, as Giddens puts it, 'the conditions of governability' may depend less on 'legitimacy', on the 'justifiability' of policies, than on mass acceptance of the daily routines shaped by administrative power, which he sees as replacing tradition within modern society (Giddens, 1985a: 322–3). For example, in this context 'anomie' (arising from widespread 'ontological insecurity' in modern societies) may be far more potent than class conflict in opening up the masses to social movements (e.g. nationalism or totalitarianism). However, this is not to my mind the main problem since Giddens does not forget agency; on the contrary his model always retains the possibility of a two-way relation between dominators and those dominated, and in *Nation-State and Violence* and elsewhere he clearly wishes to be numbered among those who see very real gains from the existence of the 'new publics', that are one outcome of the spread of literacy and new forms of mass communications.

The more serious problem in my view arises from his reluctance to think through his 'developmental' models more systematically. Giddens suggests at one point that in many respects he is happy to be called a Weberian but states clearly that he wants to avoid Weber's relativism. Yet for all this, his restrictive view of a macro-sociology, confined to analysis of episodes, would seem to leave his sociology in much the same boat as Weber's. As McLennan pointedly remarks:

> Giddens' wholesale dismissal of any version of social evolution and functional explanation thus chimes in well with post-modernist currents. Yet the very aspiration to provide a 'social theory' of any kind, especially one admitting of 'progressive' political implications, runs hard against deconstructionist logic.
>
> (McLennan, 1988: 117)

A related final point is that, although Giddens makes plain that a theory of 'the good life' ought to be a primary part of social theory (Giddens, 1981a: 248), and he is clearly prepared to use terms such as 'exploitation' and 'oppression', all this is undermined since he provides no normative theory 'capable of ordering the various goodness claims' that arise (Bertilsson, 1984: 352).

Conclusion

Notwithstanding the very great praise it has deservedly received, a central ambivalence exists in the reception of Giddens' work. A central ambivalence has also run through this commentary. On the one hand one might accept that in some respects approaches such as his point the way forward for historical sociology. This would be to recognize the undoubted value of:

- a focus on structure and agency;
- a multidimensional rather than a reductionist approach;
- an intersocietal and time–space perspective;
- aspects of his insistence on an 'episodic' characterization of historical change.

On the other hand, acceptance of the importance of accounts in terms of agency and structure, and characterization of historical change as 'multi-factoral', requiring a time–space perspective for its analysis, and as, in part, 'episodic', 'uneven', etc. is far more widespread in sociology than Giddens suggests – including today many versions of Marxist and evolutionary theory. This is so, moreover, without such viewpoints leading to either the acceptance of a purely 'episodic' view of historical change or to an assumption that multifactoral causation must imply the rejection of all forms of theory that in any way continue to grant general primacy to one or more factors. Thus, Giddens can sometimes be accused of dealing in 'strawmen', of exaggerating the weaknesses of the approaches that he rejects while also hiding some of their potential strengths compared with his own. Nothing in my commentary has been intended as simply overturning Giddens' view, but rather as indicating that this is perhaps best regarded as representing only one significant view of historical change in structurationist terms. As suggested at the outset, I would see my critique as operating within the spirit of Giddens' work, but at the same time, as seeking to avoid a premature foreclosure on key issues. At a time when structuralism on the one hand and ethnomethodology and social phenomenology on the other threatened to lead to the fragmentation of sociology on a wholly new scale, Giddens' discussion of agency and structure was widely welcomed as a way of avoiding extremes. However, that it was received thus was more an indication of a prior acceptance within sociology of the general desirability of an explanatory mix of agency and structure than of any necessary acceptance of the entirety of Giddens' particular interpretation. Giddens' discussion of these issues must be seen as instructive rather than definitive. My suggestion has been that in his historical sociology, as elsewhere, Giddens has been perhaps overzealous in proposing the elimination of alternatives to his own approach. Much of his account of the method and empirical substance of structuration theory arises from 'debate' with the work of others and usually results in a fairly sharp distinction between this work and what can be incorporated within structuration theory. There is a widespread recognition that Giddens – a master in the distanciation of his work from the work of others in this respect – often proceeds by the construction of strawman of rival approaches to his own, employing in these matters, as Smith, 1982a, has put it, a 'ruthless dichotomous logic'. To have one's work singled out by Giddens has therefore often been something of a 'mixed blessing'. My critical comments have involved asking the question: Cannot a good deal of historical sociology, while operating in a broadly 'structurationist' way, be seen as justifiably reaching conclusions that are less restrictive than his? Whatever the verdict may be in this respect, however, the fact remains that the width of interpenetration of sociological theory and historical analysis achieved by Giddens is remarkable, and will continue to stimulate other sociologists, whether this be to develop his analysis or to take issue with him.

Notes

1. In Chapter Eight of the present volume Giddens indicates that he now also plans a fourth volume in his *Critique of Historical Materialism* (1981a), dealing with critical theory. Other relevant texts and articles by Giddens are: *Sociology, A Brief*

Critical Introduction (1982d), and his two volumes of collected essays, Giddens, 1982c; 1987a. His new general text *Sociology* (1989) arrived too late for any very full consideration.

2. For a fuller identification of the many works that might be considered part of such a broader 'reform movement' see Abrams, 1982; Skocpol, 1984; Eisenstadt, 1987.

3. A particularly perceptive paper, in many ways anticipating views such as Giddens', is Martins (1974). Apart from a discussion of the neglect of time in sociological theory, this article also stresses the importance of a focus on what Martins terms 'interphenomena', his term for inter-societal systems.

4. Whether, as suggested by Layder (1981), more integral features of Giddens' conception of 'structure' – e.g. its formulation as a 'virtual' order, observable only in its instantiations – are the main problem in Giddens' approach cannot receive any very full treatment in this chapter (see also Chapter One). However, while the features identified by Layder are certainly related to an 'agency bias' in Giddens' work, and also inhibit the construction of more systematic institutional theories, the solution Layder proposes of a return to a 'dualism of structure and interaction' is, to my mind, to throw the baby out with the bathwater.

5. An important reason for suggesting this is that the 'duality of structure' is also a model of science, including both physical and social sciences. Thus, in post-empiricist terms, it can be argued that no ontological or epistemological argument can be decisive in prescribing the form in which accounts and theories may be advanced.

6. There are also complaints that there occurs 'a loss' in the treatment of 'the depth of human action as well' (Craib, 1986: 19; cf. Smith and Turner, 1986), a loss of depth in general in Giddens' work that Craib also sees as inherent in any attempt at synthesis such as Giddens'.

7. The generally restrictive viewpoint represented by Giddens' position can be further indicated by contrasting it with Martins' (1974) much more open-ended overview of the general implications of a new emphasis on 'time', or with the range of approaches that Abrams (1982) identifies as compatible with recognition of 'the mutual dependence of structure and agency'.

8. Bhaskar (1979), for example, regards Marx as quintessentially 'relational' in his treatment of agency and structure.

9. Not surprisingly, the major exception for Mann is Weber, whom he quotes with approval as follows:

Even the assertion that social structures and the economy are 'functionally' related is a biased view, which cannot be justified as an historical generalization, if an unambiguous interdependence is assumed. For the forms of social action follow 'laws of their own' as we shall see time and time again, and even apart from this fact, they may in a given case always be co-determined by other than economic causes. However, at some point economic conditions tend to become causally important, and often decisive, for almost all social groups, and those which have major cultural significance; conversely, the economy is usually also influenced by the autonomous structure of social action within which it exists. *No significant generalization can be made as to when and how this will occur.*
(Weber, 1922: 340, Mann's emphasis)

10. See also Bryant's discussion of Giddens' 'dialogical' model in the present volume, Chapter Seven.

References

Abrams, P. (1982) *Historical Sociology*, London: Open Books.

Anderson, P. (1974a) *Passages from Antiquity to Feudalism*, London: New Left Books.

Anderson, P. (1974b) *Lineages of the Absolutist State*, London: New Left Books:

Anderson, P. (1986) 'Those in authority' – Review of Mann (1986), in *Times Literary Supplement*, 12 December: 1405–6.

Bertilsson, M. (1984) 'The theory of structuration: prospects and problems', *Acta Sociologica* 27: 339–53.

Bendix, R. (1978) *Kings or People*, Berkeley: University of California Press.

Bhaskar, R. (1979) *The Possibility of Naturalism: a Philosophical Critique of Contemporary Human Science*, Brighton: Harvester.

Bhaskar, R. (1986) *Scientific Realism and Human Emancipation*, London: Verso.

Bleicher, J. and Featherstone, M. (1982) 'Historical materialism today: an interview with Anthony Giddens', *Theory, Culture and Society* 1: 63–77.

Braverman, H. (1974) *Labour and Monopoly Capital*, New York: Monthly Review Press.

Callinicos, A. (1987) *Making History: Agency, Structure and Change in Social Theory*, Cambridge: Polity Press.

Carlstein, T. (1981) 'The sociology of structuration in time and space: a time-geographic assessment of Giddens' theory', *Swedish Geographical Yearbook* 41–57.

Cohen, I. (1986) 'The status of structuration theory: a reply to McLennan', *Theory, Culture and Society* 3: 123–33.

Collins, R. (1986) *Weberian Sociological Theory*, Cambridge: Cambridge University Press.

Craib, I. (1986) 'Back to Utopia: Anthony Giddens and modern social theory', *Radical Philosophy*, No. 43: 17–23.

Eberhard, W. (1965) *Conquerors and Rulers*, Leiden: Brill.

Eisenstadt, S. (1987) 'Macrosociology and sociological theory: some new directions', *Contemporary Sociology* 16: 602–9.

Foucault, M. (1975) *Discipline and Punish*, London: Allen Lane Press (1977).

Friedland, R. (1987) 'Giddens' Golden Gloves', *Contemporary Sociology* 16: 40–2.

Fulbrook, M. and Skocpol, T. (1984) 'Destined pathways: the historical sociology of Perry Anderson', in T. Skocpol (ed.) *Vision and Method in Historical Sociology*, Cambridge: Cambridge University Press.

Gellner, E. (1964) *Thought and Change*, London: Weidenfeld & Nicolson.

Giddens, A. (1977j) 'Positivism and its critics', Ch. 2 in Giddens, *Studies in Social and Political Theory*, and in Bottomore, T. and Nesbit, R. (eds) *A History of Sociological Analysis*, London: Heinemann, Ch. 7.

Giddens, A. (1979a) *Central Problems in Social Theory*, London: Macmillan.

Giddens, A. (1981a) *A Contemporary Critique of Historical Materialism, Vol. 1: Power, Property and the State*, London: Macmillan.

Giddens, A. (1982c) *Profiles and Critiques in Social Theory*, London: Macmillan.

Giddens, A. (1982d) *Sociology – a Brief but Critical Introduction*, London: Macmillan.

Giddens, A. (1984a) *The Constitution of Society*, Cambridge: Polity Press.

Giddens, A. (1985a) *The Nation-State and Violence – Vol. 2* of *A Contemporary Critique of Historical Materialism*, Cambridge: Polity Press.

Giddens, A. (1987a) *Social Theory and Modern Sociology*, Cambridge: Polity Press.

Gregory, D. (1984) 'Space, time and politics in social theory: an interview with

Anthony Giddens', *Society and Space* 2: 123–32.

Gregson, N. (1986) 'On duality and dualism: the case of structuration and time-geography', *Progress in Human Geography* 10: 184–205.

Hall, J. (1984) Review of *Nation-State and Violence*, in *Sociological Review* 35: 430–4.

Hechter, M. (1987) Review of *Nation-State and Violence*, in *American Journal of Sociology* 93: 516–18.

Hindess, B. and Hirst, P. (1975) *Pre-Capitalist Modes of Production*, London: Routledge & Kegan Paul.

Hirst, P. (1982) 'The social theory of Anthony Giddens: a new syncretism', *Theory, Culture and Society* 1: 78–82.

Jacobs, J. (1970) *The Economy of Cities*, London: Cape.

Layder, D. (1981) *Structure, Interaction and Social Theory*, London: Routledge & Kegan Paul, pp. 62–70.

McLennan, G. (1984) 'Critical or positive theory? A comment on the status of Anthony Giddens' social theory', *Theory, Culture and Society* 2: 123–9.

McLennan, G. (1988) 'Structuration theory and post-empiricist philosophy; a rejoinder', *Theory, Culture and Society* 5: 101–9.

Mann, M. (1986) *The Sources of Social Power (Vol. 1) – A History of Power from the Beginning to A.D. 1760*, Cambridge: Cambridge University Press.

Marshall, T.H. (1973) *Class, Citizenship and Social Development*, Westport: Greenwood Press.

Martins, H. (1974) 'Time and theory in sociology', in J. Rex (ed.) *Approaches to Sociology: An Introduction to Major Trends in British Sociology*, London: Routledge & Kegan Paul.

Mumford, E. (1960) 'Universal city', in C. Kraeling and R. Adams (eds) *City Invisible*, Chicago: University of Chicago Press.

Runciman, W. (1980) 'Comparative sociology or narrative history? A note on the methodology of Perry Anderson', *Archives européenes de Sociologie* 22: 162–80.

Skocpol, T. (1987) Review of *Nation-State and Violence*, in *Social Forces* 66: 294–6.

Smith, D. (1982a) 'Put not your trust in princes: a commentary on Anthony Giddens and the absolutist state', *Theory, Culture and Society* 1: 93–9.

Smith, J. and Turner, B. (1986) 'Constructing social theory and constituting society', *Theory, Culture and Society* 3: 125–33.

Spybey, T. (1987) 'Some problems of Giddens' structuration theory', paper presented to the University of Uppsala, mimeo.

Stinchcombe, A. (1986) 'Milieu and structure updated: a critique of the theory of structuration', *Theory and Society* 15: 901–14. Reprinted in Clark *et al.* (1990), Ch. 5.

Thompson, E.P. (1967) 'Time, work-discipline and industrial capitalism', *Past and Present* 38: 56–97.

Thrift, N. (1983) 'On the determination of action in space and time', *Society and Space* 1: 23–57.

Thrift, N. (1984) Review of *Contemporary Critique, Vol. 1* in *Progress in Human Geography* 8: 131–42.

Thrift, N. (1985a) 'Bear and mouse or bear and tree? Anthony Giddens' reconstruction of social theory', *Sociology* 19: 609–23.

Tilly, C. (1981) *As Sociology Meets History*, New York: Academic Press.

Tilly, C. (ed.) (1975) *The Formation of Nation-States in Western Europe*, Princeton: Princeton University Press.

Turner, J. (1986b) 'The theory of structuration' – review essay – Review of *Constitution of Society*, in *American Journal of Sociology* 91: 969–77.

Urry, J. (1982) 'Duality of structure; some critical issues', *Theory, Culture and Society* 1: 100–6.

Wright, E. Olin (1983) 'Giddens' critique of Marxism', *New Left Review* 138: 11–33.

67

Nationalstaat und Gesellschaftstheorie: Anthony Giddens', John A. Halls und Michael Manns Beiträge zu einer notwendigen Diskussion[*]

W. Knöbl

[*]Source: *Zeitschrift für Soziologie*, vol. 22 (3), 1993, pp. 221–35.

Zusammenfassung

Nationalstaat und Krieg sind Themen, die die Soziologie über lange Zeit hinweg vernachlässigt hatte. Eine Einbeziehung dieser Phänomene in soziologische Zeitdiagnosen wäre zwar möglich und wünschenswert, doch wurde dieses Feld in letzter Zeit weitgehend nur von Politikwissenschaftlern oder Historikern bearbeitet. Mit den Werken von Michael Mann, John A. Hall und A. Giddens hat sich seit Mitte der achtziger Jahre nun auch wieder die Soziologie in dieser Debatte um Staat und Krieg in einer beeindruckenden Art und Weise zu Wort gemeldet. Unter Verwendung eines machttheoretischen Ansatzes betonen die genannten Autoren vor allem die Bedeutung militärisch-politischer Konstellationen für die Genese der europäischen Moderne. Dabei können sie deutlich machen, daß sich die Soziologie solchen Themen stellen muß, wenn sie zu einem angemessenen Verständnis dieser Moderne kommen will.

„Bringing the State Back In" – so lautete Anfang der achziger Jahre die kämpferische Parole einiger amerikanischer Sozialwissenschaftler angesichts der unverständlichen Vernachlässigung des Nationalstaates vor allem in der soziologischen Theoriebildung. Dieser mit viel Schwung und Selbstbewußtsein vorgetragene Angriff auf eine mit dem Etikett „gesellschaftszentriert" kritisierte 'herkömmliche' Sozialwissenschaft blieb nicht ohne Resonanz. Der „Staat" wurde vor allem im anglo-amerikanischen Sprachraum wieder zu einem Brennpunkt der soziologischen Diskussion.[1]

So kontrovers die *theoretische* Diskussion um den Staatsbegriff und den Stellenwert eines „neuen staatszentrierten Paradigmas" in den Sozialwissenschaften blieb (vgl. etwa Almond 1988), sie machte sicherlich eines deutlich: Die Soziologie weist klare Defizite hinsichtlich der Thematisierung der Genese des Nationalstaates und der mit dem Staat verbundenen Phänomene wie Krieg und Gewalt auf.[2]

Für eine solche Vernachlässigung in der Vergangenheit lassen sich mehrere Gründe anführen. Sie reichen von einem die Sozialwissenschaften durchziehenden aufklärerischen Fortschrittsoptimismus, der mit der Hypothese der Sinnhaftigkeit des Geschichtsprozesses schon immer auf die „Kontingenz" von Krieg und Gewalt hinweisen mußte, bis hin zu theoretischen Annahmen in vielen Spielarten des Marxismus, die etwa ein autonomes Staatshandeln prinzipiell für unmöglich oder unwahrscheinlich hielten (Skocpol 1979: Kap. 1).

Solche Annahmen und Hypothesen können heute gerade auch angesichts der aktuellen Entwicklungen in Ost- und Südosteuropa nicht mehr überzeugen, so daß es für die Soziologie eigentlich nur ein folgerichtiger Schritt wäre, sich intensiver mit Themen wie Nationalstaat, Nationalismus und Krieg auseinanderzusetzen. Damit ließen sich nämlich nicht nur innerfachliche Defizite beheben. Gleich zeitig würde die Soziologie auch thematisch Anschluß finden an Debatten, die das Interesse einer breiten Öffentlichkeit auf sich zogen, bei denen die Soziologie aber bisher ziemlich abseits stand.[3] Als etwa 1988 Paul Kennedy mit seinem „The Rise and Fall of the Great Powers" eine breite Diskussion um den „American Decline" entfachte und dabei auch jene schon genannten Themenkomplexe wie Krieg und Nationalstaat angeschnitten wurden, blieb der Beitrag der Soziologie zu dieser hauptsächlich von Politikwissenschaftlern und Historikern geführten Auseinandersetzung vergleichsweise gering. Es schien, als ob die gegenwärtige Soziologie zu solchen Themen kaum mehr etwas Substantielles beizutragen, als ob sie in diesem Bereich die noch von Klassikern wie etwa Max Weber beanspruchte Sachkompetenz inzwischen abgegeben hätte.

Doch zu einem Rückzug der Soziologie aus den eben angesprochenen Themengebieten besteht kein Anlaß. Vielmehr könnte sie hier durchaus Selbstbewußtsein demonstrieren, waren doch schon einige Jahre vor dem spektakulären Erfolg von „The Rise and Fall of the Great Powers" mit Arbeiten dreier britischer Soziologen wichtige Werke erschienen, die zentrale makrosoziologische und historische Fragestellungen behandeln und sich aufgrund ihrer theoretischen Brillanz mit Kennedys Werk durchaus messen können. Gemeint sind die Arbeiten von Anthony Giddens, Michael Mann und John A. Hall.

Zwar ist Giddens sicherlich in Deutschland kein Unbekannter mehr, zumal einige seiner Bücher etwa zur Handlungstheorie in deutscher Übersetzung vorliegen („Interpretative Soziologie", 1984; „Die Konstitution der Gesellschaft", 1988). Das noch unübersetzte „The Nation-State and Violence" aus dem Jahre 1985 hingegen ist in Deutschland wenig diskutiert, die „historisch-makrosoziologische Facette" des Theoretikers Anthony Giddens noch kaum zur Kenntnis genommen worden. Auch Michael Manns „The Sources of Social Power. Vol. 1" aus dem Jahre 1986 (dieser bisher vorliegende erste

Band eines auf insgesamt vier Bände angelegten Werkes erschien 1990 und 1991 in einer zweibändigen deutschen Übersetzung mit dem Titel „Geschichte der Macht") und John A. Halls „Powers and Liberties" (1985) haben mit ähnlichen Themen hierzulande nur sehr wenig Aufmerksamkeit erfahren.

Die eben genannten Arbeiten teilen nicht nur thematische Schwerpunkte. Ihnen ist auch die Herkunft aus einem gemeinsamen Diskussionszusammenhang anzumerken. Ausgangspunkt der Bücher von Hall und Mann war ein von ihnen selbst und Ernest Gellner 1980 an der London School of Economics veranstaltetes Seminar mit dem Titel „Patterns of History". Da auch Anthony Giddens zu diesem sich schließlich über einige Jahre erstreckenden Seminar engen Kontakt hatte, erklärt sich so die Tatsache einer zum Teil sehr ähnlichen, nämlich machttheoretischen Ausrichtung aller drei Autoren.

Diese also in enger Kooperation entstandenen Arbeiten stellen insgesamt einen beeindruckenden Beitrag zur international dringend notwendig gewordenen Debatte um Staat und Krieg dar und verdeutlichen, daß sich die Soziologie diesen Themen durchaus selbstbewußt stellen kann und sie nicht den Nachbardisziplinen allein überlassen muß.

1. Handeln und Macht

Kritik am üblicherweise von der Soziologie verwendeten Gesellschaftsbegriff ist mittlerweile nicht mehr neu (vlg. etwa Touraine 1981, Wallerstein 1985 oder Tenbruck 1989). Zum einen verstellt man sich mit der Fixierung auf den Begriff der Gesellschaft die Einsicht in die Notwendigkeit einer ausreichenden Thematisierung trans- oder internationaler Phänomene. Zum anderen wird durch das Festhalten an einer am modernen Nationalstaat orientierten *allgemeinen* Gesellschaftsvorstellung die historische Einzigartigkeit und Homogenität moderner westlicher Nationalgesellschaften unterschwellig in den Rang einer raum-zeitlichen Konstante erhoben. Wodurch und wie stark überhaupt 'Gesellschaften' integriert sind, welche historischen Entwicklungen etwa erst zum homogenen westlichen Nationalstaat geführt haben, erscheint vor allem dann nicht weiter hinterfragenswert, wenn z. B. die Rede von Funktionen und Systemen schon immer an hochintegrierte Gebilde denken läßt.

Giddens, Mann und Hall sind nun historisch und durch die Kritik am Funktionalismus auch theoretisch genügend belehrt, um weder die Bedeutung trans-gesellschaftlicher Phänomene zu verkennen, noch die Systemhaftigkeit von „Gesellschaften" einfach zu unterstellen. Handlungs- und macht theoretisch ansetzend, versuchen sie ein begriffliches Instrumentarium zu entwickeln, das der eben angeschnittenen Problematik bei der Analyse „gesellschaftlicher" Prozesse tatsächlich angemessen ist.

Giddens ist hierbei mit seinen theoretischen Anstrengungen am weitesten vorgedrungen. Seit den siebziger Jahren hat er seinen handlungstheoretischen Ansatz beständig verfeinert und schließlich in „Die Konstitution der Gesellschaft" (1988) eine vorläufige Quintessenz seiner Bemühungen vorgelegt.

In Anbetracht der Tatsache, daß das Alltagshandeln zu einem nicht unerheblichen Ausmaß in routinisierten Bahnen verläuft, dementsprechend ein starker Begriff der Intention für dieses nicht anwendbar ist, suchte Giddens nach einem allgemeinen Handlungsbegriff, der dem der Intention vorgängig ist. Der Begriff der Macht sollte diese 'tiefere' Fundierung des Handlungsbegriffes leisten, und zwar Macht im allgemeinsten Sinne eines „umgestaltenden Vermögens" (transformative capacity), der Fähigkeit, „'einen Unterschied herzustellen' zu einem vorher existierenden Zustand" (Giddens 1988: 66). Giddens – und dem schließen sich explizit dann auch Hall und Mann an – kann also behaupten, „daß Handeln Macht im Sinne eines umgestaltenden Vermögens logisch einschließt" (Giddens 1988: 66).

Dabei ist es für den Giddensschen Ansatz charakteristisch, daß er nicht nur die zeitliche, sondern auch die räumliche Dimension des Handelns (der Machtausübung) thematisiert. Der Raum wird als integraler Bestandteil des Handelns begriffen: „Der Raum ist keine leere Dimension, entlang der soziale Gruppierungen strukturiert werden, sondern man muß ihn mit Bezug auf seine Rolle für die Konstitution von Interaktionssystemen betrachten." (Giddens 1988: 427)

Der Raum ist in der Giddensschen Theorie vor allem auch deshalb für jede Interaktion konstitutiv, weil Giddens ganz stark die Leibgebundenheit des menschlichen Handelns betont. Während etwa Habermas fast ausschließlich den explizit diskursiven Charakter des Handelns thematisiert, wird von Giddens als Kontrapunkt dazu auch die eminente Bedeutung von Gestik und Ausdrucksverhalten hervorgehoben. Zugespitzt formuliert ist für Giddens Interaktion nicht nur ein Austausch von Geltungsansprüchen. Damit rückt der Raum, in und „mit" dem Handeln stattfindet, ins Zentrum der soziologischen Reflexion, denn die wechselseitige Wahrnehmung des Ausdrucksgeschehens ist elementarer Bestandteil jeder Interaktionssituation. Der konkrete Raum, in dem die Interaktionsteilnehmer zueinander „positioniert" sind und durch den die wechselseitige Wahrnehmung der Handelnden erschwert, begünstigt oder eingeschränkt wird, ist damit mehr als nur akzidentieller Bestandteil jeder Interaktion.

Damit ist aber schon eine Möglichkeit angedeutet, Interaktionsmuster danach zu unterscheiden, ob die Handelnden „*kopräsent*" sind und ihr Handeln durch die Anwesenheit anderer Personen mitbestimmt ist, oder ob Handlungsverflechtungen über das unmittelbare Umfeld der Beteiligten zeitlich und räumlich hinausreichen, also vom Einzelnen nicht mehr direkt überschaubare Handlungsketten entstehen.

Giddens nimmt diese Möglichkeit auf und definiert den Begriff der „sozialen Integration" so, daß damit auf stabile Handlungsmuster verwiesen wird, die sich unter Verhältnissen kopräsenter Akteure herausbilden. Der

Begriff der „Systemintegration" bleibt dann eine Art Restkategorie; er bezieht sich auf Handlungsmuster zwischen *nicht-kopräsenten* Akteuren, auf eine „Reziprozität zwischen Akteuren oder Kollektiven über weite Spannen von Raum und Zeit jenseits von Situationen der Kopräsenz hinweg." (Giddens 1988: 432)

Giddens macht nun deutlich, daß er mit diesem Begriff der System-integration vor allem Phänomene zu erfassen versucht, die in der herkömmlichen Gesellschaftstheorie eine eher untergeordnete Rolle spielten und noch spielen, nämlich die logistischen und organisatorischen Vor-aussetzungen weitreichender Handlungsketten und -vernetzungen.

Eben dies ist auch die Stoßrichtung der Ansätze von John A. Hall und Michael Mann, die sich ebenfalls ganz auf makrosoziologisch relevante Handlungsketten und Machtgefüge konzentrieren. Nicht auf Macht im allgemeinen richten sie ihr Augenmerk, sondern auf solche Machtmittel, die es erlauben, Menschen über Räume und Zeiten hinweg zu kontrollieren und zu organisieren: „Meine zentralen Fragen betreffen *Organisation, Kontrolle, Logistik* und *Kommunikation*, d. h. die Fähigkeit und Möglichkeit, Menschen, Materialien und Territorien zu organisieren und zu kontrollieren bzw. zu beherrschen (...) Meine Geschichte der Macht basiert auf der Messung sozialräumlicher Organisationskapazitäten und auf der Erklärung ihrer Entstehung und Entwicklung." (Mann 1990: 16; Hervorh. im Original)

Setzt man handlungstheoretisch so an, wie dies die hier behandelten Autoren tun, so wird es für die weitere Ausarbeitung dieses Programms ganz entscheidend, daß man sich die Offenheit gegenüber je unterschiedlichen, historisch sich doch auch ändernden makrosoziologischen Vergesellschaf-tungsformen bewahrt. Erforderlich ist also ein kategoriales Grundgerüst, das solchen Wandlungsprozessen gerecht wird und nicht von vornherein etwa nur einen einzigen Integrationsmechanismus in den Blick bekommt.

Die besondere Anlage seines Handlungsbegriffes ermöglicht es Giddens, dieser Forderung nachzukommen. Er hatte ja Handeln mit Macht, mit einem „umgestaltenden Vermögen" gleichgesetzt, und damit auch impliziert, daß Handeln immer die Rückgriffsmöglichkeit auf bestimmte Ressourcen zu seiner Voraussetzung hat – dies gilt für den Mikrobereich ebenso wie für den Makrobereich. Giddens unterscheidet dabei grundsätzlich zwischen allo-kativen (Verfügungsgewalt über Güter und Produktionsmittel) und autoritativen Ressourcen (Kontrolle von Informationen und Organisations-wissen), so daß sich also Handlungen (oder Machtgefüge) danach unterscheiden lassen, in welchem Ausmaß sie eher auf allokative oder autoritative Ressourcen zurückgreifen.

Mit dieser vor allem als Gegenposition zum historischen Materialismus zu verstehenden Differenzierung zwischen zwei Typen von Ressourcen will Giddens deutlich machen, daß gesellschaftliche Vernetzungen nicht ausschließlich als ökonomisch bedingte zu begreifen sind. Giddens – durch die Erfahrung des Totalitarismus und die Lektüre Foucaults belehrt – betont gerade auch administrative oder staatliche Steuerungs- und Überwachungs-kapazitäten, die durch die industrielle Verkehrs- und Kommunikationsrevolution in der Neuzeit enorm zugenommen haben und die sich nicht umstandslos auf ökonomische Verhältnisse zurückführen lassen.

Diese analytische Unterscheidung zwischen allokativen und autoritativen Ressourcen sensibilisiert für bestimmte historische Entwicklungen; sie erst eröffnet den Blick für die bedeutende Rolle staatlicher Instanzen bei der Konstituierung moderner „Gesellschaften". Erst das industrielle Zeitalter bot die Möglichkeit, raum-zeitlich weit ausgreifende Handlungsverknüpfungen herzustellen. Erst in der Moderne konnten Menschen in einem Grade organisiert werden, wie es in früheren Zeiten undenkbar gewesen wäre, und – wie Giddens zeigen wird – gerade staatliche Akteure spielten hierbei eine wichtige Rolle.

Insgesamt verhilft die von Giddens entwickelte Begrifflichkeit also dazu, sich die angesichts der Verschiedenartigkeit von „Gesellschaften" notwendige Offenheit für unterschiedliche Lösungen des ordnungstheoretischen Problems zu bewahren, sich auch die historisch wandelbaren Vernetzungsformen zu verdeutlichen.

Hatte *Giddens* auf eine Handlungs- und Machttypologie verzichtet (lediglich seine Kontrastierung allokativer und autoritativer Ressourcen hätte hier Anknüpfungspunkte geboten), so unterscheidet etwa *Michael Mann* ganz explizit zwischen ideologischen, ökonomischen, militärischen und politischen Machtnetzwerken, um die je verschiedenen Formen „gesellschaftlicher" Integration genauer fassen zu können.[4]

Nun muß man sicherlich nicht diese von Mann nicht näher begründete analytische Unterscheidung in vier Typen von Netzwerken als sehr originell ansehen, um darin den schon bei Giddens angesprochenen Erkenntnisgewinn sehen zu können. Denn durch die fast rigide Unterteilung von Machtnetzwerken bleibt sichergestellt, daß alle „gesellschaftlichen" Sphären zuerst einmal als einigermaßen autonom begriffen werden können. Politische Macht etwa läßt sich nicht auf ideologische, ökonomische oder militärische reduzieren und umgekehrt. Die pragmatische 'Auflösung' des Analyseobjekts „Gesellschaft" in verschiedene Machnetzwerke verhindert eine vorzeitige Deklaration bestimmter Bereiche zum entscheidenden Faktor, zur determinierenden Sphäre. Dadurch, daß Mann vier Bereiche oder Netzwerke im Prinzip gleichberechtigt nebeneinander stellt, diese sowohl einzeln als auch im Verhältnis zueinander untersuchen kann, erhält er ein äußerst variables Analyseinstrument, das von vornherein darauf angelegt ist, bestimmte Reduktionismen zu vermeiden. Die Bedeutung der vier Machtnetzwerke und ihr historisch sich wandelndes Wechselverhältnis kann so epochen- oder gesellschaftsspezifisch gewichtet und beurteilt werden.

Wie schon bei Giddens bleibt also auch hier die Offenheit gegenüber je verschiedenen Vergesellschaftungsformen und -mechanismen gewahrt. Welchem Ansatz zur Lösung des ordnungstheoretischen Problems man auch immer den Vorzug geben wird, dem von Giddens oder dem von Mann (bzw. Hall) – mit beiden ist es möglich, *die politische und militärische Konstitution moderner Gesellschaften zu thematisieren.*

Im folgenden nun sollen zwei Themen hervorgehoben werden, welche die drei Autoren ausführlich diskutiert haben und die für eine historische Soziologie von besonderer Bedeutung sind: Die militärisch-politische Spezifik Europas, die zu seiner Weltherrschaft führte (2.) und das Wechselverhältnis von Staat, Krieg und Kapitalismus (3.). Ihre Thesen zur Beziehung zwischen staatlicher Machtentwicklung und Demokratie bieten dann die Möglichkeit zu einer kurzen Kritik der Gesamtkonstruktion ihrer machttheoretischen Ansätze (4.).

2. Die militärisch-politische Spezifik Europas

Michael Manns „The Sources of Social Power" ist eine auf insgesamt vier Bände angelegte Weltgeschichte „sozialer Macht". Der *bisher vorliegende erste* Band (Volume 1: A history of power from the beginning to A.D. 1760) erfaßt die Zeit zwischen dem Auftreten der ersten großen Zivilisationen und dem Einsetzen der Industrialisierung in England. Der zweite und dritte Band werden dann die Geschichte bis zur Gegenwart weiterführen, der vierte Band soll ausschließlich der theoretischen Reflexion vorbehalten bleiben.

Aus der enormen Fülle des von Michael Mann aufgearbeiteten historischen Materials ragt seine Skizze der europäischen Geschichte seit dem Mittelalter heraus, weil Mann den Aufstieg des Westens im Vergleich zu den anderen Zivilisationen gerade durch das Wirken politisch-militärischer Faktoren zu erklären versucht. Dabei greift er zurück auf ein Argument, das sich schon Max Weber in seiner Studie über „Konfuzianismus und Taoismus" zu eigen gemacht hatte. Weber hob die Abgeschlossenheit, Einheit und Befriedetheit Chinas vor allem deswegen hervor, da für ihn der staatliche Konkurrenzkampf, der dort eben fehlte, eine der wesentlichen Voraussetzungen für ökonomische und bürokratische Rationalisierung war. „(...) so ließ das Aufhören der machtpolitischen Konkurrenz der Staaten miteinander die Rationalisierung des Verwaltungsbetriebs, der Finanzwirtschaft und der Wirtschaftspolitik kollabieren." (Weber 1988: 349)

In seiner Deutung der europäischen Geschichte betont Mann, daß um die Jahrtausendwende noch relativ wenig auf die zukünftige welthistorische Rolle Europas hindeutete. Zwar entwickelte sich schon vorher eine leidlich dynamische Ökonomie (man denke an die Erfindung der Wassermühle, des schweren Pfluges, der Dreifelderwirtschaft u.ä.), doch nehmen sich diese Ergebnisse wohl eher kümmerlich aus, vergleicht man sie mit den Errungenschaften etwa im islamischen oder chinesischen Machtbereich zur gleichen Zeit. Wichtiger war eine schon damals sichtbare strukturelle Besonderheit Europas: Europa bestand aus vielen kleinen Machtzentren unterschiedlichster Art, die beständig miteinander konkurrierten, eine produktive Unruhe hervorriefen und somit über kurz oder lang Innovationen erzwangen. Hinzuweisen ist hier vor allem auf eine Vielzahl politischer und militärischer Machteinheiten, die jedoch noch keine Stabilität besaßen, da der feudale Herrscher in der Regel schwach war: „Seine rituellen Aufgaben und die Infrastruktur seiner Bürokratie in Gestalt der Schriftkundigkeit wurden ihm durch die transnationale Kirche vorgegeben; seine richterliche Autorität mußte er sich mit der Kirche und lokalen Lehensgerichten teilen; seine militärische Führerschaft übte er nur in Krisenzeiten und über die Gefolgsleute anderer Lehensherren aus; und fiskalische und wirtschaftliche Redistributionskompetenzen hatte er praktisch überhaupt keine." (Mann 1991: 231)

Die politische und militärische Durchdringungsfähigkeit des feudalen „Staates" um die Jahrtausendwende war also schon wegen der Existenz zahlreicher Zwischengewalten gering; von einem Gewaltmonopol konnte keine Rede sein, dar durch die Vielzahl relativ autonomer Einheiten stets nur ein äußerst labiles Mächtegleichgewicht erreicht werden konnte.

Das ideologische Band des Christentums verhinderte dabei, daß die Konkurrenz dieser vielen ökonomischen, politischen und militärischen Machteinheiten zu einem Vernichtungskampf führte: Das Christentum – so die These Manns – sorgte für eine normative Basis, auf der die anderen Machtnetzwerke (ökonomische, politische und militärische) aufbauen und sich entwickeln konnten.

Gegen Ende des 12. Jahrhunderts aber zeigten sich Tendenzen, die zu einer Auflösung bzw. Beseitigung der Feudalstruktur führten. Der *Krieg* wurde dabei zum entscheidenden Faktor, militärische Auseinandersetzungen schufen die strukturellen Voraussetzungen für den späteren Aufstieg Europas.

An dieser Stelle scheint mir jedoch Manns Argumentation inkonsistent zu sein. Da Mann keine Hinweise für eine schwindende normative und befriedende Rolle des Christentums gibt, bleibt, unklar, wie es zu diesem von ihm behaupteten plötzlichen Einsetzen einer kriegerischen Dynamik kommen konnte. Dieses Problem ergibt sich für Mann deshalb, weil er zwei letztlich miteinander unvereinbare Faktoren zur Erklärung der europäischen Dynamik heranzieht: das Vorhandensein eines durch das Christentum befriedeten Wirtschaftsraumes *und* die durch militärische Spannungen hervorgerufene Wettbewerbssituation. Aber vernünftigerweise kann nur *einer* dieser Faktoren die Dynamik Europas begründen. Meiner Meinung nach würde Manns Argumentation an Plausibilität gewinnen, würde er weniger stark diese befriedende Funktion des Christentums herausstreichen. Denn einen normativen Rahmen boten ja wohl auch andere Weltreligionen, und somit kann diese Bedingung gerade nicht den *europäischen* Aufstieg erklären. Folgt man diesem Vorschlag, dann muß man für das 12. Jahrhundert nicht eine von Mann suggerierte Zäsur zwischen einer eher friedlichen und einer kriegerischen Periode behaupten. Vielmehr kann dann der Aufweis sich ändernder feudaler Strukturen genügen, um Wandlungen der Kriegführung innerhalb eines schon immer von militärischer Konfrontation gekennzeichneten europäischen Kulturraumes zu erklären und damit Bedingungen, die den späteren Aufstieg Europas ermöglichten.

Dieser Vorschlag wäre problemlos mit Manns weiterer Argumentation zu vereinbaren. Wie Mann ja auch ausführt, war es nämlich gerade im 12. Jahrhundert immer schwieriger geworden, das feudale Aufgebot einzuberufen, da komplexe Erbschaftsverhältnisse zu einer Besitzersplitterung unter den Lehenspflichtigen geführt hatten, die Fähigkeit zur Gefolgschaftsleistung deshalb in Frage gestellt war. Ein Ausweg eröffnete sich zuerst in einer Kombination von Söldnerheer und feudalem Aufgebot, da nur so noch die einzelnen Herrschaftseinheiten der militärischen und politischen Konkurrenz standhalten konnten.

Folge davon waren aber ständige Kämpfe und Aushandlungsprozesse zwischen Monarchen und Fürsten auf der einen Seite und ihren steuerpflichtigen Untertanen auf der anderen Seite um die Finanzierung dieser immer kostspieliger werdenden Kriege, auch wenn natürlich hinzuzufügen ist, daß diese „staatlichen" Interventionen noch keinen wesentlichen Einfluß auf die Lebensführung der Bevölkerungsmehrheit hatten. „Obwohl es kaum möglich ist, die jeweilige Bedeutung der verschiedenen Machtkämpfe im einzelnen genau zu ermessen, dürfte das politische Geschehen, das sich auf der Ebene des im Entstehen begriffenen Territorialstaates abspielte, für den größten Teil der Bevölkerung doch immer noch sehr viel weniger wichtig gewesen sein als die (an Brauchtum und Lehensgericht orientierte) Lokalpolitik einerseits und die Politik der transnationalen Kirchen andererseits (mitsamt ihrer Position dem Staat gegenüber) es waren." (Mann 1991: 296)

Dennoch zeigten sich erste Anzeichen eines territorialen Kerns für viele der späteren Nationalstaaten. Der ständige Konflikt um Steuern ließ zudem den Staat zum Adressaten der Forderungen unterschiedlichster Gruppierungen werden: die Kämpfe um Steuern und Steuerprivilegien zielten immer mehr auf den zentralisierten und immer mehr regulierenden Staat, wodurch lokale und transnationale Bindungen an Bedeutung verloren.

Diese Tendenz wurde nach Mann seit dem Ende des 15. Jahrhunderts durch neue Entwicklungen in der Waffentechnik noch beschleunigt. Mit der Einführung von Handfeuerwaffen und der zunehmenden Rolle der Artillerie wuchsen die für militärische Auseinandersetzungen notwendigen Ausgaben, so daß kleinere Provinzfürsten aus dem Wettrüsten ausscheiden mußten. Sie konnten schlicht die notwendigen Kapitalinvestitionen nicht mehr aufbringen, um Kriege im großen Stil zu führen, und verloren somit bald ihre politische Eigenständigkeit.

Durch die militärisch-technologische Revolution wurden also diejenigen Staaten in eine strategisch günstige Lage versetzt, die aufgrund ihrer finanziellen und administrativen Kapazitäten im militärisch-politischen Wettbewerb konkurrieren konnten. Zwei Staatstypen kristallisierten sich heraus:

In Gebieten mit einer florierenden Geldökonomie ließen sich Steuern leicht und ohne große Repressionen abschöpfen. Hier waren konstitutionelle Entwicklungspfade möglich (wie Mann am Beispiel Englands und Hollands verdeutlicht). In ökonomisch rückständigen Gebieten dagegen ließen sich Steuerabgaben nur unter erheblichem administrativen Aufwand erzwingen, was einen staatsabsolutistischen Weg wahrscheinlich machte, wie sich an Frankreich und später an Brandenburg-Preußen zeigen sollte.

In beiden Fällen jedoch mußten die staatlichen Akteure die ökonomische Entwicklung fördern, durften sie diese jedenfalls nicht allzu sehr behindern, wollten sie nicht ihre Stellung im militärisch-politischen Wettbewerb untergraben. Die enge Verzahnung von ökonomischer Entwicklung und militärischem Wettbewerb, von Kapitalismus und Staatensystem, war also – so diese Theorie – die Voraussetzung und die treibende Kraft für die europäische Expansion.

Die These Manns, wonach sich das vormoderne Europa gerade durch seine kriegerische Dynamik entwickeln konnte und durch diese Unruhe an den Beginn der Industrialisierung herangeführt wurde, wirft die Frage auf, ob diese Wechselbeziehung zwischen ökonomischer Entwicklung und militärischem Wettbewerb auch heute noch wirksam ist. Max Weber schien diese Frage – für seine Zeit zumindest – zu bejahen: „Der geschlossene nationale Staat also ist es, der dem Kapitalismus die Chance des Fortbestehens gewährleistet; solange er nicht einem Weltreich Platz macht, wird also auch der Kapitalismus dauern." (Weber 1985: 815). Tatsächlich deutet ja vieles darauf hin, daß nationale Rivalitäten auch heute noch enorme Innovationsschübe hervorrufen können, wenn man etwa an den japanisch-amerikanischen Wettbewerb im Bereich der Mikroelektronik denkt – Innovationsschübe, die auch aus machtpolitischen Gründen von der jeweiligen staatlichen Seite stark gefördert worden sind. Trifft dies zu, so ist die Forderung „Bringing the State Back In" natürlich auch für die Analyse gegenwärtiger ökonomischer Entwicklungen von großer Bedeutung.

John A. Halls „Powers and Liberties. The Causes and Consequences of the Rise of the West" greift die Mannsche These auf, wonach sich die politische Zersplitterung Europas letztlich produktiv auswirkte. Diese These erhält ja ihre intuitive Plausibilität vor allem dann, wenn man das zersplitterte Europa mit dem geeinten China vergleicht. Jedoch ist damit nicht die Frage beantwortet, welche Strukturen letztlich andere Zivilisationen wie die islamische oder die indische gegenüber der europäischen benachteiligten, waren diese doch ebenfalls von politischer Fragmentierung betroffen.

Diese Frage, der Mann nicht nachgegangen war, versucht Hall durch eine vergleichende Vorgehensweise zu beantworten. Er vermutet, daß unterschiedliche *staatliche Strukturen* (und *nicht allein* das Vorhandensein militärisch-politischer Konkurrenz) in den verschiedenen Zivilisationen einen entscheidenden Faktor für deren ökonomische Entwicklung bzw. Stagnation darstellten.[5]

Die Untersuchung zu China liefert Hall eine Bestätigung der These, daß Großreiche (und China war ja während eines Großteils seiner fast viertausendjährigen Geschichte politisch geeint) oftmals die ökonomischen Antriebskräfte fesseln. Über lange Perioden der chinesischen Geschichte hinweg war die Mandarinatsbürokratie eifersüchtig auf die Wahrung ihrer Vorrangstellung bedacht. Entwicklungen, die zum politischen und sozialen Aufstieg anderer gesellschaftlicher Gruppen hätten führen können (man denke etwa an ein sich bildendes Handelsbürgertum), wurden schon im Ansatz unterdrückt. Eine Abkehr von einer solchen zu politischer Erstarrung führenden Politik war nicht nötig, da China – auch durch quasi natürliche Grenzen vor äußeren Feinden geschützt – in sich selbst ruhte.

Hall bezeichnet die Regierungsform des Mandarinats als „capstone-government" oder „capstonestate", eben weil dieser Staat jegliche gesellschaftliche Aktivität erstickte: „The mandarin capstone remained in place, but control was at the cost of the longer term efficiency that could be created only by mobilizing different societal capacities." (Hall 1985: 197) Die politische Stabilität Chinas in Form einer ununterbrochen herrschenden Mandarinatsbürokratie wurde also durch wirtschaftliche Stagnation erkauft.

Chinas Ökonomie erblühte nur einmal in vollem Glanz, und zwar charakteristischerweise in der Zeit der politischen Spaltung. Die dadurch eintretende militärische Konkurrenz zwischen beiden Teilen Chinas zwang die Herrscher der südlichen Sung-Dynastie (1127–1269) dazu, Ressourcen aus der Gesellschaft zu mobilisieren, Rücksicht zu nehmen auch auf die Interessen der Kaufleute, da nur diese Klasse das für die Kriegführung so notwendige Steueraufkommen bereitstellen konnte: Die Mandarinatsbürokratie war also durch die militärische Situation gezwungen, ihren 'Druck' auf die 'Gesellschaft' zu vermindern, die wirtschaftlichen Aktivitäten dort zur Entfaltung kommen zu lassen – so lange jedenfalls, wie die staatlich-militärische Konkurrenzsituation anhielt (vgl. dazu auch Collins 1986: 58ff).

Gerade der Fall China scheint also den Zusammenhang zwischen Staatenkonkurrenz und ökonomischer Entwicklung glanzvoll zu bestätigen. Doch Halls Argument lautet, daß politische Heterogenität nur eine notwendige, jedoch keine hinreichende Bedingung für wirtschaftliche Dynamik war.

Dies läßt sich nämlich am Beispiel der indischen und islamischen Zivilisationen zeigen, die – obwohl politisch zersplittert – dennoch ökonomisch stagnierten.

In bezug auf den indischen Subkontinent verweist Hall auf die geringen Einflußmöglichkeiten der Politik auf die 'Gesellschaft', weil vorrangig die *Religion* der Garant der gesellschaftlichen Ordnung war. Die Brahmanen – so argumentiert Hall – machten letztlich Herrscherfunktionen überflüssig, sie verhinderten die Entstehung von starken *politischen* Gebilden. Die damit potentiell immer gegebene Instabilität der dortigen Staaten verführte sie zu bloßer Ausbeutung. „Kings had power for such a short period that they simply took what they could: as the state was not long lasting, there could be no conception of nurturing merchant activities with a view to long-term tax revenue." (Hall 1986: 81)

Eine solche Politik ohne langfristige Perspektiven erschwerte kontinuierliches Wirtschaften, das aufgrund des Kastenwesens (keine Gleichheit der Handelspartner durch die hierarchische Konzeption des sozialen Lebens; Verhinderung einer flexiblen und anpassungsfähigen Arbeitsteilung etc.) sowieso schon problematisch genug war.

Das Ergebnis war faktisch das gleiche wie in China: Die Ökonomie besaß keine wirkliche Autonomie, keine freie Entfaltungsmöglichkeit. Zugleich waren aber auch die Staaten zu instabil, als daß sie für die ökonomische Entwicklung der 'Gesellschaft' viel hätten leisten können: „The state floated above society, and provided none of those services – law, peace, universalism – that might have encouraged the creation of economic advance." (Hall 1986: 82)

Ähnliche Strukturen bestimmten auch den islamischen Machtbereich,[6] da dort – neben verschiedenen ethischen Postulaten – einzigartige sozialstrukturelle Gegebenheiten das Entstehen politisch stabiler Staaten verhinderten. Das Vorhandensein zahlreicher mobiler, kriegerischer und egalitär organisierter Nomadengruppen führte zu einer merkwürdigen Bipolarität dieser islamischen 'Gesellschaft': Auf der einen Seite die wirtschaftlich aktive Stadt und auf der anderen Seite die diese bedrohenden, unkontrollierbaren, kriegerischen Nomadenstämme: „Urban citizens faced a land of dissidence capable of great military surges. Not unnaturally, those who could not protect themselves looked for a professional defender and they found him in one tribe, capable both of fighting off tribal incursions and of providing an orderly sphere with which the market could function." (Hall 1986: 93)

Einzelne Nomadenstämme wurden also immer wieder von den militärisch schwachen Städten zu Schutzherren berufen, ihre Führer zu Regenten in der Stadt. Dabei konnte sich aber nie eine stabile Herrscherdynastie etablieren, denn: „(. . .) tribal organisation, once out of its customary water, withers and dies." (Hall 1986: 94) Die kulturellen Traditionen der Nomaden – so Hall – waren den Gegebenheiten des städtisch-politischen Lebens nie gewachsen, ein schneller Degenerationsprozeß setzte ein, der die Herrschaft des Stammes untergrub. Der schnelle Wechsel politischer Herrschaft war die unumgängliche Folge.

Insgesamt erwies sich also auch im Islam der politische 'Überbau' als Hemmnis für die ökonomische Entwicklung. Der Staat existierte nie lange genug, um wirklich tiefe Wurzeln innerhalb der 'Gesellschaft' zu schlagen und um eine dem Wirtschaftsleben angemessene Infrastruktur zu schaffen. Vielmehr verleitete die Instabilität des Staates diesen zu ständigen räuberischen Eingriffen in die Ökonomie, deren Autonomie daher immer in Frage gestellt und der eine kontinuierliche Entwicklung deshalb nie gestattet war.

Diese Beobachtungen Halls zur Beziehung zwischen Ökonomie und Staat veranlassen ihn nun zu folgender These: Politische Fragmentierung ist tatsächlich eine notwendige Bedingung für Marktautonomie. Jedoch – wie am Beispiel Indiens und des Islam gezeigt – auch die 'Qualität' des jeweiligen Staates ist entscheidend für die Entstehung einer dynamischen Ökonomie: Instabile und deshalb rein auf Ausbeutung fixierte Staaten und Regierungen behindern gerade eine solche Dynamik.

Hall stellt sich deshalb die Frage, was in Europa dazu führen konnte, daß sich hier ein Staaten*system* und zugleich *stabile* Staaten herausbilden konnten, die in der Lage waren, die Ökonomie langfristig zu fördern, sie nicht auszubeuten.

Einen Teil der Antwort auf diese Frage findet Hall in bestimmten Strukturmerkmalen des Christentums. Das Wirken der Römischen Kirche trug ganz wesentlich dazu bei, daß sich in Europa kein Großreich wie etwa in China etablieren konnte. Zum einen verweigerte sich diese Kirche als 'Hilfskraft' für einen Herrscher, sie schuf keine cäsaropapistische Doktrin (wie etwa in Byzanz) und lieferte somit auch nicht die geistig-spirituellen Grundlagen für ein Gott-Kaisertum. Zum anderen förderte die von Rom aus praktizierte eigenständige Machtpolitik die Formierung einzelner getrennter Staaten, da sich diese aus der Sicht Roms gut gegeneinander ausspielen ließen – so lange jedenfalls, als die weltlichen Herrschaftseinheiten noch auf die legitimatorischen und administrativen Leistungen der Römischen Kirche angewiesen waren.

Aber die Kirche war nicht nur für den Erhalt der Pluralität der Machtzentren verantwortlich. Die christlichen Lehren trugen auch wesentlich dazu bei, den Aufbau eines *stabilen* Staatsapparates zu ermöglichen. Denn zum einen unterminierten und beseitigten die christlichen Glaubensvorstellungen die Grundlagen der Sippenverfassung[7] und ermöglichten damit den direkten Zugriff des Staates auf seine Untertanen. Zum anderen legitimierten Päpste und Bischöfe das Königtum durch die Verleihung von Weiheattributen, wodurch dieses aus dem übrigen Hochadel herausgehoben und mit einer besonderen Würde versehen wurde.

Für Hall war also die Römische Kirche der entscheidende Faktor, der in Europa das Entstehen eines einheitlichen Imperiums verhinderte und die Bildung relativ stabiler Staaten möglich machte. Die Kirche selbst förderte also die Entstehung von Staaten, ihre ethischen Postulate standen nicht – wie im Islam – der politischen Macht entgegen und untergruben auch nicht – wie in Indien – staatliche Funktionen. Die vergleichsweise hohe Stabilität des politischen Lebens in Europa ermöglichte eine langfristige Planung und verhinderte ein Übermaß destruktiver Eingriffe in die Ökonomie.

Einen weiteren Grund für eine ungestörte ökonomische Entwicklung sieht Hall in der für Europa charakteristischen Phasenverschiebung zwischen ökonomischer und politisch-militärischer Dynamik: Der wirtschaftliche Aufschwung begann in Europa *vor* der Herausbildung starker politischer Gebilde.

Auch hier spielte Hall zufolge das Christentum eine entscheidende Rolle, weil es in der Zeit zwischen 800 und 1050 den normativen Rahmen abgab, innerhalb dessen sich ein reger Handel entwickeln konnte. Die Blüte der europäischen Stadt seit dem 11. Jahrhundert etwa war Ergebnis dieser Entwicklung. „(...) a decentralised market system, based on a sense of belonging to a single civilisation, came into place during those years in which there was no real government which could interfere with its workings." (Hall 1986: 135f)

Als sich dann einige Jahrhunderte später ein Staatensystem zu etablieren begann, waren die Herrscher aufgrund der einsetzenden kriegerischen Dynamik und des damit gegebenen Finanzbedarfs auf die Kooperation mit kapitalkräftigen Gruppen angewiesen und förderten von sich aus den Kapitalumlauf.

So entwickelte sich dann in Westeuropa ein Staatsaufbau, den Hall als „organisch" bezeichnet: „What is apparent is that large sections of the powerful in society were prepared in the long run to give quite high taxation revenues to the crown because they realized that their own interests were usually being served. Conflicts of course occurred, and they make up much of European history. Nevertheless the more important fact remains the organic quality of the state." (Hall 1986: 138)

Die staatliche Bürokratie und die gesellschaftlich relevanten Gruppen lernten also schon früh, miteinander zu kooperieren (das ist mit dem Begriff „organischer Staat" gemeint); es gab nicht wie in anderen Zivilisationen ein Gegeneinander oder Nebeneinander der Machtzentren („power standoff"), sondern ein Miteinander von 'Staat' und 'Gesellschaft'. Hall greift also auf die Parsonssche Einsicht zurück, wonach Macht akkumuliert werden kann und der Machtgebrauch kein bloßes Nullsummenspiel ist: Diese Akkumulation von Macht war letztlich der entscheidende Grund für den Aufstieg des Westens, für den Prozeß beschleunigter kapitalistischer Entwicklung, der dann in die Phase der Industrialisierung und letztlich der europäischen Weltherrschaft hineinführen sollte.

Halls entscheidende These ist also, daß die „organische" Qualität des Staates, d. h. ein Kooperationsverhältnis zwischen staatlichen und wirtschaftlichen Eliten die kapitalistische Entwicklung vorangetrieben hat. Es war somit auch kein Zufall, daß die Industrialisierung gerade im konstitutionellen Großbritannien begann. Die Voraussetzung der europäischen Dynamik zumindest in ihrer Anfangsphase waren nicht allein Handels- und Gewerbefreiheit, sondern auch bürgerliche Mitverantwortung, „Demokratie" in einem sehr weiten Sinn.

Hall warnt aber zugleich davor, vorschnell ein wechselseitiges Bedingungsverhältnis von Kapitalismus und entwickelter Ökonomie einerseits und Demokratie andererseits zu behaupten. Zurecht verweist er deshalb in „Powers and Liberties" auch auf andere (eben nicht liberal-kapitalistische) Modernisierungspfade, wobei er stark auf Barrington Moores Argumente in „Die sozialen Ursprünge von Diktatur und Demokratie" zurückgreift.

Ergänzend wäre zu bedenken, daß Halls Konzept des „organischen Staates" notwendigerweise nur sehr allgemein gehalten ist, da es ja entwickelt wurde vor allem im Hinblick auf den Vergleich Europas mit anderen Kulturen. Die Feinheiten nationaler historischer Strukturen und Entwicklungen können damit kaum erfaßt werden. Sie darf man aber natürlich nicht vernachlässigen.

So hat etwa Hans-Christoph Schröder (1977) darauf hingewiesen, daß in England in der Zeit zwischen 1754 und 1832 – also gerade in der Phase der industriellen Revolution – zu einem relativen Rückgang der Wahlberechtigten im Vergleich zur immens wachsenden Gesamtbevölkerung kam. Er schließt daraus, daß bestimmte Einschränkungen von Mitspracherechten in dieser Zeit für den Prozeß der Industrialisierung gerade funktional waren, und behauptet, daß ähnliche Konstellationen während der Industrialisierungsphase auch anderer europäischer Länder vorkamen. Halls Konzept des „organischen Staates" – so meine Ergänzung – ist zu grobmaschig, um politische Veränderungen innerhalb eines Staates zu fassen. Insofern sollte man vielleicht den Zusammenhang zwischen Demokratie und Kapitalismus noch stärker relativieren, als dies Hall mit seinem Aufweis unterschiedlicher Modernisierungspfade sowieso schon tat.

Dieser Hinweis erscheint mir auch notwendig angesichts der wiedergewonnenen Aktualität der Modernisierungstheorie nach dem Zusammenbruch des sozialistischen Staatensystems: Modernisierung und Demokratisierung des politischen Systems bedingen nicht automatisch die Modernisierung wirtschaftlicher Strukturen (ebensowenig gilt die umgekehrte Beziehung), sondern sind abhängig vom Kräfteverhältnis zwischen den gesellschaftlich relevanten Gruppen (vlg. etwa Tiryakian 1991 oder – von einer anderen theoretischen Perspektive – Rueschemeyer/Stephens/Stephens 1992).

3. Staat, Krieg und Kapitalismus

Mann und Hall hatten mit ihrer Betonung des politisch-militärischen Wettbewerbs auf das produktive Zusammenspiel von kapitalistischer Ökonomie und staatlichem Handel hingewiesen, wobei sie sich eng an Webers These einer engen Verbindung von Kapitalismus und Nationalstaat angelehnt hatten. Neu ist nun die Wendung, die Anthony Giddens dieser These zu geben versucht.

Nach Giddens konnte sich in der Epoche des Absolutismus mit der Durchsetzung bestimmter rechtlicher Regeln eine relativ reibungsfreie kapitalistische Praxis herausbilden, die ihrerseits wiederum durch die damit gegebene Möglichkeit höherer Steuerabschöpfung die staatlichen Instanzen stärkte. Die Zentralisierung und Vereinheitlichung der Rechtsprechung führten insgesamt zu einer stärkeren administrativen Durchdringung der 'Gesellschaft', der Souveränitäts*anspruch* des Staates im Innern konnte tatsächlich dann auch durchgesetzt werden. Der überregional bestehende und gewährleistete Schutz des Privateigentums machte eine faktische Enteignung der ländlichen Massen von ihren Produktionsmitteln möglich. Der Widerstand der Bauern gegen die 'enclosures' etwa ließ sich durch die staatliche „Rechtshilfe" brechen.

Die Tatsache nun, daß die Bevölkerungsmehrheit, ihrer Produktionsmittel beraubt, in den Arbeitsmarkt hineingetrieben wurde, ist verantwortlich für ein wesentliches strukturelles Merkmal moderner 'Gesellschaften': ihre Befriedetheit im Innern.

Denn zum einen erfolgte unter kapitalistischen Bedingungen der Ausbeutungsprozeß quasi stillschweigend, war etwa eine *gewaltsame* Aneignung agrarischer Überschüsse nicht mehr vonnöten. Im industriellen Kapitalismus hatte und brauchte auch die herrschende Klasse zwecks Mehrwertaneignung keinen Zugang mehr zu militärischen Gewaltmitteln.

Zum anderen unterlagen die Massen enteigneter Bauern in den Fabriken einem Disziplinierungsprozeß, der in seiner Wirkung über den Arbeitsplatz hinausreichte bzw. sich einreihte in eine ganze Anzahl weiterer disziplinierender Maßnahmen, die seit dem 16. Jahrhundert von staatlicher Seite ergangen sind. Zum Teil in Anlehnung an Foucault beschreibt Giddens, wie die Angst vor bäuerlichen Unruhen den Ausbau staatlicher Ordnungskräfte forcierte, wie die staatliche Überwachung sowohl im Sinne der direkten Observation als auch im Sinne der Datensammlung ständig zunahm, was dazu führte, daß direkte physische Gewaltanwendung aus der bürgerlichen Gesellschaft verdrängt und im Staat monopolisiert werden konnte. Die technische Entwicklung lieferte dabei die dazu erforderlichen Machtmittel: neuartige Verkehrs- und Transportmittel (wie z. B. die Eisenbahn) und qualitativ neue Kommunikationsmedien (wie Telegraph oder Telephon) führten zu einer bis dato ungeahnten Steigerung staatlicher Steuerungs- und Überwachungsfähigkeit.

Diese Argumentation führt zu Giddens' zentraler These, die schon der Buchtitel „The Nation-state and Violence" andeutet: Mit der inneren Befriedung der 'Gesellschaft', mit der Disziplinierung der Bevölkerung, die gerade auch unter kapitalistischen Rahmenbedingungen erfolgt ist, war es möglich, daß militärische Kräfte aus dem „Innern" der Gesellschaft abgezogen und nach außen gerichtet werden konnten. Nationalstaat *und* staatliche Gewalt sind zwei eng und keineswegs zufällig miteinander verbundene Phänomene. Die nach außen gerichtete militärische Gewalt – mehr oder minder reguliert durch die Existenz eines Nationalstaatensystems – ist für Giddens so bedeutsam, daß er sie (neben Kapitalismus, Industrialismus und innerstaatlicher Überwachung) als ein *wesentliches Strukturmerkmal der Moderne* bezeichnet. „(...) my theme will be that the correlate of the internally pacified state – class relationships that rest upon a mixture of 'dull economic compulsion' and supervisory techniques of labour management – is the professionalized standing army." (Giddens 1985: 160)

Die Armee war nicht nur zur Aufrechterhaltung des inneren Friedens praktisch überflüssig geworden, die disziplinarischen Techniken machten es gar möglich, die Massen selbst zu mobilisieren, sie im Rahmen eines Volksheeres zu bewaffnen, ohne damit die bestehende Ordnung zu gefährden. Nach Giddens erklärt sich daraus u.a. die Brutalität des modernen Krieges, in dem ein bislang unbekanntes Ausmaß auch menschlicher 'Ressourcen' (um die zynische Sprache militärischer Strategen zu verwenden) zum Einsatz kommen konnte. Der nationalstaat ist zugleich auch Machtstaat – nach innen durch seine administrativen Ressourcen, nach außen durch das stehende Heer.

Kapitalistische Entwicklung und militärische Gewalt(androhung) sind zwei eng miteinander verzahnte Komplexe. Giddens' Ausführungen dazu machen deutlich, daß eine Soziologie, die – wie meist geschehen – sich allein mit dem ersteren Komplex beschäftigt, zu einer angemessenen Interpretation der Moderne nicht in der Lage sein wird.

Ähnliches läßt sich auch in bezug auf sozialen Wandel sagen. Wer die Wirkungen und Folgen, die durch Kriege und Aufrüstung hervorgerufen oder beschleunigt wurden (die Ausdehnung des Wahlrechts zählt hierzu ebenso wie die kontinuierliche Steigerung der Staatsausgaben), nicht systematisch analysiert, wird für sich kaum die Kompetenz in Anspruch nehmen können, sozialen Wandel umfassend erklären zu können. Die Soziologie – und das ist Giddens' Schlußfolgerung daraus – muß diese Themen mehr ins Zentrum ihrer Reflexionen stellen.

Die hohe Bedeutung staatlicher Strukturen für Prozesse sozialen Wandels zeigt sich auch im Bereich der Klassenanalyse. In einigen Aufsätzen, die bereits auf die noch folgenden Bände von „The Sources of Social Power" verweisen, hat Michael Mann (1988) versucht, im Spannungsverhältnis von Krieg, Staat und Kapitalismus den Formierungsprozeß von Klassen zu beschreiben und zu erklären.

Konkret widmet er sich dem Problem der Bezugspunkte des Klassenhandelns. Ist es überhaupt sinnvoll und realistisch, z. B. vom Proletariat ein konsequent internationalistisches Bewußtsein zu erwarten, oder ist eine solche Forderung oder Erwartung angesichts entstehender Nationalstaaten eher Ausdruck einer ziemlich unbegründeten Hoffnung? Mit der Beantwortung solcher Fragen legt Mann nicht nur die Gründe für das Scheitern sozialistischer Revolutionshoffnungen in der Vergangenheit dar, sondern bereitet mit seinen Analysen und Argumenten gleichzeitig auch den Boden für eine differenziertere Nationalismus-Debatte vor.

Mann geht davon aus, daß seit dem Ende der feudalen Epoche der sich entwickelnde kapitalistische Sektor auch zu einem erheblichen Machtzuwachs des Staates beitrug: „Handels- und Grundeigentumskapitalisten initiierten und befestigten damit eine Welt eifrig sich bekriegender, jedoch regulativer, an diplomatische Regeln sich haltender Staaten. Ihr Bedürfnis nach und ihre Empfindlichkeit gegenüber staatlicher Reglementierung – innen wie geopolitisch – drängten Klassen und Staaten auf den Weg zur territorial zentralisierten Organisation." (Mann 1991: 420) Dieses Zusammengehen von großbürgerlichen Klassen und Staat in Westeuropa führte dann auch zu einer 'nationalen Segmentierung' der Ökonomie in dem Sinne, daß bis zum Beginn der industriellen Revolution transnationale Handelskompanien und andere übernationale Organisationen (mit Ausnahme der Banken) weitgehend verschwanden (Mann 1988: 119). Der Güterverkehr blieb wesentlich auf *nationale* Märkte beschränkt. Fanden dennoch internationale ökonomische Transaktionen statt, so wurden sie entweder von den betroffenen Staaten vermittelt oder doch zumindest reguliert.

Die Bourgeoisie mußte sich deshalb – ob sie wollte oder nicht – an diesem Staat orientieren, mußte versuchen, die staatlichen Akteure in ihrem Sinne zu lenken und zu beeinflussen. Eine nationale Organisationsweise war die logische Konsequenz. Das Klassenhandeln der Groß-Bourgeoisie war bezogen auf den jeweiligen Staat, der in „ihren" Handel, in „ihre" Produktion eingriff. Aber eine solche nationale Orientierung und Organisationsweise blieb keine Ausnahme.

Denn auch der europäische Adel – in der feudalen Epoche noch eindeutig eine transnational operierende Klasse – verlor seine staatenübergreifende Solidarität spätestens dann, als es zu einer Kommerzialisierung der Landwirtschaft kam. Er war nun entweder angewiesen auf eine staatliche Regulierung und Subventionierung der Agrarproduktion oder – falls der Landbesitz nicht mehr seinen Lebensunterhalt sichern konnte – auf die Besoldung seiner Leistungen im zivilen oder militärischen Staatsdienst.

Schon vor der Industrialisierung verschwand also eine transnationale Orientierung der *herrschenden* Klassen (von Bourgeoisie und Adel) angesichts der nationalen Segmentierung der Märkte (Mann 1988: 153).

In der Zeitspanne zwischen 1780 und 1945 wurde diese Segmentierung und damit die nationale Ausgerichtetheit der herrschenden Klassen weiter vorangetrieben, da der Strukturwandel der Ökonomie vermehrt Staatseingriffe erforderte. Hinzu kam, daß sich die Mittelklassen im 19. Jahrhundert mit ihren Forderungen nach politischer Mitbestimmung, religiöser Toleranz und rechtlicher Gleichheit an den staatlichen Apparat wandten und daß ihr Erfolg in diesem Kampf letztlich auch dazu führte, daß sie sich in diesen Staat integrierten (Mann 1988: 154 ff).

Eine solche Integration blieb in Europa den *Arbeitern* bis 1914 weitgehend versagt, ihr Kampf um politische und soziale Rechte verlief zumeist weit weniger erfolgreich als der der bürgerlichen Schichten. Nichtsdestoweniger richteten aber auch sie ihre Emanzipationsforderungen *an den Staat, so daß* man auch bei ihnen nicht von einer transnationalen Handlungsorientierung reden kann. Ihr Kampf war in der Hauptsache bezogen auf den 'eigenen' Staat, von dem sie Rechte und Hilfe einforderten. Ihre Organisationsform wurde ebenfalls zu einer nationalen, so daß ihr Handeln kaum jemals die Staatsgrenzen überschritt (Mann 1988: 154 ff).

Charles Tilly hat in diesem Zusammenhang auf die wichtigen psychologischen Konsequenzen einer staatlichen Gewährung von Rechten aufmerksam gemacht: Politische Rechte werden von der Bevölkerung oft nicht nur als abstrakte Möglichkeiten erfahren, sondern die Gewährleistung von Rechten bindet bestimmte Bevölkerungsgruppen auch emotional an staatliche Instanzen, so daß sich auch damit die oftmals enge Einbindung von Klassen in den jeweiligen nationalen Staat erklären läßt (Tilly 1975: 36 f).

Zusammenfassend läßt sich also sagen, daß sich aus der kapitalistischen Produktionsweise kein transnationales Produktionssystem ableiten läßt, da sich der Kapitalismus als ökonomisches System innerhalb sich verfestigender politischer Einheiten entwickelt hatte, also national segmentiert war. Dementsprechend konnten auch kollektive Handlungsorientierungen die nationalen Grenzen kaum transzendieren. Dies galt auch für das Proletariat.

Sicherlich wäre es unvollständig, wenn man versuchen wollte, das Phänomen des Nationalismus allein aus den zweckrationalen Orientierungen bestimmter Klassen, aus ihrer Stellung innerhalb der Ökonomie herzuleiten. Doch Michael Manns Analysen mahnen jedenfalls zur Vorsicht gegenüber vorschnellen Verdammungsurteilen gegenüber nationalistischen Bewegungen und ihrer vermeintlichen Irrationalität. Der Internationalismus ist jedenfalls – das kann Mann zeigen – nicht das „normale" Phänomen, gegenüber dem Abweichungen nur als pathologische Formen erscheinen dürften.

4. Staatliche Macht und Demokratie

Untersuchungen, die den modernen Nationalstaat in den Mittelpunkt stellen, können natürlich nicht umhin, auch das Thema Demokratie zu behandeln. Die atlantischen Revolutionen des 17. und 18. Jahrhunderts waren sicherlich *auch* Reaktionen auf staatsbildende Prozesse, und die durch diese Revolutionen verbreitete Idee der Selbstregierung und Demokratie hatte dann Auswirkungen auf die Staatsbildung in anderen Regionen der Welt.

Auch die drei hier vorgestellten Autoren analysieren das Verhältnis von Nationalstaat und Demokratie. Auf die von ihnen hervorgehobenen innergesellschaftlichen Auswirkungen von Krieg und staatlicher Konkurrenz wurde schon mehrfach hingewiesen. Ein bestimmter Aspekt davon soll jedoch nochmals kurz erläutert werden, weil an ihm eine grundsätzliche Schwäche ihrer Ansätze deutlich wird: die Vernachlässigung kultureller Faktoren.

John Halls Konzept des „organischen Staates", der so nur im politisch fragmentierten Okzident entstanden sei, verweist ja auf den möglichen Zusammenhang von Krieg und Demokratie im weitesten Sinn: Die Fürsten und Monarchen im politisch zersplitterten Europa waren gezwungen, bestimmte Rechte und Freiräume den ökonomisch potenten Klassen zu gewähren, weil diese das für die militärische Wettbewerbsfähigkeit so dringend benötigte Steueraufkommen lieferten.

Auch Giddens legt diesem Argument gerade für die Zeit des 19. und 20. Jahrhunderts große Bedeutung bei. Die Tatsache, daß seit dieser Epoche der

Krieg mit allen verfügbaren Mitteln geführt wurde, stärkte diejenigen, die bisher von der Politik eher vernachlässigt wurden: Denjenigen, die man an den Fronten verheizte – und das war ein Großteil der männlichen Arbeiterklasse – und den Frauen, die die heimische Produktion aufrechterhalten hatten, mußte man zumindest formale Mitbestimmungsrechte einräumen. Das allgemeine Wahlrecht war in verschiedenen europäischen Staaten zum Teil auch ein Ergebnis des Ersten Weltkrieges.

Diese durch den Krieg beschleunigte Wahlrechtsausdehnung ist für Giddens letztlich nur der Endpunkt einer Entwicklung, die er mit dem Begriff der „Dialektik der Kontrolle" erfassen will. Der sich über Jahrhunderte hinziehende Ausbau staatlicher Macht ließ sich erfolgreich letztlich nur durch eine Mobilisierung der Bevölkerung erreichen. Die Angewiesenheit der Machthaber auf die bis dato Unterdrückten gab letzteren gewisse Machtmittel in die Hand, die sie erfolgreich ausspielen konnten. Die Folge war ein Prozeß funktionaler Demokratisierung, durch den die Machtgewichte in der gesellschaftlichen Pyramide nach unten verschoben wurden.

Diesen Mechanismus haben Giddens und Hall im Sinn, wenn sie auf den Zusammenhang zwischen staatlicher Konkurrenz und Demokratisierung verweisen. Demokratie ist deshalb z. B. für Giddens auch kein ursprüngliches, nicht weiter reduzierbares Merkmal der Moderne. Damit steht er im Gegensatz zu Ferenc Feher und Agnes Heller (1983), die von drei Strukturmerkmalen der Moderne – Kapitalismus, Industrialismus und Demokratie – sprechen und damit schärfer als Giddens die Prägekraft und Originalität demokratischer Ideen und Strukturen betonen. Für Giddens dagegen läßt sich Demokratie aus der Konkurrenz der Nationalstaaten ableiten, aus der enorm gesteigerten Macht des Staates, der die soziale Mobilisierung der Massen mit demokratischen Rechten gleichsam abgelten muß. Die Angewiesenheit der Machthaber war (und ist) für die benachteiligten Klassen ein Mittel, ihre Einflußsphäre und ihre Interessen zu erweitern, also etwa Bürgerrechte durchzusetzen.

Hinsichtlich dieser Thematik bieten sich nun einige Fragen bzw. Bemerkungen an.

Natürlich ist es richtig, daß der Staat und die mit ihm verbundenen Phänomene gerade auch vor dem Hintergrund von aktuellen Nationalstaatsbildungen etwa in Ost- und Südosteuropa in die gesellschaftstheoretische Diskussion zurückgebracht werden müssen. Aber gleichzeitig ist zu berücksichtigen, daß aufgrund des Bestehens übernationaler Organisationen wie der UNO oder der EG vom klassischen Konzept des souveränen Staates nicht mehr ohne weiteres ausgegangen werden kann – wie dies ja auch Giddens in einigen Passagen von „Nation-State and Violence" zugesteht und diskutiert. Im Hinblick auf entstehende militärische Spannungen, aber auch im Hinblick auf Demokratisierungsprozesse etwa wird man in Zukunft womöglich stärker die Rolle der UNO berücksichtigen müssen.

Auch innerhalb des Bereiches der EG ist natürlich die demokratische

Frage nicht gelöst, und es bleibt abzuwarten, welche Konfliktlinien sich hinsichtlich dieser Thematik herausbilden werden. Falls sich z. B. die bisherige Entwicklung einer zunehmenden Kompetenzverlagerung nach Brüssel fortsetzt, wird zu untersuchen sein, inwieweit die v.a. von Giddens behauptete „Dialektik der Kontrolle" auch dann noch Geltung beanspruchen kann. Ist nicht mehr der Nationalstaat, sondern eine übernationale Bürokratie hauptsächlicher Adressat der Forderungen von Interessengruppen und Klassen, wird sich zeigen müssen, ob es zu transnationalen Bündnissen zwischen Gruppierungen kommt, die etwa in der Lage wären, einen Abbau sozialer Rechte oder eine Lockerung von Umweltschutzvorschriften durch diese Bürokratie zu verhindern oder gar neue Rechte von ihr einzufordern. Das Kräftefeld wird durch das Wirken transnationaler Organisationen wahrscheinlich noch komplexer, und man wird sehen, welche Akteure sich darin am besten und am schnellsten zurechtfinden. Dieser Punkt ist von den drei Autoren bisher jeweils nur kurz andiskutiert woroden, verdient aber sicherlich eine größere Aufmerksamkeit.

Das Problem funktionaler Demokratisierung, einer „Dialektik der Kontrolle" läßt sich aber noch grundsätzlicher hinterfragen, nicht nur in bezug auf die sich in bestimmten Regionen abzeichnenden Souveränitätsverluste von Nationalstaaten. Spätestens hier ergeben sich dann einige Fragen bezüglich der Vollständigkeit des Bildes der Moderne, das uns Hall, Mann und Giddens zeichnen. Denn in ihrer starken Konzentration auf staatlichadministrative Vorgänge versäumen sie es, auch zu einer angemessenen Berücksichtigung kultureller Momente bei der Genese der Moderne zu gelangen. Ein kurzer Blick auf die Auseinandersetzungen um das Habermassche Theoriengebäude soll dies verdeutlichen:

Johann P. Arnason hatte in der Diskussion über die „Theorie des kommunikativen Handelns" kritisch angemerkt, daß darin die Eigengesetzlichkeit des modernen Staates unterschätzt werde. Indem Habermas die politische Modernisierung mit dem frühbürgerlichen Staat anfangen lasse, der sich mit zunehmender Verrechtlichung entwickelt hatte, blende er Gegentendenzen zum Projekt der Demokratie aus. Diese gegenläufigen Tendenzen hätten im absolutistischen Staat ihren Ausgangspunkt, und sie ließen sich mit Stichworten wie Bürokratisierung, Verselbständigung einer normfreien Staatsraison etc. umreißen (Arnason 1986: 293 ff).

Der genau entgegengesetzte Einwand läßt sich nun gegen die Ansätze von Hall, Mann und Giddens vorbringen. Akzeptiert man nämlich den Befund einer zunehmenden Einbindung der Klassen in den Staat – ein Einbindungsprozeß, der funktionalen Erfordernissen eben dieses modernen Staates entsprechen soll –, so wird man unweigerlich auf die Frage stoßen, welche Faktoren denn für die in den jeweiligen Ländern so unterschiedlich verlaufende und sich ausgestaltende „Demokratisierung" verantwortlich sind. Die Integration der Bevölkerung – um hier die Perspektive der staatlichen Machtträger einzunehmen – kann ja bekanntlich innerhalb eines recht breiten

Spektrums verlaufen, das von Modellen aktiver Partizipation und Selbstbestimmung des „Volkes" bis hin zur ideologischen Mobilisierung „von oben" reicht.

Es stellt sich deshalb die Frage, ob man zur Erklärung dieser Unterschiede nicht *auch* bestimmte kulturelle Traditionen heranziehen muß – eine Frage, die von den drei genannten Autoren kaum ernsthaft angegangen wurde, für deren Beantwortung der bloße Verweis auf Mechanismen funktionaler Demokratisierung auch zu unspezifisch ist.

Sucht man Erklärungen dafür, daß die Idee der Demokratie gerade *in Europa* ihren Ausgangspunkt nahm, so wäre etwa auf die Übernahme und Transformation der Philosophie und Ordnungsvorstellungen antiker Autoren oder auf die im jüdischchristlichen Kulturkreis existente Idee eines Vertrages zwischen Gott und den Gläubigen zu verweisen (Turner 1986). Ein solches kulturelles Erbe erleichterte sicherlich nicht unwesentlich die Verwirklichung der Idee eines mit Rechten ausgestatteten Bürgers und kann *auch* erklären, warum Demokratisierungsprozesse außerhalb des europäischen Kulturkreises auf so große Hindernisse stießen und noch immer stoßen.

So notwendig die längst fällige Behandlung des Wirkens staatlicher Strukturen innerhalb der Soziologie ist, so wenig darf man andere Phänomene darüber vernachlässigen: „Bringing the State *and* Culture Back In" – so müßte also die Parole lauten, wollte man zu einem angemessenen Verständnis der Moderne gelangen.

Noten

1. Die Debatte wurde vor allem durch Theda Skocpols „States and Social Revolutions" (1979) angestoßen, auch wenn vorher schon einige wichtige Arbeiten zum Staatskonzept entstanden waren (vlg. insbesondere Nettl 1968, Poggi 1978 oder Stepan 1978). Skocpols Analysen zu den Revolutionen in Frankreich, Rußland und China konnten deutlich machen, daß ohne eine Berücksichtigung der bedeutenden Rolle vorrevolutionärer Staatsapparate weder Ausbruch, Verlauf noch Ergebnis der untersuchten Revolutionen erklärt werden können. Skocpol verallgemeinerte diese Einsicht und plädierte dann auch ganz grundsätzlich für eine gesellschaftstheoretische Nutzbarmachung des Staatskonzeptes. An die Skocpolsche Arbeit schlossen sich eine Reihe weiterer Veröffentlichungen an, die die Autonomie des Staates in den Mittelpunkt stellten und von denen einige hier genannt seien: Nordlinger 1981; Skowronek 1982; Evans/Rueschemeyer/Skocpol (Hg.) 1985.

2. Zwar haben Theoretiker des Imperialismus, die Totalitarismusforschung und Einzelfiguren wie Raymond Aron immer wieder Teilbereiche aus diesem Themenkomplex aufgegriffen, doch im großen und ganzen kann man wohl sagen, daß der Nationalstaat nie im Zentrum soziologischer Analysen und Debatten stand.

3. Dieses Einklinken in öffentliche Debatten sollte nun freilich nicht mittels „journalistischer Schnellschüsse" erfolgen, wie dies etwa gegenüber Karl Otto Hondrichs „Lehrmeister Krieg" (1992) einzuwenden wäre (vlg. dazu die Kritik von Joas 1992).

4. Hall faßt den militärischen und politischen Bereich zusammen, unterscheidet

also nur zwischen drei Machtnetzwerken. Sein theoretischer Ansatz ist ansonsten mit dem von M. Mann identisch.

5. Ein ähnlich breit angelegter, vergleichender Versuch, den Aufstieg Europas zur Weltherrschaft zu erklären, findet sich z. B. auch bei Eric L. Jones (1981; dtsch. 1991), der jedoch wesentlich stärker als Hall und Mann auch die ökologischen Besonderheiten Europas hervorhebt. Weitere Argumente zu dieser Thematik finden sich etwa bei Chirot 1985 oder Collins 1986.

6. Halls Argumentation klammert hier das Herrschaftsgebiet des osmanischen Reiches aus.

7. Vgl. Hintze 1962: „Die Kirche hatte sehr gewichtige Gründe, der Sippenverfassung entgegenzutreten. Denn erstens wurzelte in ihr mit der Ahnenverehrung der Rest des Heidentums. Zweitens hielt sie an der Blutrache fest oder handhabe das Bußensystem, das an deren Stelle trat, in einer ganz unrationalen, dem Geist des kirchlichen Rechts widerstreitenden Weise. Drittens besaß sie die ausschließliche Kontrolle des Familienrechts, das die Kirche selbst zu beherrschen trachtete, und konservierte vor allem auch das Gesamteigentum der Sippe unter Ausschluß der Testierfreiheit, die für die Kirche wegen der Zuwendungen an geistliche Stifter von allergrößtem Interesse war." (172) Zum deutschen Sozialhistoriker Otto Hintze (1861–1940) ist anzumerken, daß er in der deutschen Soziologie nur wenig rezipiert wurde. Im anglo-amerikanischen Raum hingegen erfuhr er spätestens seit Theda Skocpols „States and Social Revolutions" (1979), das sich stark auf Hintzes theoretische Einsichten bezogen hatte, vermehrte Beachtung. Seine brillanten Betrachtungen zu militärisch-politischen Konstellationen unter Einbeziehung auch soziologischer Konzepte machen ihn natürlich vor allem für jene Soziologen interessant, die sich um eine verstärkte Thematisierung des Staates bemühten.

Literatur

Almond, G.A. 1988: The Return to the State. American Political Science Review 82: 853–874.

Arnason, J.P., 1986: Die Moderne als Projekt und Spannungsfeld. S. 278–327 in: A. Honneth/H. Joas (Hrsg.), Kommunikatives Handeln. Beiträge zu Jürgen Habermas' „Theorie des Kommunikativen Handelns", Frankfurt/Main: Suhrkamp.

Chirot, D., 1985: The Rise of the West. American Sociological Review 50: 181–195.

Collins, R., 1986: Weberian Sociological Theory, Cambridge: Cambridge UP.

Evans, P.B./Rueschemeyer, D./Skocpol, T. (Hrsg.), 1985: Bringing the State Back In, New York: Cambridge University Press.

Feher, F./Heller, A., 1983: Class, Democracy, Modernity. Theory and Society 12: 211–244.

Giddens, A., 1984: Interpretative Soziologie. Eine kritische Einführung, Frankfurt/ New York: Campus.

Giddens, A., 1988: Die Konstitution der Gesellschaft. Grundzüge einer Theorie der Strukturierung, Frankfurt/New York: Campus.

Giddens, A., 1985: The Nation-State and Violence. Volume Two of A Contemporary Critique of Historical Materialism, Cambridge: Polity Press.

Hall, J.A., 1985: Religion and the Rise of Capitalism. Archives Européennes de Sociologie 26: 193–23.

Hall, J.A., 1986: Powers and Liberties. The Causes and Consequences of the Rise of the West, Berkeley/Los Angeles: University of California Press.

Hintze, O., 1965²: Weltgeschichtliche Bedingungen der Repräsentivverfassung. S. 140–185 in: O. Hintze, Staat und Verfassung, Göttingen: Vandenhoeck & Ruprecht.

Hondrich, K.O., 1992: Lehrmeister Krieg, Reinbek: rororo.

Joas, H., 1992: Lehrmeister Krieg? Kölner Zeitschrift für Soziologie und Sozialpsychologie 44: 538–543.

Jones, E.L., 1991: Das Wunder Europa. Umwelt, Wirtschaft und Geopolitik in der Geschichte Europas und Asiens, Tübingen: J.C.B. Mohr.

Mann, M., 1990: Geschichte der Macht. Erster Band: Von den Anfängen bis zur griechischen Antike, Frankfurt/New York: Campus.

Mann, M., 1991: Geschichte der Macht. Zweiter Band: Vom Römischen Reich bis zum Vorabend der Industrialisierung, Frankfurt/New York: Campus.

Mann, M., 1988: States, War and Capitalism. Studies in Political Sociology, Oxford: Basil Blackwell.

Moore, B., 1987: Soziale Ursprünge von Diktatur und Demokratie. Die Rolle der Grundbesitzer und Bauern bei der Entstehung der modernen Welt, Frankfurt/Main: Suhrkamp.

Nettl, P., 1968: The State as a Conceptual Variable. World Politics 20: 559–592.

Nordlinger, E.A., 1981: On the Autonomy of the Democratic State, Cambridge, Mass.: Harvard UP.

Poggi, G., 1978: The Development of the Modern State. A Sociological Introduction, Stanford: University of California Press.

Rueschemeyer, D./Stephens, E.H./Stephens, J.D., 1992: Capitalist Development and Democracy, Cambridge: Polity Press.

Schröder, H., 1977: Die neuere englische Geschichte im Lichte einiger Modernisierungstheoreme. S. 30–65 in: R. Koselleck (Hrsg.), Studien zum Beginn der modernen Welt, Stuttgart: Klett-Cotta.

Skocpol, T., 1979: States and Social Revolutions. A Comparative Analysis of France, Russia and China, Cambridge/New York: Cambridge University Press.

Skowronek, S., 1982: Building a New American State. The Expansion of National Administrative Capacities. 1877–1920, Cambridge et al.: Cambridge UP.

Stepan, A., 1978: The State and Society. Peru in Comparative Perspective, Princeton: Princeton UP.

Tenbruck, F.H., 1989: Gesellschaftsgeschichte oder Weltgeschichte?. Kölner Zeitschrift für Soziologie und Sozialpsychologie 41: 417–439.

Tilly, C., 1975: Reflections on the History of European State-Making. S. 3–83 in: C. Tilly (Hrsg.), The Formation of National States in Western Europe, Princeton: Princeton University Press.

Tilly, C., 1990: Coercion, Capital, and European States, AD 990–1990, Cambridge, Mass.: Basil Blackwell.

Tiryakian, E. A., 1991: Modernisation: Exhumetur in Pace (Rethinking Macrosociology in the 1990s). International Sociology 6: 165–180.

Touraine, A., 1981: Une sociologie sans société. Revue français de Sociologie 22: 3–13.

Turner, B., 1986: Citizenship and Capitalism. The Debate over Reformism, London: Allen & Unwin.

Wallerstein, I., 1985: Gesellschaftliche Entwicklung oder Entwicklung des Weltsystems. S.76–90 in: Soziologie und gesellschaftliche Entwicklung. Verhandlungen des 22. Deutschen Soziologentages in Dortmund. Frankfurt/New York: Campus.

Weber, M., 1985: Wirtschaft und Gesellschaft. Grundriß der verstehenden Soziologie, Tübingen: J.C.B. Mohr.

Weber, M., 1988: Gesammelte Aufsätze zur Religionssoziologie I, Tübingen: J.C.B. Mohr.

68

There Is No Such Thing As Society: Beyond Individualism and Statism in International Security Studies*

M. Shaw

*Source: *Review of International Studies*, vol. 19, 1993, pp. 159–75.

This article offers a sociological perspective on a major conceptual issue in international relations, the question of 'security', and it raises major issues to do with the role of sociological concepts in international studies. For some years now, the work of sociological writers such as Skocpol, Giddens and Mann[1] has attracted some interest in international studies. International theorists such as Linklater and Halliday[2] have seen their work as offering a theoretical advance both on realism and on Marxist alternatives. At the same time, these developments have involved the paradox that, as one critic puts it, 'current sociological theories of the state are increasingly approaching a more traditional view of the state – the state as actor model – precisely at a time when the theory of international relations is getting away from this idea and taking a more sociological form.'[3] Indeed, we can go further, and suggest – as I have argued elsewhere – that the work of Giddens and Mann, in trying to reinstate military issues in sociology, has effectively produced new theoretical supports for a realist view of the international system.[4]

This paper, in contrast, shares the assumption of many in international studies that, far from reinforcing traditional international relations concepts, it is necessary to subject them to sustained criticism. Within international political theory, one of the most fundamental signs of rethinking has been a reworking of the concept of 'security'. As Ken Booth has put it, 'The last decade or so has seen a growing unease with the traditional concept of security, which privileges the state and emphasizes military power' together with 'a frequent call for the "broadening" or "updating" of the concept of security'.[5] The end of the Cold War has undoubtedly greatly reinforced the critical tendencies, so that it is now possible to discuss West European security, for example, in largely (but, alas, not wholly) non-military terms, with reference to non-violence, democracy and human rights, population movements, economic relations and environmental issues.[6]

One of the first texts in international studies to argue comprehensively for this wider view of security was Barry Buzan's *People, States and Fear*.[7] For many, as Smith notes, 'the book marked a real breakthrough in the literature, broadening and deepening the concept of security in a way that opened up the whole subject area as never before'.[8] For Booth, it is still 'the most comprehensive analysis of the concept in international relations literature to date'.[9]

Despite this praise, both these writers oppose Buzan on the definition of security. Booth asserts that *People, States and Fear* 'can primarily be read as an explanation of the difficulties surrounding the concept. The book not only argues that security is an "essentially contested concept" defying pursuit of an agreed definition, but asserts that there is not much point struggling to make it uncontested.' Such a conclusion, Booth argues correctly, is 'unsatisfying': 'If we cannot name it, how can we hope to achieve it?'[10] Insofar as Buzan does commit himself, both Booth and Smith see him as over-privileging the state, and propose instead an *individual*-centred focus for security studies. In this paper, it is argued that while security is indeed something which appertains to individual human beings rather than states, it is mediated not just by inter-state relations but by the whole complex of social relations in which they are involved.

It is argued therefore that a critical *sociological* approach to understanding the concept of security can help to illuminate the debate which is developing within international studies. I proceed in three stages. The first part of the paper examines Buzan's discussion of security, developing a critique which demonstrates how, despite its undoubted broadening of the agenda of security studies, his work does indeed remain excessively state-bound. The second part discusses Booth's and Smith's critical comments on Buzan, and argues that they share with him a common sociological weakness which ultimately undermines the coherence of their conclusions on the crucial issue of state-*versus* individual-centred definitions of the concept. I argue that, despite the welcome extension of the *issue* agenda of security studies to include a wide range of non-military factors, its *conceptual* framework requires more radical revision than is provided by either side of this argument. What is needed is a *deepening* as well as a *broadening* of the agenda. The concept of 'social relations' (or 'society') needs to be interposed between and around the terms 'state' and 'individual' within which the debate has been conducted. Thirdly, I examine recent work by Giddens on risk and security, which suggests the nature and relevance of a sociological approach, although it does not refer to specifically international issues. Finally, I try to make the connections between this sociology and the international security studies debate, and suggest the basis on which a more adequate theoretical resolution can be achieved.

A Statist Conception of Security Studies

I begin by examining the conception of security which is offered by Buzan. I shall concentrate to a large extent on the more general issues of the meaning and referents of security, and the role of the state, which in Buzan occupy the first three chapters. I shall try to show that the broadened concept of security which he offers is still fundamentally a statist one, which suffers from central contradictions in its understanding of the state/society relationship, and is in this sense sociologically inadequate.

People, States and Fear starts from the assumption that there are three levels of security, 'individual', 'national' and 'international', and notes that concepts of 'national' security have tended to organize the other two levels (p. 1). (This is true enough within the international relations literature; but there are many other fields within the social sciences in which the concept of security is used primarily to refer to the individual or other sub-state levels: I shall return to the implications of this below.) Buzan further notes the historic 'militarization' of the concept to which this pattern generally gave rise, and the growing criticism of this notion of security 'bound to the level of individual states and military issues', which as Buzan points out is 'inherently inadequate' (p. 5). This criticism within international relations resulted, however, according to Buzan's account, more in an emphasis on the interdependence of international security relations – and thus in a resort to the 'international' level – as in a turning to the level of 'individual' security (p. 13).

Buzan uses the term 'the security of human collectivities', but viewing things from the standpoint of the international system, he assumes that one particular sort of institution is 'the standard unity of security'. This institution is 'the sovereign territorial state'. It seems Buzan regards the state as itself as a type of 'collectivity', but the state is also an institution linked to another basic type of collectivity, the nation. Ideally, however, these two go together. 'The ideal type is the nation-state, where ethnic and cultural boundaries line up with political ones ... But since nation and states do not fit neatly together in many places, non-state collectivities, particularly nations, are also an important unit of analysis' (p. 19).

This analysis leaves us with two crucial problems which are inadequately resolved, if at all. An absolutely critical issue, but one which amazingly is not clearly tackled, is whether 'national security' refers primarily to the nation or to the state; ideally, of course, these are symbiotically linked, but what happens where they are not? To continue to use the language of 'national' security implies, if it reflects more than terminological inexactness or conservatism, a preference for nations. Buzan recognizes this in writing that 'National security implies strongly that the object of security is the nation ...' (p. 70).

A difficulty of this line of argument is that it places a large onus on the concept of 'nation': however, Buzan, like most international theorists, barely defines the term, which does not even figure in his index. Certainly 'nation' is difficult, arguably much more so than state, but that very fact places a greater responsibility on the theorist – if he wishes to make 'nation' so central – to achieve at least some working definition, or explain, like Mayall, why he does not impose a single definition.[11]

In any case, Buzan's position is that 'the standard unit of security is ... the sovereign territorial state' and so ultimately he abandons a consistently national concept. He argues, indeed, that '*national* security in the strict sense is a concept with only limited application to the state' (p. 71).

Although Buzan examines some of the complexity of state–nation relationships (pp. 70–8), he does not resolve the lack of conceptual clarity on the nation long characteristic of international relations theory.[12] One could argue that a serious attempt to tackle this issue cannot really be achieved without an exploration of society and culture, but these are fields which Buzan does not enter. The sociological literature would lead us to see nations as cultural–ideological–political constructs – 'imagined communities' in Anderson's term[13] – rather than 'real' social collectivities in some prior objective sense (although one should not doubt the reality of culture, ideology, or politics). In this context, the relation between nation and state is intrinsically, rather than contingently, contradictory and problematic, so that any attempt to build a concept of security on its shifting sands is brought very severely into question.

The more fundamental problem which is revealed is that of the nature of human collectivities in general. Buzan's formulation certainly admits of the possibility that there may be other types of human collectivity than the nation-state/nation/ethnic group, to which security issues may be attached. No other type is actually indicated, however, in his discussion. A reference to 'ethno-cultural units', coupled with a definition of 'societal security' in terms of the sustainability of 'traditional patterns of language, culture and religious and national identity and custom' (p. 19), suggests that the only sorts of 'human collectivities' which are being admitted to theoretically significant status are those which approximate the basis for a nation-state. Those formed on axes other than ethnicity/nationality – on gender, class, community or lifestyle lines, for example – are not in practice considered relevant, although it may be argued that they are just as capable of generating 'security' concerns. Again, there is a good deal to suggest that while *formally* flexible, the conception is in practice tied closely to state-centred definitions of 'national' security.

Buzan stresses that his definition of the field of 'international security studies' is intended to leave it broader than that of 'strategic studies', seen as more narrowly tied to military power. He lists five major factors in 'the security of human collectives', military, political, economic, societal (as defined above) and environmental. However, it is clear from the above that broadening the *issue*-agenda of security studies from the military-strategic dimension does not necessarily involve broadening the *conceptual* base. The recognition of additional dimensions of security – however welcome this may be – may be an *ad hoc* enlargement of a still state-centred concept of security.

This critique may sound paradoxical, in view of Buzan's explicit contention that 'security has many potential referent objects' and that to identify security with the state ignores the 'amorphous multi-faceted' nature of the state as a 'collective object', and the multiplicity of states which means that 'the security of one cannot be discussed without reference to the others' (p. 26). It is not clear, however, that these statements function as anything more than *caveats* to a state-centred notion of security; complex qualifications which in the end preserve the integrity of the project more or less intact. What in the end inclines me to this view is that by defining the issue of security in terms of three levels, of which 'individuals' are the only sub-national/state level, Buzan has effectively ruled out any referents other than states or quasi-state collectivities as a serious basis for security studies.

Buzan's discussion of individual security opens with the statement that 'The idea of security is easier to apply to things than to people' (p. 35). This is curious because the things in question (money, material goods) only have meaning in relation to the people who own or use them. Their 'security' really means (as Buzan states in parentheses) 'their owners' security in possession of them'. In this sense we cannot talk at all of the 'security of things' as opposed to the 'security of individuals'.

Buzan seems to be trying to ascribe to individual security a particularly nebulous character when he writes that

> Different aspects of individual security are frequently contradictory (protection from crime versus erosion of civil liberties) and plagued by the difficulty of distinguishing between objective and subjective evaluation. Cause–effect relationships with regard to threats are often obscure and controversial (individual versus social explanations for crime). (p. 36)

Each of these statements is at least equally true, however, of 'national security' – indeed, as we have seen, it is not possible to determine at a theoretical level, within Buzan's text, exactly what is the 'referent' of national security (nation, state, or nation-state). This is a difficulty which we do not have in quite the same way with individual security.

Individual security seems to be important for Buzan principally in that it provides a basis for national security. Freedom for one individual, in a predictably Hobbesian scenario, may be an actual or potential threat to the security of others, and the problem is how to balance freedom and security. The state is justified as an instrument for achieving this balance, and thus national security can be seen, to some extent, as individual security writ large: 'The security of individuals is inseparably entangled with that of the state'

(p. 39). 'State and society become increasingly indistinguishable,' adds Buzan (p. 39), in a phrase which recalls – and compounds – the conceptual confusion over nation and state which we noted earlier.

Buzan recognizes the possible contradictions between the requirements of state and individual security, when 'the state becomes a major source of threat to its citizens' (p. 39), but he loses this point in a discussion about the 'maximalist' and 'minimalist' views of the state, defined as seeing the state as, respectively, greater than the sum of its (individual) parts, and reducible to those parts. The issue is muddled still further by an attempt to distinguish between different states as 'maximal' or 'minimal' (in which it seems to be suggested that it is principally 'maximal' states which threaten their citizens). This argument is confusing because 'maximalist' and 'minimalist' views are surely concepts of the state in general, their validity not related to whether we can distinguish between different types of state.

This whole debate suffers from the misplaced abstraction which bedevils political theory, according to which individuals are conceived, not within the context of their social relations in general, but as members of a particular institution, the nation-state;[14] and conversely, states are conceived not as the conglomerates of institutions which they really are, embedded in complex social relations, but as constructed on the basis of a notional contract with individual citizens.

Nevertheless, Buzan proceeds to provide us with a useful summary of the ways in which, even in democratic states, 'The individual citizen faces many threats which emanate directly or indirectly from the state' (p. 44). And he argues that

> just as there is a very mixed set of costs and benefits to individual security in relation to the state's civil order functions, so is there for its external security functions. The state is supposed to provide a measure of protection to its citizens from foreign interference, attack and invasion. But it cannot do so without imposing risks and costs on them ... While the principle may be firmly rooted, however the practice which develops around it can easily become an intense source of dispute on the grounds of individual versus national security ... Modern war is known to produce high risks and high casualties, and this makes decisions about what constitutes a threat to the security of the state a matter of considerable public concern. (p. 47)

Nuclear weapons obviously raise this contradiction in a particularly acute form, as Buzan shows.

This presentation of the conflicting requirements of individual and state security does not prevent Buzan from according them different theoretical priorities. He concludes that 'individual security ... is essentially subordinate to the higher-level political structures of the state and international system', and that 'Because this is so, national and international security cannot be reduced to individual security' (p. 54). Individuals are mainly to be considered because of the way in which, in pursuing their own security, they may influence the higher levels of national or international security.

It is in discussing national security and the state as such that Buzan most clearly makes explicit the issues which have been troubling us so far. He starts from the premise that 'the state is composed of individuals bound together in a collective political unit' (p. 57), which reflects the normative conception of political theory, and dismisses the 'rather inward-looking perspectives of Political Science and Sociology' (p. 59). We may agree about 'inward-lookingness', if by that is meant the tendency to define the state principally in relation to the social structure *within* the territory of the state. (It should be noted, however, that this is precisely what recent sociological theorists have rejected.)

There is, however, a much more fundamental issue, expressed by Buzan in references to what he calls 'the definition of the state in Weberian terms, where state and society are viewed as separate phenomena, and the state is seen almost entirely in politico-institutional terms'; and to how such 'narrow' definitions are reinforced by 'Marxian thinking, which also stresses the separation of government and society'. 'Although this perspective has its uses', Buzan concludes, 'it is much too narrow to serve as a basis for thinking about security ... The reduction of "state" to mean simply the institutions of central government does not work at the international level' (pp. 59–60).

I had to stop myself from putting 'sic' after that use of the word 'narrow' in the last quotation. While I suppose that a view that defines the state as distinct from society can be described as a 'narrow' view of the state – in that it does not incorporate the whole of society into the concept of state – the opposite view, which Buzan advances, is certainly a very narrow view of society – it refuses to acknowledge autonomous social relations as a factor in international relations distinct from the state and incorporates society into international theory only as an adjunct of the state.

It is not only Weberians, or Marxists, but sociologists in general who cannot but protest at this mind-boggling denial of the significance of *social relations in general*. There is a fundamental conceptual and historical point at issue here. Human beings entered into social relations of various kinds before they began to develop states. States are only one kind of human institution. The relations between states and societies have undergone immense change throughout human history and are continuing to do so. The semi-identity between nation-states and national societies which has characterized the twentieth century is historically novel, currently problematic, and is not likely to survive in the form which is assumed by much international theory. From the point of view of sociology, to object to an analytical separation of state and society is to deny oneself the tools with which to analyse the role of states in the modern world.

In this discussion we are using 'society' as a term to refer to the concept of social relations in general, rather than in the sense of a fixed unit of social organization. Although it may be the case that in the past there have been such units, which have existed in complete or near-complete isolation from each other, it is clear that in the modern world this is no longer the case. If we wish to talk of 'a' society, we can probably do this only at a global level. 'Societies' in the sense of tribal, ethnic, national or state-bound units are no more than reflections of attempts to partially, and more or less arbitrarily, define the separateness of certain groups within the global flux of social relations. While this sort of usage may be acceptable (even unavoidable) as a shorthand way of describing social realities, it is ultimately of limited theoretical value. It is not such usage which is referred to here, but 'society' in the sense of social relations in general.

Buzan lacks such a general concept of society; indeed if he has a concept of society, it is clearly of societies as the domestic fields of states, i.e., of state-bound segments of social relations. This enters into the argument as a critique of 'the traditional International Relations view of the state as a political–territorial billiard ball' as 'also too restrictive'. He states that 'Security issues within an international anarchy are highly conditioned not only by the structure of the system and by the interactions of states, but also by the domestic characteristics of states. Consequently, security analysis requires a comprehensive definition of the state which combines both of these perspectives' (p. 60).

So far so good, but the levels of society cannot be reduced to their influence on the 'domestic characteristics of states', i.e., admitted to the discussion only as an appendage to the level of states on which the discussion is focused. The unity of state and society is precisely what cannot and should not be assumed in any discussion of the state or of international relations.

Buzan clearly regards his distinction of 'strong' and 'weak' states (pp. 96–107), from which he draws major conclusions for security, as a manifestation of this recognition of society.[15] As a classification of states, it obviously has considerable value: strong states, with greater socio-political cohesion, are more capable of providing certain sorts of security to society within their territories, while weak states, with poorer socio-political cohesion, are less capable. The analysis has been vindicated by the collapse of the Soviet Union, described as 'having serious weaknesses' as a state, even though a great power (p. 98): the resulting tensions have increased security for individuals and groups of all kinds in its former territory, at many levels.

Although this discussion suggests ways in which social organization may have consequences for state cohesion and security, it still considers society only as an aspect of state organization. This is, moreover, the highpoint of Buzan's discussion of the state and society. The difficulties for his approach of dealing with sociological concepts is demonstrated further by a curious discussion of the comparability of individual and state as 'objects' (not as actors), and 'referents' of security (pp. 62–3). At no point in this does Buzan show any recognition that his problem – the nature of a collective or institutional social form (or actor?) in contrast to an individual – is a general sociological problem which applies to human groups and institutions of all kinds, and not just to states.

Buzan's approach is, it appears, irredeemably state-centred. He certainly recognizes the complexities of the state, but he fails to locate it in an adequate sociological context. Because he counterposes only individuals to states, and because the only social groups which are genuinely admitted to his discussion are state-oriented collectivities (nations, ethnic groups), his concept of security prioritizes national (and by extension, international) over individual security, generates no general concept of 'social' security, and leaves us with a notion of security centred on the manifoldly problematic notion of 'national security'.

Although there are approaches within international relations which may not share the deficiencies of his approach, Buzan's work can clearly stand as largely typical. As Booth points out, there have been surprisingly few attempts to define 'security', and Buzan's approach has the important merits of attempting to unravel concepts which most writers simply assume. What is more, it can be suggested that even those who disagree with Buzan's conclusions share much of his conceptual approach. It is significant that even Booth's powerful 'emancipatory' plea falls largely under this stricture.

Individualism: An Inadequate Basis for Anti-Statism

Critics of Buzan's statism from within international studies have largely counterposed to it an 'individualist' perspective. For Smith, the question of 'security for whom' is highly problematic in Buzan's work:

> 'the worry persists that he sees states as ontologically prior to other candidates. As a result the state gets undertheorized and privileged.' The alternative is that 'there is a strong case for placing individuals, not states, at the centre of security studies, which would result in a rather different conceptual focus.'[16]

It is Booth who has most clearly developed the 'individualist' case against Buzan. He starts from the very important rejection of states as 'the primary referent objects of security'. He argues this on three grounds: that states 'are unreliable as primary referents because whereas some are in the business of security (internal and external) some are not'; that 'it is illogical to place states at the centre of our thinking about security because even those which are the producers of security ... represent the means and not the ends' (rather, he says, as a house is to its inhabitants: it is the latter's security which is primary); and because states are 'too diverse in character to serve as the basis for a comprehensive theory of security'.[17] Of these objections, clearly the second is foremost. Booth's rejection of *People, States and Fear* is based on the 'litmus test' of the primary referent: 'is it states, or is it people? Whose security comes first? I want to argue, following the World Society School, buttressed on this point by Hedley Bull, that individual humans are the ultimate referent.'[18]

Both the content and form of this argument are interesting. Booth poses the question in very much the same way as Buzan, individual *versus* state: the difference between them lies in the answer. Empirically, he gives some pointers to the relation of individuals and states by mentioning as examples of struggles for emancipation not only 'the struggle for freedom of the colonial world', but also 'women, youth, the proletariat, appetites of all sorts, homosexuals, consumers, and thought' (p. 321). No more, however, than Buzan does Booth offer, in his critique of the former, any concepts or levels of analysis to either *explain* the relationship between individual and state, or to stand *between* them. At the same time, it is noteworthy that Booth's secondary arguments, on the unreliability (from a security point of view) and diversity of states are points also made by Buzan and readily (for the most part) accommodated within his framework. It also seems significant that Booth buttresses his individualism only with references to theorists within international relations, rather than in wider philosophical or methodological terms.

There is, of course, a much larger debate on this issue, which concerns much more than the state and is central to the social sciences as a whole. The postulate of 'methodological individualism' – according to which it is assumed that individuals are the subjects of social action – was advanced by Weber,[19] in opposition to holistic and organicist sociologies. Buzan's discussion indicates that organic analogies between the human individual and the state are still troubling international relations, and indeed recent linguistic analysis of the concept of 'security' suggests the deeply organic roots of the literature.[20]

Individualism belongs, moreover, to a perspective in which social science is concerned not with 'objects' but with 'action'. Collective action, ascribed to social groups or to institutions, is ultimately to be understood in terms of, but not necessarily or immediately reduced to, the actions of individuals. In practice social scientists are very much concerned with social groups and institutions, but we need to be aware of the abstraction necessary to analyse social life in these terms, and avoid endowing these social forms with characteristics which can only belong to individuals.

The relevance of this argument to the present discussion is that it indicates not just that we *should* be concerned, as Booth argues, with individual above state security, but that even when we talk about state security, we are ultimately talking about an institution constructed by human beings and which involves individuals in many ways. We cannot, from a methodological point of view, simply assume the fiction of political theory according to which states represent their citizens in a general sense. We have to examine the particular connections which individual members of society (we cannot simply consider them as citizens) – both those involved in running the state and those 'outside' it – really have with the state.

In practice, again, this must involve additional levels of analysis. We cannot, as a matter of practical social knowledge, examine even the individual roles of all the members of a government – let alone of all those involved in the state machine, let alone of all those in society at large who have some relationship with the state. We are forced to make assumptions about social groupings of various kinds, through which individuals act, and which interpose between individuals and the state.

In this sense, when we discuss security, it is not just a question of the security of individuals *versus* that of the state, but of a complex, multi-layered analysis, in which the security of individuals may be a starting place, but in which we have to examine security issues which affect social groups (below the state level), as well as issues of state security; and in which we have to examine the roles of individuals in relation to group and state issues, and of social groups and states in relation to individual issues, as well as of states in relation to individual and group issues. And in reality even this conception is highly simplified, since I am using the term 'social groups' to cover an enormous range of ways in which individuals are involved in social relations.

All this discussion points to the fact that social relations (or 'society') is the missing dimension of the security debate. 'There is no such thing as society', Margaret Thatcher is reported to have said, and it seems as though international relations theorists, including some who would doubtless abhor her company, have fallen into a parallel theoretical trap. 'Society', however, is as we have indicated above best regarded as a codeword for the complex of *social relations in general*, which form the fundamental context of individual and state activity, rather than a fixed entity or even a level of analysis. There is indeed 'no such thing as society', if we mean by society a specific structure which determines all else: thus 'British society' and similar concepts denote (as we have indicated) not fixed realities but partial – and more or less useful – abstractions from the flux of social life. Society in the generic sense, of the social relations between human individuals which are represented in constantly changing ways in the range of social groups and institutions, is however not merely a but *the* reality within which alone it makes sense to look at the relations of institutions like states.[21]

In another recent work, Booth has himself advanced a more sociological view, in his proposal that the concept of 'communities' should be a guiding concept of a new, more human international relations. He outlines the prospect of a 'new medievalism' based on the replacement of the 'anarchical society' of states by a 'community of communities'.[22] This concept of community is an important step beyond the individualism of his critique of

Buzan. 'Community' functions, however, primarily as a normative rather than an analytical concept. Booth discusses some instances of community, such as the moral union of the French and German peoples which underlies the peace between them, and he mentions some principles, such as multi-culturality, but he does not give any systematic suggestions about how communities are (or are to be) formed, or enter (or should enter) into world politics.

The proposal of 'communities' raises, therefore, the same sociological questions: on the basis of which sorts of social relationships (on what 'social bases') are communities being, or to be, constructed? If communities are no longer constructed, in Buzan's quasi-realist terms, simply or mainly on the basis of nationality or ethnicity – and there is of course a lot of impressive evidence that these are still important axes – what are the social bases of inter- or supra-nationalism? Class, morality, culture? While it is possible and desirable for international and social theorists to identify with the 'human community' in general, the realization of Booth's goals depends on the construction of human *communities* based on specific social relations. We need a fuller working out of the suggestive examples of a 'utopian' approach. Here a more developed sociology, as advocated in this critique, is essential.

A Sociological Approach to the Problem of Security

If, as I have argued, it is essential to recast the very language in which 'security' is discussed in terms of sociological concepts, it is important to ask whether sociology (including related social sciences like social anthropology and social policy) has anything directly to offer in terms of this project. The answer, until recently, might have been that there are a number of empirical areas in which, contrary to Buzan, considerable advances – arguably at least as great as those of international relations – have been made in defining and even measuring risk and the concomitant requirements of security for individuals and social groups. One could instance not only criminology – which is an obvious parallel[23] – but also health, traffic and of course disaster studies, not to mention the very precise actuarial assessments of risk made by accountants for insurance purposes.

Until recently, however, there was little mainstream theoretical recognition of the problem of security. This has now been remedied, however, in two books by Anthony Giddens, which should be as required reading on security as his *Nation-State and Violence* has already become for thinking about the state. Giddens discusses security and risk in terms of a fundamental conceptualization of modern society, bringing the concepts to the centre of the discipline. He has a lot to say about the implications of globalization for security, but little specifically about 'international security'. In this discussion I shall attempt a brief exposition, followed by a conclusion in which I draw together the argument and attempt to make it relevant to security in an international relations context.

Giddens' argument was first elaborated, rather briefly, in an interconnected series of lectures published as *The Consequences of Modernity*.[24] In this he makes 'security versus danger and risk versus trust' major themes of his discussion. He sees modernity – the spread of modern social institutions based on abstract systems of knowledge – as double-edged: it has 'created vastly greater opportunities for human beings to enjoy a secure and rewarding existence than any pre-modern system', but it also has a 'sombre side' symbolized by war (p. 7).

Giddens links the concept of 'risk' closely with that of 'security', and he argues that the nature of risk has changed. There is a 'globalization of risk in the sense of intensity' (e.g., nuclear war) and in terms of 'the expanding number of contingent events which affect everyone or at least very large numbers of people on the planet' (e.g., changes in the global division of labour). New risks arise from the nature of modern social organization: there is risk 'stemming from the created environment, or socialized nature: the infusion of human knowledge into the material environment, and the development of 'institutionalized risk environments affecting the life-chances of millions' (e.g., investment markets). In addition, and very importantly, there is greater 'awareness of risk as risk', well distributed throughout society, and incapable of being converted into certainties by religious or magic ideas (pp. 157–8).

In the following work, *Modernity and Self-Identity*,[25] Giddens provides what could be described, in terms of Buzan's discussion, as a sociological text on the individual level of security. He argues that in conditions of modernity, individuals face not merely empirical threats of the kind noted by Buzan, but something much more fundamental. Daily life is forever reconstituted by the operation of a bewildering array of what Giddens calls 'abstract systems', knowledge-based patterns of social behaviour, coordinated through markets as well as bureaucracies, which govern the conditions of individual existence. The spread of these systems is global: 'In high modernity, the influence of distant happenings on proximate events, and on the intimacies of the self, becomes more and more commonplace' (p. 4). The security 'threat' which individuals face is, at bottom, the threat to their very identity from the ways in which abstract systems operate. The challenge to individuals is to construct and reconstruct their own identity, which is no longer given for them by traditional institutions and cultures.

Individual identities, faced with a great variety of competing and changing social contexts determined by these new realities, are constantly at risk. Giddens discusses the dangers of disruption of ontological security experienced, in consequence, by individuals in modern society (pp. 35–70), and the ways in which individuals can develop their own 'trajectories' through therapy, choice of lifestyle, and development of 'life plans' (pp. 71–88).

Giddens argues that 'The notion of risk is central in a society which is taking leave of the past, of traditional ways of doing things, and which is opening itself up to a problematic future' (p. 111). Control of risk is an essential part of the operation of abstract systems: 'all action ... is in principle "calculable" in terms of risk – some sort of assessment of likely risks can be made for virtually all habits and activities, in respect of specific outcomes. The intrusion of abstract systems into everyday life, coupled with the dynamic diffusion of knowledge, means that an awareness of risk seeps into the actions of almost everyone' (p. 112). 'Risk assessment' is an essential component of the 'colonization of the future' which is central to modernity.

Giddens argues that there has been a huge historical transformation of the nature of risk – and security.

> Preoccupation with risk in modern social life has nothing to do with the actual prevalence of life-threatening dangers. On the level of the individual life-span, in terms of life expectation and degree of freedom from serious disease, people in the developed societies are in a much more secure position than were most in previous ages. (p. 115)

An impressive list follows (pp. 115–16) of the ways in which the physical security of human beings has been enhanced in industrial societies; but it is counter-balanced by a list of new risks: war, motor accidents, drugs, environmental pollution, etc. Both can be seen as results of the operation of the abstract systems of modernity. 'In terms of basic life security, nonetheless,' Giddens concludes, 'the risk-reducing elements seem substantially to outweigh the new array of risks' (p. 116).

The 'institutionalization of risk' is seen as a fundamental characteristic of the new role of risk in modern society. 'A significant part of expert thinking and public discourse today is made up of *risk profiling* – analysing what, in the current state of knowledge and in current conditions, is the distribution of risks in given milieux of action' (p. 119).

Giddens distinguishes between 'low-' and 'high-consequence' risks: the former potentially within the control of the individual agent (e.g., peculiarities of diet which may have certain medical consequences), the latter 'by definition ... remote from the individual agent, although – again by definition – they impinge directly on each individual's life-chances' (p. 121). Examples of high-consequence risks range from mercury in tuna fish to, at the most 'calamitous', the nuclear accident at Chernobyl. Risk assessment is a complex and constantly changing affair even in the case of low-consequence risks; it becomes highly speculative in the context of the larger high-consequence issues.

The pervasiveness of risk, Giddens repeats, is not because life is now inherently more risky:

It is rather that, in conditions of modernity, for lay actors as well as for experts in specific fields, thinking in terms of risk and risk-assessment is a more or less ever-present exercise, of a partly imponderable character. It should be remembered that we are all lay people in respect of the vast majority of the expert systems which intrude on our daily activities ... The risk climate of modernity is thus unsettling for everyone; no one escapes. (pp. 123–4)

Nevertheless, 'Thinking in terms of risk ... is also a means of seeking to stabilize outcomes, a mode of colonizing the future' (p. 133).

Substantively, Giddens argues, 'The abstract systems of modernity create large areas of relative security for the continuance of everyday life' (p. 133) but 'the wholesale penetration of abstract systems into everyday life creates risks which the individual is not well-placed to confront ... Greater interdependence, up to and including globally interdependent systems, means greater vulnerability when untoward events occur that affect these systems as a whole' (p. 136). At the limit, hypothetical events such as the breakdown of the global monetary system, or global warming (let alone nuclear war), indicate the dangers. Real socially-created disasters, such as the effects of the destruction of water and electricity systems in Iraq during the Gulf War, demonstrate the vulnerability of modern societies.

A problematic dimension of Giddens' discussion is that he gives little attention to the role of social groups in the distribution and negotiation of risk. It is ironic, from the point of view of this paper, that rather as Buzan and Booth counterpose individual and state (ignoring society), Giddens appears to counterpose the individual to society and social relations in the most general sense (with little to say, in this volume, about social groups – or the state). Giddens does, however, enter an early caveat about the role of social inequalities in the distribution of risk; and, whereas Buzan does attempt a general account of security as a concept, Giddens' aim is rather different, to examine the consequences of modernity for the individual.

The one area of Giddens' discussion where he does implicitly explore the dimensions of collective human action is in his final chapter, 'The Emergence of Life Politics'. Giddens' account of risk and security is clearly activist in its implications: for all the determining character of abstract systems, he does not believe that they leave people powerless. On the contrary, individuals have choices of lifestyle and life-plan. Social groups, *The Consequences of Modernity* makes clear, have the power to contest and organize around the axes of the modern social order. Giddens, interestingly, organizes his political perspective around the concept of 'utopian realism', using the term in a way which is very similar to Booth's apparently unconnected usage.[26]

On the specific implications of this perspective, however, Giddens' account diverges very significantly from Booth's position. Whereas Booth argues for recasting security in terms of 'emancipation', Giddens argues that 'emancipatory politics' is being historically transcended by 'life politics'. The difference is that 'While emancipatory politics is a politics of life chances, life politics is a politics of lifestyle.'[27] The politics of emancipation – which are still one axis of contemporary politics – revolve around social inequality, exploitation and oppression. Giddens argues that life politics are emerging as the dominant agenda because they reflect the more specific characteristics of the late modern society: 'a politics of life decisions', reflecting the situation of individuals in high modernity. Formally, they are defined as politics which concern

> political issues which flow from processes of self-actualization in post-traditional contexts, where globalizing influences intrude deeply into the reflexive project of the self, and conversely where processes of self-realization influence global strategies.[28]

Life politics, therefore, are politics of risk and security in a more fundamental sense even than emancipatory politics, since risk and security become uniquely pervasive in the late modern era.

Life politics are, of course, far more developed, and far greater choice is possible, in the prosperous West than in many poorer parts of the world, where emancipatory politics are more central. Clearly there is an ethnocentrist danger in Giddens' case, but he argues that even the poor in most parts of the world are increasingly incorporated, via mass media, into the culture of modernity, and are thus affected (albeit at a very different level) by the same tendencies which are developing in the West.

Life politics and emancipatory politics in fact intersect, Giddens acknowledges, with 'life-political' issues raising 'emancipatory' problems, and vice versa. He gives as an example the relationship between economic growth in the developing world and global environmental problems, and contends that 'a process of emancipation on the part of the world's poor could probably only be achieved if radical lifestyle changes were introduced in the developed countries.'[29]

Giddens' view of the role of social groups in politics thus departs from a traditional sociological view in that he sees social groups not just in terms of pre-formed social categories with a capacity for agency (e.g., the classic Marxian view of class), but as constituted *through* political action (e.g., around environmental and other 'life-political' issues). Social movements are seen, as they were in *The Nation-State and Violence*, as key collective actors around the main axes of modernity.[30] Politics, in life politics, is defined primarily in the broad sense of choice in action which affects the social order, although the secondary sense which relates to the nation-state is also recognized.[31]

In general, however, it is clear that unlike in *The Nation-State and Violence*, where a nation-state-divided global order was the focus of attention, in these new books Giddens assumes a developing global society which transcends the nation-state. This is not however explicitly discussed, and as Giddens does not supply us with the connections, we shall have to make them ourselves.

'International Security Studies' and the Sociology of Security

The most basic significance of Giddens' account is that it clearly establishes security as a general problem for individuals and groups in society. It provides a historical framework for analysing the changes in the nature of security problems between pre-modern and modern times. It provides a general account of risk and security in modern society, with a set of categories to explain this (I have concentrated, in this exposition, on certain of these – e.g., abstract systems – but the argument is richer than there has been space to convey).

The fact that Giddens' two recent works hardly mention the state, although limiting their more obvious relevance to international relations, is useful in underlining the point that it is highly possible to discuss security without doing so. Individual and collective human security do not depend irredeemably on the state context, as Buzan and others would have us believe. Security issues are faced at all levels of social life. The concept of security is a general concept of social science – rather like that of strategy, which is also seen as special to international relations, but has in fact a broad significance for the social sciences.[32]

Giddens' work is important for the current international debate in that it provides a broader argument, in a 'utopian realist' perspective similar to Booth's, which widens and underpins the case for moving away from the state level in discussing security. Giddens' conceptualization of social movements, and insistence on seeing social groups as constituted though political action rather than being objectively pre-formed, helps to clarify the nature of the 'communities' to which Booth refers, and gives one sort of sociological answer to the questions raised above.

It is useful to ask what happens to Giddens' argument about risk and security if we 'bring the state back in'. First, states become one sort of specialized bureaucracy monitoring and attempting to regulate risk; in Booth's sense, they become (but not uniquely: only alongside other institutions) 'providers' of security to individuals and groups within society. Second, however, states and the state system become a very important (but again, not by any means the only) context in which risk is generated for individuals and human groups. In both these senses, states (and international relations in the sense of what goes on between them) are specific instances of the wider processes which Giddens outlines.

There is a third point, however, which has to do with the specific character of the nation-state. States are unique, notably in claiming to represent 'sovereignty' and the monopoly of legitimate violence. In the 'reflexive monitoring' which Giddens indicates characterizes abstract systems, states have a dominant role, even if parallel activities are undertaken by many non-state organizations. As Giddens' own earlier work suggests, the combination of territoriality and legitimacy gives states a pivotal role in what he calls the 'surveillance' cluster of institutions in modern societies.[33]

At the very moment, however, at which Giddens defined this world of nation-states, each a 'bordered power container' mobilizing 'outward-pointing violence' against other states, this view – uncomfortably close to international relations realism, as we have indicated – was rapidly starting to lose much of the validity which it previously had. States began to crumble under the many pressures which had accumulated on that level of organiza-tion. Statehood began to fracture, so that some of its attributes could be seen as attaching themselves to supra-state institutions, while others were claimed by sub-state collectivities, often in the name of a plethora of newly revived nationalisms. Sovereignty no longer resided uniquely in one set of institutions easily labelled as 'nation-states', but was increasingly shared above and below.

This turmoil at and around the state level can, of course, be incorporated, as it would be by Buzan, in a sophisticated version of a relatively traditional state-centred version of international relations. It can be interpreted more productively, however, as evidence of the interpenetration of state and other levels of society. The international system of relations between states can be seen as a system which increasingly constitutes what Giddens describes as an 'institutionalized risk environment', reflexively monitored by the 'players' (states) but also by others (individuals, social groups) influenced by its operations. This system is influenced by other such environments at a global level (e.g., economic relations, monetary order, socially-created ecological systems) as well as influencing them. It also interpenetrates with systems which exist within states.

Recent sociological work can thus assist in developing a more broadly conceived 'security studies', which in turn refocuses the questions of 'international security studies' with which we began this paper. Giddens' work has, however, as we have seen, its own limitations, from a sociological as well as an international relations point of view. We can conclude, therefore, that at the moment sociology is better placed to pose conceptual challenges to international studies, than to give definitive answers. In moving beyond the statism/individualism dichotomy, we need to broaden the conceptual basis as well as the issue agenda of the study of security. In the process, we will also redefine the issues in sociological terms.

In arguing that 'society' is the missing dimension of international security studies, this paper has not given a fixed or closed conception to this concept. On the contrary, it has argued that we need to understand the global flux of social relations within which the international system floats. This conception suggests a new analytical agenda for a sociologically oriented international relations or a globally and internationally focused sociology. How far does a global society exist? What are the security concerns of individuals and groups within an emergent global society? Which sorts of groups are there and how do they articulate their concerns? What are the relationships between social movements, institutions and states? How do such concerns intersect with the international state system, and how far do concepts and policies of national and international security reflect such wider concerns within society? Related to this, of course, is a moral and political agenda: the answers to these questions will feed into concerns with the development of communities at local, national, regional and global levels, and contribute to a conception of community which is based not so much on an international community of states as on a global community of human beings.

This paper cannot, of course, provide answers to these questions. What it has tried to do is to raise conceptual issues which allow us to pose these questions, not in the context of a state-centric view of international relations, but in the context of social relations in general within our rapidly changing world.

Acknowledgements

A first version of this paper was presented to the Annual Conference of the British International Studies Association, Warwick, 1991. I am grateful to all of those who responded in the discussion, and especially to Barry Buzan for entering into a cordial debate on these issues. I am grateful to Barry, Ken Booth, the editor of this journal and an anonymous reviewer for their comments on a second draft. I am especially indebted to Nicholas Wheeler, who suggested I might write on these themes and who has been generous with his knowledge of international theory. Only I can be held responsible, however, for the arguments here presented.

Notes

1. See for example Theda Skocpol, *States and Social Revolutions* (Cambridge, 1979); Anthony Giddens, *The Nation-State and Violence* (Cambridge, 1985); Michael Mann, *States, War and Capitalism* (Oxford, 1988).

2. Andrew Linklater, *Beyond Realism and Marxism* (London, 1990); Fred Halliday, 'State and Society in International Relations', in Michael Banks and Martin Shaw (eds.), *State and Society in International Relations* (Hemel Hempstead, 1991), pp. 191–210.

3. Faruk Yalvac, 'The Sociology of the State and the Sociology of International Relations', in Banks and Shaw (eds.), *State and Society*, p. 94.

4. Martin Shaw, 'State Theory and the Post-Cold War World', in Banks and Shaw (eds.) *State and Society*, pp. 1–24.

5. Ken Booth, 'Security and Emancipation', *Review of International Studies*, 17 (1991), p. 317.

6. See, for example, the discussion in Owen Greene, 'Transnational processes and European security', in M. Pugh (ed.), *European Security: Towards 2000* (Manchester, 1992), pp. 141–61.

7. My discussion of Buzan, *People, States and Fear*, is based on the second edition, newly subtitled *An Agenda for International Security Studies in the Post-Cold War Era* (Hemel Hempstead, 1991).

8. Steve Smith, 'Mature Anarchy, Strong States and Security' (review article on Buzan), in *Arms Control*, forthcoming.

9. Booth, 'Security and Emancipation', p. 317.

10. Booth, 'Security and Emancipation', p. 317.

11. James Mayall, *Nationalism and International Society* (Cambridge, 1990), pp. 2–3.

12. Buzan mentions almost in passing that 'In modern usage a nation is defined as a large group of people sharing the same cultural, and possibly the same ethnic or racial, heritage' (p. 70). This loose formulation is hardly satisfactory.

13. Benedict Anderson, *Imagined Communities*, 2nd edn (London, 1991).

14. The inadequacy of such a view was indicated long ago in Marx's critique of 'political freedom' in his 'On the Jewish Question' (1844); see T. B. Bottomore (ed.), *Karl Marx: Early Writings* (London, 1964), pp. 1–41. While I would not uphold Marx *in toto*, his discussion of the limitations of the view which considers individuals purely from the standpoint of their participation in the state is of general sociological significance. A current attempt to make this aspect of Marx's work effective in a critical account of international relations can be seen in work in progress by Justin Rosenberg (LSE).

15. He describes it as 'a powerful modifier of the state-centric view' in a comment on an earlier version of this paper (reviewer's note).

16. Smith, 'Mature Anarchy'.

17. Booth, 'Security and Emancipation', p. 320.

18. Booth, 'Security and Emancipation', p. 321.

19. Max Weber, *The Philosophy of the Social Sciences* (Glencoe, 1949).

20. I am indebted on this point to the very interesting discussion of Paul A. Chilton, 'On the Embedding of the Term "Security" in Language and Conceptual Systems', to appear in Beer and Hariman (eds.), *Refiguring Realism*.

21. A most paradoxical feature of the debate in international studies is that while denying 'society' in the more fundamental sense in which it is used by sociology, international relations theorists do use the term 'society' in an altogether different context, in the sense of 'international society'. It is beyond the scope of this paper to enter fully into the discussion of this paradox, which is discussed more fully in my paper, 'Global society and global responsibility: the theoretical, practical and political limits of international society', *Millennium: Journal of International Studies* (forthcoming, 1993).

This conception compounds the statism of international security studies which has been criticized above. The crucial point is that the 'society' referred to is one composed of states. From the standpoint argued here, this is a highly misleading usage. The members of 'society', those involved in social relations, are human individuals. States are forms of, indeed *results* of, society, not members of it. To use the term 'society' to refer to the relations of states confirms the misplaced abstraction which fails to understand the dependence of these specific social institutions on the general complex of social relationships.

'International society' in a sociologically acceptable sense would refer to all those social relations which exist in international terms, across the boundaries of nation-states. Such international relations take many forms, which we could designate as economic, cultural and ideological as well as political. 'International society' in this sense would be a concept closer to that of 'global society', which is a commoner sociological usage, because it indicates the extent to which social relations exist not merely across nation-state boundaries, but even in disregard of them.

The sense in which 'international society' has been used in international relations thus indicates part of the problem – the attempt to separate off state relations from social relations generally – rather than a solution. There is no theoretical reason why the relations between states should not merely be described in terms of an 'international system', with growing integration among them being described in terms of stages of development of that system, rather than resorting to the term 'society' with its inherent confusion of relations among states with those among human individuals.

22. Ken Booth, 'Security in Anarchy: Utopian Realism in Theory and Practice', *International Affairs*, 67 (1991), especially pp. 540–1ff.

23. So much so that, when we renamed our Centre for Defence and Disarmament Studies at Hull as a 'Centre for Security Studies' – omitting the specializing 'International' which Buzan gives his book – we found ourself in some difficulty with the criminologists in our School!

24. Anthony Giddens, *The Consequences of Modernity* (Cambridge, 1990).

25. Anthony Giddens, *Modernity and Self-Identity: Self and Society in the Late Modern Age* (Cambridge, 1991).

26. Giddens, *The Consequences of Modernity*, pp. 154–8; Booth, 'Security in Anarchy', especially pp. 533–9.

27. Giddens, *Modernity and Self-Identity*, p. 214.

28. Giddens, *Modernity and Self-Identity*, p. 214.

29. Giddens, *Modernity and Self-Identity*, p. 230.

30. Giddens, *The Nation-State and Violence*, and *The Consequences of Modernity*, pp. 158–63.

31. Giddens, *Modernity and Self-Identity*, pp. 226–7.

32. See Lawrence Freedman's contribution to Gerald Segal (ed.), *New Directions in Strategic Studies* (London, 1989), in which he argues for what I criticize (in the same symposium) as an 'imperialistic' view of strategic studies in relation to the social sciences. There is however a difference between 'strategy' and 'security' in that the former has specifically military origins – see my 'Strategy and Social Process: Military Context and Sociological Analysis', *Sociology*, 24 (1990), pp. 465–73 – while the latter does not.

33. Giddens, *The Nation-State and Violence*.